Wall Street Words

THIRD EDITION

**Other Books on Finance and Investing
By David L. Scott**

Dictionary of Accounting
Fundamentals of the Time Value of Money
The Guide to Buying Insurance
The Guide to Investing in Bonds
The Guide to Investing in Common Stocks
The Guide to Investing for Current Income
The Guide to Investing in Mutual Funds
The Guide to Managing Credit
The Guide to Personal Budgeting
The Guide to Saving Money
The Guide to Tax-Saving Investing
How Stocks Work
How Wall Street Works
Investing in Tax-Saving Municipal Bonds
The Investor's Guide to Discount Brokers
Municipal Bonds: The Basics and Beyond
Understanding and Managing Investment Risk and Return

Wall Street Words

THIRD EDITION

AN A TO Z GUIDE TO INVESTMENT TERMS FOR TODAY'S INVESTOR

DAVID L. SCOTT
Professor of Accounting and Finance

HOUGHTON MIFFLIN COMPANY
BOSTON   NEW YORK

Library of Congress Cataloging-in-Publication Data

Scott, David Logan, 1942-
  Wall Street words: an A to Z guide to investment terms for today's investor / David L. Scott.—3rd ed.
    p. cm.
Includes bibliographical references.
  ISBN 0-618-17651-9
  1. Investments—Dictionaries. 2. Securities—Dictionaries. 3. Stock exchanges—Dictionaries. I. Title.
HG4513.S37 2003
332.6'03—dc21

2003049928

Visit our website: www.houghtonmifflinbooks.com

Manufactured in the United States of America

Book design by Melodie Wertelet
Charts by Mary Reilly

Contents

Contributors of Investment Tips   vi

Preface to the Third Edition   vii

Wall Street Words with Tips from Experts   1

Technical Analysis Chart Patterns   418

Selected Websites   423

Contributors of Investment Tips

Stephanie G. Bigwood,
  CFP, ChFC, CSA
Assistant Vice President
Lombard Securities Incorporated
Baltimore, MD

Gloria Cole
Attorney, private practice
Weston, MA

Christopher Farrell
Economics Editor
Minnesota Public Radio
Sound Money®
St. Paul, MN

Steven Flagg
Senior Vice President—Investments
UBS PaineWebber
Mount Kisco, NY

Reg Green
Editor, *Mutual Fund News Service*
Bodega Bay, CA

Jeffrey S. Levine, CPA, MST
Alkon & Levine, PC
Newton, MA

Thomas J. McAllister, CFP
McAllister Financial Planning
Carmel, IN

Henry Nothnagel
Senior Vice President—Options
Wachovia Securities, Inc.
Chicago, IL

Sharon Rich
Financial Planner
WOMONEY
Belmont, MA

George Riles
First Vice President and
  Resident Manager
Merrill Lynch
Albany, GA

Mark G. Steinberg
President
Trabar Associates
Boston, MA

Thomas M. Tarnowski
Senior Business Analyst
Global Investment Banking Division
Citigroup, Inc.—Salomon Smith Barney
New York, NY, and London, UK

Preface to the Third Edition

Hopefully, you weren't on the wrong end of a pump-and-dump scheme devised by a fourteen-year-old who earned more than three quarters of a million dollars buying stock and touting them in Internet chatrooms so he could sell at a big gain after other investors pushed up prices. You certainly weren't alone if you bit on one of these investment scams. Have you decided to invest in an exchange-traded fund that offers the performance of a mutual fund without all the expenses? Did your broker call recently and try to sell you some CoCo bonds? The world of investing often appears to move at warp speed and, some might say, spin out of control.

Every day we seem to read or hear about a new investment product, a new company offering shares of stock to the public, a new method for earning a higher return, a new scandal, or a new federal regulation related to investing. Significant changes occurred with respect to investment products, securities trading platforms, and regulations in the years between the original edition of this book in 1988 and publication of the revised edition in 1997. Changes seemed to occur at an even faster pace between publication of the revised edition and the current edition. New securities exchanges were born, new financial products were introduced, new investment scams were perpetrated, new regulations were passed, and, of course, new terminology emerged. Our Canadian neighbors revamped their securities markets with three distinct exchanges in Toronto, Montreal, and Vancouver that specialize in trading different types of securities. European exchanges merged to offer new trading platforms and new types of securities.

In the United States, the National Association of Securities Dealers purchased the American Stock Exchange and then spun off Nasdaq, whose own stock commenced trading on the over-the-counter market. The Pacific Stock Exchange altered its name, closed its two equities floors, and merged with an electronic commerce network to form a computerized registered stock exchange. One of the biggest changes was the practice of quoting stock prices in decimals rather than fractions. No longer are investors required to figure out how many dollars and cents are involved in paying an extra eighth or sixteenth for shares of stock.

While institutional changes were taking place, investment banking firms were prying additional money from institutional and individual investors with new types of securities. Exchange-traded funds—a type of mutual fund whose shares trade like a common stock—became a popular investment product that helped keep the American Stock Exchange afloat. Meanwhile, an underwriting firm successfully issued bonds secured by future music royalties of a famous rock singer. Similar debt securities followed.

New financial products, and new ways of using existing financial products, were accompanied by companies that presented ever more complicated, and often misleading, financial statements that even professional financial analysts didn't seem to fully understand. While corporate debt was sometimes hidden in secret partnerships, companies began reporting earnings without taking account of all their expenses. Some of these shenanigans were even legal! The dot-com boom took the term *hot stock* to a new level as newly issued shares of Internet-related companies rose to stratospheric heights only to fall to earth when their issuers sank in a sea of red ink and negative cash flow. Paupers who became overnight multimillionaires often saw much of their wealth disappear in a matter of days or weeks. The telecom boom and subsequent bust was even more severe. Corporate managements of telecom companies—living in a foggy universe of optimism—overbuilt everything, and their stockholders suffered the consequences. And of course there are Enron and WorldCom, poster children for financial and accounting excesses in this new century of investing.

This new edition of *Wall Street Words* addresses all these changes and events with new terminology, new investment tips, and new case studies. The third edition includes nearly 600 new terms and 75 new case studies. You will find references to new and revamped securities exchanges, new financial organizations, new investment tools and techniques, new types of securities, and new regulations. This edition includes an added appendix with the web addresses for most of the organizations included in this book. Just as you can't tell the players at a sporting event without a scorecard, you can't make intelligent investment decisions without understanding the language. *Wall Street Words* will help you understand what you read and what you hear. The next time you are browsing through an Internet chatroom and come across a glowing report about a stock that can't miss being a big winner, check out the entry for *pump and dump*.

David L. Scott
Valdosta, Georgia

A

a 1. —Used in the dividend column of stock transaction tables in newspapers to indicate a cash payment in addition to regular dividends during the year: *2.75a*. **2.** —Used in money market mutual fund transaction tables in newspapers to indicate a yield that may include capital gains and losses as well as current interest: *AmCap Reserv a*.

A An upper-medium grade assigned to a debt obligation by a rating agency to indicate a strong capacity to pay interest and repay principal. This capacity is susceptible to impairment in the event of adverse developments.

AA A grade assigned to a debt obligation by a rating agency to indicate a very strong capacity to pay interest and repay principal. Such a rating indicates only slightly lower quality than the top rating of AAA. —Also called *Aa*.

AAA The highest grade assigned to a debt obligation by a rating agency. It indicates an unusually strong capacity to pay interest and repay principal. —Also called *triple A*.

abandon To elect not to exercise an option.

abandonment —See EXPIRATION.

ABC Agreement An agreement between a firm that finances a seat on the New York Stock Exchange and the employee who purchases the seat. The agreement, approved by the exchange, permits the member to transfer the seat to another employee of the member firm, keep the seat and purchase a second membership for another individual designated by the lending firm, or sell the membership with proceeds given to the member firm. ABC Agreements are used because of an exchange restriction prohibiting organizations from becoming members.

above par Of or relating to a security that sells at more than face value or par value. For example, a $1,000 par bond that trades at a market price of $1,050 is selling above par. A fixed-income security is most likely to sell above par if market rates of interest have declined since the time the security was issued. Bonds purchased above par will result in capital loss to the buyer if held to maturity and redeemed at face value. —Compare BELOW PAR. —See also PREMIUM BOND.

absolute priority rule The principle that senior creditors are paid in full prior to any payment being made to junior creditors, and that all creditors have seniority to equity holders.

absorb To offset sell orders or a new security offering with buy orders.

abusive tax shelter A tax shelter in which an improper interpretation of the law is used to produce tax benefits that are disproportionate to economic reality.

Accelerated Cost Recovery System (ACRS) An accounting technique for calculating the depreciation of tangible assets on the basis of the estimated-life classifications into which the assets are placed. ACRS was initiated by the Economic Recovery Act of 1981. The goal was to make investments more profitable by sheltering large amounts of income from taxation during the early years of an asset's life. The initial law established classifications of 3, 5, 10, and 15 years; these classifications were subsequently modified in order to reduce depreciation and increase the government's tax revenues. The classification into which an asset is placed determines the percentage of the cost potentially recoverable in each year. —See also MODIFIED ACCELERATED COST RECOVERY SYSTEM.

accelerated depreciation An Accelerated Cost Recovery System method for writing off the cost of a capital asset by taking the largest deductions in the early years of the asset's life. The purpose of using accelerated depreciation is to delay the payment of taxes so that cash savings from the deferral can be reinvested to earn additional income. —Compare STRAIGHT-LINE DEPRECIATION.

acceleration clause A provision in a bond indenture that in the event of default allows the trustee or the holders of 25% of the principal amount of the outstanding issue to declare all of the principal and interest immediately. Calling for an acceleration is likely to cause the borrower to cure the default or seek bankruptcy protection.

acceptance —See BANKER'S ACCEPTANCE.

accommodative monetary policy The Federal Reserve policy of increasing the supply of money to make credit more readily available. An accommodative monetary policy tends to lower interest rates, especially the short-term ones, at the time credit is made plentiful. Such a policy is likely to result eventually in increased inflation and interest rates. —Compare MONETARY POLICY.

account **1.** The client of a broker, brokerage firm, or broker-dealer. The client may be a business, an individual investor, or an institutional investor. **2.** The record of a client's transactions and investment position. —See also ACCOUNT STATEMENT.

accountant's opinion —See OPINION.

account executive —See REGISTERED REPRESENTATIVE.

accounting period —See FISCAL PERIOD.

Accounting Principles Board (APB) A group of accountants appointed by the American Institute of Certified Public Accountants to determine accounting principles for financial record keeping. The APB was terminated in 1973 with the founding of the Financial Accounting Standards Board.

account number A unique code assigned to each investor's account at a brokerage firm.

accounts payable Money a business owes to others. Accounts payable are current liabilities incurred in the normal course of business as a firm purchases goods or services with the understanding that payment is due at a later date. If a firm pays cash for all of its purchases, no accounts payable will appear on that firm's balance sheet.

accounts receivable Money owed to a business by customers who have bought goods or services on credit. Accounts receivables are current assets that continually turn into cash as customers pay their bills. —Also called *receivables*.

accounts receivable turnover The number of times in each accounting period that a firm converts credit sales into cash. A high turnover indicates effective granting of credit and collection from customers by the firm's management. Accounts receivable turnover is calculated by dividing the average amount of receivables into annual credit sales. —Also called *receivables turnover*. —See also ACTIVITY RATIO; COLLECTION PERIOD.

account statement A periodic statement to an investor showing the investor's investment position at a given point in time and transactions for the investor's account during a given period of time. An account statement for an active account is generally sent at the beginning of each month, while statements for inactive accounts are sent quarterly.

accredited investor An investor with sufficient income or wealth to be exempted from the 35-person limit in contributing funds to a private limited partnership. An accredited investor must have an annual income of more than $200,000 or a net worth of $1 million, or the investor must purchase $150,000 or more of the offering with the investment representing 20% or less of his or her net worth.

accreted value The current value of an original-issue discount bond, taking into account imputed interest that has accumulated.

accretion The accumulation of capital gains on discount bonds with the expectation that the securities will be redeemed at maturity. Excluding municipals, the amount of annual accretion is taxable on an original-issue discount bond even though only a small amount of interest or no interest at all is paid each year. —See also IMPUTED INTEREST.

accrual accounting A method of accounting that recognizes expenses when incurred and revenue when earned rather than when payment is made or received. Thus, it is the act of sending the goods or receiving an inventory item that is important in determining when transactions are posted on financial statements. For example, using accrual accounting, sales are recorded as revenue when goods are shipped even though payment is not expected for days, weeks, or months. Most firms use the accrual basis of accounting in recording transactions. —Compare CASH BASIS ACCOUNTING.

⋀⋀ CASE STUDY Recording revenues that are used to calculate earnings before actually receiving those revenues can potentially misrepresent a firm's financial results and lead to financial difficulties down the road. For example, a company that ships substantial amounts of goods on credit may produce outstanding earnings in the current accounting period, but if customers who receive the goods fail to pay for the merchandise, future earnings are likely to suffer. Firms build an estimate for doubtful payments into the revenues and earnings they report, but the estimates may be understated and make earnings look better than they actually are. More than a few companies have been known to ship unusually large amounts of merchandise near the end of a fiscal year in order to make the year's sales and earnings appear favorable even though the extra sales produce an unrealistic picture of the firm's operations. In one instance, a large toy company was offering special incentives to customers that loaded up with the firm's merchandise just prior to the end of the year. This, of course, is perfectly legal. However, the company offering the incentives was accused of overstating its earnings by not properly accounting for the expense of the incentives being offered. A firm that aggressively pursues end-of-year sales may end up selling to some financially weak customers who fail to pay for the merchandise. Unfortunately, it is difficult for stockholders to know the extent to which a firm's actions serve to puff up the financial statements rather than produce real results.

accrual bond —See ZERO-COUPON BOND.

accrued expense   An expense incurred but not yet paid. A firm incurs certain expenses such as wages, interest, and taxes that are paid only periodically. From the time expenses are incurred until the date they are paid, expenses accrue in a firm's balance sheet.

accrued interest   Interest owed but not yet paid. Accrued interest is listed as a liability on corporate balance sheets. It is also added to the price at which bonds are traded. For example, if a 12% coupon bond is trading at $950 and the last record date for an interest payment was two months ago, the buyer must pay the seller $20 (two months' interest at 1% per month on $1,000 principal) in accrued interest in addition to the quoted price. This additional expense will be recovered when the new owner receives six months' interest after holding the bond only four months.

accrued market discount   The gain in the value of a bond that occurs because the bond has been bought at a discount from face value. For example, a $1,000 par bond maturing in ten years and selling at $800 can be expected to rise gradually in price throughout its remaining life. The accrued market discount is the portion of any price rise caused by the gradual increase (as opposed to an increase caused by a fall in interest rates).

accumulate   To purchase a relatively large amount of stock in a firm during a given period. —Compare DISTRIBUTE.

accumulated depreciation   The total amount of depreciation that has been recorded for an asset since its date of acquisition. For example, a computer with a 5-year estimated life that was purchased for $2,000 would have accumulated depreciation of $800 [($2,000/5) × 2] and a book value of $1,200 ($2,000 − $800) after 2 years of straight-line depreciation. —Also called *depreciation reserve*.

accumulated dividend —See DIVIDENDS IN ARREARS.

accumulated earnings tax   A federal tax on a company's retained earnings that are considered in excess of what is reasonable. The purpose of an accumulated earnings tax is to make it more difficult to defer or lower the tax rate (that is, change from ordinary income to capital gains) on income that would ordinarily be paid to stockholders in dividends. For example, stockholders in high tax brackets generally prefer earnings be retained rather than paid in dividends so that they can avoid being taxed at ordinary rates. The position of the Internal Revenue Service is that if the funds are not actually needed by the firm and are only being retained for tax reasons, the accumulated earnings should be taxed.

accumulation   The purchase of a particular security throughout a period of time. For example, the accumulation of a substantial quantity of a stock by a portfolio manager may take place over a period of several weeks or months in order to avoid driving up the price of the stock. An individual's accumulation of shares of a mutual fund may occur over a period of many years.

accumulation area In technical analysis, a rectangular-shaped chart formation produced when insiders and other knowledgeable investors purchase shares of stock from the public and characterized by little price movement but relatively heavy volume. If an accumulation area can be identified, it indicates a time to buy. —Compare DISTRIBUTION AREA. —See also RECTANGLE.

acid-test ratio —See QUICK RATIO.

acquisition The purchase of an asset such as a plant, a division, or even an entire company. For example, the Walt Disney Company made a major acquisition in 1996 when it purchased Capital Cities/ABC, Inc., in order to extend its reach in the entertainment industry.

ACRS —See ACCELERATED COST RECOVERY SYSTEM.

acting in concert Two or more investors acting together to achieve a common goal. For example, a number of relatively large investors may accumulate a major position in a security in an attempt to influence management decisions.

active Of or relating to a security in which there is a great deal of trading. Active securities appeal to many investors because they usually can be traded without affecting the price. In over-the-counter trading, an active security usually has a smaller spread between the bid and ask price. —See also MOST-ACTIVE STOCKS.

active bond crowd Members of the New York Stock Exchange who trade frequently in active bonds. —Compare CABINET CROWD.

active box —See OPEN BOX.

active investment management The management of an investment portfolio that involves active trading of securities in an attempt to produce above-average returns on a risk-adjusted basis. Active management is predicated on the belief that it is possible to beat the market averages consistently. —Compare PASSIVE INVESTMENT MANAGEMENT.

active market A securities market or the market for a particular security in which trading is relatively heavy. An active market not only results in more profits for brokers but also helps institutional investors wishing to acquire or dispose of large positions without affecting price.

activity The amount of relative trading volume in a security.

activity ratio An indicator of how rapidly a firm converts various accounts into cash or sales. In general, the sooner management can convert assets into sales or cash, the more effectively the firm is being run. —See also FIXED ASSET TURNOVER; INVENTORY TURNOVER; TOTAL ASSET TURNOVER.

actual In commodities, the physical asset (that is, the commodity) as opposed to a futures contract on that asset.

A/D —See ADVANCE-DECLINE LINE.

additional bonds test A financial standard that must be met before issuing bonds that use as security revenues or assets already pledged for outstanding bonds.

additional paid-in capital Stockholder contributions that are in excess of a stock's stated or par value. For example, if a firm issues stock with a par value of

$1 per share but sells the stock to investors at $10 per share, the firm's financial statements will show $1 in common stock and $9 in additional paid-in capital for each share issued. —Also called *capital surplus; paid-in surplus.*

add-on Funds that are added to a certificate of deposit after its date of purchase and that earn the same rate of interest as funds deposited with the original certificate. The add-ons allowed by some savings institutions provide a real benefit to investors during periods of declining interest rates.

add-on financing —See FOLLOW-ON OFFERING.

adjustable-rate preferred stock —See FLOATING-RATE PREFERRED STOCK.

adjusted basis The acquisition cost of an asset after it has been adjusted to reflect changes in cost basis that result from the occurrence of certain events following the day of acquisition. For example, stock dividends, stock splits, and dividends deemed to be returned on capital cause a downward adjustment in the cost basis of a security. Conversely, commissions result in an upward adjustment in the cost basis. Adjusted basis is used in calculating gains and losses for tax purposes.

adjusted debit balance The amount owed a broker by a customer, adjusted by paper profits on short sales and balances in a special miscellaneous account. Adjusted debit balance is used to determine whether a customer is permitted to withdraw cash or securities from a margin account.

adjusted exercise price The strike price of put and call options on Ginnie Mae pass through certificates. Ginnie Mae contracts are made up of mortgages that have interest rates that differ from the rate considered to be benchmark. These contracts must be adjusted in price to achieve that benchmark, and the exercise prices of options on the contracts must also be adjusted. This produces contracts that yield the benchmark interest rate at an exercise price.

adjusted gross income The amount of taxable income that remains after certain allowed business-related deductions—such as alimony payments, contributions to a Keogh retirement plan, and in some cases, contributions to an IRA—are subtracted from an individual's gross income. Adjusted gross income and gross income will be the same for many taxpayers.

adjustment 1. —See DIVIDEND ADJUSTMENT. 2. —See INTEREST ADJUSTMENT.

adjustment bond —See INCOME BOND.

adjustment in conversion terms An alteration in the terms under which a convertible security may be exchanged. For example, if an issuer implements a two-for-one split (resulting in a doubling of the number of shares) in the common stock into which its convertible security may be exchanged, the issuer will nearly always be required to reduce the convertible's conversion price by half. Automatic price adjustments also may be scheduled throughout the life of a convertible security. Scheduled increases in the conversion price on specific dates would be an example of an automatic adjustment.

adjustments to income Any of various amounts a taxpayer is allowed to subtract from his or her gross income when calculating adjusted gross income. These adjustments are permitted even if the taxpayer does not itemize deductions during a tax year. Allowable adjustments of particular interest to investors are interest penalties on early savings withdrawals and payments into IRAs and Keogh plans. —See also ADJUSTED GROSS INCOME.

ADR —See AMERICAN DEPOSITARY RECEIPT.

ADR Index A market-capitalization-weighted index that tracks all depositary receipts traded on the New York Stock Exchange, the American Stock Exchange, and Nasdaq. The Bank of New York publishes the index along with three regional ADR indexes (Europe, Asia, and Latin America) and three market ADR indexes (emerging markets, developed markets, and Euroland).

ADR ratio The number of foreign shares represented by one American Depositary Receipt.

ADS —See AMERICAN DEPOSITARY SHARE.

ad valorem tax A tax that is computed as a percentage of the value of specific property. For example, many states levy an annual tax on the market value of an investor's securities as of a certain date. —Also called *property tax*.

advance An increase in the price of a security.

advance-decline index A cumulative total of the daily number of stock issues advancing in price minus the daily number of stock issues declining in price. Technical analysts use the advance-decline index as a measure of breadth of market in order to determine the strength of market movements. Movement of the advance-decline index in the same direction as the market confirms the market movement and indicates the movement will continue.

advance-decline line (A/D) The line that results from plotting the advance-decline index over a period of time. The direction of the advance-decline line is used to confirm movements in a stock or the market.

advance refunding —See PREREFUNDING.

adverse opinion An opinion by a firm's auditors that the firm's financial statements do not accurately present its operating results or financial position. This unusual opinion is a strong warning that investors should be wary. —Compare CLEAN OPINION. —See also QUALIFIED OPINION; SUBJECT TO OPINION.

Advisers Act —See INVESTMENT ADVISERS ACT OF 1940.

advisers' sentiment A contrarian technical indicator derived from market forecasts regarding the future course of security prices and predicated on the theory that when most advisers expect a certain market movement, the opposite movement is most likely to occur. For example, strong bullish sentiment from investment advisers is often considered a bearish sign, while strong bearish sentiment is considered a bullish sign. —Compare SENTIMENT INDEX.

advisory account A brokerage account in which the broker may make limited investment decisions without consulting the customer. Securities traded in the account are confined to those that meet the customer's investment goals. —Compare DISCRETIONARY ACCOUNT.

advisory fee —See MANAGEMENT FEE.

affidavit of loss A notarized form detailing the circumstances relating to the loss of securities. An indemnity bond and replacement securities are not made available until an affidavit of loss is accompanied by a 2% surety premium.

affiliate An organization that is related to another organization through some type of control or ownership. For example, a U.S.-based company may have a foreign affiliate that handles overseas sales.

affiliated person A person who is in a position to influence a firm's management decisions. Affiliated persons usually include directors, officers, owners of more than 10% of the firm's outstanding stock, and family members or close associates of these groups. —Also called *control person.*

affinity fraud Investment scams that target members of identifiable groups, including elderly, ethnic, professional, and religious groups. Perpetrators of affinity fraud are often either members of the targeted group or individuals who enlist the assistance of leaders in order to exploit the trust of members of the group. —See also PYRAMID.

affirmative obligations Requirements imposed by the National Association of Securities Dealers on Nasdaq market makers who must meet certain standards, including timely reporting of price and volume data, participating in the Small Order Execution System, making a two-sided market on a continuous basis, and quoting firm prices.

after-hours trading The trading of securities after the exchanges are closed. After-hours trading often refers to trading a listed security in the over-the-counter market after the exchanges have been closed for the day. This fairly common practice is not illegal. —Also called *extended-hours trading.*

CASE STUDY | Research indicates individual investors trading outside normal market hours (9:30 A.M. to 4:00 P.M. EST) can expect to incur increased transaction expenses. The higher expense of after-hours trading stems from reduced liquidity and the resulting larger spreads between bid and ask quotations. For example, a stock that typically trades with a spread of 5¢ to 10¢ during regular market hours might have a spread of 25¢ to 50¢, or even more, in after-hours trading. Actively traded stocks during regular hours often become relatively illiquid in after-hours trading, when few orders are posted and even small transactions can result in large price fluctuations. The potential volatility and lack of liquidity in after-hours trading are likely to result in individual investors paying too high a price when buying stock and receiving too low a price when selling stock.

aftermarket —See SECONDARY MARKET.

aftertax profit —See NET INCOME.

aftertax yield The rate of return on an investment after taxes have been calculated and subtracted. Aftertax yield, as opposed to pretax yield, is generally a preferred basis for comparing investment alternatives.

CASE STUDY | Utilizing aftertax rather than pretax yield to evaluate investments is a universal rule that applies to stocks, bonds, real estate, and mutual funds. In 2001 the Securities and Exchange Commission adopted a rule requiring that mutual funds disclose in their prospectuses aftertax returns based on stipulated formulas. The SEC order also required certain funds to include standardized aftertax yields in advertisements and other sales materials. The order was prompted by the belief that many investors lack a clear understanding of the impact of taxes on their mutual fund investments. Mutual funds regularly tooted their horns regarding their pretax returns, but SEC studies indicated substantial differences existed in the extent to which these returns were taxed. The tax consequences of distributions are especially puzzling to many mutual fund shareholders who are taxed on distributions based on realized gains from which they frequently did not benefit. To provide investors with more accurate information, the SEC requires that mutual funds present aftertax returns in two ways: on fund distributions only, which would apply to investors who continued to hold their mutual fund shares, and on fund distributions and a redemption of fund shares, which would apply to investors who liquidated their mutual fund shares. In each case aftertax returns are presented as if the shareholder is in the highest applicable federal income tax rate. Pretax and aftertax returns are presented using a standard format.

after the bell Following the formal close of trading for the day. The phrase originates from the bell that rings each day to signal the close of trading on the New York Stock Exchange. For example, a company may announce important news following the close of trading or "after the bell."

against the box —See SHORT AGAINST THE BOX.

aged fail A contract between broker-dealers that remains unsettled 30 days after the settlement date. A security that is subject to an aged fail may no longer be counted as an asset by the receiving firm.

agency **1.** A security issued by a federal agency or federally sponsored corporation. —See also FEDERAL AGENCY SECURITY; FEDERALLY SPONSORED CORPORATE SECURITY. **2.** A relationship between an agent and a principal in which the agent acts for and represents the principal on the basis of the principal's instructions.

agency risk The possibility a firm's managers will not act in the best interest of its stockholders. For example, if managers attempt to ensure their job tenure by making low-risk investment decisions, such decisions may penalize the firm's profitability and the stockholders' return. Likewise, managers may spend the firm's money to benefit themselves rather than stockholders.

agent An individual or organization that acts on behalf of and is subject to the control of another party. For example, in executing an order to buy or sell a security, a broker is acting as a customer's agent.

aggregate exercise price In options trading, an option contract's exercise price multiplied by the number of securities specified in the contract. For example, a call option on 100 shares of Procter & Gamble common stock at an exercise price of $65 has an aggregate exercise price of 100 × $65, or $6,500.

aggressive Of or relating to an investment philosophy that seeks to achieve above-average returns by accepting above-average risks. An example of an aggressive investment posture would be confining one's investments to the common stocks of companies in young industries with high growth potential. Likewise, seeking high current yields by purchasing bonds issued by financially weak companies is an example of aggressive investing.

aggressive growth fund An investment company that attempts to maximize capital gains by investing in the stocks of companies that offer the potential of very rapid growth. Aggressive growth funds tend to produce very high returns in bull markets and relatively large losses in bear markets. Shares of an aggressive growth fund produce very little current income and are subject to wide variations in value. —Also called *performance fund.*

aging A technique for evaluating the composition of a firm's accounts receivables to determine whether irregularities exist. It is carried out by grouping a firm's accounts receivables according to the length of time accounts have been outstanding. For example, a financial analyst may use aging to determine whether a firm carries many overdue debtors that may never pay their bills.

agreement among underwriters A contract signed by members of an underwriting syndicate that specifies the syndicate manager, additional managers, member liability, and life of the group. —Compare UNDERWRITING AGREEMENT.

AICPA —See AMERICAN INSTITUTE OF CERTIFIED PUBLIC ACCOUNTANTS.

AIMR —See ASSOCIATION FOR INVESTMENT MANAGEMENT AND RESEARCH.

air pocket stock An equity security that falls sharply in price.

airport revenue bond Tax-exempt debt issued by a city, county, state, or airport authority with debt service guaranteed either by general revenues generated by the airport or by lease payments for facilities used by a particular airline. A second type of airport revenue bond depends on the financial strength of a private company and may be more risky than a bond guaranteed by an airport's general revenues.

Alberta Stock Exchange —See CANADIAN VENTURE EXCHANGE.

all-holders rule An SEC rule that prohibits bidders and target companies from excluding a stockholder or a group of stockholders from a tender offer. —See also EXCLUSIONARY TENDER OFFER.

allied member An officer, a partner, or a stockholder of a member firm of the New York Stock Exchange who is not individually a member. Allied members, bound by special rules, may not trade on the exchange floor.

alligator An option spread in which the commissions are so large a part of any potential profit that the investor gets eaten alive. Obviously, alligator spreads are of greater benefit to the broker than to the investor.

allocate **1.** To spread systematically a single monetary amount over a number of time periods, usually years. For example, depreciation allocates the cost of a capital asset over its useful life. **2.** To distribute cost or revenue throughout a number of operations or products. For example, a business must decide how to allocate the costs of running its headquarters over all its operations to determine the profitability of each of those operations.

all-or-none offering A securities offering in which the entire issue must be sold or the securities will be withdrawn from distribution. With an all-or-none offering, no sale is considered final until the issuer has determined that the entire issue has been distributed.

all-or-none order A limit order in which the broker is directed to attempt to fill the entire amount of the order or, failing that, to fill none of it. —See also FILL-OR-KILL ORDER.

allotment Securities apportioned to members of an underwriting syndicate for resale to investors.

allowance for doubtful accounts A balance-sheet account established to offset expected bad debts. If a firm has made a sufficient provision in its allowance for doubtful accounts, reported earnings will not be penalized by bad debts when the bad debts occur. If uncollectible accounts are larger than expected, however, the firm will have to increase the size of the account and reduce reported income. —Also called *allowance for bad debts; reserve for bad debts.*

alpha The mathematical estimate of the return on a security when the market return as a whole is zero. Alpha is derived from a in the formula $R_i = a + bR_m$ which measures the return on a security (R_i) for a given return on the market

(R_m) where *b* is beta. —See also CAPITAL-ASSET PRICING MODEL; CHARACTERISTIC LINE.

alternative minimum tax (AMT) A federal tax on taxable income as adjusted for specific tax-preference items, such as passive losses from tax shelters and interest paid on certain municipal bonds. The intent of the tax is to ensure that nearly all individuals pay at least some tax on their incomes. The alternative minimum tax is most likely to apply to individuals with high incomes when a relatively large portion of their income is sheltered from taxation under normal reporting. —Also called *minimum tax.* —See also PRIVATE ACTIVITY BOND.

CASE STUDY | Municipal debt issues sometimes contain both AMT and non-AMT bonds. This combination is especially prevalent when public housing authorities issue debt securities. In April 2000 the Georgia Housing and Finance Authority issued $40 million of single-family mortgage bonds with maturities that ranged from June 1, 2001, to December 1, 2031. The AAA-rated issue included approximately $38 million of bonds that paid interest subject to the federal alternative minimum tax. The remainder of the bonds were of the non-AMT variety. AMT bonds are less desirable to own than non-AMT bonds because of the potential tax liability resulting from interest payments received. Because interest on AMT bonds is considered a preference item in calculating the alternative minimum tax, AMT bonds tend to have higher yields compared to non-AMT bonds from the same issue. In the case of the Georgia Housing and Finance Authority issue, AMT bonds maturing on June 1, 2011, provided buyers with a yield of 5.55%, while non-AMT bonds from the same issue maturing on the same date offered a yield of 5.25%. AMT and non-AMT bonds maturing on other dates offered a similar yield difference. The 30-basis point yield advantage of the AMT bonds was a bonus for investors who did not have to worry about paying the alternative minimum tax.

alternative order A customer order that instructs a broker to complete only one of two possible transactions. For example, an investor holding shares of USX Corp. that were acquired at $45 may have a price target of $75 but may wish to limit any losses to a maximum of $5 per share. The investor would place a limit order to sell at $75 and a stop order to sell at $40. Whichever occurs first will trigger a transaction and cancel the other part of the order. —Also called *combination order; either-or order; one-cancels-the-other order.*

Ambac Assurance Corporation A subsidiary of publicly traded Ambac Financial Group that provides financial guarantees for municipal borrowers and for asset-backed and structured issues. Ambac was founded in 1971 as a subsidiary of MGIC Investment Corporation and later owned by Baldwin-United and Citibank. —Formerly called *American Municipal Bond Assurance Corporation.*

American Association of Individual Investors An organization that sponsors publications, seminars, and other educational programs for individual investors. This group, established in 1979, has its headquarters in Chicago.

American currency quotation In foreign exchange trading, the value of a foreign currency in terms of the U.S. dollar. For example, if the euro is worth 90¢, the American currency quotation would be expressed as 0.90, meaning there are 0.9 dollars to the euro. —Compare EUROPEAN CURRENCY QUOTATION. —Also called *multiplier.*

American Depositary Receipt

Are foreign securities traded in U.S. markets?

Stocks of some, especially large, foreign companies traded in the U.S. markets are traded as American Depositary Receipts (ADRs). ADRs are receipts for the shares of a foreign corporation held by a U.S. depositary bank. The receipts are traded openly on the U.S. markets, and the owner (shareholder) is entitled to all dividends and capital gains. Each ADR represents a determined ratio of the foreign stock, and the price of the ADR corresponds to the price of the stock in the home market adjusted for this ratio.

ADRs traded in the U.S. markets will clear and settle in U.S. dollars. The depositary bank will also convert, for a small fee, any dividends to U.S. dollars.

Thomas M. Tarnowski, Senior Business Analyst
Global Investment Banking Division, Citigroup, Inc.—Salomon Smith Barney, New York, NY, and London, UK

American Depositary Receipt (ADR)   The physical certificate for an American Depositary Share. American Depositary Shares trade electronically, but only American Depositary Receipts can be delivered to an investor. American Depositary Shares and their companion American Depositary Receipts always exchange on a one-for-one basis. Although American Depositary Receipts and American Depositary Shares are different, the terms are frequently used interchangeably. —See also SPONSORED AMERICAN DEPOSITARY RECEIPT; UNSPONSORED AMERICAN DEPOSITARY RECEIPT.

American Depositary Share (ADS)   A negotiable U.S. depositary share that represents securities of a non-U.S. company being held in custody. A custodian bank in the issuer's home country holds the foreign shares. An ADS is traded in U.S. dollars in the U.S. markets, and dividends are paid in U.S. dollars. American Depositary Shares are traded in lieu of the underlying foreign securities that remain in custody. —See also SPONSORED AMERICAN DEPOSITARY RECEIPT; SPONSORED AMERICAN DEPOSITARY SHARE.

◿✚ CASE STUDY | Trading of American Depositary Shares boomed in the early 2000s, largely because of the increased number of ADSs available to U.S. investors. Foreign companies issued American Depositary Shares as part of their effort to raise funds in the booming U.S. capital markets. Some ADS issues originated from foreign-based corporations with U.S. operations that wanted to offer dollar-denominated ownership shares to their U.S. employees. Foreign companies sometimes issued ADSs to use in acquiring U.S. firms in equity transactions. For example, British Petroleum paid for its acquisition of Chicago-based Amoco Corporation with newly issued American Depositary Shares. These shares offer U.S. investors the opportunity to achieve international diversification without the investors being required to convert dollars for a foreign currency and vice versa. American Depositary Shares also offer liquidity that often surpasses the liquidity of the same firm's ordinary shares. Actively traded ADSs in U.S. markets include Alcatel (France), BP (United Kingdom), Ericsson (Sweden), Nokia (Finland), Royal Dutch Petroleum (Netherlands), and Telefonica (Spain).

American Institute of Certified Public Accountants (AICPA)   A professional association for Certified Public Accountants providing guidance to members on accounting techniques and standards. The AICPA determines how financial data are calculated and reported to stockholders.

American Municipal Bond Assurance Corporation —See AMBAC ASSURANCE CORPORATION.

American option A put or call option that permits the owner to exercise the option at any time on or before the expiration date.

American Stock Exchange®️ (AMEX®️, ASE) A large floor-based securities exchange in New York City that provides facilities for trading stocks, bonds, index shares, and equity derivative securities. Listing requirements for stocks are less stringent than those of the New York Stock Exchange, resulting in the AMEX trading securities of younger and smaller firms with fairly volatile price movements. The American Stock Exchange has been a leader in introducing new investment products such as exchange-traded funds. —See also CURB EXCHANGE.

AMEX®️ —See AMERICAN STOCK EXCHANGE®️.

AMEX®️ Composite Index A market-value-weighted index (market price times shares outstanding) of all AMEX-listed securities relative to their aggregate value on December 29, 1995. Index components include common stocks and American Depositary Receipts of all AMEX-listed companies, REITs, master limited partnerships, and closed-end investment companies. The day-to-day price change of each security is weighted by the security's market value.

Amivest Liquidity Ratio A measure of liquidity calculated as the dollar volume of trading associated with a 1% change in the price of a security.

amortize To write off gradually and systematically a given amount of money within a specific number of time periods. For example, an accountant amortizes the cost of a long-term asset by deducting a portion of that cost against income in each period. Likewise, an investor will usually amortize the premium each year on a bond purchased at a price above its principal.

AMT —See ALTERNATIVE MINIMUM TAX.

analyst —See FINANCIAL ANALYST.

A-network —See NETWORK A.

angel investor A wealthy investor who provides capital for new business ventures.

animals Zero-coupon receipts on U.S. Treasury securities that have been repackaged and sold to investors under names such as CATS®️, TIGR^{SM}, and LIONS. —Also called *felines*. —See also COUPON STRIPPING.

annualized Of or relating to a variable that has been mathematically converted to a yearly rate. Inflation and interest rates are generally annualized since it is on this basis that these two variables are ordinarily stated and compared. As an example, disregarding the effects of compounding, the earning of a 3% return on an investment during a 4-month period is equal to 9% ($^{12}/_4 \times 3\%$) on an annualized basis.

annual meeting The annual gathering of a corporation's directors, officers, and shareholders during which new directors are elected, shareholder resolutions are passed or defeated, and operating and financial results of the past fiscal year are discussed.

annual report A firm's annual statement of operating and financial results. The annual report contains an income statement, a balance sheet, a statement of changes in financial position, an auditor's report, and a summary of operations. Because many annual reports are prepared with public relations as a primary focus, serious investors should obtain a copy of a firm's 10–K in order to obtain detailed financial data.

annuitant   The recipient of an annuity.

annuitize   To convert a sum of money into a series of payments. For example, an investor may pay a sum of money in return for a lifetime series of monthly payments.

annuity   A stream of equal payments to an individual, such as to a retiree, that occur at predetermined intervals (that is, monthly or annually). The payments may continue for a fixed period or for a contingent period, such as for the recipient's lifetime. Although annuities are most often associated with insurance companies and retirement programs, the payment of interest to a bondholder is also an example of an annuity. —See also ANNUITY CERTAIN; CONTINGENT ANNU-ITY; DEFERRED ANNUITY; FIXED ANNUITY; JOINT AND SURVIVOR ANNUITY; REFUND ANNU-ITY; STRAIGHT LIFE ANNUITY; TAX-SHELTERED ANNUITY; VARIABLE ANNUITY.

annuity bond   —See CONSOL.

annuity certain   An annuity that provides a fixed number of payments. If the annuitant dies prior to the completion of the contract, payments continue to the annuitant's designated beneficiary.

annuity due   An annuity in which payments are made at the beginning of each period. —Compare ORDINARY ANNUITY.

antidilution clause   A stipulation of virtually every convertible security that requires an adjustment to the conversion terms in the event of certain occurrences, such as stock splits, stock dividends, and new stock issues, that would dilute the value of the conversion privilege. As an example, a bond convertible into 40 shares of stock would have its terms changed to conversion into 120 shares if the stock split 3 for 1.

antidilutive   Of or relating to the conversion of convertible securities into common stock when such conversion would result in an increase in diluted earnings per share or a decrease in diluted loss per share. For example, it is an antidilutive conversion if outstanding warrants are assumed to be exercised in order to acquire shares of common stock at a higher price than the market price of the stock. Such a conversion would result in an increase in diluted earnings per share. Conversions that would increase earnings per share or reduce loss per share are not generally used in calculating diluted earnings per share.

antigreenmail provision   A provision in a firm's charter that prohibits management from purchasing a large shareholder's stock at a premium price without extending the same offer to other shareholders. —Compare GREENMAIL.

antitakeover measure   An action by a firm's management to block or halt a takeover by another party. Examples of antitakeover measures include a fair price amendment, staggered terms of office for directors, and a requirement for an increased number of affirmative votes from shareholders to approve a takeover. —See also SHOW STOPPER.

antitakeover statute   A state law that makes it easier for a firm based in that state to fend off a takeover hostile to the firm's management. Such a statute may actually penalize shareholders since acquisition-minded firms or individuals may be less likely to make an offer for the firm's stock.

antitrust laws Federal and state statutes designed to promote competition among businesses. Antitrust laws in the United States originated from the laissez-faire excesses that took place in the early 1900s. Effectiveness of antitrust laws is heavily dependent upon enforcement by the powers in charge—primarily the U.S. Justice Department. Thus, the success of antitrust laws has varied. —See also CELLER-KEFAUVER ANTIMERGER ACT; CLAYTON ACT; FEDERAL TRADE COMMISSION ACT OF 1914; SHERMAN ANTITRUST ACT.

any-and-all bid An offer to purchase all shares offered at a specified price until a predetermined date. A firm may make an any-and-all bid for the shares of a company it intends to acquire. —Compare TWO-TIER TENDER OFFER.

APB —See ACCOUNTING PRINCIPLES BOARD.

APB opinion A determination by the former Accounting Principles Board regarding the way a certain financial transaction is to be treated for reporting purposes. For example, APB Opinion 15 sets forth the ways in which convertible issues and common-stock equivalents are to be used in calculating earnings per share. In 1973 the Accounting Principles Board was superseded by the Financial Accounting Standards Board, thereby halting further APB opinions and initiating FASB Statements.

application of funds statement —See STATEMENT OF CASH FLOWS.

appraisal right The right of minority shareholders to obtain an independent valuation of their shares to determine a fair value in a two-tier tender offer. —See also FAIR PRICE AMENDMENT.

appreciation 1. An increase in value, as of an asset. 2. —Used to distinguish between securities that are likely to provide profits because of increases in price and those that provide dividend payments.

approved list —See LEGAL LIST.

arb —See ARBITRAGEUR.

arbitrage The simultaneous purchase and sale of substantially identical assets in order to profit from a price difference between the two assets. As a hypothetical example, if General Electric common stock trades at $45 on the New York Stock Exchange and at $44.50 on the Philadelphia Stock Exchange, an investor could guarantee a profit by purchasing the stock on the Philadelphia Stock Exchange and simultaneously selling the same amount of stock on the NYSE. Of course, the price difference must be sufficiently great to offset commissions. Arbitrage may be employed by using various security combinations including stock and options and convertibles and stock. —See also BASIS TRADING; RISK ARBITRAGE.

arbitrage bond A municipal bond issued for the purpose of investing the proceeds in securities with higher yields than those paid by the municipal bond. Generally, the arbitrage involves purchasing U.S. Treasury bonds that are used to prerefund an outstanding issue prior to the outstanding issue's call date.

arbitrage pricing theory A mathematical theory for explaining security values that holds that the return on an investment is a function of the investment's sensitivity to various common risk factors such as inflation and unemployment.

arbitrageur One who engages in arbitrage. —Also called *arb*.

arbitration A process for settling disputes between securities firms or between securities firms and their customers in which the parties submit their differences to the judgment of an impartial third party or parties. Many brokerage firms require their customers to sign an agreement for binding arbitration to resolve disputes. The agreement requires the customer to accept the arbitrator's decision and to waive the right to subsequent legal action. Pressure from the SEC and a 1990 court decision now allows investors the option of using an independent arbitration panel in place of a securities-industry panel. —Compare MEDIATION. —See also NASD DISPUTE RESOLUTION, INC.

arbitration panel   A group of individuals charged with resolving a dispute between individuals and/or organizations. Arbitration panels to resolve investment disputes are sponsored by self-regulatory organizations such as NASD.

ArcaEx —See ARCHIPELAGO.

Archipelago   An electronic communications network formed in 1996 as one of the four original ECNs approved by the SEC. The network offers what is essentially a national and visible limit order book for stocks. In 2001 Archipelago received SEC approval to launch Archipelago Exchange (ArcaEx), an electronic stock market for New York Stock Exchange, American Stock Exchange, and Nasdaq securities. ArcaEx is operated as a regulated facility of the Pacific Exchange.

Arizona Stock Exchange (AZX)   An electronic exchange for the online trading of NYSE, Nasdaq, and AMEX stocks. The exchange attempts to balance bids and offers to find a consensus price in scheduled daily auctions. All successful participants in a particular auction receive the same price.

Arms Short-Term Trading Index (TRIN)   A short-term technical index that indicates the strength of the volume of advancing stocks relative to that of declining stocks. TRIN is calculated as

$$\frac{\text{advances/declines}}{\text{up volume/down volume}}$$

An index reading of greater than one indicates more activity in declining stocks.

arrearage   An overdue payment. —See also DIVIDENDS IN ARREARS.

articles of incorporation   The document that a firm files with state authorities when establishing a corporation. This document contains the firm's name and address, the type and amount of stock to be authorized and issued, the type of business activity, a delineation of corporate powers, and other information. —Also called *charter; corporate charter.*

ascending tops   In technical analysis, a chart pattern indicating the up and down movement of a security's price and characterized by progressively higher peaks on each upturn. This pattern is considered bullish. Refer to *Technical Analysis Chart Patterns* section for an example of this chart. —Compare DESCENDING TOPS.

ascending triangle   In technical analysis, a triangle-shaped chart pattern indicating price breaks during periods of high- and low-volume trading and characterized by a left side that is nearly vertical, a top that is nearly horizontal, and a third side that slopes upward and to the right to connect with the left side and the top. This pattern is considered to be a bullish indicator especially when the price breaks upward through the top side on high volume. Refer to *Technical*

Analysis Chart Patterns section for an example of this chart. —Compare DE-SCENDING TRIANGLE.

ASE —See AMERICAN STOCK EXCHANGE®.

Asian option An option with a payoff that depends on the average price of the underlying asset during a period of time during the life of the option.

ask The price at which a security is offered for sale. —See also BEST ASK. —Compare BID 1. —Also called *offer*.

assay A test to determine the purity of gold, silver, or other precious metals. Metals used for delivery of futures contracts must be assayed to verify that they meet standards established by the exchange on which the contracts trade.

asset Something of monetary value that is owned by a firm or an individual. Assets are listed on a firm's balance sheet and include tangible items such as inventories, equipment, and real estate as well as intangible items such as property rights or goodwill. —Compare LIABILITY. —See also CURRENT ASSET; INTANGIBLE ASSET; TANGIBLE ASSET.

asset allocation The assignment of investment funds to broad categories of assets. For example, an individual allocates funds to bonds and equities. Likewise, an investment manager may allocate clients' funds to common stocks representing various industries.

asset allocation fund An investment company that varies the proportion of its portfolio devoted to stocks, bonds, and money market securities in order to reduce the variability of returns and to take better advantage of different segments of the securities markets. An asset allocation fund is designed to save individual investors from being required to alter their investment mix in response to changes in market conditions.

asset-backed security A debt security collateralized by specific assets. Although the term applies to any debt backed by identified assets, it generally refers to securities backed by short-term collateral such as credit-card receivables, car loans, and home-equity loans. Because even the most financially strapped companies can hold valuable assets, it is possible for the credit quality of asset-backed securities to be substantially better than the general credit of the company issuing the securities.

---

asset allocation

Should I expect my asset allocation plan to remain largely unchanged throughout my preretirement years, or should I anticipate occasional large-scale restructuring?

You should expect only modest shifts in your asset allocation during your working years. Two components combine to create an asset allocation plan: your own financial situation and risk tolerance, coupled with historic and expected investment performance by asset class. Unless one of these components changes dramatically, there should be only modest adjustments in your allocation. The kinds of personal change that can trigger significant allocation changes are marriage, divorce, disability, birth of children, or employment or income change. Major changes in inflation, interest rates, or unforeseen social or political shocks are the type of economic events that could trigger broad allocation shifts.

Mark G. Steinberg, President, Trabar Associates, Boston, MA

asset class   A category of investments, such as cash, near money, common equities, fixed income, international equities, and so forth.

asset management account   A comprehensive brokerage account that includes checking, a credit or debit card, margin loans, and the automatic sweep of cash balances into a money market fund. Examples of brokerage asset management accounts include Cash Management Account® by Merrill Lynch (the first firm to offer this type account), Financial Management Account® by Smith Barney, and Schwab One® by Charles Schwab. Features and fees vary by firm. —Also called *central assets account; sweep account.*

asset play   A stock with a market price considerably lower than the value of the firm's assets on a per-share basis. For example, a paper company may operate in an extremely competitive market and earn minimal profits. However, a financial analyst may believe investors are concentrating on poor earnings and are pricing the stock in a manner that does not consider extensive and valuable timber and real estate holdings and thus does not reflect the stock's current market price. Thus, the stock is an asset play.

asset redeployment   The reallocation of underused assets in an attempt to make a firm more profitable. To effect an asset redeployment, a company might sell a relatively unprofitable subsidiary and use the funds to strengthen another part of its business. Many corporate takeover attempts are based on the premise that assets will be redeployed once the acquisition has been completed.

asset stripping   The sale of selected assets of an acquired company generally for the purpose of raising money to pay off some of the debt incurred in financing the acquisition.

asset turnover   —See TOTAL ASSET TURNOVER.

asset value   —Used to refer to the stock of a company, especially a stock whose price does not necessarily reflect the full value of the firm's assets. This situation may occur when the assets are not producing much current income.   —See also ASSET PLAY.

assign   To decide which writer of an option or futures contract (the party that is short the security) will be required to perform the terms of the contract. Clearing corporations and brokerage companies usually assign this responsibility in a random manner when the holders of the contracts ask for delivery of the asset specified in the contract.

assigned dealer   —See SPECIALIST.

assignment   The transfer of a registered security from one owner to another.

associate member   A firm that is permitted certain of the advantages of membership on the American Stock Exchange but does not actually own a seat. Although an associate member may place orders through regular members, such a member is not permitted to trade for its own account on the exchange floor. —Compare REGULAR MEMBER.

Association for Investment Management and Research (AIMR)   An international nonprofit organization for investment practitioners and educators. AIMR was founded in 1990 from a merger of the Financial Analysts Federation and the Institute of Chartered Financial Analysts. The AIMR is charged with educating and examining investment managers and analysts while sustaining high standards of professional conduct.

at-risk rule A law that limits tax write-offs to the amount of money directly invested (and thus, at risk) in an asset. The purpose of an at-risk rule is to prohibit investors from deriving tax benefits that exceed the amount of money actually invested.

at-the-close order A specialized order to a broker in which the customer specifies that execution take place at the closing price of the day. In practice, execution is permitted during the 30-to-60-second period before the closing bell.

at-the-money Of or relating to a call or a put option that has a strike price equal to the price of the underlying asset.

at-the-opening order A specialized order to a broker in which the customer specifies that execution take place at the opening price of the day.

auction market A market in which buyers and sellers gather to transact business through announced bid and ask prices. The organized securities exchanges are examples of auction markets. —Compare DEALER MARKET; OPEN OUTCRY.

auction-rate preferred stock A type of floating-rate preferred stock for which dividend payments are determined at periodic auctions conducted by the issuer rather than by short-term interest rates. —Compare REMARKETED PREFERRED STOCK.

audit An examination of an organization's financial documents in order to determine whether the records and reports are valid and the information is fairly presented. An independent audit is usually conducted by a Certified Public Accountant who then issues an opinion as to whether the statements accurately and fairly represent the firm's operations and financial position. —See also EXTERNAL AUDIT; INTERNAL AUDIT.

audit committee A subcommittee of a corporation's board of directors that selects the firm's external auditors. The audit committee is responsible for hiring the auditors, resolving disputes with the auditors, and evaluating and disclosing the auditors' reports.

audited statement A financial statement that is prepared according to generally accepted auditing standards. —Compare UNAUDITED STATEMENT.

auditor A person who examines an organization's financial records and reports. If the person is an employee of the organization being audited, he or she is known as an internal auditor. If the auditor is not an employee of the organization, he or she is called an external auditor.

auditor opinion —See OPINION.

audit trail A record of business transactions that can be used by an interested party to trace an organization's activities to original documents. Audit trails are used to verify account balances.

Autex An electronic network alerting broker-dealers to the interests of other broker-dealers in buying or selling large blocks of securities. For example, a broker may have an institutional customer interested in disposing of 100,000 shares of a stock. Rather than dumping such a large order on the exchange specialist, the broker could use the Autex system to determine whether other broker-dealers are interested in, or have customers interested in, acquiring that block of stock.

authority A government organization created to perform a certain function. A state or region, for example, may establish a public power authority to provide low-cost electricity to people living in a certain geographical area. The activities of an authority and its fundraising methods are ordinarily limited.

authority bond A bond issued by an authority and having interest and principal payable from revenues generated by the authority. The quality of an authority bond is only as good as the quality of the projects sponsored by the authority. —Compare REVENUE BOND.

authorization to transfer A form signed by a customer permitting a broker to transfer funds from the customer's segregated account to that customer's non-segregated account. The purpose of the transfer is usually to cover a shortage of funds in a margin account with funds that the customer has in a separate account.

authorized capital stock The number of shares of capital stock that a business may issue. Authorized capital stock is stated in a firm's articles of incorporation; changes in it may occur only if approved by the stockholders. The number of shares authorized often greatly exceeds the number actually issued. In this way, management can issue more shares to raise additional funds, or it can use the shares to make an acquisition. —Also called *shares authorized.*

Automated Bond System A computerized system of the New York Stock Exchange information that allows for automated trading of bonds listed on the exchange. This system handles most of the bond volume on the NYSE.

Automated Search and Match A New York Stock Exchange system designed to uncover individual affiliations that might indicate possible insider trading. The system contains public data on approximately 500,000 business executives and 75,000 companies and subsidiaries.

automated stock trading The trading of securities without the direct assistance of a broker or specialist. Generally, automated stock trading involves investor trading of securities via computer. Security bid and ask prices are listed and are continually updated with executions occurring automatically when the orders are entered. Although fully automated trading has been restricted primarily to professional and institutional investors, an increasing number of brokerage firms are now offering some automation for individual investors. —Compare SMALL ORDER EXECUTION SYSTEM. —Also called *computerized investing.*

automatic dividend reinvestment —See DIVIDEND REINVESTMENT PLAN.

automatic exercise Exercise of an in-the-money option following expiration unless the holder issues instructions to the contrary.

automatic reinvestment The automatic purchase of additional shares of an open-end investment company using any dividends and capital gains distributions that are made by the firm. This option (in lieu of actually receiving payments) permits a mutual fund shareholder to increase his or her holdings in the fund. Taxes must be paid on the amount reinvested even though no funds are received directly. —See also DIVIDEND REINVESTMENT PLAN.

automatic withdrawal A feature of some mutual funds that allows a shareholder to specify that the fund remit fixed payments at periodic intervals. The payments are composed of dividends, interest, and capital gains received by the fund, and, if these are insufficient, liquidation of some shares owned by the shareholder.

AUTOPER An electronic trading and reporting system used by the American Stock Exchange for small orders. AUTOPER allows a specialist to execute an order and report the trade automatically.

available asset A person's or a firm's asset that is not being used as collateral for a loan and is therefore available for general use or for sale.

average —See AVERAGES.

average collection period —See COLLECTION PERIOD.

average cost A cost amount calculated by dividing the total cost by the units of production. Thus, if a firm produces 10,000 units of output for a total cost of $25,000, the average cost of each unit is $25,000/10,000 units, or $2.50 per unit. Average cost is made up of costs remaining unchanged throughout a range of output and costs varying directly with output. Firms with the lowest average cost in an industry have a competitive advantage in the event of severe competition and price cutting.

average-cost method **1.** A method of determining the value of an inventory by calculating unit cost, that is, the result obtained by dividing the total cost of goods available for sale by the number of units available for sale. —See also INVENTORY VALUATION. **2.** A method of valuing the cost basis of securities that are sold in order to determine the gain or loss for tax purposes. Average cost is calculated as total cost of shares owned divided by the number of shares owned. The average-cost method is particularly useful for shares acquired at varying prices in a reinvestment plan.

average daily volume The number of shares or bonds traded daily, on average, during a period of time, generally one year. Average daily volume serves as a basis to determine if trading in a security is unusually heavy.

average down To purchase shares of the same security at successively lower prices in order to reduce the average price at which the stock was acquired. If an investor buys 100 shares of Disney common stock at $40 per share and the price subsequently falls to $30 per share, the purchase of an additional 100 shares would average down the investor's cost to $35 per share. Opponents of this strategy argue that the investor is simply throwing good money after bad and would be better advised to sell the stock, having realized that a mistake had been made to begin with. —Compare AVERAGE UP.

average life —See HALF-LIFE.

average maturity The average time to maturity of all the debt securities held in a portfolio. A relatively short average maturity results in smaller price fluctuations in response to changes in market rates of interest. A short average maturity subjects the owner of a debt portfolio to the risk that maturing debt will be replaced with debt carrying a lower interest rate. Average maturity is an important consideration for investors who hold bond and money market funds.

averages Stock price measures that are calculated and distributed by a number of organizations including Dow Jones, Standard & Poor's, and organized securities exchanges. The two major stock price measures are the Dow Jones Averages and the S&P 500. —Also called *average; market averages; market index; stock average.* —See also INDEX.

average up To purchase shares of the same security at successively higher prices. When averaging up, the investor accumulates an increasingly larger position in a security while keeping the average cost of the position lower than the security's current market price. Such an investor will earn significant profits only if the stock price continues to rise. The investor will suffer substantial losses if the stock price quickly drops after he or she has established a large position at increasingly higher prices. —Compare AVERAGE DOWN.

averaging —See DOLLAR-COST AVERAGING.

away —Used to refer to a market, quotation, or trade not originating with a particular dealer. For example, a dealer quoting a stock at 15 away would be quoting a price that comes from a different market maker.

away from the market —Used to refer to a security order at a price not immediately available. A limit order to buy 100 shares of Intel at $37 is away from the market if Intel stock is currently trading at $41 per share.

AZX —See ARIZONA STOCK EXCHANGE.

B

b —Used in the dividend column of stock transaction tables in newspapers to indicate payment of a stock dividend in addition to the indicated cash dividend: *1.50b.*

B A low, speculative grade assigned to a debt obligation by a rating agency. Such a rating indicates there is considerable uncertainty as to the ability to pay interest and repay principal over a long period.

Ba —See BB.

Baa —See BBB.

Baby Bell One of several integrated-communications providers that were formerly part of AT&T but became independent in 1984 following AT&T's court-ordered divestiture. The seven original Baby Bells were once operating subsidiaries of AT&T that provided local and intrastate long-distance service.

baby bond A bond that has a principal amount under $1,000. Baby bonds may be issued by firms hoping to attract investors who do not have funds to purchase bonds with $1,000 principal. On occasion, bonds of less than $1,000 principal are issued as part of a corporate refunding. Because baby bonds are unusual, they may be more expensive to trade.

backdoor borrowing Borrowing by a public authority without voter approval. Public authorities often use backdoor borrowing when voters reject proposed debt issues. Taxpayer funds are used to repay debt accumulated in backdoor borrowing.

backdoor listing Acquisition and merger with a listed company by an unlisted company in order to gain a listing on a securities exchange.

backdating The practice of allowing a mutual fund shareholder to use previous purchases of the fund's shares so as to qualify for reduced commission charges on subsequent purchases. Backdating is used when a fund offers declining proportional sales charges on larger purchases.

back-end load —See DEFERRED SALES CHARGE.

back-end value The amount paid to remaining shareholders in the last stage of a two-tier tender offer.

back fee Payment made by the owner of a compound option to the owner of the underlying option when the compound option is exercised. —Compare FRONT FEE.

backing away The failure of a market maker to honor a previous bid for a minimum quantity of a security. The National Association of Securities Dealers considers backing away to be unethical.

back month —See FURTHEST OUT.

back office The physical location within a business where records are kept and processed. In the case of a brokerage firm, the back office includes the section where individual account records are kept, checks are processed, and security certificates are sent. —Also called *operations department.*

back testing Using historical data to determine the relationship of specific variables. For example, a researcher might use historical data to determine if changes in the money supply have influenced changes in stock prices. This relationship, if positive, can be used to develop an investment policy.

back up To swap a debt security with one maturity for another security with a shorter maturity.

backup withholding Compulsory withholding from payments to an investor in order to take care of a potential tax liability. Payments of interest, dividends, and proceeds from a sale of securities are subject to backup withholding when certain requirements are not met, including if the investor fails to provide a correct taxpayer identification number (TIN) or if dividends and interest have been underreported.

backwardation —See INVERTED MARKET.

bad delivery The delivery of a security that fails to meet all the standards required to transfer title to the buyer. —Compare GOOD DELIVERY.

bail out To sell a security, generally at a loss, in anticipation of a further price decline.

bailout The financial rescue of a faltering business or other organization. Government guarantees for loans made to Chrysler Corporation constituted a bailout.

bailout bond U.S. government-guaranteed debt issued by the Resolution Funding Corporation to pay for the rescue of bankrupt savings and loan associations.

balanced budget A budget in which the expenditures incurred during a given period are matched by revenues.

balanced fund An investment company that spreads its investments among stocks and bonds. Essentially, a balanced fund is a middle-of-the-road fund made up of investments that will achieve both moderate income and moderate capital growth.

balance of payments The record of money payments between one country and other countries. Balance of payments is more inclusive than balance of trade because balance of payments comprises foreign investment, loans, and other cash flows as well as payments for goods and services. A country's balance of payments has a significant effect on its currency value in relation to other currencies. It is of particular interest to individuals who own foreign investments or who own domestic investments in companies dependent upon exports.

balance of trade A net figure calculated by subtracting a country's imports from its exports during a specific period. If a country sells more goods and services than it purchases, its balance of trade is said to be positive, that is, exports exceed imports. Such a balance is generally considered to be favorable. Conversely, a negative balance is said to be unfavorable. A country's balance-of-trade position has great impact on its economic activity and on the profits of companies operating within it. —See also TRADE DEFICIT; TRADE SURPLUS.

balance sheet The financial statement of a business or institution that lists the assets, debts, and owners' investment as of a specific date. Assets are ordered according to how soon they will be converted into cash, and debts according to how soon they must be paid. Because balance sheets do not list items at their current monetary value, they may greatly overstate or understate the real value of certain corporate assets and liabilities. —Also called *statement of financial condition; statement of financial position.* —See also CONSOLIDATED BALANCE SHEET.

balloon interest A higher interest rate received on the longer maturity bonds of a serial bond issue.

balloon payment A final loan payment that is significantly larger than the payments preceding it. For example, a bond issuer may redeem 3% of the original issue each year for 20 years and then retire the remaining 40% in the year of maturity.

BAN —See BOND ANTICIPATION NOTE.

bandit —See SOES BANDIT.

bank-discount basis A method of calculating the quoted yield on a debt security. In a bank-discount basis calculation, the amount of discount from face value is divided by the security's face value and the result is annualized. For example, a $10,000 face-amount bond due in two months and selling for $9,900 would be quoted at ($100/$10,000) (360/60), or 6%. While this is a common way of quoting yields on certain securities such as Treasury bills and commercial paper, it actually understates the effective rate paid. —Also called *discount basis; discount yield.* —See also EQUIVALENT BOND YIELD.

banker's acceptance A short-term credit instrument created by a nonfinancial firm and guaranteed by a bank as to payment. Acceptances are traded at discounts from face value in the secondary market on the basis of the credit quality of the guaranteeing banks. These instruments have become a popular investment for money market funds. —Also called *acceptance.*

bank-grade —See INVESTMENT-GRADE.

bank holding company A corporation that owns the stock of one or more banks and thus exercises control over the bank or banks. —See also HOLDING COMPANY.

Banking Act of 1933 —See GLASS-STEAGALL ACT.

Bank Insurance Fund The federal fund administered by the Federal Deposit Insurance Corporation, which insures the deposits of individuals who invest at banks that are members of the Federal Reserve System. This includes all national banks and state banks that choose to join the Fed. The fund was created in 1989 in order to separate the insurance funds for commercial banks from those that insure thrift institutions.

bank line —See LINE OF CREDIT.

bank note Currency issued and guaranteed by a bank. The sole issuer of bank notes in the United States is the Federal Reserve Bank.

bankruptcy The financial status of a firm that has been legally judged either to have debts that exceed assets or to be unable to pay its bills. Formal bankruptcy may result in reorganization and continued operation of the firm or it may require liquidation and distribution of the proceeds. In either case, most security owners, especially shareholders, are likely to suffer losses. Stock transaction tables indicate that a company is in bankruptcy proceedings by appending *vi* or *q* immediately before the name of the stock. —See also CHAPTER 7; CHAPTER 11; REORGANIZATION.

Banks for Cooperatives (COOP) Twelve regional, privately owned, government-sponsored banks that make loans to farm cooperatives. The loans are financed primarily by the sale of debt securities issued by the Federal Farm Credit Bank.

barbell portfolio A bond portfolio heavily weighted with long and short maturities but few intermediate maturities. Bonds with short maturities provide liquidity, and those with long maturities offer higher yields.

bar chart In technical analysis, a chart pattern indicating the activity of an economic variable, usually a stock price, over time (plotted on the horizontal axis) compared with the value of that variable throughout the same period of time (plotted on the vertical axis). In a bar chart of a stock price, the high and low prices for the period are connected by a vertical line. A short horizontal slash is often drawn across the bar at the closing price. Bar charts are the graphs most frequently used by technicians. Refer to the *Technical Analysis Chart Patterns* section for an example of this chart. —Compare POINT-AND-FIGURE CHART. —Also called *vertical line chart*. —See also LINE CHART; CANDLESTICK CHART.

barometer An indicator of fluctuations. For example, the S&P 500 is a barometer for stock market movements. Likewise, long-term interest rates are a barometer of inflationary expectations.

Barron's Confidence Index A confidence indicator calculated by dividing the yield on intermediate-grade bonds into the yield on high-grade bonds. A rising ratio indicates investors are demanding a lower premium in yield for increased risk, thus expressing confidence in the economy and the securities markets. A rising index is considered bullish for stocks; a falling index is considered bearish for stocks. —Compare STANDARD & POOR'S CONFIDENCE INDICATOR.

base period The time or period of time on which an index is based. Usually, the index is established at a value of 10 or 100 in the base year. The consumer price index of 177 in early 2002 indicated that consumer prices were 77% higher than during the base period of 1982–84. The Standard & Poor's 500 Stock Index of 1300 in early March 2002 indicated that, on average, a portfolio of blue chip stocks with a market value of $10 during the period 1941–43 (the base period) had a market value of $1,300 in early 2002. The portfolio of stocks making up the S&P 500 underwent substantial changes during the intervening years.

basic earnings per share   Net income less preferred stock dividends during a given period, divided by the average number of shares of common stock outstanding during that period. —Compare DILUTED EARNINGS PER SHARE. —See also DUAL PRESENTATION.

basis **1.** In futures trading, the difference between the futures price and the spot price. The basis will narrow as a contract moves closer to settlement. **2.** In taxation, the acquisition cost of an asset adjusted for capital distributions (that is, stock dividends). A security's basis is used in calculating gains and losses for tax purposes. —Also called *cost basis; tax basis.* —See also ADJUSTED BASIS.

basis book   A book of tables giving conversions to equivalent dollar prices for bond yields having given maturity lengths and coupon rates. —Also called *bond basis book.*

basis grade   The specified grade for a commodity necessary for it to be acceptable for delivery on a futures contract.

basis point   A value equaling one one-hundredth of a percent ($1/100$ of 1%). Basis point is used to measure yield differences among bonds. For example, there is a 30 basis point difference between two bonds if one yields 10.3% and the other yields 10.6%.

⌁ CASE STUDY | On May 9, 2001, WorldCom, Inc., issued $11.9 billion of bonds in what at the time was the largest corporate debt issue in U.S. history. WorldCom's bond issue exceeded by $3.3 billion the previous largest issue, by Ford Motor Company two years earlier. Most of the proceeds from the WorldCom bond issue were to be used to pay down short-term debt, including $6 billion of commercial paper. The entire issue, which included maturities of 3 years, 10 years, and 30 years, was sold at an average interest cost of 7.6%. The 3-year bonds were sold to yield 6.566%, while the 10-year and 30-year bonds sold to yield 7.659% and 8.250%, respectively. The 30-year portion, maturing in May 2031, sold at a premium of 259 basis points, or 2.59 percentage points, above the 30-year Treasury yield of 5.66%. The 259 basis-point premium to long-term Treasuries indicated the substantial credit risk assumed by investors who purchased WorldCom bonds. The WorldCom issue took place during a painful period for telecom companies, and the firm's common stock price had declined by over 60% in the year prior to the debt issue. Intense competition caused the company's long distance operation to become a particular problem. The bonds were rated BBB + by Standard & Poor's and A-3 by Moody's. Although the issue was a success, the firm's financial position continued to deteriorate, and a little more than a year later WorldCom was bankrupt.

basis price **1.** The price of a security quoted in terms of its yield rather than its dollar price. Bonds are often quoted on a basis price reflecting yield to maturity since such information is of greatest importance to an investor deciding to buy or sell. **2.** The price selected by a specialist at which to execute an odd-lot order on an inactive stock. The large spread on inactive stocks often results in a basis price that splits the difference between the bid and ask.

basis risk   The possibility that a commodity contract's basis will move against the investor. For example, an investor may buy a spot contract and sell short a higher-priced futures contract on the same commodity in expectation of a narrowing of the basis but may find that the basis widens instead.

basis trading An arbitrage operation in which an investor takes a long position in one type of security and a short position in a similar security in an attempt to profit from a change in the basis between the two securities. For example, an investor might purchase a call with an April expiration and simultaneously sell short a call with a different expiration or strike price on the same stock. The investor expects that the values of the two positions will change over time such that a profit will ensue. Basis trading is undertaken when the investor feels one security is priced too high or too low relative to the price of another security. Because of this, the profit on one side of the trade should more than cancel out the loss on the opposite side of the trade. Basis trading may involve an index or group of securities as well as individual securities. —Compare PROGRAM TRADING. —Also called *relationship trading.*

basket A preassembled group of securities. Baskets allow individual investors to acquire a group of securities with a single trade while paying one commission.

batch trading A trading system for securities in which orders accumulate and then, at specified times, are executed all at once. Batch trading in the U.S. securities markets only is used on opening transactions when orders received after the previous day's close are executed all at one time. —Compare CONTINUOUS TRADING.

BB A grade assigned to a debt obligation by a rating agency to indicate significant speculative elements and a moderate ability to pay interest and repay principal. —Also called *Ba.*

BBB A medium grade assigned to a debt obligation by a rating agency to indicate an adequate ability to pay interest and repay principal. However, adverse developments are more likely to impair this ability than would be the case for bonds rated A and above. A BBB rating is the lowest rating a bond can have and still be considered investment-grade. —Also called *Baa.*

BD form A document containing information on a firm's officers and capital that is filed by broker-dealers with the SEC.

BEACON A Boston Stock Exchange computerized system for automatically executing orders for stocks listed on any of the U.S. securities exchanges. Executions are made based on the prices posted in the consolidated market. —Also called *Boston Exchange Automated Communications Order-Routing Network.*

bear An investor who believes a security or some other asset or the security markets in general will follow a broad downward path. An investor can often be a bear on a particular security but not on the general market and vice versa. —Compare BULL.

bearer bond A debt instrument that does not have an owner name listed in the issuer's books or inscribed on the certificate. Because no record of ownership exists, bearer bonds are favored by investors who, illegally, want to avoid paying gift, estate, and local taxes. The issuance of new municipal bonds in bearer form was prohibited beginning in 1983. —Also called *coupon bond.* —See also COUPON CLIPPING.

bearer form —Used to refer to any security that, according to the books of the issuing organization, is not registered to an owner. Essentially, a security in

bearer form is owned by the person holding the security. —Compare REGIS-
TERED SECURITY.

bearer stock Securities ownership certificates that are not registered in a
name. As with other bearer securities, bearer stock is a negotiable certificate
that can be transferred between owners without endorsement. Bearer stock is
popular in Europe but not in the United States.

bear hug A buyout offer so favorable to stockholders of a company targeted for
acquisition that there is little likelihood they will refuse the offer. Not only does
a bear hug offer a price significantly above the market price of the target company's stock, but it is likely to offer cash payments as well. —See also TAKEOVER.

⋀ CASE STUDY Following rejection by the General Motors board of an
EchoStar Communications takeover proposal for GM-
controlled Hughes Electronics, owner of DirectTV, EchoStar soon made another surprise bid to acquire Hughes. At the time of the bid Hughes's equity
was trading on the New York Stock Exchange as a tracking stock. The second
bid, announced with a public letter addressed to the GM board, was a bear
hug offer made directly to Hughes's stockholders. Believing that General Motors directors were likely to recommend a sale of Hughes to Rupert Murdoch's
News Corp., EchoStar felt it could only be successful by offering a higher price
to Hughes's shareholders. The higher price would appeal to Hughes's shareholders and make it more difficult for GM directors to recommend a sale at a
lower price to another company. GM directors rejected the earlier EchoStar offer in part because they felt the combination of DirectTV and EchoStar would
be unacceptable on an antitrust basis. Rupert Murdoch later pulled out of the
bidding for Hughes.

bearish Of or relating to the belief that a particular stock or the market as a
whole is headed for a period of generally falling prices. —Compare BULLISH.

bear market An extended period of general price declines in an individual security or other asset, such as silver or real estate; a group of securities; or the
securities market as a whole. Nevertheless, even during widespread bear markets, it is possible to have bull markets in particular stocks or groups of stocks.
For example, stocks of gold-related companies often move against major trends
in the security markets. —Compare BULL MARKET.

bear raid A concerted effort to drive down the price of a stock by selling many
shares short. The bear raid was popular among speculators in the early 1900s.
Such a raid would frequently be accompanied by unfavorable rumors and sto-
ries about the target firm that would be planted in business publications. The
goal of the raid was to involve other investors in a selling stampede that would
drive the stock's price down to a bargain level.

bear spread In futures and options trading, a strategy in which one contract is
bought and a different contract is sold in such a manner that the person undertaking the spread makes a profit if the price of the underlying asset declines.
Two contracts are used in order to limit the size of the potential loss. An example of a bear spread is the purchase of a call option and the simultaneous sale
of another call option with a lower strike price and the same expiration date as
the option purchased. A fall in the price of the underlying stock will tend to decrease the value of each option. Because the option sold carried a higher price
than the option purchased, the investor could expect to make a profit equal to

the difference between the two options if a major price decline in the stock should occur. —Compare BULL SPREAD.

bear trap An accumulation of shares being sold short by bears trying to drive down the price of a stock. The bear trap occurs when the bears find they must repurchase the shares from an individual or a group at an artificial price determined by the seller.

beat the averages To obtain superior investment returns, generally on a risk-adjusted basis, compared with popular stock price averages such as the Dow Jones Industrial Average or the S&P 500. Professional portfolio managers are generally judged by their ability to beat the averages, although many studies indicate that it is virtually impossible to do so consistently on a risk-adjusted basis.

beginning inventory Goods available for sale at the beginning of an accounting period. —Compare ENDING INVENTORY.

bell The device that sounds to mark the open and close of each trading day on an organized securities exchange.

bells and whistles Special features that are added to ordinary investments to attract investors' attention. Examples of bells and whistles include put features on bonds and floating dividends on preferred stock. Often the value of the features is more apparent than real. —Also called *kickers; wrinkles.*

bellwether A security that tends to lead the market and signal the general direction of future price movements. An increasing price for a bellwether stock is considered a bullish signal for the overall stock market.

CASE STUDY | Securities maintain their bellwether status for varying periods of time. The common stock of General Motors Corporation was considered the stock market's bellwether for many years, until the American economy transitioned from manufacturing to computers and information management and GM's status was supplanted by the stock of International Business Machines. IBM stock's perch as a market bellwether was subsequently replaced by the common stocks of Microsoft and Cisco Systems, two major players in the new Internet economy. The 30-year Treasury bond served as the bond market's bellwether for nearly two decades, until the 10-year Treasury note took its place in the early 2000s. Unlike stocks that lost their status because of their company's products or services, the 30-year bonds were replaced as a benchmark because the U.S. government redeemed a large portion of its long-term debt, causing the 30-year bond to lose its important status in the bond market. The Treasury announced in late 2001 that sales of the 30-year Treasury bonds would be discontinued.

belly up Of, relating to, or being in bankruptcy. —Used of a firm.

below par Of or relating to a security that sells at less than face value or par value. For example, a $1,000 par bond with a market price of $850 is below par. Likewise, a $100 par preferred stock with a market price of $80 is below par. Fixed-income securities usually trade below par because market rates of interest are higher than they were when the securities were issued. —Compare ABOVE PAR. —See also DISCOUNT BOND.

benchmark A standard by which something is measured. For example, bond yields are generally compared to benchmark yields on U.S. Treasury securities of similar maturity. Mutual fund performance is often compared to changes in the Standard & Poor's 500 Stock Index.

beneficial owner   The owner of a security registered in another name. For example, investors often leave securities in trust with their brokerage firms. Although the brokerage firm is shown on the issuer's books as the owner of record, the investor is the beneficial owner.

Best, Alfred M. and Company   A firm that is widely recognized for its ratings of insurers. The highest Best rating for insurers is A + +, and some financial advisers suggest that individuals limit selections to companies rated A + + and A +. Other insurance-rating companies include Duff & Phelps, Moody's, Standard & Poor's, and Weiss.

best ask   The lowest quoted price at which a security is offered for sale.

best bid   The highest price that is being offered to purchase a security.

best-efforts basis   **1.** An agreement by an investment banker to do its best to oversee but not guarantee the sale of a security issue in the primary market. —See also UNDERWRITER.   **2.** An investor's market order to buy or sell a security in which the brokerage firm agrees to obtain the best possible price.

best-execution requirement   The obligation of broker-dealers and market makers to execute customer orders at the best available price.

beta   A mathematical measure of the sensitivity of rates of return on a portfolio or a given stock compared with rates of return on the market as a whole. A high beta (greater than 1.0) indicates moderate or high price volatility. A beta of 1.5 forecasts a 1.5% change in the return on an asset for every 1% change in the return on the market. High-beta stocks are best to own in a strong bull market but are worst to own in a bear market. —See also ALPHA; CAPITAL-ASSET PRICING MODEL; CHARACTERISTIC LINE; PORTFOLIO BETA.

bid   **1.** The price that a potential buyer is willing to pay for a security. —Compare ASK. —See also BEST BID.   **2.** An offer to purchase something.

bid-ask spread   —See SPREAD 3.

bid-to-cover ratio   At an auction of Treasury securities, the dollar amount of money being bid compared with the dollar amount of securities being auctioned. A high ratio indicates strong demand and is likely to strengthen the market prices of other fixed-income securities.

bid wanted (BW)   Notice given by a security owner that a security position is available for sale and that purchase offers will be considered. A bid wanted announcement is the initial step in seeking an interested buyer with the final price to be negotiated later.

Big Bang   The date, October 27, 1986, on which the London security markets were significantly deregulated. The deregulation eliminated fixed commissions on security trades and put an end to the prohibition against securities firms acting as brokers and dealers.

Big Blue   A widely used reference to the firm, International Business Machines Corporation. The term derives from the company's logo, usually appearing in blue.

Big Board   A widely used reference to the New York Stock Exchange.

Big Four   A widely used reference to the four largest public accounting firms that perform most of the external audits in the United States for large publicly owned corporations. The Big Four include PricewaterhouseCoopers, Deloitte Touche Tohmatsu, Ernst & Young, and KPMG. The group was long known as the Big Eight until it was reduced by mergers; it was called the Big Five until the Enron scandal led to the collapse of Arthur Andersen.

BIGS An acronym for a type of municipal convertible bond.

Big Three A widely used reference to the three major automobile manufacturers in the United States: Chrysler Division of DaimlerChrysler, Ford, and General Motors.

bill 1. A Treasury bill. 2. —See DUE BILL.

black Of or relating to the profitability of a firm or the operations of a firm. The term derives from the color of ink used to enter a profit figure on a financial statement. —Compare RED.

Black and Scholes Model A relatively complicated mathematical formula for valuing stock options. The Black and Scholes Model is used in options pricing to determine whether a particular option should be selling at a price other than the one at which it currently trades.

black-box accounting Accounting methodology so complex that financial statements are nearly impossible to accurately interpret. Black-box accounting may be used to obscure unfavorable information.

Black Friday A widely used reference to September 24, 1869, the date on which stock market operator Jay Gould nearly cornered the gold market. Although eventually broken by government selling of the metal, the corner resulted in massive failures on Wall Street. Gould made considerable profits on the manipulation, but his brokers declared bankruptcy.

Black Monday A widely used reference to October 19, 1987, the day the Dow Jones Industrial Average dropped a record 508 points, or nearly 23%. Disarray in the financial markets resulted from a combination of trade deficits, budget deficits, and potential government regulation of mergers and issuance of junk bonds.

blackout period 1. The time period prior to the release of financial information during which certain employees of a public company are prohibited from trading in the firm's stock. —See also WINDOW PERIOD. 2. —See LOCKDOWN.

Black Thursday A widely used reference to October 24, 1929, the date on which security prices plunged, producing one of the most memorable days in the history of the New York Stock Exchange. During that Thursday afternoon, Richard Whitney, who was then vice president of the exchange, went to the floor with large buy orders in a successful attempt to stem the decline. Unfortunately, his success was short-lived.

Black Tuesday A widely used reference to October 29, 1929, the date of the greatest frenzy on the New York Stock Exchange during the Great Crash. Security prices plunged, volume surged to more than 16 million shares, and the ticker tape ran hours behind trading on the floor.

blank-check company A company that issues penny stock in order to finance its involvement in establishing a business in which principal operations have not yet commenced. The company either has no business plan or plans to engage in a merger or acquisition with an unspecified business entity. Essentially, the company is given a blank check with regard to investors' money. Blank-check companies are required to provide certain information prior to and after the registration of securities. In addition, funds received from a penny stock offering must be placed in an escrow account for the benefit of the purchaser. —See also RULE 419.

blanket bond —See BLANKET FIDELITY BOND.

blanket certification form —See FORM FR-1.

blanket fidelity bond A type of insurance that protects against losses from employee actions such as forgery or unauthorized trading. —Also called *blanket bond; fidelity bond.*

blanket recommendation A recommendation to buy or sell a security that is sent by a brokerage firm to all its customers. Firms do not consider individual investors' objectives before sending out a blanket recommendation.

blank stock Stock for which voting powers, preferences, and rights are determined by the issuer's board of directors after the shares have been purchased by subscribers.

blended price The weighted average price paid to shareholders in a two-tier tender offer. For example, if 60% of shares are purchased for $20 each and the remaining 40% of shares are acquired for $15 each, the blended price is (.60)$20 + (.40)$15, or $18.

blind bid An offer to purchase a basket of stocks without knowing exactly which stocks are included in the basket. Portfolio managers utilize blind bids when they risk affecting the market prices of stocks they buy and sell.

blind pool An investment vehicle that raises capital from the public without telling investors how their funds will be utilized. These pools are sometimes used to acquire and convert private companies into public companies without going through a lengthy registration process. Blind pools are risky investments in which investors should pay particular attention to the background and knowledge of the promoters and officers. Shares in these investment vehicles are often sold to the public at relatively low prices.

block A large amount of a security, usually 10,000 shares or more.

blocked account —See RESTRICTED ACCOUNT.

blockholder The owner of a large proportion of ownership shares of a company.

block house A brokerage firm that specializes in assisting with trades of blocks of securities. Block houses generally work with institutional clients such as mutual funds and pension funds that take large security positions.

---

blanket recommendation

Are blanket recommendations sent to investors in a timely enough manner to be effective?

Blanket recommendations for a specific security usually have been significantly diluted by the time the client receives a mailing from the brokerage firm. In most cases, the recommended security should be looked at as a long-term play rather than as a trading vehicle.

George Riles, First Vice President and Resident Manager, Merrill Lynch, Albany, GA

block positioner A securities dealer who is willing to take a large long or short position in a stock or bond. The block positioner expects to profit on a position by selling at a price higher than the one at which the block was purchased but will often hedge by using arbitrage or options.

block trade A trade of a block of shares that is most likely to occur between two institutions because of the large amount of money involved.

blotter An accounting book of original entry used in the back office of brokerage firms for recording clearings, fails, trades, and so forth.

blowout The nearly immediate sale of a new security issue because of great investor demand. —See also HOT ISSUE.

blue chip A very high quality investment involving a lower-than-average risk of loss of principal or reduction in income. The term is generally used to refer to securities of companies having a long history of sustained earnings and dividend payments.

Blue Room A relatively small trading room on the floor of the New York Stock Exchange that is adjacent to the main trading room and contains three posts.

blue skying —Used to refer to the determination of whether a new issue of securities meets the requirements for distribution in the various states where the issue will be sold.

blue sky laws State regulations that cover the offering and sale of securities within state boundaries. Although the laws differ among states, most include provisions relating to fraudulent activities and the licensing of individuals who sell securities. The term derives from an effort to protect investors from unwittingly buying a piece of "blue sky."

B-network —See NETWORK B.

board broker An employee of the Chicago Board Options Exchange who handles option orders that cannot be immediately executed because of price limits away from the current market price.

board of arbitration A group of three to five people selected to arbitrate disputes between securities firms. The board's rulings are final for disputes in which both parties have agreed to arbitration.

board of directors The group of people responsible for supervising the affairs of a corporation. The board of directors generally sets broad corporate policy rather than participating in day-to-day managerial decisions, although selection of the chief executive officer is the board's responsibility. Members are elected by the firm's stockholders and may or may not be stockholders themselves. —See also CHAIRMAN; CLASSIFIED BOARD; INSIDE DIRECTOR; INTERLOCKING DIRECTORATES; OUTSIDE DIRECTOR; STAGGERED TERMS.

board of governors **1.** An elected body composed of members of a stock exchange that oversees the affairs of the exchange. **2.** A group of people appointed by the President of the United States to the Federal Reserve to oversee the nation's money system. Decisions by the board have great impact on the securities markets. —See also FEDERAL OPEN MARKET COMMITTEE.

board-out clause A provision that permits a firm's board of directors to decide whether to enforce a supermajority antitakeover amendment.

board room 1. A room or section of a room in a brokerage office in which security prices are displayed. 2. The room in which a firm's board of directors meets.

bogey An index whose performance an investment manager attempts to match. For example, the S&P 500 may be the bogey for the portfolio manager of an index fund.

boilerplate Standardized technical language used in a legal document such as a prospectus or a registration statement.

boiler room An area in a sales operation in which are located personnel who are engaged in contacting prospective buyers, usually by telephone, and in using high-pressure tactics to sell securities. These operations are associated with high commissions and unethical practices.

Bollinger Bands The outer limits of the market's price variations that are used by technical analysts to determine if the market is overbought or oversold. The bands are plotted two standard deviations on each side of the moving average. The closer the market average moves to the lower band, the more oversold the market. Conversely, the closer the average to the upper band, the more overbought the market.

bond 1. A long-term promissory note. Bonds vary widely in maturity, security, and type of issuer, although most are sold in $1,000 denominations or, if a municipal bond, $5,000 denominations. 2. A written obligation that makes a person or an institution responsible for the actions of another.

bond anticipation note (BAN) A short-term municipal security that has its principal repaid from the proceeds of a long-term municipal bond issue that is sold at a later date. Essentially, BANs represent debt that is used until long-term funding is available.

bond bank A bond pool sponsored by a state.

bond basis book —See BASIS BOOK.

bond broker A broker who executes bond trades on an organized exchange or in the over-the-counter market.

Bond Buyer A comprehensive weekday publication that provides detailed information about the bond market, especially the municipal bond segment. Established in 1891, the publication includes data on yields, new issues, underwriters, and nearly everything else of interest to professional bond buyers. The *Bond Buyer* is published both in hard copy and online.

Bond Buyer's Index An index of yields for AA-rated and A-rated municipal bonds that is widely used by dealers to evaluate yields on new municipal bond issues. The Index is published in the *Bond Buyer,* a daily publication specializing in fixed-income securities.

bond calendar —See CALENDAR.

bond conversion The exchange of a convertible bond for another asset, generally shares of common stock.

bond crowd Members of a securities exchange who transact bond orders on the floor of the exchange.

bond discount —See UNAMORTIZED BOND DISCOUNT.

bond dividend A type of liability dividend paid in the dividend payer's bonds.

bond fund An investment company that invests in long-term debt securities. A bond fund may restrict its investments to certain categories of bonds, such as corporate, municipal, or foreign bonds, or it may hold many types of bonds. —See also CORPORATE BOND FUND; MUNICIPAL BOND FUND.

bondholder An individual or institution that owns bonds in a corporation or other organization.

bond indenture —See INDENTURE.

Bond Market Association A nonprofit trade association for approximately 200 securities firms that underwrite, trade, and sell debt securities. The association compiles statistics, attempts to standardize market practices, and serves as an industry advocate before legislators and regulators.

bond pool A municipal bond offering in which a sponsor sells an issue of bonds with proceeds used by a number of cities or other tax-exempt organizations. The pool permits small cities with low borrowing requirements to reduce the underwriting and interest costs inherent in a small issue. Because of the varying credit risks associated with cities in a single bond pool, nearly all bond pools are insured as to payment of interest or principal. —Also called *pool financing.*

bond power A form, separate from a bond certificate, that permits the owner of the bond to transfer ownership to another investor without endorsing the bond certificate. —Compare STOCK POWER.

bond premium risk —See RISK PREMIUM.

bond rating The grading of a debt security with respect to the issuer's ability to meet interest and principal requirements in a timely manner. The three major rating services—Fitch, Moody's, and Standard & Poor's—use AAA as their highest rating and grade down through Bs and Cs. (D is used only by Fitch.) Debts rated AAA, AA, A, and BBB are considered investment-grade. Higher rated bonds provide lower returns, the price an investor pays for greater safety. —Compare STOCK RATING. —See also INTEREST COVERAGE.

bond ratio The proportion of a firm's long-term financing that is represented by long-term debt. A bond ratio is calculated by dividing a firm's total outstanding debt by its long-term debt and owners' equity. —Compare DEBT RATIO. —See also COMMON STOCK RATIO.

bond room The room below the main trading floor of the New York Stock Exchange in which bonds listed on the exchange are traded.

bond sinking fund —See SINKING FUND PROVISION.

bond swap The selling of one bond issue and concurrently buying another issue in order to take advantage of differences in interest rates, maturity, risk, marketability, and other factors. In some instances, especially with municipals, bond swaps are undertaken in order to realize losses for tax purposes. *See Investment Tip on p. 36.* —See also INTERMARKET SPREAD SWAP; RATE ANTICIPATION SWAP; REVERSE SWAP; SUBSTITUTION BOND SWAP; TAX SWAP.

book 1. A specialist's information on limit orders to buy and sell the security in which the specialist makes a market. The orders are left by other exchange members who wish to trade at a price that differs from the current market price. The book provides the specialist with an estimate of the demand for and supply of the stock in which he or she is a market maker. —Also called *specialist's* *book.* **2.** —See BOOK VALUE PER SHARE. **3.** An organization's written accounting record. **4.** An underwriting syndicate's record of activity for a new security issue.

book In accounting, to recognize a transaction by recording an entry. For example, a financial institution books a loan when it lends money to a customer.

book building Solicitation of tentative interest from likely institutional and individual investors by the investment banking syndicate of a new security issue before the offering has been approved by the Securities and Exchange Commission.

book closure The termination of announced benefits to new shareholders. For example, a company announces a specific date on which it will close the firm's books for shareholders to receive a dividend. —See HOLDER OF RECORD.

book-entry security A security for which the purchaser receives a receipt rather than an engraved certificate. Although a certificate may exist in some instances, it is held in one location as ownership changes. The U.S. government, which issues Treasury bills only in book-entry form, uses this method as a way to reduce paperwork expenses. —See also DEPOSITORY TRUST COMPANY.

bookrunner —See LEAD UNDERWRITER.

book-to-bill ratio The dollar amount of orders on the books compared to the dollar amount of orders filled. A high ratio indicates a backlog of orders that should produce revenues and profits in future periods. The book-to-bill ratio is often used to analyze the health of technology companies.

book transfer Transfer of ownership without physical movement of the item whose ownership is being changed. For example, ownership of a bond is generally transferred without movement of the actual bond certificate.

book value **1.** The net dollar value at which an asset is carried on a firm's balance sheet. For example, a building that was purchased for $900,000 but that has depreciated $200,000 has a book value of $700,000. Book value, an accounting concept, often bears little relation to an asset's market value. —Also called *carrying value; depreciated cost.* **2.** —See BOOK VALUE PER SHARE.

---

bond swap

How can I obtain a tax benefit from a bond swap?

Bond swaps are done for many reasons (such as to improve income, improve quality, change maturity schedule, or enhance diversification). Thus, if the bond swap is worthwhile, it will be done for various economic reasons rather than simply for tax benefits. (Of course, there is nothing wrong with obtaining a tax benefit at the same time.) A tax benefit is often realized when an investor sells bonds that were acquired during a period when interest rates were lower than they were at the time of the swap. Because interest rates rose, bond prices fell, and the seller is able to generate a tax-deductible capital loss. The tax savings may be viewed as an ancillary benefit derived from the bond swap. A word of caution is in order, though: if you are considering a bond swap that will generate a tax-deductible capital loss, do not swap into a security classified by the Internal Revenue Service as basically identical to the one you sold until the appropriate time period has passed. Otherwise, the loss will be disallowed for tax purposes.

Stephanie G. Bigwood, CFP, ChFC, CSA, Assistant Vice President
Lombard Securities, Incorporated, Baltimore, MD

book value per share Common stockholders' equity determined on a per-share basis. Book value per share is calculated by subtracting liabilities and the par value of any outstanding preferred stock from assets and dividing the remainder by the number of outstanding shares of stock. —Also called *book; book value.* —See also MARKET TO BOOK.

booster shot report An analyst research report designed to prop up the price of a stock just prior to the expiration of a lock-up period.

booths Workspaces on the perimeter of the NYSE trading floor where member firms and independent brokers receive orders.

bootstrap To assist a new business in getting off the ground.

borrowing power 1. A firm's ability to borrow significant amounts of money. This term is often applied to companies having valuable assets but few outstanding debts. 2. The amount of money that may be borrowed in a margin account.

Boston Exchange Automated Communication Order-Routing Network —See BEACON.

Boston option —See DEFERRED PREMIUM OPTION.

Boston Stock Exchange (BSE) A securities exchange that makes markets in over 2,000 of the most active U.S. stocks in competition with other exchanges and approximately 125 securities that are traded only on the BSE or jointly on another exchange. The BSE was founded in 1834.

BOT —Used on transaction slips to indicate the side of a trade in which securities are bought. —Compare SLD 2.

bottom The lowest price to which a stock, market index, or another asset will sink. —Compare TOP.

bottom fishing —Used to refer to the activity of investing in securities when it is believed the market has reached bottom following a major decline.

bottom line —See NET INCOME.

bottom-up investing Making investment decisions by first focusing on individual companies. Industry analysis and economic forecasts are considered after companies of interest have been identified. —Compare TOP-DOWN INVESTING.

bought deal —See FIRM COMMITMENT.

bounce Upward movement in the price of a security following a period of price stability or price declines. For example, a stock might get a nice bounce because of a favorable comment from an influential analyst.

bourse The common name for a securities exchange located in Europe.

Bourse de Montreal, Inc. (Canadian Derivatives Exchange) The major Canadian exchange for trading derivative products, including options and futures contracts. The exchange has a history dating to 1874, and its current specialization derives from a 1999 agreement of the four principal Canadian exchanges to restructure into three specialized exchanges. —Formerly called *Montreal Stock Exchange.* —See also CANADIAN VENTURE EXCHANGE; TORONTO STOCK EXCHANGE.

boutique —See INVESTMENT BOUTIQUE.

Bowie Bonds Debt securities collateralized by future earnings of singer David Bowie's song catalog. Issued in 1997, Bowie Bonds established a new category of securitized debt in which entertainers sold future royalties to investors. Similar bonds were subsequently created for the song catalogs of James Brown, the Isley Brothers, and the estate of Marvin Gaye.

box   The physical location in which brokerage firms and banks place securities for safekeeping. —See also FREE BOX; OPEN BOX.

box spread   A combination of four options consisting of one money spread on calls (one long, one short, same expiration, different strike price) and one money spread on puts (one long, one short, same expiration, different strike price). A box spread locks in a specific dollar return at expiration (all four options have the same expiration), with the goal being to acquire the position at a sufficiently low outlay that a favorable return is guaranteed.

bracket creep   The movement of a taxpayer into higher tax brackets as his or her taxable income increases over time. Bracket creep occurs because of the progressive nature of the federal income tax structure, that is, extra income is taxed at higher and higher rates. As a result of bracket creep, more and more individuals seek tax-advantaged investments. Bracket creep was reduced significantly by 1986 tax reform, which reduced the number of tax brackets. Several additional brackets were added in the early 1990s.

bracketing   The order in which underwriters' names appear in a securities offering. The names are generally listed in the order of importance in a particular offering. —See also MAJOR BRACKET; MEZZANINE BRACKET; TOMBSTONE.

Brady bonds   Dollar-denominated bonds of developing countries backed by zero-coupon U.S. Treasury securities. Although no longer in use, Brady bonds were issued in exchange for defaulted commercial bank loans.

breadth of market   The underlying strength of stock market movements in an upward or a downward direction. Determining breadth of market is important to technical analysts when they forecast whether a given market movement is likely to persist. Among numerous measures of breadth of market, the advance-decline index is one of the most popular. —Also called *market breadth.*

break   1. A sharp price decline in a particular security or in the market as a whole. A break usually occurs when unexpected negative information is made public and investors rush to sell. —Also called *market break.*   2. A discrepancy on the books of a brokerage firm.

break   1. To dissolve an underwriting syndicate.   2. —See BUST.

breakaway gap   In technical analysis, a gap in a chart pattern of price movement indicating a stock price has broken out of a trend on high volume. A breakaway gap is bullish if the price movement is upward and bearish if the price movement is downward. Refer to the *Technical Analysis Chart Patterns* section for an example of the chart. —Compare RUNAWAY GAP. —See also EXHAUSTION GAP.

breakeven   1. The level of output or sales necessary to cover fixed expenses. Companies in industries that have high fixed costs and, consequently, high breakevens, such as automobile and steel manufacturing, are likely to exhibit large fluctuations in earnings.   2. The price at which a security position can be closed out with no profit or loss.

⸢akeven analysis   A mathematical method for analyzing the relationships ⸢ a firm's fixed costs, profits, and variable costs. Financial analysts are particularly interested in how changes in output and sales will translate into changes in earnings.

breakeven time   The number of years a convertible security must be held in order for its extra current income to cover the excess of its market price over its value in terms of common stock (that is, annual interest on the bond minus annual dividends on the stock). For example, a 10% coupon bond selling for $1,000, convertible to common stock with a market value of $600 and paying no dividend, would have a breakeven time of $400/$100, or 4 years.

breaking a buck   A decline below $1 in the share price of a money market fund. A money market fund share price may break a dollar if a major decline occurs in the value of securities owned by the fund. For example, a corporation may default on commercial paper held by a fund.

breaking the syndicate   The termination of a syndicate of investment bankers organized to underwrite an issue of securities. Following the breaking of the syndicate, its individual members are free to dispose of remaining securities without price restrictions.

breakout   The advance of a stock price above a resistance level, or the fall of a stock price below a support level. A breakout, especially one on relatively heavy volume, indicates to technicians that the security is about to make a major price movement in the direction indicated by the breakout. Thus, if a breakout is upward, a major upward price movement can be expected. A breakout on relatively low volume is suspect. —See also BREAK THROUGH; CONGESTION AREA.

breakpoint   The cumulative level of purchases of shares in a mutual fund that is required before an individual purchaser can qualify for a reduced sales commission. —Compare LETTER OF INTENT. —See also RIGHT OF ACCUMULATION.

break through   To achieve a breakout.

breakup   The division of a company into separate parts. The most famous breakup to date was the 1984 division of AT&T (formerly, American Telephone & Telegraph Company). This breakup was intended to increase competition in the communications industry.

Ⲙ CASE STUDY | In early 1996, Dun & Bradstreet management announced the firm would be divided into three publicly traded companies. Dun & Bradstreet would survive as a smaller, leaner firm while A.C. Nielsen, the media-ratings company, and Cognizant, a marketing information firm, would become separate corporations. At the time of the announcement, all three firms were part of the same parent company. In announcing the breakup, Dun & Bradstreet's chief executive officer said the decision was driven by management's desire to improve shareholder value. That statement implied management believed the three companies would be more valuable as separately owned and managed enterprises than as components of a single company.

breakup fee   A provision in a takeover agreement that requires a firm to pay the investment banker a large sum of money if another firm takes over the target company. A breakup fee tends to discourage other firms from making bids for the target. —See also TOPPER FEE.

breakup value   The market value of all the individual parts of a firm if the firm were to be broken up and the individual parts operated independently. If the breakup value of a firm exceeds the market value at which its stock trades, the firm may be managed and operated inefficiently. In such a case, stockholder holdings would increase in value if parts of the firm were divested. Many takeovers originate when raiders spot firms with breakup values that exceed the prices at which those firms' stocks are traded.

bridge loan   A short-term loan that is taken out until permanent financing can be arranged. —Also called *swing loan.*

broad-based   Of or relating to an index or average that provides a good representation of the overall market. The S&P 500 and NYSE Composite are generally regarded as broad-based stock indexes, while the popular Dow Jones Industrial Average is biased toward blue chips and is not considered broad-based. —Compare NARROW-BASED.

broad tape   The machine over which Dow Jones & Company, Inc., provides current business news to brokerage houses and other subscribers. The term derives from the width of the paper on which this news is printed compared with the width of ticker tape.

broker   **1.** An individual or a firm that brings together buyers and sellers but does not take a position in the asset to be exchanged. Some observers believe a broker provides an unbiased opinion on a security since there is little self-interest involved in the transaction. —Compare DEALER. **2.** —See REGISTERED REPRESENTATIVE.

broker call loan   —See CALL LOAN.

broker comparison   —See COMPARISON.

broker-dealer   A firm that functions both as a broker by bringing buyers and sellers together and as a dealer by taking positions of its own in selected securities. Many firms that are commonly called *brokers* or *brokerage firms* are actually broker-dealers.

brokered CD   A certificate of deposit of a commercial bank or savings and loan that is sold through an intermediary (usually a brokerage firm) rather than directly by the savings institution itself. Small investors can frequently obtain rates paid on very large certificates through brokered CDs, which are generally sold in $1,000 units.

Broker ITS   A pre-opening indication of prices sent to NYSE trading-floor broker terminals.

broker's loan   Funds borrowed by a broker, mainly from banks, for various purposes including a call loan for purchases of securities on margin, an underwriter's purchase of a new security issue for resale, or a specialist's inventory of securities. —Also called *general loan and collateral agreement.*

BSE   —See BOSTON STOCK EXCHANGE.

broker

What should I look for in a broker?

When interviewing prospective brokers, you should look for one with a clean NASD record, great referrals, and stability in his or her business. In addition, he or she should not be transaction oriented but should instead be concerned about your values and goals and be willing to realize that the best trade may be no trade. In summary, you should look for a financial advisor rather than just a "broker."

George Riles, First Vice President and Resident Manager, Merrill Lynch, Albany, GA

B2B e-commerce The conducting of commerce by companies, government agencies, and institutions with one another over the Internet.

B2C e-commerce The conducting of commerce by companies, government agencies, and institutions with consumers over the Internet. Amazon.com is typical of a company engaged in B2C e-commerce.

bubble A price level that is much higher than warranted by the fundamentals. Bubbles occur when prices continue to rise simply because enough investors believe investments bought at the current price can subsequently be sold at even higher prices. They can occur in virtually any commodity including stocks, real estate, and even tulips.

bucketing Taking the opposite side of a customer's order into the broker's account or an account over which the broker has an interest without first putting the order out for a competitive bid.

bucket shop An illegal operation in which buy and sell orders are accepted, but no executions actually take place. Instead, the operators expect to profit when customers close out their positions at a loss. A bucket shop is similar in concept to a bookie who does not lay off bets and accepts the risk of a bettor winning.

build a book —See BOOK BUILDING.

bulge-bracket firm A large investment banking firm that is considered to have an exceptional reputation and customer base. Investment bankers such as Merrill Lynch, Morgan Stanley, and Goldman Sachs are held to be among the relatively small group of firms that qualify.

bull An investor who believes the price of a particular security or security prices in general will follow a broad upward trend. An investor can often be a bull on a specific security but not on the general market, and vice versa. —Compare BEAR.

bulldog bond A sterling-denominated bond issued by a non-British firm or institution. An example of a bulldog bond is one denominated in sterling and issued in England by a U.S.–based company. Purchase of a bulldog bond by a U.S. investor would entail extra risks but also potential rewards stemming from possible changes in the value of sterling in relation to the dollar.

bullet bond A bond that is noncallable.

bullet immunization The protection of a bond portfolio so as to fund a single liability.

Bulletin Board —See OTC BULLETIN BOARD.

bullion Refined gold or silver in bulk (that is, ingots) rather than in the form of coins.

bullish Of or relating to the belief that a particular stock or the market as a whole is headed for a period of generally rising prices. —Compare BEARISH.

bull market An extended period of generally rising prices in an individual item, such as stock or gold; a group of items, such as commodities or oil stocks; or the market as a whole. Because security prices are often subject to reversals, it is sometimes difficult to know whether there has been a temporary interruption in or a permanent end to a bull market. Thus, the opinion of whether a bull market is actually in progress is often subject to individual interpretation. —Compare BEAR MARKET.

bull spread In futures and options trading, a strategy in which one contract is bought and a different contract is sold in such a manner that the person undertaking the spread makes a profit if the price of the underlying asset rises. Two contracts are used in order to limit the size of the potential loss. —Compare BEAR SPREAD.

bunch To combine a number of odd-lot orders into round-lot orders so as to avoid an odd-lot differential.

buoyant Of or relating to a market in which prices have a tendency to move upward.

burn and churn —See CHURN.

burn rate The speed with which a company consumes cash, generally stated on a monthly basis. A high burn rate indicates a firm will soon be out of business unless it can raise additional capital, dramatically increase cash sales, or reduce expenses. The burn rate was particularly high for dot-com companies that placed emphasis on capturing market share rather than profitability.

business combination —See COMBINATION.

business cycle The somewhat irregular but recurring periods of change in economic activity over time. A business cycle is generally divided into four stages: expansion, prosperity, contraction, and recession. The stage in which an economy operates has a significant impact on a firm's profitability and prospects. This impact is especially severe with respect to firms that experience large swings in sales and profits. Many analysts believe stock prices tend to lead the business cycle. Therefore, it is felt that bull markets begin before a period of expansion and that bear markets begin before a period of contraction.

business day A day on which the securities markets are open.

business fundamentals The general background within which an economy operates including earnings, sales, wage rates, taxes, and inflation. Improving business fundamentals are generally viewed as bullish for stocks, although stock prices at any given point already include some of the expected improvement of the business fundamentals.

business risk The risk that a business will experience a period of poor earnings and resultant failure. Business risk is greatest for firms in cyclical or relatively new industries. Business risk affects holders of stocks and bonds, since a firm may be unable to pay dividends and interest.

business segment —See SEGMENT.

bust To cancel an order after it has been filled. In most cases, cancellation occurs only under unusual circumstances, such as an error or a misunderstanding. —Also called *break*.

busted convertible A convertible bond on which the stock into which the bond is convertible has fallen so far below the conversion price that the convertible bond trades in the market as regular debt. For example, if a convertible bond is convertible into stock at a price of $40 per share when the stock sells at only $7 per share, the conversion feature has such little value that the bond will be priced to offer investors a yield nearly equal to that from a bond with similar risk and maturity but without a conversion feature.

-up takeover The acquisition of a firm in which the acquiring company rtain assets or segments of the target firm in order to raise funds and repay the acquisition debt. Such a takeover is most often undertaken when the target firm has a significant amount of undervalued assets and the acquiring company has little cash.

butterfly spread A combination of two long and two short call options, all with the same expiration date. The two short options carry the same strike price, which is sandwiched between a higher and a lower strike price on the long options. A hypothetical example of a butterfly spread would be to sell two April GM $60 and buy an April GM $50 and an April GM $70. The butterfly spread is designed to be profitable if the price of the underlying asset remains within a narrow trading range.

Buttonwood Agreement A historical 1792 agreement among 24 New York brokers to band together into an investment group. The name stemmed from the buttonwood tree that served as the Wall Street meeting place for members of the group.

buy A bargain-priced asset. For example, an analyst may feel that a particular firm owns valuable assets overlooked or undervalued by the financial community. In such an instance, the firm's stock is considered a buy.

buy To purchase a security or other asset. —Compare SELL.

buy-and-hold strategy The investment strategy of purchasing securities and holding them for extended periods of time. Investors using the buy-and-hold strategy select companies on the basis of their long-term outlook. Such investors are not influenced by short- or intermediate-term movements in the price of a security.

buy-and-write strategy The investment strategy often used by covered writers in which stock is purchased and call options written. A buy-and-write strategy is a fairly conservative approach to generating maximum current income from option premiums and dividends.

buy a spread In options trading, to establish a spread position in which the premium on the option purchased exceeds the premium on the option sold. A typical example would be to buy a call on Microsoft with a $60 strike price for a premium of $300 and to sell a Microsoft call with a $65 strike price for $125 (both expiring on the same date).

buy back To repurchase an asset or security. For example, a company may decide to buy back shares of its own stock from an investor in order to reduce the possibility of a takeover.

buyback A company's repurchase of a portion of its own outstanding shares. The purpose of a buyback may be to acquire a block of stock from an investor who is unfriendly to the target firm's management and is considering taking over the firm. Conversely, a buyback may be an attempt to increase earnings per share by reducing the number of outstanding shares. Regardless of the purpose of a buyback, the result is increased risk for the firm because of reduced equity in the firm's capital structure. —Also called *stock buyback; stock repurchase plan.* —See also GREENMAIL; PARTIAL REDEMPTION; SELF-TENDER.

〽️ CASE STUDY | Corporate stock buybacks generally consist of a company purchasing its shares in the open market or offering shareholders an above-market price for a certain proportion of their holdings. Either method will result in fewer outstanding shares and, hopefully, help support the market price of the firm's stock. In some instances companies sell short put options that commit the companies to buy back shares of their stock at a specified price until a certain date. Companies issuing the puts pocket premiums paid by investors who gain the right to force the company to buy back its own shares. If the stock price remains above the exercise price specified by the puts, option holders choose not to exercise the puts because they have no interest in selling stock at a below-market price. The unexercised options expire, allowing the companies to issue additional puts and pocket additional premiums. In the event puts are exercised, companies purchase shares they intended to purchase in any case. A problem develops when the company's stock price declines dramatically, in which case the company will be forced to repurchase its own shares at a price much higher than the market price. This is exactly what happened to PC maker Dell Computer during the first half of 2001, when the company was forced to repurchase some of its shares for $47 (the exercise price of the puts) at a time the stock was trading on the Nasdaq National Market in the mid-20s. In other words, Dell was being required to pay twice the market price to repurchase its shares because the company had earlier sold put options with strike prices that on the issue date seemed reasonable but later turned out to be substantially higher than the price at which the stock traded in a depressed market. According to an SEC filing, Dell had issued put contracts on 96 million of its own shares at an average exercise price of $44 per share. Unfortunately for Dell, the purchases of its stock at inflated prices came at a time when the firm's cash flow was being squeezed by a weak PC market.

buyers' market A market in which the supply of an asset swamps demand to the point that prices fall below the level expected under normal circumstances. Occasionally, several large new issues of municipal bonds will be marketed at the same time, thereby creating a buyers' market that causes underwriters to raise yields. A buyers' market in municipal bonds results in a narrowing of the gap between the yields on these tax-exempt securities and the yields on U.S. Treasury bonds, which are taxable. —Compare SELLERS' MARKET.

buy in The purchase by one broker of securities that another broker has failed to deliver on time.

buying climax A period of very high volume and sharp upward movement in the stock market. A buying climax often signals the end of a bull market or, at the least, an overbought market that can be expected to fall. —Compare SELLING CLIMAX. —Also called *climax*.

buying hedge —See LONG HEDGE.

buying panic A period of rapidly rising stock prices on very high volume as investors, speculators, traders, and institutions attempt to establish investment positions without regard to price. Buying panics occur when individuals and institutions believe they must buy securities at once before prices rise further. —Compare SELLING PANIC.

buying power **1.** The amount of liquid funds available for investing. A large amount of buying power indicates that significant funds from investors are available to fuel a bull market. **2.** The funds in an investor's brokerage account that may be used for purchasing securities. An investor's buying power includes cash balances plus the loan value on securities held in the account.

buy minus Of or relating to an order to purchase a security only when the last change in the security's price is downward. A buy-minus order may be used to acquire a position in a security during a short-term price decline.

buy on margin

What are the risks inherent in buying securities on margin?

Here one borrows money from a broker to buy securities, using securities as collateral so that more can be bought at one time. It's called leveraging, and it is wonderful—if it's an up market! You make more money because you put more money out at risk. (It's wonderful for your broker too; the broker makes more in commissions and charges you interest. Your broker also can—and does—loan out the stocks you hold in your margin account, getting in return an interest-free deposit equal to the value of your shares on loan.) But, if the market goes against you, it can be just awful, because you owe the borrowed money in full, with interest, no matter what happens to the price of the stock or bond. TIP: Margin is a little like booze: the more you drink, the better you feel—until the morning after.

Thomas J. McAllister, CFP, McAllister Financial Planning, Carmel, IN

buy on margin To buy securities by putting up only a part, or a margin, of the purchase price and borrowing the remainder. The loan is usually arranged for by the investor's broker. The securities must be kept in the account. —See also INITIAL MARGIN REQUIREMENT; MAINTENANCE MARGIN REQUIREMENT.

buy order A brokerage order to purchase a specified quantity of a security.

buy out 1. To purchase all the stock of a company or all the stock of a company owned by one investor or by a group of investors. For example, corporate management may decide to buy out an investor in order to halt a potential takeover. **2.** To terminate a contract before its scheduled termination date by reaching a monetary agreement satisfactory to the parties involved.

buyout 1. The purchase of a company. —See also LEVERAGED BUYOUT. **2.** The purchase of all the stock of a company, owned by a single investor or by a group of investors.

buy side The portion of the securities business in which institutional orders originate. In most instances, the buy side is limited to institutional buyers such as pension-fund portfolio managers. Individual investors are usually excluded from the buy side because they are not considered formal participants in the securities business. —Compare SELL SIDE.

buy signal An indication provided by a technical tool, such as a bar chart or trading volume, that a particular security or securities in general should be purchased. For example, the achievement by a stock of a new high price on heavy trading volume is often interpreted as a buy signal. —Compare SELL SIGNAL.

buy stop order A customer's order to a broker to buy a security if it sells at or above a stipulated stop price. This type of stop order can be used to protect an existing profit or to limit the potential loss on a security that has been sold short. —Compare SELL STOP ORDER.

buy the book An order to purchase all of a security offered at the current ask price. The purchase is made from the specialist, dealers, and other holders willing to sell at the specified price.

BW —See BID WANTED.

bylaws Stockholder-approved rules governing the conduct of a business. Bylaws typically include rules concerning the election of directors, selection of auditors, and amendment of existing bylaws.

C

c 1. —Used in the dividend column of stock transaction tables of newspapers to indicate that the listed dividend is a liquidating dividend: *City Inv 7.50c.* **2.** —Used in money market mutual fund transaction tables in newspapers to indicate funds that are chiefly or wholly exempt from federal income taxes: *Fld Tax Exmpt c.*

Caa —See CCC.

cabinet crowd New York Stock Exchange members who trade inactive bonds. —Compare ACTIVE BOND CROWD. —Also called *inactive bond crowd.*

cabinet security An inactive security listed on an exchange. The term derives from the type of storage unit in which limit orders for these securities are kept until needed for execution or cancellation.

CAC 40 A market-capitalization-weighted index of the 40 most actively traded stocks on the Paris Bourse. CAC is short for Cotation Assiste en Continu.

CAES —See COMPUTER-ASSISTED EXECUTION SYSTEM.

cage —See CASHIER'S DEPARTMENT.

calendar A list of upcoming bond issues. A full calendar indicating a large number of issues may force issuers to increase interest rates in order to compete for buyers. —Also called *bond calendar.*

calendar effects The impact a particular day, week, or month a security is owned has on rates of return. For example, studies indicate tax selling produces downward pressure on stock prices during the end of the calendar year followed by upward price pressure in January. —See also JANUARY EFFECT.

calendar spread In options and futures trading, the purchase of one contract and the sale of another contract that differs from the first only by its delivery or expiration date. An example of calendar spread would be the purchase of a December call with a strike price of $20 and the sale of a June call with the same strike price. An investor would use a calendar spread in order to profit from a change in the price difference as the securities move closer to maturity. —Also called *horizontal spread; time spread.*

call 1. An option that permits its holder to purchase a specific asset at a predetermined price until a certain date. For example, an investor may purchase a call option on General Electric stock that confers the right to buy 100 shares at $25 per share until October 17. Calls are sold for a fee by other investors, who incur an obligation. —Compare PUT 1. —Also called *call option.* —See also SYNTHETIC CALL. **2.** An issuer's right to repurchase an issue of bonds at a predetermined price before maturity. The feature is used when interest rates fall, so that the bonds can be repurchased and a new, lower-rate issue sold. A call feature is normal for nearly all long-term bond issues, and it operates to the detriment of bond owners. —See also CALL PRICE; CLEANUP CALL; EXTRAORDINARY CALL; OPTIONAL CALL; SINKING FUND CALL. **3.** Redemption of an issue of bonds before maturity by forcing the bondholders to sell at the call price.

call To force an option writer to sell shares of stock at a price stipulated in a contract. Stocks usually are called just before the expiration of the options.

callable bond A bond that is subject to redemption by its issuer before maturity.

callable CD A certificate of deposit that can be redeemed prior to the scheduled maturity. Many retail brokerage firms broker callable CDs issued by insured financial institutions. These CDs, often with long maturities, are traded in the secondary market and can fluctuate in value with changes in market rates of interest. —Also called *deposit note*.

> ⋀⋀ **CASE STUDY** | Although insured, callable certificates of deposit can spell trouble for unwary investors. The issuer can redeem a callable certificate of deposit prior to the scheduled maturity, but an investor holding the CD cannot redeem it prior to the scheduled maturity. The investor can only liquidate the CD through a sale in the secondary market, possibly for less than the principal or the investor's purchase price. Heads the issuer wins, tails the investor loses. The investor gains little if market interest rates fall, because the CD is likely to be redeemed early by the issuer. On the other hand, there is much to lose if market interest rates rise and the CD must be held for a long period of time. The added risk of the call feature causes issuers to pay higher interest rates on callable CDs than are paid on regular certificates of deposit. In late 2000 the New York Stock Exchange censured and fined a major brokerage firm for failing to supervise and control the sale of approximately $3 billion in callable CDs to approximately 161,000 customers. Some of the customers claimed their brokers did not inform them issuers could redeem the CDs prior to scheduled maturity. Other investors complained brokers did not warn that the CDs could not be cashed in early. The danger in owning these investments is particularly great for callable CDs with long maturities. Unlike regular certificates of deposit, which typically have maturities of six months to 5 years, callable CDs sometimes have maturities of 20 to 30 years.

callable common stock Common stock of a subsidiary that is sold by the parent company and is subject to a stock purchase option agreement. The exercise price of the call generally steps up over time. —Compare PUTTABLE COMMON STOCK.

callable preferred stock An issue of preferred stock that may be repurchased by the issuer at a specific price, usually par value or slightly above. The option to repurchase such stock is held by the issuer, not the investor. Calls can be expected when market rates of interest have fallen significantly below the yield on the preferred stock at the time the stock was issued.

call date The date on which a security can be repurchased by the issuer at a predetermined price. The call date is established by the issuer at the time a security is issued.

called away —Used to refer to the forced sale of a security by an investor because of the action of another party. For example, the writer of a call option has the underlying stock called away when the call owner exercises the option. Likewise, a bondholder may have bonds called away by the issuer if interest rates decline and the issuer decides to redeem a portion of the issue before maturity. In nearly all cases, a call works to the disadvantage of the owner of the security.

call feature —See CALL PROVISION.

call loan A loan that may be terminated at any time by either party. For investors, a call loan means bank loans to stockbrokers for the purpose of carrying customer margin borrowing, using securities as collateral. The rate of interest, similar to that on other high-quality short-term loans, varies over time. Brokerage firms usually charge customers the rate on call loans plus an additional 1% or so depending on the amount borrowed. —Also called *broker call loan.* —See also BROKER'S LOAN.

call market A market in which trading in individual securities occurs at specific times as opposed to continuously. In a call market all orders to buy and sell a particular security are assembled at one time in order to determine a price at which most of the orders can be executed. The participants then move on to a different security. Call markets are frequently used in situations in which there are few securities and participants.

call option —See CALL 1.

call premium The difference between the principal amount of a security and the price at which the security can be called by the issuer. During the first few years a call is permitted, the premium is generally equal to one year's interest. Thereafter, the premium gradually declines to zero at maturity. Calls for sinking fund requirements are usually made at par rather than at a premium. —Also called *redemption premium.*

call price The price at which an issuer may, at its option, repurchase a security for redemption before the security's maturity. For bonds, the call price often declines over the life of the security until it reaches par value at maturity. —Also called *redemption price.* —See also EXTRAORDINARY CALL; OPTIONAL CALL; PROVISIONAL CALL TRIGGER PRICE; SINKING FUND CALL.

call protection The prohibition against an issuer's calling a bond from an investor during the early years of the security's life. Municipals and industrial bonds usually have ten years of call protection, while protection on utility debt is often limited to five years. A longer period of call protection is advantageous to the investor because calls nearly always occur during periods of reduced interest rates. —Also called *cushion.* —See also NONCALLABLE; NONREFUNDABLE.

call provision The stipulation in most bond indentures that permits the issuer to repurchase securities at a fixed price or at a series of prices before maturity. This provision operates to the detriment of investors because calls on high-interest bonds usually occur during periods of reduced interest rates. Thus, an investor whose bond is called must find another investment, often one that provides a lower return. Certain preferred stock issues are also subject to call. —Also called *call feature.* —See also MAKE-WHOLE CALL PROVISION.

⋀⋀ CASE STUDY Unlike most long-term corporate and municipal bonds, U.S. Treasury bonds cannot generally be called prior to their scheduled maturity dates. The U.S. Treasury last issued callable bonds in 1984 and even these bonds could only be called in the five years prior to maturity. All U.S. Treasury bonds issued after 1984 have been noncallable. The Treasury's inability to call its bonds prior to their scheduled maturities proved to be a bonanza for investors who purchased long-term Treasury securities in the mid-1980s when interest rates were relatively high. The U.S. Treasury was required to continue paying very high interest rates on this debt into the next decade, when market interest rates had declined substantially. If these bonds

call provision

Why should I check a bond's call provision before buying it? Which types of bonds have these provisions?

Bond issuers seem to call their bonds in when bond investors least want to receive their principal back—after interest rates have already dropped. If you pay close attention to a bond's call provisions, however, you can avoid experiencing losses of principal (that is, you can avoid paying big premiums for high-coupon bonds that are about to be called in at lower premium prices or, worse yet, at par). Furthermore, if you are a short maturity buyer (let's use three years for an example), you may be able to earn a higher yield for the three-year period by purchasing a longer cushion bond that is callable in three years instead of buying a bond that matures in three years. Reason: the market will generally reward you with a higher yield to the call on the cushion bond (due to the uncertainty of its actually being called in three years) compared with the yield that the market will provide you on a similar bond that will definitely mature in three years. It is important to mention that if you invest in a cushion bond and it is not called, you will be faced with the choice of either holding a longer bond than you may have intended to hold or liquidating at market value.

Stephanie G. Bigwood, CFP, ChFC, CSA, Assistant Vice President
Lombard Securities, Incorporated, Baltimore, MD

had been issued with a call provision, the Treasury could have retired bonds with coupons of 11% and 12% and issued new bonds with coupons of 5% and 6%, thereby saving taxpayers billions of dollars in interest expense.

call risk —See PREPAYMENT RISK.

call spread An option position in which a call is purchased while another call on the same security is sold short. The two calls have different strike prices, different expiration dates, or both. —Compare PUT SPREAD. —Also called *option spread.* —See also SPREAD 1.

call watch A service provided by independent organizations that monitor the actions of bond issuers in order to inform clients, such as financial advisors, trustees, and individual investors, that their bonds have been called for redemption before maturity. A call watch is particularly valuable to holders of bearer bonds for which no records of ownership are maintained by the issuers.

Canadian Derivatives Exchange —See BOURSE DE MONTREAL, INC.

Canadian Venture Exchange (CDNX) The Canadian marketplace for trading securities of emerging companies. The CDNX resulted from a merger of the Alberta Stock Exchange and the Vancouver Stock Exchange following a 1999 agreement among Canada's four exchanges to form three specialized exchanges. The exchange specializes in trading small- and medium-cap equity issues, while the Toronto Stock Exchange serves as the Canadian exchange for large-cap issues. The Canadian Venture Exchange is headquartered in Calgary with trading facilities in Vancouver.

cancel former order A customer order to a broker that cancels and replaces an earlier, unfilled order with a new order. For example, a customer may cancel a former limit order to buy stock at $15 per share and replace it with a market order.

cancellation A broker's notice to a customer that an erroneous trade credited to the customer has been voided. For example, if a brokerage firm mistakenly purchases 200 shares of stock for an account when the customer has entered an order for only 100 shares, the firm will send the customer a cancellation for the 200-share trade to void the original confirmation and then will send a new confirmation showing the correct trade.

cancel order A customer order to a broker that cancels an earlier, unfilled order given by the customer.

candlestick chart A variation of a bar chart in which the open and close prices are represented as the top and bottom of a rectangle surrounding a vertical line connecting the high and low prices. The appearance is of a barrel around a fence post. The body of the rectangle is filled if the closing price is lower than the opening price and blank if the closing price is higher than the opening price. Refer to the *Technical Analysis Chart Patterns* section for an example of this chart. —Compare BAR CHART; LINE CHART.

cap 1. An upper limit on the interest rate to be paid on a floating-rate note. **2.** —See CAPITALIZATION.

capital appreciation An increase in the market value of a security.

capital appreciation bond —See ZERO-COUPON BOND.

capital asset An asset that has an expected life of more than one year and that is not bought and sold in the usual course of business. Buildings and machinery are examples of capital assets.

capital-asset pricing model (CAPM) A mathematical model for securities pricing in which the relative riskiness of securities is combined with the return on risk-free assets. This model, which uses beta, the widely used measure of risk, has been criticized; nevertheless, it is considered a very important element of modern investment and portfolio theory. —See also CAPITAL MARKET LINE.

capital budgeting Corporate evaluation of long-term investment proposals, generally by means of discounting estimated future cash flows.

capital dividend A dividend considered to be drawn from paid-in capital rather than from current earnings or retained earnings. Capital dividends are generally not taxable to a stockholder when paid; rather, they are used to adjust the basis of the security downward such that a larger capital gain or a smaller capital loss will result at the time the security is sold. A capital dividend is somewhat akin to tearing boards off a house to use as firewood. If the process goes on too long, the house itself will be gone. —Also called *return of capital.*

capital expenditure Funds used to acquire a long-term asset. A capital expenditure results in depreciation deductions over the life of the acquired asset. —Also called *capital outlay.*

capital flight The shifting of funds out of a country to avoid confiscation, controls, or depreciation. Capital flight results in further deterioration of a currency's exchange rate.

capital formation The creation of productive assets that expand an economy's capacity to produce goods and services. Private savings facilitates capital formation by allowing resources to be diverted to corporate investment rather than individual consumption.

capital gain The amount by which proceeds from the sale of a capital asset exceed the cost basis.

capital gains distribution Payments to investment company shareholders based on gains from securities in the firm's portfolio that have been sold. These gains are passed through to the shareholders and are taxed to the shareholders. Distributions usually occur once each year.

⋀ CASE STUDY | Capital gains distributions can produce unexpected tax problems for mutual fund shareholders, especially investors who acquire mutual fund shares following a major increase in stock values. An even greater surprise occurs when a large distribution occurs during a year of poor market performance. Mutual funds are required to distribute to their shareholders all of the net gains the funds realize through the sale of securities. Unfortunately for some investors, gains that occur during one period are realized and distributed in a subsequent period. Buy a mutual fund following a major increase in stock values and you are likely to receive distributions on gains from which you did not benefit. In 2000 Warburg Pincus Asset Management made a capital gains distribution equal to a stunning 55% of assets to the shareholders of its Warburg Pincus Japan Small Company Fund. The distribution was occasioned by a year of spectacular gains in 1999 (a return of 329%) followed by a year of poor performance with resulting shareholder redemptions that forced portfolio managers to sell stocks to raise cash. Stock sales by the fund produced capital gains that triggered the distribution by Warburg Pincus. Although mutual funds typically make distributions during the end of the calendar year, Warburg Pincus officials indicated their distribution was made early in the year to allow shareholders time to take care of any tax liability. In a similar event, in December 2000 Select Software and Computer Services Fund distributed nearly 40% of its net asset value even though the fund was down over 9% for the year. Investors who purchased shares in the fund in early 2000 received a large taxable distribution even though their shares had lost market value during the year. Woe to the investor who fails to research a mutual fund purchase.

capital gains tax The tax applicable to gains realized from the sale of capital assets, including stocks and bonds. The capital gains tax rate and holding period requirements are periodically changed by Congress. A favorable tax rate is generally applied to realized gains on assets that are sold following a holding period of over one year. Realized capital gains on assets held a year or less do not generally receive favorable tax treatment.

capital intensive Of or relating to a firm or industry that requires large amounts of fixed assets and/or cash to operate. Steel, automobile manufacturing, and mining are capital intensive industries.

capitalization The amounts and types of long-term financing used by a firm. Types of financing include common stock, preferred stock, retained earnings, and long-term debt. A firm with capitalization including little or no long-term debt is considered to be financed very conservatively. —Also called *cap; capital structure; financial structure; total capitalization.* —See also COMPLEX CAPITAL STRUCTURE; LARGE-CAP; MARKET CAPITALIZATION; RECAPITALIZATION; SMALL-CAP.

capitalization rate The rate used to convert an income stream into a present value lump sum. For example, a capitalization rate of 10% and an income stream of $2,000 annually provide a present value of $2,000/0.1, or $20,000. The capitalization rate for a particular flow of income is a function of the rate of interest on Treasury bills (the risk-free rate) and the risk associated with the flow of income. A riskier investment has a higher capitalization rate and, therefore, a lower present value.

capitalize To calculate the current value of a future stream of earnings or cash flows. For example, to calculate the current price at which a bond should sell, a financial analyst must capitalize the interest payments and principal repayment that will be made to the investor.

capital lease The long-term lease of a capital asset. To the lessee, a capital lease is the same as owning the asset. Accounting rules require that the leased asset and the present value of the lease payments be recorded on the lessee's balance sheet. For the lessor, a capital lease is treated as a sale of the asset. —Also called *financial lease.*

capital loss The amount by which the cost basis of a capital asset exceeds the proceeds from its sale.

capital market The market for long-term funds where securities such as common stock, preferred stock, and bonds are traded. Both the primary market for new issues and the secondary market for existing securities are part of the capital market.

capital market line The line used in the capital-asset pricing model to present the rates of return for efficient portfolios. These rates will vary depending upon the risk-free rate of return and the level of risk (as measured by beta) for a particular portfolio. The capital market line shows a positive linear relationship between returns and portfolio betas. —Also called *market line.* —See also ALPHA; BETA; SYSTEMATIC RISK.

capital outlay —See CAPITAL EXPENDITURE.

capital shares One of two types of stock issued by a dual purpose fund in which the owner is entitled to all of the capital value but none of the current income of the fund. Capital shares appeal primarily to aggressive investors seeking capital growth. —Compare INCOME SHARES.

capital spending Spending for long-term assets such as factories, equipment, machinery, and buildings that permits the production of more goods and services in future years.

capital stock Any of various shares of ownership in a business. These shares include common stock of various classes and any preferred stock that is outstanding. If a firm has only a single class of capital stock outstanding, the terms *common stock* and *capital stock* are often used interchangeably. —See also AUTHORIZED CAPITAL STOCK; OUTSTANDING CAPITAL STOCK; STOCK CLASS.

capital structure —See CAPITALIZATION.

capital surplus —See ADDITIONAL PAID-IN CAPITAL.

capital turnover A measure indicating how effectively investment capital is used to produce revenues. Capital turnover is expressed as a ratio of annual sales to invested capital.

CAPM —See CAPITAL-ASSET PRICING MODEL.

capped-style option An option with an established price (the cap price) at which the option will be automatically exercised. The cap price is equal to the strike price plus a predetermined interval for a call option and the strike price less a predetermined interval for a put option.

CAPS —See CONVERTIBLE ADJUSTABLE PREFERRED STOCK.

CARDS —See CERTIFICATES FOR AMORTIZING REVOLVING DEBTS.

carload In commodities trading, a railroad car or truckload of grain that ranges from 1,400 to 2,500 bushels.

carryback A business operating loss that, for tax purposes, may be deducted for a certain number of prior years, usually no more than three. A business uses a carryback to recover taxes paid on income earned in prior years. For example, if a firm experiences a year of large losses following a period of profitable operations, it may use the losses to cancel out profits from preceding years on which taxes have been paid. When the taxes a company paid on profits are canceled because of a carryback, the firm is issued a refund by the Internal Revenue Service. —Also called *carryover; tax loss carryback.*

carryforward **1.** A business operating loss that, for tax purposes, may be claimed a certain number of years in the future, often up to 15 years. Thus, a loss in one year would be carried forward to a future year and used to offset profits up to the amount of the carryforward. Carryforwards are especially useful to firms operating in cyclical industries such as transportation. —Also called *tax loss carryforward.* **2.** In taxation of individuals, net capital losses exceeding the annual limit of $3,000 that may be carried to succeeding years so as to offset capital gains or ordinary income. There is no limit on the amount of capital losses that may be used to offset capital gains in any one year, only on the amount of losses in excess of gains that may be used to offset income. —Also called *carryover.*

carrying charges **1.** The cost of owning and storing a commodity during a period of time. This cost influences the difference between the futures price and the expected future spot price. **2.** —See COST OF CARRY.

carrying value —See BOOK VALUE 1.

carryover —See CARRYBACK; CARRYFORWARD 2.

CARS —See CERTIFICATE FOR AUTOMOBILE RECEIVABLES.

cartel A group of companies or countries acting together to control the supply and price of certain goods or services. Cartels are formed to produce higher profits than would ordinarily be earned.

carve-out —See EQUITY CARVE-OUT.

cash Coins and currency on hand and in checking account balances. Because cash is a nonearning asset, firms usually attempt to keep their cash balances to the minimum level required to sustain operations.

cash account A brokerage account requiring that cash payments on purchases and deliveries on sales be made promptly. (Settlement is officially five business days after the transaction date.) The cash account is the most popular type of brokerage account even though it does not permit investor borrowing (that is, buying on margin). —Compare MARGIN ACCOUNT. —Also called *special cash account.*

cash and equivalents The sum of cash and short-term assets that can be easily converted to cash. This measure of corporate liquidity indicates a firm's ability to meet its short-term obligations.

cash balance plan A qualified employer pension plan in which the employer guarantees a contribution level and minimum rate of return.

What are the advantages or disadvantages of investing in firms that pay large cash dividends?

Income investors look for corporations that pay consistent, large dividends. Income can be predicted by purchasing one group of stocks that pays dividends quarterly beginning in January, one beginning in February, and one in March. Growth investors or investors in a high tax bracket may not want these stocks. They favor companies that forgo dividends to grow internally. Since dividends on stocks are taxable when paid, highly taxed investors postpone taxes by holding growth stocks and selling for gains later, rather than holding dividend paying stocks. Capital gains taxes may be lower than the ordinary tax rates on dividends.

Jeffrey S. Levine, CPA, MST, Alkon & Levine, PC, Newton, MA

cash basis accounting A method of accounting in which the receipt and payment of cash are the basis for recording transactions. Thus it is not the date on which goods and services are received that matters, as in accrual accounting, but the dates on which the cash changes hands for the transactions. Cash basis accounting is typically used for tax purposes by individuals but not by corporations. —Compare ACCRUAL ACCOUNTING.

cash contract A fairly unusual security transaction in which settlement with payment and security delivery are to occur on the same day as the trade date. This type of trade often occurs during the last week of a calendar year when sellers wish to settle early in order to realize a gain for tax purposes. —Compare REGULAR-WAY CONTRACT. —Also called *cash trade.*

cash conversion cycle The time required for a business to turn purchases into cash receipts from customers. A short cycle allows a business to quickly acquire cash that can be used for additional purchases or debt repayment.

cash cow A business or a segment of a business that produces significantly more cash than it consumes. As an example, a firm may sell a product that requires minimal advertising and promotional expenditures but continues to generate revenues year after year. Firms sometimes use cash cows to provide cash for financing other segments of their business.

cash dividend A dividend paid in cash (that is, by check) to holders of a firm's stock. Although the amount is usually based on profitability, it may temporarily exceed net income. Certain legal and contractual restrictions may limit a firm's ability to pay cash dividends.

cash equivalent **1.** An asset such as property or stock that has a realizable cash value equivalent to a specific sum of money. **2.** An asset that is so easily and quickly convertible to cash that holding it is essentially equivalent to holding cash. A Treasury bill is a cash equivalent.

cash flow The amount of net cash generated by an investment or a business during a specific period. One measure of cash flow is earnings before interest, taxes, depreciation, and amortization. Because cash is the fuel that drives a business, many analysts consider cash flow to be a company's most important financial statistic. Firms with big cash flows are frequently takeover targets because acquiring firms know that the cash can be used to help pay off the costs of the acquisitions. —See also FREE CASH FLOW.

CASE STUDY Financial analysts generally consider cash flow to be the best measure of a company's financial health. Increased cash flow means more funds are available to pay dividends, service or reduce debt, and invest in new assets. On the other hand, reported net income is heavily influenced by a firm's accounting practices. Reduced income generally means lower taxes and more cash, thus the same accounting practices that reduce net income can actually increase cash flow. A firm with large amounts of new investments and corresponding high depreciation charges might report low or negative earnings at the same time it has large cash flows to service debt and to acquire additional assets. Cable companies have huge investment requirements and are typical of firms that may be quite healthy in spite of reporting net losses. In early 1996, TCI Communications, at the time the nation's largest cable operator, reported fourth-quarter results that included a net loss of $70 million, more than double the loss reported in the year-earlier quarter. At the same time, the firm added more than a million new customers and reported a 25% increase in revenues. It also reported a 5% increase in cash flow. Thus, although TCI reported an additional loss, the quarter was generally considered quite successful. Operating cash flow, calculated as cash flow (the sum of net income and noncash expenses such as depreciation, depletion, and amortization) plus interest expense plus income tax expense, is an important consideration in corporate acquisitions because it indicates the cash flow that is available to service a firm's debt.

cash flow per share A value calculated by dividing a firm's cash flow by the average number of shares of capital stock that are outstanding. Cash flow per share is frequently used in valuing a firm's stock by analysts who believe the amount of net cash a firm produces is a more valid measure of its value than its reported earnings per share.

cashier's check A check drawn by a bank on itself. A cashier's check is made out to a designated institution or person and must be paid for before it is issued. —See also CERTIFIED CHECK.

cashier's department The division of a broker-dealer operation in which security certificates are processed, checks are sent or received, and dividend and interest records are kept. Essentially, the cashier's department handles the broker-dealer's money and paperwork. —Also called *cage.*

cash management bill A very short-term security (typically one having 10 to 20 days from date of issue until maturity) that is issued by the U.S. Treasury in order to manage its cash balances. A cash management bill is issued in minimum denominations of $1 million and is bought by institutional investors.

cash market The market in which trades are made for the immediate sale or purchase of a particular item. Cash market is commonly used in commodities trading to differentiate transactions involving immediate or nearly immediate delivery from transactions requiring delivery at a future time. —Also called *spot market.*

cash matching strategy A method of assembling a bond portfolio so that cash receipts from coupon and principal payments exactly meet future cash needs. —Compare DURATION MATCHING STRATEGY.

cash on delivery —See DELIVERY VERSUS PAYMENT.

cash price A price quotation in a cash market. In securities trading, a cash price distinguishes a transaction as being other than a regular five-day delivery, a difference that may be sought for tax or dividend reasons. In commodities trading, a cash price implies immediate or nearly immediate delivery as opposed to settlement in a specified future month. —Also called *spot price.*

cash ratio A type of current ratio measure that compares a firm's cash and cash equivalents with its current liabilities. A firm's cash ratio is a demanding test of its liquidity. —Compare QUICK RATIO.

cash reserves Investment funds that are held in short-term assets such as Treasury bills and certificates of deposit until more permanent investment opportunities are available. Large cash reserves, indicating a big pool of funds that eventually will be used, may force up the prices of selected investments at the time the funds are invested.

cash-secured put A put for which the writer deposits an amount of cash equal to the option's exercise price. For example, the writer of a put option on 100 shares of Sears stock at $35 per share would deposit $3,500 because the writer has agreed to buy $3,500 of Sears common stock if the put is exercised. The funds for a cash-secured put may be placed in short-term income-earning securities such as Treasury bills.

cash settlement Settlement of a futures contract in cash rather than in the asset underlying the contract. For example, stock index futures call for cash settlement because it is not feasible actually to deliver an index or the securities constituting an index.

cash surrender value The money paid by an insurance company to a policyholder who is canceling an annuity or cash-value life insurance policy. Cash value accumulates when premiums and interest on any previous cash value exceed the cost of insurance. Generally, the cash value a policyholder receives upon cancellation is not taxable unless it exceeds the sum of the premiums paid. —Also called *surrender value.*

cash trade —See CASH CONTRACT.

cash-value life insurance A type of life insurance in which part of the premium is used to provide death benefits and the remainder is available to earn interest. Thus, cash-value life insurance is both a protection plan and a savings plan. This insurance entails a significantly higher premium than protection-only insurance and, depending on the issuer and the policy, may pay a relatively small return on savings compared with other investments. —Compare TERM INSURANCE. —Also called *permanent insurance; whole life insurance.*

catastrophe bond A debt security with a payoff tied to the relative severity of a natural disaster such as a hurricane or earthquake. Bondholders are paid with insurance premiums but may have to accept reduced principal repayment in the event the specified disaster occurs during the life of the bond.

catastrophe call Redemption of a bond because of a disaster. For example, a bond issue collateralized by an airplane may be called if the plane crashes.

cats and dogs Speculative securities.

CBOE —See CHICAGO BOARD OPTIONS EXCHANGE.

CBOE Volatility Index —See VIX INDEX.

CBOT —See CHICAGO BOARD OF TRADE.

CCAB An acronym for a type of municipal convertible bond.

cash-value life insurance

Is cash-value life insurance a good investment? Why? For whom?

For many years this was a lousy investment pushed by excellent sales forces, often using deceptive practices to mask how poor it really was. In recent years the situation has changed, with the widespread offering by major companies of universal life and interest-sensitive whole life, both of which pay competitive interest rates on the cash-value portion of the policy. These policies can be an appropriate—even an excellent—investment because of the lack of federal taxation on the internal earnings of the policies. And if they are held until death, no tax is ever paid on these earnings. If the owner ever needs funds, he or she can borrow from the policy rather than cashing it in, thereby continuing to avoid taxation. TIP: Cash-value life insurance is an investment and should be treated as such. If you just need protection, buy term; 10- or 20-year level premium term policies are available.

Thomas J. McAllister, CFP, McAllister Financial Planning, Carmel, IN

CCC A very speculative grade assigned to a debt obligation by a rating agency. Such a rating indicates default or considerable doubt that interest will be paid or principal repaid. —Also called *Caa*.

CD —See CERTIFICATE OF DEPOSIT.

CDNX —See CANADIAN VENTURE EXCHANGE.

CDO —See COLLATERALIZED DEBT OBLIGATION.

Celler-Kefauver Antimerger Act A 1950 federal antitrust law that updated the Clayton Act by severely restricting anticompetitive mergers resulting from acquisition of assets.

central assets account —See ASSET MANAGEMENT ACCOUNT.

central bank A bank administered by a national government. A central bank issues money and carries out the country's monetary policy. The Federal Reserve System is the central bank of the United States.

central limit order book (CLOB) A central system that contains securities limit orders received from specialists and market makers. Such a system consolidates limit orders in a central location and bridges the gap in establishing a national market system. A hard CLOB executes orders immediately; a soft CLOB provides data to facilitate trading but does not include automatic executions. Establishment of a CLOB has generally been opposed by securities exchanges because they would stand to lose significant volume to such a system.

Central Registration Depository (CRD) A computerized database with information about most brokers, some investment advisers, their representatives, and the firms they work for. The CRD provides information about brokers' educational backgrounds, regulatory problems, and investor complaints.

CEO —See CHIEF EXECUTIVE OFFICER.

certainty equivalent The minimum sum of money a person would accept to forgo the opportunity to participate in an event for which the outcome, and therefore his or her receipt of a reward, is uncertain. For example, suppose you are told to draw one card from a full deck of cards. If you draw a red card you win $100 and if you draw a black card you win nothing. If you would accept $40 to forgo the selection and possibility of winning, $40 is the certainty equivalent of the outcome of the event. Certainty equivalents are used in evaluating risk.

certificate Evidence of ownership of a bond or shares of stock. A certificate contains detailed information relating to the issuer and the owner, including the issuer's name, particulars of the issue, the number of shares or the principal amount of the bonds, and the name and address of the owner. The back of a certificate may contain further details about the issue along with a provision for transferring ownership. —Also called *stock certificate.* —See also BOOK-ENTRY SECURITY.

certificate for automobile receivables (CARS) A short-term debt security backed by automobile loans and originating when lenders package and resell the automobile loans to the public. CARS provide lenders with more funds to use in additional lending and provide investors with relatively safe securities that pay short-term interest rates slightly above Treasury securities of similar maturity.

certificate of deposit (CD) A receipt, issued by a financial institution for a deposit of funds, that permits the holder to receive interest plus the deposit at maturity. Early withdrawal of CDs issued after October 1, 1983, results in a penalty of 30 days' loss of interest on maturities of one year or less, and loss of 90 days' interest on maturities over one year. —See also ADD-ON; CALLABLE CD; JUMBO CERTIFICATE OF DEPOSIT; NEGOTIABLE CERTIFICATE OF DEPOSIT; REAL ESTATE CERTIFICATE OF DEPOSIT; TERM CERTIFICATE; ZERO-COUPON CERTIFICATE OF DEPOSIT.

certificate of indebtedness A United States Treasury debt obligation with an original maturity of one year or less and a fixed coupon rate of interest. A certificate of indebtedness differs from a Treasury bill, which is sold at a discount from face value and has no coupon.

certificate of participation (COP) Entitlement to a participation, or share in the lease payments from a particular project. The lessor generally assigns lease payments to a trustee that distributes the payments to certificate holders.

Certificates for Amortizing Revolving Debts (CARDS) A special type of asset-backed debt security collateralized by credit card balances.

certified check A check that a financial institution draws on an individual's account and then certifies to indicate that sufficient funds are available to cover the amount of the check when cashed.

certified financial planner (CFP) A professional financial planner who has completed a series of correspondence courses and has passed examinations in subject areas such as insurance, securities, and taxes. The designation is awarded by the Institute of Certified Financial Planners. —Compare CHARTERED FINANCIAL CONSULTANT.

Certified in Financial Management (CFM) A professional designation awarded by the Institute of Management Accountants to members who demonstrate knowledge of financial management principles by passing a series of examinations. Members must meet a work experience requirement and provide evidence of continuing education.

Certified in Management Accounting (CMA) A professional designation awarded by the Institute of Management Accountants to members who demonstrate knowledge of management accounting by successfully passing a series of four computer-based examinations. Candidates for the designation must have two years of professional experience in management accounting, and individuals who earn the designation are required to present evidence of continuing education.

Certified Public Accountant (CPA) An accountant who has met certain state requirements as to age, education, experience, residence, and accounting knowledge, the latter measured by the successful completion of an extensive series of examinations. In most instances, only CPAs are permitted to render opinions on the fairness of financial statements.

cf —Used in bond transaction tables in newspapers to indicate that the certificate of a bond has matured but is still trading: *VarCp 10s99cf.*

CFA —See CHARTERED FINANCIAL ANALYST.

CFM —See CERTIFIED IN FINANCIAL MANAGEMENT.

CFP —See CERTIFIED FINANCIAL PLANNER.

CFTC —See COMMODITY FUTURES TRADING COMMISSION.

chairman The highest-ranking executive in a corporation. The chairman leads the board of directors in setting broad corporate goals and determining if managers are, in fact, pursuing and achieving those goals. In large corporations the chairman is not ordinarily involved in day-to-day operational activities, although it is likely that he or she was the chief executive officer before attaining the position of chairman. In some corporations, the chairman also serves as the president and the chief executive officer. —Also called *chairman of the board.* —See also DIRECTOR.

change —See NET CHANGE.

channel In charting, a line connecting a series of high points accompanied by a parallel line connecting a series of low points. The two parallel lines compose the channel in which the variable (for example, a stock price) has been moving and is expected to continue moving. An ascending channel indicates a bullish trend, while a descending channel represents a bearish trend. Breaking downward through an ascending series of low prices or upward through a descending series of high prices indicates a likely change in trend.

channel stuffing Artificially inflating current sales and earnings by shipping more goods than would normally be ordered. For example, an appliance manufacturer may inflate revenues and earnings in the current accounting period by shipping to retail stores more refrigerators, stoves, and dishwashers than the stores are likely to sell. The practice of channel stuffing borrows revenues and earnings from the future because overstocked customers will reduce orders in future periods.

Chapter 7 A bankruptcy option in which a bankrupt firm is liquidated after the courts have determined that reorganization is not worthwhile. A trustee is charged with liquidating all assets and distributing the proceeds to satisfy claims in their order of priority. In Chapter 7 bankruptcies the creditors often receive a fraction of the value of their claims and the stockholders receive nothing.

Chapter 11 A bankruptcy option in which a trustee is appointed to reorganize the bankrupt firm. Although the existing claims of security holders are likely to be reduced or replaced with different claims, it is expected that the firm will continue operating. Both creditors and owners must vote approval of the plan before the reorganization can be confirmed by court action and become effective. —See also PREPACKAGED BANKRUPTCY; REORGANIZATION PLAN.

⋀⋀ CASE STUDY | The turn of the century produced difficult business conditions for many companies, including one of America's technical giants, Polaroid Corporation. Founded by Edwin Land and George Wheelwright in 1937, Polaroid was best known for instant photography and glare-free sunglasses. During the 1960s and early 1970s the firm's common stock was part of the "Nifty Fifty," a collection of must-own securities for many portfolio managers and individual investors. Changing consumer preferences, a technological revolution in photography, debt incurred to fend off an attempted takeover, and faulty management decisions during the next several decades sent the firm's stock into a downward spiral until the shares traded for only 28¢ just prior to filing for Chapter 11 bankruptcy protection on October 12, 2001. At the time of the filing the company listed $1.81 billion in assets and $948 million in debts, including a $360 million bank loan that was due in one month. The stock traded as high as $60 per share in 1997. Polaroid's problems stemmed in large part from the increased popularity of digital photography, which captured substantial market share from the firm's products in instant photography. Other photographers discovered the widespread availability of one-hour processing was nearly as convenient and less costly than instant photography. Polaroid had taken on substantial debt in 1988 when it successfully fought a takeover attempt by Shamrock Holdings. The combination of large debt, high costs, and deteriorating market share doomed an American icon. At the time of the bankruptcy filing many analysts expected the firm to be liquidated and its assets sold piecemeal.

characteristic line A straight line on a graph that shows the relationship over time between returns on a stock and returns on the market. The line is used to illustrate a stock's alpha (the vertical intercept) and beta (the line's slope) and to show the difference between systematic and unsystematic risk.

charge off —See WRITE OFF.

charitable contribution deduction An itemized income-tax deduction for donations of assets to Internal Revenue Service–designated organizations. Certain qualifications on this deduction apply, such as a contribution limit of 50% of a taxpayer's adjusted gross income. Of particular interest to investors is the option to donate appreciated property (that is, securities that have increased in value since acquisition) and to deduct the entire market value of the donated assets without being obligated to pay taxes on the capital gains. Donations of appreciated property may subject the taxpayer to the alternative minimum tax.

charitable lead trust A trust that pays an income to a charity for a specific length of time then leaves the remainder of the trust to designated beneficiaries, usually family members. The purpose of the charitable lead trust is to reduce taxes on the estate of the deceased while maintaining the family's control of the estate's assets. —Compare CHARITABLE REMAINDER TRUST.

charitable remainder trust A trust that pays an income to one or more individuals for a specified length of time then leaves the remainder of the trust to a designated charity. A charitable remainder trust can produce substantial tax benefits and is particularly suitable for use by a married couple with no children. —Compare CHARITABLE LEAD TRUST.

chart   Data displayed in a diagrammatic manner, often to show relationships between different sets of numbers. Charts are used to observe the historical values of variables and, frequently, to spot trends that may provide insights for use in projecting future values. —Also called *graph*. —See also BAR CHART; CANDLESTICK CHART; LINE CHART; POINT-AND-FIGURE CHART.

charter   —See ARTICLES OF INCORPORATION.

chartered financial analyst (CFA)   A financial analyst who has met certain standards of experience, knowledge, and conduct as determined by the Association for Investment Management and Research. The successful candidate must pass examinations covering economics, security analysis, portfolio management, financial accounting, and standards of conduct.

chartered financial consultant (ChFC)   A professional financial planner who has completed a series of courses and examinations in subject areas such as economics, insurance, real estate, and tax shelters. The designation is awarded by the American College in Bryn Mawr, PA. —Compare CERTIFIED FINANCIAL PLANNER.

chart formation   A series of graphed stock prices or other market variables that form a recognizable pattern that may be used to determine future movements of the charted variable. Chart formations are not always as clearly defined as their users would like; thus, the ability to recognize and use charted data varies among technicians. —Also called *formation; pattern*. —See also INVERTED FORMATION.

charting   The graphing of market variables, especially of stock prices and market averages. Technicians also chart other variables including commodity prices, interest rates, and trading volume in an attempt to determine trends and project future values. —See also BAR CHART; CANDLESTICK CHART; LINE CHART; POINT-AND-FIGURE CHART.

chartist   An analyst, such as a market technician, who attempts to determine future stock price movements using past price movements that have been recorded on a chart. Two chartists may have different projections after viewing the same chart.

chart service   A firm selling graphs of security prices. A chart service records prices for a large number of securities or commodities and publishes charts at periodic intervals (generally on a monthly basis) for sale to investors. Subscribing to a chart service saves an investor considerable time; however, the charts often arrive a few days after the date of the last entry.

chase a stock   To attempt to buy a stock that is rising in price by placing orders at increasingly higher prices.

chattel mortgage   A mortgage loan using personal property such as automobiles, paintings, inventories, or real estate leases, but not real estate ownership, as security.

cheap   Of, relating to, or being a security that sells at a market price below what is expected given fundamental factors such as earnings, assets, and management ability. Determining whether a security is cheap is a subjective judgment. —Compare EXPENSIVE.

cheap money   —See EASY MONEY.

checking the market　To scan market maker quotations to find the lowest ask or highest bid for a security.

checkwriting privilege　The privilege of writing checks against shares held in a mutual fund. This option, which provides greater liquidity for the investor, is generally offered free of charge. The dollar amount of each check is usually subject to a minimum value—often $250 or $500—depending on the policy of the fund.

ChFC　—See CHARTERED FINANCIAL CONSULTANT.

Chicago Board of Trade (CBOT)　A derivatives exchange established in 1848 to trade forward contracts in agricultural commodities, including wheat, corn, and oats. CBOT members now trade 48 different futures and options products on agricultural commodities, U.S. Treasury bonds, and the Dow Jones Industrial Average. The exchange introduced electronic trading in 1994 after 145 years of using open outcry.

Chicago Board Options Exchange (CBOE)　A securities exchange established in 1973 as the nation's first organized floor for trading standardized options. Although its success spawned option trading on a number of other exchanges, the CBOE remains the most active options exchange in the country. Unlike most exchanges that use a specialist system of trading, the CBOE uses market makers who compete among themselves for trades. —See also BOARD BROKER.

Chicago Mercantile Exchange (CME)　A leading exchange for trading futures and options on futures in four major areas: interest rates, stock indexes, foreign currency exchange, and commodities. The CME was established in 1919 as a marketplace for agricultural futures contracts, and in 2000 became the first U.S. financial exchange to demutualize and become a shareholder-owned corporation. The exchange also operates GLOBEX, an electronic trading system for after-hour orders. —Also called *Merc*.

Chicago Stock Exchange (CHX)　A regional securities exchange that provides an auction market for equities. The CHX first opened for business in 1882 and later merged with exchanges in Cleveland, Minneapolis, and St. Louis to form the Midwest Stock Exchange. The exchange reclaimed its prior name in 1993. The CHX currently trades over 4,000 stocks, including many issues also listed on the NYSE and Nasdaq. All but very large trades are executed electronically.

chief executive officer (CEO)　The person responsible to a company's board of directors for carrying out its policies. Essentially, the CEO is the highest-ranking executive managing the firm on a day-to-day basis. —Also called *chief operating officer*. —See also CHAIRMAN.

Chinese wall　An imaginary separation placed between a brokerage firm's investment banking business and its trading and retail business. A Chinese wall prevents investment bankers who frequently are privy to information that could substantially influence the price of a client's securities from leaking that information to the firm's traders and sales personnel. The exchange of such information is legally prohibited.

chooser option　An option that permits the owner to choose whether to use the security as a put or a call after the option is purchased. The exercise price and expiration date are specified at the time of purchase.

churn To trade securities very actively in a brokerage account in order to increase brokerage commissions rather than customer profits. Brokers may be tempted to churn accounts because their income is directly related to the volume of trading undertaken by customers. Churning is illegal and unethical; suspected churning should be reported to the brokerage firm's office manager. —Also called *burn and churn; overtrade.*

CHX —See CHICAGO STOCK EXCHANGE.

Cincinnati Stock Exchange (CSE) A regional securities exchange dating to 1885 when a group of businessmen met in Cincinnati, Ohio, to auction the shares of several local companies. In 1976 the Cincinnati Stock Exchange replaced its trading floor with a geographically dispersed electronic trading system. The Cincinnati Stock Exchange is now headquartered in Chicago.

circle A process used in finding interested buyers of a new security issue before determining the final price. A potential customer will be given a preliminary price (for example, the interest rate for a bond or the selling price for a stock) and will commit to a purchase if the issue is actually priced at the preliminary estimate. A different price permits the customer to back out or to get the first chance to buy the issue at the new price. —Compare INDICATION OF INTEREST.

circuit breaker The automatic response, usually a halt or slowdown, in activity at an exchange in response to certain occurrences in trading. Circuit breakers are designed to reduce market volatility and were instituted following the large market breaks in October 1987 and October 1989. —See also RULE 80A; SUSPENDED TRADING.

class **1.** —See STOCK CLASS 1. **2.** Option contracts of the same type (put or call) and style (American or European) on the same security and expiring on the same expiration date.

class action lawsuit A lawsuit in which one party or a limited number of parties sue on behalf of a larger group to which the parties belong. For example, investors may bring a class action lawsuit against a brokerage firm that has actively promoted a tax shelter without having adequately disclosed the attendant risks. —See also SHAREHOLDER DERIVATIVE SUIT.

classified board A corporate board of directors whose members are elected to terms that expire in different years. A classified board makes it more difficult for a new owner to assume control in a takeover. —See also STAGGERED TERMS.

classified stock —See STOCK CLASS 1.

clawback **1.** A provision in an incentive stock option that requires an employee to reimburse the company for any gains from exercising options in the event the employee goes to work for a direct competitor within a specified number of months of exercise. **2.** Excessive management share of profits that must be refunded to investors of a venture capital fund. A clawback is required when managers of a venture capital fund take a contractual share of early investment gains that are subsequently reduced by losses.

Clayton Act A 1914 federal antitrust law designed to promote competition by prohibiting or severely restricting practices such as the acquisition of competitors, price discrimination, secret rebates, and interlocking directorates.

clean balance sheet A balance sheet with only a small amount of debt in relation to assets.

clean cross —See CLEAN TRADE.

clean opinion The opinion of a firm's auditors that its financial statements are fairly presented in accordance with generally accepted accounting principles. A clean opinion does not necessarily mean that the firm is financially strong or that its future is favorable, since even financially weak firms generally receive clean opinions. —Compare ADVERSE OPINION; DISCLAIMER OF OPINION; QUALIFIED OPINION. —Also called *standard opinion; unqualified opinion.* —See also SUBJECT TO OPINION.

clean price The price of a bond without accrued interest. —Compare DIRTY PRICE.

clean trade A security transaction by a broker that exactly matches customer buy and sell orders. Thus, the broker does not find it necessary either to acquire securities or to sell from inventory in order to complete the transaction. —Also called *clean cross.*

cleanup call Early redemption of the entire balance of a debt issue when a relatively small amount of the original issue remains outstanding. For example, mortgage-backed securities are gradually paid down as mortgages backing the bonds are paid off by homeowners. At some point the issuer of the mortgage-backed securities may decide to reduce its own administrative expenses by calling the balance of the issue.

cleanup merger A merger in which an acquired firm is consolidated into the acquiring firm. —Also called *take-out merger.*

clear To pay for securities delivered into an account and accept funds for securities delivered out of an account.

clear Of or relating to a trade in which the seller delivers securities and the buyer delivers funds in the prescribed manner and on time. —Compare FAIL. —See also GOOD DELIVERY.

clearing fee A charge assessed by a clearing house for clearing securities trades using its own facilities.

clearing house A corporation established by an exchange in order to facilitate the execution of trades by transferring funds, assigning deliveries, and guaranteeing the performance of all obligations. —See also CLEARING-HOUSE STATEMENT.

clearing-house statement A statement of security or commodity trades submitted by a member firm to a clearing house. The statement indicates the net balance (that is, short or long) in each security or commodity and the net amount to be paid or received to reconcile the member's account.

clearing member A member of a clearing house. Membership in such a house permits the member firm to use it for clearing security trades.

Clearstream International An international clearing and settlement organization formed in 2000 through a merger of Cedel International and Deutsche Borse Clearing.

clientele effect The tendency of different securities to attract different types of investors, depending on the dividend policy of the issuer. For example, certain investors are attracted to stocks (for example, electric utility stocks) with high dividend yields while other investors, in high income-tax brackets, prefer stocks with lower dividend yields but more capital gains potential.

📉 **CASE STUDY** | Following the close of security markets on September 25, 2001, Winn-Dixie Stores, Inc., announced the firm would slash its $1.02 annual dividend. The Jacksonville, Florida, supermarket chain was one of few large corporations that paid monthly dividends, a costly policy that attracted a clientele of investors who valued the regular current income. The monthly dividend of 8.5¢ per share was to be reduced to an expected 5¢ per quarter. The firm's policy had been to declare three monthly dividend payments at the beginning of each quarter. Under the new plan, only the quarterly dividend would be declared. At the time of the dividend announcement the firm also indicated first-quarter earnings would be in the range of 15¢ to 18¢ per share, a reduction from the previous projection of 24¢ to 30¢ per share. At the same time the company lowered its forecast for fiscal 2002 earnings. The announcement was bad news for stockholders, who saw the value of their shares fall in price during trading on the day following the news. Winn-Dixie common stock fell $7.37 to $12.41, a 37% decline on very heavy volume. The firm's chief financial officer said the new dividend policy would give Winn-Dixie more financial flexibility at the same time it placed added emphasis on capital appreciation rather than cash payments to stockholders. The large price decline indicated existing stockholders apparently didn't appreciate the new emphasis.

Clifford trust A temporary trust (established to last at least ten years and one day or until the death of the beneficiary) in which assets are irrevocably transferred to the trust and income from the trust is given to the beneficiary. When the trust is terminated, the principal passes back to the creator. Clifford trusts are used almost exclusively by people with dependent children or dependent parents. Income from trusts created before March 1, 1986, is taxed at the creator's rate until the minority child reaches 14 years of age. At that time the child's tax rate applies. For trusts created after March 1, 1986, the income is taxed at the donor's rate even after the minority child has reached 14 years of age. Tax reform passed in 1986 eliminated most of the tax advantages of Clifford trusts.

climax —See BUYING CLIMAX; SELLING CLIMAX.

clip To detach the interest coupons from a bearer bond. These coupons must be presented to a bank, a brokerage house, or the issuer's agent in order for the holder of the bearer bond to receive interest payments.

CLOB —See CENTRAL LIMIT ORDER BOOK.

clone fund A mutual fund started by another mutual fund as a result of the parent fund's large growth and management's assessment that the parent is limited as to the investments it can make. For example, a very large fund would generally be unable to establish investment positions in small or new corporations. Thus, a new, smaller fund with the same goals as the older, bigger fund is started. Although the parent fund and clone fund have the same investment objectives, they purchase different securities and generally operate under different managements.

📉 **CASE STUDY** | Many finance professionals believe that mutual funds can become so large that investment performance is hindered. Managers of mutual funds that have a huge amount of assets are restricted in the securities that can be added to their portfolios because of the large size of transactions these funds typically undertake. For example, a large fund generally cannot establish a position in the stock of a relatively small

clone fund

What are clone funds, and are they as good as the real thing?

Rocky versus Rocky II. Clone mutual funds are replicas of existing funds. They are set up for several reasons. The managers of a fund may conclude that if it becomes any bigger it will be too unwieldy (this was true of the Windsor Fund). Or the group may want to introduce a new pricing structure. (Most Massachusetts Financial Services funds now have A, B, and C shares: the first with a front-end charge, the second and third with redemption charges, depending on when they are sold, and higher annual fees but no up-front charge.) Or a new fund may have similar but slightly different objectives. Finally, when a group successfully pioneers a new type of fund, imitators inevitably follow. (Benham Target Maturities broke new ground for investors planning for retirement with a series of zero-coupon bond funds; the following year the Scudder group followed suit.) There is no reason in principle why the clone should perform worse or better than the original. Throughout the years, the Pioneer Fund often beat Pioneer II (renamed Pioneer Value Fund in 2001), but then Pioneer II often beat the Pioneer Fund! The investor should keep in mind, however, that the two funds are different. They may have different portfolio managers, perhaps some difference in investment outlook, and perhaps different fees. The simple rules then, when looking at a new clone fund, are first, take into account what the original has done—clearly that is a crucial piece of evidence. And second, research the differences.

Reg Green, Editor, *Mutual Fund News Service*, Bodega Bay, CA

firm simply because of the limited number of shares that trade. Even if the fund could acquire a stake in the firm, the amount invested would represent such a tiny proportion of the fund's assets that the fund's investment performance would be little affected. Similarly, a big fund may have difficulty unwinding a large position in a security with limited trading volume. In 1995, the manager of Fidelity's Magellan fund, America's largest equity fund, took at least two months to sell the fund's 11.8-million-share stake in Micron Technology. The manager of a relatively small fund can take investment positions in the stocks of both small and large firms without worry that the fund's transactions will have an effect on the prices of the securities. Mutual funds may also become more difficult to manage as they grow in size. More assets mean bigger trades and a larger number of securities to track. Some fund sponsors stabilize the size of a rapidly growing fund by closing the fund, thus halting the sale of shares to new investors. Closing a fund is sometimes followed by the introduction of a new clone fund that has an investment philosophy virtually identical to the closed fund. Vanguard closed its Windsor fund to new investors in 1985 and at the same time started successor Windsor II, a clone of the closed fund. Likewise, the Putnam Fund for Growth & Income was closed in 1994 when the firm launched the clone Putnam Fund for Growth & Income II.

close 1. The end of a session of trading. **2.** The last price at which a security trades during a trading session. The last price is reported in the financial media and is of particular importance to the valuation of investment portfolios. —Also called *closing price; last.*

close a position To eliminate an investment position. The most common way to close a position is to sell a security that is owned. An investor might also close a position by purchasing stock to replace shares borrowed for a short sale.

closed corporation —See CLOSELY HELD COMPANY.

closed-end investment company An investment company that issues a limited number of shares and does not redeem those that are outstanding. Closed-end investment companies are fairly rare; their shares trade on the exchanges or in the over-the-counter market. Thus, like stock of other publicly traded companies, share prices are determined by the pressures of supply and demand rather than by the value of underlying assets. —Compare MUTUAL FUND. —Also called *publicly traded fund.* —See also REGULATED INVESTMENT COMPANY.

closed-end mortgage A mortgage with a prohibition against additional borrowing using the same lien. The prohibition against additional borrowing protects the existing creditors from having the security diluted. —Compare OPEN-END MORTGAGE.

closed fund A mutual fund that no longer issues shares to nonshareholders but that may continue to sell shares to existing shareholders. A fund usually closes because its management has decided the fund has grown too large to be managed effectively.

CASE STUDY Mutual funds that have closed to new investors sometimes reopen. Managers may close a fund to new shareholders for several reasons. A fund may grow so large in assets that the portfolio becomes difficult to effectively manage. Large investment positions in individual securities can be difficult to acquire or sell without affecting the prices of securities. Thus, portfolio managers of very large funds lose flexibility because they are mostly limited to owning the stocks of large corporations with huge numbers of shares outstanding. Likewise, a mutual fund that specializes in the investments of a relatively narrow market segment may have limited investment options. A fund that concentrates on investing in small-capitalization firms or companies from developing countries is likely to face limited share availability. Investors may pour money into a successful mutual fund that the portfolio manager is unable to invest. Mutual funds often close after strong asset growth from a long bull market. For example, Janus Capital closed 7 of its 21 funds in a two-year period beginning in mid-1998. Closed funds included the popular Janus Fund, which had grown in size to $52 billion of assets. A fund that has been closed may subsequently reopen if the fund size shrinks or if the portfolio manager believes new investment opportunities have become available. A bear market may reduce the size of a fund because of reduced stock values and as a result of share redemptions by the fund's shareholders. A smaller fund means reduced income to the fund's managers, who may decide to reopen the fund to new investors. In late 2000 Fidelity Investments announced that it would reopen both its Contrafund and Growth & Income Portfolio funds to new investors after holders had withdrawn nearly $11 billion by redeeming the funds' shares.

closely held company A firm whose shares of common stock are owned by relatively few individuals and are generally unavailable to outsiders. —Also called *closed corporation.*

close market A narrow spread between the bid price and ask price of a security. A close market in a security is facilitated by active trading and multiple market makers.

closet index fund An investment company that claims to actively manage its portfolio but in reality emulates a market index such as the S&P 500. Closet index funds generally charge sales fees and annual expenses that are typical for an actively managed fund.

closet indexing An investment method in which an individual develops a widely diversified portfolio of securities that achieves a performance level nearly identical to that of a broad-based market average yet claims the performance is the result of active management based on market expertise.

closing price —See CLOSE 2.

closing purchase —See CLOSING TRANSACTION 2.

closing quote The final bid and ask price stated by the market maker or specialist at the end of a trading session.

closing range In futures trading, the range of prices at which transactions occur during the close of the market.

closing sale —See CLOSING TRANSACTION 2.

closing transaction 1. The final transaction for a particular security during a trading day. —Compare OPENING TRANSACTION 1. 2. An option order that eliminates or decreases the size of an existing option position. An investor who repurchases three options that have been sold short is entering into a closing transaction. —Compare OPENING TRANSACTION 2. —Also called *closing purchase; closing sale.* —See also CLOSE A POSITION.

CMA —See CERTIFIED IN MANAGEMENT ACCOUNTING.

CME —See CHICAGO MERCANTILE EXCHANGE.

CMO —See COLLATERALIZED MORTGAGE OBLIGATION.

CNS —See CONTINUOUS NET SETTLEMENT.

CoCo bond —See CONTINGENT CONVERTIBLE BOND.

Code of Procedure Rules of the National Association of Securities Dealers for settling disputes among members or complaints against NASD members by outsiders.

codicil A legal change made to a will.

Coffee, Sugar and Cocoa Exchange (CSCE) An organized exchange, established in 1882, that provides facilities in New York City for the trading of futures contracts on coffee, sugar, and, following its addition in 1979, cocoa. Options on sugar futures are also traded at this exchange.

coil —See TRIANGLE.

cold call A broker's telephone call to a heretofore unknown person during which the broker tries to enlist that person as a customer.

collar 1. In options, buying a put and selling short a call so as to limit the potential profit and loss from an investment position. 2. The level at which an index triggers a circuit breaker to temporarily stop trading. 3. In an acquisition, an upper and lower limit that will be paid for shares of the company to be acquired. 4. In a new issue, a limit on the price or interest rate that is acceptable. —See also ZERO-COST COLLAR.

〽 CASE STUDY | In December 2000 PepsiCo, Inc., announced it would acquire Quaker Oats Co. for $13.4 billion in PepsiCo stock. The elusive deal was sealed after Quaker spurned an earlier PepsiCo offer and a more recent offer from Coca-Cola had been withdrawn. Both soft drink giants were after Quaker's noncarbonated beverages, including Gatorade. The deal specified that PepsiCo would offer 2.3 shares of its stock for each share of Quaker. At a then-current PepsiCo stock price of $42.38, the Quaker shares were each valued at $97.46. The agreement also provided a minimum and maximum value, or collar, for the Quaker stock. PepsiCo guaranteed a minimum price of $92 per Quaker share in the event PepsiCo stock fell below $40 for ten random days during the month prior to closing. Likewise, PepsiCo would be required to pay no more than $105 per Quaker share in the event PepsiCo stock increased to more than $45.65. The collar of $92 to $105 provided a maximum and minimum value that Quaker stockholders would receive for each of their shares. The earlier PepsiCo offer specified the same 2.3-to-1 exchange rate but had been rejected by Quaker because PepsiCo was unwilling to include a collar as part of the offer. In other words, PepsiCo refused to guarantee a minimum price for the Quaker stock it wanted to acquire.

collar rule —See RULE 80A.

collateral Assets pledged as security for a loan. In the event that a borrower defaults on the terms of a loan, the collateral may be sold, with the proceeds used to satisfy any remaining obligations. High-quality collateral reduces risk to the lender and results in a lower rate of interest on the loan.

collateralize To pledge an asset as security for a loan. A loan to a broker is collateralized by pledging securities.

collateralized bond obligation A derivative security collateralized by a pool of high-yield bonds. Several classes of these obligations are issued for a single pool of bonds with different classes offering different yields and a different degree of credit risk. Interest and principal repayments received on the bond portfolio are passed through to owners of the derivative securities. —Compare COLLATERALIZED MORTGAGE OBLIGATION.

collateralized debt obligation (CDO) A debt security collateralized by a variety of debt obligations including bonds and loans of different maturities and credit quality.

CASE STUDY Collateralized debt obligations (CDOs) originated in the 1990s when financial institutions began moving debts off their balance sheets by selling new securities (CDOs) using bonds and loans—often of relatively low credit quality—as collateral. Each CDO package permits investors to choose particular securities of different risk, ranging from investment-grade to very speculative. A CDO is considered high quality when it enjoys first claim on cash flows produced by the package of loans and bonds. This safety results in high-quality CDOs promising investors relatively low rates of return. CDOs with a lower claim to a package's cash flows carry a high rate of return because of the increased likelihood that some of the payments from the underlying collateral will not occur. Many CDOs were issued with low-grade bonds as collateral at a time when junk bond defaults were in the range of 2% to 3%. The subsequent meltdown of telecommunications and other high-tech firms in 2000 and 2001 resulted in increased defaults on debt that caught many CDO investors by surprise. In fact, the sudden decline in credit quality surprised even professional investors. Financial services company American Express was forced to take pretax writeoffs of over $1 billion in the first seven months of 2001 to account for the decreased market value of the CDOs and other debt securities held in its portfolio. Bank One and insurance companies Lincoln National, American General, and Torchmark were also forced to take large writeoffs on CDO holdings.

collateralized mortgage obligation (CMO) A security collateralized with mortgage loans and issued by Freddie Mac. Although collateralized in a manner similar to a Freddie Mac pass through, a CMO provides interest and principal payments in a more predictable manner. CMOs are classed according to expected maturity ranges at the time of issue. The greater certainty of payment size is offset by slightly lower yields compared with ordinary pass throughs. —Compare COLLATERALIZED BOND OBLIGATION. —See also PLANNED AMORTIZATION CLASS; TARGETED AMORTIZATION CLASS BOND; Z-TRANCHE.

collateral trust bond A long-term debt obligation with a claim against securities rather than against physical assets. This type of bond is issued primarily by holding companies that own mainly securities of subsidiaries.

collectible An asset of limited supply that is sought for a variety of reasons including, it is hoped, an increase in value. Stamps, antiques, coins, and works of art are among the many things usually classified as collectibles. Collectibles are often regarded by investors as hedges against inflation, since their value tends to appreciate most when general prices are rising. The collectibles market represents a very tricky investment for inexperienced investors.

collection period The number of days, on average, that a firm requires for collection of a credit sale. The length of the collection period indicates the effectiveness with which a firm's management grants credit and collects from customers. A short period is desirable because the firm obtains cash more quickly for reinvestment or for paying its own bills. The collection period is calculated by dividing accounts receivable by average daily credit sales. —Also called *average collection period.*

college-savings plan A plan that allows individuals to set aside money in a special account designed to pay for future college expenses. Funds in the account grow tax-deferred, and withdrawals used for college expenses are exempt from federal income taxes. Parents are permitted to change from one state plan to another once a year with no penalty. Many states also offer tax incentives for these plans. —Also called *529 plan.*

combination A union of two or more entities, either by merging one or more of the entities into another of the entities or by consolidating the entities into a new entity.

> 〰️ **CASE STUDY** Lucas Industries PLC and Variety Corporation, two manufacturers of auto and truck brakes, agreed in June 1996 to a combination to be called Lucas-Variety PLC. Managements of both firms indicated the combination was necessary so as to remain competitive in a market that demanded a global presence. The combination also was expected to produce cost savings and to result in tax savings by allowing the new firm to benefit from Lucas's tax-loss carryforwards. Terms of the agreement called for the two firms to merge into a new company through an exchange of shares. Variety's owners would receive approximately 38% of the shares of the new firm while Lucas's owners would receive the other 62% of the shares. The market prices of both firms' shares rose following announcement of the agreement, an indication that investors agreed with managements' assessment of the financial benefits of the merger.

combination bond —See DOUBLE-BARRELED MUNICIPAL BOND.

combination option An option composed of one or more calls and one or more puts. While the original combination is sold as a single unit, each part may be sold or exercised individually. Examples of combination options are spreads, straddles, straps, and strips.

To what degree are brokerage commissions or other fees negotiable?

The ability to negotiate fees and commissions varies from firm to firm. Some firms are very flexible and give the individual advisors and brokers the ability to negotiate fees to some extent. Some firms offer a discount service via the Internet as well as a full service account. The degree of personal service and advice the investor requires will influence the amount of the discount.

George Riles, First Vice President and Resident Manager, Merrill Lynch, Albany, GA

combination order —See ALTERNATIVE ORDER.

combination security A security that combines the attributes of two or more individual securities. An example of a combination security is a convertible bond that is part debt and part common stock.

COMEX —See NEW YORK MERCANTILE EXCHANGE.

comfort letter A statement issued by a Certified Public Accountant declaring no indication of false or misleading information in the financial statements being used in connection with a securities offering.

commercial paper A short-term unsecured promissory note issued by a finance company or a relatively large industrial firm. The notes are generally sold at a discount from face value with maturities ranging from 30 to 270 days. Although the large denominations ($25,000 minimum) of these notes usually keep individual investors out of this market, the notes are popular investments for money market mutual funds. Used interchangeably with the term *paper*. —See also PRIME PAPER.

commingled fund An investment fund that consists of assets of several individual accounts. A commingled fund is established to reduce the cost and effort required to manage accounts separately.

commingled securities Customers' securities that are stored together with a brokerage firm's securities.

commission The fee levied by a broker to undertake a trade on behalf of a customer. Because the amount of the commission for a particular trade is no longer fixed, it can vary considerably among firms. —See also DISCOUNT BROKERAGE FIRM; FULL-SERVICE BROKERAGE FIRM.

commission broker An employee of a member firm of an organized securities exchange who transacts orders for the firm or its customers on the exchange floor. Orders flow to the commission broker from the firm's trading desk or from its registered representatives.

commission house A firm whose primary business is the execution of its customers' orders to buy and sell securities, activities for which it earns a fee. Commission houses earn the name from acting as brokers rather than as dealers.

Committee on Uniform Securities Identification Procedures (CUSIP) An appointed board that assigns standard identification (CUSIP) numbers for all stock certificates and registered bonds issued in the United States. —See also CUSIP NUMBER.

commodity A generic, largely unprocessed, good that can be processed and resold. Commodities traded in the financial markets for immediate or future delivery are grains, metals, and minerals. They are generally traded in very large quantities. —See also FUTURES CONTRACT.

commodity-backed bond A rare bond that has its interest payments and/or principal repayment tied to the price of a commodity such as silver or oil. Although such a bond carries a relatively low interest rate at the time of issue, it gives the investor a hedge against inflation since the price of the commodity is likely to rise. These bonds are usually issued by firms having a stake in the commodity used to back the security. —Also called *gold bond.*

commodity brokerage firm —See FUTURES COMMISSION MERCHANT.

Commodity Futures Trading Commission (CFTC) A federal agency, established in 1974, that regulates and supervises the trading of commodity futures and commodity options. Additional regulation is effected by the exchanges on which the contracts are traded. —Compare NATIONAL FUTURES ASSOCIATION.

commodity option An option either to buy or to sell a commodity futures contract at a fixed price until a specified date. —See also CALL 1; PUT 1.

commodity product spread A spread involving two commodities: a primary commodity and a byproduct of the primary commodity. For example, an investor might purchase a contract for soybeans and sell short a contract for soybean oil.

common equity The dollar amount of common shareholders' investment in a company, including common stock, retained earnings, and additional paid-in capital.

Common Market —See EUROPEAN ECONOMIC COMMUNITY.

common-size statement A financial statement that has variables expressed in percentages rather than in dollar amounts. For example, items on an income statement are shown as a percentage of revenue or sales, and balance sheet entries are displayed as a percentage of total assets. Common-size statements are used primarily for comparative purposes so that firms of various sizes can be equated. —Also called *one hundred percent statement.*

common stock A class of capital stock that has no preference to dividends or any distribution of assets. Common stock usually conveys voting rights and is often termed *capital stock* if it is the only class of stock that a firm has outstanding (that is, the firm has neither preferred stock nor multiple classes of common stock). Common stockholders are the residual owners of a corporation in that they have a claim to what remains after every other party has been paid. The value of their claim depends on the success of the firm. —See also CALLABLE COMMON STOCK; COMMON STOCK EQUIVALENT; PUTTABLE COMMON STOCK.

common stock equivalent A security viewed as basically the same as common stock, generally because the equivalent security may be exchanged for shares of common stock. Common stock equivalents include convertible bonds, convertible preferred stock, options, and warrants. Common stock equivalents are used in calculating earnings per share even though the calculation overstates the actual number of shares outstanding.

common stock fund A mutual fund that limits its investments to shares of common stock. Common stock funds vary in risk from relatively low to quite high, depending upon the types of stocks in which the funds invest.

common stock ratio The portion of a firm's capitalization that represents owner(s) equity. A relatively high common stock ratio is the mark of a conservatively financed company.

community property Property that is owned jointly by spouses. The legal concept in community property states that, with the exception of gifts and inheritance, all property acquired during a marriage is equally owned by each spouse. The community property statute is very important in the event that the marriage is dissolved or one spouse dies. In some locales, the concept of community property extends to individuals participating in unions other than marriage.

comp —See COMPARISON.

companion bond In a collateralized mortgage obligation, a class of bonds most likely to be retired early from mortgage prepayments. Companion bonds entail more payment risk and generally offer higher returns compared to other bonds from a CMO.

company risk The risk that certain factors affecting a specific company may cause its stock to change in price in a different way from stocks as a whole. For example, the profits and stock price of a firm selling an unusually large portion of its output to foreign customers are subject to certain factors, such as changes in foreign exchange rates, that are less important to other companies.

comparative financial statements Financial statements, the current statement and the statement from the previous accounting period, presented together for comparative purposes.

comparison A confirmation from one broker to another with respect to the details of a security trade. —Also called *broker comparison; comp.*

compensating balance The funds that a corporate borrower is required to keep on deposit in a financial institution in order to satisfy the terms of a loan agreement. The deposit may be in a checking account, savings account, or certificate of deposit, depending on the nature of the agreement. The net effect of a compensating balance requirement is an increase in the effective cost of the loan because the borrower is unable to use all the funds on which interest is paid.

competitive bidding 1. A method by which a corporation or government organization wishing to sell securities in the primary market chooses an investment banker for the sale on the basis of the best price submitted by interested investment bankers. Municipal governments and public utilities are often required to ask for competitive bids on new security issues. —See also NEGOTIATED OFFERING. 2. The bidding on U.S. Treasury securities in which an investor stipulates a particular price or yield.

competitive trader —See FLOOR TRADER.

completed-contract method A method of recognizing revenues and costs from a long-term project in which profit is recorded only when the project has been completed. Even if payments are received while the project is in progress, no revenues are recorded until its completion. The completed-contract method is a conservative way of accounting for long-term undertakings and is used for certain types of construction projects. —Compare PERCENTAGE-OF-COMPLETION METHOD.

complex capital structure A corporate capital structure that contains securities other than straight debt and stock. Thus, a firm that has securities outstanding such as convertible bonds, convertible preferred stocks, options, rights, or warrants is said to have a complex capital structure. Potential dilution of earnings resulting from a complex capital structure occurs in firms that report earnings per share on a primary and a fully diluted basis.

compliance department Securities exchange staff who are charged with ensuring that activity on the exchange complies with the rules of the exchange and those of the SEC.

composite tape A security price reporting service that includes all transactions in a security on each of the exchanges and in the over-the-counter market. A composite tape is structured to provide a complete picture of a security's price and volume activity rather than limiting the information to that which occurs on a single exchange.

compound growth rate The percentage rate, generally stated on an annual basis, at which a variable grows adjusted for compounding. For example, a 7% compound growth rate for ten years results in $100 growing to slightly less than $200. Without compounding, the $100 would earn $7 per year and grow to only $170. Financial analysts frequently use historical and projected compound growth rates in analyzing earnings, sales, and dividends.

compounding period The period between the points when interest is paid or when it is added to principal. For example, a quarterly compounding period indicates interest is paid or is calculated at three-month intervals.

compound interest Interest paid both on principal and on interest earned during previous compounding periods. Essentially, compounding involves adding interest to the sum of principal and any previous interest in order to calculate interest in the next period. —Compare SIMPLE INTEREST. —See also FREQUENCY OF COMPOUNDING.

compound option An option to purchase an option. Examples include, a call on a call option or a call on a put option. A fee must be paid to buy a compound option and a second payment must be made to the owner of the option in the event the compound option is exercised. —Also called *split-fee option.* —See also BACK FEE; FRONT FEE.

compound return The annual rate of return earned on an investment in which dividends or interest are reinvested at the same annual rate of return.

comptroller —See CONTROLLER.

Compustat® A registered trademark for a unit product of statistical and financial information that consists of goods and services such as computer programming services (systemizing the information and preparing data cards and tapes based on such information) and reports of the information presented as printed cards and prerecorded computer tapes. The service is provided by Investors Management Services, a subsidiary of Standard & Poor's.

computer-assisted execution system (CAES) A system for the automatic execution of broker-dealer limit and market orders by market makers in the over-the-counter market. Broker-dealers may designate a particular market maker or may have the order automatically routed to the market maker offering the best price.

Is "concept" more important overall than assets or income, when one evaluates concept companies?

Concept companies rely on investor psychology rather than fundamentals. If an investor can spot a concept or fad before it actually becomes popular, there is the possibility for gains. Warning: fundamentals become secondary for a concept stock.

Steven Flagg, Senior Vice President—Investments, UBS PaineWebber, Mount Kisco, NY

computerized investing —See AUTOMATED STOCK TRADING.

concept company A firm that attracts investors more on the basis of the type of business it is in or by the direction in which its management says it is moving than on its current earnings or dividends. For example, a company involved in sophisticated biomedical research that might achieve a major scientific breakthrough and large profits could qualify as a concept company. Concept companies of the 1990s include firms engaged in computer software development, Internet commerce, genetic engineering, and medical technology.

concession The dollar discount from a security's retail selling price received by members of an underwriting syndicate. For example, a syndicate member paying $995 for a bond to be sold at par (that is, at $1,000) is receiving a $5 concession. —Also called *selling concession.*

conditional rating —See PROVISIONAL RATING.

conduit theory The theory that states that because regulated investment companies merely act as conduits for the passage of dividends, interest, and capital gains to stockholders, these income items should not be taxed once to a company and again to the company's stockholders. If an investment company complies with certain federal regulations, the income is taxed only to the stockholders receiving the distributions. —Also called *pipeline theory.* —See also SUBCHAPTER M.

confidence indicator A measure of investors' faith in the economy and the securities market. A low or deteriorating level of confidence is considered by many technical analysts as a bearish sign. —See also BARRON'S CONFIDENCE INDEX; STANDARD & POOR'S CONFIDENCE INDICATOR.

confirmation **1.** A written acknowledgment of a security trade that lists important details of the trade such as date, size of the transaction, price, commission, taxes, and amount of money involved. A confirmation is generally mailed the day after a trade takes place. —See also CANCELLATION. **2.** The reaction of one technical indicator (such as the movement of a stock price average) that strengthens a signal given by another indicator.

congestion area In technical analysis, a horizontal band on a point-and-figure chart resulting from a stock price fluctuation within a narrow price range. Because a congestion area indicates an equality of supply and demand, technicians wait until the stock breaks through the upper or lower bound before committing funds. —See also HORIZONTAL COUNT.

conglomerate A company engaged in varied business operations, many of which seem unrelated. A conglomerate is designed to have reduced risk, since its various operations are affected differently by business conditions over time. In addition, it is possible for a conglomerate to redistribute its corporate assets depending on which operations show the most promise. Conglomerates were popular among investors during the 1960s but investors' interest in them faded during the 1970s and the 1980s.

consensus rating or consensus estimate   The average of multiple analyst ratings or estimates for a particular stock. For example, if three analysts estimate next year's earnings per share for a company at $3.00, $3.20, and $2.70, the consensus estimate is ($3.00 + $3.20 + $2.70)/3, or $2.97. Reported earnings per share different from the consensus estimate is likely to affect the stock's market price.

consent dividend   The retained earnings that are credited to paid-in surplus by a personal holding company. The consent dividend is taxed to stockholders as an ordinary dividend; however, this tax liability is partially offset by the stockholders' increasing the cost basis of the stock by the same amount.

consideration   Something of value provided by one party to another. For example, a person might provide an idea or labor to a business in exchange for shares of ownership.

consol   A debt instrument having no scheduled return of principal and therefore perpetual interest payments and no maturity. Consols fluctuate widely in price with changes in long-term interest rates. They have never been popular in the United States. —Also called *annuity bond; perpetual bond.* —See also PER-PETUITY.

consolidated balance sheet   A balance sheet in which assets and liabilities of a parent company and its controlled subsidiaries are combined, thereby presenting balance sheet items for the parent and its subsidiaries as if they were a single firm.

consolidated bond   A single bond issue used to replace two or more outstanding issues.

consolidated income statement   An income statement that combines the income statements of two or more organizations. As with other consolidated statements, a consolidated income statement eliminates any funds owed to or due from firms within the same group.

consolidated mortgage   A mortgage made to replace two or more outstanding mortgages.

Consolidated Quotation System (CQS)   An electronic system for disseminating the bid, ask, and size for a security in each market in which the security is traded. CQS was developed in 1978 by the National Association of Securities Dealers and the organized exchanges.

consolidated tape   An integrated reporting system of price and volume data for trades in listed securities in all markets in which the securities trade. Thus, the consolidated tape would report trades in General Motors stock not only from its principal market on the New York Stock Exchange but also from all the other markets in which it trades. —See also NETWORK A; NETWORK B.

consolidation   A combination of two or more firms into a completely new company. Assets and liabilities of the firms are absorbed by the new company. —Compare MERGER.

consortium A group of organizations that participate in a joint venture. Airbus Industrie, a European airplane manufacturer, is a consortium of four public and private corporations in Britain, France, Spain, and Germany.

constant dollar plan A formula plan for investing in which a constant dollar amount is kept in stocks, with other investments in bonds or short-term securities. Essentially, this plan forces the investor to sell stocks in rising markets and purchase them in falling markets.

constant dollars Dollars reported in unchanged value compared with the value reported on a previous date. For example, a company may have raised its dividends on each share of common stock from $2.00 in 1986 to $5.00 in 1996. However, after investors have adjusted for consumer price increases during the 10-year period, the 1996 dividend amounts to only $3.60 in constant dollars. In this case, the 1996 dollars are constant in terms of their 1986 purchasing power.

constant ratio plan A formula plan for investing in which the market value of all stocks in an investor's portfolio is kept at a predetermined percentage, with other investments making up the remainder of the portfolio. Thus, stocks must be sold if they rise in value more rapidly than other investments and bought if they fall in value more rapidly than other investments in the portfolio. As an example, an investor may decide upon a portfolio of 70% stocks and 30% bonds.

construction loan A short-term mortgage taken to finance the construction of a real estate project before permanent long-term financing is obtained. Because of its relatively high return, some real estate investment trusts specialize in this type of loan. Construction loans are often more risky than long-term mortgages.

constructive dividend A corporate payment to a stockholder that is characterized by the Internal Revenue Service as a dividend distribution even though the corporation calls it something else. For example, a small firm may pay an employee who is also a stockholder an excessive salary so that the payment can be used as a tax-deductible expense rather than as an aftertax dividend payment. The IRS may determine that part of the payment is a constructive dividend and then disallow it as a tax-deductible expense.

constructive receipt Receipt of items considered to be income for a given tax period even though payment is not received until later. For example, a dividend paid and mailed on December 30, 2003, but not received by stockholders until after the first of the following year is considered taxable income for 2003 because the stockholders are considered to have constructive receipt of the dividend.

consumed-income tax A tax levied only against the part of income that is spent. Proponents of this type of taxation contend that exempting the portion of income that is saved will encourage savings, provide funds for investment, and make the economy more productive.

Consumer Confidence Index A measure of consumer views regarding the current economic situation and consumer expectations for the future. Information for the index is compiled and released on the last Tuesday of each month by the Conference Board, an independent not-for-profit research group. Consumer views of the economy affect consumer spending, which makes up two thirds of the U.S. economy.

consumer durables —See DURABLE GOODS.

consumer price index (CPI) A measure of the relative cost of living compared with a base period (currently 1982–84). The CPI can be a misleading indicator of the impact of inflation on an individual because it is based on the spending patterns of an urban family of four. —Compare PRODUCER PRICE INDEX. —Also called *price index.* —See also GDP DEFLATOR.

consumption tax A tax levied on individual commodities or services and included as part of the retail price of those commodities or services paid by consumers. For example, a 25¢ tax levied on a pack of cigarettes is a consumption tax. Consumption taxes are advocated by many people as an inducement to increase savings in the economy. These people argue that the present taxation of income penalizes savers and rewards spenders. —Compare EXCISE TAX; VALUE-ADDED TAX.

contango In futures or options trading, a market in which longer-term contracts carry a higher price than near-term contracts. The premium accorded to longer maturities is a normal condition of the market and reflects the cost of carrying the commodity for future delivery. —Compare INVERTED MARKET.

contingent annuity A series of payments scheduled to begin at the time of a specified event. For example, an individual's death may set in motion an annuity payable to a designated person or organization.

contingent convertible bond A bond convertible into shares of stock only if the share price achieves a specified level. —Also called *CoCo bond.*

contingent deferred sales charge A mutual fund redemption fee that is reduced or eliminated for specified holding periods. For example, a fund might charge a 6% redemption fee for a holding period of less than one year, a 5% fee for a holding period of one to two years, and so forth. Mutual funds with a contingent deferred sales charge also generally levy an annual 12b–1 fee.

contingent issue An issue of securities that is to be distributed only when a specified event has occurred or when a given standard has been met. For example, the poison pill defense against hostile takeovers involves issuance of additional securities in the event that the raider acquires a certain percentage of the takeover target's outstanding stock.

contingent liability An obligation that may result, but is not likely to result because the event causing the obligation is improbable. For example, the award from a lawsuit against a firm is a contingent liability of the defendant if there is little likelihood the plaintiff will recover the award.

contingent order A special type of security order that instructs the broker to take some action only in the event that something else has occurred. An example would be an order to sell call options on Westinghouse common stock only after shares of Westinghouse have been purchased at a specified limit price.

contingent takedown option An option to buy a new issue, fixed-income security at a predetermined price until a specific date. The price is usually at par. Contingent takedown options typically originate as sweeteners in new debt issues to lower the interest cost to the issuers.

contingent value right (CVR) The right to a cash payment if the average price of an underlying security fails to reach a specified level by a certain date. The size of the payment to the owner of the right depends on the difference between the specified and actual prices. The CVR expires without value if the actual price of the underlying security exceeds the specified price.

contingent voting rights The entitlement to vote in a corporate election in the event of certain prescribed events. For example, owners of preferred stock may obtain the right to vote for a firm's directors in the event that preferred dividends are not paid.

continuing operations Parts of a business that are expected to be maintained as an ongoing segment of an overall business operation. Income and losses from continuing operations are reported separately if any segments have been discontinued during the accounting period. —Also called *going lines.*

continuous compounding Compounding of interest using the shortest possible interval of time. Although continuous compounding sounds impressive, in practice it results in virtually the same effective yield as daily compounding.

continuous net settlement (CNS) The settlement of securities transactions among brokers and dealers in which all transactions are netted out by the National Securities Clearing Corporation in order to minimize the movement of physical certificates and money balances. With continuous net settlement, only net settlement balances need be moved. For example, if during a day of trading, Merrill Lynch purchases 1,000 shares of SBC Communications for one customer and sells 1,000 shares of SBC Communications for another customer, Merrill Lynch will have a zero net settlement in this stock, with no movement of securities required.

continuous trading A trading system for securities in which transactions take place whenever a sell limit order equals or is less than a buy order or a buy limit order equals or is more than a sell order. Essentially, continuous trading occurs when dealers and brokers attempt to execute orders as soon as they have been received. Except for opening transactions, continuous trading is the way securities are bought and sold in the United States. —Compare BATCH TRADING.

contra broker The broker on the opposite side of a transaction. To a broker acting as an agent to buy, the contra broker is the selling broker. Conversely, to a broker on the sell side, the contra broker is the broker on the buy side.

contract 1. In futures trading, an agreement between two parties to make and take delivery of a specified commodity on a given date at a predetermined location. 2. In options trading, an agreement by the writer either to buy (if a put) or to sell (if a call) a given asset at a predetermined price until a certain date. The holder of the option is under no obligation to act.

contract grades In commodities trading, the standards that a commodity must meet in order to be used for delivery on a futures contract. For example, the Chicago Board of Trade requires silver deliveries to take place with 1,000- or 1,100-ounce bars assaying at a fineness of not less than 0.999.

contract month The month in which a futures contract requires delivery of the commodity. Most contracts are offset or closed before this time so that no delivery is necessary.

contract sheet A ledger sheet that is prepared by the Securities Industry Automation Corporation and lists, by security, information on transactions that involve broker-dealers. Contract sheets summarize the information that participating broker-dealers require to settle their accounts with other broker-dealers and with the Securities Industry Automation Corporation.

contract size In futures and options, the size or amount of an asset to be delivered. For example, stock options nearly always specify 100 shares, while a silver futures contract on the Chicago Mercantile Exchange stipulates 5,000 troy ounces.

contractual plan A program in which an investor in a mutual fund agrees to invest a fixed amount of money at regular intervals in accumulating shares. For example, an individual may contract to invest $100 per month with a selected fund regardless of what the market does or at what price the fund's shares sell throughout the period. —See also DOLLAR-COST AVERAGING; LOAD SPREAD OPTION.

contrarian An investor who decides which securities to buy and sell by going against the crowd. For example, a contrarian would tend to purchase the stock of steel companies when steel stock prices are depressed and most investment counselors are advising against them. Contrarians operate on the premise that when stocks are very popular they are overbought and when they are very unpopular they are oversold.

contributed capital Funds or property transferred to a company by its stockholders. The contribution may be made in return for stock, in which case the payment is recorded as paid-in capital, or it may be a donation, in which case it is recorded as donated capital.

contribution margin The price at which a firm sells its product less the variable cost of producing the product. A company with a large contribution margin is likely to experience substantial profit increases during an economic upswing.

contributory pension plan A pension plan in which the participating employees are required to support the plan with contributions. —Compare NONCONTRIBUTORY PENSION PLAN.

controlled account —See DISCRETIONARY ACCOUNT.

controller An organization's chief accounting officer, who is responsible for establishing and maintaining the organization's accounting system. —Also called *comptroller.*

controlling interest The ownership of a quantity of outstanding corporate stock sufficient to control the actions of the firm. Controlling interest often involves ownership of significantly less than 51% of a firm's outstanding stock because many owners fail to participate in decision making.

control person —See AFFILIATED PERSON.

control stock —See SUPERVOTING STOCK.

control value The value of shares in a firm when the number of shares available is sufficient to control the firm. If one person or a group owns 60% of a firm's outstanding stock, the shares in the controlling 60% are worth more on a per-share basis than the remaining 40% of outstanding shares.

conventional option A put or call option contract negotiated independently of the organized option exchanges. Before 1973 and the opening of the Chicago Board Option Exchange, all options originated through private negotiations. The disadvantage of conventional options is their lack of liquidity due to a limited secondary market. —See also FLEX OPTION.

convergence The process by which the futures price and the cash price of an underlying asset approach one another as delivery date nears. The futures and cash prices should be equal on the delivery date.

conversion equivalent The price at which common stock would have to sell in order to make a convertible security worth its market price in common stock value alone. The equivalent is calculated by dividing the conversion ratio into a convertible security's market price. A $1,000 face amount bond trading at $1,200 and convertible into 40 shares of stock has a conversion equivalent of $1,200/40 shares, or $30 per share.

conversion factors The rates used to adjust differences in bond values for delivery on a U.S. Treasury bond futures contract. Because the contract calls for the equivalent of an 8% coupon, 20-year maturity bond, it is necessary to convert other securities that are acceptable for delivery.

conversion parity The condition of a convertible security when it sells at a price equal to the value of the underlying asset into which it may be exchanged.

conversion period The time during which a convertible security may be exchanged for other assets. Most conversion periods extend for the lives of the convertible securities (until maturity for bonds), although some periods are limited. A conversion period occasionally may be extended by the issuer.

conversion premium The excess at which a convertible security sells above its conversion value. The conversion premium usually declines as a convertible security rises in market price. A bond trading at $1,400 and convertible into 50 shares of common stock with a current market price of $22 each sells at a conversion premium of $1,400 − (50 × $22), or $300.

conversion price The price per share at which common stock will be exchanged for a convertible security. The principal amount of a convertible security divided by the conversion price equals the number of shares that will be received upon exchange. The conversion price is usually adjusted downward for events such as stock splits and dividends. —See also ADJUSTMENT IN CONVERSION TERMS.

⋀⋀ **CASE STUDY** On April 2, 2002, GenCorp, an aerospace, defense, chemical, and automotive products manufacturer, announced it had privately sold $125 million principal amount of five-year subordinated notes that were convertible into shares of the firm's common stock. The notes carried a 5.75% coupon and were sold at their $1,000 face amount. The notes had a conversion price of $18.42, meaning each note could be converted into 54.2888 shares of stock. The number of shares per note is determined by dividing the $1,000 par value by the conversion price. The conversion price of $18.42 represented a 27% premium over the common stock that had closed the prior day on the New York Stock Exchange at a price of $14.50. The conversion price is a key element in valuing a convertible security. The lower the conversion price compared to the market price of the stock, the more valuable the conversion feature. A lower conversion price on the GenCorp issue would have allowed the firm to sell the notes with a lower interest coupon. It would also result in additional shares being issued when the notes were eventually submitted for conversion.

conversion privilege —See EXCHANGE PRIVILEGE.

conversion ratio The number of shares of stock into which a convertible security may be exchanged. The ratio for a convertible bond is calculated by dividing the principal amount of the bond by the conversion price.

conversion value The market value of the underlying asset(s) into which a convertible security may be exchanged. Generally, conversion value is calculated by multiplying the number of shares that can be obtained by the market price per share. Thus, a bond that can be converted into 30 shares of stock with a market price of $20 each has a conversion value of $600.

convert To exchange one security for a different security. For example, the owner of a convertible bond can choose to submit the bond to the issuer for conversion into a specified number of shares of stock.

convertible —See CONVERTIBLE SECURITY.

convertible adjustable preferred stock (CAPS) Preferred stock with a dividend tied to rates paid by U.S. Treasury securities. CAPS can be converted to cash or shares of stock when the following period's dividend is announced, a feature that adds liquidity and protects principal.

convertible floating-rate note A floating-rate note that gives the holder the option of exchanging it for a longer-term debt security with a specified coupon. Unlike a regular floating-rate note, the convertible feature protects investors against declining interest rates.

convertible security A security that, at the option of the holder, may be exchanged for another asset, generally a fixed number of shares of common stock. Convertible issues frequently are fixed-income securities such as debentures and preferred stock. Their prices are influenced by changes in interest rates and the values of the assets into which they may be exchanged. Convertible securities vary in price to a greater degree than straight debt but to a lesser degree than the underlying asset. —Also called *convertible.* —See also BOND CONVERSION; BUSTED CONVERTIBLE; CONVERSION PREMIUM; CONVERSION PRICE; CONVERSION RATIO; CONVERSION VALUE; MANDATORY CONVERTIBLE SECURITY.

⋀ CASE STUDY Convertible securities sometimes sport unusual features that can make these investments difficult to evaluate. In July 2001 Norvellus Systems, a manufacturer of semiconductor production equipment, issued unrated zero-coupon bonds convertible into shares of the firm's common stock at a price of $76.36 per share, a 50% premium to the market price. Zero-coupon debt securities are popular with many borrowers and investors, so the lack of a coupon on the issue was not especially unusual. The unique feature was the issue price of the bonds, which were sold at face value rather than a discount to face value. Virtually all zero-coupon bonds are issued at a discount to par value, thus attracting buyers who are assured of earning a positive return in the event the securities are held to maturity. To attract investors to this unique bond Norvellus agreed to allow bondholders to redeem their securities at par value at the end of one year. In other words, buyers of the securities were guaranteed they would be able to recoup their original investment at the end of a year if they were unhappy with the firm's stock price performance. During the first year Norvellus invested proceeds of the bond issue in U.S. government securities. The government securities collateralized its bonds and allowed the firm to earn interest income at the same time it was not paying interest to bondholders who had purchased the firm's debt. Holders of the convertibles who decided not to redeem the bonds at the end of the first year held a debt security that could be converted into common stock but paid no interest.

convexity A mathematical measure of the sensitivity of a bond's price to changing interest rates. A high convexity indicates a greater responsiveness of a bond's price to interest rate changes.

cook the books To distort a firm's financial statements. For example, a manager may intentionally overstate sales or understate expenses in order to create high net income.

cooling-off period The required waiting period between the time a firm files a registration statement for a new security issue with the SEC and the time the securities actually can be issued. The cooling-off period is usually 20 days, although the SEC may alter it for individual issues. —Also called *twenty-day period; waiting period.* —See also EFFECTIVE DATE.

COOP —See BANKS FOR COOPERATIVES.

COP —See CERTIFICATE OF PARTICIPATION.

core holding An investment expected to be part of a portfolio over a long period of time. For example, an investor may consider shares of Intel, Procter & Gamble, and General Electric as core holdings to be supplemented by other investments with short- and intermediate-term holding periods.

core inflation A measure of consumer price increases after stripping out volatile components such as energy and food. Core inflation is generally considered more accurate than changes in the Consumer Price Index in representing the economy's underlying inflationary pressures.

corner Significant control over a sufficient portion of a particular security so that it is possible to control the security's price. Others wishing to purchase the security, especially to cover short positions, are forced to buy it at an artificially high price. Corners were popular in the early 1900s when the securities markets were virtually unregulated. —See also NATURAL CORNER.

corner To acquire a big enough position in a particular security or commodity so that control over its price and supply is achieved.

corporate Of or relating to a bond issued by a corporation as opposed to a bond issued by the U.S. Treasury or a municipality.

corporate bond fund An investment company that invests in long-term corporate bonds and passes the income from these securities to its stockholders. Although these funds vary in value with changes in long-term interest rates, they usually provide a current return in excess of money market funds. Corporate bond funds are of interest primarily to investors seeking high current income or to those betting on a substantial fall in long-term interest rates.

corporate charter —See ARTICLES OF INCORPORATION.

corporate equivalent The yield that would need to be realized on a taxable bond selling at par in order to achieve the same aftertax yield to maturity of a bond selling at a premium or discount. For example, a $1,000 par, 10% coupon bond that sells for $900 and is due to mature in five years would provide a yield to maturity of 12.8%. However, after taxes have been paid at a rate of 28% on the $100 gain ($1,000 − $900) and 28% on the $100 annual interest payments, the aftertax yield to maturity is slightly under 10%. The corporate equivalent yield is $0.1/(1 − 0.28)$, or 13.9%.

Corporate Financing Committee   A council of the National Association of Securities Dealers that determines the fairness of markups made by underwriters on securities issues.

corporate raider —See RAIDER.

corporation   An organized body, especially a business, that has been granted a state charter recognizing it as a separate legal entity having its own rights, privileges, and liabilities distinct from those of the individuals within the entity. A corporation can acquire assets, enter into contracts, sue or be sued, and pay taxes in its own name. Corporations issue shares of stock to individuals supplying ownership capital and issue bonds to individuals lending money to the business. The corporation is a desirable organization for a business entity for a variety of reasons including the increased capability such an entity has to raise capital. Most large firms, especially those engaged in manufacturing, are organized as corporations. All stocks sold in the primary market and traded in the secondary market are shares of corporate ownership. —Compare PARTNERSHIP; PROPRIETORSHIP. —See also INCORPORATE; LIMITED LIABILITY; UNLIMITED LIABILITY.

corpus   **1.** The principal of a bond. For example, securities dealers create zero-coupon Treasury receipts by purchasing a regular Treasury bond and separating the interest coupons from the corpus. —See also COUPON STRIPPING. **2.** The principal amount of an estate or trust.

CORR —Used on the consolidated tape to indicate a correction in a reported transaction : CORR.LAST.GY 50 WAS 51.

correction   A sharp, relatively short price decline that temporarily interrupts a persistent upward trend in the market or in the price of a stock.

correlation   The relationship between two variables during a period of time, especially one that shows a close match between the variables' movements. For example, all utility stocks tend to have a high degree of correlation because their share prices are influenced by the same forces. Conversely, gold stock price movements are not closely correlated with utility stock price movements because the two are influenced by very different factors. The concept of correlation is frequently used in portfolio analysis. —See also SERIAL CORRELATION.

correspondent   A financial organization such as a securities firm or a bank that regularly performs services for another firm that does not have the requisite facilities or the access to perform the services directly. For example, a member of a securities exchange may execute a trade for a nonmember firm.

cost   The expenditure of funds or use of property to acquire or produce a product or service. —See also AVERAGE COST; FIXED COST; HISTORICAL COST; MARGINAL COST; REPLACEMENT COST; VARIABLE COST.

cost accounting   The field of accounting that measures, classifies, and records costs. A cost accountant, for example, might be required to establish a system for identifying and segmenting various production costs so as to assist a firm's management in making prudent operating decisions.

cost basis —See BASIS 2.

cost-benefit analysis   The comparison of benefits and costs in decision making. Dollar values are assigned to benefits and costs in most cost-benefit analyses.

cost center   A segment of a business or other organization in which costs can be segregated, with the head of that segment being held accountable for expenses. Cost centers are established in large organizations to identify responsibility and to control costs.

cost depletion   Depletion calculated as a percentage of the original cost of a natural resource that is consumed during a period. —See also PERCENTAGE DEPLETION.

cost of capital   The overall percentage cost of the funds used to finance a firm's assets. Cost of capital is a composite cost of the individual sources of funds including common stock, debt, preferred stock, and retained earnings. The overall cost of capital depends on the cost of each source and the proportion that source represents of all capital used by the firm. The goal of an individual or business is to limit investment to assets that provide a return that is higher than the cost of the capital that was used to finance those assets.

cost of carry   Direct costs paid by an investor to maintain a security position. For example, an individual purchasing securities on margin must pay interest expenses on borrowed funds. Likewise, an investor selling stock short is responsible for making dividend payments to the buyer. —Also called *carrying charges*.

cost of goods sold   The cost of purchasing materials and preparing goods for sale during a specific accounting period. Costs include labor, materials, overhead, and depreciation.

cost-push inflation   Rising consumer prices caused by businesses passing along increases in their own costs for labor and materials. Cost-push inflation does not necessarily result in rising corporate profits because businesses may be unable to pass through all of their cost increases. —Compare DEMAND-PULL INFLATION.

Council of Economic Advisers   A group of three economists appointed by the President of the United States to advise the executive branch on domestic and foreign economic issues. The influence of the Council has varied widely depending upon the views of the President in office and the use he wishes to make of its advice.

Council of Institutional Investors   An organization of approximately 120 large pension funds formed in 1985 to address investment issues affecting its members. The Council provides its members with educational seminars and a variety of legal, research, and regulatory services.

countercyclical stock   A stock that tends to increase in price during recessions and decrease in price during economic expansions. The stocks of companies with relatively stable sales and profits are generally considered countercyclical. Likewise, utility stocks, which generally have stable earnings and dividends, tend to be countercyclical. —Compare CYCLICAL STOCK.

counterparty risk   The risk that a party to a transaction will fail to fulfill its obligations. The term is often applied specifically to swap agreements in which no clearinghouse guarantees the performance of the contract.

Country Basket   An unmanaged single-country index portfolio designed to mimic the equity market of that particular country. Country Baskets trade on the New York Stock Exchange. —Compare ISHARES.

coupon 1. The annual interest paid on a debt security. A coupon is usually stated in terms of the rate paid on a bond's face value. For example, a 9% coupon, $1,000 principal amount bond would pay its owner $90 in interest annually. A coupon is set at the time a security is issued and, for most bonds, stays the same until maturity. 2. The detachable part of a coupon bond that must be presented for payment every six months in order to receive interest. —See also CLIP; COUPON CLIPPING.

coupon bond —See BEARER BOND.

coupon clipping The removal of interest coupons attached to a bearer bond in order that they might be taken to a bank or sent to a paying agent for redemption. Coupon clipping is necessary because owners of bearer bonds do not automatically receive interest checks in the mail every six months.

coupon-equivalent rate An alternative measure of yield that is used to make securities usually quoted on a discount basis comparable with those quoted on the more usual return on the amount invested. Stating interest at the coupon-equivalent rate is useful for securities, such as Treasury bills and commercial paper, sold at discounts from face value. As an example, a $10,000, 91-day Treasury bill selling for $9,750 is usually quoted at

$$\left(\$10,000 - \frac{\$9,750}{\$10,000} \right) \times \left(\frac{360 \text{ days}}{91 \text{ days}} \right) = 9.89\%$$

However, the coupon-equivalent rate calculated on the amount of money invested is

$$\left(\$10,000 - \frac{\$9,750}{\$9,750} \right) \times \left(\frac{360 \text{ days}}{91 \text{ days}} \right) = 10.14\%$$

—See also BANK-DISCOUNT BASIS.

coupon-equivalent yield The stated rate of return on bonds without accounting for any compounding. Because bonds nearly always pay interest twice a year, the coupon-equivalent yield must be compounded semiannually to produce the effective annual yield, a measure used by many banks in advertising certificates of deposit. For example, a 12% coupon, $1,000 principal amount bond pays $60 in interest each six months, resulting in an effective yield of 12.36% because the first $60 payment each year can be reinvested to earn an additional $3.60 during the latter half of the year.

coupon stripping The purchase of ordinary bonds (usually, U.S. Treasury bonds) that are then repackaged such that the receipts to interest and corpus payments are sold separately. The effect is to transform a security paying regular interest into zero-coupon receipts of varying maturities. Sold under a variety of names such as CATS®, LIONS, and TIGR^{SM}, these investments have proved popular for tax-sheltered accounts such as IRAs. Generic names for them include *animals* and *felines*. —Also called *stripping*.

covariance A statistical measure of the extent to which two variables move together. Covariance is used by financial analysts to determine the degree to which return on two securities is related. In general, a high covariance indicates similar movements and lack of diversification. —Compare VARIANCE. —See also RISK.

covenant A clause in a loan agreement written to protect the lender's claim by keeping the borrower's financial position approximately the same as it was at the time the loan agreement was made. Essentially, covenants spell out what the borrower may do and must do in order to satisfy the terms of the loan. For example, the borrower may be prohibited from issuing more debt by using certain assets as collateral. Likewise, the borrower may be required to issue reports to bondholders on certain dates. —Also called *protective covenant; restrictive covenant.* —See also NEGATIVE COVENANT; POSITIVE COVENANT.

 CASE STUDY | In February 2002 Qwest Communications issued a warning that the company was in danger of violating a bank loan covenant by the end of June. A major slump in the telecom business combined with heavy indebtedness caused concern that the firm's debt would exceed the specified maximum of 3.75 earnings before interest, taxes, depreciation, and amortization. A month later the company announced that in return for agreeing to use $608 million from a $1.5 billion bond issue to reduce bank debt, the bankers agreed to a concession that raised the covenant maximum to 4.25 until the end of September, and 4.00 during the following six months. The covenant had been included as part of the original bank loan agreement in order to help insure that Qwest could continue to meet its existing obligations before taking on additional debt.

cover —See SHORT COVER.

coverage ratio A measure of a corporation's ability to meet a certain type of expense. In general, a high coverage ratio indicates a better ability to meet the expense in question. —See also DIVIDEND COVERAGE; FIXED-CHARGE COVERAGE; INTEREST COVERAGE; PREFERRED DIVIDEND COVERAGE.

cover bid The second-highest bid in a competitive sale.

Coverdell Education Savings Account A special individual retirement account opened on behalf of a child under age 18. Contributions of up to $2,000 annually may be made by anyone who meets specified income limits. Contributions are not tax-deductible, but earnings grow tax-deferred until withdrawn. Money withdrawn prior to the child turning age 30 to pay for elementary, secondary, or postsecondary education expenses after high school is not subject to federal income tax. —Formerly called *Education IRA.*

covered call option A call option sold short by an investor owning the underlying stock. If the option is later exercised against the short seller of the option, the seller is covered by the stock that is owned. —Compare NAKED OPTION.

covered put option A put option sold short by an investor who is short the underlying stock. If the put is later exercised, the investor will be required to purchase the underlying stock from the holder of the put. The stock will then be used to cover the short position in the stock.

covered writer The seller or writer of a call option who owns the underlying asset that may be required for delivery. Covered writers are usually conservative investors seeking extra current income. —See also BUY-AND-WRITE STRATEGY.

CPA —See CERTIFIED PUBLIC ACCOUNTANT.

CPI —See CONSUMER PRICE INDEX.

CQS —See CONSOLIDATED QUOTATION SYSTEM.

cram down   Relating to a business deal in which a group of investors is forced to accept an undesirable arrangement. For example, minority shareholders of a company being bought out may have to accept less than what they consider a fair price for their stock.

crash   A protracted major decline in the securities markets.

CRD   —See CENTRAL REGISTRATION DEPOSITORY.

creation unit   The minimum number of shares of an exchange-traded fund, usually between 25,000 to 300,000, that will be delivered to authorized participants in exchange for the predefined basket of securities underlying the fund's securities. Creations and redemptions occur at end-of-day net asset values.

creative accounting   The use of aggressive and/or questionable accounting techniques in order to produce a desired result, generally high earnings per share. Creative accounting may include selling assets with a low cost basis, shipping unusually large quantities of product near the end of the year, and failure to write down inventories that have declined in value.

credit   **1.** The ability to borrow or to purchase goods and services with payment delayed beyond delivery. **2.** An accounting entry resulting in an increase in liabilities or owners' equity or in a decrease in assets. —Compare DEBIT. **3.** The balance in an account.

credit balance   Cash and the market value of securities held in a brokerage account. —Compare DEBIT BALANCE. —See also FREE CREDIT BALANCE.

credit-balance theory   The technical theory that holds that the level of credit balances in investors' brokerage accounts can be used to forecast market trends. Most technical analysts consider large credit (cash) balances bullish because credit balances represent potential buying power that will eventually be used for purchasing securities. —Compare DEBIT-BALANCE THEORY.

credit crunch   A period during which borrowed funds are difficult to obtain and, even if funds can be found, interest rates are very high. Credit crunches were particularly severe before 1980 when the ceilings on interest rates that financial institutions could pay resulted in a drying up of deposits.

credit department   —See MARGIN DEPARTMENT.

credit enhancement   An addition to a bond issue that improves the issue's safety of principal and interest. For example, the purchase of insurance guaranteeing payments on a bond issue is credit enhancement.

credit line   —See LINE OF CREDIT.

creditor   One to whom funds are owed. Holders of bonds and debentures are creditors to whom funds are owed by the issuers. —Compare DEBTOR. —See also SECURED CREDITOR; UNSECURED CREDITOR.

creditors' committee   A group of lenders who seek to protect their interests in connection with a borrower that experiences financial difficulties.

credit rating   A grading of a borrower's ability to meet financial obligations in a timely manner. Credit ratings are set by lenders and by independent agents for companies, individuals, and specific debt issues. —See also BOND RATING.

credit risk   The risk that a borrower will be unable to make payment of interest or principal in a timely manner.

credit spread The simultaneous sale of one option and purchase of another option that results in a credit to the investor's account. Thus, more funds are received from the sale than are required for the purchase. —Compare DEBIT SPREAD.

credit squeeze Restricted bank lending that is accompanied by rising short-term interest rates and a decline in economic growth. Credit squeezes are generally attributed to policy actions of the Federal Reserve.

credit union A nonprofit cooperative financial institution that provides credit to its members. Credit unions often pay slightly higher rates of interest on passbook-type savings accounts and charge lower rates on consumer loans.

credit watch The reevaluation of the credit quality of a firm's debt obligations by a rating agency. Being the object of a credit watch generally indicates the credit quality of a firm's debt has deteriorated and may be downgraded.

creeping tender offer The purchase of a target firm's stock at varying prices in the open market rather than through a formal tender offer. Most shares are often acquired in large blocks from arbitrageurs, frequently resulting in the exclusion of small stockholders from the offer. The purpose of a creeping tender offer is to gain control of a firm's stock more cheaply and quickly than an ordinary tender offer permits. —See also WILLIAMS ACT.

cross To match, by a single broker or dealer, a buy order and a sell order. For example, a floor broker may have an order to buy 500 shares of IBM at $120 and another order to sell 500 shares of IBM at the same price. Subject to certain rules, the floor broker may cross the order by matching the sell and the buy orders. Crossing of stock is common in large blocks.

crossborder bond A bond issued in a country other than the country of the issuer.

crossed market A situation in which one market maker's ask price for a security is lower than another market maker's bid price for the same security.

crossed trade The matching of a buy order with a sell order when the trade is not reported to the exchange on which it occurred. Crossed trades are prohibited.

cross hedge In futures trading, an offsetting position in a futures contract for an existing position in a related commodity in the cash market. An example would be the sale of a contract on wheat for delivery in two months in order to offset an existing cash position in oats.

cross holding The holding of securities in one another by two or more corporations. For example, firm A owns equity in firm B at the same time that firm B holds equity in firm A.

crossing session A period after the close of regular trading during which buyers and sellers may match orders.

cross option An option that permits each of two parties to purchase a specified ownership stake in the other. For example, a cross option may allow each of two companies to buy 10% ownership in the other company. Cross options are frequently used in merger agreements in order to thwart hostile takeover bids from a third party.

⋀⋀ CASE STUDY | In April 2001 First Union Corporation and Wachovia Corporation, two large commercial banking firms, announced a merger agreement under which First Union would acquire Wachovia in an exchange of stock. The price offered by First Union for Wachovia was at a relatively small premium to the premerger price, and some analysts and investors believed another bidder might emerge to make a better offer. Wachovia had previously engaged in merger discussions with SunTrust Banks, which many analysts believed was a better fit with Wachovia. To thwart another bidder, the two banks used a cross option that allowed either bank to purchase a 19.9% stake in the other. The cross option allowed First Union to purchase nearly 20% of Wachovia so that a hostile bidder would have to negotiate with First Union for a large amount of Wachovia stock. In the less likely case of a hostile offer for First Union, the bidder would be required to negotiate with Wachovia to buy a large block of First Union stock. Thus, the cross option served as a deterrent to another company interfering in the planned merger.

crossover credit Of or relating to a bond that straddles the gap between investment-grade and speculative. Crossover credits are generally rated low investment-grade by one rating agency and upper-grade speculative by another rating agency. —See also SPLIT RATING.

crossover refunding bonds Bonds issued for the purpose of paying off an existing bond issue. Crossover bonds are secured initially by the escrow of investments created from the crossover bond proceeds while the bonds to be refunded continue to be secured by the original revenue stream. On a specified date the refunded bonds are redeemed from the funds held in escrow and the crossover bonds become payable from the original revenue stream.

cross rate The rate at which two currencies exchange based on exchange rates using a third currency. For example, the cross rate of euros for yen might be based on the rate of euros for dollars and dollars for yen.

crowd Members on the floor of an exchange who are clustered around a pit or a specialist's post waiting to execute trades. —See also FOREIGN CROWD.

crowding out The borrowing of large amounts of money by the federal government—a process that soaks up lendable funds, drives up interest rates, and eliminates from the credit markets many private firms wishing to borrow money from those markets. The government is able to crowd out private borrowers because its credit rating is so high and because it is willing to pay the interest rate demanded by the market. Small firms and companies with poor credit ratings are most adversely affected by crowding out.

crown jewel **1.** A prized asset of a company. **2.** —Used to refer to a part of a business that is sought by another firm or an investor in a takeover attempt that is hostile to the target firm's management. —Compare SCORCHED EARTH.

crown jewel lockup agreement —See LOCKUP AGREEMENT.

CRSP tapes A magnetic computer tape of monthly and daily stock prices. The tape is provided as a service by the Center for Research in Security Prices at the University of Chicago.

crush A combination commodity trade in which soybean futures are purchased and soybean meal or oil futures are sold. —Compare REVERSE CRUSH.

CSCE —See COFFEE, SUGAR AND COCOA EXCHANGE.

CSE —See CINCINNATI STOCK EXCHANGE.

cubes —See QQQ.

cum dividend —Used to refer to a stock trading such that buyers qualify to receive the next dividend payment. Stocks trade cum dividend until the fifth business day before the record date. —Compare EX-DIVIDEND.

cum rights —See RIGHTS ON.

cumulative Of or relating to preferred stock and income bonds on which dividends must be paid in full before any payment of dividends is made to common stockholders. Thus, any dividends that are passed eventually must be brought up to date before common stockholders may receive payments. Nearly all issues of preferred stock are cumulative. —Compare NONCUMULATIVE. —See also DIVIDENDS IN ARREARS.

cumulative voting A type of corporate voting right in which a stockholder receives one vote per owned share times the number of directors' positions up for election. The stockholder may allocate votes among the different positions as he or she wishes. For example, an owner of 200 shares is permitted a total of 1,200 votes if six positions are to be voted on. These 1,200 votes may be cast for a single director, may be split between two directors, or may be allocated equally among all six directors. Cumulative voting, making it easier for smaller interest groups to be represented, is required by some states. —Compare MAJORITY VOTING.

Curb Exchange An early name for what is now the American Stock Exchange. The term derived from the market's beginnings on a street in downtown New York.

currency futures A contract for the future delivery of a specified amount of a major currency. Currency futures were developed in response to the substantial volatility of currency trading rates that occurred following the 1971 shift from fixed to flexible currency exchange rates.

currency futures option An option that gives the owner the right to buy (call) or to sell (put) a currency futures contract.

Currenex An independent online global currency exchange used by corporate and institutional buyers and sellers of foreign exchange products.

current asset Cash or an asset expected to be converted into cash within one year. In addition to cash, current assets include marketable securities, accounts receivable, inventories, and prepaid expenses. Current assets are typically not very profitable but tend to add liquidity and safety to a firm's operation. —Also called *gross working capital.*

current coupon Of or relating to a bond with an interest coupon very close to the coupons being carried on new issues of the same maturity. Therefore the bond must be selling at a price close to its par value. —Also called *full coupon.*

current income Investment income earned from interest, dividends, rent, premiums from option writing, and similar sources as opposed to that derived from increases in asset value.

current issue The most recently issued Treasury security of a particular type. For 13-week Treasury bills that are auctioned each Monday, the current issue is the bill issued on the most recent Monday.

cushion bond

Can a cushion bond pad the conservative investor's backside against the impact of rising interest rates?

A cushion bond can protect a conservative investor against rising interest rates because the higher the coupon rate on a bond, the less dramatic the price change for a given shift in that bond's yield to maturity. This makes sense when one considers how much greater a percentage change 25 basis points is when yields are 5%, compared with yields at 10%. Furthermore, the longer the maturity period, the greater the price change for a particular move in that bond's yield to maturity. Because cushion bonds are by definition premium-priced bonds that trade on a yield to call basis, rather than a yield to maturity basis, their price swings account for shifts in interest rates for shorter time periods. Thus their price swings should be less dramatic when interest rates rise.

Stephanie G. Bigwood, CFP, ChFC, CSA, Assistant Vice President
Lombard Securities, Incorporated, Baltimore, MD

current liability A debt due within a year. Current liabilities include accounts payable, short-term loans from financial institutions, current maturities of long-term debt, dividends declared but not paid, and expenses incurred but not paid. Current liabilities are generally met using current assets.

current market value The value of an individual's portfolio when the securities are appraised at current market prices.

current maturity The length of time before a security matures. For example, a bond issued 15 years ago that had an original maturity of 20 years, has a current maturity of 5 years. The current maturity, rather than the original maturity, is important in valuing a bond.

current production rate The maximum interest rate payable on current Ginnie Mae pass throughs. The current production rate is usually ½ of 1% under the rate of interest charged on mortgages backing the pass throughs, with the difference covering service charges to the firm processing the mortgages.

current ratio A measure of a firm's ability to meet its short-term obligations. The current ratio is calculated by dividing current assets by current liabilities. Both variables are shown on the balance sheet. A relatively high current ratio compared with those of other firms in the same business indicates high liquidity and generally conservative management, although it may tend to result in reduced profitability. —See also CASH RATIO; QUICK RATIO.

current yield The annual rate of return received from an investment, based on the income received during a year compared with the investment's current market price. For example, a bond selling at $800 and paying an annual interest of $80 provides a current yield of $80/$800, or 10%. —Also called *rate of return; running yield.*

curtesy A widower's portion of his wife's assets that were acquired during the course of their marriage. Curtesy usually amounts to one third of the assets. —Compare DOWER.

cushion —See CALL PROTECTION.

cushion bond A high-coupon bond that sells at a price only slightly above par because of a call provision permitting the issuer to repurchase the security near its current price. A cushion bond has an unusually high current yield, little chance for a price rise, and considerable protection against falling prices caused by increased interest rates.

cushion theory The theory that holds that a large short position in a stock will eventually exert upward pressure on the stock's price as investors purchase the stock to cover their short positions. The rise in the price of a stock that has been the object of substantial short selling will become more rapid as investors cover short positions to stem losses.

CUSIP —See COMMITTEE ON UNIFORM SECURITIES IDENTIFICATION PROCEDURES.

CUSIP number A unique identification number that is assigned to stock and bond certificates in an effort to improve the efficiency of clearing operations.

custodial fee The fee charged by a financial institution that holds securities in safekeeping for an investor.

custodian An organization, typically a commercial bank, that holds in custody and safekeeping someone else's assets. These assets may be cash, securities, or virtually anything of value.

custodian account An account controlled by a custodian rather than the owner of the assets. Custodian accounts are often used for minors or other individuals who are unable or unwilling to handle their own assets.

custody A safekeeping service that a financial institution provides for a customer's securities. For a fee, the institution collects dividends, interest, and proceeds from security sales and disburses funds according to the customer's written instructions.

customer's loan agreement An agreement that permits brokerage firms to borrow customers' margined securities in order to cover certain delivery failures or other customers' short sales. A customer's loan agreement must be signed by the customer before borrowing can take place. —Compare MARGIN AGREEMENT.

customer's man —See REGISTERED REPRESENTATIVE.

cut out The deletion or withholding of a trade from clearance.

cv —Used in the yield column of bond transaction tables in newspapers to indicate that a bond is convertible into some other asset, usually shares of common stock: *STERLBN 6½% cv.*

CV —Used on the consolidated tape to indentify a security as a convertible security: *AXPr. CV 25.*

CVR —See CONTINGENT VALUE RIGHT.

CXL —Used on the consolidated tape to indicate that a transaction reported earlier has been canceled: *CXL.5 SLS.BK.GY 49.*

cyclical stock

When should I invest in cyclical stocks?

With the proper crystal ball, you should buy cyclical stocks six months before the earnings in the target group begin to move up, and sell the group six months before the earnings turn down. Note: Most crystal balls are cloudy!

Steven Flagg, Senior Vice President—Investments, UBS PaineWebber, Mount Kisco, NY

cyclical Of or relating to a variable, such as housing starts, car sales, or the price of a certain stock, that is subject to regular or irregular up-and-down movements.

cyclical stock Common stock of a firm whose profits are heavily influenced by cyclic changes in general economic activity. As investors anticipate changes in profits, cyclical stocks often reach their high and low levels before the respective highs and lows in the economy. *See Investment Tip on p. 93.* —Compare COUNTERCYCLICAL STOCK.

D

d —Used in the daily or weekly low column of stock transaction tables in newspapers to indicate that the price of a security reached a new 52-week low: *d16.*

daily trading limit In commodities, the range of prices within which trades may take place during a day. The limit is usually determined on the basis of the previous day's settlement price.

daisy chain Manipulative trading among a small group of individuals or institutions that is intended to give the impression of heavy volume. As outsiders see the unusual trading activity and are drawn into the chain, the traders who started the daisy chain then sell their positions, leaving the new investors with overpriced securities.

D&O Coverage —See DIRECTORS' AND OFFICERS' LIABILITY INSURANCE.

dated date The date on which a newly issued bond begins to accrue interest. The buyer of a bond in the primary market must pay the issuer interest accruing between the dated date and the settlement date in addition to the principal amount of bonds purchased. This additional interest is returned to the buyer when the issuer makes the first interest payment. For example, a new bond issue with a dated date of July 1 and a settlement date of July 20 would require purchasers to pay 19 days' interest in addition to the face value of the bonds. —Also called *issue date.*

date of acquisition For accounting and tax purposes, the effective purchase date of an asset.

date of issue The date on which a security is issued and begins trading.

date of record —See RECORD DATE.

DAX The leading German index of equity prices based on the 30 most heavily traded stocks on the Frankfurt Stock Exchange.

day loan A one-day loan made by a bank to a broker for the purchase of securities. The loan is used until delivery allows a regular call loan to be arranged.

day order A customer order to buy or sell a security that will expire automatically at the end of the trading day on which it is entered. Day order is used when a customer prefers to reconsider an order that is not executed on the day it was placed. —See also GOOD-TILL-CANCELED ORDER.

days to cover —See SHORT-INTEREST RATIO.

day trade A trade opened and closed on the same trading day. A purchase and sale of the same security on the same day is an example of a day trade. Likewise, a short sale followed by a covering purchase on the same day is a day trade.

day trader A speculator who buys and sells securities on the basis of small short-term price movements. Day traders are thought to add a measure of liquidity to the market.

dc —Used in bond transaction tables in newspapers to indentify a bond as a deep-discount bond: *WMX dc2s05*.

dead cat bounce A sharp and likely temporary rise in the market price of a stock following an extensive decline.

dead hand poison pill A special type of poison pill antitakeover defense in which only ousted directors can rescind the poison pill. Poison pill plans are put in place in order to make a hostile takeover prohibitively expensive by issuing a huge number of new shares.

dealer An individual or a firm that buys assets for and sells assets from its own portfolio as opposed to bringing buyers and sellers together. In practice, many firms operate as broker-dealers and perform both services depending on the market conditions and on the size, type, and security involved in a particular transaction. Dealers are sometimes able to offer investors better prices, but they may tend to make recommendations based on their own ownership positions. —Compare BROKER.

dealer bank A commercial bank that buys and sells municipal securities and/or U.S. government and agency securities.

dealer loan A short-term secured bank loan to a security dealer for the purpose of financing inventory.

dealer market A market in which securities are bought and sold through a network of dealers who buy, sell, and take positions in various security issues. —Compare AUCTION MARKET; OPEN OUTCRY.

dealer paper Commercial paper that is sold by original issuers through dealers who wholesale the paper to its ultimate buyers. Individual investors are usually excluded from trading in dealer paper because of the size of the investment required, usually a minimum of $250,000. —Compare DIRECT PAPER.

death spiral The deteriorating financial condition and associated stock price of a cash-starved company that can raise capital only under the most onerous of terms. Restrictions and high interest charges on new capital cause the company to end up in an even worse financial position.

death tax **1.** —See ESTATE TAX. **2.** —See INHERITANCE TAX.

debenture A corporate bond that is not secured by specific property. In the event that the issuer is liquidated, the holder of a debenture becomes a general creditor and therefore is less likely than the secured creditors to recover in full. Because of their high risk factor, debentures pay higher rates of interest than secured debt of the same issuer. —See also SUBORDINATED DEBENTURE.

debit An accounting entry that results in an increase in assets or a decrease in liabilities or owners' equity. —Compare CREDIT 2.

debit balance The amount owed in a brokerage margin account. A debit balance occurs when an investor purchases securities on margin or borrows money from the account by using securities as collateral. Brokerage firms typically charge an interest rate on the borrowed funds that varies with the size of the debit balance. —Compare CREDIT BALANCE. —See also CALL LOAN.

debit-balance theory   The technical theory that holds that the level and change in brokerage account debit balances can be used to forecast market trends. A rise in debit balances is generally considered bullish because such balances result from the purchase of securities on margin by sophisticated investors. —Compare CREDIT-BALANCE THEORY.

debit card   A plastic card that may be used for purchasing goods and services or for obtaining cash advances for which payment is made from existing funds in a bank account. Because a debit card provides about the same float as a checking account (one to three days), it is a less desirable method of payment than a credit card. These cards are often part of the comprehensive all-in-one accounts offered by many brokers.

debit spread   The simultaneous sale of one option and purchase of another option that results in a debit to the investor's account. Thus, more funds are required for the purchase than are received from the sale. An example is the purchase of a 6-month call at a price of $500 and the simultaneous sale of a 3-month call at the same strike price for $300. This trade results in a debit of $200 plus commissions to the investor's account. —Compare CREDIT SPREAD.

debt   —See LIABILITY.

debt-based asset   An investment in the debt of another party. Savings accounts, bonds, annuities, and certificates of deposit are all debt-based assets because they represent debt of the issuer. Debt-based assets are generally conservative investments that pay a fairly predictable rate of return.

debt financing   The acquisition of funds by borrowing. For example, a business may use debt financing to raise funds for constructing a new factory. Corporations find debt financing attractive because the interest paid on borrowed funds is a tax-deductible expense. —Compare EQUITY FINANCING.

debt limit   The statutory maximum amount of debt that a municipality may have outstanding.

debt management   The regulation of the size and handling of the structure of the public debt. Actions taken to manage the debt have significant effects on the financial markets because government securities compete with private securities for limited funds in the capital market.

debt management ratio   A measure of the extent to which a firm uses borrowed funds to finance its operations. Owners and creditors are interested in debt management ratios because the ratios indicate the riskiness of the firm's position. —See also DEBT RATIO; DEBT-TO-EQUITY RATIO; FIXED-CHARGE COVERAGE.

debtor   An individual or organization that owes a debt or has an obligation to another party. —Compare CREDITOR.

debtor in possession   A company that continues to operate while in Chapter 11 bankruptcy.

debtor in possession financing   Financing arranged during the time a company is in Chapter 11 bankruptcy.

debt ratio   The proportion of a firm's total assets that are being financed with borrowed funds. The debt ratio is calculated by dividing total long-term and short-term liabilities by total assets. Assets and liabilities are found on a company's balance sheet. For example, a firm with assets of $1,000,000 and $150,000 in short-term debts and $300,000 in long-term debts has a debt ratio of $450,000/$1,000,000 or 45%. A low debt ratio indicates conservative financing with an opportunity to borrow in the future at no significant risk. —Compare BOND RATIO.

debt restructuring An exchange of one or more new debt issues for outstanding debt issues that can occur when the new issues have interest rates and/or maturities that differ from those of the outstanding issues. For example, a firm might offer holders of 9% coupon bonds with 5 years to maturity a new bond with a higher-coupon rate and a 25-year maturity. Creditors having difficulty making interest and/or principal payments often restructure their debt to reduce the size of the interest payments and to extend debt maturity. —Compare RESTRUCTURING. —Also called *troubled debt restructuring.*

debt security A security representing borrowed funds that must be repaid. Examples of debt securities include bonds, certificates of deposit, commercial paper, and debentures.

debt service Funds required to meet interest expenses, principal payments, and sinking fund requirements during a specific time period. A firm's ability to service its debt is estimated by comparing cash flow with debt service.

debt-to-equity ratio The relationship between long-term funds provided by creditors and funds provided by owners. A firm's debt-to-equity ratio is calculated by dividing long-term debt by owners' equity. Both items are shown on the balance sheet. A high debt-to-equity ratio, which indicates very aggressive financing or a history of large losses, results in very volatile earnings. A low debt-to-equity ratio, which indicates conservative financing and low risk, results in fewer possibilities of large losses or large gains in earnings.

debt warrant A security that allows the holder to buy additional bonds from the issuer at the same price and yield as the initial bond.

December effect The tendency of stock prices to move upward during the last month of the year. Historical statistics indicate December is the strongest month of the year for stock prices.

decimalization The transition of security prices being quoted in decimals rather than fractions. Decimalization in U.S. markets started in fall 2000 with exchange-listed stocks and was completed in April 2001 with Nasdaq stocks. Studies during the transition indicated that moving to decimals benefited investors by reducing the bid-ask spreads.

declaration date The date on which a firm's directors meet and announce the date and amount of the next dividend. Following the declaration, dividends become a legal liability of the firm. —See also EX-DIVIDEND DATE; INTEREST DATES; RECORD DATE.

declare To authorize a dividend formally.

declared dividend A dividend authorized by a firm's board of directors. At the time a dividend is declared, the firm creates a liability for the dividend's payment.

decline A decrease in the price of a security.

dedication —See PORTFOLIO DEDICATION.

deduction An expenditure that may legally be used to reduce an individual's income-tax liability. Potential deductions of particular interest to investors are expenditures for subscriptions to financial publications, a lock box for storing securities, and computer software for investment-related activities. These deductions, combined with employee business expenses and miscellaneous deductions, may be subtracted from a person's taxable income only to the extent their total exceeds 2% of that person's adjusted gross income. Interest paid on loans used to finance investments is deductible only against investment income. —Also called *itemized deduction; tax deduction.* —See also CHARITABLE CONTRIBUTION DEDUCTION.

deep-discount bond 1. A long-term debt security that, because of a low coupon rate of interest compared with current rates of interest, sells at a substantial discount from face value. Bonds of this type, if not originalissue discounts, are preferred by some investors because they are unlikely to be called before maturity. —See also MUNICIPAL CONVERTIBLE; ZERO-COUPON BOND. **2.** —See ORIGINAL-ISSUE DISCOUNT BOND.

deep-in-the-money —Used to describe a call (put) option that has a strike price considerably less (more) than the market price of the underlying stock. A deep-in-the-money option is almost certain to be exercised on or before its expiration.

deep market A market for a security in which there are numerous, sizable bids and offers. A deep market for a security provides an investor in that security with more liquidity. —Compare THIN MARKET; TIGHT MARKET.

deep-out-of-the-money 1. —Used to describe a call option with a strike price significantly above the market price of the underlying asset. A deep-out-of-the-money call option sells at a low price because in all likelihood it will expire without value. **2.** —Used to describe a put option with a strike price significantly below the market price of the underlying asset. A deep-out-of-the-money put option sells at a low price because in all likelihood it will expire without value.

default The failure to live up to the terms of a contract. Generally, default is used to indicate the inability of a borrower to pay the interest or principal on a debt when it is due. —See also TECHNICAL DEFAULT.

default risk The possibility that a borrower will be unable to meet interest and/or principal repayment obligations on a loan agreement. Default risk has a significant effect on the value of a bond: if a borrower's ability to repay debt is impaired, default risk is higher and the value of the bond will decline.

defeasance The extinguishment of debt. While defeasance technically refers to extinguishment by any method (for example, by payment to the creditor), in practice it is generally used to mean discharging debt by presenting a portfolio of securities (usually, Treasury obligations) to a trustee who will use the cash flow to service the old debt. This procedure permits the firm to wipe the debt off its financial statements and to show extra income equal to the difference between the old debt and the smaller, new debt. —Also called *in-substance debt defeasance.*

defensive acquisition A firm or an asset purchased by a potential target of a takeover in order to make itself less desirable to raiders. For example, a target company might purchase another firm engaged in the same business as the raider in order to create an antitrust problem for the raider. —See also RAIDER; TARGET COMPANY.

defensive buy A low-risk investment acquired for its resistance to major declines in market value. For example, an investor expecting a weak economic climate may buy stock in a pharmaceutical company or an electric utility.

defensive stock A stock that is resistant to general stock market declines. Stocks of electric utilities, gold and silver producers, and some consumer goods companies are considered defensive. Although defensive stocks resist downturns, they generally move up more slowly than other stocks during bull markets.

deferment period The period following the issue of a security during which it cannot be called by the issuer. —Also called *deferred call period; period of call protection; preferred call period.* —See also CALL PROTECTION.

deferred annuity An annuity that is not scheduled to begin payments until a given date. These annuities may be purchased with a single payment or, as is more often the case, with a series of periodic payments. Deferred annuities are most commonly purchased by individuals who want to make periodic payments during their working lives in order to receive monthly or annual income payments from the annuities during their retirement. —Compare IMMEDIATE ANNUITY. —See also PERIODIC PURCHASE DEFERRED CONTRACT; SINGLE-PREMIUM DEFERRED ANNUITY.

deferred call period —See DEFERMENT PERIOD.

deferred compensation Compensation that is being earned but not received, a process that defers the taxes on the compensation until it is actually received at a later date. Deferred compensation includes various plans, some being pensions, profit-sharing, and stock options.

deferred contracts Futures contracts that settle in months beyond the closest current trading month.

deferred credit —See DEFERRED INCOME.

deferred income Income received by a business but not yet reported as earned. For example, a business may receive payment for a service or a product that has not yet been delivered. A deferred credit is treated as a liability until reported as income earned. —Also called *deferred credit.*

deferred income tax A liability created by income recognized for accounting purposes but not for tax purposes. The liability recognizes future taxes due when earned income is later reported for tax purposes. Use of accelerated depreciation for reporting to the Internal Revenue Service and straight-line depreciation for reporting to stockholders is one of the major reasons a firm includes deferred income taxes as a liability on its balance sheet.

deferred-interest bond A bond that does not pay interest for a specified period, typically three to ten years. At the end of the initial period, the interest payments on the bond begin in accordance with its coupon rate. Deferred-interest bonds generally sell at steep discounts to par during a period of deferred interest.

deferred liability A liability that usually would have been paid but is now past due.

deferred premium option An option requiring payment of the premium at maturity rather than on the purchase date. The premium is paid whether or not the option is exercised. —Also called *Boston option.*

deferred sales charge A fee levied by some open-end investment companies on shareholder redemptions and by many insurance companies on annuities. The charge of up to 5% of the value of the shares being redeemed frequently varies inversely with the period of time the shares have been owned. A deferred sales charge is indicated in mutual fund transaction tables in newspapers by the symbol *r.* —Also called *back-end load; exit fee; redemption charge.* —See also CONTINGENT DEFERRED SALES CHARGE.

deficiency 1. The amount by which an individual's or an organization's tax liability as computed by the Internal Revenue Service exceeds the tax liability reported by the taxpayer. 2. The amount by which a firm's liabilities exceed assets.

deficiency letter A letter from the SEC indicating disapproval with one or more aspects of a security issuer's registration statement.

deficit 1. A negative retained earnings balance. A deficit results when the accumulated losses and dividend payments of a business exceed its earnings. 2. —See OPERATING LOSS.

deficit financing The sale of debt securities in order to finance expenditures that are in excess of income. Generally, deficit financing is applied to government finance because income, represented by tax revenues and fees, is often unavailable to pay expenses. As with monetizing the debt, deficit financing puts upward pressure on interest rates because government debt securities compete with private securities for limited capital.

deficit net worth —See NEGATIVE NET WORTH.

deficit spending Expenditures that are in excess of revenues during a given period of time. Deficit spending is generally applied to governmental units, but the concept is equally applicable to private businesses.

defined-asset fund An investment trust with a fixed portfolio of assets that generally has a defined lifetime at which time the trust assets are liquidated.

defined-benefit pension plan A pension plan in which retirement benefits rather than contributions into the plan are specified. Thus, a retired employee who has reached a certain age with a given number of years of service and has earned a certain income is entitled to a specific monthly pension payment.

defined-contribution pension plan A pension plan in which an employer's periodic payments into the plan, rather than eventual retirement benefits to employees, are specified. For example, a defined-contribution pension plan may require an employer to contribute 5% of its employees' gross pay into a fund with contributions earmarked for each employee upon retirement.

deflation A reduction in consumer or wholesale prices. The term generally applies to more than just a temporary decline. —Compare INFLATION. —See also DISINFLATION.

deindustrialization A shift in an economy from producing goods to producing services. Such a shift is most likely to occur in mature economies such as that of the United States. This shift has considerable impact on investors' view of the attractiveness of various industries.

delayed convertible A security with a conversion feature that does not come into effect until a specified date.

delayed delivery Delivery of a certificate after the day on which delivery would occur with a regular-way contract. Delayed delivery is sometimes specified by the seller when the order to sell is entered. —See also SELLER'S OPTION CONTRACT.

delayed opening An intentional delay in the opening transaction of a particular security. Generally, the delay occurs when unexpected developments before the opening make it difficult for the specialist to match buy and sell orders.

delayed settlement The transfer of a security or cash at a date beyond the usual settlement date. A seller may prefer delayed settlement in order to be listed on a firm's books on the record date for a dividend.

deleted Of or relating to a security that is no longer listed on a securities exchange.

delist To drop a security from trading on an organized exchange. Delisting may occur for a number of reasons including failure to meet an exchange's standards or placement of a new listing on another exchange. —Compare LIST.

⋀⋀ CASE STUDY In early 2001, Nasdaq informed Drkoop.com, a one-time high-flying Internet company, that the firm's stock was subject to being delisted from the Nasdaq Stock Market. At the time of the notice Drkoop.com stock was trading at approximately 20¢ per share, well below the $1 per share required to continue trading on the Nasdaq. Delisting can have a serious negative impact on a firm's ability to raise equity capital, since it is likely to reduce liquidity and increase the bid-ask spread quoted by dealers. Many individual investors avoid buying a delisted stock as trading volume dries up. Negatives associated with delisting are likely to cause a major decline in the market price of a stock that most likely has already experienced a major price decline. Nasdaq, which delisted 240 companies in 2000, often begins the delisting process when a stock's bid price falls below $1 per share for 30 consecutive trading days. The firm subsequently has 90 calendar days to boost its stock price above $1 per share for 10 consecutive trading days. The New York Stock Exchange has a similar price requirement plus additional minimums regarding market capitalization and shareholder equity.

deliver To relinquish possession of a security for transfer to another party.

delivering short Delivering borrowed shares in order to fulfill the requirements of an option that has been exercised.

delivery 1. The transfer of a security to an investor's broker in order to satisfy an executed sell order. Delivery is required by the settlement date. 2. The transfer of a specified commodity in order to meet the requirements of a commodity contract that has been sold.

delivery day In futures trading, the day on which delivery of the asset is to be made according to the quantity, quality, and location specified in the contract.

delivery instructions A customer's directions to a broker as to the disposition of funds and securities in the customer's account. For example, a customer must instruct the broker whether securities placed in the account should be sent to the customer or kept in street name in the account.

delivery notice In futures trading, a notice that the party having sold (short) a contract intends to make delivery of the commodity in settlement of its terms.

The quantity, quality, and point of delivery are designated by the exchange. —Also called *transfer notice.*

delivery point The specified location at which a commodity may be delivered to satisfy a futures contract. The points and procedures for delivery are established by the exchange on which the contract trades.

delivery versus payment (DVP) A settlement procedure in which a customer instructs that he or she will make immediate payment upon delivery of the purchased security. —Compare RECEIVE VERSUS PAYMENT. —Also called *cash on delivery.*

delta The change in the price of an option that results from a one-point change in the price of the underlying stock. For example, a delta of 0.5 indicates that the option will rise in price by ½ point (50¢) for each 1-point ($1) rise in the price of the underlying stock. Call options have positive deltas; put options have negative deltas.

demand deposit A checking account balance held at a financial institution. Because demand deposits constitute one of the most important segments of the nation's money supply, the financial community closely monitors their size. —Compare TIME DEPOSIT. —See also M1.

demand loan A loan due at any time the lender decides to request payment.

demand-pull inflation Rising consumer prices resulting from the demand for goods and services exceeding supply. Demand-pull inflation is likely to enhance corporate profits because businesses are able to increase the prices they charge without corresponding increases in their costs. —Compare COST-PUSH INFLATION.

denomination The face value of a security. For bonds, it is usually $1,000 ($5,000 for municipals) or multiples thereof, and for stock it is the par value.

dependent variable A variable affected by another variable or by a certain event. For example, because a stock's price is affected by dividend payments, earnings projections, interest rates, and many other things, stock price is a dependent variable. —Compare INDEPENDENT VARIABLE.

depletion The periodic cost assigned for a reduction in the quantity and indicated value of a natural resource such as a mineral deposit or timber. Thus, depletion indicates an activity such as harvesting or mining a natural resource. —See also COST DEPLETION; DEPRECIATION; PERCENTAGE DEPLETION.

depositary receipt A negotiable certificate that represents a company's publicly traded debt or equity. Depositary receipts are created when a company's shares or bonds are delivered to a depositary's custodian bank, which instructs the depositary to issue the receipts. Depositary receipts facilitate trading of foreign securities. —See also AMERICAN DEPOSITARY RECEIPT; AMERICAN DEPOSITARY SHARE.

depository —See SECURITY DEPOSITORY.

Depository Trust Company (DTC) A national depository for security certificates that records, maintains, and transfers securities for member firms. The DTC seeks to reduce the movement of certificates by arranging for computerized transfers.

deposit note —See CALLABLE CD.

depreciable Of, relating to, or being a long-term tangible asset that is subject to depreciation.

depreciate To reduce the value of a long-term tangible asset.

depreciated cost —See BOOK VALUE 1.

depreciation The periodic cost assigned for the reduction in usefulness and value of a long-term tangible asset. Because firms can use several types of depreciation, the amount of depreciation recorded on corporate financial statements may or may not be a good indication of an asset's reduction in value. Depreciation not only affects the asset's value as stated on the balance sheet, it also affects the amount of reported earnings. —See also ACCELERATED COST RECOVERY SYSTEM; ACCELERATED DEPRECIATION; ACCUMULATED DEPRECIATION; RECAPTURE OF DEPRECIATION; STRAIGHT-LINE DEPRECIATION.

depreciation recapture —See RECAPTURE OF DEPRECIATION.

depreciation reserve —See ACCUMULATED DEPRECIATION.

depressed Of or relating to a security, product, or market in which demand is weak and price continues to decline.

depth —Used to refer to a security market's ability to absorb large security purchases or sales without significant price changes. A market's depth is an important consideration in selecting securities to trade and markets in which to trade. —See also DEEP MARKET.

deregulate To reduce or eliminate control. One of the major forces in the financial markets in the 1970s and 1980s was the federal government's decision to deregulate interest rates. The commissions charged to investors on security trades were deregulated in 1975.

deregulation The act of removing controls from some sector of the economy. In nearly all cases, deregulation of a given industry has both positive and negative implications for investors. Typically, firms in a strong financial position benefit from deregulation, while firms in a weak financial position suffer.

derivative An asset that derives its value from another asset. For example, a call option on the stock of Coca-Cola is a derivative security that obtains value from the shares of Coca-Cola that can be purchased with the call option. Call options, put options, convertible bonds, futures contracts, and convertible preferred stock are examples of derivatives. A derivative can be either a risky or low-risk investment, depending upon the type of derivative and how it is used. —See also UNDERLYING ASSET 2.

derivative suit —See STOCKHOLDER DERIVATIVE SUIT.

descending tops In technical analysis, a chart pattern indicating the up and down movement of a security's price and characterized by progressively lower highs on each upturn. This pattern is considered bearish. Refer to the *Technical Analysis Chart Patterns* section for an example of this chart. —Compare ASCENDING TOPS.

descending triangle In technical analysis, a triangle-shaped chart formation indicating a downward price for a stock and characterized by a nearly vertical left side, nearly horizontal bottom, and downward sloping third side that dips to the right. A descending triangle is a bearish indicator in which a sell signal is confirmed if the price breaks through the bottom side. Refer to the *Technical*

Analysis Chart Patterns section for an example of this chart. —Compare AS-CENDING TRIANGLE.

Designated Order Turnaround (DOT)   An electronic system on the New York Stock Exchange that channels smaller orders directly from a member firm to the specialist post on the exchange floor. The system speeds the execution of orders and allows increased volume on the floor by bypassing commission brokers.

detachable warrant   A warrant issued in conjunction with another security (nearly always a bond) that can trade or be exercised separately following the issue date.

detailed audit   A thorough and complete examination of all or a selected portion of an organization's books. In a detailed audit, as opposed to a normal audit, systems of internal control, the details of all the transactions, books of account, subsidiary records, and supporting documentation may be examined for accuracy, use of generally accepted accounting principles, total accountability, and legality.

Deutsche Borse Group   A diversified German financial group that operates securities and derivatives exchanges, provides clearing services, and markets capital market information. —See also XETRA.

devaluation   A reduction in the value of one currency in relation to other currencies. For example, when Mexico devalued the peso, more pesos were required to obtain a given amount of a foreign currency. Devaluation is generally undertaken by a government in order to make its country's products more competitive in world markets. Devaluation can significantly reduce the value of investments held by foreign investors in the devaluing country. In the case of the peso devaluation, U.S. investors who held high-interest peso accounts in Mexican banks found their account balances worth very little in terms of U.S. dollars.

developmental oil and gas partnership   —See OIL AND GAS DRILLING LIMITED PARTNERSHIP.

DIA   —See DIAMOND.

diagonal spread   Any spread with different strike prices in which the purchased options have a longer maturity than the written options.

Diamond   Registered name for interest in a trust that holds all 30 stocks included in the Dow Jones Industrial Average. Ownership of a Diamond allows an investor to track the DJIA with a single investment. Diamonds are traded on the American Stock Exchange under the symbol DIA.

differential   **1.** In commodities trading, the premium or discount in the futures contract price caused by delivering a commodity that does not exactly meet the standards fixed by the exchange. Allowances for these differentials are included in the contract specifications. **2.** —See ODD-LOT DIFFERENTIAL.

digits deleted   —Used on the consolidated tape service to indicate that only the last digits and fractions of stock prices will be reported until further notice. Thus, what would ordinarily be reported as XOM 5s52.23 will be listed as XOM 5s2.23. Deleting digits is the first step in speeding the reporting process when the tape is late because of heavy volume. —See also VOLUME DELETED.

diluted earnings per share   An earnings measure calculated by dividing net income less preferred stock dividends for a period by the average number of shares of common stock that would be outstanding if all convertible securities were converted into shares of common stock. Net income is adjusted for any changes that would occur because of the conversions. Diluted earnings per share is a particularly effective method of presenting earnings-per-share data for companies with complex capital structures. —Compare BASIC EARNINGS PER SHARE. —See also DUAL PRESENTATION.

dilution A decrease in the equity position of a share of stock because of the issuance of additional shares. Dilution is usually detrimental to the position of existing shareholders because it weakens their proportional claim on earnings and assets. —See also POTENTIAL DILUTION.

dip A small, short decline in a variable such as the price of a security or interest rates. A broker may advise a customer to accumulate a particular stock on dips. When the security begins declining in price, it is difficult to know if the decline is just a dip or if it is the initial step in a more substantial price reduction.

direct-access firm A brokerage firm that enables customers to place orders directly with Nasdaq market-maker firms, electronic communications networks, and organized securities exchanges. Direct access is particularly important to investors who attempt to profit from rapid changes in stock prices.

> ᴧᴧ **CASE STUDY** | In August 2001 online brokerage firm Waterhouse announced it had agreed to purchase for cash R.J. Thompson Holdings, a direct-access firm. Thompson, a brokerage firm with approximately 13,000 accounts, catered to active traders by offering its customers direct trades to market makers and electronic communications networks. The acquisition allowed Waterhouse to be more competitive with other brokerage firms offering direct access, including Ameritrade, Datek Online, and Charles Schwab.

direct cost A cost that can be directly related to producing specific goods or performing a specific service. For example, the wages of an employee engaged in producing a product can be attributed directly to the cost of manufacturing that product. Certain other costs such as depreciation and administrative expenses are more difficult to assign and are not considered direct costs. —Compare INDIRECT COST.

directed sale The sale of a block of stock to a single buyer as part of a new issue. Shares for a directed sale are withheld by the lead underwriter from members of the underwriting syndicate.

direct (federal) government obligation A debt that is backed by the full taxing power of the U.S. government. Direct obligations include Treasury bills, Treasury bonds, and U.S. savings bonds. These investments are generally considered to be of the very highest quality. —See also FEDERAL AGENCY SECURITY.

direct financing The raising of funds without using an intermediary. For example, a firm may decide to save an underwriter's fee by offering new securities directly to investors.

director A member of a firm's board of directors. A director also may hold a management position within the firm. —See also INSIDE DIRECTOR; OUTSIDE DIRECTOR.

directors' and officers' liability insurance A type of insurance taken to protect a firm's directors and officers against lawsuits—mainly suits instituted by unhappy shareholders of the firm. Directors' and officers' liability insurance has become more expensive and more difficult to obtain in recent years as the number of lawsuits has increased dramatically. Companies find it very difficult to recruit outside directors unless the candidates are supplied with liability insurance. —Also called *D&O Coverage.*

direct paper Commercial paper sold directly by issuers to individual investors without the use of an intermediary. This method is most often used by finance companies such as General Motors Acceptance Corporation. —Compare DEALER PAPER.

direct participation program An investment program in which tax consequences and cash flows pass directly from the investment to the investors. The purpose of a direct investment program is to permit investors to enjoy certain benefits (for example, depreciation deductions) usually available to a corporation.

direct placement The sale of a new security issue to a limited number of large buyers rather than to the general public. Direct placement generally involves less expense to the issuer, although the buyer may be able to negotiate a more favorable price.

direct play The stock of a firm that concentrates its operations in a specific industry. An investor expecting favorable opportunities from a particular line of business may seek a direct play in the business itself rather than invest in the stock of a company engaged not only in that business but also in a variety of other businesses. Although a direct play has good profit potential, it is generally more risky than a security in a widely diversified company. —Also called *play.*

direct purchase To buy shares of a mutual fund directly from the fund rather than from an intermediary such as a broker or financial planner. Mutual funds that sell directly to investors do not have sales personnel and generally charge no sales fee or a relatively small sales fee.

direct stock purchase plan A plan initiated by some firms that permits investors to purchase stock directly from the issuer (thereby avoiding brokerage commissions). Although generally open only to employees and current shareholders, an increasing number of companies allow nonstockholders to make direct purchases.

direct tax A tax paid by the individual or organization on which it is levied. For example, the personal income tax is levied on individuals, who end up bearing the entire burden of the tax. A direct tax cannot be shifted from the entity on which it is levied. —Compare INDIRECT TAX.

dirty price The price of a bond including accrued interest. —Compare CLEAN PRICE.

dirty stock A security that is not in deliverable form for transfer. For example, a certificate may not be endorsed properly.

disabilities Restrictions or special handling requirements that are placed on an individual's brokerage account. For example, an employee of a financial institution involved in the securities business must have special permission from the employer in order to have a margin account.

disbursement A payment in cash or by check.

disclaimer of opinion The statement of a Certified Public Accountant that an audit opinion cannot be rendered because of limitations on the extent of the examinations. —Compare CLEAN OPINION.

disclosure The submission of facts and details concerning a situation or business operation. In general, security exchanges and the SEC require firms to disclose to the investment community the facts concerning issues that will affect the firms' stock prices. Disclosure is also required when firms file for public offerings. —See also FULL DISCLOSURE.

discontinued operation A segment of a business that has been abandoned or sold or for which plans for one or another of these actions have been approved. —See also CONTINUING OPERATION.

discount The amount by which a bond sells below face value. —See also BELOW PAR; DISCOUNT BOND.

discount 1. To adjust the value of an asset on the basis of information rather than activity or events. For example, investors may already have discounted a firm's stock price because of the anticipation of weak earnings. 2. To deduct the charge for making a loan from the loan's principal before distributing funds to the borrower.

discount basis —See BANK-DISCOUNT BASIS.

discount bond A bond selling at a price that is less than its par value. In addition to semiannual interest payments, a discount bond offers investors additional appreciation if the security is held until maturity.

discount brokerage firm A brokerage firm that discounts commissions for individuals to trade securities. Most discount brokerage firms offer limited advice but reduce their fees by 50% or more compared with full-service brokerage firms. —Compare FULL-SERVICE BROKERAGE FIRM. —See also MAY DAY.

discounted cash flow A method of estimating an investment's current value based on the discounting of projected future revenues and costs. The answer derived from the technique is only as accurate as the estimates used, which, in many cases, are far from certain.

discounting the news Adjusting a security's price so that it already reflects some anticipated event or series of events. For example, a stock price may be unaffected by a favorable earnings report because the report was expected. Likewise, a bond's price may not fall on a rating downgrade because investors anticipated the downgrade and had priced the bond to discount the event.

discount rate 1. The interest rate charged by the Federal Reserve on loans to its member banks. A change in this rate is viewed as a strong indicator of Fed policy with respect to future changes in the money supply and market interest rates. Generally, a rise in the discount rate signals increasing interest rates in the money and capital markets. 2. The rate at which an investment's revenues and costs are discounted in order to calculate its present value.

discount security 1. Any security that is issued at less than face value. —See also ORIGINAL-ISSUE DISCOUNT. 2. A money market security, such as a Treasury bill or commercial paper, that is issued at a discount but that matures at face value. The only income received by the investor is the difference between the price paid and the proceeds received at maturity or the sale of the security. —See also BANK-DISCOUNT BASIS.

discount window The lending facility of the Federal Reserve through which commercial banks borrow reserves. Federal Reserve policy toward supplying banks with reserves has a major effect on credit conditions and interest rates.

discount yield —See BANK-DISCOUNT BASIS.

discretionary account A brokerage account in which the customer permits the broker to act on the customer's behalf in buying and selling securities. The broker may decide upon securities, prices, and timing—subject to any limitations specified in the agreement. Because a discretionary account can be quite risky, it should be avoided unless the customer has a great deal of confidence in the broker. —Compare ADVISORY ACCOUNT. —Also called *controlled account.* —See also LIMITED DISCRETION.

discretionary income Individual income that is not allocated to expenditures for necessities such as food and shelter. Increasing amounts of discretionary income are especially favorable for the prospects of firms that sell luxury or leisure items and services.

discretionary order A customer order to a broker giving the broker discretion in the buying and selling of securities. Depending on the customer's instructions, the amount of discretion may vary from very limited (that is, price only) to nearly complete.

disinflation A slowdown in the rate of inflation. A drop in the inflation rate from 3% in one year to 2% in the next year is an example of disinflation. On an overall basis, disinflation is good for security prices, but it can be painful for individual companies that have made investment and borrowing decisions based upon a belief that a high rate of inflation would continue. —See also INFLATION.

disinflation stock Stock that tends to benefit from a slowdown in the rate of inflation. Disinflation stock, which includes stock of organizations such as utilities and savings and loans, are hurt by high inflation and rising interest rates.

disintermediation The withdrawal of funds from financial intermediaries such as banks, thrifts, and life insurance companies in order to invest directly with ultimate users. Disintermediation was more of a problem when financial intermediaries were limited in the returns they could pay to savers. Deregulation of financial intermediaries was intended to dampen the periodic swings toward disintermediation. —Compare INTERMEDIATION.

disinvestment Divestiture, liquidation, or sale of a segment of a firm. Disinvestment may occur for a number of reasons including a poor outlook for a particular line of business or a firm's need to raise additional capital for other more promising segments of its business.

disposable income Aftertax income, calculated quarterly, that consumers have available for spending or saving. Economists view changes in disposable income as an important indicator of the present and future health of the economy. —See also PERSONAL INCOME.

disqualifying disposition The sale, gift, or exchange of stock acquired through an employee stock purchase plan within two years of enrollment or one year of the purchase date. A disqualifying disposition results in ordinary income for tax purposes.

dissident director A director who wishes to change a firm's policies and generally acts in opposition to the wishes of the other directors.

dissident shareholders Shareholders who oppose a firm's management or management policy. For example, dissident shareholders of Hewlett-Packard opposed that firm's offer to purchase Compaq Computer.

distressed debt Debt with low junk status and a market price substantially below par value, often pennies on the dollar. Investors sometimes buy distressed debt on the possibility that management can renegotiate loan agreements and keep the issuer out of bankruptcy. Alternatively, distressed debt may offer potential value in the event the issuer is liquidated.

CASE STUDY In December 2001 communications network services company Global Crossing, Ltd., was on the ropes. With reports of shrinking liquidity and an increased likelihood of seeking bankruptcy protection, the firm's stock dropped to under a dollar a share in trading on the New York Stock Exchange. At the same time its distressed 8.7% notes with 2007 maturity were bid at 7¢ on the dollar. At this price the notes provided buyers with a yield to maturity of nearly 100%. Three months earlier the same debt traded for over 50¢ on the dollar. The debt sold at such a low price because of the company's poor operating results and lack of cash, and also because investors believed the firm's telecom assets would bring little in liquidation.

distribute To sell a relatively large amount of stock in a firm during a given period. For example, a mutual fund may liquidate a position in a security over a period of days or weeks so as not to drive down the market price of the security. —Compare ACCUMULATE.

distribution 1. —See PUBLIC OFFERING. 2. An investment company payment to its shareholders of capital gains realized from the sale of securities. Investment company shareholders, not the investment company, pay taxes on a distribution.

distribution area In technical analysis, a rectangular-shaped chart formation occurring when stock is being sold by insiders and other knowledgeable investors in anticipation of a major price decline. A distribution area is generally characterized by relatively small price movements and heavy volume. —Compare ACCUMULATION AREA. —See also RECTANGLE; REVERSAL PATTERN.

distribution fee —See 12B-1 FEE.

distribution stock A relatively large block of stock sold over a period of time in either the primary or the secondary markets.

diversifiable risk —See UNSYSTEMATIC RISK.

diversification The acquisition of a group of assets in which returns on the assets are not directly related over time. An investor seeking diversification for a securities portfolio would purchase securities of firms that are not similarly affected by the same variables. For example, an investor would not want to combine large investment positions in airlines, trucking, and automobile manufacturing because each industry is significantly affected by oil prices and interest rates. Proper investment diversification, requiring a sufficient number of different assets, is intended to reduce the risk inherent in particular securities. Diversification is just as important to companies as it is to investors. *See Investment Tip on p. 110.* —See also UNSYSTEMATIC RISK.

diversified company A company engaged in varied business operations not directly related to one another. A diversified company is less likely to suffer either

What types of mutual funds provide the best diversification?

Diversification, the notion of "not putting all your eggs in one basket," is among the most celebrated concepts in finance. Economist Harry Markowitz even got a Nobel Prize for turning your parents' oft-repeated advice into mathematical equations. Diversification both reduces investment risk and increases the odds that you'll earn a decent return over time. A big attraction of mutual funds is that they offer instant diversification. You own a portfolio holding anywhere from hundreds to thousands of stocks or bonds for an initial investment that can be as low as $100. The best way to make sure that your equity mutual fund is well diversified—and not just stuffed with the latest high flyers—is to own a broad-based equity index fund. The same goes for fixed-income securities through a bond index fund that invests in both corporate and government debt. Although the annual management is higher, an alternative is an actively managed balanced fund that owns large and small companies and value and growth stocks as well as fixed-income securities.

Christopher Farrell, Economics Editor
Minnesota Public Radio, heard nationally on Sound Money®

a collapse or a spectacular gain in earnings compared with a firm concentrating its operations in a single business. Likewise, the stock of a diversified company is unlikely to bring extraordinarily large gains or losses to its shareholders.

diversified management company An investment company with a minimum of 75% of its assets as cash, government securities, securities of other investment companies, and other securities subject to a limitation of no more than 5% of the diversified management company's assets or 10% of the voting securities of the issuing company. Most investment companies, including mutual funds and closed-end investment companies, are diversified management companies. —Compare NONDIVERSIFIED MANAGEMENT COMPANY.

diversify To acquire a variety of assets that do not tend to change in value at the same time. To diversify a securities portfolio is to purchase different types of securities in different companies in unrelated industries.

divestiture The sale, liquidation, or spinoff of a division or subsidiary. For example, a firm may decide to divest itself of a division in order to concentrate its managerial efforts on more promising segments of its business.

divided account The account of an underwriting syndicate when sales and liability are apportioned individually rather than shared jointly. —Compare UNDIVIDED ACCOUNT.

dividend A share of a company's net profits distributed by the company to a class of its stockholders. The dividend is paid in a fixed amount for each share of stock held. Although most companies make quarterly payments in cash (checks), dividends also may be in the form of property, scrip, or stock. Unlike interest on a debt, dividends must be voted on by the company's directors before each payment. —See also BOND DIVIDEND; CAPITAL DIVIDEND; CASH DIVIDEND; CONSENT DIVIDEND; CONSTRUCTIVE DIVIDEND; DECLARATION DATE; DECLARED DIVIDEND; EX-DIVIDEND DATE; FINAL DIVIDEND; ILLEGAL DIVIDEND; INTERIM DIVIDEND; LIABILITY DIVIDEND; LIQUIDATING DIVIDEND; OPTIONAL DIVIDEND; STOCK DIVIDEND.

dividend adjustment The extra proceeds sent to an investor submitting convertible preferred stock for conversion in order to compensate for dividends accrued but not received since the last date of record for a dividend payment. The dividend adjustment is an unusual practice designed to compensate holders of convertible preferred stock for dividends lost between the time of the last dividend and the time of conversion. —Also called *adjustment.*

dividend capture The trading of a stock in order to be the holder of record for dividend payment purposes. Once the right to receive the dividend payment has been earned, the stock is sold. Dividend capture is practiced chiefly by corporations; they are permitted to exclude from their taxable income 80% of dividends received. Certain specific tax rules apply to dividend capture.

dividend coverage The extent to which a firm's net income supports the company's total dividend payments. For example, a utility earning $5.00 per share and paying a dividend of $4.79 per share has relatively weak dividend coverage. Poor coverage permits a firm's management to enjoy less flexibility to raise dividends or to keep them at the same level in the event that earnings decline. —See also PREFERRED DIVIDEND COVERAGE.

dividend discount model A model used to determine the price at which a security should sell based on the discounted value of estimated future dividend payments. Dividend discount models are used to determine if a security is a good buy, such as one that sells at a lower current price than the model would indicate, or a bad buy, such as one that sells at a higher current price than the model would indicate.

dividend equivalent right In incentive stock options, the right to a credit for additional shares for the value of dividends a firm pays on its shares.

dividend exclusion For corporate stockholders, the dividends received that are exempt from taxation. A corporation that owns less than 20% of the stock in another company can exclude 70% of the dividends received from taxable income. When between 20% and 79% of the stock of another company is owned, 75% of the dividends received from that firm can be excluded from taxation. When 80% or more of another company's stock is owned, all of the dividends received from that firm can be excluded from taxation. Dividend exclusion is not applicable to individual investors.

dividend payable A dividend that has been declared by directors but not paid to stockholders. A dividend that is declared becomes a general liability of the company until paid to shareholders.

dividend payment date The date on which an issuer's paying agent will send dividend payments to stockholders. —See also EX-DIVIDEND DATE; PAYMENT DATE.

dividend payout ratio —See PAYOUT RATIO.

dividend reinvestment plan (DRIP) A plan that allows stockholders to automatically reinvest dividend payments in additional shares of the company's stock. Instead of receiving the usual dividend checks, participating stockholders will receive quarterly notification of shares purchased and shares held in their accounts. Dividend reinvestment is usually an inexpensive way of purchasing additional shares of stock because the fees are low or are completely absorbed by the company. In addition, some companies offer stock at a discount from the existing market price. Usually these dividends are fully taxable even though no cash is received by the stockholder. —Also called *automatic dividend reinvestment; reinvestment plan.* —See also SUPER DRIP.

dividend requirement Total annual preferred dividends to be paid by a company.

dividends in arrears Dividend payments on cumulative preferred stock that have been passed by a firm's directors. These dividends must be brought up to date before any payments are made to common stockholders. Any payments of dividends in arrears go to the current holders of the preferred stock regardless of who held the stock when the dividend was passed. —Also called *accumulated dividend.*

dividend test A provision in some borrowing agreements that restricts the borrower's ability to pay dividends to stockholders. This provision is supposed to protect the position of creditors against a drawdown on assets by dividend payments.

dividend yield The annual dividends from a common or preferred stock divided by that stock's market price per share. If ExxonMobil common stock trades at a price of $50 per share, its $.92 dividend provides a dividend yield of $.92/$50, or 1.84%. This figure measures the current return on a particular common stock but does not take into account potential gains and losses in the security's value.

> ⩗ **CASE STUDY** | While dividend yield can be an important measure of the current income you are likely to receive from ownership of a particular common stock, it can also signal other possibilities, some of which aren't so good. For example, a very high dividend yield is almost certainly a sign that the dividend being paid is likely to be reduced or even eliminated. In the summer of 1996, Northeast Utilities was facing rising expenses as a result of shutting a nuclear power plant located in Connecticut. The firm's stock price, reflecting investor concern about the escalating costs, had declined 50% since the beginning of the year. The reduced stock price of $12⅞ produced a dividend yield of 13.7% based on the utility's quarterly dividend of 44¢ per share. The high dividend yield stemmed from investors' expectations that the dividend would have to be reduced, perhaps substantially, because of lower earnings and cash flow related to the troubled nuclear plant. A common stock that has a dividend yield higher than the yield on long-term bonds indicates a need for caution.

divider —See EUROPEAN CURRENCY QUOTATION.

DJA —See DOW JONES AVERAGES®.

DJIA —See DOW JONES INDUSTRIAL AVERAGE®.

DK —See DON'T KNOW.

dogs of the Dow The investment strategy of purchasing the ten stocks in the Dow Jones Industrial Average that offer the highest current dividend yield. The ten-stock portfolio is continuously rebalanced as stock prices and dividends change. The theory is that Dow stocks offering the highest dividend yield are solid investments that are temporarily undervalued.

dollar bond A bond that is traded and quoted on the basis of its dollar price rather than on its yield. Dollar quotations are fairly unusual except in the case of municipal revenue bonds. Price quotes may or may not include any dealer fees; therefore, it is important for an investor to determine which is the case.

dollar-cost averaging Investment of a fixed amount of money at regular intervals, usually each month. This process results in the purchase of extra shares

dollar-cost averaging

What types of investors should use dollar-cost averaging?

When asked what the market was going to do, J. P. Morgan reportedly said, "It will fluctuate." Morgan was right! This concept refers to putting a fixed amount of money into securities periodically. In so doing, one's average price per share is lower than the mean average price during the holding period. This is basic math: $100 buys 10 shares of a stock at $10, and 5 shares at $20 when the market is higher. The mean average price is $15. But the investor owns 15 shares and paid just $200 for an average price per share of just $13.33. TIP: A good approach for smaller investors just getting started, and also for IRAs. It works particularly well with diversified mutual funds.

Thomas J. McAllister, CFP, McAllister Financial Planning, Carmel, IN

during market downturns and fewer shares during market upturns. Dollar-cost averaging is based on the belief that the market or a particular stock will rise in price over the long term and that it is not worthwhile (or even possible) to identify intermediate highs and lows. —Also called *averaging.*

dollar price The price of a bond quoted as a dollar percentage of par value rather than yield. For example, a bond selling at par would be quoted at 100.

dome In technical analysis, a chart formation indicating a market top and characterized by an upside-down U-shaped pattern. A dome is an example of a reversal pattern. Refer to the *Technical Analysis Chart Patterns* section for an example of this chart. —Also called *inverted saucer; rounded top.*

domestic corporation A firm incorporated under the laws of the country or state in which it does business. For example, a firm incorporated in the United States is considered a domestic corporation in the U.S. but a foreign corporation elsewhere. —Compare FOREIGN CORPORATION.

donated capital Funds or property given as a gift to a corporation. The donation may be from individuals or organizations not affiliated with the corporation. —See also CONTRIBUTED CAPITAL.

do not increase A directive that the number of shares in an order not be increased in the event of a stock split. The order to which such a directive is added may be either a limit order to buy stock or a stop order to sell stock.

do not reduce An addition to a limit order to buy or a stop order to sell stock that states that the price will not automatically be reduced when the stock goes ex-dividend. Without this instruction, the price is reduced by the amount of the dividend to be paid.

don't fight the tape A market axiom that asserts an investor shouldn't buy stocks during a major decline or sell stocks during a strong market advance. The guidance is based on the belief that price movements for individual stocks and the overall market gain momentum so that it is more likely to be profitable to trade with the trend than against the trend.

don't know (DK) A broker-dealer response to a transaction report when the facts of the trade are in doubt or are unknown.

DOT —See DESIGNATED ORDER TURNAROUND.

dot-com **1.** Of or relating to a company or the stock of a company engaged primarily in a business associated with the Internet. Amazon.com is the most obvious example of a dot-com company. **2.** —See INTERNET STOCK.

double auction market A market in which multiple buyers compete to purchase many items that are simultaneously offered for sale. Sales are made to buyers willing to offer the highest price by sellers who are willing to offer the lowest price. The New York Stock Exchange is an example of a double auction market.

double-barreled municipal bond A municipal obligation that is a general obligation of the issuer and is also secured by a particular revenue source outside the general fund. —Also called *combination bond.*

double bottom In technical analysis, a chart formation indicating stock price recoverability over time. It is characterized by a drop in a stock's price to a low level, a recovery in price, and a second decline to the previous low price. If the stock price recovers a second time, the low price reached at the two bottoms becomes a level of support for the stock. It is a bearish sign if the stock subsequently falls through this level. Refer to the *Technical Analysis Chart Patterns* section for an example of this chart. —Compare DOUBLE TOP.

double-declining-balance depreciation A depreciation method that records large depreciation expenses in the early years of an asset's life and reduced depreciation expenses in the later years of an asset's life. The acceleration of depreciation is designed to reduce taxable income and tax payments so that extra cash will be available for reinvestment. According to this method, depreciation is calculated by multiplying twice the straight-line depreciation rate by the asset's book value each year. —See also MODIFIED ACCELERATED COST RECOVERY SYSTEM.

double-dip recession An extended decline in economic activity following an aborted recovery from a previous recession. A relatively weak economic recovery sometimes causes investors to worry about the economy entering another recession.

double-exempt fund A mutual fund that limits its investments to tax-free bonds of issuers from a single state. Thus, a double-exempt fund pays investors residing in the same state as the issuers of the bonds with income free of federal and state income taxes. Double-exempt funds have been particularly popular in the populous, high-tax states of California and New York. If an investor lives in a city with an income tax, these funds are exempt from three taxes. —Also called *single state municipal bond fund.* —See also TRIPLE TAX EXEMPT.

double option A commodity option traded in Europe that gives its owner the right either to call (buy) or to put (sell) the underlying asset but not both. When one side of the option is exercised, the opposite side is automatically terminated.

double taxation Taxation of the same income twice by the same taxing authority. It is generally used to refer to the taxation of dividends that are taxed once at the corporate level (as income before dividends are declared) and again at the personal level (when the dividends are received).

double top In technical analysis, a chart formation indicating stock price resistance level and characterized by a stock price reaching a single high price on two different occasions. The price level represented by the double top becomes a resistance level through which the stock will later have difficulty breaking below. Refer to the *Technical Analysis Chart Patterns* section for an example of this chart. —Compare DOUBLE BOTTOM.

double up To purchase an equal number of additional shares when the price of a stock declines. For example, an investor who purchases 500 shares of a stock at $40 per share would double up by purchasing an additional 500 shares if the price of the stock drops. This investment technique can also be applied to short sales. The risk of doubling up is that a bad decision on an initial trade will be compounded when additional shares of the same stock are purchased. Imagine doubling up on high-tech stocks during the dot-com bust.

doubling option A provision in some indentures that allows the borrower, at his or her option, to retire twice as many bonds as stipulated under a sinking fund requirement. The additional retirements take place at or near par, so that the option is used during periods of low interest rates. Thus, the provision operates to the disadvantage of investors. —Compare SINKING FUND PROVISION. —See also CALL PROVISION.

Dow —See DOW JONES INDUSTRIAL AVERAGE®.

dower A widow's portion of her husband's assets that were acquired during the course of their marriage. The dower, usually amounting to one third, applies even if the deceased husband wills her a portion less than this. —Compare CURTESY.

Dow Jones & Company, Inc. A major publisher of financial data and business news. Although best-known as the publisher of *The Wall Street Journal* and compiler of the Dow Jones Averages, Dow Jones also publishes a magazine, produces a radio show and a television show, and provides an electronic news service to the financial community.

Dow Jones Averages® (DJA) A trademark for an index of the relative prices of selected industrial, transportation, and utility stocks based on a formula developed and periodically revised by Dow Jones & Company, Inc.

Dow Jones Industrial Average® (DJIA) A trademark for one of the oldest and most widely quoted measures of stock market price movements. The Average is calculated by adding the share prices of 30 large, seasoned firms such as Intel, ExxonMobil, General Electric, and GM and dividing the sum by a figure that is adjusted for such things as stock splits and substitutions. —Also called *the Dow.*

⩘ CASE STUDY The DJIA, frequently referred to as "the Dow," celebrated its 100th birthday in 1996. Although academics and many finance professionals do not hesitate to cite the deficiencies of the average as a measuring device for the overall stock market, the Dow persists as the most widely recognized market yardstick. An announcement on the evening news of a 25-point market decline almost certainly refers to a decline of 25 points in the Dow. The extent of any price movement in the Dow should be put in perspective by comparing the price change to the value of the average. For example, a 25-point decline in the average from a base of 5,000 amounts to a percentage decline of only 25/5,000 or 0.5%. The DJIA is a price-weighted average of 30 stocks, meaning that only the prices of the component stocks are considered in the Dow's calculation. Market value, or stock price multiplied by shares outstanding, is used in calculating some other indexes such as the S&P 500. The original DJIA comprised only 12 stocks, including long-forgotten companies such as American Cotton Oil, Distilling & Cattle Feeding

Co., Tennessee Coal, Iron & Railroad Co., and U.S. Leather, and was calculated by dividing the sum of the 12 stock prices by 12. The divisor has changed many times during the past century as stock splits have taken place and components of the average were adjusted. (For example, IBM was added in 1932, dropped in 1939, and added back in 1979. General Electric is the only original stock that remains in the average.) The result is a divisor that has declined from the original 12 to a 2002 level of .14452124. Thus, in mid-2002 the Dow was calculated by dividing the sum of the 30 component stock prices by the then current divisor of .14452124. The fractional divisor causes a price decline of $2.00 in one of the component stocks to produce a decline of approximately 14 points in the Dow. Of course, the average is also affected by price changes in the other component stocks. With a relatively small number of component stocks making up the average, large price movements in a few stocks sometimes overwhelm smaller price movements in many other component stocks.

Dow Jones Transportation Average® A trademark for a stock average that uses the share prices of 20 large companies in an effort to show overall price movements in the stock of transportation-related firms. This average, which used to be limited to the stock of railroads, now includes those of airlines and trucking companies.

Dow Jones Utility Average® A trademark for a stock average of 15 large electric and gas utility companies that attempts to show overall price movements of utility stock. The direction that this average takes is heavily influenced by changes in long-term interest rates.

down-and-in option An option that is created when the value of the underlying asset falls to a predetermined level. —Compare DOWN-AND-OUT OPTION.

down-and-out option An option that terminates when the value of the underlying asset falls to a predetermined level. —Compare DOWN-AND-IN OPTION.

downgrading A reduction in the quality rating of a security issue, generally a bond. A downgrading may occur for various reasons including a period of losses, or increased debt service required by restructuring a firm's capital to include more debt and less equity. For example, takeover targets that engage in stock buybacks to prop up the price of their shares are subject to debt issue downgrading by the rating agencies. —Compare UPGRADING 1.

ᴧᴧ CASE STUDY | In late 2000 Moody's Investors Service, a major bond rating agency, downgraded the debt of Imax Corportion, the well-known big-screen movie company. The downgrading occurred amid bad times for the movie industry. Carmike Cinemas, a major theater company, had recently filed for bankruptcy, and Regal Cinemas, America's biggest theater chain, announced it might follow Carmike's lead. Concerned about Imax's financial viability, Moody's reduced its rating for the firm's senior notes from Ba2 to B2. It also lowered the rating for Imax's convertible subordinated notes from B1 to Caa1. The downgrading of Imax debt made it more difficult for the firm to obtain additional financing.

downside protection An investment position that seeks to reduce losses resulting from the decline of a stock or a fall in the overall market. For example, put options provide downside protection against a decline in the price of the underlying stock. Likewise, writing covered call options can provide partial downside protection against price declines.

downside risk The potential losses that may occur if a particular investment position is taken. For example, the downside risk from holding Treasury bills is quite small. —Compare UPSIDE POTENTIAL.

downsize To reduce the size of a company, often by eliminating one or more divisions. Management may decide to downsize a firm in order to improve efficiency and to increase the returns to shareholders. Downsizing can cause a firm to grow smaller and more valuable at the same time.

downstream Of or relating to earnings or operations at a firm that are near or at the final stage of consumption. For example, marketing and transportation are downstream operations for a large, integrated oil company. —Compare UPSTREAM.

downstream merger A type of merger in which a parent firm is absorbed into one of its subsidiaries.

downtick A downward price movement for a security transaction compared with the preceding transaction of the same security. —Compare UPTICK. —Also called *minus tick*.

downtrend A series of price declines in a security or the general market. Many analysts feel that investors should avoid securities in a downtrend until the pattern is broken. —Compare UPTREND.

downturn A decline in security prices or economic activity following a period of rising or stable prices or activity. Even strong bull markets are subject to occasional downturns.

Dow theory A technical trading theory that holds that stock market price trends can be forecast based on price movements of the Dow Jones Averages (industrials and transportation). The theory classifies price movements into individual components of primary, secondary, and daily. Only when both averages reach new highs or lows (one average confirms the other) is a major trend in progress.

draft A written order by one party for a second party to make payment to a third party. A check is an example of a draft drawn by a depositor (first party) on a financial institution (second party) and payable to an individual or organization (third party). —See also OVERDRAFT; SIGHT DRAFT; TIME DRAFT.

drag-along rights The right of majority shareholders to force minority shareholders to join in a sale of a company. These rights allow majority shareholders to complete a sale in the event a buyer wants to own 100% of the firm.

dragon bond A long-term debt security issued in Asia and denominated in U.S. dollars.

dressing up a portfolio —See PORTFOLIO DRESSING.

DRIP —See DIVIDEND REINVESTMENT PLAN.

drive-by deal A short-term investment by a venture capitalist in a start-up company.

droplock bond A floating-rate bond that automatically converts to a fixed-rate bond if the interest rate used to peg the floating rate falls to a predetermined level. The new fixed rate stays in place until the droplock bond reaches maturity.

DTC —See DEPOSITORY TRUST COMPANY.

dual-class recapitalization The issue of a second class of common stock, generally with reduced voting power, in exchange for already outstanding shares of common stock. This type of recapitalization typically results in the entrenchment of management that enjoys increased control over corporate affairs.

dual-class stock —See STOCK CLASS.

dual coupon bond —See STEPPED COUPON BOND.

dual-currency bond A debt security that pays coupon interest in one currency and the principal in a different currency. Several variations of dual-currency bonds are issued, including some that specify the exchange rate at which currencies are converted for payments.

dual fund —See DUAL PURPOSE FUND.

dual listing The listing of a security on more than one exchange. Many stocks are traded on the New York or the American stock exchanges and on one or more of the regional exchanges. For example, the common stock of General Motors is listed on the New York Stock Exchange, but it also enjoys a large amount of activity on regional exchanges. Although dual listing theoretically should improve the liquidity of a stock thereby benefiting investors, most dual listed securities trade chiefly on one exchange.

dual presentation The presentation of a firm's earnings per share on a basic and a diluted basis. Dual presentation of earnings per share is required only for firms with complex capital structures.

dual purpose fund A special-purpose, unusual type of closed-end investment company offering two classes of stock in approximately equal amounts. One class, called income shares, is entitled to all the portfolio's income, while the second, called capital shares, is entitled to appreciation in investments in the firm's portfolio. At the time a dual purpose fund is established, a date is set on which the fund will be liquidated. At that time, income shareholders receive preference up to the par value of their shares and capital shareholders receive any excess. —Also called *dual fund; leveraged investment company.*

due Of or relating to an obligation or receivable that is outstanding and payable.

due bill A statement of a liability by one party to another party following a transaction. In the case of a security transaction, a due bill reflects money or securities owed by one broker to the other broker. For example, stock purchased on the ex-dividend date gives the seller rather than the buyer the right to receive the subsequent dividend. However, because the actual payment date of the dividend may follow the ex-dividend date by as much as a month, the buyer will be required to sign a due bill indicating that the dividend belongs to the selling party. —Also called *bill.*

due-diligence meeting A meeting between officials of the organization that will be issuing securities and members of the syndicate that will be distributing the securities. A due-diligence meeting is held for the purpose of discussing the terms of the issue, preparing a final prospectus, and negotiating a final agreement between the issuer and syndicate members.

dummy director The director of a firm who acts and votes according to the wishes of another party who is not a member of the board.

dummy stockholder An individual or firm holding stock in its own name when the stock is really owned by another party.

dumping 1. The selling of large amounts of a stock or stocks in general at whatever market prices are in effect. For example, investors might dump stocks upon hearing of an outbreak of fighting in some part of the world. **2.** The selling of a product in one market at an unusually low price while selling the same product at a significantly higher price in another market. For example, a firm may sell a product in its home market at a price covering all costs and then sell the product in a foreign market at a significantly lower price covering only variable costs.

durable goods Goods, such as appliances and automobiles, that have a useful life over a number of periods. Firms that produce durable goods are often subject to wide fluctuations in sales and profits. —Also called *consumer durables.*

durable power of attorney A legal document conveying authority to an individual to carry out legal affairs on another person's behalf.

duration The number of years required to receive the present value of future payments, both interest and principal, from a bond. Duration is determined by calculating the present value of the principal and each coupon and then multiplying each result by the period of time before payment is to occur. The concept of duration is used to relate the sensitivity of bond price changes to changes in interest rates. —Also called *mean term.*

duration matching strategy A method of assembling a bond portfolio so that the duration of the portfolio equals the duration of the investor's liability stream. —Compare CASH MATCHING STRATEGY.

Dutch auction An auction in which the seller reduces the offering price until a level can be found that clears the market. This is the price at which all sales will take place. The auction for Treasury bills is similar to this except that the Treasury accepts the highest bids first and works through progressively lower bids until an issue is completely sold. Thus, in a Treasury bill auction, various prices are accepted.

> **⩔ CASE STUDY** Whittaker Corporation announced plans in 1986 to sell several of its business units and use the proceeds to repurchase a significant proportion of its own outstanding stock. The stock buyback was to occur through a process by which Whittaker's shareholders could submit offers for varying numbers of shares at various prices. A shareholder might submit an offer to sell 500 shares at $35; 500 shares at $34; and 500 shares at $33, for example. Depending on the number of available shares and the prices offered by the shareholders, Whittaker would then set a price at which it would purchase the stock. Thus, if Whittaker set a price of $34.75, the shareholder would sell 1,000 shares (those offered at $34.75 or less) at a price of $34.75 each. Whittaker undertook the Dutch auction to determine the lowest price at which it could buy back the desired number of shares.

duty —See TARIFF.

DVP —See DELIVERY VERSUS PAYMENT.

E

e **1.** —Used in the dividend column of stock transaction tables in newspapers to indicate the dividend that was declared and paid in the preceding 12 months: *1.75e*. **2.** —Used in mutual fund transaction tables in newspapers to indicate that the shares trade ex-distribution.

early exercise The exercise of an option before it expires. Although somewhat unusual, an option holder may decide on early exercise in order to receive an upcoming dividend (in the case of a stock option) or in order to satisfy another commitment.

early settlement The transfer of a security or cash on a date prior to the usual settlement date. A buyer of stock may prefer an early settlement in order to be listed on a firm's books on the record date for a dividend. The buyer of a municipal bond may desire an early settlement in order to begin earning tax-free interest on an earlier date.

earned income Individual income, such as commissions, salaries, and bonuses, that is derived as compensation for personal services. —Compare UN-EARNED INCOME.

earned surplus —See RETAINED EARNINGS.

earning power **1.** The earnings that an asset could produce under optimal conditions. For example, AT&T may currently be earning $2.50 per share; however, under optimal conditions each share could have earnings of $3.75. **2.** The expected yield on a security.

earnings The income of a business. Earnings usually refers to aftertax income but may occasionally be used synonymously with pretax income or even revenues.

earnings before interest and taxes (EBIT) —See OPERATING INCOME.

earnings before interest, taxes, depreciation, and amortization (EBITDA) One popular measure of cash generated from the operation of a company. Financial analysts frequently use EBITDA to evaluate the ability of a company to service its debt obligations. EBITDA is also used as a measure of profitability in valuing a company and in comparing a company's financial performance with other firms. Critics contend EBITDA can be a misleading financial tool, in part because companies have wide discretion in determining the dollar amount of the components used in calculating EBITDA. In addition, EBITDA does not consider the funds a company is likely to require for capital investments. —See also also CASH FLOW; FREE CASH FLOW.

⋀⋀ CASE STUDY | Belgian brewer Interbrew NV announced in summer 2001 a deal to purchase Germany's fourth largest brewer, Brauerei Beck & Co. Interbrew was interested in an expanded presence in Germany and Italy, and also in the U.S. market, where Beck's was a major import brand. At the time of the announcement Interbrew's flagship brand, Stella Artois, was a minor player in the U.S. market. Some analysts criticized Interbrew for paying too high a price based on Beck's earnings before interest, taxes, depreciation, and amortization (EBITDA). The DM 3.5 billion ($1.58 billion) price represented 13 times Beck's EBITDA in the most recent fiscal year, substantially more than the 11.3 times EBITDA paid by another firm for the major French brewer Kronenbourg in an earlier deal.

earnings before taxes —See PRETAX INCOME.

earnings capitalization rate —See EARNINGS-PRICE RATIO.

earnings momentum The increase of earnings per share at an increasing rate. For example, a company is said to have earnings momentum if its reported earnings per share increases 10%, 15%, and 25% in successive years.

earnings multiple —See PRICE-EARNINGS RATIO.

earnings per share (EPS) An earnings measure calculated by subtracting the dividends paid to holders of preferred stock from the net income for a period and dividing that result by the average number of common shares outstanding during that period. EPS is the amount of reported income, on a per-share basis, that a firm has available to pay dividends to common stockholders or to reinvest in itself. As with other financial measures, EPS can vary with differing accounting techniques; therefore, reported EPS may give a very misleading signal as to how the firm is really doing. —Also called *income per share; net income per share.* —See also BASIC EARNINGS PER SHARE; DILUTED EARNINGS PER SHARE.

⋀ CASE STUDY | Companies often release several versions of earnings per share to the investment community. In October 2001 telecommunications company Convergys Corporation, a 1998 spinoff from Cincinnati Bell, announced its third-quarter operating earnings rose 12% to 31¢ per share from the prior year's 27¢ per share. At the same time the firm announced that cash earnings per share, excluding goodwill amortization and special items, increased 13%, to 35¢ from 31¢ during the year earlier period. However, earnings per share calculated according to generally accepted accounting principles specified by the Financial Accounting Standards Board were reported as 2¢ per share, down over 90% from 27¢ per share a year before. The shareholders' quandary is determining which measure of earnings per share most accurately represents the company's performance. Companies would like you to focus on the earnings report that is most favorable to the company and its management. In this instance investors must have considered operating income the most important measure of the firm's performance because Convergys stock closed up $1.80 at $28.00. A month later the stock was trading in the low 30s.

earnings-price ratio (E/P ratio) A measure indicating the rate at which investors will capitalize a firm's expected earnings in the coming period. This ratio is calculated by dividing the projected earnings per share by the current market price of the stock. A relatively low E/P ratio anticipates higher-than-average growth in earnings. Earnings-price ratio is the inverse of the price-earnings ratio. —Also called *earnings capitalization rate; earnings yield.*

earnings quality The extent to which a firm's reported earnings accurately reflect income for that period. Firms using conservative accounting practices tend to penalize current earnings and are said to have high earnings quality. At least over the short run, the earnings reported by a firm are as much a function of its accounting methods as they are a measure of its business success. —Also called *quality of earnings.* —See also INVENTORY PROFIT.

earnings report —See INCOME STATEMENT.

earnings retention ratio —See RETENTION RATE.

earnings statement —See INCOME STATEMENT.

earnings surprise Earnings reported by a company that are different from the earnings that had been expected by the investment community. An earnings surprise often produces a sharp increase or decrease in the market price of a stock.

earnings variability Fluctuations in a corporation's net income or earnings per share during a given period. Past earnings variability is generally considered undesirable because it makes investors less certain of future earnings per share and dividends. As such, a history of earnings variability may be expected to penalize a firm's stock with a lower-than-average price-earnings ratio.

earnings yield —See EARNINGS-PRICE RATIO.

earnout A contingency component of an acquisition agreement in which the acquiring company agrees to additional payments in the event certain performance-based goals are achieved. For example, Sylvan Learning Systems in 1995 acquired Drake Prometric for $20 million in cash plus 5.9 million restricted Sylvan common shares. The deal included an additional 2.7 million Sylvan shares to be released to the sellers in the event stipulated revenue goals were met through 1998.

easy money A condition of the money supply in which the Federal Reserve permits substantial funds to accrue in the banking system, thereby cutting interest rates and facilitating the acquisition of loans. In the resultant period when borrowing is relatively easy and inexpensive, security prices may be initially stimulated. But an extended period of easy money eventually may depress security values as investors begin to fear inflation. —Compare TIGHT MONEY. —Also called *cheap money.*

EBIT —See EARNINGS BEFORE INTEREST AND TAXES.

EBITDA —See EARNINGS BEFORE INTEREST, TAXES, DEPRECIATION, AND AMORTIZATION.

EBS —See ELECTRONIC BLUE SHEET.

ECN —See ELECTRONIC COMMUNICATIONS NETWORK.

e-commerce The buying and selling of goods and services over the Internet.

economic activity The production and distribution of goods and services at all levels. Economic activity and expected future levels of it have an important influence on security prices because of the interrelationship between economic activity and corporate profits, inflation, interest rates, and other variables. One frequently used measure of economic activity is the gross domestic product.

economic growth An increase in the production levels of goods and services. If measured in monetary terms, the increases must occur after adjustments for inflation have been made.

economic indicator A variable such as the unemployment rate or volume of help-wanted advertising that indicates the direction of the economy.

economic life The period of time during which a fixed asset competitively produces a good or service of value. The economic life of an asset may be particularly short in a rapidly changing field such as electronics where new developments often render an asset obsolete shortly after it is purchased. Companies sometimes continue to carry assets with expired economic lives on their balance sheets because they do not wish to penalize their earnings by writing off the assets. —See also PHYSICAL LIFE.

ECU —See EUROPEAN CURRENCY UNIT.

EDGAR (Electronic Data Gathering, Analysis, and Retrieval) A Securities and Exchange Commission computer database utilized by companies to electronically transmit required SEC filings for securities offerings and disclosure statements.

Edge Act corporation A corporation established under the 1919 Edge Act to undertake activities in international banking and investing. The Act gives U.S. firms more flexibility in competing effectively with foreign firms. Corporations established under the Edge Act are often organized in order to finance foreign trade or to own foreign securities.

Education IRA —See COVERDELL EDUCATION SAVINGS ACCOUNT.

EEC —See EUROPEAN ECONOMIC COMMUNITY.

effective date The date on which a new offering registered with the SEC may be sold by underwriters. There is usually a 20-day cooling-off period between the filing of a registration and the effective date.

effective rate of interest The rate of interest that incorporates compounding in the calculation used to determine the amount of interest to be credited to an account. For amounts invested during an entire year, the annual effective rate of interest multiplied by the principal will equal the amount of earned interest.

effective sale The trade that determines the price for an odd-lot order. For odd-lot market orders, the effective sale is the first trade following the specialist's receipt of the odd-lot order. For an odd-lot limit order, the effective sale is the trade that permits an odd-lot differential. —See also ELECTING SALE.

effective spread The spread actually paid by investors whose orders are routed to a particular market.

efficient market A market in which security prices reflect all available information and adjust instantly to any new information. If the security markets are truly efficient, it is not possible for an investor consistently to outperform stock market averages such as the S&P 500 except by acquiring more risky securities. Significant evidence supports the premise that security markets are very efficient. —Also called *market efficiency.* —See also RANDOM-WALK HYPOTHESIS; STRONG FORM; WEAK FORM.

efficient portfolio A combination of investments that offer either the highest possible yield at a given risk level or the lowest possible risk at a given yield level. Although the concept of an efficient portfolio is important to understand, in practice it is more academic than practical.

EFT —See ELECTRONIC FUNDS TRANSFER.

eighth One eighth of a point. With bond quotes, an eighth represents $1/8$ of a percent. For example, a quote of $90$1/8$ indicates $90$1/8$% of par, or usually, $901.25 per bond.

8–K A report filed with the SEC by any firm seeking to provide information on a material event that affects its financial condition. The report must be filed by any firm with shares traded on a national exchange or in the over-the-counter market. The SEC makes 8–Ks available to the public. —Also called *Form 8–K.*

either-or order —See ALTERNATIVE ORDER.

elastic Of or relating to the demand for a good or service when the quantity purchased varies significantly in response to price changes in the good or service. For example, the demand for a product with many close substitutes is elastic because a small price rise will cause consumers to switch to competing brands. —Compare INELASTIC.

elasticity The responsiveness of the quantity purchased of an item to changes in the item's price. If the quantity purchased changes proportionately more than the price, the demand is elastic. If the quantity purchased changes proportionately less than the price, the demand is inelastic. For example, price increases by cigarette manufacturers have a relatively small effect on cigarette consumption, thus, the demand for cigarettes is inelastic.

elect To convert a stop limit order or a stop order to a limit order or a market order.

electing sale The round-lot transaction that activates an odd-lot or round-lot stop order. The first transaction after the electing sale is the effective sale for determining the price of the odd-lot order. An electing sale can take place only when the price of a security is at or through the price specified on the order. For example, if a customer enters an order to buy at 15 stop, the electing sale will be the first sale at which the stock trades at a price of $15 or more.

election cycle —See PRESIDENTIAL ELECTION CYCLE.

electronic blue sheet (EBS) The electronic format for clearing firms to submit security trading records to the Securities and Exchange Commission. Information was submitted manually on blue paper until the late 1980s. The SEC and self-regulatory organizations use the EBS format to conduct surveillance and enforcement inquiries.

electronic communications network (ECN) A computerized trading network that matches buy and sell orders entered electronically by customers. Orders that cannot be immediately matched are posted for viewing by investors who may wish to take an offsetting position. Instinet became the first ECN when it started business in 1969. Archipelago and Island are two other large electronic communications networks. One study indicated that in January 2001 ECNs handled over 50% of all Nasdaq transactions.

Electronic Data Gathering, Analysis, and Retrieval —See EDGAR.

electronic funds transfer (EFT) The transfer of funds, as from one account to another or from buyer to seller, by telephone or computer. The use of EFT results in the instantaneous movement of money. The additional time that the funds are available to earn income can more than offset the fees charged by institutions for this service. —Also called *wire transfer.*

Electronic Quotation Service An Internet-based quotation service operated by Pink Sheets LLC for brokers and market makers of over-the-counter equities and bonds.

elephant An institutional investor that controls a substantial amount of funds and that makes investment decisions that can have a major impact on a security's market price.

eligible margin Collateral that is specified by a firm or an exchange as acceptable for satisfying margin requirements. For example, certain low-priced stocks may not be acceptable as margin.

emerging markets

Are the stocks of companies in emerging markets particularly risky?

Investing in emerging markets is considered very risky. The financial markets of developing countries are typically small, with a short operating history. Emerging markets exist in undeveloped regions of the world, which are very volatile and therefore have great growth potentials but also pose significant risks. Corruption, political instability, illiquidity, and currency collapse are just some of the significant risks of emerging regions. Argentina's economic collapse is the latest example of the risk involved in emerging countries.

Thomas M. Tarnowski, Senior Business Analyst
Global Investment Banking Division, Citigroup, Inc.—Salomon Smith Barney, New York, NY, and London, UK

Elliott Wave Theory A technical tool developed in the 1930s by R. N. Elliott for explaining stock price movements in terms of the sociological factors of investor optimism and pessimism. The theory holds that market movements occur in five waves in a given direction (up or down) followed by a correction of three waves in the opposite direction. According to the theory the wave patterns repeat themselves and can be used for forecasting market movements.

embedded option A provision within a security giving either the issuer or the security holder the right to take a specified action against the other. For example, a call provision is an embedded option in a bond that gives the issuer the right to redeem the bond prior to the scheduled maturity.

embezzle To take illegally something of value being held in custody for someone else.

EMCC —See EMERGING MARKETS CLEARING CORPORATION.

emerging growth stock The common stock of a relatively young firm that is operating in an industry that has very good growth prospects. Although this kind of stock offers unusually large returns, it is very risky because the expected growth may not occur or the firm may be swamped by the competition.

emerging markets Security markets in countries such as Mexico and Malaysia that are still developing their industrial base. Investments in emerging markets entail substantial risk with the potential for above-average returns.

Emerging Markets Clearing Corporation (EMCC) An industry-owned company that assists in the clearance and netting of emerging market debt products. Founded in 1998, EMCC reduces dealer risk by becoming a counter party to trades in emerging market debt.

emerging growth stock

Keys to spotting a good emerging growth stock

Keep these points in mind:

- High percentage of management ownership. If management has a vested interest, its commitment to succeed will be all the stronger.
- What stage is the overall industry in?
- More important, where is the target stock focusing its efforts within the industry?
- What will be the industry leader's reaction to another player?

Steven Flagg, Senior Vice President—Investments, UBS PaineWebber, Mount Kisco, NY

Emerging Markets Traders Association —See EMTA.

Employee Retirement Income Security Act (ERISA) A 1974 act that protects the retirement income of pension fund participants by setting standards for eligibility, performance, investment selection, funding, and vesting. The Act was designed to curb abuses by pension fund managers so as to ensure that retirement funds would actually be available at the time of the workers' retirement.

employee stock option —See INCENTIVE STOCK OPTION.

Employee Stock Ownership Plan (ESOP) A qualified retirement plan in which employees receive shares of the common stock of the company for which they work and the company receives an investment tax credit. The purpose of this type of plan is to give employees a vested interest in the company, thereby providing them with an additional incentive toward greater productivity. —See also LEVERAGED ESOP.

employment cost index A closely watched economic report by the Bureau of Labor Statistics that indicates the total cost of employing a civilian worker. A larger-than-expected increase in the index is likely to place downward pressure on both bond and equity prices.

EMTA The principal trade group for emerging markets trading. Originally formed in 1990 in response to debt reschedulings by Mexico and Venezuela, the group later expanded its interests to market practices and documentation. —Formerly called *Emerging Markets Traders Association.*

encryption The manipulation of data to prevent accurate interpretation by all but those for whom the data is intended. Financial institutions use encryption to increase the security of data transmitted via the Internet.

encumbrance 1. A liability on real property. For example, a mortgage encumbers title to real estate because the lender has an interest in the property. —Compare UNENCUMBERED. **2.** A commitment within an organization to use funds for a specific purpose. Thus, a college may encumber funds for later payment to cover expenses associated with a faculty member's trip to recruit new professors.

ending inventory Goods available for sale at the end of an accounting period. —Compare BEGINNING INVENTORY.

endorse To sign a negotiable instrument in order to transfer it to another party. For example, investors holding securities must endorse the certificates before delivery to the broker.

endorsement An owner's signature that serves to transfer the legal rights to a negotiable certificate to another party.

endorsement in blank An endorsement of a security by the owner without any transferee being named. Such an endorsement is risky because anyone coming into possession of the security may become its new owner.

endowment life insurance A life insurance policy that provides benefits for a specified period (for example, 20 years or until age 65) and that may be redeemed at face value if the insured is alive at the end of the specified period. Thus, payment is made regardless of whether the insured lives or dies, although the cost of the policy is quite high compared with other types of life insurance.

energy stock The stock of a company engaged in an energy-related business such as coal mining, oil refining, or electric power generation. Because of the diverse nature of this industry, the stocks do not always move together.

enhanced indexing A technique for making relatively small adjustments to an indexed portfolio in order to increase the return slightly above the return on the index. Employing enhanced indexing, the manager of an indexed portfolio may weight the portfolio slightly toward market sectors the manager feels are under-priced. —See also SECTOR NEUTRAL INDEX FUND.

entrepreneur A risk-taker who has the skills and initiative to establish a business.

E/P ratio —See EARNINGS-PRICE RATIO.

EPS —See EARNINGS PER SHARE.

equalizing dividend A dividend payment that is intended to compensate for a change in regular dividend dates. For example, a firm may move back its dividend payment dates by one month and compensate its shareholders with a one-time equalizing dividend to account for the four-month, instead of the normal three-month, interval before the first payment under the new schedule.

equipment Fixed assets that are acquired as additions or supplements to more permanent assets. Equipment includes lighting fixtures in a building, for example. Equipment, unlike real estate, is generally moveable.

equipment leasing limited partnership A partnership in which investors' funds are used to acquire equipment that is leased to businesses. Lease payments are passed through to partners with much of the income sheltered from taxation by depreciation and interest expense. At the termination of a lease, the equipment is sold and a cash distribution is made to the partners.

equipment trust certificate An intermediate- to long-term security that pays a fixed return based on payments received from the lease of equipment. These certificates are frequently used by railroads and airlines to finance rolling stock and aircraft, respectively.

equity **1.** In a brokerage account, the market value of securities minus the amount borrowed. Equity is particularly important for margin accounts, for which minimum standards must be met. **2.** Stock, both common and preferred. For example, an investor may prefer investing in equities instead of in bonds. —Also called *equity security.* **3.** In accounting, funds contributed by stockholders through direct payment and through retained earnings. —See also OWNERS' EQUITY.

equity arbitrage —See RISK ARBITRAGE.

equity carve-out The initial sale of common stock by a corporation of one of its business units. The initial public offering generally involves less than the entire amount of the stock in the unit so the parent company retains an equity stake in the subsidiary. An equity carve-out is sometimes followed by a distribution of the remaining shares to the parent's stockholders. —Also called *carve-out; split-off IPO.*

⋀⋀ CASE STUDY | Phillip Morris's 2001 equity carve-out of a portion of its ownership in subsidiary Kraft Foods resulted in what to that time was the second largest initial public offering in U.S. history. The $8.7 billion raised from the issue of 280 million shares was second only to the prior year's $10.6 billion initial public offering of AT&T Wireless tracking stock by AT&T. Demand for the Kraft issue was strong enough to allow the managers, Credit Suisse First Boston and Salomon Smith Barney, to increase the issue price to $31 per share from an earlier estimate of $27 to $30. Kraft, owner of well-known products including Maxwell House coffee, Post cereals, and Planters peanuts, was wholly owned by Phillip Morris prior to the IPO. Subsequent to the carve-out, Phillip Morris held slightly less than 50% of Kraft's class A common stock but controlled nearly all of the firm's voting shares. Proceeds from the stock issue were to be used to reduce Kraft's immense debt, which was incurred when the company in late 2000 purchased Nabisco Holdings for nearly $20 billion.

equity commitment note   Corporate debt that eventually will be repaid by issuing stock.

equity financing   The acquisition of funds by issuing shares of common or preferred stock. Firms usually use equity financing when they are unable to raise sufficient funds through retained earnings or when they have to raise additional equity capital to offset debt.   —Compare DEBT FINANCING.

equity-indexed annuity   A contract with an insurance company that promises periodic payments keyed in a specified manner to a stock market index. Unlike variable annuities, equity-indexed annuities specify a guaranteed minimum return that is typically 3%. These contracts may also specify an upper limit (cap) on the return that is paid. Indexing methods vary, and surrender charges often apply to early withdrawals.

equity kicker   An addition to a fixed-income security that permits the investor to participate in increases in the value of equity ownership. Two common types of equity kickers are a convertible feature on some bonds that allows the bonds to be exchanged for shares of stock, and warrants to purchase stock that are sold in combination with a new bond issue.   —Compare REAL ESTATE CERTIFICATE OF DEPOSIT.

equity method   A method of accounting for an investment in another company in which the book value of the investment reflects a share of the acquired firm's increases in retained earnings. Thus, if Firm A purchases 20% of Firm B's stock and Firm B earns $3 million after taxes during the next year, Firm A will increase the carrying value of its investment by 20% of $3 million, or $600,000. If Firm B pays half its earnings in dividends, Firm A will increase its investment by $300,000.

equity note   Intermediate-term debt that is automatically converted into common stock at maturity.

equity option   An option for which the underlying asset is stock.   —Compare NONEQUITY OPTION.

equity participation loan   A loan in which the lender obtains or has the right to obtain an ownership interest in the project being financed.

equity REIT   A real estate investment trust that purchases property with investors' money. Investors in an equity REIT earn dividend income from rental income earned by the REIT on property it owns. The investors also participate in increases in value of the owned real estate.   —Compare MORTGAGE REIT.

equity risk premium   The extra return expected from investments in common stocks compared to the return from U.S. Treasury securities.

equivalent taxable yield

Does the purchase of tax-free securities make sense?

Analyze investments for risk related to return (payout and growth) and yield. Tax-free securities have less risk, but their return is usually lower than riskier growth investments, corporate bonds, or preferred stocks. Determine the equivalent taxable yield of a tax-free security (yield divided by the difference of one minus your marginal tax bracket). Compare the investment to alternative securities with similar or higher yields or returns. Invest for a higher return if you are comfortable with the risk. Tax-free securities make sense for high-income taxpayers looking for safer, certain returns.

Jeffrey S. Levine, CPA, MST, Alkon & Levine, PC, Newton, MA

equity security —See EQUITY 2.

equity swap An exchange of the potential appreciation of an equity's value and dividends for a guaranteed return plus any decrease in the value of the equity. An equity swap permits an equity holder a guaranteed return but demands the holder give up all rights to appreciation and dividend income.

equity warrant —See WARRANT.

equivalent bond yield The annual yield on a short-term security that is usually quoted on a bank-discount basis to make the yield comparable with quotations on other interest-bearing debt.

equivalent taxable yield The taxable return that must be achieved in order to equal, on an aftertax basis, a given tax-exempt return. Equivalent taxable yield is calculated by dividing the available tax-exempt yield by one minus the investor's marginal tax rate. For example, a tax-exempt return of 9% for an investor in a 40% marginal tax bracket would require a taxable return of .09/0.6, or 15%, to produce the same aftertax equivalent.

ERISA —See EMPLOYEE RETIREMENT INCOME SECURITY ACT.

ERR —Used on the consolidated tape to indicate that an error has been made when reporting a transaction in the indicated security: ERR.LAST.IBM. The previous report, therefore, should be disregarded.

escheat The right of the state to claim a deceased person's property when there are no individuals legally qualified to inherit it or to make a claim to it. This occurrence is fairly unusual even when the deceased leaves no will.

escrow The holding of assets (that is, securities) by a third party.

escrowed to maturity —Used to describe a bond that has been prerefunded to the degree that cash flows will match the debt obligation to the retirement date.

ESOP —See EMPLOYEE STOCK OWNERSHIP PLAN.

essential function bond A bond issued by a municipality when funds from the bond issue are used for traditional government purposes such as government office buildings, libraries, parks, prisons, roads, and schools. The interest on municipal essential function bonds is exempt from federal income tax and is not subject to the alternative minimum tax. —Compare PRIVATE ACTIVITY BOND. —Also called *traditional governmental purpose bond.* —See also MUNICIPAL BOND.

estate The assets owned by a person at the time of death. —See also GROSS ESTATE.

Why is estate planning important?

A well-drafted estate plan is your assurance that the taxes and costs associated with your death will be minimized. A good estate plan also keeps the process of settling your estate as simple and efficient as possible. Most importantly, your estate plan will ensure that your assets will be used to benefit the people or institutions that you choose, in the amounts that *you* choose.

Gloria Cole, Attorney, private practice, Weston, MA

estate planning   The preparation for the orderly administration and disbursement of a person's estate. The preparation includes taking actions that will minimize taxes and distribute assets to the appropriate heirs.

estate tax   A tax on the estate of the deceased before any distribution is made to the heirs. A federal unified gift and estate tax provides an exemption before any tax is paid. Although some states also levy an estate tax, it is generally at a much lower rate than the federal tax. —Compare INHERITANCE TAX. —Also called *death tax.*

estimated tax   The estimated tax liability on income that is not subject to withholding. Individuals with even moderate investment income are generally expected to file a declaration of estimated tax and to pay quarterly installments on the estimated tax liability.

ETF   —See EXCHANGE-TRADED FUND.

ethical fund   A mutual fund that limits investment alternatives to securities of firms meeting certain social standards. For example, an ethical fund might exclude securities of companies that are known to practice discrimination, that operate in certain countries, or that produce specific products (for example, those having to do with nuclear weapons or nuclear power plants). Ethical funds include the Dreyfus Third Century Fund, the New Alternatives Funds, and the Working Assets Fund, among others. —See also SOCIAL INVESTING.

ethical investing   —See SOCIAL INVESTING.

e-trade   To buy or sell a security via computer. Brokerage firms route computer-generated customer orders to appropriate dealers and exchange specialists.

euro   A common currency used by many European countries. The euro was established in 1999 when 11 European countries adopted a common currency in order to facilitate global trade and encourage the integration of markets across national borders. Euro banknotes and coins began circulating in January 2002.

Eurobond   A type of foreign bond issued and traded in countries other than the one in which the bond is denominated. A dollar-denominated bond sold in Europe by a U.S. firm is a Eurobond.

Euro CD   A certificate of deposit issued primarily in London by a foreign bank or a foreign branch of a U.S. bank.

Euroclear   The world's largest settlement system for international and domestic bond and equity transactions. Euroclear provides a variety of financial services, including securities lending, settlement, and clearing.

Eurocurrency   Funds deposited in a bank when those funds are denominated in a currency differing from the bank's own domestic currency. Eurocurrency applies to any currency and to banks in any country. Thus, if a Japanese company deposits yen in a Canadian bank, the yen will be considered Eurocurrency.

Eurodollar   A dollar-denominated deposit made in foreign banks or foreign branches of U.S. banks. Depositors sometimes transfer their funds to European banks in order to take advantage of higher interest rates. The Eurodollar is one type of Eurocurrency.

Eurodollar bond   A dollar-denominated bond sold to investors outside the United States. These securities allow buyers to benefit, or lose, from variations in currency exchange rates. A Eurodollar bond is an example of a Eurobond.

Eurodollar CD   A certificate of deposit denominated in U.S. dollars and issued by a financial institution outside the United States.

European currency quotation   In foreign exchange trading, the value of a dollar in terms of a foreign currency. For example, if the euro is worth 90¢, the European currency quotation would be expressed as 1.11, meaning that there are 1.11 euros to the dollar. —Compare AMERICAN CURRENCY QUOTATION. —Also called *divider.*

European Currency Unit (ECU)   A weighted index of the currencies of ten European Economic Community members. For bonds denominated in ECUs, U.S. investors risk not only the possibility of interest-rate increases but also the chance that the dollar will rise relative to the ECU (that is, one ECU will buy fewer dollars). On the plus side, these securities provide investors with the opportunity of overseas diversification without reliance on the currency of a single country.

European Economic Community (EEC)   A group of Western European countries that have joined together to promote trade and economic and political cooperation. Essentially, the EEC represents an attempt to combine a group of countries into a single economic unit. —Also called *Common Market.*

European option   An option that can be exercised only on its expiration date, in contrast to the option available in the United States whereby the owner may exercise any time up to and including the expiration date.

evaluator   An expert who appraises and assigns a worth to assets for which it is difficult to determine market value.

even lot   —See ROUND LOT.

event risk   The risk that some unexpected event will cause a substantial decline in the market value of a security. For example, a leveraged buyout that entails huge amounts of new debt will cause a decline in the market value of the target company's outstanding debt.

◿◿ CASE STUDY The September 11, 2001, terrorist attacks with hijacked airliners on New York's World Trade Center and Washington's Pentagon caused death and destruction on a monumental scale. The tragic events also had an effect on numerous businesses, including insurance companies, hotels, cruise lines, and brokerage and investment banking firms that conducted much of their activities from the impacted area of New York City. Trading of stocks in the United States was halted from September 11 until September 17. On a national scale no industry was affected more than commercial airlines. Four large passenger jets lost to suicidal terrorists were only the tip of the iceberg for an industry that was already on a downward economic slide. The hijackings on the morning of September 11 caused the Federal Aviation Administration to ban all commercial airline traffic in the United States for most of three days, an expensive proposition for airlines that experts estimated did business at a quarter of a billion dollars daily. The airlines were already experiencing a major decline in profitable business travel, and the hijackings caused fearful leisure travelers to cancel existing bookings and reduce their own airline travel. Analysts were expecting industry losses in 2001 of $2.5 to $3.5 billion prior to the attack. Following the attack these estimates ranged upward to $5 billion with some forecasts of several industry bankruptcies. One smaller firm, North Carolina–based Midway Airlines, threw in the towel and permanently shut down all of its operations on the day following the terrorist attack. Continental Airlines was the first airline to announce large layoffs of 12,000 employees. Other airlines soon followed with employment and schedule reductions of their own at the same time as they requested billions of dollars in federal financial assistance. Airlines incur substantial fixed expenses, including salaries and lease payments, that must be taken care of regardless of how many people purchase tickets. High fixed costs mean that reduced load factors (a smaller percentage of filled seats by paying passengers) have a major impact on the firms' income. When equity markets reopened on Monday following the disaster, airline stock declines from the prior Monday included 52% for US Airways, 49% for Continental, 44% for Delta, 42% for UAL (parent of United Airlines), and 39% for AMR (parent of American Airlines). One terrible event resulted in unexpected financial distress and extensive shareholder losses in an already troubled industry.

event studies   Research that attempts to determine if particular events produce abnormal returns from stock investments. For example, researchers have conducted event studies in an attempt to determine if stock splits, dividend increases, and earnings announcements produce abnormal returns.

even up   To buy or sell a security in a quantity that offsets an existing position in that security.

ex —Used in combination to refer to a security that trades without something, such as a dividend, warrant, or some other distribution. For example, when a stock trades ex-dividend, it trades without the right to receive the next dividend payment.

exception   An auditor's qualification of a financial report that indicates disagreement with an item in the report or limitations to the extent of the audit.

excessive trading   The act of churning.

excess margin   The dollar amount of equity in an investor's brokerage margin account that is in excess of what is necessary for meeting either initial margin or maintenance margin requirements. An investor with $30,000 of unmargined securities has an excess initial margin of $15,000 (with Regulation T margin of 50%) and an excess maintenance margin of $22,500 (if the maintenance requirement is 25%). Excess margin may be withdrawn or used to purchase more securities. —See also SPECIAL MISCELLANEOUS ACCOUNT.

excess profits tax   A temporary tax levied on business profits during a period of national emergency. For example, the federal government may levy an additional corporate income tax during wartime to generate extra government revenues.

excess reserves   The reserves held by banks and thrifts in excess of what is required by the Federal Reserve. Large excess reserves indicate a potential for credit expansion and reduced interest rates that could prove beneficial to the security markets. Conversely, small excess reserves indicate reduced possibilities for credit expansion and a relatively tight monetary policy by the Federal Reserve. —Compare REQUIRED RESERVES.

excess return   The return on an asset or a portfolio in excess of the risk-free return. If short-term corporate debt provides a return of 4½% while U.S. Treasury bills are yielding 3½%, excess return on the corporate debt is 1%. Excess return is usually correlated with the riskiness of an investment.

exchange   —See SECURITIES EXCHANGE.

exchange   —See SWAP.

exchangeable bond   A special type of convertible security that permits the holder to exchange the bond for shares of a company in which the issuer has an ownership position. An exchangeable bond differs from an ordinary convertible bond in that a convertible permits the holder to convert it into shares of stock of the issuer.

exchange acquisition   The filling of a large buy order on the floor of an exchange in which a member solicits numerous sellers whose orders are then lumped together. This group of transactions is reported as a single transaction. —Compare EXCHANGE DISTRIBUTION. —See also SPECIAL BID.

exchange distribution   The sale of a large block of stock on the floor of an exchange in which a member solicits numerous buyers, each of whom takes a portion of the block. All the buy orders are combined, crossed with the orders to sell, and reported as a single trade. An exchange distribution is facilitated by the fact that buyers usually do not have to pay a commission. —Compare EXCHANGE ACQUISITION.

exchange fund   An open-end investment company that swaps its own shares for an equal value of securities owned by an individual investor. Although the exchange is tax-free, the fund assumes the stockholder's basis on the securities it obtains. Thus, exchange funds ordinarily have large potential capital gains liabilities. Because of a 1967 Internal Revenue Service ruling, shares of these funds are no longer offered.

exchange offer   An offer by a firm to exchange its own securities for those of another firm or for a different series of the same firm's securities. For example, a firm may offer a new bond issue in exchange for an older series currently outstanding. Depending on the type of securities included in the offer, the security holder may be taxed for the exchange.

> **⋀⋀ CASE STUDY** | In April 2001 AT&T offered its stockholders shares in AT&T Wireless Group in exchange for shares of AT&T Corp. The exchange offer was intended to split off AT&T Wireless from the parent company as part of the firm's planned restructuring into three separate and independent corporations. At the time of the offer, AT&T owned approximately 70% of AT&T Wireless that traded on the New York Stock Exchange as a tracking stock. Japan's Nippon Telegraph & Telephone had earlier paid nearly $10 billion for 16% of AT&T Wireless. According to terms of the exchange offer, AT&T would issue 1.176 shares of AT&T Wireless Group for each share of AT&T stock. The exchange ratio represented a 6.5% premium

How do currency exchange rates influence investment values?

When the exchange rate between the foreign currency of an international investment and the U.S. dollar changes, it can increase or reduce your investment return. Because foreign companies trade and pay dividends in the currency of their local market, you will need to convert the cash you receive from dividends or the sale of the investment into U.S. dollars. Therefore, if the exchange rate changes significantly between the time you buy and the time you sell, it can sometimes turn a positive return in the investment itself into a loss for the investment in total, or vice versa.

International investment returns increase when the dollar weakens in value against another currency, because each unit of foreign currency translates into more U.S. dollars. On the other hand, if the U.S. dollar strengthens against the foreign currency, it translates each foreign currency unit into fewer U.S. dollars and therefore diminishes your returns.

Thomas M. Tarnowski, Senior Business Analyst, Global Investment Banking Division, Citigroup, Inc.—Salomon Smith Barney, New York, NY, and London, UK

compared to AT&T's common stock, which was then trading for $22 per share. AT&T announced it would accept up to 427.7 million shares of its common stock in the exchange, which would be conducted on a pro rata basis in the event AT&T stockholders tendered more than 427.7 million shares.

exchange privilege The right to exchange shares in one mutual fund for shares in another fund managed by the same firm. The rate at which shares are exchanged is determined by differences in relative values. There is usually a nominal charge for each transfer. This privilege is designed to allow investors to move their money among funds without incurring additional sales fees as their investment goals change. —Also called *conversion privilege.*

exchange rate The price of one currency expressed in terms of another currency. For example, if the U.S. dollar buys 1.40 Canadian dollars, the exchange rate is 1.4 to 1. Changes in exchange rates have significant effects on the profits of multinational corporations. Exchange rate changes also affect the value of foreign investments held by individual investors. For a U.S. investor owning Japanese securities, a strengthening of the U.S. dollar relative to the yen tends to reduce the value of the Japanese securities because the yen value of the securities is worth fewer dollars. —Also called *foreign exchange rate.* —See also DEVALUATION; FIXED EXCHANGE RATE; FLOATING EXCHANGE RATE; FOREIGN EXCHANGE RISK.

exchange rate risk —See FOREIGN EXCHANGE RISK.

exchange-traded fund (ETF) A mutual fund whose shares trade on a securities exchange, generally at or very near net asset value per share. Unlike ordinary mutual funds that continually issue and redeem their own shares, exchange-traded funds are similar to closed-end investment companies whose shares trade among investors. The share price is maintained at or near net asset value because of the ability of large investors to convert ETF shares to the underlying stocks or to trade underlying stocks for shares of the ETF.

⎰⎱ **CASE STUDY** | The exchange-traded fund has become a very popular investment, in large part because of the low expenses and great flexibility. Annual expense ratios for ETFs are often lower than even the lowest-cost index funds. ETFs can be used either to buy or short the overall market or a specific segment of the market. These funds can also be used to hedge an investment position. For example, an investor holding a diversified portfolio of stocks can hedge an expected market decline by shorting shares of an exchange-traded fund that replicates the S&P 500. Investors with more specialized portfolios have the option of using other ETFs that track a more focused index. The market price of an ETF efficiently tracks a stock index because large investors are permitted to swap ETF shares (generally, 50,000 shares) for the underlying stocks that compose the index, and vice versa. If an ETF market price moves below its net asset value, investors will swap the ETF shares for shares of stock composing the ETF portfolio. Conversely, if an ETF market price moves above its net asset value, investors will swap shares of stock that underlie the index tracked by the ETF for shares of the ETF. The swapability of ETF shares for shares that compose the index keeps the market price of the exchange-traded fund near its net asset value.   —See also CRE-ATION UNIT.

exchange-traded security   —See LISTED SECURITY.

excise tax   A tax on the manufacture, purchase, or sale of a good or service. The tax may be based on the number of units or on value.   —Compare CONSUMP-TION TAX.

exclusionary tender offer   An offer to purchase shares of a firm's stock on a pro rata basis while excluding the offer from one or more specific shareholders. The SEC has prohibited exclusionary tender offers.

ex-distribution   Of or relating to a stock, such as a spinoff of a subsidiary's stock, that no longer carries the right to a specific distribution. A mutual fund trading on an ex-distribution basis is indicated in transaction tables in newspapers by the symbol *d*.

ex-distribution date   The first day of trading when the seller, rather than the buyer, of a stock will be entitled to a recently announced distribution of an asset. The price of the stock can be expected to fall by approximately the value of the distribution on this date since the stock no longer carries the right to the distribution.

ex-dividend   —Used to refer to a stock no longer carrying the right to the next dividend payment because the settlement date occurs after the record date. If, for example, GenCorp common stock goes ex-dividend on May 31, an investor purchasing the stock on or after that date will not receive the next dividend check. A stock trading ex-dividend is indicated in stock transaction tables by the symbol *x* in the volume column.   —Compare CUM DIVIDEND.

⋀⋀ CASE STUDY | A stock's ex-dividend date should be of more interest to an investor than the dividend record date or dividend payment date. A stock must be purchased one day prior to the ex-dividend date for the buyer to claim a dividend that has been announced but not yet paid. Buy shares of stock on the ex-dividend date and the seller, not you, will receive the upcoming dividend. The ex-dividend date is two business days prior to the record date because three days are required for regular settlement of a stock transaction. Buy stock on Tuesday and you will be listed as the owner of record on Friday, the day that payment is required for the purchase. If a firm's directors have declared that a dividend will be paid to stockholders of record on Friday, you must buy the stock the stock on Tuesday in order to have a right to the dividend. In this case the ex-dividend date is Wednesday, two days prior to the record date. Relevant dates for the stock of international petroleum giant BP are illustrated below.

	Quarter 1	Quarter 2	Quarter 3	Quarter 4
Announcement date	Feb 13	May 8	August 7	Nov 6
Ex-dividend date	Feb 21	May 16	August 15	Nov 14
Record date	Feb 23	May 18	August 17	Nov 16
Payment date	March 19	June 11	Sept 10	Dec 10

Notice that the record date follows the ex-dividend date by two business days for each quarterly dividend. In the first quarter you must have purchased the stock by February 20 to be listed as a stockholder on February 23 and receive the dividend on March 19. Purchasing the stock on February 21 meant you would not have been listed as a stockholder of record until February 24, one day beyond when the company determined who was to receive the dividend. A weekend or holiday between the ex-dividend and record dates lengthens the time difference to four days or three days, respectively. The schedule for BP indicates owners of the stock on the day prior to the ex-dividend date must wait nearly a month for actual payment of the dividend.

ex-dividend date The first day of trading when the seller, rather than the buyer, of a stock will be entitled to the most recently announced dividend payment. The length of time ensuing between the ex-dividend date and the date of actual payment may be up to a month.

execution The consummation of a security trade.

executor or executrix The person or institution that administers and disburses the assets of an estate. The executor is charged with various duties, including identifying assets, paying taxes, taking care of debts, and distributing the balance to appropriate individuals and organizations. Executor is masculine and executrix is feminine.

exemption An annual deduction permitted a taxpayer and each dependent for use in computing taxable income. An extra exemption is allowed for being blind or for being 65 years of age or older. The size of the annual exemption is altered each year according to the level of inflation. —Also called *personal exemption.*

exempt security A security that is exempt from registration under the Security Act of 1933 or from margin requirements of the Securities Exchange Act of 1934. Examples of exempt securities are small issues, intrastate issues, and direct placements.

exercise To require the delivery (for example, a call option) or to force the purchase (for example, a put option) of the option's underlying asset. Many options expire without being exercised because the strike price stated in the option is unfavorable to the holder.

exercise limit The maximum number of option contracts that a holder can exercise during a specified period. This limit is established by the exchange on which the option trades.

exercise loan A loan from an employer to an employee to pay for the exercise of incentive stock options. Exercise loans are sometimes forgiven in the event that specified performance goals are met.

exercise notice A notice sent by an option holder to the Options Clearing Corporation, calling for fulfillment of the option's terms. The OCC will then assign fulfillment to someone short the same option.

exercise price The dollar price at which the owner of a warrant or an option can force the writer to sell an asset (in the case of a call option or warrant) or to buy an asset (in the case of a put option). The exercise price is set at the time the option is issued and, except for unusual instances that include warrants, remains constant until the option expires. A market price of an asset above, or expected to be above, an option's exercise price gives the option value. —See also AGGREGATE EXERCISE PRICE; STEP-UP.

exhaustion gap In technical analysis, a chart formation in which a gap in a price range occurs when a stock declines following a rapid rise. The exhaustion gap usually occurs on relatively low volume as demand, at least temporarily, falls off. Technical analysts generally believe that an exhaustion gap eventually will be filled when the stock resumes its upward push. Refer to the *Technical Analysis Chart Patterns* section for an example of this chart.

exhaust price The price at which a broker must sell a margined security that has declined in price.

exit fee —See DEFERRED SALES CHARGE.

exit strategy The method by which an investor plans to cash out of an investment. For example, a venture capitalist may intend to utilize an initial public offering to liquidate an investment in a closely held company.

ex-legal Of or relating to a municipal bond that is traded without the benefit of the legal opinion of a bond counsel. The trading of ex-legal municipal bonds is permitted as long as the buyers are informed about the lack of legal opinion.

exotic option An option with a nonstandard feature. A lookback option that allows the owner flexibility in selecting an exercise price is an example of an exotic option. Exotic options are traded in the over-the-counter market.

expectations hypothesis The explanation that the slope of the yield curve is attributable to expectations of changes in short-term interest rates. The yield curve relates bond yields and maturity lengths.

expected rate of return The rate of return expected on an asset or a portfolio. The expected rate of return on a single asset is equal to the sum of each possible rate of return multiplied by the respective probability of earning on each return. For example, if a security has a 20% probability of providing a 10% rate of return, a 50% probability of providing a 12% rate of return, and a 25% probability of providing a 14% rate of return, the expected rate of return is $(.20)(10\%)$ + $(.50)(12\%)$ + $(.25)(14\%)$, or 12%.

expense ratio The proportion of assets required to pay annual operating expenses and management fees of a mutual fund. If a fund charges an annual fee of 50¢ per $100 of net assets, the expense ratio will be 0.5%. Expense ratios range from 0.4% to 1.0%, depending on the size of the fund and the degree of cost control employed by its managers. The expense ratio is independent of any sales fee.

expensive Of, relating to, or being a security that sells at a market price above what is expected, given fundamental factors such as earnings, assets, and management ability. Deciding whether a security is expensive is a subjective judgment. —Compare CHEAP.

expiration The relinquishment of the rights of an options contract by permitting the contract to terminate on the expiration date. —Also called *abandonment*.

expiration effect

What should individual investors know about expiration effect?

Investors can cushion themselves from the expiration effect by adjusting their stock trading strategies to accommodate the volatility that can occur on expiration days. The major market moves triggered on these days can cause problems for investors who enter market orders at the open or close. This is especially true when buying or selling the blue chip stocks that make up the major indexes and therefore reflect the most volatility. Limit orders can help investors protect themselves and even profit from expiration day volatility. A limit order indicates the maximum price at which an investor will buy a stock or the minimum price at which he or she will sell it. That order will be executed only if the stock reaches the specified price. An investor who expects the stock price to fall on expiration day could enter a limit order to buy the stock at a lower price. An investor who expects the stock price to rise on expiration day could enter a limit order to sell the stock if it moves higher than its original price. If the stock reaches the limit order price, the broker will execute the order. If the stock doesn't reach the price set by the investor, the limit order won't be executed and the investor will retain his or her original position.

Henry Nothnagel, Senior Vice President—Options
Wachovia Securities, Inc., Chicago, IL

expiration cycle The dates on which options on a particular underlying security are scheduled to expire. Options other than LEAPS are assigned one of three cycles, January, February, or March. At any time options with four expiration dates will trade, the two near months and two later months. For example, in early March options on ExxonMobil shares had expiration dates of March, April, July, and October.

expiration date The last day on which an option holder may exercise an option. This date is stated in the contract at the time the option is written.

expiration effect The effect on securities, options, and futures prices and volume as traders unwind their positions shortly before expiration of the options and futures contracts. Trading near the expiration dates often produces a flurry of activity and large price changes.

expiration Friday The Friday once each quarter when stock index futures, index options, and stock options simultaneously expire. Investors tend to close out positions in futures, options, and stocks on expiration Friday with the result being extremely volatile prices on this day. —See also TRIPLE WITCHING HOUR.

expiration series A group of options or futures that expire on the same monthly cycles.

ex-pit Of or relating to a futures transaction that takes place away from the trading floor. For example, a person long a futures contract on coffee may agree to take delivery of the commodity from an investor who is short an identical contract. The two parties have to close out their respective obligation away from the trading floor.

exploration cost The cost of searching for and drilling exploratory gas and oil wells.

exploratory oil and gas partnership —See OIL AND GAS DRILLING LIMITED PARTNERSHIP.

export A good or service that is produced in one country and then sold to and consumed in another country. Because many companies are heavily dependent on exports for sales, any factors such as government policies or exchange rates that affect exports can have significant impact on corporate profits. —Compare IMPORT. —See also BALANCE OF TRADE.

ex-rights —Used to describe a stock that trades without giving the stockholder the privilege to receive rights to buy shares of a new stock issue. Because new shares are sold at below market price to rights holders, the rights have value. Thus, a stock trading ex-rights is worth less than the same stock with rights attached. A stock trading ex-rights is indicated in stock transaction tables in newspapers by the symbol x near the volume column. —Compare RIGHTS ON. —Also called *rights off*. —See also RIGHTS OFFERING.

ex-rights date The first day of trading on which new buyers of a firm's stock will not be entitled to receive recently declared rights to buy shares in a new security issue.

extendable bond A long-term debt security that permits the owner to extend the maturity such that interest payments continue and the principal repayment is delayed beyond the original date. This relatively rare type of bond works to the advantage of investors during periods of declining interest rates.

extended-hours trading —See AFTER-HOURS TRADING.

extension risk The possibility that rising interest rates will slow the rate at which loans in a pool will be repaid, thereby slowing the return of principal to investors who have committed funds to the pool. For example, rising interest rates will reduce the rate at which holders of mortgage-backed securities have their principal returned.

extension swap The exchange of a bond or note for another virtually identical security having a longer maturity.

external audit An examination of a company's records and reports by an outside party. —Compare INTERNAL AUDIT. —Also called *independent audit; outside audit*.

external funds The funds that are raised from sources outside a firm. The monies that are received from the sale of stock and bonds are external funds. Firms seek external funds when they are unable to finance expenditures with money generated from operations. External funds are particularly important for a young, fast-growing company that has capital requirements that greatly outstrip its ability to generate funds internally. —Compare INTERNAL FUNDS.

extra dividend A nonrecurring additional payment to stockholders that is brought about by special circumstances. An extra dividend may be issued when a firm in a cyclical industry has an especially profitable period and wishes to distribute some extra funds to its stockholders. —Also called *extra; special dividend*.

extraordinary call Redemption of a debt security due to unusual circumstances. For example, some bond issues can be redeemed prior to the scheduled maturity because of the destruction of the facility that was financed by the bonds. Extraordinary calls are most frequently used to retire single-family mortgage revenue bonds when homeowners refinance their mortgages. Extraordinary calls, generally made at par, nearly always work to the disadvantage to bondholders. —Also called *extraordinary redemption.* —See also OPTIONAL CALL.

extraordinary gain Income from an unusual, infrequently occurring event or transaction. For example, a firm might sell a subsidiary at a price significantly higher than the value at which that subsidiary's assets are carried on the firm's balance sheet. An extraordinary gain is reported separately from regular income to emphasize the fact that it is nonrecurring.

extraordinary item An infrequently occurring transaction or event that, if material, is reported separately from continuing operations.

extraordinary loss A loss caused by an unusual, infrequently occurring event or transaction. For example, a firm might sell a money-losing business at a price lower than the value at which the business is carried on its balance sheet.

⋀⋀ CASE STUDY | Sometimes the ordinary is extraordinary and the extraordinary becomes ordinary. A task force of the Financial Accounting Standards Board (FASB) announced on October 1, 2001, that the September 11, 2001, terrorist attacks on the World Trade Center and Pentagon were not considered "extraordinary" events for accounting purposes. The FASB decision meant companies affected by the airplane hijackings could not treat disaster-related expenses as extraordinary, but rather would have to record costs as part of normal business operations in reporting income according to generally accepted accounting principles. Choosing to view the costs as ordinary rather than extraordinary was an important and controversial decision because investors tend to view extraordinary expenses as one-time events that are less relevant to a company's ongoing financial health. If income from continuing operations and pretax income are substantially different in a reporting period, analysts and investors generally view the former, rather than the latter, as the most important information. In part, the task force made its decision on the basis that the disaster affected nearly all businesses during what had become a poor business environment, so it was difficult to determine whether expenses were directly related to the disaster or to the deteriorating economy. The accounting group was concerned that many companies would attempt to take advantage of the disaster and classify all sorts of charges as extraordinary even though the firms had been planning to take many of these same charges prior to the disaster. The FASB decision prevented firms from doing this.

extraordinary redemption —See EXTRAORDINARY CALL.

ex-warrants —Used to refer to a stock that no longer carries the right to a distribution of declared warrants. The buyer of a stock trading ex-warrants therefore will not receive the warrants. A stock trading in this manner is indicated in stock transaction tables by the symbol *xw.* —Compare WITH WARRANTS.

F

f 1. —Used in bond transaction tables in newspapers to indicate a bond that trades flat: *Datpnt 8⁷/₈ 06f.* **2.** —Used in mutual fund transaction tables in newspapers to indicate that the price quotation is derived from the previous day's trading: *Gro Inc f.*

face-amount certificate Debt issued by a face amount certificate company obligating the issuer to redeem the certificate at face value at maturity. The buyer makes installment payments that earn interest over the life of the certificate.

face value —See PAR VALUE 1.

factor A firm that purchases accounts receivable from another firm at a discount. The purchasing firm then attempts to collect the receivables.

factor To sell accounts receivable to another party at a discount from face value. Thus, a firm in need of cash to pay down short-term debt may decide to factor its accounts receivable to another firm.

fail Of or relating to a trade in which the seller does not deliver securities or the buyer does not deliver funds in the prescribed manner at the prescribed time, usually on the settlement date. —Compare CLEAR.

fail float Funds available for short-term investing beyond the usual settlement date when securities are not delivered within five business days of a transaction. —See also FAIL.

fail to deliver —Used to refer to the nondelivery of securities from a selling broker to a buying broker by the settlement date.

fail to receive —Used to refer to the failure of a buying broker to receive delivery of securities by the settlement date. As a result, the buying broker does not have to make payment until the securities have been delivered.

fair market value The price at which a buyer and a seller willingly consummate a trade.

fairness opinion An independent opinion characterizing the fair value of a firm's stock. A fairness opinion is frequently obtained by a majority owner of a company that is attempting to buy out the interests of minority shareholders. For example, Royal Dutch Petroleum, the 70% owner of Shell Oil, sought a fairness opinion from Morgan Stanley in an attempt to set a price on the shares it wished to purchase from Shell's minority stockholders. —See also SQUEEZE-OUT.

fair price amendment An addition to a company's bylaws that prevents an acquiring firm or investor from offering different prices for the shares held by different stockholders during a takeover attempt. The amendment tends to discourage takeover attempts by making them more expensive. —See also APPRAISAL RIGHT.

fallen angel A once-popular security that has lost investor favor and has declined in value. For example, a high-growth company may hit a period of heavy competition or saturated markets such that its stock declines in price and becomes a fallen angel.

falling knife A stock with a rapidly declining price.

family of funds A group of mutual funds operated by the same investment management company. Investors are often able to transfer money between mutual funds within a particular family of funds at only a nominal charge. Thus, an investor with shares in a growth fund could move funds out of the growth fund and into a money market fund or a bond fund without paying a new sales charge if each of these funds is managed by a single investment firm. Investing money with a company permitting this flexibility is advantageous to the investor. —Also called *fund group; group of funds.* —See also FUND SWITCHING.

family trust A trust established for the purpose of passing assets to children or other heirs rather than to a surviving spouse. —See also SPRINKLING TRUST.

Fannie Mae 1. A private, shareholder-owned company created by Congress in 1938 to bolster the housing industry during the depression. Fannie Mae facilitates homeownership by adding liquidity to the mortgage market when it purchases loans from lenders who use the funds received to make additional loans. Fannie Mae finances mortgage purchases by issuing its own bonds or by selling mortgages it already owns to financial institutions. The firm's common stock trades as FNM on the New York Stock Exchange. —Formerly called *Federal National Mortgage Association.* —See also QUASI-PUBLIC CORPORATION. 2. A security issued by this company that is backed by insured and conventional mortgages. Monthly returns to holders of Fannie Maes consist of interest and principal payments made by homeowners on their mortgages.

far month In futures and options, the longest settlement or expiration month of a currently traded contract.

farther in Of or relating to an option contract with an earlier expiration date than a contract that is currently owned or being considered.

farther out Of or relating to an option contract with a later expiration date than a contract that is currently owned or being considered. For example, a contract with a May expiration date is farther out than a contract with a February expiration date of the same year.

FASB —See FINANCIAL ACCOUNTING STANDARDS BOARD.

FASB Statement A standard set by the Financial Accounting Standards Board regarding a financial accounting and reporting method. Essentially, FASB statements determine the acceptable accounting practices that Certified Public Accountants use in reporting corporate financial information to stockholders, the SEC, and the general public. —See also APB OPINION.

fast market A market in which sudden increases in the demand or supply of shares cause sharp price movements of a stock. Market orders in a fast market are subject to being executed at prices substantially different from the prices in effect at the time the orders were entered.

favorite fifty —See NIFTY FIFTY.

F/C —See FIRST COUPON.

FCM —See FUTURES COMMISSION MERCHANT.

FDIC —See FEDERAL DEPOSIT INSURANCE CORPORATION.

Fed —See FEDERAL RESERVE SYSTEM.

federal agency security The debt obligation of a government-owned agency such as the Export-Import Bank and Ginnie Mae. Federal agency securities offer higher yields than direct Treasury obligations even though, with the exception of U.S. Postal Service and Tennessee Valley Authority issues, they are guaranteed by the U.S. government. Certain issues are exempt from state and local taxes. —Compare FEDERALLY SPONSORED CORPORATE SECURITY. —Also called *indirect government obligation.*

Federal Deposit Insurance Corporation (FDIC) The federal agency that insures deposits at commercial banks to a limit of $100,000 per depositor or combination of depositors at each insured bank. This insurance also applies to certificates of deposit sold through retail brokerage houses. The insurance fund is financed by a small fee paid by the banks based on the amount of their insured deposits.

Federal Farm Credit Bank A federally sponsored financing organization intended to consolidate operations of the Banks for Cooperatives, the Federal Intermediate Credit Banks, and the Federal Land Banks. The Federal Farm Credit Bank issues short-term securities that trade in the secondary market.

federal funds Reserve balances that are maintained by commercial banks in the Federal Reserve System at amounts above what is required. These excess reserves are available for lending to other banks in need of reserves. Although the loans are usually made on a single-day basis, they may be renewed. The availability of and the rate paid for federal funds are important indicators of Federal Reserve policy; hence, both are watched closely by financial analysts in order to forecast changes in the credit markets. —Also called *fed funds.*

federal funds rate The rate of interest on overnight loans of excess reserves made among commercial banks. Because the Federal Reserve has significant control over the availability of federal funds, the rate is considered an important indicator of Federal Reserve monetary policy and the future direction of other interest rates. A declining federal funds rate may indicate that the Federal Reserve has decided to stimulate the economy by releasing reserves into the banking system. Care is needed in using this indicator, however, because a declining rate may simply mean that the banks have weak demand for commercial loans and little need for borrowing reserves.

CASE STUDY The Federal Reserve announced in early December 2001 it was lowering its target federal funds rate from 2.00% to 1.75%, the lowest level in 40 years. The quarter-point decline represented the 11th reduction in the benchmark short-term interest rate since the beginning of the year and established a target rate lower than the rate of inflation. The federal funds rate represents the rate that banks pay to borrow reserves from other banks. This rate influences other short-term rates, including the prime rate and the interest rate on U.S. Treasury bills. The aggressive Federal Reserve policy toward reducing interest rates was intended to stimulate a weak economy that had produced rising unemployment and business failures, especially following the September 11 terrorist attacks in New York City and Washington, D.C. The Federal Reserve has tools available to affect short-term interest rates but not long-term rates, which are influenced by inflation expectations of lenders and borrowers. Thus, an aggressive policy by the Federal Reserve to reduce short-term rates and stimulate the economy can actually result in higher long-term rates as investors become concerned that increased economic activity will be accompanied by rising inflation.

Federal Home Loan Bank System (FHLBS) A government-sponsored enterprise established in 1932 to improve the supply of funds to lenders, including credit unions, thrifts, banks, and insurance companies that finance loans for home mortgages. With an AAA credit rating the system is able to borrow funds at relatively low cost and pass the savings through to borrowers in the housing market.

Federal Home Loan Mortgage Corporation —See FREDDIE MAC 1.

Federal Housing Administration (FHA) A government-sponsored organization insuring mortgage loans made by private lenders.

Federal Intermediate Credit Banks Privately owned, government-sponsored organizations that provide short-term loans to the agricultural sector. Federal Intermediate Credit Banks obtain funds from debt issues of the Federal Farm Credit Bank.

Federal Land Banks Privately owned, government-sponsored organizations that make funds available for farm-related activities. Federal Land Banks secure funds from the Federal Farm Credit Bank, which issues debt securities.

federally sponsored corporate security A security issued by a privately owned, government-sponsored firm such as Fannie Mae or the Federal Land Banks. These securities, primarily debt obligations, are not guaranteed by the U.S. government but are generally considered relatively safe. —Compare FEDERAL AGENCY SECURITY.

Federal National Mortgage Association —See FANNIE MAE 1.

Federal Open Market Committee (FOMC) A policy-making committee within the Federal Reserve that has the responsibility for establishing and carrying out open-market operations. Policies and decisions of the committee have a substantial impact on interest rates and the securities markets. The FOMC is composed of the 7 members of the Board of Governors of the Federal Reserve System and presidents from 5 of the 12 Federal Reserve Banks. —Also called *Open Market Committee.*

Federal Reserve Board The seven governing members of the Federal Reserve System who are appointed by the President for 14-year terms. Board members play an important role in determining the country's monetary policy which, in turn, strongly influences economic activity.

Federal Reserve System The independent central bank that influences the supply of money and credit in the United States through its control of bank reserves. Federal Reserve actions have great impact on security prices. For example, restriction of bank reserves and lending ability in an attempt to restrain inflation tends to drive up interest rates and drive down security prices over the short run. —Also called *Fed.* —See also FEDERAL OPEN MARKET COMMITTEE.

Federal Trade Commission (FTC) A federal agency responsible for maintaining the competitive markets, thereby discouraging restraint of trade and monopoly. The clout and aggressiveness of the FTC vary greatly depending on its membership and the incumbent Presidential administration.

Federal Trade Commission Act of 1914 The federal law that established the Federal Trade Commission and provided it with limited power to investigate corporate conduct, hold hearings, and issue cease-and-desist orders. In a 1938 amendment, the FTC was given expanded powers in halting merger activities. —See also CLAYTON ACT; SHERMAN ANTITRUST ACT.

fed funds —See FEDERAL FUNDS.

fed wire A high-speed communications system for transferring funds and ownership of book-entry securities between banks. The fed wire is used to move bank reserves and to make credit available without delay.

felines —See ANIMALS.

fence An investment position consisting of being long (or short) a stock or commodity, being long (or short) an out-of-the-money put, and being short (or long) an out-of-the-money call. Both options have the same expiration date.

FGIC —See FINANCIAL GUARANTY INSURANCE CORPORATION.

FHA —See FEDERAL HOUSING ADMINISTRATION.

FHLBS —See FEDERAL HOME LOAN BANK SYSTEM.

fictitious credit The dollar amount credited to an investor's brokerage account following a short sale. The credit, which represents both the proceeds of the sale and the margin required under Regulation T, is used as collateral for the borrowed shares and may not be withdrawn by the investor.

fidelity bond —See BLANKET FIDELITY BOND.

fiduciary A person, such as an investment manager or the executor of an estate, or an organization, such as a bank, entrusted with the property of another party and in whose best interests the fiduciary is expected to act when holding, investing, or otherwise using that party's property.

FIFO —See FIRST-IN, FIRST-OUT.

fight the tape To trade securities against the trend. A trader fights the tape if he or she continues to buy stock in a declining market or sell stock in a rising market. One of the axioms of stock market trading is to not fight the tape. Of course, the premise is that a trader is actually able to determine what the tape is really saying.

FIGS An acronym for a type of municipal convertible bond.

fill To complete a customer's order to buy or sell a security. —See also PARTIAL EXECUTION.

fill-or-kill order An order sent to the floor of an exchange, demanding that it either be filled immediately and in full or be canceled.

filter rule A technical trading rule in which an investor buys and sells stocks if their price movement reverses direction by a minimally acceptable percentage. For example, a technician may decide on a filter of 10%. If a stock being followed by the technician subsequently reverses a downtrend and rises by 10% from its low price, the filter rule indicates that the stock should be bought. A 10% decline from a high price indicates that a stock should be sold or sold short. The size of the filter is determined by the technician. The filter rule is supposed to permit an investor to participate in a security's major price trends without being misled by small fluctuations.

final dividend 1. The final dividend payment from a firm that is liquidating. **2.** The last dividend of a firm's fiscal year. The final dividend is declared when management is able to estimate rather accurately the firm's earnings and its dividend-paying ability. —Compare INTERIM DIVIDEND. —Also called *year-end dividend.*

Financial Accounting Standards Board (FASB) The independent accounting organization that determines the standards for financial accounting and reporting. The rules set by FASB play a large role in determining the numbers that companies show the financial analysts and stockholders. —See also FASB STATEMENT.

financial analyst A person with expertise in evaluating financial investments. Financial analysts, who serve as investment advisers and portfolio managers, use their training and experience to investigate risk and return characteristics of securities. —Also called *analyst; securities analyst.* —See also CHARTERED FINANCIAL ANALYST.

Financial and Operational Combined Uniform Single Report —See FOCUS REPORT.

financial asset A financial claim on an asset that is usually documented by some type of legal representation. Examples include bonds and shares of stock but not tangible assets such as real estate or gold.

financial condition —See FINANCIAL POSITION.

financial contagion A financial problem that spreads among companies or regions. For example, Russia's 1998 default triggered sharp declines in the market values of debt issued by emerging countries.

financial futures Obligations to buy or sell particular positions in financial instruments. The features of financial futures are identical to those of any futures contract except that the asset for delivery is of a financial nature. Financial futures are traded on certificates of deposit, commercial paper, Ginnie Mae certificates, foreign currencies, Treasury bills, and Treasury bonds. —See also FUTURES MARKET.

Financial Guaranty Insurance Corporation (FGIC) A private insurer of interest and principal payments on municipal bond issues. As with other insurers, the municipality issuing the bond pays the required premium to FGIC in order to obtain a higher rating on the issue. In this way, the bonds can be sold at a lower interest rate.

financial highlights The section of a corporate report providing investors with an overview of the firm's performance during the period covered by the report. For example, a report's highlights may note a major acquisition made by the firm during the period and it may discuss the implications of the acquisition relative to future sales and corporate earnings.

Financial Institutions Reform, Recovery, and Enforcement Act of 1989 (FIRREA) Federal legislation that revamped regulation and insurance of depository financial institutions in response to the savings and loan crisis. The Act created several new organizations, including the Resolution Trust Corporation that closed and merged troubled institutions and the Bank Insurance Fund that replaced the Federal Savings and Loan Insurance Corporation as the insurer of thrift deposits.

financial intermediary A financial institution such as a commercial bank or thrift that facilitates the flow of funds from savers to borrowers. Financial intermediaries profit from the spread between the amount they pay for the funds and the rate they charge for the funds. —Also called *intermediary*. —See also INTERMEDIATION.

financial lease —See CAPITAL LEASE.

financial leverage The extent to which interest on debt magnifies changes in operating income into even greater proportionate changes in earnings after taxes. Financial leverage magnifies increases in earnings per share during periods of rising operating income but adds significant risks for stockholders and creditors because of added interest obligations. —Compare OPERATING LEVERAGE. —See also DEBT MANAGEMENT RATIO; DEBT-TO-EQUITY RATIO.

⋀⋀ CASE STUDY | Financial leverage results from utilizing debt to finance assets. The greater the ratio of funds contributed by creditors compared to funds contributed by stockholders, the greater a firm's financial leverage. Financial leverage magnifies changes in net income compared to changes in operating income. For example, financial leverage might cause a firm's reported net income to increase by 30% when operating income increases by 20%. Without financial leverage the 20% increase in operating income would produce an equal percentage increase in net income. The magnification operates both upward and downward, which means stockholders benefit from financial leverage when times are good and operating income is increasing but their investment in the firm can be at substantial risk when times are bad and operating income is falling. In late 2001 Italian automaker Fiat announced a restructuring intended to reduce financial leverage by halving the firm's debt of nearly €7.5 billion. As part of the restructuring Fiat said it would sell €2 billion of assets, undertake a €1 billion rights offering to sell new stock, and issue $2.2 billion in bonds exchangeable for the firm's holding of General Motors Corporation common stock. The restructuring package was intended to increase equity at the same time it reduced the firm's debt, both of which would decrease financial leverage and dampen fluctuations in net income. At the time, Fiat was struggling as Europe's fifth-largest automaker.

financial planner   A person who counsels individuals and corporations with respect to evaluating financial status, identifying goals, and determining ways in which the goals can be met. Although many people call themselves financial planners, a large number are primarily interested in selling a limited number of products they represent. A full-time professional planner, including a certified financial planner, an investment manager, or a tax attorney, may be better able to provide unbiased advice to the investor. —See also CERTIFIED FINANCIAL PLANNER; CHARTERED FINANCIAL CONSULTANT.

financial portal   An Internet entry to comprehensive financial information and tools for portfolio analysis.

financial position   The state of and the relationships among the various financial data found on a firm's balance sheet. For example, a company with fairly valued and relatively liquid assets, combined with a small amount of debt compared to owner's equity, is generally described as being in a strong financial position. —Also called *financial condition*.

financial ratio —See RATIO.

financial risk   The risk that a firm will be unable to meet its financial obligations. This risk is primarily a function of the relative amount of debt that the firm uses to finance its assets. A higher proportion of debt increases the likelihood that at some point the firm will be unable to make the required interest and principal payments.

financial statement   A report providing financial statistics relative to a given part of an organization's operations or status. The two most common financial statements are the balance sheet and the income statement. —See also COMPARATIVE FINANCIAL STATEMENTS.

financial structure —See CAPITALIZATION.

financial supermarket   A financial services company that offers customers a wide variety of financial products, generally including insurance, stocks, bonds, real estate services, and annuities. Financial supermarkets are convenient but may not offer the best deals on each of the financial products they sell.

finder A person who puts deals together. A finder may locate funds for a corporation seeking capital, bring together firms for a merger, or find a takeover target for a company seeking an acquisition.

finder's fee The charge levied by a person or firm for putting together a deal. For example, a finder may receive a fee equal to 3% of the principal amount paid for a corporate acquisition.

fineness A measure of the purity of a precious metal. Fineness is quoted in parts per thousand, with 1,000 fine being equivalent to 24-karat gold and 583.3 fine being equivalent to 14-karat gold.

FINEX A futures and options exchange for the trading of financial contracts on currencies and U.S. Treasury securities. The FINEX, with trading floors in New York City and Dublin, Ireland, is a division of the New York Board of Trade.

fingerprint In technical analysis, the individual way that a particular stock trades. Technical analysts believe that an understanding of a security's fingerprint allows the investor to detect unusual variations in volume or changes in price that would signal a buying or selling opportunity.

firm commitment In securities offerings, a commitment by the underwriter to purchase securities from the issuer for resale to the public. Thus, the sale is guaranteed by a firm commitment to the issuer. With a firm commitment, the risk of being unable to sell an entire issue at the offering price is transferred from the issuer to the underwriter. —Also called *bought deal.*

firm order 1. An investor's order to buy or sell that is not conditional on any additional instruction. 2. An order placed on behalf of a broker-dealer firm rather than on behalf of the firm's client.

firm quote A quotation from a market maker to buy and sell a security at firm bid and ask prices. —Compare NOMINAL QUOTE.

FIRREA —See FINANCIAL INSTITUTIONS REFORM, RECOVERY, AND ENFORCEMENT ACT OF 1989.

First Call The best-known segment of Thomson Financial, a major provider of financial information. First Call provides current and historical data on broker recommendations, insider transactions, financial ratios, and earnings estimates. Consensus earnings estimates from First Call are often utilized for comparison purposes by the financial press when corporations report quarterly earnings.

first call date The earliest date on which a security may be redeemed by the issuer. This date is particularly important to an investor who holds a security that is selling above or near its call price. The first call date is likely to be either five years or ten years after the date of issue; however, the timing varies by bond issue. Information regarding the first call date may be found on the bond certificate or it may be obtained from the brokerage firm holding the security. Bonds selling at a premium are often quoted at the yield to first call. —See also YIELD TO CALL.

first coupon (F/C) The date on which a bond's initial interest payment will be made by the issuer.

first-in, first-out (FIFO) An accounting procedure for identifying the order in which items are used or sold. With FIFO, the oldest remaining items are assumed to have been sold first. During a period of inflation this procedure tends to keep costs low for accounting purposes; it results in higher reported profits and a greater tax liability, however. —Compare LAST-IN, FIRST-OUT.

first mortgage A real estate loan with the right to payment in full before payments to other lenders are made. First mortgages are generally considered low-risk investments, although the quality of real estate pledged as collateral is of crucial importance in determining the riskiness of the mortgage.

first position day The initial day on which the investor who is short a commodity futures contract may notify the clearing corporation of an intention to deliver the commodity. The first position day occurs two business days before the first date on which delivery may be made. —Compare POSITION DAY.

first preferred stock A class of preferred stock with a preferential claim over common stock and other preferred stock from the same issuer with respect to dividends and assets.

first section The area in each of Japan's three largest securities exchanges where more seasoned securities are traded.

fiscal agent The organization responsible for paying the interest and principal of another organization's debt. For example, Valdosta State Bank may be fiscal agent for, and make interest and principal payments on, debt incurred by Scott Motors Corporation.

fiscal period The period covered by financial reports. For example, an annual report covers a fiscal period of one year, but a quarterly report includes accounting data for three months. —Also called *accounting period.*

fiscal policy The existing policy the government has for spending and taxing. Fiscal policy directly affects economic variables, such as tax rates, interest rates, and government programs, that influence security prices. —See also MONETARY POLICY.

fiscal year (FY) The 12-month accounting period for an organization. Because many firms end their accounting year on a date other than December 31, the fiscal year often differs from the calendar year.

Fisher effect The direct relationship between inflation and interest rates. Increasing inflationary expectations result in increasing interest rates.

fit A condition in which a security fulfills an investor's portfolio needs. For example, an investor may select a new municipal bond because that bond's maturity makes it a good fit in the investor's portfolio.

Fitch Investors Service A financial services company best known for the bond ratings it provides investors.

Fitch Ratings An international rating agency for financial institutions, insurance companies, and corporate, sovereign, and municipal debt. Fitch Ratings has headquarters in New York and London and is wholly owned by FIMALAC of Paris. —Formerly called *Fitch Investors Service.*

five-hundred-dollar rule The SEC provision that prohibits brokers from instituting punitive measures against an investor's margin-deficit account if the amount of the deficiency is under $500. The five-hundred-dollar rule is intended to preclude brokers from having to sell part of a client's investment position because of a relatively small cash deficiency in the client's account.

501(c)(3) bond A bond issued by a nonprofit college or hospital that pays tax-exempt interest not subject to the alternative minimum tax. Interest from municipal bonds used to finance private activity are either fully taxable or are subject to the alternative minimum tax.

529 plan —See COLLEGE-SAVINGS PLAN.

five-percent rule A National Association of Securities Dealers rule that requires its members to use ethical and fair standards when setting commissions and establishing quotation spreads. Although members may set markups and markdowns in excess of 5%, they must be able to justify the commissions and spreads if complaints are filed.

fix To set the price of a commodity. For example, commodity traders in London fix the price of gold on a daily basis.

fixed annuity A stream of unchanging payments for a specific period or for an individual's lifetime, depending on the terms of the annuity contract. Fixed annuities are sold by insurance companies to people who desire a fixed income. —Compare VARIABLE ANNUITY. —Also called *guaranteed-dollar annuity.* —See also HYBRID ANNUITY.

fixed asset An asset not readily convertible to cash that is used in the normal course of business. Examples of fixed assets include machinery, buildings, and fixtures. A firm whose total assets are made up primarily of fixed assets is in a less liquid financial position, thus entailing greater risk of a big tumble in profits if its revenues fall.

fixed asset turnover A financial ratio that indicates a firm's ability to generate sales based on its long-term assets. Fixed asset turnover is calculated by dividing annual sales by the dollar amount of fixed assets. A high fixed asset turnover indicates management's effective use of the firm's fixed assets.

fixed-charge coverage The number of times that a firm's operating income exceeds its fixed payments. Fixed-charge coverage is a measure of a firm's ability to meet contractually fixed payments, with high coverage indicating significant flexibility for making payments in the event that business conditions deteriorate and earnings decline. Expenses used in calculating fixed-charge coverage usually include interest, lease payments, preferred dividends, and principal payments on debt. —Compare INTEREST COVERAGE. —Also called *times fixed charges.*

fixed cost A cost that remains unchanged even with variations in output. An airline with 20 airplanes has the fixed costs of depreciation and interest (if the planes are partially financed with debt), regardless of the number of times the planes fly or the number of seats filled on each flight. Firms with high fixed costs tend to engage in price wars and cutthroat competition because extra revenues incur little extra expense. These firms tend to experience wide swings in profits. —Compare VARIABLE COST.

fixed exchange rate An exchange rate between currencies that is set by the governments involved rather than being allowed to fluctuate freely with market forces. In order to keep currencies trading at the prescribed levels, government monetary authorities actively enter the currency markets to buy and sell according to variations in supply and demand. —Compare FLOATING EXCHANGE RATE. —See also DEVALUATION.

fixed-income security A security, such as a bond or preferred stock, that pays a constant income each period. Price changes in a fixed-income security are caused primarily by changes in long-term interest rates.

fixed price —See OFFERING PRICE.

fixed trust —See UNIT INVESTMENT TRUST.

flag —See TRIANGLE.

flash price The price of a selected security reported out-of-order on the consolidated tape when market volume becomes so heavy that the tape runs six or more minutes late. Flash prices are intended to provide traders and investors with up-to-date information on widely held stock.

flat **1**. Of, relating to, or being a market maker's inventory position that is neither long nor short; that is, the inventory is zero. **2**. Of, relating to, or being a bond that trades without accrued interest. For example, bonds of a company in bankruptcy proceedings trade flat. A bond trading flat is indicated in bond transaction tables by the symbol *f*.

flat loan A loan without interest to the lender. A firm lending securities for a short sale is often compensated by the borrowing firm with a flat loan. Thus, the lending firm has use of the funds without charge.

flat market A securities market in which there has been no tendency either to rise or to fall significantly. —Also called *sideways market.*

flat scale A municipal bond offering in which similar yields are available at all the various maturities.

flat tax An income tax that has a single rate of taxation. For example, a taxing authority may levy a flat tax of 3% against gross income. —See also GRADUATED FLAT TAX.

flat yield curve At a particular time, similar yields on bonds of similar risk at all maturity lengths. During a period of a flat yield curve an investor would receive approximately the same yield on a long-term bond as he or she would on a short-term bond, although the former would be subject to greater price fluctuations.

flexible exchange rate —See FLOATING EXCHANGE RATE.

flexible income fund A mutual fund that invests in several types of bonds, including high-yield corporate bonds, foreign bonds, and U.S. government bonds. Flexible income funds attempt to earn high current returns without being subject to the risks of a single segment of the bond market.

FLEX option Registered name for a customized equity option with unique characteristics including expiration date, strike price, and exercise style. Unlike regular options, FLEX options do not have standardized features and do not trade in continuous markets.

flight to quality A movement by investors to purchase higher-quality securities. For example, an investor might sell bonds rated lower than BBB and invest the proceeds in bonds rated AA or AAA. A flight to quality occurs when investors expect a deterioration in political stability or in economic activity.

flip-over pill An entitlement granted by a firm's management to its stockholders giving them the right to purchase shares of an acquiring company's stock at a bargain price in the event of a merger. The flip-over pill is a variation of the poison pill.

flipper   A trader who attempts to make a small profit by very quick in-and-out buying and selling. For example, a flipper might try to take advantage of a hot market for new issues by purchasing a new issue at the offering and then selling it on the first day of trading.

flipping   The immediate selling of shares purchased in an initial public offering. Flipping is especially popular in a hot IPO market when newly issued shares can soar in price when they hit the secondary market. Investment banking firms underwriting new issues generally discourage flipping, in large part because it can depress a stock's price in the secondary market.

⋀⋀ CASE STUDY In late 2001 UBS PaineWebber issued a memo to its branch offices that the firm intended to fine its brokers whose customers engaged in flipping shares purchased in initial public offerings underwritten by the firm. According to the policy, brokers would be required to pay a fine equal to 200% of their original commission. Following complaints from the firm's brokers, PaineWebber withdrew the proposal but indicated it would monitor the investment activity of clients who participated in new issues and adjust future allocations of shares in subsequent IPOs. Investment banking firms dislike flipping because it tends to destabilize trading and depress the stock's price, both of which are likely to anger management of the issuing company.

float   1. Funds that are on deposit at two institutions at the same time because of inefficiencies in the collection system. This situation permits a person or firm to earn extra income because the two institutions are paying interest on the same funds. As an example, a person writes a check on a money market fund in order to make a deposit in a local financial institution. Until that check gets back to the bank on which it was written (a transit often entailing two or three days), the investor receives interest on his or her funds from both institutions. —See also FAIL FLOAT. **2.** The number of shares in public hands and available for trading. Institutional investors require that a security have a large float before they will take a position in it. The large float guards against a substantial price change in the security while the institution is buying. —Also called *floating supply.*

float   To permit a country's currency to change freely in value against foreign currencies.

float an issue   To sell a security issue in the primary market. For example, a firm may decide that it needs to expand its manufacturing facilities and float a new issue of common stock to pay for the expansion. Issuers generally employ an investment banker to assist in floating an issue.

floater   —See FLOATING-RATE NOTE.

floating debt   Short-term debt that is subject to continual refunding by the issuer.

floating exchange rate   An exchange rate between two currencies that is allowed to fluctuate with the market forces of supply and demand. Floating exchange rates tend to result in uncertainty as to the future rate at which currencies will exchange. This uncertainty is responsible for the increased popularity of forward, futures, and option contracts on foreign currencies. —Compare FIXED EXCHANGE RATE. —Also called *flexible exchange rate.*

floating-rate note An unsecured debt issue with an interest rate that is reset at specified intervals (usually every six months) according to a predetermined formula. Floating-rate notes usually can be redeemed at face value on certain dates at the holder's option. Floating-rate notes pay short-term interest and generally sell in the secondary market at nearly par value. Floating-rate notes are indicated in bond transaction tables in newspapers by the symbol *t*. —Also called *floater; variable-rate note*. —See also CONVERTIBLE FLOATING-RATE NOTE; DROPLOCK BOND; VARIABLE-RATE DEMAND OBLIGATION; YIELD CURVE NOTE.

floating-rate preferred stock A special and unusual type of preferred stock with a dividend that is reset at specified intervals according to a predetermined formula. Floating-rate preferred stock contrasts with most preferred stock issues that pay a fixed quarterly dividend. Floating-rate preferred stock issues do not generally fluctuate much in price because the dividend is automatically adjusted to keep the shares selling near to par. —Also called *adjustable-rate preferred stock; variable-rate preferred stock*.

floating supply —See FLOAT 2.

floor The area of an organized exchange where securities are traded. Customer orders are transferred to the floor, where they are executed by members of the exchange.

floor broker A member of a securities exchange who executes orders on the exchange floor. For example, commission brokers and two-dollar brokers are floor brokers.

floor give-up The announcement of the names of the principal organizations represented by participants after a transaction has taken place on the floor of a securities exchange. Thus, when a transaction has been completed, exchange members must inform one another which firms they are representing.

floor official An exchange member or employee who mediates disputes among members on the floor of the exchange. For example, two floor brokers may disagree as to which one of them has priority on an order. The floor official would then umpire the dispute.

floor ticket A ticket that summarizes a customer order ticket and that is used by a floor broker in executing the customer's order at the trading post on the exchange floor.

floor trader An independent trader on a securities exchange who trades primarily for his or her own account. Floor traders generally attempt to profit from short-term price swings. They tend to add liquidity to the market and are required to make at least 75% of their trades against the last price change in the security traded. Thus, the majority of a floor trader's purchases must occur when the last price change in the security is a downtick. —Also called *competitive trader; registered competitive trader; registered trader*.

flotation cost The expense involved in selling a new security issue. This expense includes items such as registration of the issue and payment to the investment banker. Flotation costs depend on the size and riskiness of an issue as well as on the type of security to be sold.

flower bond Any of a limited series of U.S. government bonds that may be used at par to pay federal estate taxes. The bond is unique because there is no minimum time for which it must be held; further, its holder does not have to wait until maturity to use it at par for paying the tax. Flower bonds have not been issued since 1971.

flow of funds statement 1. For municipal bond issues, a listing of priorities for municipal revenues, including the relative position of debt service and sinking fund requirements. 2. —See STATEMENT OF CASH FLOWS.

FOB —See FREE ON BOARD.

FOCUS Report A monthly and quarterly report on net capital position submitted by members of the New York Stock Exchange to the exchange. —Also called *Financial and Operational Combined Uniform Single Report*.

folio A personalized collection of stocks an investor can assemble or purchase as a preselected basket. Investors can sell and replace individual stocks in a folio, generally as often as desired, for a single monthly or annual fee. Choosing when to replace stocks allows an investor substantial control over the tax consequences of owning folios compared to owning mutual funds.

follow-on offering A stock issue that follows an initial public stock offering from a firm. The follow-on offering can consist of primary and/or secondary shares. Companies will sometimes authorize additional shares that are issued at a higher price following a successful initial public offering. —Also called *add-on financing; piggyback*.

FOMC —See FEDERAL OPEN MARKET COMMITTEE.

footnote A detailed explanation of an item in a financial statement. Footnotes are nearly always located at the end of a statement. For example, a company is likely to attach footnotes to its annual report to expand on the depreciation and inventory valuation methods used by its accountants. Many financial analysts consider footnotes the most important information in an annual report. —Also called *note*.

Footsie —See FTSE 100 INDEX.

Forbes 500 The annual listing of the 500 largest publicly traded firms published by *Forbes* magazine. The Forbes 500, a compilation of separate lists categorized by assets, market value of shares, profits, and sales, is constructed somewhat differently from the Fortune 500, which lists firms on the basis of industry segment and amount of assets owned.

forced conversion The call for redemption of a convertible security at a price lower than the market value of the underlying asset into which the convertible may be exchanged. The investor finds it more favorable to exchange the convertible for the underlying asset than to give up the security for cash at the call price. For instance, suppose a $1,000 principal bond with a call price of $1,080 is converted into 20 shares of stock selling at $70 each. The bond is worth $1,400 in underlying stock. If the issuer calls the bond, the investor will be forced to convert before the call becomes effective.

foreign bond A debt security issued by a borrower from outside the country in whose currency the bond is denominated and in which the bond is sold. A bond denominated in U.S. dollars that is issued in the United States by the government of Canada is a foreign bond. A foreign bond allows an investor a measure of international diversification without subjection to the risk of changes in relative currency values. —See also EUROBOND.

foreign bond

Is it risky to invest in foreign securities?

Investing in foreign securities can actually reduce your overall portfolio risk and at the same time modestly increase the potential for returns. The U.S. stock market still remains the largest in the world; however, foreign markets now account for approximately 50% of the global stock market capitalization. Consequently, it is becoming more important to diversify portfolios globally, taking advantage of growth rates in different regions and countries. Proper international diversification can help balance out your returns by reducing or avoiding losses when the U.S. markets are underperforming.

Thomas M. Tarnowski, Senior Business Analyst
Global Investment Banking Division, Citigroup, Inc.—Salomon Smith Barney, New York, NY, and London, UK

foreign corporation A firm that conducts business in states or countries other than the state or country in which it is incorporated. For example, a firm incorporated in Canada but conducting business throughout North America is considered a foreign corporation in the United States. —Compare DOMESTIC CORPORATION.

Foreign Corrupt Practices Act A 1977 amendment to the Securities Exchange Act that sets penalties for those engaging in bribery of foreign government officials or foreign personnel and that requires adequate records and internal controls in all publicly held companies.

foreign crowd Members of the New York Stock Exchange who trade foreign bonds on the exchange floor.

foreign currency future A contract for the delivery of a specified amount of a foreign currency. A U.S. business selling products in Germany may decide to sell futures contracts on the euro in order to guarantee an exchange rate of the euro to dollars on a specific date.

foreign currency option The right to buy (a call option) or to sell (a put option) a foreign currency futures contract at a fixed price until a specified date.

foreign currency translation —See TRANSLATION.

foreign exchange controls Restrictions that are imposed by a nation on the free exchange and convertibility of its own currency. Foreign exchange controls are most often instituted by countries whose currencies are weak and whose citizens prefer to hold and use the currencies of other nations. Institution of foreign exchange controls hinders foreign investors who wish to extricate their funds.

foreign exchange rate —See EXCHANGE RATE.

foreign exchange risk The risk that the exchange rate on a foreign currency will move against the position held by an investor such that the value of the investment is reduced. For example, if an investor residing in the United States purchases a bond denominated in Japanese yen, a deterioration in the rate at which the yen exchanges for dollars will reduce the investor's rate of return, since he or she must exchange the yen for dollars. —Also called *exchange rate risk.*

Foreign Restricted List An SEC index of foreign companies whose securities are being offered for public sale in the United States in possible violation of registration requirements. Promoters sometimes illegally offer these securities directly to investors by mail, telephone, or personal solicitation.

foreign tax credit   The reduction in a U.S. tax liability because of taxes accrued or paid to a foreign government during the same taxable year.

Form ADV   An SEC form for reporting information about an investment adviser, including education, business, regulatory problems, services, and fees. The form has two parts, and an investor should read both prior to employing the services of an investment adviser.

Form BD   An SEC form to apply for registration as a broker or dealer of securities, or as a government securities broker or dealer, and to amend a registration. Form BD provides background information on the applicant.

Form F–1   An SEC form for foreign issuers of securities to be offered in the United States.

Form F–6   An SEC form for the registration of depository securities represented by American Depository Receipts.

Form FR–1   A National Association of Securities Dealers form that requires foreign securities dealers who are purchasing new issues for resale to comply with NASD rules for hot issues. The form helps to ensure that foreign broker-dealers will not sell a stock intended for public offering above the offering price or to individuals associated with those broker-dealers. —Also called *blanket certification form.*

Form N–1A   An SEC form for the registration of mutual funds.

Form N–2   An SEC form for the registration of closed-end investment companies.

Form N–SAR   An SEC form for semiannual and annual filing by registered investment companies with regard to sales charges, 12b–1 fees, sales of shares, portfolio turnover rate, and so forth.

Form PD 4632   A Federal Reserve form that investors must complete in order to buy Treasury bills at auction from a Federal Reserve bank. The form may be submitted by mail or in person to any of the 12 Federal Reserve banks or any of the 25 branch banks. The form has three categories, depending on whether a 13-week, 26-week, or 52-week bill is sought.

Form PD 4633-1   A Federal Reserve form that investors must complete in order to roll over a matured Treasury bill into a newly issued Treasury bill. This form must be in the hands of the Federal Reserve 20 business days before the maturity of currently held bills.

Form S–1   A statement that a firm must file with the SEC before its securities can be listed for trading on a national securities exchange. This form contains information on the firm's business, financing, and directors. It also includes a description of the securities listed.

Form S–2   A simplified registration form filed with the SEC by firms that have already reported under the Securities and Exchange Act of 1934.

Form S–3   An SEC form for companies with publicly traded stock to sell additional shares. Form S–3 is frequently used for resale of restricted securities.

Form S–4   An SEC form for the registration of securities to be issued in connection with business combinations.

Form S–6 An SEC form for the registration of securities to be issued by unit investment trusts.

Form S–11 An SEC form for the registration of securities to be issued by real estate investment trusts.

Form S–18 An SEC registration form for use by issuers of securities having a market value of $7.5 million or less.

Form SB–1 An SEC form used by small businesses to register offerings of up to $10 million of securities, provided the company has not registered over $10 million in securities offerings during the preceding 12 months.

Form X17–A5 An audited financial statement filed annually with the SEC by brokers and dealers.

Form 3 An SEC form that directors, officers, and holders of 10% or more of a firm's stock are required to file. This form requires disclosure of all shares and all securities convertible into shares that are directly or beneficially owned by these people.

Form 4 An SEC form used when reporting changes in the holdings of a firm's common stock or stock equivalents. A reporting of changes is required of holders of more than 10% of a firm's stock and of all directors and officers. This form must be filed with the SEC within ten days of the end of the month in which the change took place.

Form 8–K —See 8-K.

Form 10–K —See 10-K.

Form 10–Q —See 10-Q.

Form 13–F A quarterly report of security holdings filed with the SEC by large institutional investors.

Form 6781 An Internal Revenue Service tax form used by an investor to disclose open option positions showing gains and to calculate the unrecognized gain in each open position.

formation —See CHART FORMATION.

formula plan The buying and/or selling of securities according to a predetermined formula. This approach to investment decisions is intended to eliminate the investor's emotions and instead to follow a mechanical set of rules. A huge number of formula plans have been developed over the years.

Fortune 500® A trademark for a well-known, widely quoted annual listing by *Fortune* magazine of the largest industrial corporations in the United States. Firms are listed along with their assets, sales, and profits. Subsequent issues include the largest retailers, utilities, financial institutions, transportation companies, foreign corporations, and the second 500 largest industrial firms.

for valuation only (FVO) —See FOR YOUR INFORMATION.

forward contract An agreement between two parties to the sale and purchase of a particular commodity at a specific future time. Although forward contracts are similar to futures, they are not easily transferred or canceled. Thus, they are not liquid.

forward federal funds Federal funds traded for delivery at a future date.

forward-looking statement A projected financial statement based on management expectations. A forward-looking statement involves risks with regard to the accuracy of assumptions underlying the projections. Discussions of these statements typically include words such as *estimate, anticipate, project,* and *believe.*

forward P/E The price-earnings ratio of a firm's common stock calculated as the current stock price divided by estimated earnings per share for the coming year. —Compare TRAILING P/E.

forward pricing The pricing of mutual fund shares on the basis of the next net asset valuation following receipt of a customer's order to buy or sell. While the price is based on net asset value, this value is adjusted for any applicable redemption or sales fee. Forward pricing is required by the SEC.

forward rate 1. The expected yield on a given fixed-income security at a particular time in the future. For example, if the yield on 6-month Treasury bills is expected to be 10.5% in a year, this yield is the forward rate on 6-month bills. **2.** The rate at which a particular currency or commodity may be purchased on a forward contract.

for your information (FYI) Of or relating to a market maker's quotation for trading purposes when the price is not firm. For example, a market maker might supply an FYI quote for valuation purposes. —Also called *for valuation only; throwaway.*

401(k) plan —See SALARY REDUCTION PLAN.

403(b) plan —See TAX-SHELTERED ANNUITY.

fourth market The market for securities in which large investors bypass exchanges and dealers in order to trade directly among themselves. —Compare SECONDARY MARKET; THIRD MARKET. —See also AUTEX; INSTINET®.

fractional discretion order A customer's order to buy or sell a security, giving the broker limited discretion as to price. For example, an order to sell 200 shares at $75, 25¢ discretion, informs the broker that the customer would like a price of $75 per share but will accept a price as low as $74.75 per share.

fractional share Less than one share of stock, that is, one-third or one-half a share. Fractional shares are generally created from dividend reinvestment plans or stock dividends. For example, if a firm's directors declare a 2% stock dividend, an owner of 70 shares would be entitled to 1.4 additional shares. Because corporations do not issue certificates including fractional shares, the stockholder would receive one share and the cash equivalent for the fractional share. Fractional shares are credited to dividend reinvestment plans.

fragmentation The lack of full interconnection of the various securities markets. Fragmentation can result in customer orders being sent to markets that do not offer the best available price. Critics claim the inefficiencies of fragmentation can be cured with a central order book that includes orders from all markets.

franchise 1. An agreement between a firm and another party in which the firm provides the other party with the right to use the firm's name and to sell or rent its products. Selling franchise rights is a method of expanding a business quickly with a minimum of capital. —See also FRANCHISEE; FRANCHISOR. **2.** A right granted to another party by a government to engage in certain types of business. For example, a firm may obtain a government franchise to supply certain public services within a limited geographic region.

franchisee An individual or a company that has the right to sell or rent another firm's products and to use its name. —Compare FRANCHISOR.

franchise tax A tax on the right of a firm to do business within a certain geographic region.

franchisor A firm that sells to others the right to sell or rent its products and to use its name. —Compare FRANCHISEE.

Frankfurt Stock Exchange (FWB Frankfurter Wertpapierborse) One of the world's largest securities exchanges that provides both floor and electronic trading facilities. The Frankfurt Stock Exchange was founded in 1585 and is operated by Deutsche Borse AG.

fraud Deception carried out for the purpose of achieving personal gain while causing injury to another party. For example, selling a new security issue while intentionally concealing important facts related to the issue is fraud.

Freddie Mac 1. A stockholder-owned corporation chartered by Congress in 1970 to help supply funds to mortgage lenders such as commercial banks, mortgage bankers, savings institutions, and credit unions that in turn make funds available to homeowners and multifamily investors. Freddie Mac purchases mortgages from lenders and then packages the mortgages into guaranteed securities that are sold to investors. The firm's common stock trades as FRE on the New York Stock Exchange. —Formerly called *Federal Home Loan Mortgage Corporation.* **2.** A security that is issued by this corporation and is secured by pools of conventional home mortgages. Holders of Freddie Macs receive a share of the interest and principal payments made by the homeowners.

free box The site in brokerage firms where securities that are fully owned by customers are located. Securities in the free box are free of encumbrances. —Compare OPEN BOX.

free cash flow The cash flow that remains after taking into account all cash flows including fixed-asset acquisitions, asset sales, and working-capital expenditures. The definition of free cash flow varies depending on the purpose of the analysis for which it is being used.

free credit balance Cash held in a brokerage account that may be withdrawn or used to acquire additional securities. Free credit balances generally originate from dividends, interest payments, and security sales. Many firms automatically send balances to customers on the first day of each month. Investors may also request placement of the funds in a money market mutual fund. —See also DEBIT BALANCE.

freed up To have released members of an underwriting syndicate from the obligation of selling a security at the fixed issue price.

free on board (FOB) —Used in commodities contracts to indicate the geographical point to which delivery is included in the price. After this point, the buyer is responsible for all risks and delivery costs. The FOB point is only important to someone who sells or buys a futures contract with the intention of making or taking delivery of the specific commodity.

freeriding 1. An action taken by a syndicate member to withhold a portion of a new security issue from sale because of a belief that a later reselling of the withheld security will yield a higher price. Freeriding is prohibited by the SEC. **2.** The purchase and sale of a security in a short period of time without putting up any money. Freeriding by investors is prohibited by Federal Reserve Board's Regulation T. —Compare FROZEN ACCOUNT.

free right of exchange   The ability of an investor to transfer a security from one form to another without charge. For example, free right of exchange permits a security owner to transfer a certificate from registered to bearer form or from street name to registration in the investor's name without paying a charge.

free stock   Securities that are held by brokerage firms or in a margin account and can be loaned or used for hypothecation.

free supply   In commodities trading, the amount of a commodity that is available for trading.

freeze out provision   A clause in a corporate charter that permits an acquiring firm to buy the shares of noncontrolling stockholders at a fair price after a specified period of time, generally two to five years.

frequency of compounding   The number of times interest is calculated and added to the sum of the principal and any interest added during a particular period (nearly always one year). More frequent compounding results in a more rapid buildup of funds. For example, $1,000 deposited at 12% compounded twice a year equals $1,000(1.06)(1.06), or $1,123.60 at the end of one year, while compounding four times a year results in $1,000(1.03)(1.03)(1.03)(1.03), or $1,125.51.

friendly takeover   The acquisition of a firm with approval of the acquired firm's board of directors. —Compare UNFRIENDLY TAKEOVER.

friends and family stock   The shares of an initial public offering that are allocated to individuals designated by executives of the firm being taken public.

front-end load   —See LOAD.

front fee   The payment made to acquire a compound option. A second payment must be made in the event the compound option is exercised. —Compare BACK FEE.

frontier markets   Securities markets in the least developed of the emerging markets. Mexico and Taiwan are generally considered emerging markets while Zimbabwe, Jamaica, and Kenya are considered frontier markets. Political factors are especially important to the trading and valuation of securities traded in frontier markets.

front running   Entering into a trade while taking advantage of advance knowledge of pending orders from other investors. For example, an exchange specialist may step in front and buy stock for slightly more than the price offered by other investors. The 2001 change to pricing stocks in pennies rather than fractions facilitated front running by reducing the extra amount that must be offered to step in front of other orders. —Also called *pennying; stepping in front.*

⋀⋀ **CASE STUDY** | The switch to pricing stocks in decimals rather than fractions brought narrower bid-ask spreads at the same time it raised new concerns about front running by specialists and market makers. With penny intervals in decimal pricing, market makers found it less expensive to step ahead of a large order. Suppose an institutional investor has placed a limit order to buy 50,000 shares of XYZ stock at $35.50. Knowledge of the limit order allows the exchange specialist or Nasdaq market maker to step ahead of the institutional order and offer $35.51 with little risk of incurring a big loss. In the event the stock price doesn't rise, the market maker can sell the stock for $35.50 to the institution that placed the limit order. On the other hand, a rise in the stock price produces a nice profit for the front-running market maker that offered minimal price improvement. Front running was considerably more expensive with fractional pricing, which resulted in price intervals of ¹⁄₁₆ (6.25¢) to ⅛ (12.5¢). Thus, decimalization benefited investors who profited from reduced spreads at the same time it increased the possibility that limit orders would not be executed.

frozen account A brokerage account in which a customer must pay in full before securities are bought and must deliver certificates before securities are sold. An account is frozen when a customer fails to maintain the proper margin required by Regulation T. —Compare FREERIDING 2.

frozen asset An asset that may not be liquidated.

frozen collateral Collateral that the lender is unable to seize in order to satisfy repayment of a debt. For example, a lender may find that there is a legal question as to who actually owns the asset pledged as collateral.

FTC —See FEDERAL TRADE COMMISSION.

FTSE 100 Index A market-weighted index of the 100 leading companies traded in Great Britain on the London Stock Exchange. The *Financial Times* calculates several other indexes, although financial commentators typically refer to the FTSE 100 when they say "Footsie." The full name is Financial Times-Stock Exchange 100 Share Index.

full coupon —See CURRENT COUPON.

full disclosure The disclosure of all relevant financial and operating information. For example, the SEC requires public corporations to make full disclosure when they issue securities.

full-faith-and-credit bond —See GENERAL OBLIGATION BOND.

full-faith-and-credit pledge In a municipal obligation, a pledge of the full financial resources and taxing power of the issuer. A full-faith-and-credit pledge is an important element of general obligation bonds. —See also SPECIAL ASSESSMENT BOND.

full price Fair price as applied to a security or an acquisition. For example, if a firm's stock is selling at close to full price, the firm is less likely to be a candidate for a takeover.

full-service brokerage firm A brokerage firm that provides a wide range of services and products to its customers, including research and advice. —Compare DISCOUNT BROKERAGE FIRM.

full trading authorization The allowance of full discretion to a broker or financial adviser trading in a particular account.

fully depreciated Of or relating to a fixed asset that has been depreciated to a book value of zero. An asset can be fully depreciated and still be used.

fully distributed Of or relating to a new issue of securities that has been sold out.

fully invested To have committed nearly all available funds to assets other than short-term investments such as savings and money market accounts. Fully invested is generally used in reference to institutional investors such as mutual funds or trust departments and indicates that these investors are very bullish.

---

fund manager

I choose a particular mutual fund both because I am impressed with its performance or potential and because it strengthens the diversity of my portfolio. Should I also add an assessment of the fund's manager to this equation? If so, what should I consider?

With some 8,000 (and climbing) mutual funds to choose from, it has become a daunting task for individual investors to figure out which is the right one for them. Check out the fees. Read the prospectus. Gather short- and long-term performance data. Compare a fund's historic rate of return against those of its peers—mutual funds that invest in a similar asset class. And, yes, check out the fund manager. As every mutual fund prospectus tells us, past performance is no guarantee of future results. But at least you should know whether those total return figures were achieved by the current money manager or by someone who has moved on. What's more, experience matters in the world of money management, and investors should do a little digging to find out if a fund manager has weathered a bear market as well as a bull market.

Christopher Farrell, Economics Editor
Minnesota Public Radio, heard nationally on Sound Money®

---

fully valued   Of or relating to a stock that is selling at a price most analysts believe fully reflects the company's asset values and earnings potential. If a stock is in fact fully valued, it generally has limited appreciation potential.

fund   —See MUTUAL FUND.

fundamental analysis   Analysis of security values grounded in basic factors such as earnings, balance sheet variables, and management quality. Fundamental analysis attempts to determine the true value of a security, and, if the market price of the stock deviates from this value, to take advantage of the difference by acquiring or selling the stock. Fundamental analysis may involve investigating a firm's financial statements, visiting its managers, or examining how a particular industry is affected by changes in the economy. —Compare TECHNICAL ANALYSIS.

fundamentalist   An investor who selects securities to buy and sell on the basis of fundamental analysis. —Compare TECHNICIAN.

fundamentals   The basic economic, financial, and operating factors that influence the success of a business and the price of its securities. Fundamentals of a security include the price-earnings ratio, dividend payout, and earnings-per-share growth.

funded debt   Long-term interest-bearing debt, such as that for bonds and debentures.

fund group   —See FAMILY OF FUNDS.

fund manager   The supervisor of a pool of investment capital such as that held by a mutual fund, pension fund, or closed-end investment company. The fund manager is charged with making investment decisions that adhere to stated investment objectives.

fund of funds   An open-end investment company that invests only in the shares of other open-end investment companies. This type of mutual fund was popular during the 1960s but subsequently fell into disfavor with investors. Many analysts consider it more of a gimmick than a useful investment vehicle.

fund supermarket   A financial institution that offers a large number of mutual funds from many different sponsors. The term is often used to refer to brokerage firms that offer customers a very large number of no-load funds.

funds statement   —See STATEMENT OF CASH FLOWS.

fund switching   An investment activity in which shares in one mutual fund are sold and the proceeds from the sale are reinvested in another mutual fund. Fund switching results from an investor's changed perception of investment opportunities. For example, an individual may become bearish and switch money from a growth fund to a money market fund. Because of the high sales charges involved in purchasing some funds, fund switching is practical only if no-load funds are used or if the investor switches within a family of funds.

fungible   Of or relating to assets that are identical in quality and are interchangeable. Commodities, options, and securities are fungible assets. For example, an investor's shares of Xerox left in custody at a brokerage firm are freely mixed with other customers' Xerox shares. Likewise, stock options are freely interchangeable among investors, and wheat stored in a grain elevator is not specifically identified as to its ownership.

funnel sinking fund   A special type of bond retirement system in which an issuer has the option to make all its outstanding bonds subject to one annual sinking fund requirement. Thus, the issuer may take the annual sinking fund requirements for all outstanding issues and concentrate them into retiring an unusually large amount of a high-coupon issue. A funnel sinking fund generally operates to the disadvantage of bondholders and to the advantage of the issuer.

furthest out   In futures and options trading, the contract month with the most distant delivery or expiration. —Compare NEARBY. —Also called *back month.*

futures commission merchant (FCM)   A firm that carries out futures transactions for another party. Essentially, futures commission merchants are to futures trading what ordinary brokerage firms are to stock and bond trading. Some futures commission merchants are full-line brokerage firms in which futures trades make up only a small part of their business. —Also called *commodity brokerage firm; futures commission firm.*

futures contract   An agreement to take (that is, by the buyer) or make (that is, by the seller) delivery of a specific commodity on a particular date. The commodities and contracts are standardized in order that an active resale market will exist. Futures contracts are available for a variety of items including grains, metals, and foreign currencies. —See also SECTION 1256 CONTRACTS.

futures market   A market in which futures contracts are bought and sold. The various organized futures exchanges specialize in certain types of contracts. For example, corn, oats, soybeans, and wheat are traded on the Chicago Board of Trade, while the Commodity Exchange in New York handles trades in copper, gold, and silver. Other futures markets include the Chicago Mercantile Exchange, the Coffee, Sugar and Cocoa Exchange, the International Monetary Market, the Kansas City Board of Trade, the Minneapolis Grain Exchange, the New York Cotton Exchange, the New York Futures Exchange, and the New York Mercantile Exchange.

futures option   A put or call option on a futures contract. Because of the price volatility of futures contracts, options on these contracts are high-risk investments. —See also SECTION 1256 CONTRACTS.

future value   The amount to which a specific sum or series of sums will grow on a given date in the future. The sums are assumed to earn an annual return that is related to the market rate of interest. For example, $1,000 has a future value of $1,120 in one year, assuming an annual return of 12%. —Compare PRESENT VALUE.

FVO   —See FOR VALUATION ONLY.

FWB Frankfurter Wertpapierborse   —See FRANKFURT STOCK EXCHANGE.

FY   —See FISCAL YEAR.

FYI   —See FOR YOUR INFORMATION.

G

g   —Used immediately following the stock name in stock transaction tables of newspapers to indicate that dividends and earnings are in Canadian currency but that the stock price is in U.S. dollars: *Dome g .12.*

G-8   The world's eight largest industrial countries, including Canada, France, Germany, Great Britain, Italy, Japan, Russia, and the United States. G-8 finance ministers meet annually to evaluate and coordinate economic policy.

GAAP   —See GENERALLY ACCEPTED ACCOUNTING PRINCIPLES.

GAAS   —See GENERALLY ACCEPTED AUDITING STANDARDS.

gain   The excess of the amount received as opposed to the amount expended in a transaction. For example, receipt of $4,500 from the sale of an asset with a book value of $3,000 results in a gain of $1,500. —Compare LOSS.

gainer   A security that has risen in price during a specified period. —Compare LOSER.

GAINS®   A trademark for a type of municipal convertible bond that combines the features of a zero-coupon bond with those of interest-bearing bonds.

gamma   The sensitivity of an option's delta to changes in the price of the underlying asset. The gamma of an option is greatest when an option is near the money (strike price close to market price of underlying asset) and near zero when an option is deep out of the money.

gap   A price range in which no shares are traded. A gap on a chart is created when the lowest price at which a security trades on one day is above the highest price at which the same security was traded on the previous day. Thus, if a stock trades between a low of $51 and a high of $52.50 on Monday and between $53.50 and $54 on the following day, a gap from $52.50 to $53.50 is created on a chartist's graph. A gap may have varying degrees of significance, depending on the general formation and the volume at the time the gap occurs. —Also called *price gap.* —See also BREAKAWAY GAP; EXHAUSTION GAP; RUNAWAY GAP.

gap opening   The opening trade of a security in which the opening price shows a significant increase or decrease compared with that security's closing price of the previous day.

Garage An annex floor to the main trading floor of the New York Stock Exchange.

GARP —See GROWTH AT A REASONABLE PRICE.

gather in the stops To sell shares in order to drive down the price of a stock to a level that will activate stop orders that place additional downward price pressure on the stock.

GATT —See GENERAL AGREEMENT ON TARIFFS AND TRADE.

GDP —See GROSS DOMESTIC PRODUCT.

GDP deflator A price index used to adjust gross domestic product for changes in prices of goods and services included in the GDP. The GDP deflator is a more broadly based and, many economists argue, a better measure of inflation than the consumer price index or the producer price index. —Also called *gross domestic product deflator.*

GDR —See GLOBAL DEPOSITARY RECEIPT.

general account —See MARGIN ACCOUNT.

General Agreement on Tariffs and Trade (GATT) A 1947 multilateral trade agreement designed to establish rules, reduce tariffs, and provide a setting for a solution to international trade problems. GATT agreements are of particular importance to industries and firms heavily involved in international trade. Changes or even discussion of changes in these agreements can have a significant effect on the prices of the securities of affected companies.

general creditor A lender with an uncollateralized loan, such as the owner of a debenture. In the event that a borrower goes bankrupt, its general creditors are likely to recover a smaller proportion of what is owed them than secured creditors will.

general loan and collateral agreement —See BROKER'S LOAN.

generally accepted accounting principles (GAAP) Guidelines and rules for use by accountants in preparing financial statements. These principles, which evolved over a period of years, are designed to help ensure that financial data are presented fairly and are comparable from firm to firm and from industry to industry. In expressing an opinion on financial statements, certified public accountants are required to stipulate whether their statements have been prepared according to generally accepted accounting principles.

generally accepted auditing standards (GAAS) Guidelines established by the American Institute of Certified Public Accountants for use by public accountants when conducting external audits of financial statements. —See also AUDITED STATEMENT; UNAUDITED STATEMENT.

general obligation bond (GO) A municipal debt obligation on which interest and principal are guaranteed by the full financial resources and taxing power of the issuer. This broad promise makes a general obligation bond of higher quality than issues secured by a particular project or a more limited guarantee. It also results in lower returns to bondholders. —Also called *full-faith-and-credit bond.* —See also REVENUE BOND.

general partnership A partnership in which each of the partners is liable for all of the firm's debts and the actions of one partner are binding on each of the other partners. —Compare LIMITED PARTNERSHIP.

general price level accounting —See INFLATION ACCOUNTING.

General Securities Registered Representative Examination —See SERIES 7.

General Utilities Doctrine An Internal Revenue Service provision that permits a firm to liquidate its assets at more than book value and to pass the proceeds of the liquidation through to stockholders without making the firm pay income taxes on the gains. Rather, stockholders receiving the distribution are required to report the gain (but not the entire liquidation) as income. The General Utilities Doctrine was repealed in 1986 tax reform. As a result of the repeal, any gain from liquidation is taxed twice: once to the liquidating firm and again to the stockholders.

ghosting Illegal collusion among market makers to manipulate the market price of a stock.

ghost stock Stock that has been sold short but that has not been borrowed and therefore cannot be delivered to the buyer.

GIC —See GUARANTEED INVESTMENT CONTRACT.

gift tax A federal tax that is imposed on the giver and determined on the basis of a unified gift and estate tax schedule. Annual gifts above a specified amount per recipient are deducted from a lifetime exemption. This exemption applies jointly to accumulated gifts and to the taxable estate left at death. In most cases, only relatively large gifts incur a tax. —See also UNIFIED CREDIT.

Gilded Age The years between the Civil War and World War I when institutions undertook financial manipulations that went virtually unchecked by government. This era produced many infamous activities in the security markets.

gilt A bond issued through the United Kingdom Treasury and guaranteed by the British government. The market for gilt-edged securities is similar to the market for U.S. Treasury securities, with a high degree of safety, liquidity, and maturity selection.

gilt-edged security Any high-quality security in which the chance of default or failure is quite slim.

Ginnie Mae A wholly owned government association that operates the mortgage-backed securities program designed to facilitate the flow of capital into the housing industry. Ginnie Mae–approved private institutions issue mortgage-backed securities with payments that are guaranteed even if borrowers or issuers default on their obligations. Ginnie Mae was created in 1968 when the Federal National Mortgage Association was partitioned into two parts. —Formerly called *Government National Mortgage Association.* —See also GINNIE MAE PASS THROUGH; MOBILE HOME CERTIFICATE.

Ginnie Mae mutual fund A mutual fund that invests exclusively in Ginnie Mae certificates and passes through the interest payments to owners of the fund's shares. Because the fund continually invests in new certificates, the yield on the fund varies over time. In addition, the value of a fund will change as long-term interest rates change. The primary advantage of buying a fund over buying Ginnie Mae certificates directly is that the fund is sold to investors in smaller denominations. Furthermore, a fund's investments are spread over a large number of certificates so that prepayment of principal is not as much of a problem. The main disadvantage of a fund is that it may entail a sales fee of from 4 to 6% of the amount invested and will charge an annual investment fee.

Ginnie Mae pass through　A security backed by the Federal Housing Administration, Veterans Administration, and the Farmers Home Administration mortgages that is guaranteed by Ginnie Mae. The issuers of the securities service the mortgages and pass through interest and principal payments to the security holders. During periods of declining interest rates, holders of Ginnie Mae pass throughs are likely to receive extra principal payments as mortgages are refinanced and paid off early. —Also called *Ginnie Mae.* —See also ADJUSTED EXERCISE PRICE; CURRENT PRODUCTION RATE.

Ginnie Mae trust　A unit trust that invests in Ginnie Mae certificates and passes through interest and principal repayments to the trust's owners. Ginnie Mae trusts differ from Ginnie Mae mutual funds in that the trusts do not continually invest in new certificates. As principal is returned, the trust's owner will receive progressively smaller interest payments. Essentially, owning a Ginnie Mae trust is much like owning a certificate itself. A sales fee is charged, but, unlike Ginnie Mae funds, a trust charges no management fee because no management is involved once the trust has been set up and has become operative.

giveback　The relinquishment by employees of certain existing benefits or contract provisions. For example, many companies engaged in manufacturing have asked for employee givebacks on the premise that lower costs are needed in order for the companies to be more competitive with foreign producers. Givebacks are good news for investors because they result in higher profits or smaller losses for the company obtaining the concessions.

give-up　**1.** A prohibited practice in which a large investor would direct that a portion of the commission charged in a security trade be handed over to another broker. Give-ups were popular when commission rates were fixed and when large trades produced artificially high commissions that were transferrable to firms that provided the investor with valuable services such as research information. **2.** The reduction in yield when a bond position is swapped for bonds with a lower coupon.

glamor stock　A widely held stock that receives a considerable amount of favorable publicity in the financial press. Glamor stocks typically represent firms with strong earnings growth and bright futures. Glamor stocks, which tend to sell at relatively high price-earnings ratios, are found in most institutional portfolios.

Glass-Steagall Act　A 1933 act that prohibited commercial banks from undertaking investment banking activities such as underwriting the securities of private corporations. The legislation was passed to keep banks from entering into nonfinancial businesses (for example, owning corporate stock) and more risky activities. The Glass-Steagall Act was repealed in 1999. —Also called *Banking Act of 1933.*

Global Depositary Receipt (GDR)　A receipt on shares of a foreign company when funds are simultaneously raised in two or more markets.

global fund　A mutual fund that includes at least 25% foreign securities in its portfolio. The value of the fund depends on the health of foreign economies and exchange rate movements. A global fund permits an investor to diversify internationally. —Compare INTERNATIONAL FUND. —Also called *world fund.*

global shares　Stock that trades in multiple currencies. For example, shares of DaimlerChrysler trade in dollars in the United States, euros in Germany, yen in Japan, and in the home currencies of several other countries. Global shares are uncommon and are different from American Depositary Shares that are claims on a firm's ordinary shares.

GLOBEX　—See CHICAGO MERCANTILE EXCHANGE.

GO　—See GENERAL OBLIGATION BOND.

go-go fund　An investment company that concentrates on short-term investment performance through frequent trading of highly speculative securities. Such funds were very popular during the late 1960s but lost favor following the market decline of the early 1970s that produced large price drops in the types of stock held by the go-go funds.

going away　The purchase by institutional investors of large amounts of a serial bond issue in a particular maturity.

going concern　A business expected to continue operating in the foreseeable future. A going concern is valued differently from a firm for which liquidation is expected.

going-concern statement　An auditor's statement that there is concern whether the company being audited can remain in business. A going-concern statement indicates equity investors are at substantial risk.

going lines　—See CONTINUING OPERATIONS.

going long　Buying an investment.

going private　The process by which a publicly held company has its outstanding shares purchased by an individual or by a small group of individuals in order to obtain complete ownership and control. The group wishing to take the firm private may feel that the market is undervaluing the shares. In addition, the purchaser(s) may not wish to meet the various requirements imposed on a publicly held company. —Also called *management buyout.*

going public　The process by which a privately held company sells a portion of its ownership to the general public through a stock offering. Owners generally take their firms public because they need additional large sums of equity funding that they are unable or unwilling to contribute themselves.

going short　Selling an investment asset that is not owned. An example of such an asset would be shares of stock you borrowed through your broker. Going short means you owe what you have sold.

going south　—Used to describe the direction of prices for a security or the general market during a period of declining prices.

gold bond　—See COMMODITY-BACKED BOND.

gold bug　An individual who thinks that investors should keep all or part of their assets in the form of gold. The tendency to recommend gold nearly always stems from the gold bug's expectation of rapid or uncontrolled growth of the money supply accompanied by high rates of inflation. Some gold bugs also predict economic collapse with gold becoming the standard of payment.

gold certificate　A receipt of ownership for a stated quantity of gold. A certificate, usually issued by a major bank, allows an investor to own gold without actually taking possession of the metal. A commission is generally charged at the time of purchase.

golden boot A lucrative financial package offered an employee who is being involuntarily terminated.

golden handcuffs A lucrative incentive offered to a firm's executive in order either to keep him or her from moving to a job at another company or to buy the executive's longer-term cooperation after departure.

golden parachute An employment agreement that provides a firm's key executives with lucrative severance benefits in the event that control of the firm changes hands and that shifts in management subsequently occur. A golden parachute benefits management more than the stockholders. —Also called *golden umbrella*. —See also SILVER PARACHUTE.

CASE STUDY | After a rocky year that included embarrassing financial disclosures and a plummeting stock price, one-time high-flying Enron Corporation was forced in November 2001 to seek a major cash infusion to shore up its balance sheet. Improper accounting caused the Houston-based energy trading company to disclose that the firm would reduce four years of previously reported income by over half a billion dollars. The company was also forced to write down assets and reduce shareholders' equity. Competitor Dynegy, Inc., came to Enron's aid by proposing an all-equity $8.85 billion takeover. Enron's chairman, Kenneth Lay, was eligible for severance benefits under certain circumstances, including a change in management that resulted in a termination of his employment. Lay had worked at the firm since 1984, when it was a regional pipeline company operating under as Houston Natural Gas Company. The golden parachute was to pay Lay a lump sum of $20.2 million for each year remaining on his contract. The chairman had three years remaining at the time of the Dynegy offer, meaning he was entitled to receive a lump-sum payment of over $60 million. To the surprise of many, Lay announced at a meeting with Enron employees that he would waive his right to the severance pay. As it turned out, the Dynegy offer was shortly withdrawn and a month later Enron was in bankruptcy. Information released following the bankruptcy indicated that Enron executives had personally profited in financial dealings with the firm.

golden umbrella —See GOLDEN PARACHUTE.

gold fix The setting of the price of gold by dealers so as to establish values for gold bullion, gold products, and gold-related products. The price of gold is fixed twice a day in each of the world's gold centers. —See also FIX.

gold fund An investment company with all or a major part of its assets in gold or gold-related securities. A gold fund's price, which is closely related to the value of gold, frequently moves opposite the prices of other securities and stock market indexes.

gold standard A monetary system under which a country's money is defined in terms of gold and convertible into a fixed quantity of gold. A gold standard effectively takes monetary policy out of the hands of government policymakers. While use of the gold standard reduces the likelihood of inflation, the accompanying inability to pursue other economic goals, such as full employment or reduced interest rates, has resulted in the gold standard's fall from favor.

good delivery Delivery of a security that meets all the standards required to transfer title to the buyer. Thus, a certificate must be delivered on time with proper denomination, endorsements, and endorsement guarantee. —Compare BAD DELIVERY.

good faith deposit **1**. A sum of money required of an investor who is placing an order when that investor is not known to the brokerage firm. A good faith deposit ensures that the customer will follow through with proper payment for a buy order or with delivery of securities for a sell order. **2**. A sum of money deposited by competing underwriters of a new municipal bond issue. The deposit is a relatively small proportion (usually under 5%) of the value of the issue being underwritten.

goods in process —See WORK IN PROCESS.

good-this-month order —See MONTH ORDER.

good-till-canceled order (GTC) An order either to buy or to sell a security that remains in effect until it is canceled by the customer or until it is executed by the broker. —Also called *open order.*

goodwill **1**. The amount above the fair net book value (adjusted for assumed debt) paid for an acquisition. Goodwill appears as an asset on the balance sheet of the acquiring firm and must be reduced in the event the value is impaired. **2**. The discounted value of a larger-than-normal return on tangible assets. A business may build goodwill over time as loyalty builds among its customer base.

⋀⋀ CASE STUDY | The Financial Accounting Standards Board (FASB), the body charged with establishing generally accepted accounting standards, in 2001 changed the method by which companies account for goodwill. Goodwill is posted as an asset to a firm's balance sheet when the firm makes an acquisition for above net asset value. In other words, goodwill is created when a firm pays more than the accounting value of a firm's assets adjusted for its debts. Huge amounts of goodwill were created in the late 1990s and early 2000s when the merger and acquisition business was progressing at full steam. Prior to 2002 companies were required to write down, or deduct, a prescribed amount of goodwill each accounting period. Thus, firms that engaged in major acquisitions at high prices posted large amounts of goodwill that had to be written off over a period of years. Goodwill writeoffs increase expenses and reduce reported earnings to shareholders. Prior to the change in accounting standards, companies were required to amortize goodwill regardless of how much the acquired assets were actually worth. Under the new standard imposed by the FASB in 2001 goodwill does not have to be reduced in value until it is determined the acquisition that created goodwill is no longer worth the purchase price. This change was expected to result in substantially higher reported earnings for companies with large amounts of goodwill on their balance sheets. For example, AOL Time Warner had $127 billion in goodwill on its balance sheet at the time of the change and was expecting to report substantially higher earnings because of the change in standards. On the downside, the firm announced in March 2001 it would incur record charges of $54 billion in goodwill impairment in the first quarter.

Government National Mortgage Association —See GINNIE MAE 1.

governments All bonds issued by the U.S. Treasury or other agencies of the U.S. government. —Also called *United States government securities.* —See also FEDERAL AGENCY SECURITY; SAVINGS BOND; TREASURIES.

Government Securities Clearing Corporation (GSCC) A nonprofit organization that provides clearing and settlement of U.S. government securities.

GSCC was established in 1986 as a subsidiary of the National Securities Clearing Corporation.

grace period The period during which the issuer of a bond is not required to make interest payments. For example, a bond issued this year might only start paying interest five years from now. Bonds with grace periods are sometimes issued during a corporate restructuring.

graduated flat tax An income tax having a minimal number of progressively higher rates. For example, a taxing authority may levy a tax of 10% on all income up to $15,000, 15% on income from $15,000 to $25,000, and 20% on all income above $25,000. The graduated flat tax is a compromise between a flat tax and a progressive tax.

Graham and Dodd Authors of *Security Analysis,* one of the more well known and durable works dealing with investment philosophy. Graham and Dodd stressed the importance of value investing, that is, buying shares of companies with undervalued assets and low price-earnings ratios.

grandfathering An alteration of the rules that apply to a certain investment or investment technique while stipulating that investment actions taken before a certain date remain subject to the old rules. For example, Congress may change the law by stipulating that certain types of municipal bonds no longer pay tax-free interest while at the same time grandfathering the municipal bonds issued before the date on which the new law is to take effect.

grantor An investor who sells short a call option or a put option. The grantor of a call option agrees to sell stock at a fixed price and the grantor of a put option agrees to buy stock at a fixed price.

graph —See CHART.

graveyard market A declining market with low prices that discourage investors from selling and with little interest among investors to buy.

gray knight A company, neither friendly nor hostile, that outbids another firm in an acquisition attempt.

gray market trade An open-market transaction in a when-issued security through brokers outside the selling syndicate.

Great Crash The major declines in economic activity and stock prices that occurred in 1929 and the early 1930s.

greater fool theory The theory that no matter what price an investor pays for a security, someone else with less sense will be willing to buy it later. The greater fool theory reaches its height of popularity near the end of a bull market when speculation is high.

green investing The choosing of investments of companies that have a positive environmental record. Green investing is a special category of social investing.

greenmail A defensive maneuver aimed at thwarting a potential takeover in which the target firm purchases shares of its own stock from a raider at a price above that available to other stockholders, who are ordinarily excluded from the transaction. Funds to finance greenmail are often borrowed, in which case the target company may end up with substantial additional debt. —Compare ANTIGREENMAIL PROVISION. —Also called *negotiated share repurchase.* —See also FAIR PRICE AMENDMENT.

greenshoe An underwriting agreement provision that permits syndicate members to purchase additional shares at the original offering price. Shares in the greenshoe may consist of additional shares from the issuing company or may come from existing shareholders as a secondary offering. For example, the 2002 IPO of CIT Group included 200 million shares plus a greenshoe of 20 million additional shares that could be purchased by syndicate members at the $23 offering price within 30 days. —Also called *overallotment option.*

gross domestic product (GDP) The dollar output of final goods and services in the economy during a given period (usually one year). GDP is one measure of the economic vitality of a country and provides some indication of the health of near-term corporate income. —See also ECONOMIC ACTIVITY.

gross domestic product deflator —See GDP DEFLATOR.

gross estate The total dollar value of all the assets in an estate before paying debts and taxes.

gross income 1. For a business, its total revenues exclusive of any expenses. **2.** For an individual, all income except as specifically exempted by the Internal Revenue Code. For example, an inheritance is specifically excluded from gross income.

gross lease A lease in which the costs of maintaining the leased asset, including its insurance and taxes, are paid by the lessor. —Compare NET LEASE.

gross margin —See GROSS PROFIT MARGIN.

gross per broker The number of commissions produced by a broker during a given period. The productivity of a registered representative and a brokerage office is often measured by the gross commissions per broker. Registered representatives are generally allowed to keep about one third of their gross commissions.

gross profit Total revenue of a business minus the cost of goods it sold. Gross profit does not include income from incidental sources and also excludes selling and administrative expenses. —Compare NET INCOME.

gross profit margin A measure calculated by dividing gross profit by net sales. Gross profit margin is an indication of a firm's ability to turn a dollar of sales into profit after the cost of goods sold has been accounted for. —Compare NET PROFIT MARGIN. —Also called *gross margin; margin of profit.* —See also RETURN ON SALES.

gross sales Total sales for a period before discounts, returns, and freight expenses have been deducted. —Compare NET SALES.

gross spread The difference in the price that an investor pays for a new security issue and the price paid the issuer by the lead underwriter. The gross spread is a function of a number of variables including the size of the issue and the riskiness, or price volatility, of the security. —Also called *underwriting spread.*

gross working capital —See CURRENT ASSET.

group of funds —See FAMILY OF FUNDS.

group rotation —See SECTOR ROTATION.

group sales The distribution of a new security issue to institutional clients.

growth and income fund An investment company that invests in the common stock of growing companies that have a history of paying dividends. This type of fund is a compromise between a growth fund that concentrates on capital gains and an income fund that concentrates on maximizing current income.

growth at a reasonable price (GARP) The strategy of investing in stocks with growth potential but only when the stocks are reasonably priced relative to the overall market. GARP investors generally search for a favorable combination of earnings growth (higher is better) and price-earnings ratio (lower is better).

growth fund An investment company whose major objective is long-term capital growth. Growth funds offer substantial potential gains over time but vary significantly in price during bull and bear markets. This type of fund is most appropriate for someone who will not need to withdraw funds in the near future.

growth rate The annual rate at which a variable, such as gross domestic product or a firm's earnings, has been or is expected to grow. One common method of estimating future growth rate is simply to measure a variable's past growth rate and then project a continuation of the trend.

growth recession An economy in which the output of goods and services slowly expands but unemployment remains high or grows.

growth stock The stock of a firm that is expected to have above-average increases in revenues and earnings. These firms usually retain most earnings for reinvestment and therefore pay small dividends. The stock, often selling at relatively high price-earnings ratios, is subject to wide swings in price. Examples include Intel, General Electric, and Dell.

GSCC —See GOVERNMENT SECURITIES CLEARING CORPORATION.

GTC —See GOOD-TILL-CANCELED ORDER.

guaranteed account A brokerage account that has its margin requirements or losses guaranteed by the assets of another account.

guaranteed bond A bond that is issued by one firm and guaranteed as to interest and principal by one or more other firms. Such bonds, often resulting from joint ventures, are particularly common among railroads that lease tracks to and from each another.

guaranteed-dollar annuity —See FIXED ANNUITY.

guaranteed investment contract (GIC) An investment product sold by life insurance companies that guarantees a return for a specific length of time on a large, lump-sum premium. Most GICs are funded by transfers from some other pension plan. The return of principal is dependent on the insurance company's ability to satisfy its obligation.

guaranteed mortgage certificate A pass through issued by Freddie Mac in which conventional mortgages purchased by Freddie Mac are resold to investors in $100,000, $500,000, and $1,000,000 principal amounts. Interest is paid semiannually and principal repayments are made annually. —See also PASS-THROUGH SECURITY.

guaranteed stock Preferred stock that is issued by one company and guaranteed as to dividends by one or more other companies. Guaranteed stock issues, like guaranteed bonds, are most prevalent among railroads.

guarantee letter A letter that is issued by a commercial bank guaranteeing that an investor who is writing a put option will pay the required sum in the event that the put is exercised against the investor.

guarantee of signature A certificate that verifies the authenticity of the signature of the registered owner of a bond or stock. The guarantee of signature is attached to the assignment of a bond or stock certificate.

gun jumping 1. The trading in a security before inside information has been released to the public. **2.** Solicitation of orders for a new security underwriting before the SEC has approved the registration statement.

gunslinger An aggressive investor who purchases speculative securities. The term is often used to refer to portfolio managers who choose risky investments with the potential for major gains in value.

H

H —Used in stock transaction tables in newspapers to indicate that during the day's activity the stock traded at a new 52-week high price.

haircut A deduction in the market value of securities being held by brokerage and investment banking firms as part of net worth for calculating their net capital. The size of a haircut varies with the particular type of security held.

half One half of one point. For stock quotes, a half represents one half of $1, or 50¢. For bond quotes, a half represents one half of 1% of par, or $5. For option quotes, a half represents $50.

half-life The length of time before half the principal on a debt is expected to be repaid through amortization or sinking fund payments. For example, a 25-year bond issue may require the issuer to retire 5% of the beginning principal commencing 5 years after the issue date. Thus, the bond issue has a half-life of 5 years plus the number of years required to retire half the issue, or 15 years. Mortgage-backed securities often have a relatively short half-life because many homeowners pay off or refinance their mortgages early. —Also called *average life*.

half-year convention The assumption for tax purposes that a newly acquired asset is placed in service halfway through the year regardless of when the asset is actually acquired and placed in service. The half-year convention affects annual depreciation, taxation, and earnings calculations.

hammering the market The heavy selling of securities, driving down prices. Unexpected bad news such as disclosure of corporate fraud, a terrorist attack, or the outbreak of armed hostilities can cause a hammering of the market.

handle The whole dollar price of a bid or offer. A bid of $91.10 and an ask of $91.15 would have a handle of $91.

Hang Seng Index A market-weighted index of 33 stocks making up approximately 70% of the market value of all stocks traded on the Stock Exchange of Hong Kong. HSI Services Limited, a subsidiary of Hang Seng Bank, calculates the index. The firm also calculates several other indexes including an Asian index, a mid-cap index, and an index for companies traded in Hong Kong and headquartered in mainland China.

hard asset —See TANGIBLE ASSET.

hard dollars Cash payment to a brokerage firm for goods or services provided by the firm. Thus, individual investors are usually required to pay cash for a market letter. —Compare SOFT DOLLARS.

head-and-shoulders In technical analysis, a chart pattern indicating the rise and fall of a stock's price throughout a given period and characterized by a peak followed by a decline, a second peak that rises above the first peak followed by a decline, and finally a third rise to a level below the second peak followed by a decline. The first and third peaks are shoulders while the second peak is the pattern's head. Technical analysts generally consider a head-and-shoulders pattern to be a very bearish indicator if the second shoulder declines below a line connecting the bottom points of the two intermediate declines. An upside-down formation is said to be an inverted head-and-shoulders formation and is considered to be a bullish indicator. Refer to the *Technical Analysis Chart Patterns* section for an example of this chart. —See also NECKLINE; REVERSAL PATTERN.

headline risk The possibility a negative news story will spread to other media outlets and cause a significant change in the value of an investment. For example, an unconfirmed report of a corporate management shakeup might be picked up by competing newspapers and television networks, thus causing a sharp decline in the company's stock price. The firm's stock price is likely to be subject to substantial volatility even though the story eventually proves false.

heart bond A bond issued by a private nonprofit corporation such as a church, hospital, or school. The term refers to the type of sales pitch used for such bonds; it often appeals more to buyers' hearts than to their pocketbooks.

heavy market A declining market.

hedge A security transaction that reduces the risk on an already existing investment position. An example is the purchase of a put option in order to offset at least partially the potential losses from owned stock. Although hedges reduce potential losses, they also tend to reduce potential profits. —See also PERFECT HEDGE; RISK HEDGE; SHORT HEDGE; SPECIAL ARBITRAGE ACCOUNT.

⋀ **CASE STUDY** A hedge that limits potential losses is also likely to limit potential gains. In May 1997 Georgia entrepreneur and billionaire Ted Turner entered into an arrangement whereby Mr. Turner had the right to sell four million of his Time Warner shares to a brokerage firm at a price of $19.815 per share. At the same time the brokerage firm acquired the right to buy the same four million shares at a price of $30.45. This particular hedge, called a collar, established a minimum and maximum value for four million shares of Time Warner owned by Mr. Turner. In other words, the former owner of the Atlanta Braves, Atlanta Hawks, CNN, and superstation WTBS acquired the right to obtain at least $19.815 per share by agreeing to give up any increase in value above $30.45. Time Warner stock subsequently skyrocketed when America Online acquired the firm at a price nearly triple the $30.45 stipulated in the agreement. Thus, the hedge ended up costing Mr. Turner approximately a quarter of a billion dollars. On a positive note, the four million shares represented less than 4% of Mr. Turner's total holdings of Time Warner stock he had acquired when the firm bought his Turner Broadcasting several years earlier.

hedge clause A statement in an advertisement, a market letter, or a security report indicating that the information therein is believed to be accurate and that it has been obtained from usually reliable sources, with nothing, however, guaranteed. Essentially, a hedge clause indicates to readers that the writer believes the information is accurate and that reasonable care has been taken to ensure its accuracy.

hedged tender   An investor's tender of securities accompanied by the short sale of a portion of the securities tendered. The short sale hedges the possibility that not all the tendered securities will be accepted by the buyer and that the value of those securities not accepted will be less than the tender price.

hedge fund   A very specialized, volatile, open-end investment company that permits the manager to use a variety of investment techniques usually prohibited in other types of funds. These techniques include borrowing money, selling short, and using options. Hedge funds offer investors the possibility of extraordinary gains with above-average risk.

> ⩓ **CASE STUDY** | Even hedge fund managers with an excellent track record sometimes decide to throw in the towel. In March 2000 well-known hedge fund investor Julian Robertson announced that he had decided to close hedge funds managed by Tiger Management LLC, a firm he started in 1980. Saying he didn't understand the booming market for Internet stocks, the value investor who had accumulated an impressive record for beating the market indicated he would return approximately $4.5 billion to investors and retain nearly $1.5 billion of his own funds. Tiger Management had produced a loss of 19% in 1999 and an additional loss of 13% in 2000 up to the date of the announcement. Liquidation of the funds required that investment positions in Tiger Management's holdings, including U.S. Airways Group and Normandy Mining, would be gradually sold so that cash could be returned to Tiger's investors. Robertson announced the closing of his hedge fund just as Internet stocks had peaked and were heading for a major decline in value.

hedge margin   In commodities trading, a special low-margin rate for hedgers such as manufacturers and dealers. The hedge margin is lower because of offsetting positions.

hedge ratio   The number of options required to offset the change in value due to a price change in 100 shares of common stock. For example, if two options are needed to offset value changes for 100 shares of stock, the hedge ratio is 2.

heir   A person who by will or statutory law receives or is scheduled to receive a portion or all of the assets of an estate.

held   Temporarily unavailable for trading. —Used of a security.

hemline theory   The theory that holds that stock prices tend to move in the same direction as the length of hemlines on dresses. Thus, rising hemlines are a bullish sign and falling hemlines are a bearish sign.

hidden assets   Items of value that are owned by a firm but do not appear on its balance sheet. For example, a trademark or patent may be a firm's most valuable owned asset; yet, it would not appear as such on its balance sheet.

hidden load   A mutual fund sales fee that is not readily apparent to investors. The term generally applies to an annual 12b–1 fee that is charged by many mutual funds.

hidden reserve   The amount by which a firm's net worth is understated. For example, overdepreciation results in assets and net worth being carried on the firm's financial statements at less than market value.

high flyer A heavily traded stock that sells at a high price-earnings ratio. High flyers go through a period of rapidly rising prices when something about the firms or the industries in which they operate catches the investing public's fancy. Unfortunately, however, most high flyers eventually come to earth with plunging prices when investors' expectations are shattered.

high-grade Of, relating to, or being a bond with little risk of default on the part of the issuer. High-grade is usually reserved for bonds rated AAA or AA by the rating services. —Compare INVESTMENT-GRADE.

high-low index A cumulative tabulation of the number of stocks reaching new highs minus the number of stocks reaching new lows. Technical analysts use the high-low index to measure the strength of the market's movement. In general, movement of the high-low index in the same direction as the market confirms the market's movement and indicates that this movement is likely to continue in the same direction.

highly confident letter An investment bank's statement that it can raise the necessary capital to complete a deal based on current market conditions and its analysis of the deal. Highly confident letters are useful for companies that want to convince the investment community they can raise the necessary capital to finance an acquisition.

highs The number of stocks that exceed the highest price reached by each stock during the most recent 52-week period. Technicians consider an increasing number of highs to be a bullish sign, especially if accompanied by other favorable indicators. Conversely, record high market averages not accompanied by an increasing number of individual highs would be suspect. —Compare LOWS. —Also called *new highs*.

high-technology stock The stock of a company that is involved in sophisticated technology, such as electronics, computer software, robotics, or life sciences companies. High-technology stock often offers large potential gains but tends to be quite risky because of intense competition and uncertain success.

high-yield bond —See JUNK BOND.

high-yield bond fund An investment company that attempts to produce unusually high income for its shareholders by maintaining a corporate bond portfolio that contains at minimum two thirds lower-rated bonds (Baa by Moody's; BBB by S&P).

high-yield financing —See JUNK FINANCING.

historical cost The amount of money that was originally used to pay for an asset. A company records assets on a balance sheet at historical cost, which often bears little relation to the market value of the assets after they have been owned several years. —Also called *original cost*.

historical trading range The highest and lowest prices at which a security has traded since going public.

historical yield The yield that a money market mutual fund has provided during a specified period. Investors frequently compare historical yields among firms when trying to select a fund to purchase. Historical yields are more useful when comparing funds than when estimating future yields.

hit 1. To sell a security at a bid price quoted by a dealer. For example, a trader will hit a bid. 2. To lose money on a trade. For example, a dealer may take a hit on the holdings of Moore's Fried Foods' common stock.

holder The owner of a security.

holder of record A security holder listed in a firm's books as having ownership of the security on the record date. This list is used in determining who will receive dividends, interest, proxies, financial reports, and so on. —Also called *owner of record; shareholder of record; stockholder of record.* —See also RECORD DATE.

holding company A type of parent company that exists primarily to exercise control over other firms. The control is exercised through ownership of a majority of the controlled firm's shares. Earnings of the holding company are derived from earnings of the controlled firms, which pay dividends on the shares. —Compare SUBSIDIARY. —See also OPERATING UNIT.

Holding Company Depositary Receipts —See HOLDRS.

holding period The length of time during which a security is owned.

holding period return (HPR) The return achieved on an investment including current income and any change in value during an investor's holding period. This measure proves useful in comparing expected returns on different investments. —Also called *holding period yield.*

holding the market —See PEG 1.

HOLDRS (Holding Company Depositary Receipts) Exchange-traded receipts representing beneficial ownership of a fixed basket of common stocks in a particular sector or industry. Owners of these securities can choose to have HOLDRS converted to the underlying stocks so that individual shares can be sold. Stocks represented by HOLDRS are selected prior to the initial issue of HOLDRS and remain unchanged except for unusual circumstances such as corporate mergers and spinoffs. HOLDRS are originated by Merrill Lynch and traded on the American Stock Exchange.

> **CASE STUDY** Unlike mutual funds and most unit trusts, HOLDRS represent beneficial interest in the underlying stocks. As such, owners of HOLDRS are entitled to receive dividends, annual reports, proxy statements, and other correspondence from each firm included in the portfolio represented by a particular class of HOLDRS. Owners of HOLDRS are also permitted to vote on corporate affairs of firms whose stocks are included in the HOLDRS portfolio. Agile Software Corporation, a firm whose stock traded on the New York Stock Exchange, became concerned with the expense of servicing all of its new shareholders who owned B2B Internet HOLDRS. Agile had approximately 15,000 shareholders prior to the creation of the B2B HOLDRS in which the firm's stock was included. Creation of the HOLDRS caused Agile to incur the additional expense of servicing nearly 50,000 additional shareholders. In April 2001 Agile Software filed a federal lawsuit seeking to force the American Stock Exchange, Bank of New York (the trustee for HOLDRS), and Merrill Lynch (originator of HOLDRS) to pick up Agile's expense of servicing the additional shareholders. Agile claimed that all three of these companies were earning a profit from HOLDRS and should be responsible for the expenses of servicing its owners.

holiday effect The unusually good performance by stocks on the day prior to market-closing holidays.

hospital revenue bond

Are hospital revenue bonds so risky that my portfolio and I will land in traction?

Before you buy a hospital revenue bond, you need to review carefully the financial and demographic characteristics of the issuing hospital and have some understanding of how it might be influenced by competition from other health care providers in its market. Although many hospitals represent reasonable credit risks, they are certainly not all alike, and the group should not be painted with a broad brush in the same manner that municipal bond investors sometimes paint other types of bonds (such as water and sewer revenue bonds or school district bonds). Many hospitals are struggling as a result of numerous factors, several of which are overbuilding of capacity relative to community needs, tightening reimbursement policies on the part of Medicare and other insurers, rising costs as hospitals are forced to update equipment to keep up with leaps in health care technology, and growing competition, including that from nonmedical facilities. Of course, these industry problems have been compounded by cuts in federal aid to states and municipalities. Although these problems are greater for the nonprofit hospitals, the for-profit hospitals are clearly not immune to them. In reviewing a hospital to determine its relative creditworthiness, financial analysts focus on institutional characteristics and market position, management factors, medical staff characteristics, financial indicators, and legal covenants. Because of the greater risks often associated with hospital revenue bonds, most bonds of this type are issued with some kind of credit enhancement, usually in the form of insurance, but sometimes via letter-of-credit facilities.

Stephanie G. Bigwood, CFP, ChFC, CSA, Assistant Vice President
Lombard Securities, Incorporated, Baltimore, MD

home run An investment that produced a large return in a short period of time for its purchaser. For example, an investor might purchase shares in an initial public offering that moves sharply upward in subsequent trading in the secondary market.

horizon —See TIME HORIZON.

horizontal analysis Comparison of financial statements or specific items in a financial statement that covers two or more periods. —Compare VERTICAL ANALYSIS.

horizontal count A measure of the horizontal width of a congestion area on a point-and-figure chart. Technical analysts use the horizontal count to determine a price target for a stock once it breaks out of the congestion area.

horizontal merger A merger between firms that provide similar products or services. Merging one steel manufacturer into another steel manufacturer is an example of a horizontal merger. Horizontal mergers permit the surviving firm to control a greater share of the market and, it is hoped, gain economies of scale. —Compare VERTICAL MERGER.

horizontal price movement The movement of the price of a security or the market in a narrow range day after day. On a chart this price movement appears as a horizontal line or a horizontal bar across the page.

horizontal security exchange The exchange of one security for a like security (that is, stock for stock, debt for debt). Exchange offers involving horizontal exchanges are generally tax-free, although a taxable event will occur if and when the new securities are sold.

horizontal spread —See CALENDAR SPREAD.

hospital revenue bond Tax-exempt debt issued by a city, county, state, or hospital authority with debt service guaranteed by hospital revenues. While the facility that the bond issue is used to finance may be leased or sold to the hospital, it is the financial strength of the hospital, not the issuer, that backs the debt. Hospital bonds are generally more risky than general obligation or water and sewer bonds because the hospital has no taxing power. *See Investment Tip on p. 179.* —See also 501(C)(3) BOND.

hostile leveraged buyout The purchase of a firm, against the wishes of the acquired firm's managers, in which a small group of investors finances the purchase primarily by borrowing. Although leveraged buyouts have become quite common, hostile leveraged buyouts are unusual because lenders financing takeovers generally prefer that the acquired firms' managements remain, albeit under new ownership.

hostile takeover —See UNFRIENDLY TAKEOVER.

hostile tender offer An offer to purchase shares from a firm's stockholders when directors of the target firm have recommended that stockholders not sell their stock. Hostile tender offers sometimes cause the directors of the target company to seek a better offer from another party. —Compare TENDER OFFER. —See also UNFRIENDLY TAKEOVER.

hot issue A new security issue for which investor demand exceeds securities available in the issue. National Association of Securities Dealers rules forbid members from taking advantage of the likelihood that these securities will rise in price immediately after issue. —See also FORM FR-1; INVESTMENT HISTORY; NORMAL INVESTMENT PRACTICE.

∿ **CASE STUDY** The stock market boom of the late 1990s produced some spectacular price gains, especially in new issues of dot-com companies. The quick and seemingly effortless road to riches of buying hot issues in the primary market and then quickly selling these same stocks in the secondary market resulted in substantial profits and was often accompanied by questionable dealings. In January 2002, following a ten-month investigation, NASD Regulation announced that it had censured and fined Credit Suisse First Boston (CSFB) $50 million for taking millions of dollars from customers in inflated commissions in exchange for allocations of "hot" IPOs. NASD claimed the inflated commissions amounted to an illegal profit-sharing arrangement with CSFB. The settlement also included CSFB paying an additional $50 million to the Securities and Exchange Commission. According to the charges CSFB instructed employees to give greater stock allocations to accounts that agreed to share their profits with CSFB. The profit sharing was disguised as inflated brokerage commissions on transactions unrelated to the IPOs. For example, in one instance a CSFB customer obtained an allocation of 13,500 shares in a VA Linux IPO. The customer subsequently sold two million shares of Compaq and paid CSFB 50¢ a share, or $1 million in brokerage commissions. The customer immediately repurchased the same Compaq shares at the normal commission rate of 6¢ per share. The customer's $880,000 in excess commissions paid to CSFB for the Compaq sale were more than offset when the VA Linux PIO shares were sold for a one-day profit of $3.3 million. In another instance, a CSFB customer paid a $650,000 commission to purchase one million shares of Disney shortly after receiving allocations of IPO shares of both VA Linux and FogDog. The 65¢ per share commission was substantially more than the client subsequently paid a different broker-dealer to immediately sell the Disney shares.

hot money Funds that are controlled by investors who seek high short-term yields when the funds are likely to be reinvested somewhere else at any time. Some financial institutions attract hot money by offering above-average yields on certificates of deposit. However, if the rate is lowered, the funds are likely to be lost to another institution or investment.

hot stock A stock that has large price movements on very heavy volume. Hot stocks often run in cycles depending on the investing public's interest in particular industries or particular concepts. Hot stocks are usually quite risky and are suitable for speculators involved in short-term trading.

house An organization that acts as a broker-dealer or an underwriter.

house account A brokerage account managed by a firm's main office or by an executive of the firm.

house maintenance requirement The minimum equity that must be kept in a customer's margin account as determined by the firm holding the account. A house maintenance requirement is imposed when a brokerage firm desires a more strict maintenance margin requirement than the one required by an exchange or by the National Association of Securities Dealers.

house of issue —See LEAD UNDERWRITER.

house rules A brokerage firm's regulations regarding customer accounts and practices. For example, the firm must establish rules concerning margin requirements, the handling of customers' checks, and good faith deposits on new accounts. House rules must be at least as strict as industry regulations require.

house stock A stock that a brokerage firm buys and sells as a market maker or has in its inventory.

housing bond —See MORTGAGE-BACKED REVENUE BOND.

HPR —See HOLDING PERIOD RETURN.

Hulbert Financial Digest A monthly newsletter devoted to information about investment advisory letters. The publication includes a top-five ranking of advisory letters during short and extended periods, along with commentary and detailed overviews of advisory letters providing the most profitable recommendations.

hybrid annuity A single annuity in which a part of an investor's payments purchase units of a variable annuity and the remaining funds purchase units of a fixed annuity.

hybrid security A security that has features characteristic of two or more securities. A convertible bond, for example, is a hybrid security in that it has the features (that is, interest, maturity, and principal) of an ordinary bond but is heavily influenced by the price movements of the stock into which it is convertible.

hyperinflation A very high level of inflation that tends to result in the breakdown of the monetary system, the hoarding of goods, and difficulty in achieving real economic growth. The classic case of hyperinflation occurred in Germany during the 1920s. Hyperinflation, which tends to motivate people to own real goods, adversely affects security prices.

hypothecate To pledge securities as collateral for a loan without giving up ownership of the securities. —See also REHYPOTHECATE.

hypothecation agreement A written agreement between a customer opening a margin account and a brokerage firm that pledges stock in the account as collateral for margin loans. The brokerage firm is permitted to sell the stock in the event that equity in the account falls below a stipulated level.

I

i —Used in the dividend column of stock transaction tables to indicate that the dividend was paid after a stock dividend or split: *Lehigh s.20i.*

IASB —See INTERNATIONAL ACCOUNTING STANDARDS BOARD.

ICAA —See INVESTMENT COUNSEL ASSOCIATION OF AMERICA.

ICI —See INVESTMENT COMPANY INSTITUTE.

identify shares To distinguish which shares among those that are owned are to be sold. An investor may buy shares of a company or mutual fund at many different prices over a period of years. If a portion of those shares are to be sold, the investor may identify shares so as to control the profits or losses that are realized. In addition, an investor who identifies shares having the highest cost basis often can minimize the taxes associated with such a sale.

idle funds Money, as the funds in a checking account, that is not invested and therefore earns no income. Investors wishing to increase their income try to keep idle funds to a minimum.

illegal dividend A declared dividend that violates the corporate charter or the laws of the state in which the firm is incorporated.

illiquid 1. Of or relating to an asset that is difficult to buy or sell in a short period of time without its price being affected. For example, a large block of stock or a small amount of an infrequently traded stock is likely to be difficult to sell without a reduced price being offered to potential buyers. —Compare LIQUID 1. **2.** Of, relating to, or being an investment position in which a low proportion of assets is in cash or near-cash, thereby creating difficulty for the investor who is trying to raise funds for another purpose.

IMA —See INSTITUTE OF MANAGEMENT ACCOUNTANTS.

imbalance of orders —See ORDER IMBALANCE.

IMF —See INTERNATIONAL MONETARY FUND.

immaterial Of so little importance or relevance as to have no significant impact on an outcome. For example, a firm may be engaged in a lawsuit involving such an insignificant amount of money that the lawsuit's outcome will not appreciably affect the firm. Thus, the lawsuit and its potential results are immaterial to the preparation of the firm's financial statements. —Compare MATERIAL.

immediate annuity An annuity that is purchased with a lump sum and that begins making payments one period after the purchase. Immediate annuities are most commonly purchased by people who have accumulated a sum of money and are ready for retirement. —Compare DEFERRED ANNUITY.

immediate family Close relatives by birth or marriage including siblings, parents, children, in-laws, and any financial dependents. The National Association of Securities Dealers restricts financial transactions between a broker-dealer and his or her immediate family.

immediate-or-cancel order A customer order that not only specifies a price but also requires the broker to fill immediately as much of the order as possible and cancel any part remaining. This type of order differs from a fill-or-kill order, which disallows a partial fill.

immunization A technique of investing in bonds such that the portfolio's target return is protected against interest rate fluctuations. Changes in returns at which cash flows can be reinvested are offset by changes in the value of the securities in the portfolio. —See also BULLET IMMUNIZATION.

impairment Reduction in a firm's capital as a result of distributions or losses.

import A good or service brought into a country from another country and offered for sale. While some imported items originate in foreign subsidiaries of domestic companies, large increases in imports tend to hurt sales and profits of many firms located in the importing country. —Compare EXPORT. —See also BALANCE OF TRADE; QUOTA.

improvement An increase in the value of real estate achieved by changing its configuration or by adding to it. —Also called *land improvement.*

imputed interest Interest on an investment that is assumed for certain purposes to be paid even though no interest payment is physically received by the investor. For example, the Internal Revenue Service considers annual accretion on a zero-coupon corporate or a zero-coupon Treasury bond to be imputed interest for tax purposes even though investors holding these bonds receive no annual interest payments from the issuers.

imputed interest rate A minimum market rate of interest assumed by the government for tax purposes regardless of the actual rate charged on a loan. The imputing of interest was included as part of the 1984 tax act in order to stop tax avoidance by people making loans at artificially low interest rates.

inactive account A brokerage account in which few transactions take place. Some brokerage firms levy a fee on accounts in which securities are deposited but no activity occurs during a specified time.

inactive bond crowd —See CABINET CROWD.

inactive post The location on the floor of an exchange where inactive securities are traded. —See also POST 30 STOCK.

inactive security A security that has a relatively low trading volume. A particularly inactive security may not trade for days or weeks at a time, although bid and ask quotations for it are generally available. Inactive securities are often difficult to buy or sell in any significant quantity without affecting the price.

in-and-out The purchase and sale of an investment within a short period of time.

incentive fee —See PERFORMANCE FEE.

incentive stock option An option that permits an employee to purchase shares of the employer's stock at a predetermined price. No tax is due on any gain until the time of sale if the sale date is at least one year subsequent to the date on which the option was granted. —Also called *employee stock option; option.*

income averaging   A technique for calculating personal income taxes in which an individual with large variations in annual taxable income is allowed to average income over a specified period. Income averaging was eliminated by 1986 tax reform.

income bond   A long-term debt security in which the issuer is required to pay interest only when interest is earned. This rare security, issued principally as part of a corporate reorganization, offers an investor a relatively weak promise of payment. Some issues require that unpaid interest be accumulated and made up in periods that earnings permit. —Also called *adjustment bond.*

income-bond fund   An investment company that maintains a portfolio of corporate and government bonds that produce a high level of current income.

income dividend   A distribution of dividends, interest, and short-term capital gains by an investment company to its shareholders. This type of dividend is taxed at the recipient's marginal rate. —See also CAPITAL GAINS DISTRIBUTION.

income-equity fund   An investment company that invests primarily in the equities of companies with good records of paying dividends so as to produce a high level of current income for shareholders.

income fund   An investment company, the main objective of which is to achieve current income for its owners. Thus, it tends to select securities such as bonds, preferred stocks, and common stocks that pay relatively high current returns. This type of fund is most appropriate for someone seeking high current income rather than growth of principal. —Also called *income-mixed fund.*

income per share   —See EARNINGS PER SHARE.

income property   Real estate that produces current income, typically from rental payments. Apartments, office buildings, and rental homes are considered income property.

income shares   One of the two types of stock issued by a dual purpose fund in which the owner is entitled to all the income earned by the portfolio plus the return of the stock's par value (if sufficient funds remain) at the time the fund dissolves. These shares appeal mainly to investors seeking high current income since the chance for capital gain is negligible. —Compare CAPITAL SHARES.

income statement   A business financial statement that lists revenues, expenses, and net income throughout a given period. Because of the various methods used to record transactions, the dollar values shown on an income statement often can be misleading. —Also called *earnings report; earnings statement; operating statement; profit and loss statement.* —See also CONSOLIDATED INCOME STATEMENT.

income stock   A stock that has a relatively high dividend yield. The stock's issuer is typically a firm having stable earnings and dividends and operating in a mature industry. The price of an income stock is heavily influenced by changes in interest rates.

income tax   A tax levied on the annual earnings of an individual or a corporation. Income taxes are levied by the federal government and by a number of state and local governments. One set of rules applies to individual income and another to corporate income. The size and structure of an income tax greatly influence security prices and investor decisions.

incorporate To obtain a state charter establishing a corporation. Owners of proprietorships and partnerships incorporate in order to obtain limited liability for themselves and for potential investors. The limited liability makes it easier for the firm to raise additional equity capital.

incremental cost —See MARGINAL COST.

incubator An organization designed to assist start-up companies, generally with respect to providing knowledge and technical assistance.

indenture A legal contract between a bond issuer and its lenders that specifies the terms of the issue. Typical provisions are the amount and dates of interest payments, name of the trustee, maturity date, collateral, restrictions on dividends or other borrowing, and specifics of a sinking fund or potential calls. It is the trustee's job to ensure that the terms of the indenture are fulfilled. —Also called *bond indenture; trust deed.* —See also COVENANT.

indenture qualification statement A statement presented to the SEC by the issuer of debt securities detailing the terms of the borrowing arrangement. An indenture qualification statement is required of debt securities exempt from the Securities Act of 1933 but subject to the Trust Indenture Act of 1939.

independent audit —See EXTERNAL AUDIT.

independent broker —See TWO-DOLLAR BROKER.

independent variable A variable that is not affected by any other variables with which it is compared. For example, in comparing the price of an electric utility stock with interest rates, the interest rates are an independent variable because they are not affected by utility stock prices. —Compare DEPENDENT VARIABLE.

index The relative value of a variable in comparison with itself on a different date. Many security price indicators such as the Standard & Poor's series and the New York Stock Exchange series are constructed as indexes. —Also called *stock index.* —See also BASE PERIOD.

index To adjust a variable by a selected measure of relative value. For example, it has been proposed that an investor's basis on a security be indexed for changes in consumer prices so that only real increases in value will be taxed. —Also called *tax indexing.* —See also SUBINDEX.

index arbitrage An investment strategy that takes advantage of the price discrepancies between an asset or group of assets and an index futures contract on the asset. For example, a money manager might attempt to earn a profit for shareholders by selling an overpriced stock index futures index and buying the underlying stock. —See also STOCK-INDEX ARBITRAGE.

index arbitrage tick test —See RULE 80A.

index-based offer An offer either to buy or to sell a security at a price based on an index. For example, in 1985 Exxon Pipeline Company offered to purchase up to $100 million principal amount of two of its bond issues at a price that would provide a yield to maturity of 170 points less than the *Bond Buyer*'s 40-Bond Index.

index fund A mutual fund that keeps a portfolio of securities designed to match the performance of the market as a whole. The market is represented by a market index such as the S&P 500. An index fund has low administrative expenses and appeals to investors who believe it is difficult or impossible for investment managers to beat the market. —Also called *market fund.*

index futures   Futures contracts on stock indexes such as the S&P 500. Index futures are settled in cash.

indexing   A strategy for choosing securities so that a portfolio mimics the market as represented by some chosen market index. Most stock index funds attempt to mimic Standard & Poor's 500 Stock Index. —See also ENHANCED INDEXING.

index of industrial production   —See INDUSTRIAL PRODUCTION.

index of leading economic indicators   An index that is compiled by the Conference Board, a private-sector consulting firm. The index is designed to indicate the future direction of economic activity. A rising index signals that economic activity can be expected to increase in the near future. Although variations in this index are of interest to stock analysts, stock market price movements are also considered as a separate leading indicator; therefore, the series is not particularly useful in forecasting stock price changes.

index option   A call option or put option with a specific index as the underlying asset. For example, a call option on the S&P 500 gives the option buyer the right to purchase the value of the index at a fixed price until a predetermined date. Index options provide a means to leverage a bet on the future direction of the market or of a particular industry segment without purchasing all the individual securities. Use of the option can entail considerable risk for an investor.

indication   **1.** An estimate of the bid and ask when a security begins trading. Brokers, dealers, or investors may seek an indication before a security begins trading to help them establish a trading strategy in that security. **2.** A nominal quote disseminated by a stock exchange that gives the range in which a stock will open or reopen. —Also called *preopening indication.*

indication of interest   An investor's expression of interest in purchasing part of a new security issue before the issue comes to market. Brokers frequently seek indications of interest from clients even though the indications are not firm commitments to purchase the security. —Compare CIRCLE. —See also UNDERBOOKED.

indicator   A variable used to forecast the value or change in the value of another variable. For example, changes in the producer price index are used to forecast subsequent changes in the consumer price index. Likewise, some financial analysts believe a change in the money supply is an indicator of the direction of the stock market. —See also TECHNICAL INDICATOR.

indirect convertible   A convertible security that may be exchanged into another convertible. The market price of the indirect convertible is actually a function of the value of the shares underlying the second convertible. As an example, a bond may be convertible into 10 shares of a convertible preferred stock, each of which may be exchanged for 5 shares of common stock. Thus, the bond trades indirectly on the basis of the value of 50 shares of common stock.

indirect cost   A cost that is not directly related to the production of a specific good or service but that is indirectly related to a variety of goods or services. For example, the cost of administering a large company is an indirect cost that must be spread over a number of products or services. —Compare DIRECT COST. —Also called *overhead.*

indirect government obligation —See FEDERAL AGENCY SECURITY.

indirect tax A tax paid by an entity other than the one on which it is levied. For example, a retail sales tax is collected and remitted to the government by a business even though the tax is ultimately paid by the consumers. —Compare DIRECT TAX.

individual account A brokerage account opened in the name of one person. —Compare JOINT ACCOUNT.

individual retirement account —See IRA.

industrial Of or related to companies engaged in the manufacture of products. The word also can refer to firms engaged in distribution. For example, Sears is classified as an industrial company for purposes of calculating the Dow Jones Averages, but it is included as a retailer rather than as an industrial in *Fortune* magazine's annual survey of America's largest firms.

industrial bond A long-term debt security issued by a corporation engaged in industrial activities such as manufacturing or refining.

industrial development bond A type of municipal revenue bond in which interest and principal payments are secured by the credit of a private firm rather than by the municipality. —Also called *industrial revenue bond.* —See also PRIVATE ACTIVITY BOND.

industrial production A measure of the country's economic health judged by its output from manufacturing, mining, and utility industries. Industrial production is calculated by the Federal Reserve, which publishes a monthly index of industrial production. Rising industrial production is generally more favorable for stockholders than for bondholders because it can signal rising inflationary pressures and higher interest rates. —Also called *index of industrial production.*

industrial revenue bond —See INDUSTRIAL DEVELOPMENT BOND.

industry life cycle The stages of evolution through which an industry progresses as it moves from conception to stabilization and stagnation. The stage in which a particular industry (and thus, a firm within the industry) currently exists plays a major role in the way investors view its future.

industry segment An identifiable component of a business. The segment may be identified by product line, geographic region, division, or other divisible part of the company. Firms often evaluate performance on a segment basis. Segments also may be sold as the firm reevaluates its product lines or territories.

inelastic Of or relating to the demand for a good or service when quantity purchased varies little in response to price changes in the good or service. For example, the demand for medicines and medical services is generally inelastic because the quantity purchased by consumers is unresponsive to price changes. Producers of products and services facing inelastic demand curves have an easier time passing on price increases. —Compare ELASTIC.

inflation A general increase in the price level of goods and services. Unexpected inflation tends to be detrimental to security prices, primarily because it forces interest rates higher. A point to keep in mind is that a certain amount of inflation is already embodied in security prices. —Compare DEFLATION. —See

also CONSUMER PRICE INDEX; CORE INFLATION; COST-PUSH INFLATION; DEMAND-PULL IN-
FLATION; GDP DEFLATOR; PRODUCER PRICE INDEX; PURCHASING POWER RISK.

inflation accounting   Alteration of a firm's financial statements to account for
changes in the purchasing power of money. With inflation accounting, gains
and losses from holding monetary items during periods of changing prices are
recognized. Likewise, long-term assets and liabilities are adjusted for changing
price levels. Inflation accounting is used to supplement regular financial statements in order to illustrate how changing price levels can affect a firm. —Also
called *general price level accounting*.

inflationary psychology   Consumers' belief that prices will inevitably rise, a
belief that drives them to speed up purchases especially of real assets (that is,
gold, diamonds, and real estate) and avoid investment in financial assets (that
is, stocks and bonds). As a result, the consumers themselves can cause the inflation that they fear will occur.

inflation hedge   An investment with a value directly related to the level of general price changes. Among securities, the common stock of natural resource
companies (such as gold, timber, and oil) is often considered an inflation hedge
because the value of the companies' assets should rise during a period of inflation.

inflation-indexed security   A security with a rate of return linked to some
specified measure of inflation. For example, Series I U.S. savings bonds pay
holders a specified fixed rate adjusted for changes in the consumer price index.

inflation premium   The portion of an investment's return that compensates for
expected increases in the general price level of goods and services. The expectation of rising inflation results in higher long-term interest rates as lenders and
borrowers build in an increased inflation premium.

inheritance tax   A state tax levied on the recipient of an estate rather than on
the estate itself. The tax varies by state and its severity in a given state usually
depends on the kinship between the deceased and the heir. Some states levy a
tax on the estate instead of a tax on the amount inherited. —Compare ESTATE
TAX. —Also called *death tax*.

in-house trade   Execution of a customer order within a brokerage firm rather
than on an exchange. For example, a brokerage firm might match a customer
order to buy at $10½ with another customer order to sell the same stock at
$10⅝. An in-house trade is likely to be profitable for the brokerage firm but
does not necessarily result in customers obtaining the best price. —Compare
PREFERENCE. —See also RULE 19C–3.

---

inheritance tax

How can I minimize inheritance tax?

Estate and gift tax law is in a state of flux. An estate planning attorney will have the
most up-to-date information available to assist you in minimizing your tax liability.
Avoiding probate should also be a goal. Joint ownership, revocable living trust, irrevocable trusts, and life insurance may be useful tools to avoid or eliminate the estate
tax and costs of probate, but only an experienced estate planning attorney can help
you decide which of these tools will suit your needs best.

Gloria Cole, Attorney, private practice, Weston, MA

initial delivery —See ORIGINAL DELIVERY.

initial margin requirement The minimum portion of a new security purchase that an investor must pay for in cash. For example, with an initial margin requirement of 60%, the most an investor can borrow is $2,000 on a $5,000 purchase. This requirement is determined by the Federal Reserve Board. —Also called *margin requirement.*

initial public offering (IPO) A company's first sale of stock to the public. Securities offered in an IPO are often but not always those of young, small companies seeking outside equity capital and a public market for their stock. Investors purchasing stock in IPOs generally assume very large risks for the possibility of large gains. —See also PRE-IPO.

in play Of or relating to a company that has been, or is widely rumored to be, the target of a takeover attempt. After a firm is in play, additional offers may be forthcoming.

inside buildup The cash value increases in a life insurance policy. Inside buildup is free of income taxation during the period of buildup, thus making cash-value insurance a more desirable investment vehicle for people in high income-tax brackets.

inside director A member of a firm's board of directors who is also employed in another capacity by that firm. An example is a chief executive officer who also sits on the board. —Compare OUTSIDE DIRECTOR.

inside information Details of a company's affairs that are known by its directors and officers but are not yet released to the public. For example, initial data on an oil strike that has not been publicized is inside information.

inside market A market involving price quotes for a security trade between dealers. Price quotes between dealers usually entail a higher bid and a lower ask than quotes on the same security made to individual investors. —Compare RETAIL MARKET. —See also WHOLESALE.

insider **1.** A person who, because of his or her position within a firm, has access to proprietary information unavailable to the general public. Although the term obviously includes corporate officers, it also may extend to relatives of these officers or to employees of other firms having a special relationship with the firm in question. **2.** Officially, an officer, a director, or the owner of 10% or more of a firm's securities. —See also FORM 3.

insider trading The illegal buying or selling of securities on the basis of information that is generally unavailable to the public. An example is the purchase by a director of shares of his or her firm's stock just before the release of surprisingly good earnings information.

> **⋀⋀ CASE STUDY** In November 2001 the Securities and Exchange Commission charged 15 individuals with insider trading in the shares of Nvidia Corporation, a California maker of graphics chips. According to the SEC, in March 2000 Nvidia's president used e-mail to inform employees the firm had won a major contract to supply chips for Microsoft Corporation's new Xbox video game system. News of the contract was not announced to the public until five days following the employee e-mail. The time lag allowed the 15 individuals—11 employees plus 4 people tipped by the employees—to profit by purchasing Nvidia shares prior to the public announcement of the

contract. The case was relatively unusual in that the individuals charged with insider trading were low-level employees rather than high-level executives.

Insider Trading Sanctions Act of 1984 The federal legislation that increased sanctions against individuals who buy or sell securities while in possession of information that is pertinent to the transaction and not available to the public.

Insider Trading and Securities Fraud Enforcement Act of 1988 The federal legislation that increased the potential liabilities associated with insider trading and other fraudulent activities. This act provides informers with cash awards, allows individuals who claim damages to file suit, and encourages companies to implement improved internal controls.

insolvent Unable to meet debts or discharge liabilities. —Compare SOLVENT.

installment A partial payment on a financial obligation. For example, an annual or monthly payment to the seller of an asset, such as a farm, on a long-term contract is an installment. Installments are composed partly of principal and partly of interest. If all the installments are of equal size, each subsequent payment incorporates an increasing amount of principal and a decreasing amount of interest.

installment method The accounting method of treating revenue from the sale of an asset on installments such that profits are recognized in proportion to the percentage of the sale price collected in a given accounting period. For example, if an asset with a book value of $12,000 is sold for $15,000 and payment is to occur in 5 equal installments of $3,000 each, the seller would record annual profits of ($15,000 − $12,000)/5, or $600. The installment method is a conservative way of treating an installment sale because profit is not recognized until receipt of payment.

installment sale A sale in which the buyer is scheduled to make a series of payments over a period of time. An installment sale can offer certain tax advantages; however, the seller may have a lengthy wait before receiving the entire proceeds. Virtually any asset, including securities, may be disposed of through an installment sale.

Instinet® A registered securities exchange in the form of an electronic network that links subscribers who wish to display bid and ask quotations for equity and debt securities. Instinet also offers research and clearing and settlement services. The firm was founded in 1969 and was acquired by Reuters Holdings in 1987.

Institute of Management Accountants (IMA) A professional organization for individuals employed in management accounting and financial management. IMA provides educational resources, establishes a set of ethical standards, and awards professional certification to members who pass a series of examinations and provide proof of continuing education. —See also CERTIFIED IN FINANCIAL MANAGEMENT; CERTIFIED IN MANAGEMENT ACCOUNTING.

institutional account A brokerage account of an investment management organization.

institutional broker A broker specializing in security trades for institutions such as banks and pension funds. Institutions usually trade in large blocks that require special handling.

institutional favorites —See NIFTY FIFTY.

institutional investor An entity such as an insurance company, an investment company, a pension fund, or a trust department that invests large sums in the securities markets. Institutional investing has had an increasing impact on securities trading: as the institutions buy and sell huge blocks of the same securities during short periods of time, large security fluctuations ensue.

institutional ownership The ownership of a company's stock by mutual funds, pension funds, and other institutional investors, generally expressed as percentage of outstanding shares. A high proportion of institutional ownership may result in relatively large changes in a stock's price, as institutions tend to buy and sell the same stocks at the same time.

Institutional Shareholder Services (ISS) A private organization that provides proxy voting and corporate governance services to institutional investors. The firm evaluates proxy proposals and makes voting recommendations to its clients. ISS was an important player in the proxy fight over Hewlett-Packard's proposed acquisition of Compaq.

instrument A legal document, such as a check, a security, or a will.

in-substance debt defeasance —See DEFEASANCE.

insubstantial quantity The limited amount of stock or bonds from a new security issue that may be allocated to certain people involved in or related to other people involved in the distribution of the security issue.

insured bond A municipal debt obligation for which interest and principal are guaranteed by a private insurance company. Municipal issuers pay a premium to purchase the insurance in order to obtain a higher credit quality rating and a lower rate of interest on the debt.

intangible asset An asset such as a patent, goodwill, or a mining claim that has no physical properties. Since intangible assets are often difficult to value accurately, such assets when included on a corporate balance sheet may have a true value significantly different from the dollar amounts indicated there. —Compare TANGIBLE ASSET.

intangible drilling costs Expenses incurred while exploring for gas, geothermal, or oil reserves. These items may be expensed in the year incurred, or they may be capitalized and deducted throughout a period of years. Intangible drilling costs are an effective means of reducing taxes because they can be used to offset income in a single year even though the costs were incurred in order to produce or develop a capital asset (energy reserves) that will in turn generate income for many years. Costs for fuel, preparation of a site, and wages are examples of intangible drilling costs.

intangible tax A tax imposed by some states or local governments on the value of intangible assets such as stocks, bonds, money market funds, and bank account balances.

integrated market making —See SIDE-BY-SIDE TRADING.

intercommodity spread An investment position in which an investor purchases one commodity and sells short a related but different commodity. An example of an intercommodity spread would be the purchase of a futures contract in silver and the sale of a contract in gold.

interdelivery spread In options or futures, the purchasing of contracts expiring in one month and the selling of contracts expiring in a different month but on the same stock or commodity. For example, an investor might buy a June coffee contract and sell a September coffee contract.

interest 1. Payment for the use of borrowed money. 2. An investor's equity in a business.

interest adjustment Extra proceeds going to an investor who submits a convertible bond for conversion to account for interest accrued since the last date of record for an interest payment. —Also called *adjustment.*

interest coverage A measure of a firm's ability to meet required interest obligations. A high coverage ratio indicates enhanced ability to make timely interest payments. Interest coverage is calculated by dividing the firm's operating income by its required interest payments. —Compare FIXED-CHARGE COVERAGE. —Also called *times interest earned.* —See also DEBT MANAGEMENT RATIO.

interest dates The dates on which interest is paid to bondholders, nearly always involving two payments per year on either the first or the fifteenth of the month. Interest dates are set at the time of issue and remain unchanged throughout the life of the bond. —See also PAYMENT DATE.

interest equalization tax A tax, no longer in effect, that was levied on income received from foreign securities owned by U.S. residents. By discouraging investment in foreign securities, the tax was intended to prevent an outflow of U.S. dollars.

interest-only (IO) Of or relating to a derivative mortgage security scheduled to receive interest only from a pool of mortgages. An IO derivative security has no par value, and the owner of the security can lose money because of mortgage prepayments that reduce or eliminate interest payments. —Compare PRINCIPAL-ONLY.

interest rate future A contract on the future delivery of interest-bearing securities, primarily U.S. Treasury bills (on the Chicago Mercantile Exchange) or Treasury bonds (on the Chicago Board of Trade), although contracts on certificates of deposit, Ginnie Mae certificates, and Treasury notes are also available. As with other futures contracts, interest rate futures permit a buyer and a seller to lock in the price of an asset (in this case, a specified package of securities) for future delivery. The contracts are large in amount ($1 million for bills and $100,000 for bonds) and lend themselves to sophisticated analysis. Amateurs beware!

interest rate option An option contract on interest-bearing securities or on a futures contract on interest-bearing securities. These options are generally used as a means to manage the risk of a bond portfolio.

interest rate parity The interrelationship between currency exchange forward rates and spot rates that result from interest rate differentials. If interest rates are higher in the United States than in a foreign country, the forward dollar value of the foreign currency will exceed the spot dollar value of the foreign currency.

interest rate risk The risk that interest rates will rise and reduce the market value of an investment. Long-term fixed-income securities, such as bonds and preferred stock, subject their owners to the greatest amount of interest rate risk. Short-term securities, such as Treasury bills, are influenced much less by interest rate movements. Common stock prices are also affected by changes in interest rates, although the linkage is less clear than is the case with debt securities and preferred stock.

interest rate swap —See SWAP.

interest-sensitive stock A stock whose price tends to move in the opposite direction from that of interest rates. Interest-sensitive stocks include nearly all preferred stocks and the common stocks of industries such as electric utilities and savings and loans. A common stock may be interest-sensitive either because its dividend is relatively fixed (as with an electric utility) or because the firm raises a large portion of its funds through borrowing (as with a savings and loan or a commercial bank).

interim dividend A dividend declared before a firm's annual earnings and dividend-paying ability are accurately known by its management. An interim dividend is ordinarily paid in each of the first three quarters of the fiscal year. These payments are followed by a final dividend at the time that earnings can be accurately determined. —Compare FINAL DIVIDEND 2.

interim financing The financing that supports a transaction until permanent financing can be arranged.

interim report A financial statement that has a date other than that of the end of a fiscal year. Interim reports, generally unaudited, are intended to indicate the level of a firm's performance, usually during quarterly intervals of the fiscal year.

interlocking directorates Boards of directors of different firms that have one or more of the same people serving as directors. Interlocking directorates are illegal among competing firms.

intermarket spread swap The sale of one bond combined with the purchase of another bond that has entirely different features in order to improve the investor's position.

Intermarket Surveillance Information System A system for storing options and equity trade information from eight national securities exchanges, including the New York Stock Exchange and the National Association of Securities Dealers. Included in the system is information on trades, the places where they occurred, the firms involved, and the brokers making the trades.

intermarket trading Trading that occurs between two or more markets. For example, an individual might engage in arbitrage by purchasing stock index futures on one exchange and then selling options on the same futures on another exchange.

Intermarket Trading System (ITS) An interconnection of security trading floors that allows brokers and market makers to trade securities in additional markets. The system is intended to allow customers to obtain the most favorable price available on any of the participating exchanges. —See also NATIONAL SECURITIES TRADING SYSTEM.

intermediary —See FINANCIAL INTERMEDIARY.

intermediate bond A debt security with a maturity of 7 to 15 years. —Also called *medium-term bond.* —See also LONG BOND; SHORT BOND.

intermediate-term Of or relating to an investment with an expected holding period somewhere between short-term and long-term. For bonds, collectibles, and real estate, intermediate-term usually refers to a holding period that ranges between one and seven years. For stocks, intermediate-term indicates a somewhat shorter period of six months to several years. For futures and options contracts, intermediate-term ranges from one month to several months.

intermediation The flow of funds through financial intermediaries (such as banks and thrifts) on its way to borrowers. Money deposited at financial institutions that make the money available to corporate borrowers is an example of intermediation. This process tends to facilitate saving and investing in sophisticated financial systems. —Compare DISINTERMEDIATION.

internal audit The examination of a company's records and reports by its employees. Internal audits are usually intended to prevent fraud and to ensure compliance with board directives and management policies. In contrast, the financial statements presented to stockholders are typically prepared by outside parties to ensure absolute objectivity. —Compare EXTERNAL AUDIT.

internal financing The financing of asset purchases with funds generated in the usual course of operations rather than funds that are borrowed or raised from the issuance of stock.

internal funds Funds that are raised within a firm. For example, income after taxes and noncash expenses, such as depreciation, provide a firm with funds to use in the acquisition of investments. Companies that are able to finance expenditures with internal funds are not required to rely on borrowing or the sale of additional shares of stock. —Compare EXTERNAL FUNDS.

internalize To send a customer order from a brokerage firm to the firm's own specialist or market maker. Internalizing an order allows a broker to share in the profit (spread between the bid and ask) of executing the order.

internal rate of return (IRR) The rate of discount on an investment that equates the present value of the investment's cash outflows with the present value of the investment's cash inflows. Internal rate of return is analogous to yield to maturity for a bond.

Internal Revenue Code The tax law of the United States.

Internal Revenue Service (IRS) The agency of the U.S. Treasury Department that administers the Internal Revenue Code.

International Accounting Standards Board (IASB) A privately funded, London-based organization whose goal is to establish a single set of enforceable global financial reporting standards. The IASB was originally formed in 1973 as the International Accounting Standards Committee.

International Federation of Stock Exchanges —See WORLD FEDERATION OF EXCHANGES.

international fund A mutual fund that invests in the equity securities of companies located outside the country in which the fund is located. —Compare GLOBAL FUND.

International Monetary Fund (IMF) An international financial agency that is affiliated with the United Nations and has as goals the stabilization of foreign exchange rates, lowering of trade barriers, and correction of trade imbalances among countries. The IMF, which was established in 1944, works with countries much as a credit counselor works with individuals having financial difficulties.

international fund / global fund

What is the best method of investing in foreign securities?

Investing directly in international markets can be very expensive, as transaction fees are generally higher than in the United States. Additionally, smaller foreign markets often charge a higher premium when trading stocks. Other considerations are lack of liquidity and information in some foreign markets, different market operations, and withholding taxes. It is therefore recommendable that the novice investor invests in either global or international mutual funds. Although fund companies also pay transaction and exchange fees, they get better rates because of larger transaction sizes. Finally, international fund managers have the expertise it takes to maneuver through foreign economic, political, and currency trends. Also, fund managers have the ability to hedge against currency risks, thereby "insuring" part of your investment.

Thomas M. Tarnowski, Senior Business Analyst
Global Investment Banking Division, Citigroup, Inc.—Salomon Smith Barney, New York, NY, and London, UK

International Organization of Securities Commissions (IOSCO) An association of securities commissions and similar bodies with responsibility for securities regulation in their home countries. IOSCO promotes the development and efficiency of securities markets and encourages cooperation in the establishment and maintenance of regulatory standards relative to world securities and futures markets. The IOSCO Secretariat is permanently based in Madrid, Spain.

International Securities Exchange (ISE) An SEC-registered securities exchange that commenced operation in 2000 for electronic trading of options. The exchange has ten designated trading areas, each staffed by market makers who make orderly markets including firm bid and ask prices for designated options. The ISE was funded by a consortium of broker-dealers and is based in New York City.

Internet stock The equity security of a company engaged primarily in a business associated with the Internet. —Also called *dot-com.*

interpositioning The involvement of a third party between a broker-dealer and the best available market price that results in the customer paying a bigger markup or markdown than would have been the case if the third party had not been present. For example, Dealer A satisfies a customer order to buy a security by purchasing the security through Dealer B who in turn purchases the security from the market maker. Dealer B marks up the security to Dealer A, who then marks up the security again when selling it to the customer. Interpositioning is considered unethical by the National Association of Securities Dealers.

inter vivos trust —See LIVING TRUST.

intestate Of, relating to, or being an individual who has died without leaving a valid will. In such a case, the estate of the deceased is distributed according to the laws of the state in which he or she resided.

in-the-money —Used to describe a call (put) option that has a strike price that is less (more) than the price of the underlying asset. If Convergys common stock is trading at $40 per share, a call option on Convergys with a strike price of $35 is in-the-money.

in the tank —Used to describe a security or a securities market during or following a period of large price declines.

intraday In the course of a day. For example, during trading on March 8, 2002, AT&T Corp., common stock reached an intraday low of $15.73 before closing at $15.88.

intrastate offering A security offering in which the issue is offered and sold only to persons within the state in which the issuer is incorporated. Intrastate offerings are exempt from registration under the Securities Act of 1933.

intrinsic value The value of a security, justified by factors such as assets, dividends, earnings, and management quality. Intrinsic value is at the core of fundamental analysis since it is used in an attempt to calculate the value for an individual stock and then compare it with the market price. Because analysts view facts differently, there is often a wide disparity in estimates of a particular stock's intrinsic value.

invasion powers A provision in a trust that permits the trustee to use the principal of the trust if its income is insufficient to fulfill the requirements of the beneficiary. However, trustees are usually prohibited from exercising this power without prior authorization.

inventory The amount of raw materials, work in process, and finished goods being held for sale at a given time. Diamonds held by a jeweler, engines owned by General Motors, and canned and frozen foods in a grocery store chain's warehouse are examples of inventory. Inventory is generally the least liquid item listed by a firm in the current asset account of its balance sheet. —See also BEGINNING INVENTORY; ENDING INVENTORY.

inventory profit Profit that results from the increase in value that assets undergo during the time they are held in inventory. Inventory profit, ordinarily due to general inflation, is not considered to be of high quality because it is incidental to the firm's main business. —See also FIRST-IN, FIRST-OUT; LAST-IN, FIRST-OUT.

inventory turnover A measure indicating the number of times a firm sells and replaces its inventory during a given period and calculated by dividing the cost of goods sold by the average inventory level. A relatively low inventory turnover may indicate ineffective inventory management (that is, carrying too large an inventory) or carrying out-of-date inventory to avoid writing off inventory losses against income. A high inventory turnover is generally desirable.

inventory valuation The cost assigned to inventory for the purpose of establishing its current value. Inventory valuation is determined according to the basis by which a firm assumes inventory units are sold. If the first units acquired are assumed to be the first units sold (first-in, first-out), costs of the last units purchased are used for valuing inventory remaining in stock. Conversely, if the last units acquired are assumed to be the first units sold (last-in, first-out), the costs of the first units purchased are used for valuing the inventory remaining in stock.

inverse floater A derivative security that has a yield that is inversely related to interest rates. Inverse floaters are one part of a long-term bond. A portion of the bond's current interest income is used to pay money market rates to holders of the regular floating-rate notes. The remainder of current interest and changes in the bond's market value are earned by holders of the inverse floaters. Holders of this type of security can have major losses as a result of increases in interest rates. These securities are used primarily, although not always successfully, by professional portfolio managers.

inverted formation   In technical analysis, a chart pattern that is upside down from its usual configuration. For example, a saucer pattern is a U-shaped curve indicating a market bottom. An inverted saucer is an arched formation indicating a market top. When a chart formation is inverted, it indicates the opposite future stock movement of the basic formation. Thus, while a head-and-shoulders formation is a bearish indicator, an inverted head-and-shoulders formation is a bullish indicator.

inverted market   In futures or options trading, a market with nearby contracts having a price that is higher than more distant contracts. This unusual situation may occur when the underlying asset is heavily in demand.   —Compare CON-TANGO.   —Also called *backwardation.*

inverted saucer   —See DOME.

inverted scale   An issue of serial bonds having yields on short-term securities that exceed yields on long-term securities. An inverted scale is generally caused when investors judge interest rates to be unusually high and expect them to fall.

inverted yield curve   —See NEGATIVE YIELD CURVE.

invested capital   An investment measure calculated by adding an investor's net worth and long-term liabilities.

investment   **1.** Property acquired for the purpose of producing income for its owner. Just as plants and equipment are investments for manufacturers, stocks and bonds are investments for individuals.   **2.** Expenditures made for income-producing assets.

investment adviser   A person who offers professional investment advice. Investment advisers are required to register with the SEC.

Investment Advisers Act of 1940   A federal act that defines what an investment adviser is, requires such advisors to register with the SEC, and sets standards for advertising, disclosure, fees, liability, and record keeping. The Act was passed to protect investors.   —Also called *Advisers Act.*

investment banker   A firm that functions as an intermediary between organizations that need additional funds and individuals and organizations having surplus funds to invest. An investment banker, an expert in the financial markets, sells its expertise to organizations wishing to raise funds.   —See also PRI-MARY DISTRIBUTION; STANDBY UNDERWRITING.

investment boutique   A relatively small, specialized brokerage company. —Also called *boutique.*

investment climate   The overall environment for investments. A favorable investment climate is likely to include low inflation, falling interest rates, growing corporate earnings, political stability, and a high degree of consumer confidence.

investment club   A group of people who meet regularly and pool their funds to invest in securities. In many instances, a club is formed as much for social and educational reasons as for making profits. Since most investment clubs are formed as partnerships, their dividends, realized capital gains, and losses are passed through for tax reporting by the individual members. *See Investment Tip on p. 198.*

investment club

Are investment clubs a good idea? Why?

Investment clubs offer many benefits with few drawbacks. The individual investor joins with a group of peers to invest in stocks and other securities. The clubs focus on education: each member learns from and teaches the others. The monthly meetings create a comfortable social setting to help the individual stay focused on investment goals. Members are usually required to contribute a minimum amount each month to the investment pool as well as commit time to do investment research. And the clubs' financial returns are often very successful. To get started, contact the National Association of Investors Corporation (www.better-investing.org), which offers guidance to new clubs, or visit www.bivio.com and register to connect with others.

Sharon Rich, Financial Planner, WOMONEY, Belmont, MA

investment company A firm in which investors pool their funds to allow for diversification and professional management. Because individual firms often specialize in particular types of investments, the potential returns and risks vary considerably among firms. Charges to investors—both to acquire shares in a firm and to pay management for operating the company—vary significantly from investment company to investment company. —Also called *management company.* —See also CLOSED-END INVESTMENT COMPANY; CONDUIT THEORY; MANAGEMENT FEE; MUTUAL FUND; PERFORMANCE FEE; REGULATED INVESTMENT COMPANY.

Investment Company Act A 1940 act that regulates the management of investment companies in relation to items such as financial statements, stated investment goals, personnel, debt issuance, and directors. The goal of the Act was to provide adequate disclosure and to curb the management abuses prevalent during the 1920s and 1930s.

Investment Company Amendments Act of 1970 An act that regulates sales charges and penalties on withdrawals from mutual fund accumulation plans. This Act sets the maximum load fee that may be charged to buyers of mutual funds and determines how the fees may be set in accumulation plans.

Investment Company Institute (ICI) A national association for mutual funds, closed-end investment companies, and unit investment trusts. ICI, established in 1940, collects and publishes industry data, represents its members in matters of regulation and taxation, and promotes the interests of the industry and its shareholders.

Investment Counsel Association of America (ICAA) A nonprofit organization founded in 1937 to represent the interests of federally registered investment adviser firms. ICAA establishes standards of practice for its members and serves as an advocate in dealings with Congress, the SEC, and state securities commissions.

investment-grade Of, relating to, or being a bond suitable for purchase by institutions under the prudent man rule. Investment-grade is restricted to those bonds graded BBB and above by Standard & Poor's and graded Baa3 and above by Moody's. —Compare HIGH-GRADE. —Also called *bank-grade.*

investment history The past relationship between a broker-dealer and an investor. Rules of the National Association of Securities Dealers require a consideration of investment history in making judgments concerning the adequacy of an underwriter's performance in issuing securities. For example, sale of a hot issue to certain accounts generally must conform to the investment history of those accounts.

investment letter   A letter from the buyer of a private placement stating that the securities are for investment purposes and not for resale within two years. An investment letter is supposed to assure the SEC that the issue is not the first stage of a regular public offering subject to normal registration requirements. —See also RESTRICTED SECURITY.

investment objective   The financial goal or goals of an investor. An investor may wish to maximize current income, maximize capital gains, or set a middle course of current income with some appreciation of capital. Defining investment objectives helps to determine the investments an individual should select.

investment philosophy   The investment ideology practiced by a professional money manager. For example, a portfolio manager may seek maximum capital gains at the expense of volatile and uncertain returns. An individual investor should choose a money manager with an investment philosophy that coincides with the individual's investment objectives.

investment vehicle   A specific investment having attributes that are intended to accomplish certain goals. Examples of investment vehicles include common stock, preferred stock, bonds, options, futures, annuities, and collectibles.

investor   A person who purchases income-producing assets. An investor—as opposed to a speculator—usually considers safety of principal to be of primary importance. In addition, investors frequently purchase assets with the expectation of holding them for a longer period of time than speculators.

involuntary bankruptcy   Bankruptcy that is forced by creditors instead of being initiated by the firm or individual. —Compare VOLUNTARY BANKRUPTCY. —See also CHAPTER 7; CHAPTER 11.

IO —See INTEREST-ONLY.

IOSCO —See INTERNATIONAL ORGANIZATION OF SECURITIES COMMISSIONS.

IPO —See INITIAL PUBLIC OFFERING.

IRA   A custodial account or trust in which individuals may set aside earned income in a tax-deferred retirement plan. For individuals who earn under a specified amount or who are not in an employer-sponsored retirement plan, contributions to an IRA (subject to an annual maximum) are deferred along with any income the contributions earn. Withdrawals at retirement are fully taxable. For individuals in an employer-sponsored plan and having an adjusted gross income above a specified amount, all or part of the contribution may be taxable although any income earned in the IRA is tax deferred. The rules governing IRAs were significantly altered in the 1986 tax reform. IRA investment opportunities include certificates of deposit, mutual funds, and securities purchased through brokerage accounts. *See Investment Tip on p. 200.* —Also called *individual retirement account.* —See also COVERDELL EDUCATION SAVINGS ACCOUNT; KEOGH PLAN; ROTH IRA; SELF-DIRECTED IRA; SIMPLIFIED EMPLOYEE PENSION PLAN.

IRA rollover   Reinvestment of a lump-sum distribution from an IRA when physical receipt of funds has been taken by the investor. The lump-sum distribution must be deposited in an IRA rollover account within 60 days of receipt to escape taxation. —Compare IRA TRANSFER.

IRA

Is it a good idea to name my estate as the beneficiary of my IRA?

Generally speaking, this is not advisable. If you name your estate as the beneficiary of your IRA, then the assets held inside your IRA must be distributed according to your last will and testament and the proceeds of your IRA will go through probate. Most IRA owners like to keep assets inside their IRA for the longest time period allowed by law, thereby maximizing the dollars that can be accumulated on a tax-deferred basis while also delaying the payment of income taxes for as long as possible. IRAs are subject to annual required minimum distribution requirements once the IRA owner reaches age 70½. These requirements are based upon either the individual life expectancy of the IRA owner or the joint life expectancy of the IRA owner and his beneficiary. Because your estate has no life expectancy, there is no way to stretch out the period during which your IRA assets can remain inside your IRA and grow tax-deferred even if this is what your IRA beneficiaries want. Thus, if you die prior to age 70½, naming your estate as your beneficiary, the assets held in your IRA will have to be liquidated and proceeds disbursed over a five-year period to the beneficiaries you named in your will. If your IRA was a traditional IRA, your beneficiaries will have to include every IRA disbursement in their taxable income for the year during which the disbursement was received. If your IRA was a Roth IRA, your beneficiaries won't owe any income tax on your IRA disbursements, but they will still be forced to withdraw your IRA assets by the end of the five-year period, whereas they could have kept your IRA assets inside of your IRA for many more years if you had named specific beneficiaries for your IRA. If you die after age 70½, naming your estate as your beneficiary, your IRA beneficiaries will have to take annual minimum distributions from your IRA that are based on what the federal government's actuaries have determined would have been your remaining life expectancy if you were still alive, reduced by one for each year thereafter. From a financial planning viewpoint, the biggest disadvantage of naming your estate as the beneficiary of your IRA is the basic inability to stretch out the distributions from your IRA to maximize the buildup of value and delay the payment of income taxes, as described above.

Stephanie G. Bigwood, CFP, ChFC, CSA, Assistant Vice President
Lombard Securities, Incorporated, Baltimore, MD

IRA transfer The direct transfer of assets in an individual retirement account from one trustee to another. With an IRA transfer, the investor does not take physical possession of the IRA assets; thus, there are no tax consequences to the movement of the funds. A direct transfer may result in some lost income to the investor since the funds could remain in transit for a number of days. —Compare IRA ROLLOVER.

IRR —See INTERNAL RATE OF RETURN.

irregular coupon A bond interest payment for more or less than six-months' interest. The first coupon on many bonds is irregular because payment is other than six months from the dated date. —Also called *odd coupon.*

irrevocable trust A trust in which the grantor gives up any right to amendments or termination. Income from an irrevocable trust is taxable to the beneficiary if disbursed or to the trust if not disbursed. —Compare REVOCABLE TRUST.

IRS —See INTERNAL REVENUE SERVICE.

ISE —See INTERNATIONAL SECURITIES EXCHANGE.

iShares Exchange-traded funds with portfolios based on a series of stock indexes including the S&P indexes, the Dow Jones indexes, and the Russell indexes. iShares are also available for MSCI foreign indexes. Shares of each fund represent proportional ownership of individual stocks that make up the index on which the fund is based. iShares were developed by Barclays Global Investors and are mostly traded on the American Stock Exchange.

Island A major electronic communications network that attempts to match investor orders to buy and sell NYSE, ASE, and Nasdaq National Market System and SmallCap securities. Orders that cannot be immediately matched are displayed as limit orders until matched, cancelled, or expiration. Only limit orders placed by subscribing broker-dealers are accepted by Island.

ISS —See INSTITUTIONAL SHAREHOLDER SERVICES.

issue A particular grouping of an organization's securities. For example, General Motors has a number of different issues of preferred stock listed on the New York Stock Exchange.

issue To sell securities in the primary market. For example, in late 1996, Florida Panthers Holdings, Inc., owner of the NHL hockey team, issued 2,700,000 Class A shares of common stock at a price of $10 per share.

issue date —See DATED DATE.

issued capital stock Capital stock that has been authorized and issued but that may have been reacquired in part. Issued capital stock reacquired as Treasury stock or stock that has been retired is not included in earnings-per-share calculations.

issuer An organization that is selling or has sold its securities to the public.

itemized deduction —See DEDUCTION.

ITS —See INTERMARKET TRADING SYSTEM.

J

j —Used in the dividend column of stock transaction tables to indicate that the listed dividend was paid earlier in the year but that the latest board meeting voted an omitted or a deferred dividend or decided to take no action on the dividend: *ChockFull j.*

January effect The tendency of stocks to perform better in January than at any other time of the year. Some analysts speculate that the stock market tends to become oversold in December when investors sell to establish losses for tax purposes or to obtain money for holiday spending.

CASE STUDY One investment strategy that uses stock index futures or stock index options to profit from the January effect assumes that equities of small firms continue to outperform equities of large firms during the early part of each calendar year. Using this strategy, an investor could take advantage of the higher returns offered by small-caps by purchasing options or futures on the Value Line Composite Index, which includes more than 1,700 stocks, and simultaneously selling options or futures on a blue chip index such as the S&P 500 or the Major Market Index. This spread should produce a profit regardless of an increase or decrease in the overall market so long as small-caps outperforms large-caps. This same spread will be a losing investment if the January effect doesn't hold and small-caps underperforms large-caps.

joint account

Is a joint account preferable for investing couples?

Joint ownership occurs when more than one person has rights and privileges to an account. It is practical to invest jointly in many situations, as access or availability of the assets occurs almost immediately upon death of either of the parties. By law, ownership passes directly to the surviving joint owner, even if a will states otherwise. However, for larger estates (over $1 million), other forms of ownership may be preferred. Proper estate planning to lower estate taxes or to transfer assets to trusts rather than to an individual would call for assets to be moved out of joint ownership.

Jeffrey S. Levine, CPA, MST, Alkon & Levine, PC, Newton, MA

January indicator The tendency of stock market movement in January to set the market trend for the entire year. Thus, if a market average is higher at the end of January than it is at the beginning of January, chances are that the year will produce a rising market.

job lot In commodities trading, the quantity of a commodity that is smaller than what is specified in a standard contract.

joint account A brokerage account in which two or more individuals hold joint interests. Joint accounts may be established in a number of different forms that produce very different results. —Compare INDIVIDUAL ACCOUNT. —See also PARTNERSHIP ACCOUNT.

joint account agreement A form that is required when opening a brokerage account or bank account in the names of two or more individuals.

joint and survivor annuity An annuity that pays a lifetime income to the annuitant and to another person, generally a spouse. The payments may be scheduled to decrease at the death of either recipient. —Also called *joint life annuity*.

jointly and severally Of or relating to a securities offering in which the underwriter is responsible for its own allocation and for a proportionate share of any securities that remain unsold. Thus, a syndicate member allocated 10% of the securities to be sold would also be responsible for 10% of any unsold securities. —Compare SEVERALLY BUT NOT JOINTLY. —Also called *severally and jointly*.

joint life annuity —See JOINT AND SURVIVOR ANNUITY.

joint ownership Ownership of an asset, such as property, by two or more parties. Joint ownership of property has advantages and disadvantages compared with individual ownership. For example, the property automatically passes to the co-owners upon the death of one of the other owners. Also, with one type of joint ownership, one owner can sell the property without the permission of the other owners. —See also JOINT TENANCY WITH RIGHT OF SURVIVORSHIP; TENANCY BY THE ENTIRETY; TENANCY IN COMMON.

joint return A single income-tax return filed commonly by a husband and wife. In a joint return, the tax liability is calculated on the premise that each spouse has contributed equally to the reported income. A joint return is especially advantageous for couples in which one spouse has considerably more taxable income than the other spouse. —Compare SEPARATE RETURN.

joint-stock company A rare type of business organization characterized by some features of a partnership and some features of a corporation. Shares are transferrable and the company is assessed taxes according to corporate tax rates. However, the liability of each owner is unlimited. Joint-stock companies are established primarily because of the ease with which they are formed.

joint tenancy with right of survivorship (JTWROS)   Asset ownership for two or more persons in which each owner holds an equal share and may give away or sell that share without the permission of the other owner(s). In the event of death, an owner's share is divided equally among the surviving co-owners. —Compare TENANCY IN COMMON. —Also called *right of survivorship.* —See also TENANCY BY THE ENTIRETY.

joint venture   A business undertaken by two or more individuals or companies in an effort to share risk and use differences in expertise. For example, oil companies often enter into joint ventures on particularly expensive projects carrying a high risk of failure. —See also CONSORTIUM.

Jonestown defense   Defense against a corporate takeover in the form of a poison pill so strong that it threatens the survivability of the target company. The name comes from the mid-1970s Jonestown massacre.

JTWROS   —See JOINT TENANCY WITH RIGHT OF SURVIVORSHIP.

jumbo certificate of deposit   A certificate of deposit with a denomination of $95,000 or more. Jumbo certificates of deposit are negotiable and ordinarily carry slightly higher interest rates than smaller certificates.

junior debt   A class of debt that is subordinate to another class of debt issued by the same party. Junior debt is more risky for an investor to own, but it pays a higher rate of interest than debt with greater security. Debentures are junior debt. —Compare SENIOR DEBT.

junior security   A security having a subordinate claim to assets and income with respect to another class of security. For example, preferred stock is a junior security compared with a debenture, and a debenture is a junior security compared with a mortgage bond. In general, a junior security entails greater risk but offers higher potential yields than securities with greater seniority.

junk bond   A high-risk, high-yield debt security that, if rated at all, is graded less than BBB by Standard & Poor's or BBB3 by Moody's. These securities are most appropriate for risk-oriented investors. —Also called *high-yield bond.*

junk financing   The raising of funds by issuing unsecured high-yield securities, for example, during takeover attempts in which the acquiring firm has little cash and must issue unsecured debt to finance the acquisition. —Also called *high-yield financing.*

junk muni-bond fund   A mutual fund or unit trust that invests in relatively low-grade tax-exempt bonds in order to earn a higher return. Bonds purchased for the fund are rated below investment-grade (that is, lower than BBB), or they are not rated at all.

K

k —Used in the dividend column of stock transaction tables of newspapers to indicate dividends that have been paid so far during the year on an issue of preferred stock with dividends in arrears: *pf 1.75k.*

K —Used frequently in the financial literature as a symbol for 1,000.

Kansas City Board of Trade A commodities exchange chartered in 1876 that is primarily known for trading futures and options on hard red winter wheat, the primary ingredient in bread. The exchange also trades stock index futures and options on the Value Line Index, and in 1999 it commenced trading in ISDEX Internet stock index contracts.

karat A measure of the purity of gold. Pure gold is indicated by the label 24 karat. —See also FINENESS.

Keogh plan A federally approved retirement program that permits self-employed individuals to set aside for savings up to a specified amount. All contributions and income earned by the account are tax deferred until withdrawals are made during retirement. Investment opportunities include certificates of deposit, mutual funds, and self-directed brokerage accounts.

kickers —See BELLS AND WHISTLES.

kiddie tax A federal income tax levied on the investment income of children under 14 years of age. Investment income above a specified amount is taxed at the parent's top, or marginal, tax rate. The kiddie tax is designed to make it less advantageous for parents to shift income to their children.

kill To halt a trade before sending a confirmation of it.

killer bee An individual or organization that assists a firm in repelling a takeover attempt, especially by devising defensive strategies.

knock-out option An option that loses its entire value in the event the underlying asset crosses a predetermined price level.

know-your-customer rule A requirement that brokers understand the financial needs and circumstances of a customer before providing investment advice.

Krugerrand A gold coin minted in South Africa.

L

L —Used in stock transaction tables in newspapers to indicate that during the day's activity the stock traded at a new 52-week low: *L53½.*

laddering An investment strategy in which bonds or certificates of deposit that have different maturities are assembled for a portfolio. For example, an investor with $50,000 might invest $10,000 in bonds with a two-year maturity, $10,000 in bonds with a four-year maturity, $10,000 in bonds with a six-year maturity, and so forth. Principal from matured bonds or CDs is either spent or reinvested in additional bonds or CDs with longer maturities at the top of the ladder. A laddered portfolio hedges interest rate changes by providing liquidity with short-term securities while at the same time providing a relatively steady source of income with long-term, fixed-income investments. —Also called *liquidity diversification; staggering maturities.*

laddering a stock Price manipulation in which a stock is purchased at escalating price levels in order to push the price even higher.

lagging economic indicator An economic or a financial variable, the movements of which tend to follow the movement of overall economic activity. Thus, a lagging economic indicator would reach a peak after a peak in economic activity and would hit bottom after a bottom in economic activity. —Compare LEADING ECONOMIC INDICATOR.

laissez-faire Of, relating to, or being an economy devoid of government interference.

land A firm's dollar investment in real estate.

land improvement —See IMPROVEMENT.

lapsed option An option that remains unexercised after its expiration. A lapsed option has no value.

large-cap 1. Of or relating to the common stock of a big corporation that has considerable retained earnings and a large amount of common stock outstanding. Large-cap stocks, which are generally well known, include the ones listed in the Dow Jones Averages. —See also MID-CAP 1. 2. Of or relating to a mutual fund that chooses to hold a portfolio of large-cap stocks. Large-cap funds tend to have a more stable net asset value than either microcap or mid-cap funds.

last —See CLOSE 2.

last-in, first-out (LIFO) An accounting method for identifying the order in which items are used or sold. With last-in, first-out, the most recently acquired items are assumed to be sold first. During a period of inflation, last-in, first-out accounting tends to result in high costs that reduce reported profits. The reduced profits result in a lower income-tax liability. —Compare FIRST-IN, FIRST-OUT.

last notice day The final day to issue a notice of intent to deliver on a futures contract.

last sale The most recent transaction in a particular security.

last sale rule A National Association of Securities Dealers rule that permits investors to obtain information other than just the bid and ask on an actual trade.

last trading day 1. The day on which a trader must liquidate a futures position or else be required to receive (if long) or make delivery (if short). Following this day, the particular contract will cease trading. 2. The last day on which a particular option is traded. Currently, this day is the third Friday of the expiration month.

late tape Delayed reporting of stock transactions because of unusually heavy volume. —See also DIGITS DELETED; FLASH PRICE; VOLUME DELETED.

layoff The allocation of unsold shares to syndicate members from a new issue rights offering by the managing underwriter.

LBO —See LEVERAGED BUYOUT.

LDC —See LESS DEVELOPED COUNTRY.

leader An active stock that tends to lead the general market in price movements. For example, strength and activity may have made a stock a leader in a recent upward market movement.

leadership —See MARKET LEADERSHIP.

leading economic indicator An economic or a financial variable that tends to move ahead of and in the same direction as general economic activity. —Compare LAGGING ECONOMIC INDICATOR. —See also INDEX OF LEADING ECONOMIC INDICATORS.

lead month —See NEARBY.

lead underwriter The main underwriter of a new security issue. The lead underwriter forms a distribution system to sell the security issue and is generally responsible for the largest part of the offering. —Also called *house of issue; managing underwriter.*

LEAPS —See LONG-TERM EQUITY ANTICIPATION SECURITIES.

lease An agreement that permits one party (the lessee) to use property owned by another party (the lessor). The lease, which may be written either for a short term or for a long term, often results in tax benefits to both parties. —See also CAPITAL LEASE; GROSS LEASE; LEVERAGED LEASE; NET LEASE; OPERATING LEASE.

leaseback —See SALE AND LEASEBACK.

lease fund An investment company that invests the shareholders' money in lease obligations. A lease fund is very similar to a bond fund except that the maturities of its investments are shorter. Because leases do not have an active secondary market, the fund manager must secure outside agreements to buy the leases in case the shareholders redeem their shares.

leasehold improvement An improvement of a leased asset that increases the asset's value. The expense of a leasehold improvement is carried as an asset that declines in value over time as the value is depreciated over the life of the lease or the improvement.

lease-rental bond A long-term state or municipal obligation, the proceeds of which are used to finance public-purpose projects such as police stations and public office buildings. Debt service, along with maintenance and operational expenses, is covered by rental or lease payments from the facilities, although some bonds are also general obligations of the respective issuers.

leg One side of a combination option. —See also LEG LIFTING; LEG ON; LONG LEG; SHORT LEG.

legacy cost The financial expense of supporting retiree benefits, including pensions, heath care, and insurance. Legacy cost is especially burdensome for mature companies with declining markets and a shrinking labor force.

legal —See LEGAL INVESTMENT.

LEGAL A New York Stock Exchange data bank of enforcement actions, investor complaints, and member audits.

legal capital Capital that by law or resolution must remain within a firm and that is restricted for purposes of dividends or other distributions. Legal capital is generally equal to the par or stated value of all outstanding stock. —Also called *stated capital.*

legal investment An investment that is eligible for purchase by a fiduciary. —Also called *legal; statutory investment.*

legal list The list of securities designated eligible as investments by institutions such as life insurance companies, restricted trust funds, and commercial banks. Such lists are generally limited to relatively high-grade securities of issuers exhibiting little chance of default. —Also called *approved list.*

legal list state A state with laws that restrict investment of certain funds only to securities included in a legal list.

legal opinion The statement of a bond counsel that a municipal bond issue is legal under the laws and restrictions of the issuing jurisdiction, and which indicates whether interest on the bonds is exempt from federal income taxes. A legal opinion is generally necessary to bring an issue to market. —See also EX-LEGAL.

legal transfer The transfer of a registered security when more than an endorsed bond or stock power is required for legal change of ownership. For example, transfer of securities registered to a deceased person usually requires submission of a death certificate.

legging out The closing of one side of a hedged position while leaving the other side of the hedge position open. For example, an investor might buy an October call on ExxonMobil and sell short a November call on the same stock. Subsequently buying the November call to cover the short position while continuing to hold the October call results in the investor legging out.

leg lifting The selling of one part of a combination option while retaining possession of the remaining part. For example, an owner of a straddle may sell one part (either the put or the call) when the premium is sufficient to make the entire investment profitable. —Also called *lifting a leg; taking off a leg.*

leg on To put together a combination option (that is, a straddle or a spread) one side at a time.

lemon A poorly performing investment. Many technology stocks became lemons during the 2000 and 2001 bear market.

lending at a premium The imposition of an extra fee when securities are lent by one broker to another to cover a customer's short sale. Although lending at a premium is fairly unusual, it may occur when a particular security is difficult to borrow.

lending at a rate The payment of interest by a broker-dealer on a customer's credit balance from a short sale. When the investor sells short, the broker holds the proceeds from the sale in escrow to secure the securities borrowed for the short sale. In certain instances the broker may pay the customer interest on this balance.

less developed country (LDC) A country with relatively low per capita income and little industrialization. Less developed countries have been major borrowers from a number of banks worldwide.

lessee A party using under lease an asset owned by another party. —Compare LESSOR.

lessor The owner of an asset who permits another party to use the asset under a lease. —Compare LESSEE.

letter bond —See RESTRICTED SECURITY.

letter of credit　A promise of payment in the event that certain requirements are met. A letter of credit essentially substitutes the credit of a third party (usually a large bank) for that of a borrower. In the case of municipal bonds, an LOC generally permits a trustee to draw six months' interest and sufficient funds to retire outstanding bonds at par in the event of default.

letter of guarantee　A letter from a bank stating that a customer owns a particular security and that the bank will guarantee delivery of the security. A letter of guarantee is used by an investor who is writing call options when the underlying stock is not in his or her brokerage account.

letter of intent　An agreement by a mutual fund shareholder to invest a specific sum over a defined period in order to qualify for reduced sales fees. The reduced fee may apply to an individual fund or to all the funds operated by an investment management group. —Compare BREAKPOINT. —See also RIGHT OF ACCUMULATION.

letter ruling　—See REVENUE RULING.

letter security　—See RESTRICTED SECURITY.

letter stock　—See RESTRICTED SECURITY.

level-load fund　A mutual fund that charges a relatively high 12b–1 fee.

Level 1 Service　A service providing real-time inside bid-ask quotes for securities traded on the Nasdaq system and for the OTC Bulletin Board. Level 1 Service is intended for securities firms not actively engaged in trading Nasdaq and OTC Bulletin Board stocks for themselves or for their customers.

Level 2 Service　A service providing real-time access to market maker quotations for every Nasdaq-listed security and for OTC Bulletin Board securities. Level 2 Service is intended for firms trading significant amounts of Nasdaq and OTC Bulletin Board securities for themselves or for their customers.

Level 3 Service　A service providing Level 2 Service plus the ability to enter quotes and send information. Access to Level 3 Service is limited to NASD members who are registered market makers in Nasdaq, exchange-listed, or OTC Bulletin Board securities.

leverage　The use of fixed costs in order to increase the rate of return from an investment. One example of leverage is buying securities on margin. While leverage can operate to increase rates of return, it also increases the amount of risk inherent in an investment. —See also FINANCIAL LEVERAGE; OPERATING LEVERAGE.

leveraged　Of, relating to, or being an investment situation for which borrowed funds are used. A highly leveraged investor or firm is in a relatively risky position if interest rates rise or if the investment yields are disappointingly low.

leveraged buyout (LBO)　The use of a target company's asset value to finance most or all of the debt incurred in acquiring the company. This strategy enables a takeover using little capital; however, it can result in considerably more risk to owners and creditors. —See also HOSTILE LEVERAGED BUYOUT; REVERSE LEVERAGED BUYOUT.

⋀⋀ CASE STUDY｜Leveraged buyouts (LBOs) became popular in the 1980s when firms such as Beatrice Companies, Swift, ARA Services, Levi Strauss, Jack Eckerd, and Denny's were acquired and then were taken private. With an LBO, a firm's management often borrows funds using the firm's assets as collateral. The borrowed money is used to purchase all the firm's outstanding stock. As a result, a small group of individuals is able to take control of the firm without using any or much of the group members' own money. Following the buyout the new owners frequently attempt to cut costs and sell assets in order to make the increased debt more manageable. Because the group initiating the LBO must pay a premium for the stock over the market price, an LBO nearly always benefits the stockholders of the firm to be acquired. However, investors holding bonds of the acquired company are likely to see their relative position deteriorate because of the increased debt taken on by the company. For example, the leveraged buyout of R. H. Macy & Co. produced a $16 jump in the price of its common stock at the same time the price of its debt securities fell. Most bondholders have no recourse to the increased risks they face because of the greater resultant debt.

leveraged company A company that uses borrowed money to help finance its assets. Leveraged companies often have more volatile earnings than firms that rely solely on equity financing. This volatility is offset, however, by the possibility of a higher return to stockholders if the firm is able to earn more on its assets than the cost of the money used to finance those assets.

leveraged ESOP An Employee Stock Ownership Plan that borrows funds to purchase securities of the employer.

leveraged investment company 1. An investment company that uses borrowed money to acquire securities. Leveraged investment companies produce more volatile returns for their shareholders than do investment companies not employing debt financing. 2. —See DUAL PURPOSE FUND.

leveraged lease A long-term lease in which a major part of the purchase price of the to-be-leased asset is financed by a third party. Thus, the lessor uses a combination of its own funds and borrowed money in order to purchase the asset that is then leased to another party.

leveraged recapitalization A corporate reorganization in which borrowed funds are used to pay a large one-time dividend to shareholders. The result is a company with greater financial risk because of increased debt and reduced equity. In some instances the dividend is paid in shares of stock rather than cash to inside shareholders who increase their proportional ownership and control.

leverage up To increase the portion of debt in a firm's capital structure by issuing debt and using the proceeds to repurchase stock or by financing any new expansion through debt. In the mid-1980s, firms decided to leverage up in an attempt to improve the market price of their stock, thereby fending off takeover attempts.

liability An obligation to pay an amount in money, goods, or services to another party. The balance sheet lists the liabilities. —Compare ASSET. —Also called *debt*. —See also CONTINGENT LIABILITY; CURRENT LIABILITY.

liability dividend A dividend paid with a type of debt, such as a bond. Liability dividends are usually paid when a firm is short of cash. —Compare SCRIP DIVIDEND. —See also BOND DIVIDEND.

LIBOR —See LONDON INTERBANK OFFERED RATE.

lien The legal right of a creditor to sell mortgaged assets when the debtor is unable or unwilling to meet requirements of a loan agreement. A lien makes a bondholder's claim more secure.

---

limited partnership

What type of investor should participate in a limited partnership?

The target market for investors who could participate in most limited partnerships is composed of high net worth clients who have tax problems and significant income. An investor who participates in such a partnership should understand that most limited partnerships are illiquid investments having no public market. In addition, the investor must ask himself or herself whether use can be made of the anticipated benefits and whether the high economic risk can be sustained.

George Riles, First Vice President and Resident Manager, Merrill Lynch, Albany, GA

---

life annuity A stream of payments intended to continue during the annuitant's lifetime and to cease automatically at the annuitant's death.

life-cycle fund A mutual fund that maintains a certain mix of stocks and bonds in order to attract investors of a given age and risk preference. Mutual fund families sometimes offer several different life-cycle funds with various asset allocations so as to appeal to investors of different ages.

life of contract In futures or options trading, the period of time in which trading can occur before the expiration or settlement. In general, a longer life makes an option more valuable.

life tenant A person entitled to the use of or the income from an asset during his or her lifetime. As an example, a person may stipulate in a will that all of his or her assets are to go to a charity but that the surviving spouse, designated as life tenant, is to have the use of the income from the deceased's estate for his or her lifetime, following which the remainder of the assets in the estate are to pass to the charity.

LIFFE —See LONDON INTERNATIONAL FINANCIAL FUTURES AND OPTIONS EXCHANGE.

LIFO —See LAST-IN, FIRST-OUT.

lifting a leg —See LEG LIFTING.

lighten up To reduce, but not eliminate, a particular security position when the investor feels that the security constitutes too much of the portfolio's total value, or when the investor is feeling less bullish on the security. In either case, a residual position in the security is maintained.

limited company (Ltd.) A firm registered in such a manner as to give its owners limited liability. Limited companies are most often associated with British registration, much as incorporated firms are primarily associated with U.S. registration.

limited discretion The authority given a broker to make certain investment decisions without first getting in touch with the investor. The investor must sign a written agreement providing the broker with limited discretion. —Also called *limited trading authorization.*

limited liability The liability of a firm's owners for no more capital than they have invested in the business. Essentially, the legal separation of ownership and liability means that a stockholder can lose no more than he or she has paid for the shares of ownership regardless of the firm's financial obligations. Limited liability is one of the major advantages of organizing a business as a corporation. —Compare UNLIMITED LIABILITY.

limited partnership A partnership in which some of the partners have a limited liability to the firm's creditors. —Compare GENERAL PARTNERSHIP. —See also MASTER LIMITED PARTNERSHIP.

limited-tax general obligation bond A municipal bond that is secured by some limited taxing power of the issuer. For example, a bond may be secured by a municipality's property tax subject to a maximum rate at which the tax may be levied. Although a limited-tax general obligation bond is considered a general obligation of the issuer, because of the limited taxing power, this bond is somewhat more risky than a general obligation bond secured by full taxing power.

limited trading authorization —See LIMITED DISCRETION.

limited-voting stock A class of stock that provides its holders with smaller than proportionate voting rights in comparison with another class of stock issued by the same firm. Limited-voting shares allow another class of stock effectively to control the election of a firm's directors even though the limited-voting shareholders may have contributed a majority of the firm's equity capital. —Compare SUPERVOTING STOCK.

limit move The maximum price change in a commodity futures contract permitted during a single trading session.

limit on close Of or relating to an order to sell or purchase a security at the closing price but only if the order can be executed at a specified price or better.

limit order An order to execute a transaction only at a specified price (the limit) or better. A limit order to buy would be at the limit or lower, and a limit order to sell would be at the limit or higher. Limit orders are used by investors who have decided on the price at which they are willing to trade. —Compare MARKET ORDER. —See also ELECT; OR BETTER; STOP ORDER 1.

limit order display rule An SEC requirement that better-priced customer limit orders (higher bid or lower ask) be included in market maker quotes. This rule improves transparency by allowing market participants to view and access the best available price.

Limit Order Information System An electronic system that lists specialists' price and size quotes for exchange-listed securities. The Limit Order Information System is used by specialists and other subscribers to locate the best market for making a trade.

limit price The price specified by an investor for a limit order. With a limit order to buy, the price represents the highest price the investor will pay. The price of a limit order to sell represents the lowest price the investor will accept.

line In technical analysis, a horizontal pattern on a price chart indicating a period during which supply and demand for a security are relatively equal. Technical analysts generally look for the price to break away from the line, at which time they are likely to take a position in the direction of the movement. —See also MAKING A LINE.

line chart In technical analysis, a chart pattern indicating successive variable stock values over time. For example, a line chart of a stock would display the stock's closing prices over a period of time, connected by a line. Line charts for graphing stock prices are useful if an analyst is interested only in a single value each time. But if high, low, and closing prices all are required, a bar chart is used. Refer to the *Technical Analysis Chart Patterns* section for an example of this chart. —Compare POINT-AND-FIGURE CHART. —See also 200-DAY MOVING AVERAGE.

line-of-business reporting —See SEGMENT REPORTING.

line of credit A credit arrangement in which a financial institution agrees to lend money to a customer up to a specified limit. A line of credit, generally arranged before the funds are actually required, provides flexibility for the customer in that it ensures the ability to meet short-term cash needs as they arise. —Also called *bank line; credit line; revolver; revolving credit agreement.*

LIONS An acronym for a packaging vehicle for investments that have had their coupons stripped. —See also COUPON STRIPPING.

liquid **1.** Of, relating to, or being an asset that may be bought or sold in a short period of time with relatively small price changes engendered by the transaction. A U.S. Treasury bill is an example of a very liquid asset. (Many issues of municipal bonds are not very liquid.) —Compare ILLIQUID 1. **2.** Of, relating to, or being an investment position in which most of the assets are in money or near money. This kind of position generally earns a relatively low return but allows the investor to take advantage of other investment opportunities.

liquid asset fund —See MONEY MARKET FUND.

liquidate a position To sell all the stock or debt securities of a particular type. For example, a portfolio manager might decide to liquidate a position in a stock by selling all the shares of that stock held in the portfolio. A variety of reasons may induce the investor to do this, but the most common one is simply a belief that the security price will fall.

liquidating dividend A pro rata distribution of cash or property to stockholders as part of the dissolution of a business. For example, a firm may be liquidated because the officers believe its stock price does not adequately reflect the value of its assets. All debts and other obligations usually must be satisfied before issuance of a final liquidating dividend. A stock paying a liquidating dividend is indicated in stock transaction tables in newspapers by the symbol *C*, next to the dividend column. —See also FINAL DIVIDEND 1; GENERAL UTILITIES DOCTRINE.

liquidating value The estimated value of a firm in the event that its assets are sold and its debts paid. This value is often stated on a per-share basis so as to indicate some kind of minimum value for a given share of the stock. Liquidation value above the stock's market price indicates the firm is worth more dead than alive.

liquidation **1.** The conversion of assets into cash. Just as a company may liquidate an entire subsidiary by selling it to another firm, so too may an investor liquidate by selling a particular type of security. **2.** The paying of a debt. **3.** The selling of assets and the paying of liabilities in anticipation of going out of business.

> **⋀⋀ CASE STUDY** If eliminating dividends, laying off employees, selling subsidiaries, restructuring debt, and, finally, reorganization under Chapter 11 bankruptcy fail to resuscitate a business, the likely outcome is liquidation. Early 2001 witnessed the end of the line for Tennessee-based retailer Service Merchandise, a 42-year-old chain of catalog showrooms that proved unable to compete with large discounters such as Wal-Mart. Following a three-year attempt at reorganization under Chapter 11 bankruptcy,

the firm announced it would close all 216 stores and liquidate its inventories and real estate. It was expected the asset liquidation would result in creditors being paid only a portion of their claims while stockholders of the company would receive nothing. The firm's stock was trading over the counter for 2¢ per share at the time of the announcement.

liquidity   A large position in cash or in assets that are easily convertible to cash. High liquidity produces flexibility for a firm or an investor in a low-risk position, but it also tends to decrease profitability.

liquidity diversification   —See LADDERING.

liquidity premium   The extra return demanded by investors as compensation for holding assets that may be difficult to convert into cash. For example, bonds that seldom trade should offer a higher yield to maturity compared to actively traded bonds of similar maturity and credit risk.

liquidity ratio   **1**. A measure of a company's ability to meet its short-term obligations achieved through a comparison of financial variables. —See also CURRENT RATIO; QUICK RATIO; WORKING CAPITAL. **2**. The value of trading in a stock that is required to change the stock's price by 1%. A high ratio indicates the stock has considerable liquidity. A stock's liquidity ratio is of primary importance to institutions and traders that deal in large volume and that wish to avoid securities with a lack of liquidity.

liquidity risk   The risk of having difficulty in liquidating an investment position without taking a significant discount from current market value. Liquidity risk can be a significant problem with certain lightly traded securities such as unlisted options and municipal bonds that were part of small issues. —Also called *marketability risk.*

list   To admit a security for trading on an organized exchange. In order to be listed, the security and the issuer must meet certain minimal standards established by the exchange. These standards may relate to assets, earnings, market value, and stock voting rights. —Compare DELIST. —See also FORM S-1.

listed security   A security traded on any of the national or regional securities exchanges. Listed securities are generally more liquid than securities that trade only in the over-the-counter market. —Compare UNLISTED SECURITY. —Also called *exchange-traded security.*

listing department   —See STOCK LIST.

listing requirements   Requirements that are made of a firm and the firm's security before the security can be listed for trading on an exchange. Each exchange has its own listing requirements, covering things such as the minimum shares outstanding, the number of shareholders, and the earnings history.

⋀⋀ CASE STUDY | The New York Stock Exchange imposes distribution and quantitative criteria that companies must meet in order to list stocks on the Big Board. The exchange also states that it maintains broad discretion regarding a firm's listing and may deny listings or apply additional or more stringent criteria as circumstances warrant. Below are domestic standards for listing securities on the New York Stock Exchange (separate standards apply to affiliated companies and non-U.S. companies).

Minimum Distribution Criteria

1.   a) 2,000 round-lot (generally, 100 shares) shareholders, or

    b) 2,200 total shareholders together with 100,000-share average monthly trading volume during the most recent 6 months, or

    c) 500 total shareholders together with one-million-share average monthly trading volume during the most recent 12 months.

2.   One million public shares.

3.   a) $100 million market value of public shares for a public company, or

    b) $60 million market value for a spinoff, carve-out, or IPO.

Minimum Quantitative Standards

4.   a) Aggregate pretax earnings the last three years of $6.5 million achieved as $2.5 million in the most recent year and $2 million in each of the two preceding years, or

    b) Pretax earnings of $4.5 million in the most recent year, although each of the last three years must be profitable, or

    c) $25 million of aggregate operating cash flow for the last three years (each year must report a positive amount) for companies with over $500 million in global market capitalization and over $100 million in revenues of the last 12 months, or

    d) $100 million in revenues during the last fiscal year and average global market capitalization of $1 million.

living trust A trust created for the trustor and administered by another party during the trustor's lifetime. The living trust may be formed because the trustor is either incapable of managing or unwilling to manage his or her assets. The trust can be revocable or irrevocable, depending upon the trustor's wishes. —Also called *inter vivos trust*.

LME —See LONDON METAL EXCHANGE.

load The sales fee the buyer pays in order to acquire an asset. This fee varies according to the type of asset and the way it is sold. Many mutual funds impose a sales charge. As a result of the load, only a portion of the investor's funds go into the investment itself. —Also called *front-end load; sales load*.

load fund A mutual fund with shares sold at a price that includes a sales charge—typically 4 to 9.3% of the net amount invested. Thus, load funds are sold at a price exceeding net asset value, but they are redeemed at net asset value. There is no reason to expect an investment company with a sales charge to outperform one without a sales charge. —See also LOAD; LOW-LOAD FUND; NO-LOAD FUND.

⋀⋀ CASE STUDY | Mutual fund distributors sometimes offer two, three, or four classes of shares for the same fund. Fund classes differ with regard to the fees charged to investors who purchase and own the shares. Class A shares typically entail a sales charge that ranges between 3% and 6%, while class B shares for the same fund entail a higher annual fee plus a redemption charge, or exit fee, in place of an initial sales charge. The redemption fee generally declines the longer shares are held before being redeemed. A third class of mutual fund shares may have no sales or redemption charge, but entail a higher annual fee. One major brokerage firm offers an aggressive growth fund with the following charges:

Class	A	B	C
Initial Sales Charge	Up to 5.00%, reduced for large purchases; no charge for purchases over $1 million	None	1.00%
Deferred Sales Charge	1.00% on purchases over $1 million or more if redeemed within one year of purchase	Up to 5.00% with reduction over time; no deferred charge after six years	1.00% if redeemed within one year
Annual Distribution Fee	0.25% of average daily assets	1.00% of average daily assets	1.00% of average daily assets

Individuals who invest a substantial amount of money and expect a long holding period are generally better off choosing class A shares because the lower annual expenses will, over time, more than offset the initial sales charge. In addition, investors who purchase a substantial number of shares often qualify for a reduced sales charge. In summer 2001 one major brokerage firm instructed its brokers to limit sales of class B shares to clients who invested $100,000 or less.

load spread option The allocation of sales charges on mutual fund shares purchased on a contractual plan over a period of years. Sales charges may amount to as much as 20% of any single year's payments during the first four years, provided the total charges for the four years do not exceed 64% of any single year's payments. Also, the total sales charge cannot exceed 9% of contributions of the total value of the contract.

loan consent agreement A part of a margin account agreement between a brokerage firm and a client that permits the brokerage firm to lend securities owned by the client.

loaned flat The practice of lending securities from one broker to another to cover a customer's short sale when no interest is charged by the lending broker.

loan portfolio Loans that have been made or bought and are being held for repayment. Loan portfolios are the major asset of banks, thrifts, and other lending institutions. The value of a loan portfolio depends not only on the interest rates earned on the loans, but also on the quality or likelihood that interest and principal will be paid.

loan value The maximum amount that may be borrowed, using a security as collateral. If the Federal Reserve specifies an initial margin requirement of 50% under Regulation T, $5,000 in securities would have a loan value of $2,500.

LOC —See LETTER OF CREDIT.

local listing A security listing at a regional exchange when the same security is not also listed on another exchange.

lockdown A prohibition against a firm's employees making changes in the asset composition of their retirement plan. Corporate officials may lock down a retirement plan during a period of administrative changes in the plan. —Also called *blackout period; quiet period.*

⋀⋀ CASE STUDY | The term *lockdown* became a familiar component of the finance lexicon following Enron's bankruptcy on December 2, 2001. The company's management had locked down the employees' 401(k) retirement plan five weeks earlier on October 26, when Enron stock traded at a price of $15.40 per share. The lockdown was initially scheduled by directors in March 2001 to facilitate upcoming administrative changes in the retirement plan, a perfectly legal reason. Employees were notified in early October of the coming restriction on changes to the retirement plan. Unfortunately for Enron employees who chose to maintain most of their funds in Enron shares, the firm's stock price declined to $9.98 by the time the lockdown ended on November 13. Thus, employee investments in the firm's stock decreased by approximately 33% during the two-and-a-half-week lockdown period. Some employees claimed to have been misled with regard to the last day they were allowed to make changes to the retirement plan. Other critics claimed Enron's management had knowledge of the firm's severe financial difficulties and, as a result, had a fiduciary responsibility to the employees to postpone the lockdown until the news had been released. Many of the firm's employees maintained a substantial portion of their retirement funds in Enron stock, which by the end 2001 traded for less than $1 per share. The stock had traded above $80 per share early the same year.

locked in To have a large paper, or unrealized, profit in a security position, with the result being that sale of the security would engender substantial taxation.

locked market A somewhat unusual occurrence in which the bid price and ask price for a security are equal.

lock in To guarantee, as a return or cost. For example, an investor who purchases a noncallable 10% coupon Treasury bond at par locks in a return of 10% annually until the bond matures. The Treasury also locks in a 10% cost for the funds raised through the sale of this bond issue.

lock-in amendment Amendment to a corporate charter that makes it more difficult to void previously approved amendments. For example, a lock-in amendment may require 60% approval to change an existing antitakeover amendment.

lockup agreement A contractual offer of valuable assets or stock made by a takeover target to the suitor deemed most acceptable to management. A lockup agreement tends to discourage unwanted suitors, but it may penalize the target firm's stockholders because it eliminates counteroffers. —Also called *crown jewel lockup agreement.*

lockup period The time during which employees and other early investors are prohibited from selling stock in a newly listed company. Investment banks that bring the securities to market establish lockup periods to protect investors in a new issue from large insider selling that can have a major price impact because of a relatively small number of shares available for trading. Lockup periods are usually 180 days from the date of the initial public offering.

Lombard rate The rate of interest at which the Bundesbank, Germany's central bank, lends funds to the country's commercial banks. The Lombard rate is an important indicator of Germany's monetary policy.

London Commodity Exchange —See LONDON INTERNATIONAL FINANCIAL FUTURES AND OPTIONS EXCHANGE.

London interbank offered rate (LIBOR) The basic short-term rate of interest in the Eurodollar market and the rate to which many Eurodollar loans and deposits are tied. The LIBOR is similar in concept to that of the prime rate in the United States except that it is less subject to individual bank management.

London International Financial Futures and Options Exchange (LIFFE) A profit-seeking, shareholder-owned exchange that offers trading in a wide range of derivative securities, including futures and options on interest rates, equity options, and agricultural commodity contracts. LIFFE merged with the London Traded Options Market in 1992 and with the London Commodity Exchange in 1996. The exchange was established in 1982 as an open outcry market but by 2000 had transferred all of its contracts to an electronic platform known as LIFFE CONNECT.

London Metal Exchange (LME) A major London trading facility formed in 1877 that currently trades futures and option contracts for six major metals: aluminum, copper, lead, nickel, tin, and zinc. The LME also trades futures and option contracts on a base metals index.

London Stock Exchange (LSE) The United Kingdom's largest equity exchange, founded in 1760 by 150 brokers who were kicked out of the Royal Exchange for rowdiness. The LSE provides a market for stocks, bonds, and depositary receipts of U.K. and foreign companies. The London Stock Exchange launched an electronic trading platform, SETS (Stock Exchange Electronic Trading), in 1997 and became a publicly traded corporation in 2000.

London Traded Options Market —See LONDON INTERNATIONAL FINANCIAL FUTURES AND OPTIONS EXCHANGE.

long —See LONG POSITION.

long bond A debt security with a relatively long period remaining until maturity. *See Investment Tip on p. 218.* —Compare SHORT BOND. —Also called *long coupon.*

long hedge The purchase of a futures contract or call option to protect a short position against possible increases in the prices of commodities, currencies, indexes, or securities. For example, an investor might purchase a futures contract on fixed-income securities to protect against a decline in interest rates. —Also called *buying hedge.*

long leg The side of an option spread (that is, one option bought long and one option sold short) that an investor is long. With a spread that involves owning a June 20 put and being short a March 20 put, the June 20 put represents the long leg. —Compare SHORT LEG.

long position The net ownership position in a particular security. If an investor owns 500 shares of Wal-Mart common stock, that person is said to be long 500 shares of Wal-Mart. Likewise, the more unusual situation of owning 1,000 shares of a particular stock at a time when 300 shares of the same stock have been sold short produces a long position of 700 shares. Being long indicates an expectation of rising share prices. —Compare SHORT POSITION 1. —Also called *long.*

long-term **1.** Of or relating to a gain or loss in the value of a security that has been held over a specific length of time. —Compare SHORT-TERM 1. —See also HOLDING PERIOD. **2.** Of or relating to a liability for which a long period of time (usually one year) remains until payment of the face amount comes due. A long-term bond is a long-term liability.

long bond

What are the advantages and disadvantages of buying long bonds rather than short bonds?

The advantages of buying long bonds rather than short bonds are:

- you get to keep attractive interest rates longer;
- yields generally are higher on long bonds versus the yields you can obtain on short bonds;
- price swings are more significant, and thus profits are more substantial when interest rates fall;
- price swings are more dramatic when you hold a longer bond and its credit rating is upgraded, permitting it to trade at a lower yield to maturity regardless of what interest rates in general are doing.

The disadvantages of buying long bonds as opposed to short bonds are:

- you are stuck with unattractive rates longer (unless you want to take your lumps and move on);
- if the yield curve begins to take on a negative shape, or even if it simply begins to rise, as a holder of long bonds you probably will have much larger capital losses than you would have if you had chosen to buy shorter maturities instead;
- price swings are more dramatic when you hold a deteriorating credit and the bond's maturity is longer.

Stephanie G. Bigwood, CFP, ChFC, CSA, Assistant Vice President
Lombard Securities, Incorporated, Baltimore, MD

long-term equity anticipation securities (LEAPS) Options that carry expiration dates of up to two years.

look A price and size quotation for a security. For example, a floor broker may ask for a look at General Motors.

lookback call option A specialized option that gives its owner the right to purchase the underlying asset at the lowest price at which it traded between the effective date and the expiration date of the option. The added advantage of being able to look back makes this option command a relatively high premium.

lookback put option A specialized option that gives its owner the right to sell the underlying asset at the highest price at which it traded between the effective date and the expiration date of the option.

loser A security that has fallen in price during a specified period. —Compare GAINER.

loss The deficiency of the amount received as opposed to the amount invested in a transaction. —Compare GAIN. —See also NET LOSS.

lot The number of bonds or shares of stock in a single trade. —See also ODD LOT; ROUND LOT.

lowball Of, relating to, or being an unrealistically low bid. —Compare PRICEY.

lower of cost or market A method for determining an asset's value such that either the original cost or the current replacement cost, whichever is lowest, is used for financial reporting purposes. For example, an inventory item originally purchased for $50 that has a current market value of $30 would appear on the firm's balance sheet at $30. The use of lower of cost or market is considered a conservative method of valuing assets.

lump-sum distribution

When is lump-sum distribution desirable? To whom?

Lump-sum distributions from retirement plans are desirable when their special tax savings (capital gain treatment on some, ten-year tax averaging on some) are favorable when compared with taxes that may be due if the distributions were rolled over to an IRA and taxed later. Someone who needs money now to payoff debts or purchase a retirement home, or someone who will always need money from the distribution and will always be in a low tax bracket, may find the lump-sum distribution tax rules to benefit them now rather than taking their distributions over time.

Jeffrey S. Levine, CPA, MST, Alkon & Levine, PC, Newton, MA

low-grade Of or relating to debt that has a credit rating of B or below. Low-grade debt offers an above-average yield but entails substantial risk because promised payments may not be made in a timely manner.

low-load fund An open-end investment company with a sales charge ranging from 1 to 3% of the net amount invested by a shareholder, as opposed to charges of up to 9.3% on regular load funds and no charges on no-load funds. Low-load funds gained popularity in the mid-1980s, a period that witnessed renewed public interest in investment companies of all types.

lows The number of stocks that drop below the lowest price reached by each stock during the most recent 52-week period. Falling stock market averages accompanied by a large number of new lows tend to confirm that a bear market is in progress. Technicians consider an increasing number of lows to be a bearish sign, especially if accompanied by other bearish indicators. Conversely, record lows by market averages not accompanied by an increasing number of individual lows would be suspect. —Compare HIGHS. —Also called *new lows.*

LSE —See LONDON STOCK EXCHANGE.

Ltd. —See LIMITED COMPANY.

lump-sum distribution With retirement plans, the disbursement of an individual's benefits in a single payment. A lump-sum distribution has important income-tax implications; therefore, the individual must investigate this option thoroughly before choosing a single payment.

M

m **1.** —Used in bond transaction tables in newspapers to indicate a bond that has matured and is no longer drawing interest: *Cuba 4½ 77m.* **2.** —Used in the dividend column of stock transaction tables of newspapers to indicate an annual dividend rate that is reduced on the last declaration date: *.20m.*

M1 The most restrictive measure of the domestic money supply that incorporates only money that is ordinarily used for spending on goods and services. M1 includes currency, checking account balances (including NOW accounts and credit union share draft accounts), and travelers' checks. This money measure is closely watched by financial observers because it is a key indicator of past and future Federal Reserve actions.

M2 A measure of the domestic money supply that includes M1 plus savings and time deposits, overnight repurchase agreements, and personal balances in money market accounts. Basically, M2 includes money that can be used for spending (M1) plus items that can be quickly converted to M1.

M3 A very broad measure of the domestic money supply that includes M2 items plus any large time deposits and money market fund balances held by institutions.

macaroni defense A defensive tactic against a hostile takeover in which the potential target company issues a large number of bonds that must be redeemed at a substantial premium to par in the event the company is taken over. The required redemption substantially expands the cost of a hostile takeover just as macaroni expands when placed in boiling water.

MACRS —See MODIFIED ACCELERATED COST RECOVERY SYSTEM.

maintenance and replacement call A special provision of some bond indentures (especially those of utilities) that permits the borrower to pay off the issue (usually at par) before maturity if the collateral is replaced or disposed of.

maintenance call A call to an investor for additional funds when the market value of securities in the investor's margin account has fallen to the point that the investor's equity (that is, the value of the securities minus the amount owed) does not meet an established minimum. If the investor does not supply the required money or securities, the firm will sell a certain number of securities sufficient to bring the account into conformity. A maintenance call is a type of margin call.

maintenance fee The fee charged by a financial institution to keep an investor's account. For example, some brokerage firms levy a maintenance fee on accounts that have been inactive during a year. Nearly all firms offering sweep accounts charge an annual maintenance fee.

maintenance margin requirement The minimum equity in an account as a percentage of the value of the account. For example, if the maintenance requirement is 25%, the account equity (the market value of the securities minus the amount owed) must equal at least one-quarter the value of the securities in the account. The maintenance margin requirement becomes important when securities purchased on margin fall in price. —Also called *margin requirement; minimum maintenance.* —See also HOUSE MAINTENANCE REQUIREMENT; INITIAL MARGIN REQUIREMENT.

major bracket The listing of the primary underwriters in a securities offering. The major bracket appears immediately under the names of the issue's comanagers.

majority-owned subsidiary A firm in which more than 50% of outstanding voting stock is owned by the parent company.

majority stockholder A single stockholder or a group of stockholders working in concert who control more than 50% of a corporation's voting stock. —Compare WORKING CONTROL.

majority voting A type of voting right in which stockholders are granted one vote for each director's position for each share held. Thus, the holder of 100 shares would have the right to cast 100 votes for each position for which an election is held. Under this system, any stockholder or group holding 51% of the shares voting is able to control every position up for election. —Compare CUMU-LATIVE VOTING. —Also called *statutory voting*.

Major Market Index An index of 20 bellwether stocks that closely tracks changes in the Dow Jones Industrial Average. Nineteen of the stocks in the Major Market Index are also included in the Dow Jones Industrial Average. The Major Market Index is used primarily by program traders who take a long or short position in the stocks included in the index and the opposite position in a futures contract on the index. The Major Market Index was developed in 1983 by the American Stock Exchange.

major turn A significant change in an intermediate- or long-term trend. For example, an analyst may look for a major turn in stock prices following an extended bull market.

make a market To quote a bid price at which a security will be purchased and an ask price at which the security will be sold. An individual makes a market by quoting the prices at which he or she will buy and sell.

make-whole call provision A stipulation in a bond indenture that permits the borrower to redeem a bond prior to maturity by making a lump-sum payment equal to the present value of future interest payments that will not be paid because of the early call. The provision makes the bondholder whole by providing compensation for interest payments that are missed because of an early redemption.

making a line In technical analysis, movement of a stock price in such a way that it traces a relatively thick line across a graph. The thickness of the line is determined by the size of the upward and downward price movements. A breakout from the line in an upward direction is bullish and a breakout in a downward direction is bearish.

Maloney Act A 1935 act that provides for the self-regulation of security brokers and dealers in the over-the-counter market. The only organization currently registered under the Act is the National Association of Securities Dealers, with approximately 5,000 members. As an incentive to join, members receive discounts on securities traded among themselves.

managed account An investment account that is managed by a broker or other professional. Managed accounts are designed for investors lacking the time or expertise to make their own decisions.

managed earnings Corporate earnings that have been manipulated in order to produce a desired result. Earnings can be managed utilizing a variety of both acceptable and questionable accounting methods. For example, a company might time gains and losses from asset sales in order to produce steadily rising earnings.

management audit A detailed audit that concentrates on analysis and evaluation of management procedures and the overall performance of an organization. A management audit is undertaken to discover weaknesses and to institute improvements within the organization. —Also called *operational audit; performance audit*.

management buyout —See GOING PRIVATE.

management company —See INVESTMENT COMPANY.

margin account

Are there any advantages to opening a margin account as opposed to a cash account?

A margin account provides the flexibility to borrow funds using your securities as collateral. This can be an advantage if used properly. Funds from a margin loan can be used to purchase other securities, or they can be utilized for consumption. The risk is that a decrease in the market value of the account can create a "margin call," which requires the deposit of additional securities, the deposit of cash, or the liquidation of some securities held in the account.

George Riles, First Vice President and Resident Manager, Merrill Lynch, Albany, GA

management fee   The money paid to the managers of an investment company. The fee is generally based on a percentage of the net asset value of the fund, with the percentage becoming smaller as the fund's assets grow larger. Fees vary considerably among firms but average about one half of 1% of assets. A fund's management fee must be listed in its prospectus and can be found in a number of publications. —Also called *advisory fee.*

managing underwriter   —See LEAD UNDERWRITER.

mandatory convertible security   A debt security that automatically converts to another security, generally shares of common stock, on a specified date. A mandatory convertible differs from most convertible securities in that it does not permit the owner to choose whether or not to convert.

mandatory tender bond   A bond with a long maturity but a shorter-term (generally six months to five years) mandatory tender date. Unlike an ordinary put bond, a mandatory tender bond is put back to the bondholder who does not take action to roll the bond into the next tender period. The interest rate is adjusted on the mandatory tender date.

manipulate   To cause a security to sell at an artificial price. Although investment bankers are permitted to manipulate temporarily the stock they underwrite, most other forms of manipulation are illegal.

CASE STUDY | Manipulation of security prices is not limited to industry professionals out for a quick buck. In early 2001 the Securities and Exchange Commission settled securities fraud charges with former burrito vendor Yun Soo Oh Park IV, known to his Internet followers as "Tokyo Joe." As part of the settlement Park agreed to return nearly a quarter of a million dollars in trading profits. According to SEC charges, to which Park did not admit or deny wrongdoing, the 50-year-old Korean native engaged in stock manipulation by recommending on Internet message boards stocks he already owned. He then sold his own shares as the recommended stocks rose in price. As Park's legend grew several thousand people agreed to pay an annual fee to receive an advance notice of his postings. The SEC also charged that Park was paid by a firm to recommend its stock. Park's lawyers claimed their client's actions were protected by free speech and not subject to federal securities regulation.

maple leaf   A gold coin minted in Canada.

margin   **1.** The amount of funds that must be deposited when purchasing securities. —See also INITIAL MARGIN REQUIREMENT. **2.** The equity in an investor's account. —See also MAINTENANCE MARGIN REQUIREMENT.

margin account A brokerage account that permits an investor to purchase securities on credit and to borrow on securities already in the account. Buying securities on credit and borrowing on securities are subject to standards established by the Federal Reserve and/or by the firm carrying the account. Interest is charged on any borrowed funds and only for the period of time that the loan is outstanding. —Compare CASH ACCOUNT. —Also called *general account.* —See also INITIAL MARGIN REQUIREMENT; MAINTENANCE MARGIN REQUIREMENT.

margin agreement The written document that describes the functioning of a margin account and permits a customer's broker to pledge securities in the account as collateral for loans. A customer must sign a margin agreement before undertaking trades on credit in an account. —Compare CUSTOMER'S LOAN AGREEMENT.

marginal cost The additional cost needed to produce or purchase one more unit of a good or service. For example, if a firm can produce 150 units of a product at a total cost of $5,000 and 151 units for $5,100, the marginal cost of the 151st unit is $100. Industries with sharply declining marginal costs tend to be made up of firms that engage in price wars to gain market share. For example, the airlines often discount fares to fill empty seats with customers from competing airlines. —Also called *incremental cost.*

marginal revenue The extra revenue generated by selling one additional unit of a good or service. For example, if a firm can sell 10 units of a product at a price of $25 per unit, total revenue is $250. If, in order to sell 11 units, it must reduce the price to $24, total revenue rises to 11 × $24, or $264. Thus, the marginal revenue of the 11th unit is $264 − $250, or $14.

marginal tax rate The percentage of extra income received that must be paid in taxes. It is crucial for an investor to know his or her marginal tax rate in order to make intelligent investment decisions. For example, a decision whether or not to purchase municipal bonds is primarily a function of the investor's marginal tax rate. —Also called *tax bracket.* —See also PROGRESSIVE TAX.

margin call A call for additional funds or securities in a margin account either because the value of equity in the account has fallen below a required minimum (also termed a maintenance call) or because additional securities have been purchased (or sold short).

margin department The section of a brokerage firm's back office operation that is responsible for overseeing customer credit accounts. The margin department ensures that investors meet the margin standards determined by the Federal Reserve, the various exchanges, and the brokerage firm itself. —Also called *credit department.*

margin exercise The use of a margin loan to pay for exercising an incentive stock option. The amount of the loan is limited to 50% of the market value of the stock.

margin of profit —See GROSS PROFIT MARGIN.

margin requirement —See INITIAL MARGIN REQUIREMENT; MAINTENANCE MARGIN REQUIREMENT; OPTION MARGIN.

margin stock A stock with qualifications such that it is considered to have loan value in a margin account. This kind of stock usually includes all listed stocks and selected over-the-counter stocks meeting Federal Reserve criteria. Stocks not on the margin list must be paid for in full. —Also called *OTC margin stock.*

margin trading The buying and selling of securities in an account in which money is owed to the brokerage firm.

marital deduction The deduction for tax purposes of property transferred between spouses. For estate and gift purposes, all transfers between spouses are free of federal taxation.

marital-deduction trust A trust designed to pass assets to a spouse. The trust is used instead of leaving the assets to the spouse directly. The beneficiary receives income from the trust until his or her death, at which time the trust's assets are distributed or the trust is included in the deceased's estate. —See also QTIP TRUST.

markdown 1. A decrease in a security price made by a dealer because of changing market conditions. For example, a bond trader may take a markdown in long-term bonds held in inventory when market interest rates rise. —Compare MARKUP 1. **2.** The difference between the price paid by a dealer to a retail customer and the price at which the dealer can sell the same security to a market maker. —Compare MARKUP 3.

marketability The ease with which an investment may be bought and sold in the secondary market. Poor marketability tends to reduce the value of a security.

marketability risk —See LIQUIDITY RISK.

marketable security A security that may be resold by one investor to another. Most securities are marketable; they develop secondary markets for trading. —Also called *negotiable security.*

market averages —See AVERAGES.

market bottom The low point of stock prices measured by one or more of the stock averages or indexes. —Compare MARKET TOP.

market breadth —See BREADTH OF MARKET.

market break —See BREAK 1.

market capitalization The total value of all of a firm's outstanding shares, calculated by multiplying the market price per share times the total number of shares outstanding. For example, at a current price of $50 for each of its 20 million shares of outstanding stock, a firm has a market capitalization of $50 × 20 million, or $1 billion. —Also called *market value.*

market efficiency —See EFFICIENT MARKET.

market fund —See INDEX FUND.

market if touched (MIT) An order to buy or sell that becomes a market order as soon as a specified price has been reached. Execution does not have to occur at the specified price but at the first available price once the specified price has been touched. Market if touched orders are most frequently used in commodities trading.

market index —See AVERAGES.

market-indexed CD A certificate of deposit that provides a return based on a specified stock index such as the S&P 500. These CDs are issued by commercial banks but are generally marketed by brokerage companies. Terms vary by issuer, but investors are generally guaranteed the return of their principal at maturity.

market leadership The stocks that tend to dominate trading volume during a given period. Some people believe the quality of market leadership indicates future trends for market movement. For example, poor quality leadership (that is, leadership exhibited by low-priced, speculative stock) may indicate excessive speculation and forecast a major decline in stock prices. —Also called *leadership*.

market letter A newsletter containing information on topics such as market trends, security recommendations, economic forecasts, and virtually anything else having impact on security prices and investor profits. Market letters are provided by most full-service brokerage companies, often for a fee, and by individual investment advisers registered with the SEC.

market line —See CAPITAL MARKET LINE.

market maker 1. One (as a person or firm) that, on a continuous basis, buys and sells a security for one's own account. Market makers usually try to profit from a rapid turnover in security positions rather than from holding those positions in anticipation of gradual price movements. Specialists on the organized exchanges and dealers in the over-the-counter market are market makers. —See also MAKE A MARKET. 2. A dealer in options on the floor of an options exchange who makes a market in one or more options. The Chicago Board Options Exchange uses market makers.

market multiple —See PRICE-EARNINGS RATIO.

market-neutral investing An investment strategy of attempting to assemble an investment portfolio with a return that is unaffected by returns in the overall market. For example, an investor might buy shares of a petroleum company the investor considers undervalued and sell short an equal value of shares of a different petroleum company the investor considers overvalued. The investor expects to profit regardless of whether the overall market rises or declines. Market-neutral investing utilizes hedging in an attempt to profit from market inefficiencies.

market not held order —See NOT HELD.

market order A customer order for immediate execution at the best price available when the order reaches the marketplace. This, the most common type of order, has the advantage of nearly always being filled because no price is specified. —Compare LIMIT ORDER. —See also ELECT; STOP ORDER 1.

market timing

Is market timing best left to the experts, or can I use it when determining when to buy or sell securities?

To put it bluntly, the most important investment advice for the serious investor is that it is "time in the market," not "timing the market," that is the key to long-term successful investing.

George Riles, First Vice President and Resident Manager, Merrill Lynch, Albany, GA

market-out clause An addition to an underwriting agreement that permits the underwriters to opt out of their commitment to distribute securities in the event of serious market disruptions.

market outperform An analyst recommendation that a stock is expected to outperform the overall market.

market price The price at which a security trades in the secondary market.

Market Reform Act of 1990 Federal legislation that allows the SEC to influence trading practices such as program trading during periods of extraordinary market volatility. This legislation was enacted in response to the October 1987 market decline.

market risk 1. The risk that because general market pressures will cause the value of an investment to fluctuate, it may be necessary to liquidate a position during a down period in the cycle. Market risk is highest for securities with above-average price volatility and lowest for stable securities such as Treasury bills. Market risk is of little consequence to a person who purchases securities with the intention of holding them for long periods. 2. —See SYSTEMATIC RISK.

market segmentation theory The theory that certain groups of investors are interested in particular types of investments to the exclusion of all others. For example, some investors purchase only short-term debt securities while others are interested only in long-term bonds. Likewise, certain individuals or institutions may limit their investments to common stock.

market sentiment The intuitive feeling of the investment community regarding the expected movement of the stock market. For example, if market sentiment is bullish, then most investors expect an upward move in the stock market.

market share The proportion of industry sales of a good or service that is controlled by a company. Some investors prefer companies with relatively large market shares because they are generally less likely to be squeezed by competitors.

market sweep —See STREET SWEEP.

market technician —See TECHNICIAN.

market timing The purchase and sale of securities based on short-term price patterns as well as on asset values. Some analysts use fundamental analysis to select the securities to purchase or sell; then they rely on market timing to decide when to trade those securities. —Also called *timing*.

market to book A ratio comparing the market price of a firm's common stock with the stock's book value per share. Essentially, the market to book ratio relates what the investors believe a firm is worth to what the firm's accountants say it is worth according to accepted accounting principles. A low ratio indicates investors' belief that the firm's assets have been overvalued on its financial statements. —Also called *price-to-book-value ratio.*

market tone The condition of a securities market with respect to trading activity and strength of prices. An active market with steady or strong prices has a good tone.

market top The high point of stock prices measured by one or more of the stock averages or indexes. —Compare MARKET BOTTOM.

market value 1. The price at which a security currently can be sold. 2. —See MARKET CAPITALIZATION.

market-value-weighted average A measure of security prices adjusted according to the market value of each security included in the average. The greater a firm's number of shares outstanding and the higher the price of the shares, the greater the weight of that security in a market-value-weighted average. The S&P 500 is a market-value-weighted average. —Compare PRICE-WEIGHTED AVERAGE.

mark to the market The adjustment of an account to reflect gains and losses at the end of a trading period. This adjustment is especially relevant in accounts that trade commodity futures because it is used daily to determine whether the appropriate margin is being maintained. —Compare TAX STRADDLE.

> **⋀⋀ CASE STUDY** | Unrealized gains from derivatives that had been marked to the market made up approximately half of 2000 reported earnings for both Enron and Dynegy, two large energy-trading companies. Corporations are required to mark to the market derivative contracts that are owned or owed. Changes in market values of these contracts must be included in reported earnings even though the contracts have not reached the settlement or expiration date and no money has changed hands since the original transaction. For example, a baking company that hedges price fluctuations by purchasing contracts for future delivery of wheat must include in reported income any changes in the value of the contracts that are held during the reporting period, even if the gains and losses are unrealized. The Financial Accounting Standards Board grants companies considerable flexibility in determining how derivatives are valued and, as a result, how earnings are impacted. This discretion allows companies to occasionally abuse the mark-to-the-market rule, especially when contracts are seldom traded and difficult to value. Energy companies are typically heavy users of derivatives.

markup 1. An upward revaluation of a security by a dealer because of a rise in the security's market price. For example, a dealer may decide that a markup on a security issue held in inventory is appropriate because of a rising stock market. —Compare MARKDOWN 1. 2. —See SPREAD 3. 3. The difference between the price charged by a dealer to a retail customer and the prevailing price at which the same security is being offered by market makers. —Compare MARKDOWN 2.

married put A put and stock that are purchased at the same time so that a hedge position can be established. This purchase provides the investor with unlimited upside potential, with the put acting as insurance against losses from a declining stock price. —See also PROTECTIVE PUT.

marry a stock To hold a stock for a long period regardless of other investment opportunities or indications that the security should be sold. Most investment advisers consider it unwise to marry a stock, because an investor's needs and the desirability of a particular stock will change over time.

master limited partnership (MLP) A limited partnership that provides an investor with a direct interest in a group of assets (generally, oil and gas properties). Master limited partnership units trade publicly like stock and thus provide the investor significantly more liquidity than ordinary limited partnerships. —See also ROLL-UP.

matched and lost A report to a customer from a broker that an order was not executed because it lost out to another broker with an order of equal priority. When two or more orders are considered equal, the brokers must match to determine which one is executed.

matched book The position of a broker-dealer when funds borrowed are equal to funds lent to customers.

matched orders 1. The purchase and sale of the same security by an individual or organized group of individuals with the intention of giving the impression of unusual trading activity in the security. Matching orders is intended to get other investors interested in a particular security, but it is illegal. 2. A balance of buy orders and sell orders before the opening of trading in a security.

matching —See PORTFOLIO DEDICATION.

material Of sufficient importance or relevance as to have possible significant influence on an outcome. For example, the possibility that a firm might lose its right to operate a number of television stations because competitors have filed with the Federal Communications Commission for those licenses would be a material fact in preparing the firm's financial statements. —Compare IMMATERIAL.

matrix trading Swapping bonds of different classes or risk levels to take advantage of unusual differences in yield. For example, during a period when the difference between yields on AAA and AA bonds is especially small, an investor swaps AA bonds for AAA bonds to pick up added safety at a small sacrifice in yield. When the difference in yields widens, the investor then swaps back to the higher-risk, higher-yielding AA-rated bonds.

mature industry An industry in which future growth is so limited that firms in it must grow by taking sales from competitors or by diversifying. The stock of firms in mature industries often has high dividend yields and sells at low price-earnings ratios. Because of their limited growth prospects, these stocks are most appropriate for conservative investors seeking high current income. The automotive, petroleum, and tobacco industries are examples of mature industries.

maturing liability A debt that is to be paid within a short period of time.

maturity The date on which payment of a financial obligation is due. In the case of a bond, the maturity date is the one on which the issuer must retire the bond by paying the face value of the bond to its owners. Shares of stock do not have specific maturity dates.

Ⓜ **CASE STUDY** In late 1995, BellSouth became only the fifth company in 40 years to issue bonds with 100-year maturities. The AAA-rated bonds carried a 7% coupon that was 70 basis points higher than 30-year Treasury bonds yielded when the BellSouth bonds were priced. Because it is impossible to know what the next 100 years will bring, bonds with such long maturities subject investors to substantial risk. Renewed inflation, for example, could undermine the purchasing power of the interest payments a bondholder received. Likewise, competition in the communications industry might shake the financial stability of a company long protected by regulation. In addition, changes in market rates of interest have a significant impact on the price of bonds with long maturities. On the plus side though, this Bell-South bond presented investors with a chance to lock in for a long period what at the time appeared to be an attractive yield. If inflation and interest rates remain low for decades, the bonds could turn out to be a profitable investment.

maturity basis In calculating yield, the premise that a bond will be held to maturity.

maturity value The amount to be paid to the holder of a financial obligation at the obligation's maturity. In the case of a bond, the maturity value is the principal amount of the bond to be paid by the issuer to the owner at maturity.

May Day A widely used reference to May 1, 1975, the date on which brokerage commissions on securities became negotiable. May Day ushered in discount brokerage firms that charge investors reduced fees.

MBIA, Inc. A private corporation that provides financial guarantees and investment management products and services. MBIA was formed as a consortium of five casualty insurance companies in 1974 to guarantee principal and interest payments on municipal debt. It has since expanded its scope to guarantee structured asset-backed and mortgage-backed transactions, corporate bonds, and obligations of financial institutions. Borrowers pay MBIA a fee and, in return, issue debt that receives a higher rating and carries a lower interest rate.

MBSCC —See MBS CLEARING CORPORATION.

MBS Clearing Corporation (MBSCC) A registered clearing agency with the SEC that provides automated post-trade comparison, netting, risk management, and pool notification services for the mortgage-backed securities market. MBSCC provides services to firms engaged in programs involving Ginnie Mae, Freddie Mac, and Fannie Mae.

mean term —See DURATION.

mediation A process for settling a dispute between an investor and a broker. The two sides employ a third party who attempts to find common ground that will resolve the dispute. Mediation is a less lengthy and less expensive alternative to arbitration. Each side must agree to mediation and either side may walk away from the process at any time. —Compare ARBITRATION. —See also NASD DISPUTE RESOLUTION, INC.

medium-term bond —See INTERMEDIATE BOND.

medium-term note (MTN) A corporate debt security offered intermittently or continuously by an agent of the issuer. Medium-term notes are issued under the SEC's Rule 415. Despite being called notes, these debt securities generally offer a wide range of maturities.

member An individual who owns a seat on a commodities or securities exchange. —See also ALLIED MEMBER.

member firm A securities firm with officers or partners who are members of an organized securities exchange. National brokerage firms are generally members of a number of organized exchanges. Organized exchanges have established standards of conduct and financial conditions. —See also ABC AGREEMENT.

member short sale ratio A ratio comparing shares sold short by New York Stock Exchange members with total short sales. Because exchange members are thought to be knowledgeable about market conditions and trends, a high member short sale ratio is considered bearish and a low member short sale ratio is considered bullish.

Merc —See CHICAGO MERCANTILE EXCHANGE.

merchant bank An investment bank that commits its own funds by taking a creditor position or equity interest in another firm. For example, a merchant bank may provide temporary financing for a leveraged buyout.

Mergent, Inc. A major publisher of financial information in print and online. Formerly the publications department of Moody's Investors Service, publications include the popular Mergent manuals, *Mergent Bond Record* and *Mergent's Handbook of Common Stocks.*

merger A combination of two or more companies in which the assets and liabilities of the selling firm(s) are absorbed by the buying firm. Although the buying firm may be a considerably different organization after the merger, it retains its original identity. —Compare CONSOLIDATION. —See also DOWNSTREAM MERGER; SYNERGY.

mezzanine bracket The list of underwriters who play a moderately important role in a securities offering.

mezzanine financing High-yield debt issued in connection with a leveraged buyout.

microcap **1.** Of or relating to the common stock of a company with a small capitalization, usually between $50 million and $250 million. Microcap stocks tend to experience volatile price movements and are subject to investment fraud schemes. In addition, information about the small companies that issue these stocks may be difficult to obtain. Many microcap stocks trade over the counter and are quoted on the OTC Bulletin Board or the Pink Sheets. **2.** Of or relating to a mutual fund that holds mostly microcap stocks in its portfolio. Microcap funds tend to exhibit large changes in net asset value.

microlender A company or organization that makes small loans to businesses that are generally unable to obtain financing from a regular source. Microlender loans often range from $5,000 to $25,000 at interest rates higher than those charged by commercial banks.

mid-cap **1.** Of or relating to the common stock of a company with a middle level of market capitalization, usually within the range of $2 billion to $10 billion, although the cutoff points are fuzzy on both ends. **2.** Of or relating to a mutual fund that holds mostly mid-cap stocks.

Midwest Stock Exchange —See CHICAGO STOCK EXCHANGE.

MIG —See MOODY'S INVESTMENT GRADE.

minicoupon bond A bond with a coupon lower than the market rate of interest at the time of issue, resulting in sale of the bond at a discount from face value at issuance. A zero-coupon bond is a special type of minicoupon bond. —Compare ORIGINAL-ISSUE DISCOUNT BOND. —See also DEEP-DISCOUNT BOND.

mini manipulation The manipulation of the price of a security that is underlying an option so as to influence the market value of the option. Because stock price changes often produce magnified changes in the value of options, mini manipulation, although illegal, can produce enhanced profits for the manipulators.

minimum investment　The least amount of money required to invest or open an account in a mutual fund. Different funds impose different minimum investments, and a fund may impose different minimum investments for different types of accounts. For example, many mutual funds require lower minimum investments for individual retirement accounts compared to regular accounts.

minimum maintenance　—See MAINTENANCE MARGIN REQUIREMENT.

minimum tax　—See ALTERNATIVE MINIMUM TAX.

minimum tick　The smallest possible price movement of a security or contract. For example, equity options with premiums of 3 points and greater are traded in eighths of a point, while equity options with premiums less than 3 points may be quoted at sixteenth-of-a-point intervals. —Also called *trading variation.*

mini-tender offer　An offer to purchase less than 5% of a company's stock. Investors are at greater danger in a mini-tender offer because it is not subject to many of the SEC disclosure and procedural protections that apply to traditional tender offers. For example, tendering shares in a mini-tender offer generally means an investor cannot change his or her mind even though the tender has not closed.

minority interest　**1.** In accounting, the ownership by the parent company of less than 100% of an affiliated firm. **2.** A proportional ownership of a firm that is insufficient to constitute control. Generally, minority interest is viewed as ownership of less than 50% of the voting shares.

minority squeeze-out　The elimination of minority shareholders by controlling shareholders.

minus (–)　**1.** —Used in the net change column of security transaction tables to indicate a closing price that is lower than the previous closing price on the day that the security was last traded. **2.** —Used in reporting closed-end investment company share prices to indicate the percentage amount by which net asset value exceeds market price. —Compare PLUS 2.

minus tick　—See DOWNTICK.

MIPS　—See MONTHLY INCOME PREFERRED SECURITIES.

missing the market　Failing to execute a customer's order at an available price that was favorable to the customer. For example, through oversight on the part of the broker, a customer's limit order to purchase stock at $20 might not be executed even though the stock traded at less than $20 after the order was entered. The broker who misses the market is generally responsible for making good on the order.

MIT　—See MARKET IF TOUCHED; MUNICIPAL INVESTMENT TRUST.

mixed account　A brokerage account that includes long and short security positions.

mixed lot　A combination of one or more round lots plus an odd lot.

MLP　—See MASTER LIMITED PARTNERSHIP.

mobile home certificate　A security issued by Ginnie Mae that is secured by mortgages on mobile homes. Mobile home certificates pass through interest payments and principal repayments to investors.

MOB spread The difference in yield between municipal bonds and U.S. Treasury securities of the same maturity. The yield difference is important to investors who are considering the tax benefits of municipal bonds. *MOB* is an acronym for *municipals over bonds*.

model An abstraction of reality, generally referring in investments to a mathematical formula designed to determine security values. Economists also use models to project trends in economic variables such as interest rates, economic activity, and inflation rates.

modern portfolio theory —See PORTFOLIO THEORY.

Modified Accelerated Cost Recovery System (MACRS) A depreciation system in which assets are classified according to a prescribed life or recovery period that bears only a rough relationship to their expected economic lives. MACRS represents a 1986 change to the Accelerated Cost Recovery System that was instituted in 1981. The depreciation rates in MACRS are derived from the double-declining-balance method of depreciation.

momentum The tendency of a security to continue movement in a single direction. Momentum is the underlying factor in trend analysis of stock prices.

Monday effect The tendency of stocks to produce lower-than-average returns on Mondays compared to other days of the week. One study indicated most of the poor performance during Mondays occurs during the first hour of trading.

monetarism An economic theory, the proponents of which argue that economic variations, such as changes in prices and output, are primarily the result of changes in the money supply. (Thus, the Federal Reserve Board is the most important economic policymaker in the country.) Proponents of monetarism believe that changes in the money supply precede changes in other economic variables, including stock prices, and that a rational policy calls for moderate, steady increases in the money supply.

monetarist A proponent, usually an economist, of monetarism. Milton Friedman is probably America's best-known monetarist.

monetary gain The gain in purchasing power that is derived from holding monetary assets and/or monetary liabilities during a period of changing prices. An increase in prices tends to devalue monetary assets and monetary liabilities. Thus, if a firm's monetary liabilities exceeded its monetary assets, inflation would tend to produce monetary gains.

monetary items Assets on a firm's balance sheet that are fixed in dollar amount. Cash, short-term loans, and long-term bonds are monetary items.

monetary policy The Federal Reserve actions that are designed to influence the availability and cost of money. Specific policy includes changing the discount rate, altering bank reserve requirements, and open-market operations. In general, a policy to restrict monetary growth results in tightened credit conditions and, at least temporarily, higher rates of interest. This situation can be expected to have a negative impact on the security markets in the short run, although the long-run effects may be positive because of reduced inflationary pressures. —Compare ACCOMMODATIVE MONETARY POLICY.

monetize the debt To convert government debt from interest-bearing securities into money. Although both the securities and the money are considered government debt, the latter can be used to purchase goods and services. Thus, monetizing the debt is considered an inflationary process and, although it may temporarily depress interest rates, it is likely to result in higher interest rates and lower bond prices in the long run.

money A generally accepted medium for the exchange of goods and services, for measuring value, or for making payments. Many economists consider the amount of money and growth in the amount of money in an economy very influential in determining interest rates, inflation, and the level of economic activity. There is some disagreement among economists as to what types of things actually should be classified as money; for example, should balances in money market funds be included. —See also MONEY SUPPLY.

money center bank —See MONEY MARKET CENTER BANK.

money manager —See PORTFOLIO MANAGER.

money market The market for trading short-term, low-risk securities such as commercial paper, U.S. Treasury bills, bankers' acceptances, and negotiable certificates of deposit. The market is made up of dealers in these securities who are linked by electronic communications.

money market center bank A big commercial bank located in a large metropolitan center. Money market center banks play a leading role in trading financial instruments, determining market interest rates, and providing leadership to commercial banks located outside the money centers. —Also called *money center bank.*

money market deposit account A savings account at a commercial bank or thrift institution that pays a return competitive with money market funds. The number of transactions that may take place each month is limited. Institutions offering the accounts may require a minimum balance in order to receive money market yields. Because of their liquidity and adequate returns, these accounts are ideal temporary repositories for funds awaiting more permanent investment.

money market fund A mutual fund that sells shares of ownership and uses the proceeds to purchase short-term, high-quality securities such as Treasury bills, negotiable certificates of deposit, and commercial paper. Income earned by shareholders is received in the form of additional shares of stock in the fund (usually priced at $1 each). Although no fees are generally charged to purchase or redeem shares in a money market fund, an annual management charge is levied by the fund's advisers. This investment pays a return that varies with short-term interest rates. It is relatively liquid and safe but varies in yields and features. Both taxable and tax-exempt varieties of money market funds are offered. —Also called *liquid asset fund.* —See also AVERAGE MATURITY.

⋀⋀ **CASE STUDY** Choosing between a taxable and tax-exempt money market fund is a function of an investor's marginal tax rate and the difference in yields between the two types of funds. A higher marginal tax rate makes it more likely an investor will earn a higher aftertax return from owning a tax-exempt fund as opposed to a taxable fund. Likewise, the smaller the difference in yields between the two funds, the more likely an investor will benefit from choosing a tax-exempt money market fund. In late November 2001 the largest taxable money market fund managed by Smith Barney paid an average seven-day annualized yield of 1.88%. At the same time the firm's main tax-exempt fund offered a yield of 1.36%. An investor in the 35% federal tax bracket who owned the taxable fund earned an aftertax return of 1.88 × (1 − .35), or 1.22%. This investor paid the Internal Revenue Service 35% of the 1.88 taxable yield, leaving a return of only 1.22% after taxes. Thus, an investor in the 35% tax bracket would have been better off owning the tax-exempt money market fund that paid an aftertax yield of 1.31%. On the other hand, an investor who faced a marginal tax rate of 27% earned an aftertax return of 1.88 × (1 − .27), or 1.37%, by owning the taxable money fund, somewhat better than the return provided by the firm's tax-exempt fund. The yield difference between taxable and tax-exempt funds is constantly changing, so it is important for an investor to remain alert and consider transferring money from one type of fund to the other as yields warrant.

money purchase plan A defined-contribution pension plan in which the employer contributes a specified amount of cash rather than shares of stock or a percentage of profits.

money spread In options trading, the combination of buying one option and selling another option identical to it except for the strike price. For example, purchasing a January call with a strike price of $30 and selling a January call with a strike price of $25 is a money spread. —Also called *price spread; strike spread; vertical spread.*

money supply The amount of money in the economy. Since the money supply is considered by many to be a critical element in determining economic activity, the financial markets attach great importance to Federal Reserve reports of changes in the supply. For example, consistently large increases in the money supply bring fears of future inflation. There are a variety of measures of the supply of money depending on how strictly it is defined. —Also called *money stock.* —See also M1; M2; M3; MONETARISM.

monopoly A business that is the sole supplier of a particular good or service. Regulated monopolies, such as electric utilities, are generally restricted as to the returns they are permitted to earn. Other monopolies such as firms with unique products or services derived from patents, copyrights, or geographic location may be able to earn very high returns. —Compare OLIGOPOLY.

monopoly Of, relating to, or being a market in which there is a single seller of a particular good or service. For example, electric utilities nearly always operate in monopoly markets. —Compare MONOPSONY.

monopsony Of, relating to, or being a market in which there is a single buyer of a particular good or service. Businesses selling in a market characterized by monopsony are likely to suffer below-average profitability because of the lack of alternative outlets for their products. —Compare MONOPOLY.

Monthly Income Preferred Securities (MIPS) A type of preferred stock issued by a special-purpose partnership with the intent of lending the proceeds of the stock issue to a corporate parent. Interest received by the partnership is used to pay dividends to the preferred stockholders. The relatively complicated structure of such a stock issue provides a tax deduction to the corporate parent, which pays interest rather than dividends. MIPS offer higher yields than regular preferred stock and can generally be redeemed in five years.

month order A security order that, if it has not been executed, is automatically canceled at the end of the calendar month during which it is entered. Month orders are monitored by the brokerage firms handling the orders rather than by specialists on the floor of an exchange. —Also called *good-this-month order.*

Montreal Stock Exchange —See BOURSE DE MONTREAL, INC.

Moody's Investors Service A leading firm engaged in credit rating, risk analysis, and research of fixed-income securities and their issuers. Moody's ratings help investors judge the credit risks of investing in fixed-income securities. The financial publications department of Moody's was spun off in 1998 to form a new company. —See also MERGENT, INC.

Moody's Investment Grade (MIG) A rating system used by Moody's Investors Service for municipal notes. The rating system classifies notes into four grades: MIG 1, best quality; MIG 2, high quality; MIG 3, favorable quality; and MIG 4, adequate quality.

moral obligation debt Government or municipal debt that carries an implied pledge of support but that is not explicitly guaranteed by the full faith and credit of the guarantor organization. Moral obligation debt is generally issued in order to circumvent legal restrictions on borrowing. The securities are rated lower and carry higher yields than general obligation bonds of the same issuer.

Morningstar, Inc. A Chicago-based financial information service best known for its mutual fund publication and mutual fund rating system. The firm's star-based rating system is widely utilized by individual investors in selecting mutual funds. Morningstar ratings are frequently included in mutual fund advertising.

mortgage A pledge of specific property as security for a loan. —See also FIRST MORTGAGE; REVERSE ANNUITY MORTGAGE; SECOND MORTGAGE.

mortgage-backed revenue bond A municipal bond, the proceeds of which are used to provide funds to financial institutions for making mortgage loans at relatively low interest rates. Interest and principal on the bond are backed by borrower payments on the mortgages. As with other revenue bonds, the quality varies significantly among different issues of these securities. —Also called *housing bond.*

mortgage banker An organization that makes real estate loans that are then resold to another party. The mortgage banker's income derives from the fees it charges to originate and service the mortgages. Sale of the mortgages gives the mortgage banker more funds to use in making additional loans.

mortgage bond A long-term debt security that is secured by a lien on specific assets, usually on fixed assets such as real estate. —See also CLOSED-END MORTGAGE; OPEN-END MORTGAGE.

mortgage participation certificate A pass-through security that represents ownership in a pool of conventional mortgages put together by Freddie Mac. Principal and interest on the certificates are guaranteed by Freddie Mac and the income is subject to federal, state, and local taxation. —See also PASS-THROUGH SECURITY.

mortgage pool A combination of similar mortgages used as collateral for loans or for participation certificates sold to investors. —Also called *pool.*

mortgage purchase bond A housing revenue bond, the proceeds of which have been used to purchase mortgages from lending institutions. Interest and principal payments are derived from payments on the mortgages underlying the bond issue.

mortgage REIT   A real estate investment trust that combines investors' funds with other borrowed money to make loans on real estate. The return earned by the investors depends on the spread between the interest rates charged on the loans made and the interest rates paid on the loans taken out. Earnings on a mortgage REIT are subject to wide fluctuations if the REIT makes short-term loans and takes out long-term loans. —Compare EQUITY REIT.

most-active list   The list of the most-active securities in a specific market during a defined period. The most-active list is viewed with interest by analysts because it includes unusually active stocks frequently accompanied by large price movements.

most-active stocks   Stocks with trading volume high enough to warrant inclusion on the most-active list. Some widely held stocks with many shares outstanding, such as AT&T and Intel, routinely make the list. Other stocks make the list because of special circumstances such as a tender offer or an unexpected news item about the issuer.

moving average   A series of successive averages of a defined number of variables. As each new variable is included in calculating the average, the last variable of the series is deleted. Suppose a stock's price at the end of each of the last 6 months is $40, $44, $50, $48, $50, and $52. The 4-month moving average in the fifth month is: ($44 + $50 + $48 + $50)/4, or $48. At the end of the sixth month, the 4-month moving average is ($50 + $48 + $50 + $52)/4, or $50. Technical analysts frequently use moving averages to discover trends in stock prices. —See also 200-DAY MOVING AVERAGE.

MSB   —See MUTUAL SAVINGS BANK.

MSRB   —See MUNICIPAL SECURITIES RULEMAKING BOARD.

MTN   —See MEDIUM-TERM NOTE.

multimaturity bond   —See PUT BOND.

multinational   Of, relating to, or being a company with subsidiaries or other operations in a number of countries. The diversity of operations of such companies subjects them to unique risks (for example, exchange rate changes or government nationalization) but at the same time offers them unique profit opportunities closed to domestic companies.

multiple   **1.** In stock-index futures, the number multiplied by the futures price to determine the value of the contract. For example, the $500 multiple of the Standard & Poor's Midcap Index is multiplied by the futures price to determine the value of one contract. Thus, a futures price of $230 would yield a contract value of $115,000 ($500 × $230). **2.** —See PRICE-EARNINGS RATIO.

multiple compression   A decline in a stock's price-earnings ratio in the face of unchanged fundamentals regarding the company. Multiple compression may be caused by a change in investors' view of risk or an increase in market rates of interest. Long-term interest rates and price-earnings ratios tend to move in opposite directions.

multiple management   The apportionment of a large portfolio's assets among several managers. This process permits the managers more flexibility, allows for closer monitoring of investments, and creates a competitive atmosphere among the managers. The major disadvantages are higher cost and the potential lack of coordination in meeting the fund's overall investment goals.

multiple option strategy The use of more than a single option on the same underlying security at the same time. For example, an investor might buy a call on IBM at $135 with a May expiration and sell a call on IBM at the same strike price with an August expiration. A multiple option strategy may be as simple as buying a call and a put at the same time or it may be as complex as the investor desires (or can comprehend).

multiple round lots Stock transactions of 200 shares and more in units of 100 shares.

multiplier —See AMERICAN CURRENCY QUOTATION.

muni —See MUNICIPAL BOND.

municipal —See MUNICIPAL BOND.

municipal bond The debt issue of a city, county, state, or other political entity. Interest paid by most municipal bonds is exempt from federal income taxes and often from state and local taxes as well. The tax exemption stems from the use to which the funds from a bond issue have been devoted. Municipal bonds with tax-exempt interest appeal mainly to investors with significant amounts of other taxable income. —Also called *muni; municipal; tax-exempt bond.* —See also BOND BUYER'S INDEX; EX-LEGAL; 501(C)(3) BOND; GENERAL OBLIGATION BOND; REVENUE BOND; TAXABLE MUNICIPAL BOND.

> **⋀⋀ CASE STUDY** Municipal debt, like corporate debt, ranges in credit quality from investment-grade to very speculative. On November 9, 2001, bond trustee State Street Bank and Trust informed holders of $9.7 million of bonds issued by Marineland Foundation, a nonprofit corporation established by the city of Marineland, Florida, that they would receive $245 for each $1,000 of principal amount. Unfortunately for bondholders the debt was being repaid at slightly less than 25¢ on the dollar. The unrated Marineland bonds had been issued at yields of 8.5% in 1995 to institutional investors and remarketed in 1996 to individuals. Funds raised from the bond issue were used to purchase one of Florida's oldest tourist attractions. Opened south of St. Augustine, Florida, in 1937 as an underwater movie studio, Marineland opened to the public with dolphin and sea lion shows one year later. Attendance suffered beginning in the 1970s following the opening of Disney World, Sea World, Universal Studios, Circus World, and a host of other bigtime Florida attractions. Revenues at the refurbished oceanside aquarium proved too small to cover variable and fixed expenses, including interest on the debt. Marineland had been sold yet again at the time the agreement was reached with bondholders. The new owners intended to promote the attraction as a research resort where visitors could scuba-dive, hike, and learn about marine life.

municipal bond fund A mutual fund that invests in tax-exempt securities and passes through tax-free current income to its shareholders. Some municipal bond funds purchase long-term securities that provide a relatively high current yield but vary substantially in price with changes in interest rates. Other funds choose short-term securities that have lower yields but fluctuate little in value. Municipal bond funds differ from municipal bond unit trusts in that the funds manage the bond portfolios and charge an annual management fee. —See also DOUBLE-EXEMPT FUND; JUNK MUNI-BOND FUND; TAX-EXEMPT MONEY MARKET FUND.

municipal bond insurance A guarantee from a third party that principal and interest will be paid to a bondholder. Municipal bond insurance is written by private corporations for a fee paid by issuers hoping to obtain higher ratings and lower interest costs. Investors purchasing insured bonds or insured trusts obtain increased safety at the cost of lower yields.

municipal bond unit trust An unmanaged portfolio of municipal securities that is put together at the time the units are initially sold. Tax-free interest and repayments of principal are passed through to the owners, who are charged a fee of around 4% to acquire the units. This investment allows individuals to have a diversified portfolio of municipal bonds without investing large sums of money. —See also UNIT INVESTMENT TRUST.

municipal convertible A unique municipal bond that is issued at a large discount from face value because it pays no interest until a specified date, at which time interest payments begin and continue until maturity. For example, a bond issued in 1988 and due in 2015 might begin paying interest in 1998. Essentially, a municipal convertible is a combination of a zero-coupon bond and an ordinary interest-paying bond. Municipal convertibles are traded under a variety of acronyms including BIGS, CCAB, FIGS, GAINS, PACS, STAIRS®, and TEDIS, depending upon the underwriter of the particular issue.

municipal investment trust (MIT) A unit investment trust that holds a portfolio of municipal bonds. Interest and principal received by the trust are passed to the trust's owners. Payments are generally free of federal income taxes and may be free of some or all state income taxes.

municipal note A temporary debt incurred by states, local governments, and special jurisdictions. Municipal notes are usually issued with a maturity length of 12 months, although maturities can range from 3 months to 3 years.

Municipal Securities Rulemaking Board (MSRB) A 15-member self-regulatory board that sets and oversees the standards and practices of the municipal securities industry. The board is of particular importance since the issuing and trading of municipal securities are not subject to much of the federal regulation affecting other security transactions.

municipals-over-bonds spread —See MOB SPREAD.

mutilated security A stock or bond certificate that, because of damage or improper printing, cannot be transferred. The owner of a mutilated security must obtain a guarantee to ownership from the transfer agent before delivering the security to a buyer.

mutual company A company owned by its customers rather than by a separate group of stockholders. Many thrifts and insurance companies (for example, Metropolitan and Prudential) are mutual companies. —Compare STOCK COMPANY.

mutual fund An investment company that continually offers new shares and stands ready to redeem existing shares from the owners. Because the shares are purchased directly from and are sold directly to the mutual fund, there is no secondary market in these companies' stock. Individual mutual funds vary substantially in terms of the types of investments, their sales charges (many have none), and their management fees. —Compare CLOSED-END INVESTMENT COMPANY. —Also called *fund; open-end investment company.* —See also CLONE FUND; FAMILY OF FUNDS; LOAD FUND; REGULATED INVESTMENT COMPANY.

⋀⋀ CASE STUDY | Most research indicates a mutual fund's short-term performance is not an accurate indicator of long-term performance. In other words, it is generally a mistake to choose a mutual fund based on the fund's investment performance during the past quarter or the past year. Even consistent long-term performance may not be a fool-proof guide to selecting a fund. Fidelity's Magellan is considered the outstanding success story among the thousands of mutual funds that have been formed. Peter Lynch, the manager of Magellan for 13 years, became an almost mystical figure among institutional investors before voluntarily stepping down as manager in 1990. A reputation for excellent investment performance over many years caused the fund to grow to the point where, by mid-1996, it had 4.4 million shareholders and managed $56 billion in assets. Jeff Vinik, who took over the fund's reins following the departure of Lynch also produced some excellent results. In early 1996, however, Vinik turned bearish and placed nearly 30% of Magellan's assets in cash and long-term U.S. Treasury bonds. The conservative portfolio caused the fund to underperform in a market that exploded in initial public offerings and technology stocks. In May 1996, Fidelity announced Vinik would be leaving Magellan. His replacement was the manager of one of Fidelity's other mutual funds. Although Vinik apparently erred in becoming too conservative, many market watchers thought the real problem was that Magellan had become so large it was impossible to manage effectively.

mutual fund cash-to-assets ratio   A ratio expressing the proportion of total assets held in cash by mutual funds. Because cash indicates liquidity and potential buying power on the part of mutual funds, a high ratio is generally considered bullish and a low ratio is considered bearish. —See also SENTIMENT INDEX.

mutual fund custodian   An organization that holds in custody the securities owned by a mutual fund. —See also CUSTODIAN.

mutual savings bank (MSB)   A deposit-gathering thrift institution that chiefly makes mortgage loans. Mutual savings banks, typically located in the northeastern states, are organized much like savings and loan associations. MSBs are technically not depositor-owned, although all are state-chartered. —Also called *savings bank*.

N

n —Used in stock transaction tables in newspapers to indicate a new stock that has been listed within the past 52 weeks. The high and low prices are for a period of less than a year: *WeinR n*.

na —Used in bond transaction tables in newspapers to indicate a bond that trades on a nonaccrual basis (that is, on the basis of no obligation to repay any back interest owed).

NAIC —See NATIONAL ASSOCIATION OF INVESTORS CORPORATION.

naked option   An opening transaction in an option when the underlying asset is not owned. An investor writing a call option on 100 shares of IBM without owning the stock is writing a naked option. If the stock is called by the option holder, the writer must purchase shares in the market for delivery and is therefore caught naked. —Compare COVERED CALL OPTION. —Also called *uncovered option.*

naked position A security position, either long or short, that is not hedged. For example, an investor short 500 shares of IBM with no other position in IBM stock (such as ownership of calls) has a naked position in that security. Because a naked position subjects the investor to large potential gains or losses, it is an aggressive investment position.

naked short The investment position of the underwriting firm for a new issue when the underwriting firm has sold more shares short than will be issued. A short position prior to the issue permits the underwriter group to stabilize the price of the stock by becoming buyers immediately following the deal. A naked short allows the underwriting firm greater stabilization ability. —See also GREENSHOE.

naked writer The writer or seller of an option who does not also own the underlying security.

narrow-based Of or relating to an index composed of a limited number of securities or securities representing a particular segment of the whole. For example, the Dow Jones Transportation Average is narrow-based because it is composed only of the stocks of transportation companies. —Compare BROAD-BASED.

narrow basis A market condition in which only a small difference exists between a spot price and futures prices for the same type of contract. —Compare WIDE BASIS.

narrow the spread To reduce the difference between the bid price and ask price for a security. Market makers will narrow the spread as trading in a particular security becomes more active and competition increases.

NASAA —See NORTH AMERICAN SECURITIES ADMINISTRATORS ASSOCIATION.

NASD —See NATIONAL ASSOCIATION OF SECURITIES DEALERS.

Nasdaq The world's largest electronic stock market, with trades executed through a computer and telecommunications network connecting market makers, electronic communications networks, and order-entry firms. Nasdaq trading commenced in 1971, when the system was owned by the National Association of Securities Dealers. NASD members voted in 2000 to spin off Nasdaq into a shareholder-owned, for-profit company. —Formerly called *National Association of Securities Dealers Automated Quotation System.*

Nasdaq Liffe Markets (NQLX) An electronic exchange formed in 2001 for trading single stock futures contracts on the most actively traded Nasdaq and NYSE equities. The exchange is a joint venture of Nasdaq and the London International Financial Futures and Options Exchange.

Nasdaq 100 Index A market-capitalization-weighted index of the largest and most active nonfinancial domestic and international issues listed on the Nasdaq Stock Market. The index was launched in 1985 to represent Nasdaq's largest companies across major industry groups. —See also QQQ.

Nasdaq Composite Index An index that indicates price movements of securities in the over-the-counter market. It includes all domestic common stocks in the Nasdaq System (approximately 5,000 stocks) and is weighted according to the market value of each listed issue. The Index was initiated in 1971 with a base of 100. Specialized industry indexes are also published.

Nasdaq small-cap companies Any of several thousand relatively small companies whose stocks are reported separately by the National Association of Securities Dealers. These securities tend to have more risk and lower trading volumes than stocks that are part of Nasdaq's National Market System.

NASD Dispute Resolution, Inc. A NASD subsidiary that administers arbitration, mediation, and other dispute resolution services. The subsidiary was initiated on July 17, 2001, as a replacement for NASD Regulation Office of Dispute Resolution.

NASDR —See NASD REGULATION, INC.

NASD Regulation, Inc. (NASDR) A subsidiary of the National Association of Securities Dealers established in 1996 in order to separate the regulation of broker-dealers from the operation of the Nasdaq Stock Market. NASDR oversees the activities of securities firms and registered securities professionals and has the power to censure, fine, and suspend NASD members. In addition, it oversees and regulates all trading on the Nasdaq Stock Market and the over-the-counter markets.

National Association of Investors Corporation (NAIC) A nonprofit organization founded in 1951 to provide investment information, education, and support to investment clubs and individual investors. NAIC encourages a long-term approach to investing in growth companies.

National Association of Securities Dealers (NASD) An association of over-the-counter brokers and dealers that establishes legal and ethical standards of conduct for its members. NASD was established in 1939 to regulate the OTC market in much the same manner as organized exchanges monitor actions of their members. One major advantage to membership is that members sell securities at wholesale to other members but at retail to nonmembers. —See also RULES OF FAIR PRACTICE; UNIFORM PRACTICE CODE.

National Association of Securities Dealers Automated Quotation System —See NASDAQ.

National Clearing Corporation (NCC) A subsidiary of the National Association of Securities Dealers through which transactions in the over-the-counter market are compared by broker-dealers. The National Clearing Corporation is similar in concept to the Securities Industry Automation Corporation, which is used for comparisons of exchange transactions.

National Futures Association (NFA) A futures industry self-regulatory body that was established in 1982. The NFA serves a variety of functions including making rules, registering brokers, and arbitrating disputes. The NFA is to the futures industry what the National Association of Securities Dealers is to the securities industry. —Compare COMMODITY FUTURES TRADING COMMISSION.

nationalization A government takeover of private property or operations. The government may or may not compensate the property owners. Multinational companies with operations in developing countries have frequently seen their assets nationalized.

national list Securities that are included in the national market system.

national market system (NMS) **1.** A centralized system for reporting transactions and quotations from all qualified market makers. A national market system has been encouraged by the SEC as a trading system that would increase competition among exchanges and market makers, thus providing investors with more liquidity and better prices. Essentially, a national market system is envisioned as a single large market in which market makers are linked by telecommunications with information being freely available. Customer orders would be automatically filled at the best available prices. **2.** —See NASDAQ.

National Quotation Bureau A private organization that compiles and distributes dealer bid and ask prices for securities traded in the over-the-counter market. Corporate bond quotes are distributed on the Yellow Sheets, while stock quotes appear on the Pink Sheets.

National Securities Clearing Corporation (NSCC) A jointly owned firm of the New York Stock Exchange, the American Stock Exchange, and the National Association of Securities Dealers that settles accounts among brokerage firms. NSCC nets trades among the firms and directs payments and security transfers appropriate to each participant. —See also CONTINUOUS NET SETTLEMENT.

National Securities Trading System (NSTS) An automated centralized quotation system used by the Cincinnati Stock Exchange that permits brokers to enter orders for certain securities and expose them to other brokers and dealers around the country. This experiment in developing a national market for securities differs from the Intermarket Trading System in that the Intermarket Trading System connects only specialists on exchanges. —See also AUTOMATED STOCK TRADING.

natural corner A corner in a security that is not the result of manipulation. If two groups are secretly attempting a takeover of a firm while speculators are shorting the stock, the raiders may achieve a corner without having intended to squeeze the short sellers. This maneuver differs from most corners in which the buyers lend stock to the short sellers with the intention of making the short sellers repurchase the shares at an artificially high price.

NAV —See NET ASSET VALUE PER SHARE.

NC —See NONCALLABLE.

NCC —See NATIONAL CLEARING CORPORATION.

nearby In futures and options trading, the contract month that has the closest delivery or expiration. —Compare FURTHEST OUT. —Also called *lead month.*

near money Assets that can be converted quickly and easily into cash with virtually no loss in value. Examples of near money are savings account balances and Treasury bills.

neckline The line that connects the two lowest points on the intermediate declines of a head-and-shoulders chart pattern. In an inverted head-and-shoulders

negative yield curve

What should investors do when short-term rates exceed long-term rates?

By its very existence, a negative yield curve should be viewed as a market consensus or prediction that interest rates are going to fall, because the market in general has commanded a higher yield for short maturity periods than it has required to attract investment dollars for longer maturity periods. A negative yield curve is usually followed by a flattening and then by a positive yield curve. When this happens, yields on short maturities would probably fall substantially. This shift could occur for various reasons. For example, it could happen as a result of the market coming to expect an easing of inflation; then, yields on longer maturities would also be expected to decline. The longer the maturity, the greater the profit potential for a given decline in yields.

Stephanie G. Bigwood, CFP, ChFC, CSA, Assistant Vice President
Lombard Securities, Incorporated, Baltimore, MD

---

formation, the neckline connects the two intermediate tops. If the second shoulder breaks through the neckline, it is an indication of a major price movement in the direction of the breakout.

negative carry The net cost of an investment position when the investment's cost of carry exceeds its current income. For example, buying a bond with a current yield of 10% and financing the purchase with money borrowed at 13% will result in a negative carry. —Compare POSITIVE CARRY. —See also CARRYING CHARGES 1.

negative covenant A clause in a loan agreement that prohibits the borrower from an activity. For example, a negative covenant may restrict the payment of dividends or the issuance of new debt. —Compare POSITIVE COVENANT.

negative net worth An excess of liabilities over assets. If the assets are fairly valued, a firm with negative net worth could sell all its assets and then be unable to pay all its outstanding loans. Thus, nothing would remain for the owners. —Also called *deficit net worth*.

negative pledge clause A restriction in a borrowing agreement that limits a borrower's ability to issue new debt having a priority claim on the firm's assets. A negative pledge clause, a part of some debenture agreements, protects the creditors against a dilution of security.

negative yield curve An unusual relationship between bond yields and maturity lengths that results when interest rates on long-term bonds are lower than interest rates on short-term bonds. Negative refers to the downward slope of the curve that is drawn to depict this relationship. —Compare POSITIVE YIELD CURVE. —Also called *inverted yield curve*.

neglected-firm effect The theory that investments in the stocks of firms that are not regularly followed by security analysts outperform the stocks of firms that receive considerable attention from analysts.

negotiable **1.** Of, relating to, or being a price that is not firmly established. **2.** Of or relating to an instrument that is easily transferable from one owner to another owner. With proper endorsement, most securities are negotiable.

negotiable certificate of deposit A large denomination ($100,000 and larger) certificate of deposit that is issued in bearer form and that can be traded in the secondary market. Negotiable CDs appeal mainly to companies and institutional investors interested in low-risk investments with a high degree of liquidity. —See also MONEY MARKET.

negotiable order of withdrawal —See NOW ACCOUNT.

negotiable security —See MARKETABLE SECURITY.

negotiated commission A fee for trading securities that is subject to bargaining between the customer and the brokerage firm. Negotiated commissions began to become widespread in the United States in 1975. —See also DISCOUNT BROKERAGE FIRM; MAY DAY.

negotiated offering A method by which a securities issuer selects an investment banking firm to assist in or guarantee the sale of securities on the basis of discussions and factors including the best price.

negotiated share repurchase —See GREENMAIL.

Nellie Mae —See STUDENT LOAN MARKETING ASSOCIATION.

net 1. For the closing transaction in a security, the difference between net proceeds from the sale and the total outlay for the purchase. 2. —See NET INCOME.

net assets —See OWNERS' EQUITY.

net asset value per share (NAV) A valuation of an investment company's shares calculated by subtracting any liabilities from the market value of the firm's assets and dividing the difference by the number of shares outstanding. This factor illustrates the amount a shareholder would receive for each share owned if the fund sold all its assets (stocks, bonds, and so forth) at their current market value, paid off any outstanding debts with the proceeds, and then distributed the remainder to the stockholders. In general, net asset value per share is the price an investor would receive when selling a fund's shares back to the fund. Net asset value per share is similar in concept to book value per share for other types of firms.

⋀ CASE STUDY Net asset value, the Holy Grail for mutual fund investors, isn't always what it indicates. A mutual fund's shares are issued and redeemed at a price based on the fund's net asset value. Net asset value, in turn, is based on the value of securities held in a fund's portfolio. A mutual fund with 100,000 shares outstanding and holding a portfolio valued at $1 million has a net asset value of $10. An accurate net asset value depends on an accurate valuation of assets in the portfolio. Valuation isn't a problem when a mutual fund owns large publicly traded securities. Valuation can be a problem when a mutual fund holds securities that are seldom traded. In 2000 two high-yield municipal bond funds operated by Heartland Advisors, Inc., of Minneapolis slumped in value when the funds reduced the values at which bonds were being carried in the two funds' portfolios. The one-day declines amounted to a mind-boggling 77% for one fund and 44% for the other fund. During the next month the two funds increased in value by 24% and 7%, respectively, after Heartland directors assumed the responsibility of pricing the funds' bonds, which had earlier been priced by an independent firm. Accurate pricing of securities can be particularly difficult in cases in which liquidity is limited, as is the case with many small issues of nonrated debt. Heartland fund shareholders filed numerous federal lawsuits alleging that the funds were carrying the bonds at inflated values.

net capital requirement The minimal ratio of cash and assets readily convertible to cash as a proportion of total indebtedness that broker-dealers must maintain. The net capital requirement is set and monitored by the SEC. —See also RULE 15C3-1.

net change The points or dollars by which the closing price of a security or a security average has changed from the closing price on the last previous day it traded. For example, a net change of −.50 indicates a 50¢-per-share decline from the last previous closing price to the present closing price. —Also called *change; price change.*

net current assets —See WORKING CAPITAL.

net income Income after all expenses and taxes have been deducted. Net income, the most frequently viewed figure in a firm's financial statements, is used in calculating various profitability and stock performance measures including price-earnings ratio, return on equity, earnings per share, and many others. —Compare GROSS PROFIT. —Also called *aftertax profit; bottom line; net; net profit; profit.*

net income per share —See EARNINGS PER SHARE.

net investment income per share For investment companies, income from dividends, interest, and net realized short-term gains, adjusted for management fees and administrative expenses and divided by shares outstanding. Net investment income is paid to shareholders as a dividend. —See also NET REALIZED CAPITAL GAINS PER SHARE.

net lease A lease in which the costs of maintaining the asset, including taxes and insurance, are paid by the lessee. —Compare GROSS LEASE.

net loss The operating result when expenses exceed revenues for a given period.

net margin —See NET PROFIT MARGIN.

net plant and equipment —See PLANT AND EQUIPMENT.

net present value The discounted value of an investment's cash inflows minus the discounted value of its cash outflows. To be adequately profitable, an investment should have a net present value greater than zero. For investment in securities, the initial cost is usually the only outflow.

net proceeds The revenues from the sale of an asset that have been reduced by commissions or other expenses directly related to the sale. Net proceeds from a security's sale are calculated by multiplying the security's price by the result derived from subtracting the brokerage commission and any taxes or other fees realized from the sale from the number of shares sold.

net profit —See NET INCOME.

net profit margin Aftertax net income divided by net sales, a measure of management's ability to carry a dollar of sales down to the bottom line for the stockholders. In other words, net profit margin refers to that which is left for the owners from a dollar of sales after all expenses and taxes have been paid. —Compare GROSS PROFIT MARGIN; RETURN ON SALES. —Also called *net margin.*

net quick assets Current assets readily convertible into cash minus current liabilities. A large amount of net quick assets often characterizes a conservative firm with a very liquid financial position.

net realized capital gains per share For an investment company, the excess of realized long-term capital gains over realized long-term capital losses per share outstanding. —See also NET INVESTMENT INCOME PER SHARE.

net sales Gross sales for a period after cash discounts, returns, and freight expenses have been deducted. —Compare GROSS SALES.

net tangible assets per share An assets measure calculated by dividing the difference of tangible assets minus liabilities and the par value of preferred stock by the number of common shares outstanding. Net tangible assets per share is frequently used by investors and raiders seeking undervalued stock.

net transaction A transaction in which no additional fees are paid. For example, securities that are part of a new issue are priced to include all fees.

Network A The reporting service of the consolidated tape that includes price and volume data for trades on the New York Stock Exchange and on regional exchanges and the over-the-counter market in NYSE-listed stock. The service is carried in brokerage offices, on cable television, and by the reporting exchanges. —Also called *A-network.*

Network B The reporting service of the consolidated tape that includes price and volume data for round-lot trades on the American Stock Exchange, on regional exchanges, and on the over-the-counter market in AMEX-listed stock. —Also called *B-network.*

net working capital —See WORKING CAPITAL.

net worth A measure calculated by subtracting total liabilities from total assets. For an individual, total assets are recorded at current market value. For a company, net worth uses assets as recorded on the balance sheet at historical cost minus any depreciation. —See also OWNERS' EQUITY.

neutral **1.** An investment opinion that is neither bullish nor bearish. A neutral opinion for an individual stock generally indicates the stock should not be purchased or sold. **2.** Of or relating to an investment position that is likely to produce the best results if the market does not exhibit a major upward or downward movement.

neutral hedge ratio The number of options contracts necessary to offset exactly any changes in the price of a contract's underlying asset. This ratio varies depending on the time to expiration and the difference between the asset's market price and the option's strike price. It approaches one when the option is near maturity and is in-the-money.

new account report A form listing investment objectives, income, net worth, and other personal financial information that brokers must complete for each new customer. The information in a new account report is supposed to assist the broker in choosing the types of investments appropriate for a particular investor.

new highs —See HIGHS.

new issue A security that is being initially offered to the public. New stock issues are often quite risky; the securities may change significantly in price shortly after the initial sale has been completed. The greatest number of new issues generally appear near the end of an extended bull market. —See also OFFERING PRICE.

new issue market —See PRIMARY MARKET.

new listing A security that has recently been added to an organized exchange's trading list. The security may have been moved from the over-the-counter market or from a different exchange, or it may be the stock of a firm that recently went public.

new lows —See LOWS.

new money In corporate or U.S. Treasury debt refunding, the amount by which the par value of new securities exceeds the par value of the securities being refunded. The new money is the additional funds borrowed from the refunding operation.

new money preferred Preferred stock issued after October 1, 1942. Corporate owners of new money preferred are permitted to exclude 80% of the stock dividends from taxation.

New York Board of Trade (NYBOT) The parent company of the Coffee, Sugar, and Cocoa Exchange and the New York Cotton Exchange.

New York Cotton Exchange (NYCE) An organized securities exchange located in New York City that provides facilities for trading futures and futures options in cotton and frozen orange juice.

New York Futures Exchange (NYFE) A wholly owned subsidiary of the New York Cotton Exchange formed in 1979 as part of the New York Stock Exchange to provide facilities for trading futures and futures options contracts. Most trading on this exchange is in NYSE composite stock index futures.

New York Mercantile Exchange (NYM) A commodity futures and options exchange with two divisions: the NYMEX Division, trading contracts for crude oil, heating oil, gasoline, natural gas, propane, platinum, and palladium, and the COMEX Division, trading contracts for gold, silver, copper, and the Eurotop 100 stock index. The current exchange is the result of a 1994 merger of the New York Mercantile Exchange and the Commodity Exchange (COMEX). The New York Mercantile Exchange opened NYMEX ACCESS, an after-hours trading system.

New York Stock Exchange® (NYSE®) The trademarked name of the largest and oldest organized securities exchange in the United States. The NYSE, founded in 1792, currently trades a substantial portion of the nation's listed securities. Most large publicly traded firms' stock, including all but two of those listed in the Dow Jones Averages, list their stock on the NYSE. The NYSE operates as an auction market in which orders are brought to the trading floor for execution. Specialists at various locations on the floor are assigned stocks for trading. The specialists bring buyers and sellers together. They also buy and sell for their own accounts. The exchange, which has 1,366 members, lists more than 3,000 equity securities and more than 2,000 bonds. —See also BOND ROOM; GARAGE; SECURITIES EXCHANGE.

New York Stock Exchange Composite Index A composite index made up of all the stocks listed on the New York Stock Exchange and weighted according to the market value (stock price multiplied by shares outstanding) of each security. The base was set at 50 when the Index was established in 1966. Four specialized indexes for industrial, transportation, finance, and utility issues are also computed and published.

next day Of or relating to a transaction that requires settlement one business day after the trade date. For example, options require next day settlement.

next-out In futures trading, the contract month immediately after the nearest available delivery.

NFA —See NATIONAL FUTURES ASSOCIATION.

nifty fifty Fifty large growth stocks that tend to be favorite holdings of institutional investors. These stocks typically have large numbers of shares outstanding and a history of consistently rising earnings and dividends. Examples include DuPont, General Electric, and Procter & Gamble. —Also called *favorite fifty; institutional favorites.*

Nikkei Stock Average A price-weighted average of the stock of 225 large companies listed in the First Section of the Tokyo Stock Exchange. The Nikkei Stock Average is the most widely quoted average of Japanese equities. —Formerly called *Nikkei–Dow Jones Average.*

nine bond rule A requirement of the New York Stock Exchange that members' customer orders for nine or fewer bonds be sent to the trading floor in an attempt to secure an execution. Although the rule does not guarantee execution, it at least permits small orders temporary exposure to the marketplace. —Also called *Rule 396.*

19c–3 stock A stock that may be traded by an exchange member as well as on an exchange because it was listed after April 26, 1979. Prior to this date, exchange members were prohibited from making a market in exchange-listed securities. Thus, the change permits a member of an exchange to act as principal in making a market in a 19c–3 stock as well as to act as an agent in trading on the floor. This stock is named for SEC Rule 19c–3 that permits off-board trading.

N.L. —Used in the offer price column of the mutual fund transaction tables in newspapers to indicate the shares of a no-load fund: *Welsley 14.83 N.L. +.04.*

NMS —See NATIONAL MARKET SYSTEM 1.

no-action letter A response from the SEC staff to an individual inquiry, stating that the staff will recommend to the Commission that no action be taken on a specific transaction if the transaction is carried out in the fashion indicated.

NOB spread The difference in price between ten-year Treasury note futures and Treasury bond futures. Profits realized from using a NOB spread depend on changes in the difference between intermediate-term and long-term interest rates. —Also called *notes over bonds.*

noise Random market fluctuations that make it difficult to forecast the market's direction.

no-load DRIP —See SUPER DRIP.

no-load fund An open-end investment company, shares of which are sold without a sales charge. No-load funds sell directly to customers at net asset value with no intermediate salesperson charging a fee. No-load funds can be expected to perform on a par with other funds that do charge a sales fee. —See also LOW-LOAD FUND.

⋀⋀ CASE STUDY | No-load mutual funds that for many years could only be purchased directly from fund sponsors are increasingly being offered through retail financial establishments such as discount brokerage companies. Even some full-service brokerage firms that once only offered funds that imposed a sales charge are now getting in on the act and are offering a selection of no-load funds to customers. No-load funds purchased from a brokerage firm remain no-load. That is, investors avoid the direct sales fee they would be assessed when buying a load fund. If brokerage firms sell no-load mutual funds that don't charge a sales fee, why do they offer these products to their customers? After all, brokerage firms have never been known to intentionally operate as nonprofit organizations. The answer is that fund sponsors pay brokerage firms a distribution fee to sell their funds. The fee typically ranges between 0.25% and 0.35% of the assets that are involved. The sponsors might justify the extra expense on the basis that a large volume of shares can be sold without the cost of marketing the product to individual investors. On the other hand, these no-load funds often tack on an annual 12b–1 distribution fee to help cover the cost of paying the brokerage firms. Thus, an investor who buys shares of these funds without paying a sales fee may end up paying a series of annual fees instead. The distribution fee will be charged to all the fund's investors, even those who bypass the brokerage firm and buy shares directly. For long-term investors, the extra annual expense could easily exceed the amount of the sales charge that would have been levied. The bottom line is, you may be better off buying no-load funds that are not offered by brokerage firms because you are likely to incur lower distribution charges. It is important to check for annual fees as well as sales or redemption charges when deciding on which mutual fund to buy.

nominal exercise price The price at which an option on a Ginnie Mae certificate can be exercised. This price is calculated by multiplying the adjusted exercise price of the option by the unpaid principal balance on the Ginnie Mae certificate. —See also GINNIE MAE PASS THROUGH.

nominal interest rate The stated rate of interest, exclusive of any compounding, that is paid on an investment. Annual interest of $80 on a $1,000 investment is a nominal rate of 8% whether the interest is paid in $20 quarterly installments, in $40 semiannual installments, or in an $80 annual payment. Use of nominal rates can be misleading when comparing returns from different investments. —See also EFFECTIVE RATE OF INTEREST.

nominal quote The approximate price of a security although no firm bid or ask price is implied. —Compare FIRM QUOTE. —Also called *subject quote.*

nominal return The rate of return on an investment without adjustment for inflation. While nominal return is useful in comparing the returns from different investments, it can be a very misleading indication of true investor earnings on an investment. —Compare REAL RETURN.

nominee A person or an organization in whose name a security is registered even though true ownership is held by another party.

nonassessable capital stock Capital stock for which owners cannot be assessed additional funds to cover any liabilities of the firm. Thus, an owner of nonassessable capital stock can lose no more than his or her original investment. Nonassessable stock is the dominant kind issued in the United States.

noncallable (NC) A provision of some bond and preferred stock issues that prohibits the issuer from redeeming the security before a certain date, or, in some cases, until maturity. A noncallable provision operates to the advantage of the investor. —Compare NONREFUNDABLE.

nonclearing member A member of a securities exchange that does not belong to the exchange's clearing facility. Rather, the nonclearing member pays another firm to provide the service.

noncompetitive bid A method of purchasing U.S. Treasury bills at the weekly public auction without having to submit a price. With a noncompetitive bid, the investor agrees to purchase a given amount of securities (a minimum of $10,000 and a maximum of $500,000) at the average price set at the auction. Noncompetitive bids permit small investors to participate in the auction.

noncontributory pension plan A pension plan in which the participating employees are not required to support the plan with contributions. —Compare CONTRIBUTORY PENSION PLAN.

noncumulative Of or relating to a relatively unusual kind of preferred stock on which missed dividends do not have to be made up. —Compare CUMULATIVE.

noncurrent asset An asset that is not expected to be turned into cash within one year during the normal course of business. Noncurrent assets include buildings, land, equipment, and other assets held for relatively long periods. Noncurrent assets are generally more profitable than current assets, but they also entail more risk because they are more difficult to turn into cash and are likely to fluctuate in value more than current assets.

noncurrent liability A liability not due to be paid within one year during the normal course of business. A long-term debt issue is a noncurrent liability.

nondiversifiable risk —See SYSTEMATIC RISK.

nondiversified management company An investment company that does not agree to be subject to the investment limitations required of a diversified management company. Many venture capital funds, not wishing to be subject to diversification requirements, are classed as nondiversified management companies. —Compare DIVERSIFIED MANAGEMENT COMPANY.

nonequity option An option for which the underlying asset is anything other than stock. Nonequity options include commodity options, currency options, debt options, and stock index options. —Compare EQUITY OPTION. —See also SECTION 1256 CONTRACTS.

nonessential function bond —See PRIVATE ACTIVITY BOND.

no-net-sales policy An unscrupulous brokerage practice of discouraging or preventing investors from selling shares of a stock in order to artificially prop up the market price of a stock.

nonmarketable security A security that may not be sold by one investor to another. This type of security is generally redeemable by the issuer, although within certain limitations. U.S. Treasury savings bonds and most certificates of deposit are nonmarketable securities. —Also called *nonnegotiable security*.

nonmember firm A firm that is not a member of an organized securities exchange. Nonmember firms must work through member firms to have their orders executed on the exchange floor.

nonnegotiable security —See NONMARKETABLE SECURITY.

nonoperating income Income derived from a source other than a firm's regular activities. For example, a firm may record as nonoperating income the profit gained from the sale of an asset other than inventory.

nonoperating unit A firm or a firm's subsidiary that operates no assets on its own but distributes income received from other firms that operate assets leased from the nonoperating company. For example, a railroad may lease its line and equipment to other railroads and merely distribute net income received from the lease payments to the nonoperating railroad's stockholders. —Compare OPERATING UNIT.

nonparticipating 1. Of, relating to, or being a class of preferred stock that does not have the right to participate with common stock in earnings growth through increases in dividends. Nearly all preferred stock issues are nonparticipating. —Compare PARTICIPATING 1. 2. Of or relating to a type of life insurance policy in which policyholders do not share in the investment successes or failures of the insurer. —Compare PARTICIPATING 2.

nonperforming asset An asset that produces no income. For example, a loan on which the borrower is not making payments is often described as a nonperforming asset. Firms often continue to include these assets, which are of questionable value, on their financial statements because they do not wish to show the losses entailed in writing them off. —Compare UNDERPERFORMING ASSET. —Also called *nonperforming loan.*

nonprice competition Competition among firms that choose to differentiate their products by nonprice means, for example, by quality, style, delivery methods, locations, or special services. Nonprice competition is often practiced by firms that desire to differentiate virtually identical products. Companies producing cigarettes, over-the-counter medications, and food products spend large sums on nonprice competition.

nonprobate property An asset, such as one held in joint tenancy, that does not have to pass through probate in order to be transferred.

nonpublic information Information about a company that is unknown to the public. Insiders, including corporate officers and directors, are prohibited from buying or selling their firm's securities on the basis of nonpublic information.

nonpurpose loan A loan that uses securities as collateral, with proceeds from the loan being used to purchase something other than additional securities. A person may prefer a nonpurpose loan over a regular installment loan because of the lower interest rate. Nonpurpose loans are not subject to margin requirements as regular margin loans are. —Compare PURPOSE LOAN.

nonqualifying annuity An annuity not approved by the Internal Revenue Service for tax-deferred pension contributions. A nonqualifying annuity permits the investor to defer taxes on income earned by the annuity but not to reduce taxable income for contributions made to the annuity. —Compare QUALIFYING ANNUITY.

nonqualifying stock option An option to purchase stock that does not meet certain requirements established by the Internal Revenue Service for favorable tax treatment. Acting on a nonqualifying stock option results in taxable ordinary income on any gain made during the year the option is exercised.

nonrated bonds —See NOT RATED.

nonrecourse loan A loan in which the lender cannot claim more than the collateral as repayment in the event that payments on the loan are stopped. Thus, a group of investors may purchase an asset with a down payment and the proceeds from a nonrecourse loan. In the event that the investment turns sour, the investors are not apt to lose more than the down payment and payments already made on the loan. The unpaid balance on the loan will be absorbed by the lender. —Compare RECOURSE LOAN.

nonrecurring charge   An expense that is not expected to be encountered again in the foreseeable future.

nonrefundable (NR)   A provision of some bond issues that prohibits the issuers from retiring the bonds before a specified date on which funds for the retirement will be raised externally (that is, from outside the issuing firm). Essentially, this provision restricts a borrower from taking advantage of lower interest rates by replacing a bond issue that carries a high coupon rate of interest with a new bond issue that carries a reduced coupon rate of interest. Most bonds are nonrefundable for five to ten years from the date of issue. However, when the funds are raised internally, the bonds ordinarily may be called for some other reason such as a reorganization or merger. A nonrefundable feature works to the advantage of the investor because the bonds are usually not refunded unless interest rates have fallen below the coupon. —Compare NONCALLABLE.

nontaxable income   Income items specifically exempted from taxation. On federal returns, the interest from most municipal bonds, life insurance proceeds, gifts, and inheritances is generally nontaxable income.

nonvoting stock   Stock in which the holder has no vote in the election of directors, the appointment of auditors, or other matters that may be brought up at the annual meeting. Corporations sometimes create a special class of nonvoting stock to restrict corporate control only to certain groups. Most preferred stock is nonvoting. —Compare VOTING STOCK.

no par   Of or relating to a stock with no specific value assigned to it at the time of issue. Whether a stock has a par value or not is no longer of any consequence to investors.

normal investment practice   The history of security purchases recorded in a customer account for purposes of allocating hot issues. The National Association of Securities Dealers prohibits underwriters from overallocating hot issues to customers based on the customers' normal investment practice.

normalized earnings   Past or forecasted earnings that have been adjusted for cyclical variations. Earnings are generally normalized by using a moving average of earnings per share over a number of successive periods.

normal trading unit   —See ROUND LOT.

North American Securities Administrators Association (NASAA)   An international voluntary organization of state, provincial, and territorial securities administrators devoted to investor protection.

note   **1.** A written promise to pay a specific sum of money on a certain date. —Also called *promissory note.* **2.** —See FOOTNOTE.

note payable   A debt owed to a lender and evidenced by a written promise of payment. Note payable, an entry on the liabilities side of many corporate balance sheets, indicates that a certain dollar amount of loans will be repaid to the lenders at a future time.

note receivable   A debt due from borrowers and evidenced by a written promise of payment. Note receivable, an entry on the asset side of many corporate balance sheets, indicates the dollar amount of loans due to be repaid by borrowers.

notes over bonds —See NOB SPREAD.

not held A customer instruction that permits an exchange member to use personal judgment in executing either a market or limit order with respect to the time and/or the price of execution. In theory, this instruction is designed to obtain a more favorable price since the floor broker may have a feel for whether prices are likely to rise or decline. Unlike a regular market order, however, a market not held order does not guarantee that the order will be filled. —Also called *market not held order.*

notice of intention day In futures trading, the day on which the clearing firm matches the investor who has declared an intention to deliver on a contract with the investor who must accept delivery. This situation occurs one day after the person holding the short position has declared his or her intention to the clearing firm and one day before delivery is to occur. —See also DELIVERY DAY; FIRST POSITION DAY; POSITION DAY.

not rated (NR) Of or relating to an issue of fixed-income securities that has not been rated by an agency such as Moody's or Standard & Poor's. The fact that an issue is not rated does not necessarily mean the securities are risky. —Also called *nonrated bonds.*

not reoffered (NRO) Of or relating to an issue or a portion of an issue of securities that already has a buyer and is not being resold to the public by the underwriter.

novation The substitution of one debt with another debt.

NOW account An interest-bearing account on which checks may be written. Authorized on a national scale in 1981, these accounts pay a relatively small return. Therefore, the balances in NOW accounts should be kept at the minimum necessary to provide needed funds without incurring service charges. —Also called *negotiable order of withdrawal.* —See also SUPER NOW ACCOUNT.

NQLX —See NASDAQ LIFFE MARKETS.

NR 1. —See NONREFUNDABLE. **2.** —See NOT RATED.

NRO —See NOT REOFFERED.

NSCC —See NATIONAL SECURITIES CLEARING CORPORATION.

NSF check A check not honored by the bank on which it was written because of insufficient funds in the drawer's account. An NSF check is an overdraft.

NSTS —See NATIONAL SECURITIES TRADING SYSTEM.

numbered account An account identified by something other than the owner's name.

NYBOT —See NEW YORK BOARD OF TRADE.

NYCE —See NEW YORK COTTON EXCHANGE.

NYFE —See NEW YORK FUTURES EXCHANGE.

NYM —See NEW YORK MERCANTILE EXCHANGE.

NYMEX —See NEW YORK MERCANTILE EXCHANGE.

NYSE® —See NEW YORK STOCK EXCHANGE.

O

OARS —See OPENING AUTOMATED REPORTING SERVICE.

OB —See OR BETTER.

OCC —See OPTIONS CLEARING CORPORATION.

odd coupon —See IRREGULAR COUPON.

odd lot A unit of trading in securities that is made up of fewer than 100 shares of stock or $25,000 face amount of bonds. —Compare ROUND LOT. —Also called *lot*. —See also EFFECTIVE SALE; ON-THE-QUOTATION ORDER.

odd-lot dealer A member of an organized securities exchange that buys and sells in less than round lots. On most exchanges, this dealer is the specialist in a particular stock.

odd-lot differential The extra markup on odd-lot purchases and markdown on odd-lot sales to compensate the brokerage firm or specialist for dealing in less than round-lot transactions. The differential usually does not apply to odd-lot executions on market opening or to odd lots submitted with round-lot orders for the same security (that is, 260 shares). —Also called *differential*. —See also BASIS PRICE 2; WITH OR WITHOUT.

odd-lot short sale ratio A measure calculated by dividing the odd-lot short sales by the total short sales occurring during a given period. Technical theory holds that a high odd-lot short sale ratio indicates a bullish market because small investors tend to do the wrong thing.

odd-lot short sales The number of shares sold short in less than round lots. Because investors trading odd lots are viewed by many market analysts as unsophisticated, many odd-lot short sales are interpreted as bullish. The number of shares sold short in odd lots is sometimes used to construct an index to gauge small investor speculative activity. The index is calculated by dividing odd-lot short sales by total odd-lot sales. A rising index, indicative of increased speculation by less sophisticated investors, is a bearish sign.

odd-lotter An investor who buys and sells securities in less than the standard unit of trading. Odd-lotters are generally small investors lacking the financial resources to engage in larger trades.

odd-lot theory The technical theory that holds that an investor should make investment decisions contrary to what the odd-lotters, on balance, are doing. For example, if odd-lot sales exceed odd-lot purchases, the odd-lot theory says that the smart investor should buy. Conversely, if odd-lot purchases exceed odd-lot sales, the theory says that the smart investor should sell. The odd-lot theory is based on the premise that small investors who trade in odd lots tend to make the wrong decisions.

OEX Ticker symbol for the S&P 100.

off-balance-sheet financing An accounting technique in which a debt for which a company is obligated does not appear on the company's balance sheet as a liability. Keeping debt off the balance sheet allows a company to appear more creditworthy but misrepresents the firm's financial structure to creditors, shareholders, and the public. The sudden collapse of energy-trading giant Enron Corporation is attributed in large part to the firm's off-balance-sheet financing through multiple partnerships.

⩗⩗ CASE STUDY | The sudden collapse of energy-trading giant Enron Corporation caught regulators, politicians, lenders, analysts, and the public by surprise. In large part the surprise resulted from the billions of dollars of debt the company had been able to hide by using off-balance-sheet financing through hundreds of partnerships. The hidden liabilities allowed Enron to maintain the appearance of a rapidly growing but financially stable company until near the very end, when bankruptcy was imminent. Enron's financial arrangements were complicated and sometimes entailed transferring overvalued assets to partnerships which it had a controlling interest in but was not required to include on its own balance sheet. The partnerships, with minimal equity capital from outside investors, raised most of their capital from loans using Enron stock, transferred assets, or pledges from Enron as collateral. Although Enron used aggressive accounting methods, many of the accounting techniques it employed were not illegal. For this the accounting profession was called to task.

off-board trade   The purchase or sale of securities, particularly those that are listed on an exchange, without using an exchange. An example is trading 10,000 shares of Federal Express common stock (listed on the New York Stock Exchange) in the over-the-counter market. —See also RULE 19C-3; THIRD MARKET.

offer —See ASK.

offering —See PUBLIC OFFERING.

offering circular   An abbreviated prospectus that describes a new securities issue.

offering date   The date on which a new securities issue is to be sold.

offering price   The price at which an investment is offered to buyers. This price, including any sales fee, is fixed by the underwriting syndicate. —Also called *fixed price*.

offering scale —See SCALE.

offer wanted (OW)   A notice by a broker-dealer who is interested in purchasing a security in which there are no current offers.

off-floor order   An order that originates outside an exchange to trade a security. Orders entered by individual investors with brokers are off-board orders because they originate off the exchange. Off-floor orders have precedence over orders originating on the exchange floor. —Compare ON-FLOOR ORDER.

Office of Compliance Inspections and Examinations   An SEC office that administers nationwide examinations and inspections for registered self-regulatory organizations, broker-dealers, transfer agents, clearing agencies, investment companies, and investment advisers. The office is charged with detecting and correcting compliance problems.

official notice of sale   An announcement by a municipality that it is accepting bids from underwriters for a proposed bond issue.

official rate   In foreign exchange trading, the lawful rate at which an exchange rate is set.

official statement   A disclosure of financial and operating information relevant to a municipal bond issue. This statement is similar to the registration statement required of private issuers of securities.

offset The liquidation of a futures or option position by purchasing (for a short position) or selling (for a long position) an equal number of identical contracts so that no further obligation exists.

offshore Of or relating to a financial organization whose headquarters lies outside the United States. Although offshore institutions must abide by U.S. regulations for operations carried on within the U.S., other activities generally escape domestic regulation.

off-the-run issue A security issue that is not included in a dealer's list of offerings. —Compare RUN 1.

OID —See ORIGINAL-ISSUE DISCOUNT.

oil and gas drilling limited partnership A partnership in which investors' funds are used to look for new oil and gas sources. Developmental programs search in areas of proven reserves, while more risky exploratory programs limit their activities to virgin areas. —Also called *developmental oil and gas partnership; exploratory oil and gas partnership.*

oil and gas income limited partnership A partnership in which investors' funds are used to buy oil and gas royalty interests or to buy producing oil and gas properties. This partnership ordinarily provides investors with a stream of sheltered or partially sheltered income.

oligopoly A market in which a limited number of sellers follow the lead of a single major firm. For example, the domestic automobile market was long characterized as an oligopoly, with American Motors, Chrysler, and Ford following the pricing lead of industry giant General Motors. —Compare MONOPOLY; OLIGOPSONY.

oligopsony A market in which a limited number of buyers follow the leadership of a single large firm. For example, in a town or region, a large bank may set rates on certificates of deposit that are then adopted by smaller banks and savings and loan associations on their own certificates of deposit. —Compare OLIGOPOLY.

omitted dividend —See PASSED DIVIDEND.

omnibus account An account carried by a member firm for a nonmember correspondent firm.

on-balance volume A measure of volume distinguished as to whether trades take place on rising prices or on falling prices. Technical analysts consider great volume on rising prices bullish because it indicates the possibility that large traders are accumulating investment positions in a security. Conversely, the technicians consider greater volume on falling prices bearish.

one-cancels-the-other order —See ALTERNATIVE ORDER.

OneChicago LLC An electronic exchange formed in 2001 for trading futures contracts on narrow-based indexes and individual common stocks. Each contract is assigned a lead market maker who is responsible for providing a continuous two-sided market. OneChicago is a joint venture of the Chicago Mercantile Exchange, the Chicago Board Options Exchange, and the Chicago Board of Trade.

one-decision stock A stock that can be bought and held indefinitely such that no second decision to sell is required. Selecting one-decision stock was a popular investment philosophy during the 1970s when institutional investors concentrated their funds on a limited number of high-quality growth stock such as IBM, Kodak, and Procter & Gamble. The essence of this investment philosophy is that, although temporary aberrations in the stock's price may occur, the stock should outperform the market over an extended period.

one hundred percent statement —See COMMON-SIZE STATEMENT.

one-sided market The market for a security in which only a single side, either the bid or the ask, is quoted. —Compare TWO-SIDED MARKET. —Also called *one-way market.* —See also WITHOUT.

on-floor order An order to trade a security that originates from an exchange member on the exchange floor. On-floor orders are subordinated to off-floor orders. —Compare OFF-FLOOR ORDER.

on-the-quotation order A customer odd-lot market order to sell instructing that the order be executed at the existing bid price of the security. An order to buy is at the prevailing ask price. An on-the-quotation order is unusual because most odd-lot orders are executed on the basis of the price of the next round-lot transaction.

on the sidelines Of or relating to investors who, having assessed the market, have decided to avoid committing their funds. These investors keep their money in short-term investments, such as money market funds, and wait for a more opportune time to invest. —Also called *sideline.*

OPD —Used on the consolidated tape to indicate an opening transaction that is being reported late: *GY.OPD 2s51$^{1}/_{2}$.*

open box The physical location within brokerage firms of securities that are available for use as collateral for loans. —Compare FREE BOX. —Also called *active box.*

open-end investment company —See MUTUAL FUND.

open-end mortgage A mortgage that permits the issuer to sell additional bonds under the same lien. If the amount of additional bonds is restricted, the mortgage is referred to as a limited open-end mortgage. —Compare CLOSED-END MORTGAGE.

opening **1.** The beginning of a trading session. **2.** The initial price at which a security trades for the day. —Also called *opening price.*

Opening Automated Reporting Service (OARS) A computerized system that determines imbalances between buy and sell orders for individual securities before the opening of the market. The Service is used by specialists to assist in fixing opening prices for the securities assigned to them.

opening balance The balance in an account at the beginning of a period.

opening price —See OPENING 2.

opening transaction **1.** The initial transaction during a trading day for a particular security. The price at which an opening transaction takes place is important to investors who have placed market orders before the market opens or who have placed at-the-opening orders, because the price at which the opening transaction takes place is the price that these investors will pay for or the price they will receive for the security. —Compare CLOSING TRANSACTION 1. **2.** An option order that establishes a new investment position or that increases the size of an existing investment position. —Compare CLOSING TRANSACTION 2.

open interest The number of contracts for particular futures or an option which, at a given time, are outstanding. A large open interest indicates more activity and liquidity for the contract.

Open Market Committee —See FEDERAL OPEN MARKET COMMITTEE.

open-market operations The purchase and sale of government securities from a primary dealer in the open market by the Federal Reserve in order to influence the money supply, credit conditions, and interest rates. For example, large purchases of securities will release funds into bank reserves which, in turn, will be used for lending. This action increases the supply of money, and, at least temporarily, pushes down interest rates. Open-market operations have significant effects on security prices. —See also FEDERAL OPEN MARKET COMMITTEE.

open-market purchase The buying of stocks and bonds in the securities markets. For example, in order to satisfy the sinking fund requirement of a bond indenture, the issuer may call securities from investors or make open-market purchases. Likewise, a firm wishing to reduce the number of its shares outstanding may make a tender offer to the firm's stockholders or purchase shares in the open market.

open on the print Of or relating to a block trade that has been completed by a block positioner and printed on the consolidated tape. The block positioner is left in a risky position because, depending on which side of the transaction he or she was on, the block positioner is either long or short the security.

open order —See GOOD-TILL-CANCELED ORDER.

open outcry A public auction in which trading is conducted by calling out bids and offers. Open outcry retains its popularity on futures and options exchanges such as the Chicago Board of Trade and the New York Board of Trade despite the introduction of electronic trading systems. Some traders contend that open outcry offers better liquidity with the chance to obtain a better price. —Compare AUCTION MARKET; DEALER MARKET.

open position An option or futures contract that has been bought or sold and that has not yet been offset or settled through delivery.

open repo A repurchase agreement without a fixed term.

operating company A business that engages in transactions with outsiders.

operating cycle The average length of time between when a company purchases items for inventory and when it receives payment for sale of the items. A long operating cycle tends to harm profitability by increasing borrowing requirements and interest expense.

operating expense An expense incurred in transacting normal business operations. Operating expenses include administrative and selling expenses but exclude interest, taxes, and cost of goods sold.

operating income The excess of revenues over expenses derived from normal business operations. Operating income, representing income from ordinary business activities, excludes expenses, such as interest and taxes. Unusual non-recurring items, such as gains from selling a subsidiary or losses from closing a plant, are not included in the calculation of operating income. —Compare OPERATING LOSS. —Also called *earnings before interest and taxes; operating profit.* —See also OPERATING REVENUE.

operating lease A short-term lease (such as that of a cable television connection box on a monthly basis) in which rental payments are made by the lessee and full ownership rights are kept by the lessor. An operating lease contrasts with a capital lease in which ownership of the asset effectively passes from the lessor to the lessee.

operating leverage The extent to which fixed operating costs magnify changes in sales or revenues into even greater proportionate changes in operating income. For example, a company that substitutes robots or other machinery for laborers also substitutes fixed costs for variable costs and increases its operating leverage. High operating leverage tends to produce volatile earnings. —Compare FINANCIAL LEVERAGE.

operating loss The excess of operating expenses over revenue. As with operating income, operating losses exclude revenues and expenses from operations that are not considered a regular part of the business. —Compare OPERATING INCOME. —Also called *deficit*.

operating profit —See OPERATING INCOME.

operating rate The portion of capacity at which a business operates. For example, an operating rate of 80% indicates that the business is producing 80% of the output that could be produced at a maximum with existing resources. A low operating rate is generally accompanied by losses or small profits, although the opportunity for profit growth is still great. Conversely, a high operating rate is generally accompanied by high profits but limited opportunity for further profit improvement.

operating ratio A financial ratio that measures the portion of revenue going to operating expenses.

operating revenue Revenue from any regular source. Revenue from sales is adjusted for discounts and returns when calculating operating revenue. —Compare OTHER REVENUE.

operating statement —See INCOME STATEMENT.

operating unit A type of operating company that engages in transactions with outsiders and that is owned by another business. For example, in 1995 the stockholders of Capital Cities/ABC approved a $19 billion merger with the Walt Disney Company, whereupon Capital Cities/ABC became an operating unit of Disney. A decade earlier Capital Cities had acquired ABC. —Compare NONOPERATING UNIT.

operational audit —See MANAGEMENT AUDIT.

operations department —See BACK OFFICE.

opinion A Certified Public Accountant's written attestation as to the fairness of presentation of financial statements. Anything other than an opinion that the statements have been presented fairly is a matter of serious concern to investors. —Also called *accountant's opinion; auditor opinion.* —See also ADVERSE OPINION; CLEAN OPINION; DISCLAIMER OF OPINION; QUALIFIED OPINION; SUBJECT TO OPINION.

opinion shopping The search for an accounting firm that will provide the desired opinion for a financial statement. Firms sometimes opinion shop when their current auditors consider their accounting practices questionable or unacceptable. Investors should spend extra time investigating firms that have recently changed auditors.

opportunity cost The best alternative that is forgone because a particular course of action is pursued. An example is the interest income that is given up when large balances are kept in a checking account. Likewise, purchasing a home means that less money is available for another investment.

option 1. A contract that permits the owner, depending on the type of option held, to purchase or sell an asset at a fixed price until a specific date. An option to purchase an asset is a call and an option to sell an asset is a put. Depending on how an investor uses options, the risks can be quite high. Investors in options must be correct on timing as well as on valuation of the underlying asset to be successful. —See also ASIAN OPTION; CHOOSER OPTION; COMBINATION OPTION; CONVENTIONAL OPTION; EUROPEAN OPTION; EXERCISE PRICE; EXOTIC OPTION; EXPIRATION DATE; KNOCK-OUT OPTION; LAPSED OPTION; LONG-TERM ANTICIPATION SECURITIES; RESTRICTED OPTION; STOCK OPTION. **2.** —See INCENTIVE STOCK OPTION.

option account A brokerage account that is approved for buying and selling options. Opening an option account requires that an investor complete an option agreement and receive a brochure describing the risks of trading standardized options.

option agreement A formal written document that must be signed by an investor and put into the possession of the brokerage firm before the investor may trade options. The purpose of the agreement is to help assure that the investor has the financial resources and appropriate goals to qualify for trading options and that sufficient information in the form of an Options Clearing Corporation prospectus has been supplied so that the investor can understand the rules and risks.

optional call The call of a bond by an issuer who wishes to terminate a loan, generally because interest rates have declined since the time of issuance. Optional calls are frequently made at prices slightly higher than par value. Some bond issues are not subject to call; most issues provide a period of years after issuance during which optional calls are prohibited. —See also CALL PROTECTION.

optional cash purchase The buying of shares of stock through a dividend reinvestment plan that are in addition to shares purchased with the dividend. Most dividend reinvestment plans place an upper dollar limit on each shareholder's optional cash purchases.

optional dividend A dividend in which the shareholder may choose among two or more forms of payment. For example, a firm's directors may give the shareholders a choice between cash or an equal dollar amount of stock.

option chain A listing of option premiums for all the options of a given security, including expiration dates, strike prices, and class (put or call).

option cycle The series of months during which option contracts expire. Options for a particular stock or index generally expire on the same four months every year plus the current and following month.

option exchange An organized securities exchange, the primary purpose of which is to provide a location and framework for trading standardized option contracts. An option exchange handles its trading much as a stock exchange handles its trading in stocks and bonds. Until 1973, with the opening of the Chicago Board Options Exchange, all options were traded through a limited number of firms specializing in them. Most of the options traded at that time were so unique that it was difficult or impossible to close a position in one before its expiration.

option-growth fund A mutual fund that invests at least 5% of its portfolio of securities in options.

option holder The owner of an option to purchase (call) or sell (put) an asset such as shares of common stock or a further contract. The option holder pays the premium and has the alternative of using the option or allowing it to expire. An option holder's loss is limited to the amount of the premium required to purchase it.

option margin The margin requirement to open and maintain an option position. Federal Reserve Regulation T sets minimum option margins, although individual brokerage firms may establish more strict requirements.

option premium —See PREMIUM 1.

option pricing model A mathematical formula for determining the price at which an option should trade. The model expresses the value of an option as a function of the value of the underlying asset, length of time until maturity, exercise price, yields on alternative investments, and risk. —See also BLACK AND SCHOLES MODEL.

Options Clearing Corporation (OCC) An organization established in 1972 to process and guarantee the transactions in options that take place on the organized exchanges. The OCC substitutes its own credit for that of the parties undertaking the options transactions.

option series All option contracts on a stock that have an identical expiration date and strike price. An example of a series is March options on IBM with a $130 strike price. —Also called *series*.

options-income fund A mutual fund that attempts to increase current income by writing covered call options on securities held in the fund's portfolio.

option spread —See CALL SPREAD; PUT SPREAD.

option tender bond —See PUT BOND.

option writer The seller of a call option or a put option in an opening transaction. The option writer receives a premium and incurs an obligation to sell (if a call is sold) or to purchase (if a put is sold) the underlying asset at a stipulated price until a predetermined date. —See also WRITING.

or better (OB) —Used as a designation on a limit order ticket to indicate that the limit, in the case of a buy order, is higher than the market price, and, in the case of a sell order, is lower than the market price.

order A customer's instructions to buy or sell securities.

order flow Aggregated small orders for securities sent to dealers by brokers. —See also PAYMENT FOR ORDER FLOW.

order imbalance An excess of buy or sell orders such that it is impossible to match one type of order with its opposite. Order imbalances usually occur after unexpected news causes a rush to buy or sell a security. In extreme cases, an order imbalance may cause suspension of trading in a security for a limited time. —Also called *imbalance of orders*.

orderly market   A market in which bid and ask prices are continually provided and price changes between transactions are relatively small. It is the specialist's job to maintain an orderly market in assigned securities on the floor of an exchange.

order period   The period of time during which syndicate members take orders for a new security issue.

order ticket   A paper form on which a security order is written. —Also called *ticket*.

ordinary annuity   An annuity that makes payments at the end of each period. —Compare ANNUITY DUE.

ordinary income   Income that does not qualify for special tax treatment. Wages, dividends, and interest are ordinary income.

ordinary shares   The European equivalent for shares of common stock. Ordinary shares are held in trust as backing for American Depositary Receipts.

organized securities exchange   —See SECURITIES EXCHANGE.

original capital   Funds contributed to a business by the owners of the business at the time of its incorporation.

original cost   —See HISTORICAL COST.

original delivery   The delivery of a new security issue by the issuer to the original purchaser. —Also called *initial delivery*. —See also DATED DATE.

original-issue discount (OID)   The amount by which a bond is sold below its par value at the time of issue. With the exception of usually tax-free securities (that is, municipals), investors must report a certain portion of the discount as income for tax purposes each year.

original-issue discount bond   A bond issued at a discount from par value. The discount occurs when the coupon on the bond is less than the market rate of interest for a bond of similar risk and maturity. —Compare MINICOUPON BOND. —Also called *deep-discount bond*. —See also ZERO-COUPON BOND.

original maturity   The period between a security's maturity date and issue date. A bond issued 15 years ago that has an additional 10 years to maturity had an original maturity of 25 years. —See also CURRENT MATURITY.

originator   A financial institution that makes loans that are then resold.

orphan   Of or relating to a security that is not regularly covered by security analysts. An orphan security is likely to attract little investor interest and to sell at a relatively low price compared with other securities of the same type. For example, an orphan stock is likely to sell at a low price-earnings ratio and an orphan bond will offer a relatively high yield.

ᴧᴧ **CASE STUDY** | Many individuals in the financial community believe investment banking firms have an obligation to provide continuing research coverage of companies they take public. Research coverage increases a firm's exposure to the investment community, an important benefit for the firm and its shareholders, especially investors who acquired stock during the initial public offering. Dropping coverage of a small company and causing the stock to become an orphan can have a devastating effect on the stock's liquidity and market price. In some instances coverage is discontinued because of a loss of investor interest, in which case any remaining investor interest can virtually disappear. Orphan stocks became more common in the tech stock meltdown of 2000–01. In October 2001 Credit Suisse First Boston dropped coverage of Evolve Software, a software and fiber optics company that CSFB took public for $9 a share in August 2000. Although the stock quickly tripled in price following the initial public offering, it soon got caught in the downdraft of the bear market for technology stocks and had declined to approximately 25¢ per share by the time CSFB dropped its coverage of the firm. The analyst at Credit Suisse First Boston remained bullish on the stock until coverage was suddenly dropped a little more than a year after his firm managed the initial public offering.

OTC —See OVER-THE-COUNTER MARKET.

OTCBB —See OTC BULLETIN BOARD.

OTC Bulletin Board (OTCBB) A real-time quotation service for over-the-counter equity securities not listed or traded on a national securities exchange or on Nasdaq. In 2001 the OTCBB included over 330 market makers that provided firm quotations for over 3,600 domestic securities, foreign securities, and American Depositary Receipts. In January 1999 the SEC began requiring companies whose stocks are traded on the OTC Bulletin Board to report current financial information to the SEC. Securities delisted from the OTC Bulletin Board generally start trading through the Pink Sheets.

OTC margin stock —See MARGIN STOCK.

other assets Assets of relatively small value. For financial reporting purposes, firms frequently combine small assets into a single category rather than listing each item separately.

other liabilities Small and relatively insignificant liabilities. For financial reporting purposes, firms often combine small liabilities into this single category rather than listing each liability separately.

other revenue Revenue from sources other than regular ones. For example, a steel manufacturer would classify interest on customers' overdue accounts as other revenue. —Compare OPERATING REVENUE.

out-of-the-money —Used to describe a call option with a strike price above the price of the underlying asset or a put option with a strike price below the price of the underlying asset. For example, a put option to sell 100 shares of Cisco Systems stock at $50 per share is out-of-the-money if the stock currently trades at $70. Even though an out-of-the-money option has no intrinsic value, it may have market value.

outside audit —See EXTERNAL AUDIT.

outside director A member of a firm's board of directors who is not employed in another capacity by that firm. An example is the president of one firm who serves as a director of another firm. Some people believe that at least some outside directors are needed to give a board balance and to protect stockholders' interests. —Compare INSIDE DIRECTOR.

outstanding capital stock The number of shares of capital stock that have been issued and that are in public hands. Outstanding stock excludes shares issued but subsequently repurchased by the issuer as Treasury stock. Outstanding stock is used in the calculation of book value per share and earnings per share. —Also called *shares outstanding; stock outstanding*.

overallotment option —See GREENSHOE.

overbooked —See OVERSUBSCRIBED 1.

overbought Of, relating to, or being a stock market that has risen very rapidly in the recent past and is likely to suffer short-term price declines in the near future. Determining whether a market is overbought is difficult and is subject to individual interpretation.

overdepreciation 1. Depreciation that is more than sufficient to allow for the eventual replacement of the asset being depreciated. —Compare UNDERDEPRECIATION 1. 2. Depreciation that causes an asset to be carried on a firm's books at a lesser value than it would be worth if it were sold. Overdepreciation produces understated earnings and assets on financial statements. —Compare UNDERDEPRECIATION 2.

overdraft A draft for more than the balance in the account on which the draft is drawn. A bank may honor an overdraft, depending on the importance of the customer and on prior arrangements (if any) to cover overdrafts. —See also NSF CHECK.

overgrowth Rapid growth in the sales of a mutual fund's shares to the extent that the fund has difficulty finding promising new investments or it must take such large positions in individual investments that its trading flexibility is reduced. In other words, a very successful fund may grow so large that the fund may have trouble sustaining its success.

overhanging supply A relatively large block of a security that may or will be sold under certain circumstances. For example, a large stockholder may announce a secondary offering of a security. Overhanging supply is of interest to technical analysts who consider a resistance level to be caused by unhappy investors who are determined to sell the security if it reaches a certain price. There is an overhanging supply of the security at the resistance level. Overhanging supply tends to be bearish for a security because investors feel the security will have difficulty rising in price.

overhead —See INDIRECT COST.

overhead resistance level —See RESISTANCE LEVEL.

overlapping debt Debt of a municipality that is shared with another political entity. For example, a city may share responsibility with the county in which the city is located for bonds issued by the county to finance a facility such as a public auditorium. —Compare UNDERLYING DEBT.

overmargined Of or relating to an account in which the market value of the collateral in a brokerage account is above the minimum amount determined by the initial margin requirement.

overnight deal A secondary offering, follow-on offering, or sale of shares from a shelf offering in a large block trade. Compared to a public offering, an overnight deal can save on underwriting expenses and avoid downward pressure on a stock's price prior to the issue.

overnight position A broker-dealer's net security position at the end of a trading day. A large overnight position leaves the broker-dealer vulnerable to events occurring before the market opens the next day.

overnight repo A repurchase agreement in which securities are sold provided that they will be repurchased on the following day. Financial institutions use overnight repos as a means of raising short-term money for financing inventories.

overriding royalty interest   A third-party interest in royalty income derived from oil and gas rights.

oversold   Of, relating to, or being a stock market that has declined rapidly and steeply in the recent past and is likely to exhibit short-term price increases in the near future. Determining whether a market is oversold is difficult and is subject to individual interpretation.

oversubscribed   **1.** Or, relating to, or being a new security issue for which there are more requests to purchase securities than are securities available for sale. For example, brokers may take a sufficient number of preliminary orders for a new issue of stock for which there are insufficient shares available to satisfy the demand. —Also called *overbooked.* **2.** Of, relating to, or being a buyback or takeover attempt in which more securities are offered than the purchaser has agreed to buy. In such a case the purchaser may decide to buy the additional securities or may buy the agreed-upon number on a pro rata basis.

oversubscription privilege   The opportunity to purchase, on a pro rata basis, any remaining shares not already subscribed to in a new stock offering. In a typical new offering using stock rights, new shares are priced below the market price in order to ensure a successful sale. Generally, however, some stockholders will neither use nor sell their rights to buy the new shares, thus leaving some stock unsold even at the bargain price. The issuer therefore allows the stockholders to oversubscribe in anticipation of extra available shares. It is generally in the stockholder's interest to use the oversubscription privilege. —Compare SUBSCRIPTION PRICE.

over-the-counter market (OTC)   A widespread aggregation of dealers who make markets in many different securities. Unlike an exchange on which trading takes place at one physical location, OTC trading occurs through telephone or computer negotiations between buyers and sellers. Although stocks traded over the counter are often more speculative than listed stocks, virtually all government and municipal bonds and most corporate bonds are traded in the OTC market. —See also NATIONAL QUOTATION BUREAU; OTC BULLETIN BOARD; THIRD MARKET.

over-the-counter stock   A stock not listed on an exchange and trading only in the over-the-counter market.

overtrade   **1.** To purchase a client's securities at an above-the-market price in return for the client's purchase of part of a new issue. **2.** —See CHURN.

overvalued   Of, relating to, or being a security that trades at a price higher than it logically should. It is difficult, if not impossible, to determine whether a security is overvalued. —Compare UNDERVALUED.

overwriting   In options trading, the writing of more options than one expects to have exercised. Investors overwrite call options because they consider the underlying stock overvalued. Investors overwrite put options because they consider the underlying stock undervalued.

OW   —See OFFER WANTED.

owner of record   —See HOLDER OF RECORD.

owners' equity The owners' interest in the assets of a business. Owners' equity includes the amount invested by the owners plus the profits (or minus the losses) in the enterprise. Owners' equity and liabilities are used to finance a firm's assets. —Also called *net assets; shareholders' equity; stockholders' equity.*

P

p 1. —Used in the dividend column of stock transaction tables in newspapers to indicate an initial dividend: .50p. **2.** —Used in mutual fund transaction tables in newspapers to indicate that a distribution cost is charged.

PAC —See PLANNED AMORTIZATION CLASS.

Pacific Exchange (PCX) A major marketplace for stock options and equities. The PCX formerly operated trading floors in both Los Angeles and San Francisco, but it closed the L.A. floor in 2001 when equities trading was moved to the Archipelago Exchange, the nation's first electronic national stock market. Trading in equity options of over 800 companies continues on the San Francisco options floor.

Pac Man defense A defensive antitakeover tactic in which the target firm attempts to take over the acquiring firm. The target hopes that the acquiring firm will call off the takeover attempt and look for easier pickings.

PACS^{SM} A service mark for a type of municipal convertible bond.

paid-in capital Funds and property contributed to a firm by its stockholders. Paid-in capital is generated when a firm issues stock in the primary market, not when the stock is traded in the secondary market. —See also ADDITIONAL PAID-IN CAPITAL; CONTRIBUTED CAPITAL.

paid-in surplus —See ADDITIONAL PAID-IN CAPITAL.

painting the tape 1. Illegal trading of a security by manipulators among themselves in order to create the illusion of heavy trading activity, perhaps the kind generated by insiders. The increased trades are then reported on the consolidated tape, a situation that often lures unwary investors into the action. Once the market price of the security escalates, the manipulators will sell out, hoping to make a profit. **2.** Breaking down larger orders into more numerous smaller orders to have more trades appear on the tape and attract investor interest.

paired shares Shares of two firms under common management that are sold as a single unit. A single certificate may be issued to represent ownership in both firms. —Also called *stapled stock.*

pairs trade An investment strategy that matches a short position with a comparable long position in the stock of a company in the same industry. For example, an investor might buy 500 shares of Delta Airlines and sell short a comparable principal amount of the stock of UAL, Inc. The offsetting positions allow an investor to attempt to profit by selecting the best value in an industry without worrying about changes in the valuation of the sector or the overall market.

panda A gold coin minted in the People's Republic of China.

P&L —See PROFIT AND LOSS STATEMENT.

P&S —See PURCHASE AND SALES DEPARTMENT.

panic buying A flurry of security purchases accompanied by high volume and sharp price increases. During a period of panic buying, buyers do not have time to evaluate fundamental or technical factors because their primary goal is to acquire securities before the prices rise even more. For example, panic buying occurred on the day following President Lyndon B. Johnson's announcement of his decision not to run for reelection.

panic selling A flurry of selling in a particular security or in securities as a whole. Panic selling is accompanied by particularly heavy volume and sharp price declines as owners scramble to sell before prices drop even more. Panic selling is generally set off by an unexpected event viewed by traders as particularly negative. For example, uncertainty surrounding the outbreak of serious hostilities and a cutoff of oil supplies in the Middle East might be sufficient to cause panic selling.

paper A short-term unsecured note. This is generally used interchangeably with the term *commercial paper.*

paper company A corporation formed in order to accomplish a specific financial task rather than to produce a good or service. Such a firm usually has few assets other than those of a financial nature.

paper gain —See UNREALIZED GAIN.

paper loss —See UNREALIZED LOSS.

paper profit —See UNREALIZED GAIN.

par —See PAR VALUE 1, 2.

PAR —See PUBLIC AUTOMATED ROUTING SYSTEM.

par bond A bond that sells at a price equal to its par value, usually $1,000.

parent company A company that controls or owns another company or other companies. For example, Union Pacific Corporation is the parent company of the trucking firm Overnite Transportation Company. —Compare SUBSIDIARY. —See also HOLDING COMPANY.

parity The state of an option when its premium plus the strike price is equal to the market price of the underlying stock. If Amazon.com stock is selling at $17 per share, an option to buy the stock at $15 would be selling at parity if its premium is $2. —See also CONVERSION PARITY.

parking 1. Placing idle funds in a safe, short-term investment while awaiting the availability of other investment opportunities. Many investors end up parking proceeds from a security sale in a money market account while searching for other securities to purchase. 2. Transferring stock positions to another party so that true ownership of the stock will be hidden. For example, an investor involved in the takeover of a company may park securities of the company with other investors so that the management of the target company will not know the extent of the investor's stock ownership. Parking for this purpose is generally illegal.

Part B —See STATEMENT OF ADDITIONAL INFORMATION.

partial delivery Delivery by a broker of less than the quantity stipulated in the contract. A broker who delivers 200 shares of a stock when 500 shares are due is making a partial delivery.

partial execution Execution of less than the full amount of an order. An investor may place an order to buy 500 shares of GenCorp at $15 or less and get a partial execution if the broker is able to buy only 300 shares at that price. —Also called *partial fill*.

partial redemption Redemption by an issuer of less than an entire issue of its securities. For example, a corporation may redeem a portion of an outstanding bond issue.

partial spinoff Distribution to stockholders or sale to the public of shares that represent a minority interest in a firm's subsidiary. A firm may undertake a partial spinoff when it considers the subsidiary is not properly valued by the public as part of the parent firm, or when it wishes to raise funds without giving up total control of the subsidiary.

partial tender offer An offer to purchase less than all the shares of a company by specifying a maximum number of shares that will be accepted.

participate but do not initiate A customer instruction on a large order to a broker when the customer does not want the order to affect the price of the security. The instruction indicates that the broker should handle the order in such a way that no price change will be initiated by the broker.

participating 1. Of, relating to, or being an unusual class of preferred stock that participates with common stock in dividend increases according to a specified formula. For example, a participating preferred issue might require that any increases in dividends on common stock above $2 per share be shared equally with preferred. —Compare NONPARTICIPATING 1. **2.** Of or relating to a type of life insurance in which the insured shares in the insurer's investment success or lack of success. Owners of participating policies receive dividends from the insurer. —Compare NONPARTICIPATING 2.

Participating Equity Preferred Shares (PEPS) A special type of preferred stock that includes a conversion feature and a maturity date.

participation certificate A certificate indicating ownership in a pool of assets, generally mortgages.

partner A member of a partnership.

partnership A business owned by two or more people who agree on the method of distribution of profits and/or losses and on the extent to which each will be liable for the debts of one another. A partnership permits pass through of income and losses directly to the owners. In this way, they are taxed at each partner's personal tax rate. —Compare CORPORATION; PROPRIETORSHIP. —See also GENERAL PARTNERSHIP; LIMITED PARTNERSHIP; SILENT PARTNER.

partnership account A brokerage account in which two or more individuals are equally liable. A partnership account differs from a joint account in that the partnership account may include a written agreement defining the interest of each partner.

par value 1. The stated value of a security as it appears on its certificate. A bond's par value is the dollar amount on which interest is calculated and the amount paid to holders at maturity. Par value of preferred stock is used in a similar way in calculating the annual dividend. —Also called *face value; par*. **2.** The minimum contribution made by investors to purchase a share of common stock at the time of issue. Par value is of no real consequence to investors; in fact, many new common stock issues have no stated par value. —Also called *par.* —See also NO PAR.

passed dividend A regular dividend that is omitted by a firm's board of directors. Passed dividends on most issues of preferred stock, but not on common stock, eventually must be made up. —Also called *omitted dividend; unpaid dividend.* —See also DIVIDENDS IN ARREARS.

passing the book —Used to refer to the transfer of information on a firm's trading position from one office to another. For example, a New York brokerage firm may pass the book at the end of the trading day to an office in Los Angeles or Tokyo.

passive activity 1. An activity involving a trade or business in which the taxpayer does not materially participate. 2. Any engagement in real estate rental activity.

passive income (loss) A special category of income (loss) derived from passive activities, including real estate, limited partnerships, and other forms of tax-advantaged investments. Investors are limited in their deduction of passive losses against active sources of income, such as wages, salaries, and pension income.

passive investment management A method of managing an investment portfolio that seeks to select properly diversified securities that will remain relatively unchanged over long periods of time. Passive investment management involves minimal trading, based on the belief that it is impossible to beat the averages on a risk-adjusted basis consistently. —Compare ACTIVE INVESTMENT MANAGEMENT.

passive market making The offering by a market maker to purchase a firm's securities at the same time the market maker is acting as an underwriter of the securities in a secondary offering. The market maker is not permitted to offer a higher bid than a competing non-underwriting market maker.

passive portfolio A portfolio of securities that is altered only when another variable, such as market index, is altered.

pass-through security A security that passes through payments from debtors to investors. Packages of loans are assembled and sold to investors by private lenders. Although pass-through securities have stated maturities, the actual lives of the securities are likely to be shorter, especially during periods of falling interest rates when borrowers pay off mortgages early. The security derives its name from the fact that interest and principal payments made by borrowers are passed through monthly after deduction of a service fee. —Also called *pass through.* —See also GINNIE MAE PASS THROUGH; PRODUCTION RATE; WEIGHTED-AVERAGE COUPON RATE; WEIGHTED-AVERAGE MATURITY.

Patriot Bond A specially inscribed Series EE savings bond issued by the U.S. Treasury beginning December 11, 2001, three months following the September 11 terrorist attacks, to call attention to the country's war effort.

pattern —See CHART FORMATION.

payable That which is owed to another party as a debt.

payback period 1. The length of time needed for an investment's net cash receipts to cover completely the initial outlay expended in acquiring the investment. 2. The number of years the higher interest income from a convertible bond (compared with the dividend income from an equivalent investment in the underlying common stock) must persist to make up for the amount above conversion value paid for the convertible. —Also called *premium recovery period.*

paydown   In a corporate or U.S. Treasury refunding, the amount by which the face value of the bonds being refunded exceeds the par value of the new bonds being sold. The paydown represents the amount by which the debt is reduced.

paying agent   A financial institution that makes the payments to the holders of an issuer's securities. For example, an indenture will name a paying agent responsible for making interest and principal payments on a bond issue.

payment date   The date on which a dividend will be paid to stockholders or on which interest will be paid to bondholders by the issuers' paying agents. In some cases, the issuers will have the payments made a day early so that the security holders will receive payment on the payment date.

payment for order flow   The payment by a dealer to a broker acknowledging the broker's routing of customer orders to the dealer. For example, a specific market maker on a regional exchange might agree to pay a brokerage firm 2¢ per share for orders directed to the market makers. Payment for order flow has been criticized as an incentive to brokers to send orders to dealers from whom the brokers will receive the highest payment rather than to dealers who would provide the customer with the best available price.

    ⋀ **CASE STUDY** | In October 1995, Charles Schwab Corporation announced the firm would end the practice of payment for order flow. Schwab officials said the firm had been paying about 125 brokerage firms an average of 2¢ per share to route customer orders to its Mayer & Schweitzer subsidiary, which at the time was processing approximately 8% of Nasdaq's daily volume. The announcement came at least partly in response to pressure from both the Justice Department and the Securities and Exchange Commission. The concern was that payment for order flow raised questions about whether customer orders were receiving fair treatment; brokerage firms might send the orders to dealers who offered the highest payment for order flow rather than to dealers offering the best price to the customer. Shortly after the Schwab announcement, Merrill Lynch disclosed that the firm would stop automatically sending small orders for New York Stock Exchange–listed securities to the Boston and Pacific stock exchanges where it maintained dealer operations. Merrill said it would continue to send customer orders to the regional exchanges but only if these exchanges offered the best prices.

payment-in-kind security (PIK)   A relatively unusual type of security that allows the issuer to pay the investor with additional shares (in the case of PIK preferred) or with bonds (in the case of PIK bonds) rather than with cash. Payment-in-kind bonds and preferred stock may cause cash flow problems for investors who must pay income taxes on the market value of the additional securities received. PIK securities nearly always originate as a result of a leveraged buyout.

payout ratio   The ratio from which the percentage of net income a firm pays to its stockholders in dividends is calculated. Companies paying most of their earnings in dividends have little left for investment to provide for future earnings growth. Stock of firms with high payout ratios appeals primarily to investors seeking high current income and limited capital growth. —Also called *dividend payout ratio.* —See also DIVIDEND COVERAGE; RETAINED EARNINGS.

payup Additional funds required when an investor swaps a current holding for higher-value securities. For example, a person might swap low-interest bonds for higher-coupon bonds of equal face value but of higher market value.

P/CF ratio —See PRICE-TO-CASH-FLOW RATIO.

PCX —See PACIFIC EXCHANGE.

peg 1. To fix the price of a new security issue during the issuance period through buying and selling it in the open market in order to ensure that the price in the secondary market will not fall below the offering price. —Also called *holding the market; price stabilization; stabilize.* —See also STABILIZATION PERIOD. **2.** To fix the rate at which foreign currencies exchange with one another.

PEG ratio —See PRICE-EARNINGS/GROWTH RATIO.

penalty bid A financial penalty sometimes imposed by the underwriter of a new securities issue against a broker whose customer(s) sold shares of the issue immediately after purchase. Penalty bids are imposed in order to keep the price of a newly issued security from declining.

penalty plan A mutual fund accumulation plan in which sales fees for the entire obligation are deducted from shares purchased in the first few years that the plan is in effect. In the event that the investors redeem the shares after a short time, only a small portion of the purchase price will be refunded. Sales charges and penalty plans are regulated by the Investment Company Amendments Act of 1970.

penetration In charting, breaking through a trendline, resistance level, or support level. The direction of the penetration provides an indication of future price movement.

pennant —See TRIANGLE.

pennying —See FRONT RUNNING.

penny stock A low-priced, speculative stock. Although the maximum price at which a security may sell and still be classified as a penny stock is subject to individual interpretation, $1 is probably the most commonly recognized limit. Many penny stocks are traded in the over-the-counter market and on smaller exchanges.

Penny Stock Reform Act A 1990 congressional act that expanded the SEC's authority over previously unregulated promoters who associate with broker-dealers to sell penny stocks. The act also placed restrictions on blank check offerings and required broker-dealers to disclose more information about penny stocks to customers. Perhaps most importantly, the act called for the creation of an automated quotation system for OTC stocks.

Pension Benefit Guaranty Corporation A government agency that insures certain corporate pension funds. The Corporation, established under the Employee Retirement Income Security Act, is funded by charging companies a premium based on the number of covered employees.

pension cost The annual cost incurred by a firm in providing its employees with a pension plan.

pension fund A financial institution that controls assets and disburses income to people after they have retired. Pension funds, which invest in a variety of securities, control such enormous sums that their investment decisions can have significant impact on individual security prices.

pension parachute A pension agreement stating that, in the event of an unfriendly takeover, a firm can use any surplus pension assets to increase pension benefits. A pension parachute is used to make the firm less attractive to takeover, for it prevents the acquiring company from using the excess pension assets to help finance the acquisition.

pension plan An arrangement for paying death, disability, or retirement benefits to employees. Payments into the plan are ordinarily a tax-deductible expense for the firm, but any contribution by employees may or may not be deductible on personal tax returns. Likewise, retirement benefits paid to employees will be wholly or partially taxable. —Compare VESTED BENEFITS. —See also DEFINED-BENEFIT PENSION PLAN; DEFINED-CONTRIBUTION PENSION PLAN.

pension reversion Termination of a pension plan by an employer that wishes to capture the amount by which the plan is overfunded. Pension reversions are generally accomplished by using funds in the plan to purchase a fixed annuity from an insurance company. Excess funds beyond the cost of the annuity revert to the company.

pension rollover Reinvestment of a lump-sum pension payout into an individual retirement account. The rollover permits a pension beneficiary to defer taxation until funds are paid out of the individual retirement account. A pension rollover is an alternative to paying taxes on a lump-sum payout, either in one year or by averaging over a number of years.

PEPS —See PARTICIPATING EQUITY PREFERRED SHARES.

PER —See POST EXECUTION REPORTING SYSTEM.

P/E ratio —See PRICE-EARNINGS RATIO.

per capita debt The total debt of a municipality divided by the municipality's population. Financial analysts use per capita debt when evaluating a municipality's ability to repay its debt.

percentage depletion Depletion calculated as a percentage of gross income derived from a natural resource. Percentage depletion is independent of the cost of the resource.

percentage-of-completion method A method of recognizing revenues and costs from a long-term project in relation to the percentage completed during the course of the project. Thus, the percentage-of-completion method allows a business profits (or losses) on a project before its completion. —Compare COMPLETED-CONTRACT METHOD.

percentage order A customer order to purchase or sell shares of a stock after a specified number of shares of the same stock have been traded.

perfect hedge A hedge that exactly offsets any gains or losses from an existing investment position. An example of a perfect hedge is the short sale of an owned security in order to lock in an existing profit and transfer it to a subsequent tax year. Because very few hedges are perfect, most of them operate merely to offset a portion of losses or gains. —See also RISK HEDGE.

performance audit —See MANAGEMENT AUDIT.

Performance Equity-Linked Redemption Quarterly-Pay Securities^{SM}
(PERQS^{SM}**)** Intermediate-term debt securities with a maturity value dependent on the value of the underlying stock to which the security is linked. PERQS pay fixed quarterly interest and represent debt of their issuers. These securities issued by Morgan Stanley represent debt of the issuer and are not subject to early redemption.

performance fee A fee paid to an investment manager based on the performance of a client's portfolio, determined by a specified standard. For example, an investment manager might be paid a regular fixed fee plus an incentive fee based on the change in value of the client's portfolio. —Also called *incentive fee.*

performance fund —See AGGRESSIVE GROWTH FUND.

performance stock A stock that investors believe has an excellent chance for significant price appreciation. Performance stock tends to be issued by growth-oriented firms that retain most or all income for reinvestment. The stock usually sells at above-average price-earnings ratios and experiences large price swings. Performance stock is judged more on the basis of fundamental analysis than are glamour stock and hot stock, which are more subject to investor psychology.

periodic payment plan A plan in which an investor agrees to make monthly or quarterly payments to a mutual fund as a method of accumulating shares over a period of years. The periodic payment plan's stipulation of fixed periodic contributions results in dollar-cost averaging for the investor. —See also PLAN COMPLETION INSURANCE.

periodic purchase deferred contract A deferred annuity purchased with a series of premium payments. For example, an individual might obtain a lifetime monthly income by making annual premium payments to an insurance company prior to retirement. —Compare SINGLE-PREMIUM DEFERRED ANNUITY.

period of call protection —See DEFERMENT PERIOD.

PERLS —See PRINCIPAL EXCHANGE-RATE-LINKED SECURITY.

permanent financing The long-term financing that supports a long-term asset.

permanent insurance —See CASH-VALUE LIFE INSURANCE.

perpendicular spread A combination of options with the same expiration date but different strike prices.

perpetual bond —See CONSOL.

perpetual warrant A warrant that has no expiration date. Although many warrants have relatively long maturities, few are perpetual.

perpetuity A stream of payments that is expected to last indefinitely.

PERQS^{SM} —See PERFORMANCE EQUITY-LINKED REDEMPTION QUARTERLY-PAY SECURITIES^{SM}.

personal exemption —See EXEMPTION.

personal income The pretax income of individuals and unincorporated businesses. Personal income is an inferior measure of the economy compared with disposable income; however, personal income is easier to compute and is made available on a monthly basis, while disposable income is calculated on a quarterly basis.

petrodollars The funds that are controlled by oil-exporting countries and have been used to pay for oil imports. Petrodollars are a huge pool of funds available for investment and the purchase of goods and services. Although stated in terms of dollars, the term generally refers to all currencies.

pf —Used in stock transaction tables in newspapers to indicate the stock is a preferred issue. Issues without any designation are common stock. A capital letter (that is, an *A*, *B*, or *C) beside pf* indicates the particular issue of preferred listed: *GaPc pfC2.24.*

phantom stock plan An incentive plan for a firm's executives in which the executives are offered bonuses based on increases in the market price of the firm's stock. A phantom stock plan is supposed to induce the executives to act in the best interests of the shareholders.

Philadelphia Board of Trade The futures subsidiary of the Philadelphia Stock Exchange.

Philadelphia Stock Exchange (PHLX) The oldest organized securities exchange in the United States (founded in 1790), the PHLX serves as a marketplace for stocks, equity options, index options, and currency options. The exchange offers trading in both standardized and customized currency and equity options.

PHLX —See PHILADELPHIA STOCK EXCHANGE.

physical life The potential service life of an asset before it physically becomes unable to produce a good or service. An asset is often physically able to continue operating but at a cost or rate that renders it economically obsolete. The economic life, as opposed to the physical life, is most important in valuing the asset.

physical option An option on a physical commodity, such as a currency, commodity, or U.S. Treasury debt, rather than on stock or futures.

pickup A gain in yield that is achieved from swapping bonds. For example, a pickup of 30 basis points comes about when bonds with a 9.70% basis are traded for bonds with a 10.00% basis.

pickup bond A bond with a relatively high coupon and a short period remaining until it is likely to be called by the issuer. If interest rates fall and the bond is called, the investor will pick up a premium equal to the difference between the call price and the purchase price.

picture The bid and ask price at which a dealer is willing to buy or sell a security.

piece A part of a large security offering.

piggyback 1. A broker trading in his or her personal account after trading in the same security for a customer. The broker may believe the customer has access to privileged information that will cause the transaction to be profitable. 2. —See FOLLOW-ON OFFERING.

piggyback registration The registration of a new issue and already outstanding stock of the same issuer for a single public offering. Thus, a single registration suffices for the primary and secondary offering.

PIK —See PAYMENT-IN-KIND SECURITY.

Pink Sheets The registered name for a privately owned company that operates a centralized quotation service that collects and distributes market maker quotations for securities traded in the over-the-counter market. The service is named for the color of the sheets on which the National Quotation Bureau distributed bid and ask quotations for OTC securities. In 1999 Pink Sheets introduced its Electronic Quotation Service, which provides real-time quotes for OTC equities and bonds. —See also OTC BULLETIN BOARD; YELLOW SHEETS.

PIPE —See PRIVATE INVESTMENT IN PUBLIC EQUITIES.

pipeline The process through which security issues pass before their distribution to the public. If securities are being readied for distribution, they are said to be in the pipeline.

pipeline theory —See CONDUIT THEORY.

pit A location on a commodities exchange trading floor where the futures of a particular commodity are traded. —Also called *ring*.

place To sell a new securities issue.

placement ratio The percentage of municipal bonds brought to market during the past week that have been sold by underwriters. Only issues greater or equal to $1 million are included in this calculation published by the *Bond Buyer*.

plain-vanilla Of or relating to the uncomplicated version of a particular type of security. For example, a plain-vanilla derivative is typically exchange-traded and void of bells and whistles. Likewise, a plain-vanilla bond is not convertible and cannot be called.

plan company A company that receives customer payments and purchases mutual fund shares when the customers wish to purchase shares in a fund on a periodic payment plan. Thus, the plan company acts as middleman in collecting the payments and crediting customer accounts.

plan completion insurance A life insurance policy for people who purchase mutual fund shares as part of a periodic payment plan. In the event of the participant's death before completion of the contract, plan completion insurance pays an amount sufficient to complete the remaining payments.

planned amortization class (PAC) A type of collateralized mortgage obligation with a predetermined principal paydown schedule that provides investors with greater cash-flow certainty and a more specific average life. The greater payment certainty comes at the expense of a lower yield to investors.

plant and equipment The fixed assets that are used to produce the goods and services that a firm sells to its customers. On a corporate balance sheet, plant and equipment are valued at original cost. Plant and equipment become net plant and equipment when adjusted for accumulated depreciation. —Also called *net plant and equipment*.

plastic bonds The bonds that are backed by credit card receivables. These securities are generally high quality and offer yields that are nearly equal to the yields on certificates of deposit.

play 1. An investment. **2.** —See DIRECT PLAY.

pledged asset An asset used as security for a loan.

plow back To reinvest earnings in additional income-producing assets. Firms that plow back earnings rather than paying the earnings in dividends tend to experience more rapid increases in earnings per share.

plowback ratio —See RETENTION RATE.

plus (+) **1.** —Used in the net change column of security transaction tables to indicate a closing price higher than the closing price on the last previous day on which the security was traded. **2.** —Used in reporting closed-end investment company share prices to indicate the percentage amount by which market price exceeds net asset value. —Compare MINUS 2. **3.** An addition of one sixty-fourth either to the bid or to the ask price for a government bond. Government securities are usually quoted in thirty-seconds of a dollar; therefore, a quote of $91.03 + indicates a price of $91^3/$_{32}$ + ^{1}/$_{64}$, or $91^7/$_{64}$.

plus-cash convertible An unusual type of convertible security that requires a fixed cash payment in addition to surrender of the convertible in order to exercise the conversion privilege and obtain the shares of common stock. A plus-cash convertible has built-in leverage that produces relatively large price swings in the convertible compared with the underlying common stock.

plus tick —See UPTICK.

PN —See PROJECT NOTE.

PO —See PRINCIPAL-ONLY.

point A change in the value of a security or a security index or average. For common and preferred stocks a point represents a change of $1. For bonds a point represents a 1% change in face value. For example, a one-point decline in a $1,000 principal amount bond translates to a $10 decline in price. For stock averages and indexes a point represents a unit of movement and is best interpreted as a percent of the beginning value. For example, a 100-point decline in the Dow Jones Industrial Average that started the day at 10,000 represents a 1% fall in the average.

point-and-figure chart In technical analysis, a chart pattern, peculiar to securities, in which only the significant value changes of a security, a futures contract, or a market average are recorded. The vertical axis represents price, but, unlike nearly all other charts, no variable, including time, is plotted on the horizontal axis. Entries on a point-and-figure chart are made only when a variable changes by a predetermined amount, for example, by one point or two points. A period of days may pass before an entry is recorded. Refer to the *Technical Analysis Chart Patterns* for an example of this chart. —Compare BAR CHART; LINE CHART.

poison pill An antitakeover tactic in which warrants are issued to a firm's stockholders, giving them the right to purchase shares of the firm's stock at a bargain price in the event that a suitor hostile to management acquires a stipulated percentage of the firm's stock. The poison pill is intended to make the takeover so expensive that any attempt to take control will be abandoned. —See also FLIP-OVER PILL; JONESTOWN DEFENSE; MACARONI DEFENSE; SUICIDE PILL.

poison-put bond A bond that allows an investor to cash in a security before maturity if the issuer becomes the target of a takeover hostile to its management. Poison-put bonds make it expensive for the bidder to buy the target firm because the bidder will have to raise cash to pay off the owners of the bonds. The bonds can benefit the bondholders because they permit the holders to cash in the securities if the takeover spawns a new, more leveraged high-risk corporate entity. —See also POISON PILL.

pollution control bond A municipal revenue bond in which debt service is secured by payments from a private firm using pollution control equipment that the bond was used to finance. Thus, the guarantee of repayment is made by the private firm rather than by the municipal issuer. For pollution control bonds issued before August 8, 1986, interest is free from federal taxation. Tax reform passed in 1986 eliminated this exemption. Interest on pollution control bonds issued on or after August 8, 1986, is fully taxable.

Ponzi scheme —See PYRAMID.

pool 1. A temporary affiliation of two or more people in an attempt to manipulate a security's price and/or volume. The pool is necessary in order to acquire the capital needed to manipulate a stock having a large market value. Pools were especially popular in the 1920s and early 1930s but now have been regulated out of existence. —See also BLIND POOL; TRADING POOL. 2. —See MORTGAGE POOL.

pool financing —See BOND POOL.

pooling of interests An accounting method for combining unchanged the assets, liabilities, and owners' equity of two firms after a merger or combination. Before being discontinued in 2001, pooling was a preferred method of accounting for mergers because it generally produced the highest earnings calculations for the surviving company.—See PURCHASE METHOD.

poop and scoop The illegal practice of spreading negative information in order to drive down a stock price with the goal of purchasing shares at a bargain price. —Compare PUMP AND DUMP.

> ᴍᴀ **CASE STUDY** | Many investment scams involve inflating the price of a stock that is owned in order to dump shares on the public at a profit. In some instances, however, the fraudulent activity involves deflating the market price of a stock that has been sold short so that the stock can be bought back at a lower price. In late 2000 a 23-year-old man pleaded guilty to securities fraud for issuing fake negative press releases for Emulex Corporation. The man had sold short 3,000 shares of the stock in order to profit from an expected decline in price. When the stock price started rising, he used knowledge gained as a former employee of an online distributor of press releases to write and distribute a phony release that stated Emulex's chief executive had quit and the firm was restating its quarterly earnings from a profit to a loss. The press release caused the shares of Emulex to plunge until trading was halted on the Nasdaq. According to government charges, the man made a profit of nearly a quarter of a million dollars by covering his short position and subsequently purchasing additional shares of the company at the artificially low price resulting from the fraudulent press release.

portability agreement The ability of an investor to transfer a proprietary brokerage product, such as a mutual fund, to an account at a different brokerage firm.

PORTAL A NASD trading system for unregistered foreign and domestic securities.

portfolio A group of investments. The more diversified the investments in a portfolio, the more likely the investor is to earn the same return as the market. —See also DIVERSIFICATION.

portfolio beta The relative volatility of returns earned from holding a specific portfolio of securities. A high portfolio beta indicates securities that tend to be more volatile in their price movements than the market taken as a whole. Portfolio beta is calculated by summing the products of each security's beta times the proportional weight of the security in the portfolio. For example, if a portfolio consists of two securities, one valued at $15,000 and having a beta of 0.9 and the other valued at $10,000 and having a beta of 1.5, the portfolio beta is (0.9)($15,000/$25,000) + (1.5)($10,000/$25,000), or 1.14.

portfolio dedication The synchronization of returns on an investment portfolio with known future liabilities. Portfolio dedication applies primarily to investment decisions by institutions such as pension funds and insurance companies. These institutions can estimate future liabilities fairly accurately, then try to minimize the outlay to satisfy the liabilities. —Also called *dedication; matching.*

portfolio dressing The addition and deletion of securities by an institutional investor before a financial reporting period in order to make the portfolio appear acceptable to investors. Typically, portfolio dressing involves the sale of big losers and the addition of big gainers to convey the impression that the portfolio manager is competent. —Also called *dressing up a portfolio.*

portfolio effect A reduction in the variation of returns on a combination of assets compared with the average of the variations of the individual assets. This effect measures the extent to which variations in returns on a portion of assets held are partially canceled by variations in returns on other assets held in the same portfolio.

portfolio insurance The futures or option contracts that serve to offset in whole or in part changes in the value of a portfolio. For example, a portfolio manager might sell short stock-index futures to hedge an expected decline in the market value of a portfolio.

portfolio manager A person who is paid a fee to supervise the investment decisions of others. The term is usually used in reference to the managers of large institutions such as bank trust departments, pension funds, insurance companies, and mutual funds. —Also called *money manager.*

portfolio pumping The end-of-period trading by a mutual fund in order to raise the fund's performance results. For example, a mutual fund may purchase additional shares of a thinly traded stock it already owns with the intention of driving up the stock price and increasing the value of the stock in the fund's portfolio.

portfolio theory The theory that holds that assets should be chosen on the basis of how they interact with one another rather than how they perform in isolation. According to this theory, an optimal combination would secure for the investor the highest possible return for a given level of risk or the least possible risk for a given level of return. Although individual investors can use some of the ideas of portfolio theory in putting together a group of investments, the theory and the literature relating to it are so complex and mathematically sophisticated that the theory is applied primarily by market professionals. —Also called *modern portfolio theory.*

POSIT An electronic system launched in 1987 that matches institutional buy and sell orders for individual stocks and for portfolios of stocks. Trades are priced from the stock's primary market at the time the match is run, and matches take place at the midpoint of the best asking price and the best selling price. POSIT is a joint venture between Investment Technology Group and BARRA, a financial data provider.

position The ownership status of a person's or an institution's investments. For example, a person may own 500 shares of Sun Microsystems, 350 shares of Boeing, and a $10,000 principal amount of 9% bonds due in 2001. —See also LONG POSITION; SHORT POSITION.

position To buy or sell securities in order to establish a net long or a net short position. —Also called *take a position.*

position building The continual and gradual accumulation of a firm's shares for a long position or the borrowing and sale of the shares for a short position.

position day The day on which an investor with a short position in a commodity (that is, the investor who must make delivery) declares an intention to make delivery if the day is other than the first day permitted. —Compare FIRST POSITION DAY.

position limit In futures and options trading, the maximum number of contracts that an individual or a group of individuals working together may hold. The position limit is determined by the Commodity Futures Trading Commission for futures or by the exchange on which the particular contract is traded. —Compare TRADING LIMIT.

position trader A security trader who holds a position overnight, and, in some cases, for even longer periods. Position traders differ from day traders and scalpers who operate within shorter time frames.

position trading The purchase or sale of an inventory by a dealer.

positive carry The current net income from an investment position when the current income from the investment exceeds its cost of carry. A Treasury bond with a current yield of 14% has a positive carry if its purchase can be financed at 12%. —Compare NEGATIVE CARRY. —See also CARRYING CHARGES 1.

positive covenant A clause in a loan agreement that requires a specified action by the borrower. For example, a positive covenant may mandate that the borrower maintain a specific level of working capital or issue periodic reports to creditors. —Compare NEGATIVE COVENANT.

positive yield curve The normal relationship between bond yields and maturity lengths that results from higher interest rates on long-term bonds than on short-term bonds. Positive refers to the slope of the curve drawn to depict this relationship. —Compare NEGATIVE YIELD CURVE. —See also FLAT YIELD CURVE.

post A location on the floor of an organized exchange at which assigned securities are traded. Posts are numbered and staffed by specialists. A single location may accommodate the trading of a number of different securities. —Also called *trading post.*

post To enter information in an account. For example, if a customer sends money to a broker, the brokerage firm will post a credit to the customer's account.

Post Execution Reporting System (PER)　An automated switching system on the American Stock Exchange that transmits orders electronically to the appropriate specialist on the exchange floor.

Post 30 stock　A stock listed on the New York Stock Exchange that is traded in ten-share units. The name derives from the location at which these stocks are traded on the exchange floor.

pot　The securities from a new issue that are returned to the lead underwriter by syndicate members for sale to institutional investors. —See also POT IS CLEAN.

potential dilution　The decrease in the proportional equity position of a share of stock that will occur eventually if additional authorized shares are actually issued. This term generally refers to outstanding options and convertible securities likely to be exchanged for shares of common stock at a future time.

pot is clean　—Used as an indication from the lead underwriter of a new issue that the securities set aside for sale to institutional investors have been sold.

power of attorney　A legal document in which a person gives another the power to act for him or her. The authority may be general or it may be restricted to activities such as the handling of security transactions.

Pr　—Used on the consolidated tape to indicate preferred stock: *GMPr 80¹/₂.*

precedence　The sequence in which orders are executed on an exchange floor. For example, the order with the lowest ask or highest bid has precedence over other orders. With orders at an identical price, the one entered earliest has precedence. The precedence of orders is established by the rules of each exchange.

precious metals/gold fund　An investment company that maintains a portfolio that contains a two-thirds minimum of investments in securities connected with silver, gold, and other precious metals.

preemptive right　A stockholder's right to keep a constant percentage of a firm's outstanding stock by being given the first chance to purchase shares in a new stock issue in proportion to the percentage of outstanding shares already held. Not all firms provide the preemptive right, which is more important to stockholders owning a significant part of a company. —Compare PRIVILEGED SUBSCRIPTION. —Also called *subscription privilege.* —See also SPECIAL SUBSCRIPTION ACCOUNT.

preference　The practice of matching customers' buy and sell orders away from the primary exchange. Preferencing is opposed by the New York Stock Exchange because it claims the practice unfairly benefits brokerage firms and doesn't give customer orders the chance to see other customer orders in a public market. —Compare IN-HOUSE TRADE.

preference stock　—See PRIOR PREFERRED.

preferred call period　—See DEFERMENT PERIOD.

preferred creditor　A creditor having priority to payment over one or more other classes of creditors. For example, holders of first mortgage bonds must be paid by the borrower before payments are made to holders of second mortgage bonds on the same collateral. First mortgage bondholders are the preferred creditors.

preferred dividend coverage　The measure of a firm's ability to meet its dividend obligations on preferred stock. The greater the coverage the less the chance that management will pass a dividend. This ratio is calculated by dividing earnings before taxes and fixed charges by fixed charges plus preferred dividends (divided by one minus the firm's tax rate).

preferred stock A security that shows ownership in a corporation and that gives the holder a claim prior to the claim of common stockholders on earnings and also generally on assets in the event of liquidation. Most preferred stock issues pay a fixed dividend set at the time of issuance, stated in a dollar amount or as a percentage of par value. Because no maturity date is stipulated, these securities are priced on dividend yield and trade much like long-term corporate bonds. As a general rule, preferred stock has limited appeal for individual investors. —See also AUCTION-RATE PREFERRED STOCK; CALLABLE PREFERRED STOCK; CUMULATIVE; FLOATING-RATE PREFERRED STOCK; MONTHLY INCOME PREFERRED SECURITIES; NEW MONEY PREFERRED; PARTICIPATING; PREFERRED DIVIDEND COVERAGE; PRIOR PREFERRED; REMARKETED PREFERRED STOCK; SECOND PREFERRED.

preferred stock ratio The proportion of preferred stock, valued at par, in a firm's total capitalization. The preferred stock ratio is calculated by dividing the par value of a firm's outstanding preferred stock by its net worth and long-term debt.

pre-IPO An offering of a company's shares prior to the firm's initial public offering. Investing in a pre-IPO tends to be very risky, in part because the planned IPO may never take place. In addition, shares from a pre-IPO are unregistered and are likely to be very difficult to sell until the public offering is completed.

> **CASE STUDY** Acting Securities and Exchange Commission chairman Laura Unger told a congressional subcommittee in July 2001 that 16 of 57 analysts reviewed by SEC staffers had invested in 39 pre-IPOs of companies they subsequently covered. In most cases shares offered in pre-IPOs are priced substantially lower than the subscription price in the subsequent IPO, meaning that many analysts who participated were able to acquire shares at very low prices. The conflict of interest is clear: analysts are likely to have a personal interest in promoting stocks they own, thus tainting the independence of their recommendations. Corporations are anxious to have analysts come on board as shareholders, in part because of the creditability analyst ownership conveys to the investing public. Analyst ownership may also result in positive investment recommendations that become a marketing campaign for the firm's stock.

preliminary prospectus —See RED HERRING.

preliminary scale The initial yields and prices for an upcoming bond issue prior to submission of a bid.

premature exercise Exercise of an option by the owner before the expiration date. Although most options are exercised near expiration, an owner occasionally finds it advantageous to exercise prematurely. Such an action will often foul up the option writer's plan, in which instance the writer must sell (with a call) or purchase (with a put) the stock earlier than expected.

premium **1.** The price at which an option trades. The size of the premium is affected by various factors including the time to expiration, interest rates, strike price, and the price and price volatility of the underlying asset. —Also called *option premium.* **2.** The amount by which a bond sells above its face value. **3.** The excess by which a warrant trades above its theoretical value. **4.** The amount by which a convertible bond sells above the price at which the same bond without the convertible feature would sell.

premium bond A bond that sells at a price above its par value. An investor must be careful about purchasing a bond that is selling at a premium because of the possibility of a call by the bond's issuer for sinking fund requirements or for refunding. Except for convertible bonds, the size of a bond's premium usually can be expected to decline as the bond approaches maturity, at which time it will be paid off at par.

premium income Fees in the form of premiums received by an investor who sells short a call option or put option. For example, an investor holding shares of BP can earn premium income by writing covered call options that give the buyer of the calls the right to purchase the option writer's BP shares at a fixed price until a stated date.

premium put A put price on a bond that is above par value. An example would be a $1,000 principal amount bond with a put price of $1,100 ten years after issue. The purpose of including a premium put is to reduce the coupon rate of interest that must be paid to sell the issue. —Compare YIELD TO PUT.

premium recovery period —See PAYBACK PERIOD 2.

prenuptial agreement A written agreement by a couple who plan to marry in which financial matters, including rights following divorce or the death of one spouse, are detailed.

preopening indication —See INDICATION 2.

prepackaged bankruptcy A Chapter 11 bankruptcy settlement in which the reorganization and main provisions have been agreed to by creditors and stockholders in advance of the filing.

prepaid expense An expenditure for an item that will provide future benefits. For example, a firm may pay an insurance premium only once a year, resulting in an expense that provides benefits throughout a 12-month period. The unexpired part of the premium is carried on the firm's balance sheet as a prepaid expense.

prepaid interest The interest on a loan that has been paid but is not due until a following period. The Internal Revenue Service does not permit taxpayers to claim an itemized deduction on tax returns for prepaid interest.

prepayment A payment made before the day it is due. For example, sending a check on the transaction date for securities bought with regular-way delivery will almost surely result in prepayment.

prepayment risk The risk to a lender that part or all of the principal of a loan will be paid prior to the scheduled maturity. For a bondholder, prepayment risk refers to the possibility the issuer will redeem a callable bond prior to maturity. Prepayments generally occur when market rates of interest decline following the loan origination. Prepayment generally results in reduced cash flow for a bondholder when proceeds from the redemption are reinvested at a reduced interest rate. —Also called *call risk*.

prerefunded bond A bond secured by an escrow fund of U.S. government obligations that is sufficient to pay off the entire issue of refunded bonds at maturity. The rating of the refunded bond generally assumes the rating of the government obligations (highest rating) at the time the fund is established. —See also ARBITRAGE BOND.

prerefunding The placing of funds with a trustee in order to retire a bond issue as a liability before the call date. —Also called *advance refunding.* —See also ARBITRAGE BOND.

presale order An order to buy a portion of a new municipal bond issue before the time at which certain information concerning the issue, such as the coupon, has been determined. Presale orders are permitted with municipal bond issues but not with other security issues because municipal bond issues are exempt from requirements of the SEC.

present value (PV) The current value of future cash payments when the payments are discounted by a rate that is a function of the interest rate. For example, the present value of $1,000 to be received in two years is $812 when the $1,000 is discounted at an annual rate of 11%. Conversely, $812 invested at an annual return of 11% would produce a sum of $1,000 in two years. —Compare FUTURE VALUE. —See also NET PRESENT VALUE.

president A leading decision maker of a company. The president is sometimes the company's chief executive officer.

presidential election cycle The tendency of the stock market to move in four-year cycles with rising markets occurring during the period before presidential elections. The presidential election cycle is based on observation of past market movements and on the theory that holds that incumbent presidents manipulate the economy before elections in such a way that bull markets ensue. —Also called *election cycle.*

presold Of, relating to, or being a new security issue that is sold out before all the specifics of the issue have been announced. In the case of a bond issue, this term usually means that sufficient orders for the issue have been placed before announcement of the coupon rate(s).

pre-syndicate bid A stabilization bid prior to the effective date of a secondary offering.

pretax income Reported income before the deduction of income taxes. Pretax income is sometimes considered a better measure of a firm's performance than aftertax income because taxes in one period may be influenced by activities in earlier periods. —Also called *earnings before taxes; pretax.*

pretax loss A loss reported before tax benefits are considered.

pretax writedown An accounting reduction in the value of an asset, measured before any effect by income taxes.

pretax yield The rate of return on an investment before taxes have been considered. As with other measures of yield, pretax yield is usually stated on an annual basis.

price The dollar amount at which a security trades. Stocks are nearly always quoted fully (that is, $25 means $25 per share), while bonds are ordinarily quoted as a percentage of par value (that is, 98 represents $980 per $1,000 par bond).

price change —See NET CHANGE.

price continuity Of or relating to a security that experiences minimal price changes between trades. Price continuity signifies a liquid market with substantial depth.

price-earnings/growth ratio (PEG ratio) A valuation tool that compares a stock's price-earnings ratio with the firm's expected growth in earnings per share. Most advocates of this tool believe choosing a stock with a PEG ratio of less than one will tend to produce above-average returns.

price-earnings ratio (P/E ratio) A common stock analysis statistic in which the current price of a stock is divided by the current (or sometimes the projected) earnings per share of the issuing firm. As a rule, a relatively high price-earnings ratio is an indication that investors believe the firm's earnings are likely to grow. Price-earnings ratios vary significantly among companies, among industries, and over time. One of the important influences on this ratio is long-term interest rates. In general, relatively high rates result in low price-earnings ratios; low interest rates result in high price-earnings ratios. —Also called *earnings multiple; market multiple; multiple; P/E ratio.* —See also FORWARD P/E; TRAILING P/E.

price-earnings relative The price-earnings ratio of a stock in relation to the price-earnings ratio of the overall stock market, generally as measured by the S&P 500. This ratio is used as a tool to help determine if a stock's P/E ratio is reasonable.

price gap —See GAP.

price improvement The execution of an order at a price better than what is currently quoted publicly.

price index —See CONSUMER PRICE INDEX; PRODUCER PRICE INDEX.

price limits For a given futures contract, the maximum price change from the previous day's settlement price that is permitted during a trading session. These limits are sometimes adjusted in fast-moving markets.

price range —See RANGE.

price-sales ratio (P/S ratio) A financial ratio that compares a firm's stock price with its sales per share (or its market value with total revenue). It is used by some analysts to find companies that may be temporarily undervalued in the stock market. A low P/S ratio is thought to characterize a firm with the potential for a significant turnaround because sales are already being made and improvement need only take place in the margin the firm is able to earn on each dollar of sales.

price spread —See MONEY SPREAD.

price stabilization —See PEG 1; STABILIZATION PERIOD.

price talk The range within which an offering of securities is expected to be priced.

price target The projected price of a security.

price-to-asset ratio A ratio that compares a firm's stock price with its book value per share. A low ratio indicates the firm's assets are not being fully valued by investors or the assets are being overvalued on the firm's financial statements. If the former is the case, the company may be a candidate for a takeover attempt.

price-to-book-value ratio —See MARKET TO BOOK.

price-to-cash-flow ratio (P/CF ratio) A stock valuation measure calculated by dividing a firm's cash flow per share into the current stock price. Financial analysts often prefer to value stocks using cash flow rather than earnings because the latter is more easily manipulated.

price-weighted average A security average that is weighted by the market price of each security included in the average. Thus, securities that have high market prices tend to be more heavily weighted and to have more influence on changes in a price-weighted average. The Dow Jones Averages are examples of price-weighted averages. —Compare MARKET-VALUE-WEIGHTED AVERAGE.

pricey Of, relating to, or being an unrealistically high offer. An offer to sell a security at $50 when the current market price is $47 is pricey. —Compare LOW-BALL.

pricing The determination of the price at which stock will sell or the yield at which bonds will sell as new issues. If the price is set too high or the yield is set too low, the issue will not sell out. If the price is set too low or the yield is set too high, the issuer will pay more than necessary in dilution or interest to sell it.

primary dealer A government securities firm to which the New York Federal Reserve Bank sells directly and from which it buys directly in an attempt to control the money supply. —Compare REPORTING DEALERS. —See also OPEN-MARKET OPERATIONS.

primary distribution A sale of a new issue of securities in which the funds go to the issuer. —Compare SECONDARY DISTRIBUTION. —Also called *primary offering.*

primary market The market in which new, as opposed to existing, securities are sold. Investors who purchase shares in a new security issue are purchasing them in the primary market. Investors who buy stocks and bonds in the primary market usually are not required to pay brokerage commissions because fees for selling the issue are built into its price and are absorbed by the issuer. —Compare SECONDARY MARKET. —Also called *new issue market.*

primary offering —See PRIMARY DISTRIBUTION.

primary shares Shares in a stock offering in which proceeds go to the issuing company. Primary shares have not been previously traded and are not included in shares outstanding prior to the offering. —Compare SECONDARY SHARES.

primary trend The main direction in which security prices are moving. An upward primary trend is a bull market while a downward primary trend is a bear market. —See also SECONDARY TREND.

prime 1. Of or relating to a debt security rated AAA or Aaa. **2.** —See PRIME RATE.

prime bank scam A fraudulent investment scheme in which a promoter claims guaranteed high yields are available through investments in "prime" banks or other financial institutions. These scams generally amount to a pyramid scheme in which money from new investors is used to pay interest to prior investors. Prime bank scams can be identified by excessive guaranteed returns and claims by the promoter that the transactions should remain confidential.

prime broker The broker-dealer who maintains a record of the orders executed by several broker-dealers for a particular institutional or professional trader.

prime paper The highest grades of commercial paper as determined by the rating agencies. Prime paper includes those having Moody's ratings of P-3 and above.

prime rate A short-term interest rate quoted by a commercial bank as an indication of the rate being charged on loans to its best commercial customers. Even though banks frequently charge more and sometimes less than the quoted prime rate, it is a benchmark against which other rates are measured and often keyed. For various reasons, a rising prime rate is generally considered detrimental to security prices. —Also called *prime.*

prime-rate fund A mutual fund that invests in short-term bank loans that have been made to companies that often have less than prime credit ratings. Yields from owning these funds change regularly as loan interest rates are reset. Prime-rate funds generally provide substantially higher yields than money market funds.

principal 1. The face amount of a bond. Once a bond has been issued, it may sell at more or less than its principal amount, depending upon changes in interest rates and the riskiness of the security. At maturity, however, the bond will be redeemed for its principal amount. —Also called *principal amount.* 2. Funds put up by an investor. 3. The person who owns or takes delivery of an asset in a trade. For example, an investor is the principal for whom a broker executes a trade.

principal exchange-rate-linked security (PERLS) Dollar-denominated debt in which the amount of principal that is to be repaid is determined by the exchange rate that exists between a specified foreign currency and the U.S. dollar at the time the security reaches maturity.

principal market The main market in which a security trades. The principal market for the common stock of most large corporations in the United States is the New York Stock Exchange, even though most of this stock also trades on one or more other exchanges and in the over-the-counter market. —See also CONSOLIDATED TAPE.

principal-only (PO) Of or relating to a derivative mortgage security scheduled to receive all the principal but none of the interest payments in a pool of mortgages. The security is purchased at a large discount from par value. In addition, the owner of the security can benefit from a higher yield if mortgage prepayments are made, thus returning the principal to the investor at an earlier date. —Compare INTEREST-ONLY.

principal risk The possibility an investment will be worth less when it is sold than when it was purchased. Principal risk is high for common stocks compared to most fixed-income investments such as bonds, preferred stock, and certificates of deposit.

principal stockholder A stockholder who owns a large number of voting shares in a firm. For SEC purposes, a person who owns 10% or more of a firm's voting stock is considered a principal stockholder.

principal trade A securities transaction in which the executing brokers are trading from inventory and are thus acting as dealers.

print The appearance of securities transactions on the composite tape.

priority The preference received by a bid or offer entered first in an auction market. Regardless of size, the first offer has priority if a transaction occurs at the price specified by the order.

prior-lien bond A bond with a priority claim over other bonds, both secured and unsecured, of the same issuer.

prior period adjustment Correction of a material mistake in reported income in an earlier financial statement. Although prior period adjustments affect retained earnings, they are not used to alter income in the current period.

prior preferred A class of preferred stock that has preference over one or more other classes of preferred stock of the same issuer. Preference may be with respect to payment of dividends and/or claims on assets. —Compare SECOND PREFERRED. —Also called *preference stock.*

private activity bond A type of municipal bond issued when funds are to be used for a nonessential purpose. Private activity bonds pay taxable interest unless specifically exempted by the federal government. Private activities for which tax-exempt bonds may be issued include airports, electric and gas distribution systems, government mass transportation systems, hazardous waste disposal facilities, solid waste disposal facilities, and student loans. Small issues of industrial development revenue bonds and nonprofit college and hospital bonds are also permitted. Except for nonprofit college and hospital bonds, interest from tax-exempt private activity bonds is subject to the alternative minimum tax. —Compare ESSENTIAL FUNCTION BOND. —Also called *nonessential function bond; private purpose municipal bond.* —See also 501(C)(3) BOND; MUNICIPAL BOND; SMALL-ISSUE BOND.

privately held company A firm whose shares are held within a relatively small circle of owners and are not traded publicly.

private investment in public equities (PIPE) Private equity deals in which major investors purchase substantial amounts of the stock of public corporations, generally at significant discounts to market prices. PIPEs are especially popular during periods when financial markets are difficult to tap for public funding.

private placement The sale of an issue of debt or equity securities to a single buyer or to a limited number of buyers without a public offering. The placement is generally conducted by an investment banker who acts as an agent in bringing together the seller and the buyer(s).

> **⋀⋀ CASE STUDY** For companies needing investment capital, private placements often save time and fees compared to public offerings. In early 2000 Healtheon/WebMD Corporation issued $930 million of new stock directly to the Janus funds. From Healtheon's standpoint, the issue was taken care of quickly without the need to pay a hefty fee to the firm's investment banker, Morgan Stanley Dean Witter (now Morgan Stanley). From Janus's standpoint, the firm was able to obtain a small discount on a sizeable block of stock it wanted to buy. In addition, Janus wasn't required to take a chance on bidding up the price of Healtheon stock by buying shares in the open market. Shares included in the private placement increased Janus's stake in Healtheon from 3% to 12%, a relatively large position for a mutual fund.

private placement memorandum The documentation that provides information on a new security issue. It is similar to but less extensive than a prospectus.

private purpose municipal bond —See PRIVATE ACTIVITY BOND.

privatization The conversion of a public enterprise to a private enterprise. For example, a government-owned railroad or airline may undergo privatization if ownership shares of the enterprise are sold to individual and institutional investors.

privileged subscription The issuance of new stock in which existing stockholders are given preference in purchasing new shares up to the proportion of shares they already own. Thus, an owner of 5% of all the issuing firm's outstanding stock would be permitted to buy up to 5% of the new issue at a special price below the current market price. —Compare PREEMPTIVE RIGHT. —See also RIGHTS OFFERING.

probability distribution The distribution of possible outcomes to an event along with the probability of each potential outcome. This statistical tool is used to measure the risk associated with events such as shooting craps, playing cards, or investing in securities.

probate The proof that a will is valid and that its terms are being carried out. Probate is accomplished by an executor/executrix who is paid a fee based on the size of the estate that passes through the will. Certain trusts and jointly owned property pass to beneficiaries without being subject to probate and the attendant fee. —See also NONPROBATE PROPERTY.

proceeds The amount received from the sale of an asset. The term usually refers to the amount received before deduction of commissions or other costs related to the transaction. —See also NET PROCEEDS.

proceeds sale A transaction in which funds received from selling a security are immediately reinvested in another security. The National Association of Securities Dealers regards a proceeds sale as a single transaction; therefore, the member's commission or markup cannot exceed 5% of the principal of the trade.

producer price index A comprehensive index of price changes at the wholesale level. Because wholesale price changes eventually find their way into consumer prices, the producer price index is closely watched as an early indicator of future retail price changes. —Formerly called *wholesale price index.* —Compare CONSUMER PRICE INDEX. —Also called *price index.* —See also GDP DEFLATOR.

production rate The coupon rate of interest at which pass-through securities issued by Ginnie Mae are issued. The production rate is set 0.5% below the maximum rate permitted on residential mortgages that are insured by the Federal Housing Administration. —See also GINNIE MAE PASS THROUGH.

productivity The efficiency with which output is produced by a given set of inputs. Productivity is generally measured by the ratio of output to input. An increase in the ratio indicates an increase in productivity. Conversely, a decrease in the output/input ratio indicates a decline in productivity.

product mix The composition of goods and services produced and/or sold by a firm. A limited product mix tends to increase the firm's risk at the same time it increases the potential for large profits. Thus, a firm specializing in a niche market in electronics is likely to experience great success or large losses depending on how demand and competition develop for its specialized output. —Also called *sales mix.*

profit —See NET INCOME.

profitability ratio   A comparison of two or more financial variables that provide a relative measure of a firm's income-earning performance. Profitability ratios are of interest to creditors, managers, and especially owners. —Compare RETURN ON COMMON STOCK EQUITY; RETURN ON EQUITY; RETURN ON INVESTMENT; RETURN ON SALES. —See also COMMON-SIZE STATEMENT; GROSS PROFIT MARGIN; NET PROFIT MARGIN.

profit and loss statement (P&L)   —See INCOME STATEMENT.

profit center   A segment of a business for which costs, revenues, and profits are separately calculated, with the manager of the segment being responsible for and judged on the performance of that segment. A large corporation with diversified interests in paper manufacturing, trucking, and fast food may regard each of these three businesses as a profit center.

profit margin   1. The relationship of gross profits to net sales in a business. Net sales are determined by subtracting returns and allowances from gross sales, whereupon the cost of goods sold is then subtracted from net sales to obtain gross profit. Gross profit is divided by net sales to obtain the profit margin—an excellent indicator of a firm's operating efficiency, its pricing policies, and its ability to remain competitive. —See also GROSS PROFIT MARGIN. 2. Net profit margin of a business, which is calculated by deducting operating expenses and cost of goods sold and dividing the result by net sales. This term is less often used to indicate net profit margin.

profit range   The range of potential profitable outcomes that result from a given investment position. Profit range is used extensively in putting together complicated option strategies in which gains or losses or both are limited to an established level.

profit-sharing plan   A savings plan offered by many firms to their employees in which a part of the firm's profits is funneled into a tax-deferred employee retirement account. These plans give employees additional incentive to be productive.

profit squeeze   A reduction in earnings perhaps caused by a poor business climate, increased competition, or rising costs.

profit taking   The general widespread selling of securities or of a particular security after a significant price rise as investors realize, or take, their profits. Although profit taking depresses prices, it does so temporarily. The term usually implies that the market is trending upward. —Also called *taking profits*.

pro forma earnings   Income not necessarily calculated in accordance with generally accepted accounting principles. For example, a company might report pro forma earnings that exclude depreciation expense and nonrecurring expenses such as restructuring costs. In general, pro forma earnings are reported in an effort to put a more positive spin on a company's operations.

> **M̆ CASE STUDY** | Unlike net income reported in audited financial statements according to generally accepted accounting principles, pro forma earnings are calculated in any number of ways because there is no generally accepted definition for this measure of earnings. Companies may inflate pro forma earnings by omitting certain expenses, such as stock compensation, interest payments, and amortization of intangible assets. The result is a hodgepodge of earnings calculations that are not consistent from company to company or, for the same company, from year to year. In early

2001 Amazon.com released quarterly pro forma results that omitted write-downs of impaired assets, interest expense, and losses on equity investments. The latter item had been a particularly important source of income for many Internet and technology-based companies when the stock market was booming rather than swooning. According to Amazon.com officials, the firm's quarterly U.S. pro forma operating loss narrowed to $16 million while its overall pro forma operating loss amounted to $60 million. At the same time the company reported that the net loss calculated according to generally accepted accounting principles was $545 million. Critics contended that companies were emphasizing whichever measure of earnings produced the most favorable result. The controversy over reported earnings caused a group of financial executives to begin work on developing a standard for pro forma earnings. The group was at work at the time the Amazon.com results were released. In late 2001 the Securities and Exchange Commission issued a warning that companies issuing misleading pro forma earnings could face civil fraud suits. On January 16, 2002, the SEC instituted its first enforcement action addressing the abuse of pro forma earnings when it initiated proceedings against Trump Hotels & Casino Resorts, Inc., for making misleading statements in the firm's third-quarter 1999 earnings release. The SEC found that the release cited pro forma figures to tout the firm's purportedly positive results of operations while failing to disclose that the results were primarily attributable to an unusual one-time gain rather than to operations. The SEC also found that the company, through its chief executive officer, chief financial officer, and treasurer, violated the antifraud provisions of the Securities Exchange Act by knowingly or recklessly issuing a materially misleading press release.

pro forma financial statement   A financial statement constructed from projected amounts. A firm might construct a pro forma income statement based on projected revenues and costs for the following year. Likewise, a firm may wish to develop a set of pro forma statements to determine the effect of a projected stock buyback.

program trading   An arbitrage operation in which traders take a long or short position in a portfolio of stock and the opposite position in one or more futures contracts on the same portfolio. Program trading is undertaken in order to take advantage of a difference in market values between two essentially identical portfolios of securities. Both sides of the trade are closed out on or near the day the futures contract expires when the values of the positions should be equal. Because of the size of the trades and the complexity of the technique, program trading is practiced almost exclusively by large institutions. Program trading has been blamed for many of the occasionally occurring big movements in the market. —Compare BASIS TRADING.

᠕᠕ **CASE STUDY** Program trading is the sophisticated trading of a large portfolio of securities in combination with an offsetting position in a futures contract. The ability to pursue this strategy for earning a risk free return depends on integrating computer programs with trades involving one of the many new products in the securities markets—stock index futures. High-powered computer programs determine the point at which the value of a portfolio of securities that is identical to the securities constituting a stock index is out of line with the value of a futures contract on that same stock index. Thus, the value of all the stocks included in the S&P 100 Index may be determined to be either overvalued or undervalued relative to the price at which a futures contract on the index is selling. Program traders take one position in the securities constituting the index and, at the same time, take an offsetting position in a futures contract on the index. Because the two positions must be of equal value on the date that the futures contract expires, the program trader profits by the difference in values when the position was established. The greater the initial divergence of values and the shorter the wait until the values converge, the more profitable the trade. The profitability of the trade must be compared with the rate of return that can be earned on other risk free investments to determine if the arbitrage operation is profitable enough to be worthwhile. Because most positions in program trading are closed out near the settlement date of the futures contract when the value of the securities is at or close to the value of the futures contract, considerable trading, volatility, and turmoil in the markets can occur on the expiration dates. Big price changes involving the stock included in the averages and indexes frequently take place, especially late in the day on the settlement date. Although there has been considerable criticism of program trading as the stimulus to volatility in the security markets, some analysts claim that program trading has a favorable effect in that it makes for more efficient markets. Program trading can be used profitably only when values in the market are out of line. Because program trading involves such huge sums and such sophisticated trading practices, it is generally undertaken only by a limited number of traders with access to large pools of capital: establishing a position at one time in 100 or more stocks is not small potatoes. Offsetting the need for investing huge sums, however, is the fact that program traders establish what is essentially a riskless investment position. It is left to the remainder of the investment community to absorb the added risk of a more volatile market.

progressive tax A tax with a rate that increases as the amount to be taxed increases. For example, a taxing authority might levy a tax of 10% on the first $10,000 of income and increase the rate by 5% per each $10,000 increment up to a maximum of 50% on all income over $80,000. A progressive tax often uses high rates on relatively large incomes and tends to encourage tax shelters. The federal income tax, many state income taxes, and the unified gift-estate tax are progressive taxes. —Compare REGRESSIVE TAX.

project note (PN) A short-term debt security issued by a municipality to finance a federally sponsored real estate project with repayment guaranteed by a pledge from the United States Department of Housing and Urban Development. These securities are considered very high-grade.

promissory note —See NOTE 1.

property dividend A stockholder dividend paid in a form other than cash, scrip, or the firm's own stock. For example, a firm may distribute samples of its own product or shares in another company it owns to its stockholders. In general, a property dividend is taxable at its fair market value.

property tax —See AD VALOREM TAX.

proportionate redemption A partial stock buyback in which a stockholder maintains the same ownership percentage after selling a portion of his or her shares back to the issuer.

proprietor The owner of a one-person business.

proprietorship A firm with a single owner, chiefly one who acts as the manager of the business. Income, expenses, taxes, liability for debts, and contractual obligations are inseparable with respect to differentiating the owner from

What is the most important information to be found in a mutual fund prospectus?

The mutual fund prospectus is a legal document that contains valuable information for the investor. Now, it's easy to make fun of a prospectus. It's boring, and, yes, reading one is a cure for insomnia. But the prospectus is worth a close look, and a lot of investment mistakes could be avoided with a careful reading of the whole text. But several sections should be highlighted. First is the expense table. All mutual funds have to lay out in a standardized format all the fees associated with owning a fund. If there is a fee to buy and sell a fund, it's there, plus all the ongoing charges imposed by the fund. Thoroughly scrutinize the financial highlights. It's a lot of numbers, but these figures give a reading on how the fund has done over time and in different markets. The investment objective section is critical. Is this the kind of fund you are looking for? Is it run, say, to generate dividend income, or is the money manager striving for long-term capital appreciation in high-tech stocks? The management page tells you whether the fund is run by an individual or by a committee.

Christopher Farrell, Economics Editor
Minnesota Public Radio, heard nationally on Sound Money®

the business. —Compare CORPORATION; PARTNERSHIP. —See also UNLIMITED LIABILITY.

pro rata —Used to refer to something on a proportional basis. For example, in a rights offering, rights are distributed to stockholders on the basis of the number of shares already held by each stockholder. Thus, the pro rata distribution enables the stockholders to purchase new shares in proportion to the old shares they already own.

proratable factor The proportion of shares tendered by each stockholder that will be accepted for purchase or exchange.

prospect To look for customers. For example, a registered representative may join a civic organization to prospect for new customers.

prospect list A list of prospective customers. A broker might acquire a list of physicians, dentists, or owners of private aircraft, assuming that at least some of these people have money to invest and would consider becoming customers.

prospectus A formal written document relating to a new securities offering that delineates the proposed business plan or the data relevant to an existing business plan—information needed by investors to make educated decisions whether to purchase the security. The prospectus includes financial data, a précis of the firm's business history, a list of its officers, a description of its operations, and mention of any pending litigation. A prospectus is an abridged version of the firm's registration statement filed with the SEC. —See also OFFERING CIRCULAR; RED HERRING.

protected strategy An investment strategy with a goal of limiting risk. For example, purchasing a stock and a put on the stock establishes a limit on the amount of money that may be lost since the put protects against losses derived from a declining value of the stock. Although protected strategies limit losses, they also generally penalize potential profits.

protectionism The establishment of barriers to the importation of goods and services from foreign countries in order to protect domestic producers. Protectionism generates higher consumer prices. It is also likely to penalize domestic exporters because foreign countries are apt to retaliate with trade barriers of their own.

protective covenant —See COVENANT.

protective put A put option owned in conjunction with the corresponding stock. A protective put guarantees the holder will receive at minimum proceeds that equal the exercise price of the put. For example, an investor could hold 100 shares of Coca-Cola while also holding a put on Coca-Cola stock. The protective put shelters the investor in case the stock's price declines in the market. —Also called *married put*.

protective stop A stop order that protects gains or limits losses of an existing investment position.

proved reserves The quantity of minerals expected to be recoverable under current economic and operating conditions. The amount of proved reserves is important in valuing the stock of a company with significant holdings in natural resources.

provisional call trigger price The price at which the issuer of a convertible security may call the security during a period of call protection. For example, a convertible bond may allow a provisional call if the underlying common stock trades at 150% (the trigger price) of the conversion price for 30 consecutive days.

provisional rating A bond rating conditional upon the successful completion of a specific project or the fulfillment of a stipulated condition. —Also called *conditional rating*.

proxy The written authority to act or speak for another party. Proxies are sent to stockholders by corporate management in order to solicit authority to vote the stockholders' shares at the annual meetings.

proxy fight A contest among two or more opposing forces to solicit stockholders' proxies and, in effect, to gain control of the firm through the election of directors. It is usually quite difficult to wrest control from the existing management through a proxy fight, but the tactic has been used, for example, by some suitors in takeover attempts.

proxy statement The material accompanying solicitation of a proxy from stockholders. The proxy statement lists the items to be voted on including nominees for directorships, the auditing firm recommended by directors, the salaries of top officers and directors, and resolutions submitted by management and stockholders. Proxy statements are required by the SEC.

prudent man rule A federal and state regulation requiring trustees and portfolio managers to make financial decisions in the manner of a prudent man, that is, with intelligence and discretion. The prudent man rule requires care in the selection of investments but does not limit investment alternatives. —See also INVESTMENT-GRADE; LEGAL LIST.

P/S ratio —See PRICE-SALES RATIO.

Public Automated Routing System (PAR) A computer-based system used by the Chicago Board Options Exchange to speed the flow of orders for execution and reporting.

public distribution The sale of a new securities issue to individual investors. The sales fee for the distribution, usually absorbed by the issuer, is included in the offering price.

public housing authority bond A bond that is issued by a local public housing agency and its proceeds used to construct or repair low-rent housing. Public housing authority bonds are backed by the federal government and pay federally tax-exempt interest.

publicly held 1. Of, relating to, or being securities that are freely transferable among investors. For example, stock owned by institutional investors is publicly held, but unregistered stock held by a firm's founder is not publicly held. 2. Of, relating to, or being a publicly traded company.

publicly traded company A company whose shares of common stock are held by the public and are available for purchase by investors. The shares of publicly traded firms are bought and sold on the organized exchanges or in the over-the-counter market. Such companies are regulated by the SEC.

publicly traded fund —See CLOSED-END INVESTMENT COMPANY.

public offering The sale of an issue of securities to the public, an activity that usually occurs with the assistance of an investment banker that purchases the securities from the issuer and then resells them to the public. —Also called *distribution; offering.*

public offering price The price at which securities are offered for sale to the public. The price usually includes any sales commission.

public power bond Debt that is issued by a public power agency such as the Municipal Electric Authority of Georgia. Interest on such a bond is usually tax-exempt federally. Interest and principal payments are derived from revenues generated by the sale of electricity.

Public Securities Association A trade group of banks, brokers, and dealers engaged in underwriting and trading federal, state, and local government securities.

Public Utility Holding Company Act The 1935 act that gives the SEC authority over the security issues, the accounting systems, the corporate structures, and the intercompany transactions of public utilities. This act was a response to serious abuses of utility managements uncovered during the depression years.

pump and dump Market manipulation in which a thinly traded stock is accumulated, promoted, and subsequently sold at an artificially high price to unsuspecting investors. Internet chat rooms where investors gather investment information from unknown parties facilitate this illegal practice. —Compare POOP AND SCOOP.

punter —See SPECULATOR.

purchase and sales department (P&S) The department of a brokerage firm that compares details of a trade with the firm identified on the other side of the transaction. In addition, this department processes and mails confirmations to customers.

purchase group —See SYNDICATE.

purchase method A method of accounting for a merger or combination in which one firm is considered to have purchased the assets of the other firm. If the price paid for the acquired firm exceeds the market value of the acquired firm's assets, the difference is recorded as goodwill on the acquiring firm's bal-

ance sheet. The goodwill must be written off over a period of years. —Compare
POOLING OF INTERESTS.

purchasing power **1.** Consumer ability to purchase goods and services. Increased purchasing power represents proportionately larger increases in income than increases in the cost of goods and services. **2.** The ability to purchase goods and services with a fixed amount of money. Within this narrower
application, purchasing power is inversely related to the consumer price index.
Increased purchasing power is a signal that future increases in economic activity are likely.

purchasing power risk The risk that unexpected changes in consumer prices
will penalize an investor's real return from holding an investment. Because investments from gold to bonds and stock are priced to include expected inflation
rates, it is the unexpected changes that produce this risk. Fixed income securities, such as bonds and preferred stock, subject investors to the greatest amount
of purchasing power risk since their payments are set at the time of issue and
remain unchanged regardless of the inflation rate.

pure play An investment that is concentrated in a particular industry or operation. An investor who believes that snowmobiles are the wave of the future will
search for a pure play in snowmobiles. In other words, the investor seeks out a
company that does nothing other than manufacture and sell snowmobiles. Likewise, Maytag Corporation is more of a pure play in household appliances than is
General Electric, even though General Electric has a larger share of the appliance market than Maytag. Reason: General Electric generates much of its revenues from its other operations.

purpose loan A loan using securities as collateral with proceeds from the loan
being used to purchase additional securities. —Compare NONPURPOSE LOAN.

purpose statement A document that states the use to which proceeds of a loan
that is backed by securities are to be put. The borrower agrees not to use the
funds to purchase securities in violation of Federal Reserve credit regulations.

put **1.** An option that conveys to its holder the right, but not the obligation, to
sell a specific asset at a predetermined price until a certain date. In most cases,
puts have 100 shares of stock as the underlying asset. For example, an investor
may purchase a put option on GenCorp common stock that confers the right to
sell 100 shares at $15 per share until September 21. Puts are sold for a fee by
other investors who incur an obligation to purchase the asset if the option
holder decides to sell. Investors purchase puts in order to take advantage of a
decline in the price of the asset. —Compare CALL 1. —Also called *put option.*
—See also GUARANTEE LETTER; SYNTHETIC PUT; TRANSFERABLE PUT RIGHT. **2.** Sale of
an issue of bonds before maturity by forcing the issuer to buy at par. Few bond
issues permit the holder this option.

put To force the seller of a put option to purchase shares of stock at the stipulated price. Puts are exercised by the owner only when the market price of the
underlying stock is less than the strike price. *See Investment Tip on p. 296.*
—Also called *put to seller.*

put bond A relatively unusual bond that allows the holder to force the issuer to
repurchase the security at specified dates before maturity. The repurchase
price, usually at par value, is set at the time of issue. A put bond allows the in-

put

Putting things into perspective: How to hedge, using puts. How to speculate, using puts.

A put option has an inverse relationship to the underlying security. As the value of the stock increases, the value of the put decreases. Like calls, puts can be used for both hedging and speculation. Puts can be purchased in conjunction with stock ownership as a form of insurance (that is, a hedge) against downside loss on a stock. If the stock price declines, the put holder can either sell the put and keep the stock, or exercise the put and sell the stock at the put's strike price. In either case, the increased value of the option will offset the stock loss to some degree. If the stock price rises beyond a certain level, the put will expire worthless. In this case, the put holder will lose the premium paid for the option but will still participate in the upward stock movement. The break-even point occurs when the stock price advances beyond the put's strike price plus the premium. Puts also can be used speculatively without a position in the underlying security. Instead of selling a stock short, an investor who anticipates a decline in the price of a stock can buy an at-the-money put. If the stock price rises, causing the put to expire worthless, the maximum loss is the premium paid for the put. But if the stock price declines substantially, the investor could make profits that far exceed the initial cost of the put.

Henry Nothnagel, Senior Vice President—Options
Wachovia Securities, Inc., Chicago, IL

vestor to redeem a long-term bond before maturity, but the yield generally equals the one on short-term rather than long-term securities. —Also called *multimaturity bond; option tender bond.* —See also MANDATORY TENDER BOND; POISON-PUT BOND; PREMIUM PUT; YIELD TO PUT.

CASE STUDY A put option on a bond benefits bondholders who are able to force the issuer to redeem its bonds prior to the scheduled maturity. Forced redemptions typically occur following a period of rising interest rates, when bondholders can reinvest their funds at a return higher than the return paid by the bond. Bondholders may also choose an early redemption in the event the issuer runs into serious financial difficulties and bondholders become concerned about whether the issuer will be around on the scheduled maturity date for the bonds. A large issue of put bonds can place the issuer at substantial risk in the event funds are unavailable to pay for a forced redemption. This was the case with Polish conglomerate Elektrim in late 2001 when nearly all of its bondholders decided to exercise a mid-December put on €440 million worth of convertible bonds. Redemption would occur at a premium to par and entail accrued interest requiring the power and telecom company to come up with €488 million. At the time Elektrim said it had €276 million in cash, substantially less than the amount required to pay its bondholders. Likelihood of the redemption caused the firm to search for short-term financing and consider emergency asset sales in order to raise additional funds. Put bonds are uncommon and are generally issued to gain a lower interest cost for the borrower. The risk of put bonds is substantial for the borrower in the event proceeds are invested in long-term assets and the issuer has limited liquidity to redeem the bonds on short notice.

put-call ratio A ratio that compares the trading volume in put options with the trading volume in call options. Technicians use the put-call ratio to forecast market turns. A high ratio with heavy trading in puts indicates strong bearish sentiment and the possibility of a market bottom. A relatively low put-call ratio with heavy trading volume in calls indicates very bullish sentiment and a probable market top. As with many other technical indicators, use of the put-call ratio assumes that most investors are wrong.

CASE STUDY Like most technical indicators, the put-call ratio can prove very misleading when it is influenced by unusual factors. In February 1996, the ratio nearly reached five, meaning that put options were nearly five times as active as call options. This high ratio would usually be interpreted as reflecting very bearish investment sentiment, and it caused many investors to view the stock market with great caution. Contrarians, who believe the majority of investors are usually wrong, would consider the unusually high ratio to be very bullish. In fact, the ratio was artificially high and was providing false signals to both groups of investors. The heavy trading in put options was largely the result of the owners of puts selling existing holdings of these contracts and simultaneously purchasing different put contracts. For example, a holder of March put options would sell those contracts and replace them with April put options. Rolling the options forward caused a great deal of activity in put options even though a large portion of this activity represented the trade of existing holdings of puts for different puts.

put option —See PUT 1.

put spread An option position in which a put option is purchased while another put option on the same security is sold short. The two puts have different strike prices, different expiration dates, or both. —Compare CALL SPREAD. —Also called *option spread.*

puttable common stock The shares of common stock that are sold with rights to put the shares back to the issuer at a specified price. —Compare CALLABLE COMMON STOCK.

put to seller —See PUT.

PV —See PRESENT VALUE.

pyramid A classic investment fraud in which the operator pays promised high returns to current investors from the contributions made by new investors. Thus, funds are never invested in any productive assets but are simply paid out as a return to existing owners. The operator must continue to attract more and more investors in order to pay a return to those who have already committed their funds. —Also called *Ponzi scheme.*

pyramid To use profits derived from a profitable security position in combination with borrowed money in order to acquire an even larger investment position. Pyramiding, which is very risky, allows an investor the possibility of greater profits by using a given amount of funds to control the maximum amount of securities.

Q

QQQ The ticker symbol and Wall Street name for the popular exchange-traded fund based on the Nasdaq 100 Index. This fund, traded on the American Stock Exchange and the New York Stock Exchange, serves as a proxy for large-cap Nasdaq stocks, including Microsoft, Oracle, Cisco, and Intel. —Also called *cubes.*

Q ratio The ratio of stock prices to the current replacement values of the firms' underlying assets. Some analysts believe a relatively high Q ratio (higher than 1.0, although the level is subjective) indicates an overbought market. —Also called *Tobin's Q.*

QTIP trust A marital-deduction trust in which the surviving spouse receives income from the trust's assets for life but the trust's principal is left to someone else, usually children. A QTIP trust controls the eventual beneficiaries while at the same time taking advantage of the marital deduction and providing an income for the surviving spouse.

qualified institutional investor An institutional investor that is permitted by the Securities and Exchange Commission to trade private placement securities without registering the securities with the SEC.

qualified opinion The opinion of a Certified Public Accountant that a firm's financial statements deviate in some respect from a clean opinion according to generally accepted accounting principles. —Compare CLEAN OPINION.

qualified plan An employer-sponsored tax-deferred employee benefit plan that meets the standards of the Internal Revenue Code of 1954 and that qualifies for favorable tax treatment. Contributions by an employer and an employee accu-

---

QTIP trust

Should my spouse and I consider setting up a QTIP trust? Why?

A QTIP trust is a marital deduction trust that limits the surviving spouse's access to and control of the trust property. QTIP, or Qualified Terminable Interest Property, is property "qualified" by your executor to take advantage of the federal and state estate tax marital deduction(s).

A QTIP trust may be appropriate if you or your spouse has serious concerns about the following:

- A surviving spouse remarrying and then benefiting the new spouse.
- A surviving spouse benefiting someone other than your children.
- A surviving spouse's creditors attaching the trust property.
- A surviving spouse who is unsophisticated or vulnerable.

A QTIP trust addresses these concerns, but the "cost" for such control is that the trust requires the services of a professional or highly sophisticated executor who will make the QTIP election on time and in consideration of all the tax and estate planning circumstances existing at the time of the death. A mistake or missed deadline could cost the estate thousands of dollars and lose the marital deduction for the estate.

Gloria Cole, Attorney, private practice, Weston, MA

mulate without being taxed until payouts are made at the employee's retirement or termination.

qualifying annuity An annuity approved by the Internal Revenue Service in which the contributions may be deducted from taxable income. The effect of contributing to a qualifying annuity is deferred taxes on the contributions from the time the contributions are made to the time any withdrawals are made. Qualifying annuities are used for individual retirement accounts, Keogh plans, and profit-sharing plans. —Compare NONQUALIFYING ANNUITY.

qualifying dividends The dividends that meet Internal Revenue Service regulations for exclusion or partial exclusion from federal income taxation. For example, corporations are permitted to exclude a portion of all of the qualifying dividends received from stock owned in domestic corporations. There are no qualifying dividends for calculating individual income taxes.

quality of earnings —See EARNINGS QUALITY.

quant A person who has strong skills in mathematics, engineering, or computer science, and who applies those skills to the securities business. For example, a pension fund may employ a quant to put together an optimal portfolio of bonds to meet the fund's future liabilities. —Also called *rocket scientist.*

quant fund A mutual fund having a stock portfolio that is managed according to decisions made by a computer model. The investment performance of a quant fund is only as good as the computer model that drives the fund's investment decisions.

quarter 1. One quarter of a point. For bond quotes, a quarter represents one quarter of 1% of par, or $2.50. Thus, a bond quoted at $91\frac{2}{4}$ is being offered for $917.50. 2. A 3-month period that represents 25% of a fiscal year.

Quarterly Income Preferred Securities (QUIPS) Preferred stock that represents interest in a limited partnership formed for the sole purpose of lending proceeds of the equity issue to the parent company. Dividends to holders of QUIPS are paid from tax-deductible interest paid by the parent corporation.

quasi-public corporation A privately operated firm having legislatively mandated public responsibilities. A quasi-public corporation may have publicly traded shares of stock. Fannie Mae is a quasi-public corporation established to make a secondary market in mortgages. The firm is privately owned but publicly traded and its shares of common stock are listed on the New York Stock Exchange.

quick asset A current asset that is easily convertible into cash with no loss of value. Quick assets are often calculated as current assets minus inventories. —See also NET QUICK ASSETS.

quick ratio A relatively severe test of a company's liquidity and its ability to meet short-term obligations. The quick ratio is calculated by dividing all current assets with the exception of inventory by current liabilities. Inventory is excluded on the basis that it is the least liquid current asset. A relatively high quick ratio indicates conservative management and the ability to satisfy short-term obligations. —Compare CASH RATIO. —Also called *acid-test ratio.* —See also CURRENT RATIO; NET QUICK ASSETS.

quick turn   The purchase or short sale of a security followed in a short time by a closing transaction. A quick turn is intended to earn a relatively small profit in a short period of time.

quid pro quo   An equal exchange that a person or firm makes with another person or firm. In the securities industry institutional investors provide orders to brokerage firms as a quid pro quo for in-depth research.

quiet period   **1.** The period of time during which a security issue is in registration and the issuer is not permitted to promote the issue. The quiet period begins during the filing period and ends 25 days after the security begins trading.   **2.** —See LOCKDOWN.

QUIPS   —See QUARTERLY INCOME PREFERRED SECURITIES.

quota   A maximum or minimum limit on quantity. Applied to imports, a quota designates the maximum quantity of a product that may be brought into a country during a specified period of time. Quotas can have significant impact on certain industries and companies. The establishment of a quota or a change in an existing quota can influence the price of the affected firm's securities.   —See also TARIFF; TRIGGER PRICE.

quotation   A statement or listing of the price at which a security trades. A quotation is often the last price at which the trade took place, but occasionally it is the current bid and ask. For example, a quotation of $15–$15.25 means that the market maker is willing to buy at $15 per share (the bid) and sell at $15.25 per share (the ask).   —Also called *quote*.

Quote Rule   An SEC rule that requires specialists and market makers to maintain and provide continuous, firm quotations for the securities in which they make a market.

R

r   **1.** —Used in the dividend column of stock transaction tables in newspapers to indicate the amount of dividends declared or paid in the preceding 12 months plus a stock dividend: *PE Cp .25r*.   **2.** —Used in mutual fund transaction tables in newspapers to indicate funds that levy a deferred sales charge when shares are sold: *IDS Inc r*.   **3.** —Used in bond transaction tables in newspapers to indicate a registered security. Although most bonds are registered, this symbol is used when a distinction is necessary, as when a bond trades in registered and in bearer form: NoPac 3.47r.

R4   —See REGISTERED REPRESENTATIVE RAPID RESPONSE SERVICE.

raider   A person or firm that attempts a takeover of a company.   —Compare TARGET COMPANY; WHITE KNIGHT. —Also called *corporate raider*. —See also GREENMAIL; JUNK FINANCING; SHARK REPELLENT.

raiding   An attempt to purchase a sufficient number of shares of a company's stock through a tender offer so that control of the target's operations can be taken away from its current management.   —Also called *venture arbitrage*.

rainmaker   A brokerage firm employee who brings a wealthy client base to the business.

rally A fairly sharp, short-term general rise in security prices after a period of little movement or of declining prices.

RAN —See REVENUE ANTICIPATION NOTE.

R&D costs —See RESEARCH AND DEVELOPMENT COSTS.

random-walk hypothesis The hypothesis that states that past stock prices are of no value in forecasting future prices because past, current, and future prices merely reflect market responses to information that comes into the market at random. In short, price movements are no more predictable than the pattern of the walk of a drunk. This controversial hypothesis implies that technical analysis is useless in its attempts to predict future price movements in the market.

range The high and low prices reached by a security within a given period. A large range in relation to a security price tends to indicate greater price volatility, making the security a better candidate for trading purposes but not necessarily for investment purposes. —Also called *price range.*

rate anticipation swap The sale of one bond combined with the purchase of another bond of different maturity in order to take maximum advantage of expected changes in interest rates. For example, an investor would want to trade short-term bonds for long-term bonds if interest rates were expected to fall, because the price of the long-term bonds would rise more than the price of the short-term bonds.

rate base The valuation of a utility's assets for the purpose of determining the rates the utility is permitted to charge its customers. Exactly what a utility should be permitted to include in its rate base is often a point of contention between it and its customers.

rate covenant A provision for a municipal revenue bond issue that sets requirements for charging revenue on the facility that is being financed by the bond issue. For example, a rate covenant might require that the rates from customers of a city sewage plant be sufficient to ensure adequate maintenance and repair for the facility. A rate covenant is included in a bond agreement to protect the bondholders' interests.

rate of return 1. —See CURRENT YIELD; TOTAL RETURN. 2. —See RETURN ON INVESTMENT.

rate relief An action taken to allow a regulated company, such as a utility, to charge higher rates (that is, the prices it charges its customers) so that it can generate greater revenues. Public utilities frequently seek rate relief by filing a request for rate increases with public regulatory bodies. The utility's success in obtaining rate relief has a very heavy impact on the value of its shares.

rating The grading of a security with respect to a characteristic or a set of characteristics such as safety and growth. Rating is most often applied to debt securities, which are graded according to the issuer's ability to pay interest and principal when due. —See also BOND RATING; DOWNGRADING; MOODY'S INVESTMENT GRADE; NOT RATED; STOCK RATING; UPGRADING 1.

rating agencies Companies that grade securities so as to indicate the quality of the securities for investors. The two major rating services are Moody's Investor Services and Standard & Poor's Corporation. Two lesser known rating firms are Duff & Phelps and Fitch Investors Service.

rating trigger A provision in a loan agreement that initiates a specific action in the event of a change in a firm's credit rating. For example, a downgrade in a firm's credit rating may set off accelerated debt repayment in a backup credit line.

> **⋀⋀ CASE STUDY** Selling in a regulated market and buying in an unregulated market caught up with California electric utility PG&E in 2000 and 2001 when wholesale electric prices skyrocketed on the West Coast. Unable to raise the price of its product in the face of rising wholesale electric prices, the firm began defaulting on its debts when rating triggers from a rating downgrade allowed financial institutions to stop funding the company's commercial paper. The lack of funding for PG&E's commercial paper caused the company to default on its pollution-control bonds and a variety of short- and medium-term notes. The importance of the rating trigger in PG&E's subsequent bankruptcy caused one major rating agency to indicate that it would consider the negative consequence of triggers in evaluating whether a company would be able to survive a rating downgrade. Some corporations began to reconsider the inclusion of rating triggers in borrowing agreements when they discovered the rating agencies would consider these triggers in evaluating the credit quality of corporate debt.

ratio The relation between two quantities when compared mathematically with one another. For example, the most frequently used ratio among investors is the price-earnings ratio. Financial analysts, investors, and managers use ratios to evaluate many factors such as the attractiveness of a stock or the operating efficiency of a company. —Also called *financial ratio.* —See also ACTIVITY RATIO; DEBT MANAGEMENT RATIO; LIQUIDITY RATIO; PROFITABILITY RATIO.

ratio analysis A study of the relationships between financial variables. Ratios of one firm are often compared with the same ratios of similar firms or of all firms in a single industry. This comparison indicates if a particular firm's financial statistics are suspect. Likewise, a particular ratio for a firm may be evaluated over a period of time to determine if any special trend exists. —Compare TREND ANALYSIS. —See also HORIZONTAL ANALYSIS; VERTICAL ANALYSIS.

ratio writing —See VARIABLE RATIO OPTION WRITING.

raw material The goods used in the manufacture of a product. For example, a furniture manufacturer is likely to have raw materials such as hardware, lumber, and metal tubing on hand. Raw material is carried as an inventory item in the current assets section of a firm's balance sheet.

reaction A decline in security prices following a period of rising security prices.

read the tape To observe security price and volume information as it appears on the consolidated tape. Some traders read the tape in an attempt to spot irregular trades or price movements that signal buying or selling opportunities.

real asset A physical asset such as gold or timber. Real assets tend to be most desirable during periods of high inflation. —See also FINANCIAL ASSET.

real estate The land, buildings, and improvements thereto. —Also called *real property.*

real estate certificate of deposit A certificate of deposit that provides a guaranteed rate of interest as well as the possible rent revenues and capital gains that may be derived from the property that the funds from the certificate are used to acquire. The guaranteed rate of interest is usually lower than the rate paid on regular certificates of deposit. —Compare EQUITY KICKER.

real estate investment trust (REIT) A company that purchases and manages real estate and/or real estate loans. Some REITs specialize in purchasing long-term mortgages while others actually buy real estate. Income earned by a trust is generally passed through and taxed to the stockholders rather than to the REIT. —See also EQUITY REIT; MORTGAGE REIT.

real estate mortgage investment conduit (REMIC) A type of pass-through mortgage-backed security established in the Tax Reform Act of 1986. REMICs can vary in both maturity and risk and are backed by mortgage or participation loans.

real income Income, as of a person, group, or country, that has been adjusted for changes in the prices of goods and services. Real income measures purchasing power in the current year after an adjustment for changes in prices since a selected base year. If money income increases more than consumer prices, real income increases. If money income increases less than consumer prices, real income declines. Declines in real income are unfavorable for those suffering the declines and for firms selling goods and services to them.

real interest rate The nominal current interest rate minus the rate of inflation. For example, an investor holding a 10% certificate of deposit during a period of 6% annual inflation would be earning a real interest rate of 4%. The real interest rate is a more valid measure of the desirability of an investment than the nominal rate is.

realization principle An accounting standard that recognizes revenue only when it is earned. Generally, realization occurs when goods are sold or a service is rendered.

realized gain The amount by which the net proceeds from the sale of an asset exceed its cost of acquisition. When gains are realized, they become income for tax purposes. —Compare UNREALIZED GAIN.

realized loss The amount by which an investment's acquisition cost exceeds the net proceeds from its sale. A realized loss, as opposed to a paper loss, may be used to reduce taxable income. —Compare UNREALIZED LOSS.

real market The quotes from a dealer who is willing to buy and sell a security in relatively large volume. Dealers uninterested in trading a security may provide quotes but do not expect anyone to act on them.

real property —See REAL ESTATE.

real return The inflation-adjusted rate of return on an investment. If an investor earns a return of 12% during a year when inflation is 4%, the real return is 8%. —Compare NOMINAL RETURN.

real-time Of or relating to the actual time during which something occurs; that is, current as opposed to delayed. For example, real-time stock price quotations are generally available to investors with Internet brokerage accounts.

real yield security A debt security on which the coupon rate is periodically reset to a level that reflects changes in the consumer price index plus a real yield spread. A real yield security transfers the risk of unexpected inflation from the creditor to the borrower.

rebalance an account

When is it time to rebalance a portfolio?

Most investment pros I know recommend rebalancing once every year. The theory behind rebalancing is to allow automatic implementation of the age-old axiom "Buy low, sell high." It is important not to get nervous and react to short-term market activity or to rebalance so often that you do not give your winning investments a chance to grow. Despite the axiom and the recommendations of investment professionals, though, some people never rebalance, believing instead that whatever has happened in the recent past will continue indefinitely into the future. So rebalance once a year, and let the markets work for you, not against you.

Mark G. Steinberg, President, Trabar Associates, Boston, MA

rebalance an account To buy and sell securities so as to maintain a predetermined ratio of selected categories in an investment account. Following an extended bull market in equities, for example, an investor who wishes to own a portfolio of 60% equities and 40% bonds would need to rebalance the account by selling stock and buying bonds.

recapitalization A change a company makes in the long-term financing mix it uses. For example, a firm may borrow long-term funds (that is, it may sell bonds) in order to acquire the money needed to repurchase a block of its outstanding stock. Because recapitalization will often affect the level and the volatility of earnings per share, it is of interest to stockholders. Recapitalization often occurs when a firm attempts to reorganize while in bankruptcy proceedings.

recapture of depreciation The extent to which the price received from selling a depreciated asset represents recovery of depreciation taken in prior years. For example, an asset purchased for $10,000, depreciated to a book value of $6,000, and sold for $9,000 would result in a recapture of $3,000. —Also called *depreciation recapture.*

receivables —See ACCOUNTS RECEIVABLE.

receivables turnover —See ACCOUNTS RECEIVABLE TURNOVER.

receiver A person assigned by a court to handle affairs and assets of a business in bankruptcy proceedings. The receiver is charged with overseeing the firm for the benefit of its creditors and stockholders.

receiver's certificate The short-term debt that is issued by the receiver of a firm in bankruptcy proceedings. Receivers' certificates are of high quality because they have first claim on the bankrupt firm's assets.

receive versus payment (RVP) A settlement procedure in which a customer instructs that the delivery of a security will be made immediately upon receipt of proceeds from the sale of the security. —Compare DELIVERY VERSUS PAYMENT.

recession An extended decline in general business activity. The National Bureau of Economic Research formally defines a recession as three consecutive quarters of falling real gross domestic product. A recession affects different securities in different ways. For example, holders of high-quality bonds stand to benefit because inflation and interest rates may decline. Conversely, stockholders of manufacturing firms will probably see company profits and dividends drop.

CASE STUDY | After nearly a year of falling commodity prices, rising unemployment, increasing personal and corporate bankruptcies, falling stock prices, and declining public confidence, the National Bureau of Economic Research made it official and on November 26, 2001, declared a recession. The announcement wasn't a surprise to hundreds of thousands of people who had lost their jobs and an even greater number of investors who had experienced substantial losses in the stock market. The bureau's Business Cycle Dating Committee of six academic economists determined the recession commenced in March 2001, when economic activity stopped growing. Although many economists use declines in gross domestic product to define a recession, the NBER Dating Committee examined employment, industrial production, manufacturing and trade sales, and personal income. The country's last previous recession lasted eight months and ended in March 1991. The subsequent ten-year period of uninterrupted growth between March 1991 and March 2001 was the longest in America's history.

reciprocal immunity The tax immunity that interest payments on federal securities have against state and local authorities and that interest payments on state and local securities have against federal authorities. Although not specifically stated as such in the U.S. Constitution, reciprocal immunity has been recognized by the U.S. Supreme Court.

reclamation The recovery of losses by either party in a securities transaction in which there has been a bad delivery.

record date The date on which a firm's books are closed during the process of identifying the owners of a certain class of securities for purposes of transmitting dividends, interest, proxies, financial reports, and other documentation to them. For example, only the common stockholders who are listed on the record date will receive the dividends that are to be mailed on the payment date. —Also called *date of record.* —See also EX-DIVIDEND; INTEREST DATES.

recoup To sell an asset at a price sufficient to recover the original outlay or to offset a previous loss.

recourse loan A loan in which the lender can claim more than the collateral as repayment in the event that payments on the loan are stopped. Thus, a recourse loan places the borrower's personal assets at risk. —Compare NONRECOURSE LOAN.

recovery 1. The rising price of an asset. For example, following an extended decline in the price of precious metals, investor expectations of future inflation may generate recoveries in gold and silver prices. 2. Increased economic activity during a business cycle, resulting in growth in the gross domestic product.

recovery period The stipulated period during which a company fully depreciates an asset. Recovery periods for various kinds of assets are established by the government and often bear only a loose relationship to the profitable life of an asset.

rectangle In technical analysis, a chart pattern in which the price of a security bounces back and forth between two horizontal lines. Because a rectangle is thought to occur when stock is being distributed or accumulated by knowledgeable investors, a major price movement is expected once the stock breaks out of the rectangle formation. Refer to the *Technical Analysis Chart Patterns* section for an example of this chart.

red Of or relating to a firm or the operations of a firm that are deemed unprofitable. The term derives from the color of ink used to show losses on financial statements. —Compare BLACK.

redemption The retirement of a security by repurchase. Although generally used in reference to the repurchase of a bond before maturity, the term also applies to stock and mutual fund shares. —See also PARTIAL REDEMPTION.

redemption charge —See DEFERRED SALES CHARGE.

redemption date The date on which a debt security is scheduled to be redeemed by the issuer. The redemption date is the scheduled maturity date or, if applicable, a call date.

redemption premium —See CALL PREMIUM.

redemption price 1. The price at which an open-end investment company will buy back its shares from the owners. In most cases, the redemption price is the net asset value per share. 2. —See CALL PRICE.

red herring A prospectus that is given to potential investors in a new security issue before the selling price has been set and before the issuer's registration statement has been approved for accuracy and completeness by the SEC. This document, which provides details of the issue and facts concerning the issuer, is so named because of a statement on it, printed in red, that the issue has not yet been approved by the SEC. —Also called *preliminary prospectus.*

rediscount To discount a negotiable instrument a second time.

REFCORP —See RESOLUTION FUNDING CORPORATION.

refinance 1. To extend the maturity of a loan. 2. —See REFUND.

refund To retire securities with the funds that have been raised through the sale of a new security issue. Refunding usually occurs after a period of falling interest rates when firms issue new debt in order to retire existing debt having high coupon rates of interest. Refunding works to the disadvantage of existing bondholders, who must sell their securities before maturity (usually at a slight premium over face value) when proceeds can only be reinvested at a reduced yield. —Also called *refinance.* —See also CALL PROVISION; NONREFUNDABLE; PRE-REFUNDED BOND.

refund annuity An annuity that provides fixed payments as long as the annuitant lives and that guarantees repayment of the amount paid in. If the annuitant dies before receiving the amount paid in for the annuity, the balance is paid to the beneficiary.

refunding bond A bond that is issued for the purpose of retiring an outstanding bond. Issuers refund bond issues to reduce financing costs, eliminate covenants, and alter maturities. —See also CROSSOVER REFUNDING BOND; PREREFUNDING.

regional exchange A securities exchange that specializes in the stocks and bonds of companies with a regional, rather than a national, interest. The regional exchanges provide the only organized trading in many of these securities. They also list and trade many of the securities traded on one or more of the national exchanges; in recent years, the majority of trading on the regional exchanges has been in these dual-listed securities. The major regional exchanges in the United States are the Boston, Chicago, Cincinnati, and Philadelphia stock exchanges.

registered bond —See REGISTERED SECURITY.

registered company A corporation that has filed an SEC registration form and that is subject to SEC reporting requirements.

registered competitive market maker **1.** A dealer registered with the National Association of Securities Dealers to make a market in one or more securities. A registered competitive market maker must give the market firm bid and ask prices. **2.** A floor trader on the New York Stock Exchange.

registered competitive trader —See FLOOR TRADER.

registered equity market maker A floor trader on the American Stock Exchange.

registered exchange A securities exchange that has filed, and has had accepted, a registration statement with the SEC. All the larger securities exchanges in the United States are registered with the SEC, as required by the Securities Exchange Act of 1934. —Compare UNREGISTERED EXCHANGE.

registered investment adviser A professional investment adviser who is registered with the SEC as part of the Investment Advisers Act of 1940. Registered investment advisors are required to register annually with the SEC and to disclose any conflicts of interest they have concerning transactions executed for their clients.

registered investment company An investment company that is registered with the SEC and meets the requirements of the Investment Company Act of 1940 with respect to income distribution, fee structure, and diversification of assets.

registered options trader A member of an organized options exchange who is a market maker in certain options assigned by the exchange. A registered options trader holds a position similar to a specialist on a stock exchange.

registered representative An employee or a partner in a brokerage firm who is registered to handle customer accounts. —Also called *account executive; broker; customer's man; stockbroker.*

Registered Representative Rapid Response Service (R4) An automated stock trading system used on the New York Stock Exchange that provides immediate execution for a limited list of stocks at the best quoted price.

registered retirement savings plan (RRSP) A personal tax-sheltered retirement plan for Canadians that is similar to individual retirement accounts offered in the United States. Contributions may be deducted from taxable income, and earnings on contributions are exempt from taxation until withdrawals are made.

registered secondary distribution The sale of a block of previously issued securities following registration with the SEC. Securities sold in a registered secondary offering are likely to come from an institutional investor that acquired the securities in a private placement.

registered security A security, the certificate of which has the owner's name imprinted on its face. A record of current owners is kept by the issuer for purposes of transmitting checks, proxies, reports, and so forth. Nearly all securities are registered. —Compare BEARER FORM. —Also called *registered bond.*

registered trader —See FLOOR TRADER.

registrar A firm that updates stock records using information sent by the transfer agent. Essentially, the registrar makes certain that the issued certificates correspond with those that have been canceled.

registration The preparation of a security issue for public sale. For registration, the issuer hires an underwriting firm to prepare a registration statement that is submitted to the SEC or to a state authority. As part of this process, an investment banker brings in a public accounting firm to audit the issuer's financial condition. —See also COOLING-OFF PERIOD; GUN JUMPING; PIGGYBACK REGISTRATION.

registration fee The fee paid to the SEC by a firm issuing securities.

registration statement A document filed with the SEC containing detailed information about a firm that plans to sell securities to the public. Required data include financial statements, the reason for the issue, and details on the firm's business. Certain issues (such as under $500,000, intrastate sales only, private placements, and bank securities) are exempt from this requirement. —See also DEFICIENCY LETTER; OFFICIAL STATEMENT; PROSPECTUS.

regression analysis The measurement of change in one variable that is the result of changes in other variables. Regression analysis is used frequently in an attempt to identify the variables that affect a certain stock's price.

regression coefficient A mathematical measure of the relationship between a dependent variable and an independent variable. For example, a financial theorist might attempt to determine the effect of increased dividends on a stock's price by calculating the regression coefficient between the price of the stock and its dividends per share. In this instance, the stock price is the dependent variable and the dividend payment is the independent variable.

regressive tax A tax that has a rate that declines as the amount to be taxed increases. In terms of income, federal and state taxation of cigarettes is regressive because low-income smokers pay a higher rate of taxation in terms of their income than high-income smokers do. A system of regressive taxation tends to free more funds for investment because high-income individuals tend to save a greater portion of their income. However, a regressive tax is often considered socially and politically unacceptable. —Compare PROGRESSIVE TAX.

regular member A full member of a securities exchange, who is entitled to all privileges and subject to all regulations of the exchange. —Compare ASSOCIATE MEMBER.

regular-way contract A security transaction in which delivery of the certificate by the selling broker and delivery of cash by the buying broker are to occur three business days after the trade date. A regular-way contract is the usual method for handling stock and corporate and municipal bond transactions. Government securities and options settle one business day following the trade date. —Compare CASH CONTRACT. —See also SELLER'S OPTION CONTRACT.

regulated investment company An investment company that meets certain standards and, as a result, does not have to pay federal income taxes on distributions of dividends, interest, and realized capital gains. Essentially, this income is passed through to the stockholders, who, in turn, are taxed. To qualify as a regulated investment company a firm must derive at least 90% of its income from dividends, interest, and capital gains. It also must distribute at least

90% of the dividends and interest received. It must have a minimum diversification of its assets.

Regulation A An SEC regulation that permits companies raising less than $5 million in a 12-month period to file with the SEC a printed copy of an offering circular in place of a regular registration statement.

Regulation A issue A type of new security issue that requires a much shorter prospectus and carries with it reduced officer and director liability for misleading and/or false statements.

Regulation D An SEC regulation that permits some smaller companies to offer and sell securities without registering the transaction. The regulation applies to companies that seek to raise less than $1 million in a 12-month period and to companies that raise up to $5 million so long as the securities are sold to accredited investors or to 35 or fewer individuals.

Regulation FD An SEC regulation that mandates a company must release material information to all investors simultaneously. Material information released inadvertently must be made publicly available within 24 hours. Some critics contend Regulation FD causes increased volatility in stock prices.

Regulation G A Federal Reserve regulation that extends control over credit to purchase and carry listed stocks to firms other than brokers, dealers, and banks.

Regulation S An SEC regulation that permits companies to not register stock they sell outside the United States to foreign investors.

Regulation T A Federal Reserve regulation that specifies the maximum initial credit extension that may be given to investors in securities. The initial margin requirement has varied from 40 to 100% since the regulation was established under provisions of the Securities Exchange Act of 1934. Listed stocks, convertible bonds, and many over-the-counter stocks are covered by Regulation T. —See also FREERIDING 2; FROZEN ACCOUNT; SPECIAL MISCELLANEOUS ACCOUNT.

Regulation U A Federal Reserve regulation that controls bank loans made to customers for the purpose of purchasing and carrying listed stocks.

regulatory climate The extent to which a regulated firm or industry is permitted to earn an adequate return on the stockholders' investment. This term is nearly always used in reference to utilities, which are required to obtain approval for rate changes. A favorable regulatory climate generally causes investors to value a company more highly because they expect its earnings to be greater.

rehypothecate To repledge stock as collateral for a loan. In practice, this term means to pledge securities (by a brokerage firm) for a bank loan when the securities have already been pledged to the firm by one of its customers. The brokerage firm essentially passes along the collateral in order to obtain a loan to finance the customer's account.

reinvestment plan —See DIVIDEND REINVESTMENT PLAN.

reinvestment privilege The prerogative of a mutual fund shareholder to have dividends used to purchase additional shares in the fund. Most mutual funds give their shareholders reinvestment privileges and most do not charge fees for the purchase of the new shares.

reinvestment rate The annual yield at which cash flows from an investment can be reinvested. The reinvestment rate is of particular interest to people holding short-term investments, such as certificates of deposit or Treasury bills, or long-term investments that produce large annual cash flows, such as high-coupon bonds.

reinvestment risk The possibility that the cash flows produced by an investment will have to be reinvested at a reduced rate of return. For example, the owner of a certificate of deposit faces the risk that lower interest rates will be in effect when the certificate matures and the funds are to be reinvested.

REIT —See REAL ESTATE INVESTMENT TRUST.

rejection The refusal to accept a security that has been delivered by a customer or broker. A questionable certificate or an improper endorsement are reasons for rejection.

relationship trading —See BASIS TRADING.

relative strength The price strength of an individual stock compared with the strength of an industry index or a general market index. In general, a stock that acts stronger than its industry or the market as a whole shows a bullish sign for that stock. Likewise, an industry index that acts stronger than a market index is bullish for stock in that industry. Relative strength is typically used when calculating an index of a stock's price to its industry or market index over a period of time. —Also called *strength*.

relative strength indicator In technical analysis, an indicator that provides buy and sell signals by indicating whether a stock is oversold or overbought, respectively. Relative strength is calculated using a ratio of positive to negative price changes.

remainderman A person or organization that is to receive the remaining interest in a property or estate after prior interests have been satisfied.

remargin To deposit additional cash or securities in a margin account when equity in the account is judged to be insufficient to meet the maintenance margin requirement.

remarketed preferred stock A type of preferred stock in which the dividend rate is determined periodically by a remarketing agent. The agent resets the dividend rate so that the preferred stock can be tendered at par or resold at the original offering price. —Compare AUCTION-RATE PREFERRED STOCK.

REMIC —See REAL ESTATE MORTAGE INVESTMENT CONDUIT.

remit To send payment for goods or services.

reopen an issue In U.S. Treasury financing, to sell additional securities of an existing issue rather than to offer a new issue with different terms. If the market for debt has changed since the existing issue was sold, reopening the issue will require a revised selling price to make the securities competitive in the current market.

reopening The opening of trading in a security or futures contract in which trading was earlier suspended. For example, exchange officials may suspend trading in a security until certain information is made public. Following a public announcement of the information, trading in the security will resume.

reorganization The restatement of assets to current market value along with a restructuring of liabilities and equity to reflect the reduction in asset values and negotiations with creditors. Reorganization is used as an attempt to keep a financially troubled or bankrupt firm viable. —See also CHAPTER 11.

reorganization plan A plan filed with a bankruptcy court judge by a company in Chapter 11 proceedings in which the disbursement of assets is stipulated. The plan must be approved by the firm's creditors and by the court. A reorganization plan results in new securities being given to creditors in trade for old securities.

repatriate To bring home assets that are currently held in a foreign country. Domestic corporations are frequently taxed on the profits that they repatriate, a factor inducing the firms to leave overseas the profits earned there.

repeat prices omitted A notice on the consolidated tape that only the initial trade at a given price will be reported. Subsequent trades in a security are reported only when there is a price change. A repeat prices omitted notice is used when heavy trading volume requires increased speed in reporting transactions.

replacement cost The current cost of replacing an asset with an equivalent asset.

replacement cost accounting An accounting system that values assets and liabilities according to their replacement cost rather than their historical cost. Replacement cost accounting incorporates the effects of changing prices and the resultant changing values of the items that are listed in a firm's financial statements.

repo —See REPURCHASE AGREEMENT.

repo rate The rate of interest (annualized) on a repurchase agreement.

report A confirmation of a transaction at the time of execution.

reporting dealers Any of various independent dealers in government securities who report their trading activity and security positions to the Federal Reserve. Because the Federal Reserve uses purchases and sales to influence the money supply, information from reporting dealers plays an important part in monetary policy. —Compare PRIMARY DEALER. —See also OPEN-MARKET OPERATIONS.

repricing The exchanging of newly issued incentive stock options priced at the current market price for previously granted options that are out-of-the-money. Repricing rewards managers of companies with stock prices that have declined.

repurchase agreement (RP) The sale of an asset at the same time an agreement is made to repurchase the asset at a specified price on a given date. Essentially, this process involves taking out a loan and using the asset as collateral. —Compare REVERSE REPURCHASE AGREEMENT. —Also called *repo*. —See also OVERNIGHT REPO.

required rate of return 1. The minimum rate of return that an investment must provide or must be expected to provide in order to justify its acquisition. For example, an investor who can earn an annual return of 11% on certificates of deposit may set a required rate of return of 15% on a more risky stock investment before considering a shift of funds into stock. An investment's required return is a function of the returns available on other investments and of the risk level inherent in a particular investment. 2. The minimum rate of return required by an investor, a stipulation that limits the types of investments the investor can undertake. For example, a person with a required rate of return of 15% would generally have to invest in relatively risky securities.

required reserves The reserves against deposits that commercial banks and thrifts are required to hold either in cash or in deposits at the Federal Reserve. —Compare EXCESS RESERVES. —See also RESERVE REQUIREMENT.

rescission The cancellation of a previous exercise of an incentive stock option, generally because of a substantial drop in the price of the stock acquired through the exercise. Rescission results in the employee surrendering stock in exchange for money that was paid for the stock.

research and development costs (R&D costs) The costs that are incurred during the development and introduction of new products to market or during the improvement of existing products. Although R&D costs tend to penalize current profits, they eventually benefit the firm's future profits when new products developed as a result of the research become profitable themselves. Many analysts regard a high proportion of sales revenue devoted to R&D as a positive sign relative to a firm's profit potential and future stock price.

research department The group of individuals in a brokerage firm or institutional investment house that analyzes companies, economic matters, and securities. The research departments in institutional investment houses assist in selecting investments and devising investment strategies. Brokerage firm research departments assist the registered representatives in making customer purchase suggestions.

reserve The funds that are earmarked by a firm from its retained earnings for future use, such as for the payment of likely-to-be-incurred bad debts. The existence of such a reserve informs readers of the firm's financial statements that at least a part of the retained earnings will not be available to the stockholders. —See also ALLOWANCE FOR DOUBTFUL ACCOUNTS; RESERVE FOR CONTINGENCIES.

reserve deficiency A shortage in funds set aside as a reserve for a specific purpose. For example, during a recession a firm may find the reserve fund covering allowance for bad debts deficient when the amount of bad debts exceeds expectations. A reserve deficiency will penalize the firm's profits if the firm has to set aside additional funds to offset the deficiency.

reserve for bad debts —See ALLOWANCE FOR DOUBTFUL ACCOUNTS.

reserve for contingencies A part of retained earnings that are set aside for potential future losses. For example, a firm may establish a reserve account to cover the possibility of losing a lawsuit to which it is a party.

reserve requirement The required percentage of reserves (deposits) that banks and thrifts must hold in cash or in deposits at the Federal Reserve. This requirement is set by the Fed. Any changes in the required percentage are used to influence credit conditions. An increased percentage requirement means fewer funds available for lending and a resultant rise in interest rates. —See also MONETARY POLICY.

reset note A debt security with terms that can be reset on one or more dates during the life of the note. At the time the terms are changed, the holder usually has the right to redeem the security.

residual security A security with the potential for diluting earnings per share. A convertible bond is a residual security because conversion of the bond by an investor will result in more shares of common stock outstanding and a reduction in earnings per share.

residual value The price at which a fixed asset is expected to be sold at the end of its useful life. Residual value is used in calculating some types of depreciation. —Also called *salvage value; scrap value.*

resistance An increased supply of a security. —Compare SUPPORT.

resistance level A price at which a security or the market itself will encounter considerable selling pressure. A resistance level is formed when investors purchase large amounts of a security just before a decline and then resolve to sell the security should it again reach the level at which it was purchased. Technical analysts believe that an additional supply of a security will tend to keep its price from rising above the resistance level. —Compare SUPPORT LEVEL. —Also called *overhead resistance level.* —See also OVERHANGING SUPPLY.

Resolution Funding Corporation (REFCORP) The federal agency responsible for issuing up to $40 billion of long-term debt required to finance activities of the Resolution Trust Corporation, a group that closed and merged insolvent thrift institutions during the late 1980s and early 1990s. The principal of REFCORP debt is backed by zero-coupon Treasury bonds.

resource recovery revenue bond A debt obligation, usually issued by a municipality or local government agency, the proceeds of which are used to construct a facility that converts solid waste into some sort of salable item. Debt service is generally covered through fees paid by firms disposing of garbage and through revenues from the sale of an end product such as energy or fuel.

restatement The altered presentation of a portion or all of an earlier financial statement. For example, a firm may issue a restatement of its previously published balance sheet and income statement because it has discovered some heretofore unknown information that should have been included on it.

restricted account A margin account in which the customer cannot purchase any additional stock on margin without putting up more equity. An account is restricted when its debit balance is greater than the loan value of the securities within the account. —Also called *blocked account.*

restricted option An option in which an uncovered opening transaction cannot be made. An option becomes restricted when it closes at a price under $50 (½ point) and is out-of-the-money by more than 5 points. Restricted options are not prohibited for covered transactions or spreads.

restricted retained earnings The retained earnings that are unavailable for the payment of dividends to common stockholders. For example, dividend arrearages on cumulative preferred stock must be paid before any dividend payments can be made to common stockholders. Therefore, the arrearages will result in restricted retained earnings. —Also called *restricted surplus.*

restricted security A security that has not been registered with the SEC and therefore may not be sold publicly. These securities frequently enter portfolios of institutional investors through private placements and are sometimes registered at a later date. —Also called *letter bond; letter security; letter stock; unregistered security.*

restricted stock grant An offer, sometimes extended to corporate managers, that allows the purchase of stock generally at a bargain price if specified conditions are met. Restrictions may include a minimum length of employment or a specified rate of earnings growth. Voting rights and dividends revert to the recipient at the time of the grant.

restricted surplus   —See RESTRICTED RETAINED EARNINGS.

restrictive covenant   —See COVENANT.

restructuring   A significant rearrangement of a firm's assets and/or liabilities. A firm's restructuring may include discontinuing a line of business, closing several plants, and making extensive employee cutbacks. A restructuring generally entails a one-time charge against earnings. —Compare DEBT RESTRUCTURING.

restructuring charge   The expense of reorganizing a company's operations. A restructuring charge is an infrequent expense that generally results from asset writedowns or facility closings. It is not considered an extraordinary item and must be considered when calculating a firm's income from continuing operations.

> ⋀⋀ **CASE STUDY** │ In August 2001 Procter & Gamble Co. reported the first quarterly loss in nearly a decade. The $320 million quarterly loss resulted from a $1.16 billion restructuring charge to account for corporate streamlining and altering the firm's portfolio of brands. Procter & Gamble was in the process of divesting most of its food and drink business, mostly by entering into a joint venture with Coca-Cola, a plan that was later abandoned. The company reported it planned to continue taking restructuring charges through mid-2004. At the same time P&G reported the net loss, it announced that operating income increased 12% to 60¢ per share. Restructuring charges are often given little weight by investors and analysts who evaluate a company's financial performance, because these charges are considered one-time expenses. The market price of Procter & Gamble's common stock experienced no significant price change on the day the loss was announced.

retail   The sale of securities to individual investors, as opposed to sales to institutions and transactions among broker-dealer firms for eventual sale to retail clients. —Compare WHOLESALE.

retail house   A brokerage firm that primarily attracts individual investors. A retail house frequently has numerous offices, large office staffs, and high overhead; produces research reports targeted to individuals; and has brokers who earn relatively high commissions.

retail investor   An individual investor who buys and sells securities for his or her own account. Some brokerage firms specialize in serving retail investors while other brokerage firms strive to attract business from institutions that engage in large trades.

retail market   A market composed of price quotes for a security made by a broker or a dealer to an individual investor. A quote at the retail level entails a higher ask and a lower bid than a quote on the same security for another dealer. —Compare INSIDE MARKET.

retained earnings   The accumulated net income that has been retained for reinvestment in the business rather than being paid out in dividends to stockholders. Net income that is retained in the business can be used to acquire additional income-earning assets that result in increased income in future years. Retained earnings is a part of the owners' equity section of a firm's balance sheet. —Also called *earned surplus; surplus; undistributed profits.* —See also ACCUMULATED EARNINGS TAX; RESTRICTED RETAINED EARNINGS; STATEMENT OF RETAINED EARNINGS.

retained earnings statement —See STATEMENT OF RETAINED EARNINGS.

retention The securities that are distributed to members of an underwriting syndicate after accounting for the portion of the new issue retained for sales to institutions and members of the selling group who are not also part of the syndicate.

retention rate The proportion of net income that is not paid in dividends. A firm earning $80 million after taxes and paying dividends of $20 million has a retention rate of $60 million/$80 million, or 75%. A high retention rate makes it more likely a firm's income and dividends will grow in future years. —Also called *earnings retention ratio; plowback ratio.*

retirement **1.** The disposal of a fixed asset at the end of its useful life. Retirement may result in a gain or loss, depending upon any compensation received for the asset and whether the asset is carried at a positive book value. **2.** The voiding of a firm's own stock that has been reacquired and is being held as Treasury stock.

retractable bond A Canadian term for a put bond.

return —See YIELD.

return of capital —See CAPITAL DIVIDEND.

return on assets (ROA) —See RETURN ON INVESTMENT.

return on common stock equity A measure of the return that a firm's management is able to earn on common stockholders' investment. Return on common stock equity is calculated by dividing the net income minus preferred dividends by the owners' equity minus the par value of any preferred stock outstanding. For firms with no preferred stock, return on common stock equity is identical to return on equity. —Compare PROFITABILITY RATIO.

return on equity (ROE) A measure of the net income that a firm is able to earn as a percent of stockholders' investment. Many analysts consider ROE the single most important financial ratio applying to stockholders and the best measure of performance by a firm's management. Return on equity is calculated by dividing net income after taxes by owners' equity. —Compare PROFITABILITY RATIO. —See also RETURN ON COMMON STOCK EQUITY.

return on investment (ROI) A measure of the net income a firm's management is able to earn with the its total assets. Return on investment is calculated by dividing net profits after taxes by total assets. —Compare PROFITABILITY RATIO. —Also called *rate of return; return on assets.*

return on sales The portion of each dollar of sales that a firm is able to turn into income. Because of severe competition, regulation, or other factors, some firms or industries have low returns on sales. This is generally the case for grocery chains, for example. In some instances, a low return on sales can be offset by increased sales. Return on sales varies significantly from industry to industry. —Compare NET PROFIT MARGIN; PROFITABILITY RATIO.

revenue The inflow of assets that results from sales of goods and services and earnings from dividends, interest, and rent. Revenue is often received in the form of cash but also may be in the form of receivables to be turned into cash at a later date.

revenue anticipation note (RAN) A short-term municipal obligation with repayment to be made from a revenue source other than taxes.

revenue bond A municipal debt on which the payment of interest and principal depends on revenues from the particular asset that the bond issue is used to finance. Examples of such projects are toll roads and bridges, housing developments, and airport expansions. Revenue bonds are generally considered of lower quality than general obligation bonds, but there is a great amount of variance in risk depending on the particular assets financed. —Compare AUTHORITY BOND.

revenue enhancement An increase in revenues, especially by way of increased taxes. Revenue enhancement includes reducing taxpayer deductions and eliminating tax credits.

revenue ruling The written guidance that is provided taxpayers by the Internal Revenue Service. Although revenue rulings apply to individual situations, they are often of general interest because of the manner in which the IRS interprets a particular tax problem. —Also called *letter ruling; ruling.*

reversal effect The theory that stock prices overreact to relevant news so that extreme investment performance tends to reverse itself. Some studies indicate that short-term overreaction may lead to long-term reversals as investors recognize and correct past pricing errors.

reversal pattern In technical analysis, a chart formation that indicates a market top or a market bottom. A reversal pattern, which usually occurs after a major movement in the price of a stock or in the entire market, is an indication that investors should adjust their positions to take advantage of the coming change in market direction. A saucer and a head-and-shoulders are reversal patterns.

reverse —See REVERSE REPURCHASE AGREEMENT.

reverse acquisition An acquisition in which the company taken over becomes the surviving entity. A reverse acquisition is sometimes used to acquire and convert a private company into a public company without being required to go through a lengthy registration process.

reverse annuity mortgage A mortgage in which a homeowner's equity is gradually depleted by a series of payments from the mortgage holder to the homeowner. Thus, a reverse annuity mortgage increases in size as the annuity payments continue. A reverse annuity mortgage is used primarily by elderly homeowners who wish to convert the equity in their homes into a stream of retirement income payments.

reverse crush A combination commodity trade in which soybean meal and oil futures are purchased and soybean futures are sold. —Compare CRUSH.

reverse leveraged buyout An equity investment in a company that is troubled by excessive debt. The equity infusion produced by the buyout is intended to reduce debt to a more manageable level.

reverse repurchase agreement The purchase of an asset with a simultaneous agreement to resell the asset on a given date at a specified price. The result is simply a loan at a prescribed rate for a predetermined period while holding the asset as collateral. —Compare REPURCHASE AGREEMENT. —Also called *reverse.*

reverse stock split A proportionate reduction in the shares of stock held by shareholders. For example, a one-for-four split would result in stockholders owning one share for every four shares owned prior to the split. A reverse stock split has no effect on a firm's financial and operational performance and is often designed only to boost the market price of the stock so it won't be delisted from trading on an exchange that imposes a minimum share price requirement. —Compare SPLIT. —Also called *split down.*

reverse swap The exchange of one bond for another such that an earlier investment position is reestablished to the investment position that existed before an earlier swap. For example, an investor might swap intermediate-term bonds for long-term bonds to take advantage of a steeply sloped yield curve. As the yield curve flattens, the investor might engage in a reverse swap by exchanging the long-term bonds for intermediate-term bonds.

reversing trade In futures trading, a trade that brings an investor's position in a particular contract back to zero. For example, the purchase of a stock index contract that has previously been sold short is an example of a reversing trade.

revisionary trust A trust that is irrevocable for a predetermined period (at least ten years or until the death of the beneficiary), after which it becomes revocable. During the time the trust is irrevocable it will not be included as part of the donor's estate for tax purposes.

revocable trust A trust that may be terminated by the grantor or that is set up to terminate automatically at a specific date. Revocable trusts are often used to turn daily decisions regarding certain assets over to someone else. They are also used to reduce probate fees, to reduce delays in distributing assets, and to keep assets from becoming a matter of public record. A revocable trust—an important estate-planning tool—may serve to reduce federal estate taxes but generally will have no effect on income taxes. —Compare IRREVOCABLE TRUST.

revolver —See LINE OF CREDIT.

revolving credit agreement —See LINE OF CREDIT.

rich Of, relating to, or being a security price judged by some investors to be too high. For example, a new issue of stock may carry an offering price that many analysts consider rich. If too many investors and analysts believe the price is rich, the offering may be unsuccessful.

riding the yield curve The purchase of a security with a longer term to maturity than the investor's expected holding period in order to produce increased returns by taking advantage of a positive yield curve. For example, a $10,000, 26-week Treasury bill that yields 10% annually will sell for $9,524, while a 13-week bill that yields 9% will sell for $9,780. Buying the longer-term security, holding it for 13 weeks, and selling it at the existing 13-week bill price will produce a profit of $256, for an annualized yield of ($256/$9,524) × 4, or 10.75%. This yield is considerably higher than what might be obtained by simply purchasing a 13-week bill. Riding the yield curve increases yield only when longer-term interest rates are higher than shorter-term rates.

right A certificate that permits the owner to purchase a certain number of shares, or, frequently, a fractional share of new stock from the issuer at a specific price. Rights are issued to existing stockholders in proportion to the number of shares the stockholders already own. Rights then may be combined with cash to purchase the new shares or they may be sold to other investors. Rights usually have value because they permit the owner to purchase shares of stock at less than the market price. A right is indicated in stock transaction tables by the

Should rights be sold or used?

Rights offerings refer to the right of an investor to maintain his or her percentage ownership in a company when the company decides to issue new stock. Generally the company will do so at a discount to its market price to attract buyers, thus the existing stockholders' rights have value. The decision a rights holder must make is whether to put more money into the stock of this company or to sell the rights in the open market as compensation for the dilution of his or her percentage ownership in the company. TIP: Such a purchase depends completely on the individual's circumstances, goals, prejudices, and objectives—just as in any other stock purchase—and should be approached accordingly.

Thomas J. McAllister, CFP, McAllister Financial Planning, Carmel, IN

symbol *rt*, appearing after the stock's name. —Also called *stock right; subscription right.* —See also EX-RIGHTS; PREEMPTIVE RIGHT.

right of accumulation The right that is granted to buyers by some mutual funds permitting the buyers to count existing holdings of the fund along with new purchases when determining the size of the sales fee on the new shares. This right applies to funds that charge fees on a sliding scale, whereby the more shares that are purchased, the lower the fee that is charged on a percentage basis. Thus the fee charged on succeeding purchases is determined by all purchases, past and present, not just by new purchases.

right of survivorship —See JOINT TENANCY WITH RIGHT OF SURVIVORSHIP.

rights off —See EX-RIGHTS.

rights offering The distribution to existing owners of rights to purchase shares of stock as part of a new stock offering. A company uses a rights offering when it sells new shares to existing shareholders rather than selling new shares to the entire investment community. The rights are used as a means to distribute new shares to existing holders on the basis of the shares each holder already owns. —See also OVERSUBSCRIPTION PRIVILEGE; PREEMPTIVE RIGHT.

rights on Of or relating to stock that trades so that new buyers, rather than sellers, will receive rights that have been declared but not yet distributed. —Compare EX-RIGHTS. —Also called *cum rights.*

ring —See PIT.

ring fencing The legal walling off of certain assets or liabilities within a corporation. For example, a firm may form a new subsidiary to protect, or ring-fence, specific assets from creditors.

⋀ CASE STUDY California's electricity deregulation of the late 1990s resulted in the state's electric utilities hitting the financial wall by 2001. Unable by law to raise the rates it charged its customers, the utilities lost billions of dollars buying electricity at rising wholesale prices during an energy shortage in the western United States. To protect one part of the company, publicly traded PG&E, parent of Pacific Gas & Electric, in January 2001 ring-fenced its National Energy Group, which was then able to obtain its own credit rating and borrow money when the remainder of the company was shut out of the financial markets. In April 2001 Pacific Gas & Electric filed for bankruptcy while protected National Energy Group continued to borrow funds for trading power and purchasing turbines. The ring-fencing protected

National Energy Group from Pacific Gas & Electric's creditors, which, in turn, allowed the company access to the capital markets. Critics claimed the financial maneuver was an abuse that unfairly shielded assets from creditors.

rising-coupon security —See STEPPED COUPON BOND.

risk The variability of returns from an investment. The greater the variability (in dividend fluctuation or security price, for example), the greater the risk. Because investors are generally averse to risk, investments with greater inherent risk must promise higher expected yields.

risk adjusted Of or relating to a variable, such as the return on an investment, that has been altered in order to account for the differences in risk among variables of the same type. For example, financial managers adjust expected returns on various investment projects for risk in order to make them comparable.

risk arbitrage The simultaneous purchase and sale of assets that are potentially, but not necessarily, equivalent. For example, Firm A may make an offer to acquire Firm B by exchanging one share of its own stock for two shares of Firm B's stock. If the stock of Firm A is trading at $50 and the stock of Firm B is trading at $23, the risk arbitrager would buy shares in Firm B and sell short one-half this number of shares in Firm A. If the buyout offer is approved, the two stocks will exchange on a one-for-two basis and the arbitrage position will be profitable. The risk is that the buyout will be unsuccessful and the exchange of stock will not take place. Risk arbitrage is also used in situations involving reorganizations and tender offers. —Also called *equity arbitrage.*

risk aversion The tendency of investors to avoid risky investments. Thus, if two investments offer the same expected yield but have different risk characteristics, investors will choose the one with the lowest variability in returns. If investors are risk averse, higher-risk investments must offer higher expected yields. Otherwise, they will not be competitive with the less risky investments.

risk capital —See VENTURE CAPITAL.

risk-free return The annualized rate of return on a riskless investment. This is the rate against which other returns are measured. —See also EXCESS RETURN.

risk hedge The taking of an offsetting position in related assets so as to profit from relative price movements. For example, an investor might purchase futures contracts on gold and sell futures contracts on silver in the belief that gold will become relatively more valuable compared with silver over the life of the contracts.

riskless investment An investment with a certain rate of return and no chance of default. Although various investments (for example, savings accounts and certificates of deposit at insured institutions) meet these requirements, a Treasury bill is the most common example of a riskless investment.

riskless transaction A dealer transaction in which the dealer makes a purchase or sale to offset a customer order. Thus, if a customer wishes to purchase 500 shares of Rushville Exterminators, Inc., at $80 per share, the dealer may purchase the 500 shares from another source at $79.25 and resell the stock to the customer at a markup of 75¢. The dealer has entered into a riskless transaction because the purchase will be offset by an existing customer order. The markup on riskless transactions is regulated by the National Association of Securities Dealers. —Also called *simultaneous transaction.* —See also FIVE-PERCENT RULE.

---
risk profile

What questions should I ask myself as I prepare to develop my risk profile?

Ask yourself when you plan to use your investment—in a few years to buy a home, start a business, or pay for college, or in the future for retirement. After you have decided how long your money will work, the focus of your preparation should shift to personal preferences:

- Is capital preservation more important to you than outpacing inflation?
- Are you willing to accept fluctuating values when investing for the long term?
- Are you more comfortable with dividends and income, or with growth through capital appreciation?
- Will you accept above-average risk to generate above-average returns?

Mark G. Steinberg, President, Trabar Associates, Boston, MA

---

risk premium   The extra yield over the risk-free rate owing to various types of risk inherent in a particular investment. For example, any issuer other than the U.S. government usually must pay investors a risk premium in the form of a higher interest rate on bonds to account for the fact that the risk of default is less on U.S. government securities than on securities of other issuers.   —Also called *bond premium risk.*

risk profile   The degree to which various risks are important to a particular individual.

ROA   —See RETURN ON ASSETS.

road show   A series of presentations to investors describing an upcoming issue of securities. A road show is designed to drum up interest in the issue among potential investors.

rocket scientist   —See QUANT.

ROE   —See RETURN ON EQUITY.

ROI   —See RETURN ON INVESTMENT.

roll   —See ROLL OVER.

rolling down   The liquidation of an option position by an investor at the same time that he or she takes an essentially identical position with a lower strike price.

rolling forward   The liquidation of one option position by an investor at the same time that he or she takes an essentially identical position with a more distant maturity. An example would be repurchasing an option with a May expiration and selling an option on the same asset with an identical strike price but with a November expiration date.

rolling stock   Any of various readily movable transportation equipment such as automobiles, locomotives, railroad cars, and trucks. Rolling stock generally makes good collateral for loans because the equipment is standardized and easily transportable among firms or locations.   —See also EQUIPMENT TRUST CERTIFICATE.

rolling up   The liquidation of an option position by an investor at the same time that he or she takes an essentially identical position with a higher strike price.

roll over   To reinvest funds from a maturing security into a similar security. —Also called *roll.*

Roth IRA

Should I choose a regular IRA or a Roth IRA?

The hands-down favorite is a Roth IRA. Now, the money that goes into a regular IRA isn't taxed until withdrawal after age 59½ A Roth IRA is funded with aftertax dollars, but no taxes are levied on the gains when the money is taken out during retirement. One way to look at the tradeoff is to decide whether you'll be in a lower tax bracket in your golden years. If so, you might want to lean toward the regular IRA. However, you will accumulate more savings in a Roth if your tax bracket remains the same or ticks up. The Roth carries other advantages that weigh heavily in its favor. Among them: With a regular IRA you must start withdrawing money at age 70½. Not with a Roth. You can take out aftertax contributions in a Roth free of tax and penalty (but not the gains) at any time and for any reason. The income eligibility requirements for a Roth IRA are more generous than for the traditional IRA. There are a number of calculators on the Internet for comparing the two products.

Christopher Farrell, Economics Editor
Minnesota Public Radio, heard nationally on Sound Money®

rollover   The reinvestment of money received from a maturing security in another similar security. Rollover usually applies to short-term investments such as certificates of deposit, commercial paper, and Treasury bills. For example, investors often want a rollover of the proceeds from a maturing certificate of deposit into a new certificate of deposit.   —See also IRA ROLLOVER; PENSION ROLLOVER.

roll-up   A master limited partnership in which a number of existing limited partnerships are pooled into a single partnership.

Roth IRA   A special type of individual retirement account in which contributions are made with aftertax dollars but distributions are tax-free so long as certain requirements including holding period and age are met. All earnings within the account are free of taxation.

⋀⋀ CASE STUDY   Roth IRAs allow an annual contribution to a retirement account, but unlike a regular IRA the contribution is never tax-deductible. Rather, distributions from a Roth IRA are generally tax-free, so long as certain criteria are met. Individuals and their spouses are eligible to invest in a Roth so long as their adjusted gross income meets stated guidelines. Tax-free withdrawals are permitted if the investor holds the account for at least five years from the date the account was opened and is at least age 59½. A tax-free withdrawal of up to $10,000 is permitted for a first-time home purchase so long as the required five-year minimum holding period is met. Distributions prior to age 59½ are not taxable only with respect to contributions. In other words, you can always withdraw prior contributions without tax or penalty, a substantial advantage compared to a regular IRA. Withdrawals of interest are taxable and subject to a 10% penalty unless the money is withdrawn because of death, total disability, the purchase of a first home (up to $10,000), higher-education expenses, medical expenses in excess of 7.5% of adjusted gross income, or health insurance premiums for certain unemployed individuals.

rounded bottom   —See SAUCER.

rounded top   —See DOME.

round lot   The standard unit of trading in a particular type of security. For stocks, a round lot is 100 shares or a multiple thereof, although a few inactive issues trade in units of 10 shares. For corporate, municipal, and government bonds, a round lot is usually considered to be $100,000 of principal amount of securities per trade. Customers involved in securities transactions in lots other than round lots are often penalized somewhat because the trades require more broker and dealer effort. —Compare ODD LOT. —Also called *even lot; lot; normal trading unit.*

round trip The purchase and sale of the same security. Some brokerage firms offer a discounted commission if a round trip is completed within a certain length of time. —Also called *round turn.*

round turn In futures trading, a completed trade involving the purchase and subsequent sale of a position, or the sale and subsequent covering purchase.

royalty The compensation that is paid to the owner of an asset based on income earned by the asset's user. For example, an oil company pays royalties to the owners of mineral rights, and a book publisher compensates its authors with royalty payments.

royalty interest The proportional ownership interest by the owner of oil and gas rights in income produced by the asset. —See also OVERRIDING ROYALTY INTEREST.

royalty trust An ownership interest in certain assets, generally crude oil or gas production and real estate. Unlike the usual corporate organization, a trust arrangement permits income and tax benefits to flow through to the individual owners. Thus, some investors argue that a trust produces more value for the owners.

RP —See REPURCHASE AGREEMENT.

RRSP —See REGISTERED RETIREMENT SAVINGS PLAN.

^r_t —Used on the consolidated tape to indicate the transaction of a right: AEP^r_t $50s^{1/4}$.

rt —Used in stock transaction tables in newspapers to indicate a listing for rights. No dividend, yield, or price-earnings ratio is listed for a right because dividends are not paid and earnings are not applicable: *ContIl rt.*

Rule 3b–3 An SEC rule that defines short sales.

Rule 5 An American Stock Exchange rule that prohibits members of the exchange from trading listed stocks off the exchange floor. —Compare RULE 390. —See also RULE 19C-3.

Rule 10a–1 A 1939 SEC rule that prohibits the short sale of a security at or below the last price at which that security was traded, unless the last price was higher than the previous different price. Rule 10a–1 was instituted to keep short sellers from battering down the price of a stock.

Rule 10b–2 An SEC rule that prohibits firms engaged in a primary or secondary distribution from soliciting orders for the security in distribution by any means other than by the prospectus.

Rule 10b–4 An SEC rule that prohibits the tendering of stock by means of a short sale. —See also SHORT TENDER.

Rule 10b–6 An SEC rule that prohibits brokers, dealers, issuers, or underwriters participating in a securities distribution from purchasing the securities before they have been offered to the public.

Rule 10b–7 An SEC rule that limits the use of stabilizing bids by underwriters of a new security issue.

Rule 10b–8 An SEC rule that prohibits market manipulation during a rights offering.

Rule 10b–10 An SEC rule that sets disclosure requirements for confirmations sent by broker-dealers to customers.

Rule 10b–13 An SEC rule that prohibits persons who make a tender or an exchange offer from acquiring the security from other sources until the offer has expired.

Rule 10b–16 An SEC rule that sets minimum disclosure requirements for margin accounts that are opened by brokerage firms.

Rule 10b5–1 An SEC rule that permits an employee to adopt a written plan to sell shares when the employee is not in possession of material nonpublic information. Shares can then be sold according to the plan on a regular basis, regardless of subsequent nonpublic information received by the employee. —Also called *selling plan.*

Rule 11A An SEC rule that establishes requirements for trades made on the floor of an exchange by exchange members.

Rule 13d An SEC rule that establishes disclosure requirements for investors who acquire a beneficial interest of 5% or more of an equity issue registered with the SEC.

Rule 13e An SEC rule that regulates repurchase by a corporation of its own securities.

Rule 14a An SEC rule that sets minimum standards for proxy materials distributed by a corporation to its shareholders.

Rule 15c2–1 An SEC rule that regulates the safekeeping of a customer's securities by the broker-dealer.

Rule 15c3–1 An SEC rule that sets minimum net capital requirements for broker-dealers. Firms are expected to have liquid assets equal to or greater than a certain percentage of total liabilities. If the ratio falls below this minimum, the broker-dealer may face restrictions on soliciting new business or on keeping existing business.

Rule 15c3–2 An SEC rule that requires broker-dealers to inform customers who have free credit balances that their balances may be withdrawn.

Rule 15c3–3 An SEC rule that regulates the manner in which broker-dealers handle customers' fully paid securities and security values in excess of margin requirements. Fully paid securities must be segregated by broker-dealers.

Rule 17f–1 An SEC rule that requires financial institutions that process securities to promptly report counterfeit, lost, missing, or stolen securities to the proper authorities.

Rule 19b–3 An SEC rule that prohibits the fixing of commission rates.

Rule 19c–3 An SEC rule that permits exchange member firms to trade stock listed after April 26, 1979, off the exchange. Rule 19c–3, which became effective in 1980, is intended to promote competition among market makers. —See also 19C–3 STOCK.

Rule 80A A New York Stock Exchange rule that restricts program trading orders for Standard & Poor's stocks as part of index arbitrage strategies in the event the Dow Jones Industrial Average moves up or down 2% from its previous closing value. The rule requires that executions take place in a manner that stabilizes share prices. Rule 80A is intended to dampen large market-wide swings. —Also called *collar rule; index arbitrage tick test; uptick/downtick rule.*

Rule 80B A New York Stock Exchange rule that restricts trading for specified periods in the event the Dow Jones Industrial Average experiences one of three specified percentage declines. —See also CIRCUIT BREAKER.

⋏⋏ CASE STUDY | New York Stock Exchange Rule 80B is a circuit breaker designed to limit panic selling during serious market declines and extreme volatility. The rule provides for brief trading halts during a severe market decline as measured by a single-day decrease in the Dow Jones Industrial Average. Circuit breakers on the NYSE are currently in effect for three thresholds: 10%, 20%, and 30% declines in the Dow.

10% decline in the Dow
  One-hour trading halt if the decline occurs prior to 2 P.M.
  Half-hour trading halt if the decline occurs between 2 and 2:30 P.M.
  No trading halt if the decline occurs after 2:30 P.M.

20% decline in the Dow
  Two-hour trading halt if the decline occurs prior to 1 P.M.
  One-hour trading halt if the decline occurs between 1 and 2 P.M.
  The market closes if the decline occurs after 2 P.M.

30% decline in the Dow
  The market closes for the day regardless of the time.

Rule 104 A New York Stock Exchange rule that prohibits specialists from trading for their own accounts except when such trades are necessary to maintain a fair and orderly market.

Rule 105 A New York Stock Exchange rule that prohibits specialists from having an interest in a pool involving a stock in which the specialists are registered.

Rule 144 An SEC rule that permits a corporate executive who owns a large amount of his or her firm's stock that has not been bought in the open market to sell a portion of the stock every six months following a holding period of two years without having to file a formal registration statement with the SEC.

Rule 144A A 1990 SEC rule that facilitates the resale of privately placed securities that are without SEC registration. The rule was designed to develop a more liquid and efficient institutional resale market for unregistered securities.

Rule 145 An SEC rule that permits investors who acquire certain securities from consolidations, mergers, or reclassifications to transfer those securities without having them registered.

Rule 156 An SEC rule that regulates investment company sales literature. Essentially, investment companies are prohibited from distributing sales literature that contains false or misleading statements.

Rule 209 A New York Stock Exchange rule that requires all signatures on a security certificate to be guaranteed by a bank, trust company, or exchange member when the certificate is presented for registration.

Rule 254 An SEC rule that established simplified registration requirements for issuers selling relatively small amounts of a security.

Rule 390 A former New York Stock Exchange rule that stipulated that, unless exempted by the exchange, members must receive permission before trading an exchange-listed security off the exchange floor. Rule 390 was scrapped in 2000 by the New York Stock Exchange under pressure from the Securities and Exchange Commission. —Compare RULE 5. —See also RULE 19C-3.

Rule 396 —See NINE BOND RULE.

Rule 405 The "know your customer" rule of the New York Stock Exchange that requires member firms to obtain significant facts from customers when opening new accounts. These facts are supposed to give the broker and the firm some background on the customers.

Rule 415 A 1982 SEC rule that permits corporations to register a security issue and then sell the securities piecemeal throughout a two-year period as conditions and needs warrant. —See also SHELF REGISTRATION.

Rule 419 An SEC rule that stipulates that funds received by a blank-check company from an issue of penny stock must be placed in an escrow account for the benefit of the purchaser.

Rule 500 A New York Stock Exchange rule that sets requirements for listed companies that wish to delist their stock from the exchange. Companies cannot delist and move trading elsewhere unless at least two thirds of the shares are cast in favor of the move. In addition, no more than 10% of the shares can be cast in opposition to the move.

rule of 72 The mathematical rule used in approximating the number of years it will take a given investment to double in value. The number of years to double an investment is calculated by dividing 72 by the annual rate of return. Thus, an investment expected to earn 10% annually will double the investor's funds in 72/10, or 7.2 years. Dividing 72 by the number of years in which the investor wishes to double his or her funds will yield the necessary rate of return.

Rules of Fair Practice The rules of conduct that have been established for members of the National Association of Securities Dealers and that require, among other things, fair prices, reasonable charges, firm quotations, and ethical practices. Failure to follow these rules may result in fines or expulsion from NASD.

ruling —See REVENUE RULING.

run 1. A dealer's list of security offerings with respective bid and ask quotes. —Compare OFF-THE-RUN ISSUE. 2. A sequence of security price movements in the same direction. Five straight days in which a stock price closes higher is an example of a run. Runs have been evaluated in order to determine if the charting of stock is a worthwhile way to earn an above-average return.

runaway gap In technical analysis, a chart pattern that indicates the rapid price movement of a security and is characterized by a gap that forms for a range of prices in which no trading occurs. Runaway gaps occur during strong bull or bear movements on high volume. In general, technical analysts believe a security's price will return to the price range at which a gap occurs to fill in the missing prices. Thus, a strong upward movement with a runaway gap is likely to be followed by a downward correction to the price at which the gap occurred.

A downward runaway gap signals the opposite correction. Refer to the *Technical Analysis Chart Patterns* section for an example of this chart. —Compare BREAKAWAY GAP. —See also EXHAUSTION GAP.

rundown   A list of available bonds in a municipal issue of serial bonds.

running ahead   The illegal purchase or sale of a security by a broker for his or her personal account before execution of customer orders in the same security. If a brokerage firm issues a negative report on a company, a broker acting on the report for his or her own account before telling clients about the report would be running ahead. —See also FRONT RUNNING.

running yield   —See CURRENT YIELD.

runup   A sharp, short-term increase in the price of a stock or the stock market.

Russell Indexes   Any of three market-value-weighted indexes of U.S. stocks: Russell 1000, Russell 2000, and Russell 3000. Russell 1000 includes the 1,000 largest capitalization U.S. stocks. Russell 2000 consists of the next 2,000 largest capitalization U.S. stocks and is often used as a measure of small stock performance. Russell 3000 is composed of all the stocks included in the two other indexes.

RVP   —See RECEIVE VERSUS PAYMENT.

S

s   1. —Used in stock transaction tables in newspapers to indicate that the stock has been split or that the firm has paid a stock dividend of at least 25% within the past 52 weeks: *Getty s.*   **2.** —Used on the consolidated tape to indicate the size of a transaction as a multiple of 100 shares: *Gy 9s81.*   **3.** —Used in bond transaction tables in newspapers to separate a bond's coupon and year of maturity: *Deere 9s01.*

safe harbor   1. A regulation that protects individuals or corporations from the legal consequences of certain actions they undertake. For example, firms filing forecasts with the SEC have a safe harbor from individuals or businesses that use the forecasts and are subsequently damaged (that is, they lose money), as long as the forecasts were prepared in good faith.   **2.** A tactic in which the target of an unfriendly takeover makes itself less attractive by taking a specific action.

safekeeping   The keeping of assets, including securities, by a financial institution.

SAIF   —See SAVINGS ASSOCIATION INSURANCE FUND.

salary reduction plan   A retirement plan that permits an employee to set aside a portion of salary in a tax-deferred investment account selected by the employer. Contributions made to the account and income earned by the contributions are sheltered from taxes until the funds are withdrawn. —Also called *401(k) plan.*

Ⱳ CASE STUDY Salary reduction plans offer substantial tax benefits, yet at the same time they can place employee contributions at considerable risk depending on what type of investments are used to fund the plans. Especially risky are plans that invest all or most of the contributions in the employer's common stock. Consider the example of energy conglomerate Enron Corporation, whose stock tumbled nearly 99% to 60¢ per share in the 12 months ending November 2001. At of the end of 2000 approximately half of Enron's $2.1 billion 401(k) plan was invested in Enron common stock. Enron's policy was to match employee contributions at 50¢ on the dollar, for up to 6% of an employee's salary. Like many major corporations, Enron made its contributions to the firm's plan in company stock. Employees were permitted to select alternative investments, but many chose to use Enron shares to fund their contributions. As Enron shares plummeted many employees of the company saw virtually the entire value of their individual 401(k) plans evaporate at the same time as they faced the possibility of losing their jobs in a company that filed for bankruptcy.

sale and leaseback   The sale of a fixed asset that is then leased by the former owner from the new owner. A sale and leaseback permits a firm to withdraw its equity in an asset without giving up use of the asset. —Also called *leaseback.*

sales   The revenue from the sale of goods and services. Sales exclude other types of revenue such as dividends, interest, and rent.

sales, general, and administrative expenses (SG&A)   Corporate overhead costs for a period including expenses such as advertising, salaries, and rent. SG&A is found on a corporate income statement as a deduction from revenues in calculating operating income.

sales load   —See LOAD.

sales mix   —See PRODUCT MIX.

Sallie Mae   —See STUDENT LOAN MARKETING ASSOCIATION.

salvage value   —See RESIDUAL VALUE.

same-day substitution   Changes in a margin account that offset such that there is no change in the total value of the account. For example, an increase in the market value of one security may offset the market decline in another security so that no margin call is required.

Samurai bond   A yen-denominated bond issued by a non-Japanese firm or institution.

S&L   —See SAVINGS AND LOAN ASSOCIATION.

S&P®   —See STANDARD & POOR'S®.

S&P 100   —See STANDARD & POOR'S 100 STOCK INDEX.

S&P 400   —See STANDARD & POOR'S 400 STOCK INDEX.

S&P 500   —See STANDARD & POOR'S 500 STOCK INDEX.

S&P Effect   The change in the price of a stock because the stock is added to or dropped from the Standard & Poor's 500 Stock Index. Index funds based on the popular S&P 500 must purchase shares of any stock that is added to the index, thus creating added demand that is likely to drive up the price of the stock. Conversely, stocks dropped from the S&P 500 must be sold by these same index funds.

⋀ CASE STUDY   High flyer Yahoo! received an added boost in late 1999 when the stock was added to the Standard & Poor's 500 Stock Index. On December 7, the day before Yahoo! was to be included in the popular index, the Dow Jones Industrial Average and the S&P 500 each declined by about 1%. On the same day, Yahoo! increased in price by $65 to $348 per share on a trading volume of 62 million shares. Nearly a third of the volume occurred near the end of the trading day as portfolio managers of mutual funds that track the index adjusted their portfolios to include the stock.

savings bond

Do U.S. savings bonds have a place in a portfolio?
Probably not, at least for most serious investors. Higher yields are available in various other government obligations that also offer marketability with no penalties if you want your money. TIP: For a beginning investor or for individuals of modest means, U.S. savings bonds are often a better investment than certificates of deposit, because taxes are not due until the bonds are redeemed.

Thomas J. McAllister, CFP, McAllister Financial Planning, Carmel, IN

Because Yahoo! enjoyed such a high market capitalization, the portfolio managers were required to reduce their holdings of the other 499 stocks in the index as well as dispose of all of Laidlaw, the stock Yahoo! replaced. According to a report by a major research firm, portfolio managers bought $5 billion of Yahoo! stock and sold an equal amount of other stocks in the index.

sandbag An action taken by a company to stall an anticipated takeover attempt.

Santa Claus rally A rise in security prices that occurs during the last week of the calendar year and during the first few days of the new year. —Also called *year-end rally.*

Sarbanes-Oxley Act The congressional legislation that regulates certain corporate financial activities and improves the accuracy of financial statements. Among other things, the act prohibits personal company loans to directors and officers, requires certification of financial statements by a firm's chief executive officer and chief financial officer, protects employee whistle-blowers, increases criminal penalties for securities law violations, requires disclosure of off-balance-sheet financing, and calls for improvement in the accuracy of pro forma financial statements. The act was passed in 2002 in response to widely publicized corporate accounting scandals.

Saturday night special A hostile tender offer in which shareholders of the target company have a relatively short time to respond.

saucer In technical analysis, a U-shaped chart pattern that indicates a market bottom for the security or market index being graphed. Refer to the *Technical Analysis Chart Patterns* section for an example of this chart. —Also called *rounded bottom.* —See also REVERSAL PATTERN.

savings and loan association (S&L) A deposit-gathering financial institution that is primarily engaged in making loans on real estate. Although many S&Ls are owned by their depositors, some are organized as profit-making institutions with stock that is publicly traded. —See also THRIFT.

Savings Association Insurance Fund (SAIF) The federal fund that insures deposits at savings and loan associations. SAIF was created in 1989 as a successor to the Federal Savings & Loan Insurance Corporation and is administered by the Federal Deposit Insurance Corporation.

savings bank —See MUTUAL SAVINGS BANK.

savings bond A nonmarketable security issued by the U.S. Treasury in relatively small denominations for individual investors. Three categories of bonds are available. Interest on these bonds is exempt from state and local, but not federal, taxation. —Also called *United States savings bond.* —See also SERIES EE SAVINGS BOND; SERIES HH SAVINGS BOND; SERIES I SAVINGS BOND.

scale The schedule of yields (or prices) at which a serial bond issue is offered to the public by the underwriter. The schedule reflects yields at the various maturities being offered. —Also called *offering scale.* —See also INVERTED SCALE; PRELIMINARY SCALE.

scale order A specialized brokerage order that requests multiple executions at varying prices for the same security; for example, when an investor who wishes to liquidate a security position in a rising market spaces orders to sell specified numbers of shares at half-point price intervals.

scalper **1.** A market maker who assigns excessive markups or markdowns on security transactions. Such activity is in violation of National Association of Securities Dealers rules. **2.** An investment adviser who takes a position in a security before publicly recommending the security for purchase. The scalper then sells the security at a profit after the recommendation has caused investors to buy the security and push its price higher. This type of activity must be disclosed to buyers. **3.** An in-and-out trader who attempts to profit on relatively small price changes.

Schedule B The federal income tax form for listing gross dividends and/or gross taxable interest income payments that total more than $400 during the tax year.

Schedule D The federal income tax form for listing gains and losses from capital assets that have been sold (or bought, in the case of a short sale) during the tax year. —See also 1099-OID.

Schedule 13D An SEC form required of anyone who acquires ownership of 5% or more of any publicly traded corporation's equity securities. The schedule must be filed with the SEC within ten business days of the date on which the 5% threshold has been reached.

Schedule 13E–3 An SEC form that must be filed when a company is taken private. —See also GOING PRIVATE.

Schedule 13E–4 An SEC form that must be filed by issuers making a tender offer for their own securities.

Schedule 14B An SEC form that must be filed by participants in a proxy contest.

Schedule 14D–1 An SEC form that must be filed by an individual making a tender offer for securities if a successful tender would result in the individual's ownership of more than 5% of the class of securities.

scorched earth An antitakeover strategy in which the target firm disposes of those assets or divisions considered particularly desirable by the raider. Thus, by making itself less attractive, the target discourages the takeover attempt. Such a strategy is almost certain to penalize the shareholders of the target firm. —Compare CROWN JEWEL.

scrap value —See RESIDUAL VALUE.

screen To examine various securities with the goal of selecting a limited number that meet certain predetermined requirements. For example, an investor might screen all electric utilities for stock that offers a dividend yield of 8% or more and a price-earnings ratio of 8 or less.

scrip A certificate that can be exchanged for a fractional share of stock. Scrip is distributed as the result of a spinoff, a stock dividend, or a stock split in which the stockholder would be entitled to a fractional share of stock. For example, the owner of a single share would receive scrip for one-half a share in the event the issuer declared a three-for-two stock split.

scrip dividend An unusual type of dividend involving the distribution of promissory notes that call for some type of payment at a future date. Scrip dividends generally signal that a firm is short of cash. —Compare LIABILITY DIVIDEND.

scripophily The collecting of old securities certificates. Certificates are often valuable as collectors' items apart from any redemption value they may have.

seasonal variation A regularly recurring change in the value of a variable. For example, electric utilities generally experience significant seasonal sales variations in electricity. Likewise, toy manufacturers have sales increases before Christmas.

seasoned Of, relating to, or being a security issue that has traded in the secondary market long enough to establish a track record for price variability and trading volume.

seat Membership on an organized securities exchange. Because the number of seats on an exchange is generally fixed, membership may be acquired only by purchasing a seat from an existing owner at a negotiated or an offered price.

SEC —See SECURITIES AND EXCHANGE COMMISSION.

SEC fee The SEC fee levied on sellers of listed equity securities.

secondary distribution The sale of a block of existing, not newly issued, securities with the proceeds going to the present holders rather than to the issuing firm. An especially large secondary distribution may put pressure on the security's price until the additional shares or bonds have been assimilated in the market. —Compare PRIMARY DISTRIBUTION. —Also called *secondary offering.* —See also REGISTERED SECONDARY DISTRIBUTION; SPECIAL OFFERING; SPOT SECONDARY DISTRIBUTION.

secondary market The market in which existing securities are traded among investors through an intermediary. Organized exchanges such as the New York Stock Exchange facilitate the trading of securities in the secondary market. —Compare FOURTH MARKET; PRIMARY MARKET; THIRD MARKET. —Also called *aftermarket.*

secondary offering —See SECONDARY DISTRIBUTION.

secondary shares Shares in a stock offering in which proceeds go to other investors rather than the issuing company. Secondary shares have been previously traded and will not result in an increase shares outstanding. —Compare PRIMARY SHARES.

secondary stock The stock of a smaller firm listed on the New York Stock Exchange or nearly any stock traded on the American Stock Exchange, the regional exchanges, or in the over-the-counter market. These generally volatile stocks often exhibit price movements different from those of the large blue chips. —Also called *second-tier stock.*

secondary trend A movement of a security or of the entire market that is opposite the primary trend. For example, even during a bull market when the primary trend of stock prices is upward, downward secondary trends frequently occur. Although it is easy to differentiate primary and secondary trends in graphs that illustrate past price changes, it is much more difficult, and some people believe impossible, to determine if a trend is of a primary or secondary nature during the period in which it is being established.

second mortgage A real estate mortgage with a subordinate claim to another mortgage on the same property. The second mortgage is more risky to the lender than the first mortgage; thus, it carries a higher rate of interest.

second preferred A class of preferred stock that has a subordinate claim to dividends and assets relative to another class of preferred stock of the same issuer. —Compare PRIOR PREFERRED.

second-tier stock —See SECONDARY STOCK.

Section 31 fee A Securities and Exchange Commission fee on the registration and trading of securities. The fee was first levied in the 1930s to finance the government's cost of regulating the securities markets. In early 2001 the fee amounted to 1/300 of 1% of the principal amount of a stock sale.

Section 1256 contracts Any of several types of futures and options contracts that are subject to a special tax rule of the Internal Revenue Service. Named for a section of the IRS Code, these contracts must generally be treated as if they are sold at fair market value on the last business day of the tax year. Section 1256 contracts include regulated futures contracts, foreign currency contracts, nonequity options, dealer equity options, and dealer securities futures contracts.

sector A group of securities (such as airline stocks) that share certain common characteristics. Stocks that are particularly interest-sensitive are considered a sector.

sector fund An investment company that concentrates its holdings among securities or other assets sharing a common interest. For example, a sector fund may limit its holdings to foreign securities from a particular country or geographic region (for example, Korea Fund or Pacific Fund). Likewise, it may specialize in the securities of energy-related firms or in companies that produce precious metals. Sector funds permit investors to concentrate on a specific investment segment and yet diversify their investments among various issuers. Sector funds entail more risk but offer greater potential returns than funds that diversify their portfolios. —Also called *special-purpose fund; specialty fund.*

sector neutral index fund A mutual fund that maintains a portfolio with sector weights identical to a particular stock index while attempting to earn returns higher than the index by managing stocks within each sector. A sector neutral index fund is a special kind of enhanced index fund. —See also ENHANCED INDEXING.

sector rotation An investment strategy involving the movement of investments from one industry sector to another in an attempt to beat the market. For example, an investor might rotate investments among consumer durables, technology, and energy securities as economic fundamentals and valuations in each of these sectors change. —Also called *group rotation.*

sector swap A bond trading strategy that is used to gain profit by changing yield spreads among different sectors of the bond market. The sectors may be defined by type of industry, public versus private issuer, coupon size, and so forth. With a sector swap, one trades a type of bond currently in favor for a type currently out of favor in the belief that the yield differences are only temporary. The sale of utility bonds and subsequent use of the funds for the purchase of industrial bonds is a sector swap.

secular trend The relatively consistent movement of a variable over a long period. A stock in a secular uptrend is an indicator that the security has experienced an extended period of rising prices.

secured bond A bond that is guaranteed with a pledge of assets. A bond might be secured with real estate.

secured creditor A creditor having a claim that is protected by specific assets. For example, the owner of a mortgage bond can force the sale of or can take possession of a particular asset if the borrower fails to meet the terms of the lending agreement. —Compare UNSECURED CREDITOR.

secured lease obligation bond (SLOB) A debt obligation serviced by lease payments on a single asset. The debt may be secured only by the lease or by a combination of the lease and a lien on the asset being leased. SLOBs are used primarily by electric utilities to finance power stations.

secured liability A debt for which specific assets have been pledged to guarantee repayment.

Securities Act Amendments of 1975 The legislation that gives the SEC authority to develop a national market in securities, thereby making the system more competitive and more efficient. The Amendments have had limited success in producing a fully integrated market system.

Securities Act of 1933 A landmark securities law intended to improve the flow of information to potential investors in new security issues and to prohibit certain selling practices relating to those issues. Issuing firms are required to register their securities with the federal government, and investment bankers must provide investors with a prospectus. Secondary issues, private offerings, and certain small issues are usually exempted from requirements of the Act.

securities analyst —See FINANCIAL ANALYST.

Securities and Exchange Commission (SEC) The U.S. government agency, established in 1934, charged with protecting investors and maintaining the integrity of the securities markets. The SEC requires public companies to disclose meaningful financial information to the public, and it oversees participants in the securities business including stock exchanges, broker-dealers, investment advisors, mutual funds, and public utility holding companies. The commission is composed of 5 presidentially appointed commissioners, 4 divisions, and 18 offices.

securities exchange A facility for the organized trading of securities. The major national exchanges are the American Stock Exchange, Chicago Board Options Exchange, and New York Stock Exchange. In addition, a number of regional exchanges are to be found throughout the country. —Also called *exchange; organized securities exchange; stock exchange.*

Securities Exchange Act of 1934 Landmark legislation that established the SEC and that gives it authority over proxy solicitation and registration of organized exchanges. In addition, the Act sets disclosure requirements for securities in the secondary market, regulates insider trading, and gives the Federal Reserve authority over credit purchases of securities. When established, the Act reflected an effort to extend and overcome shortcomings of the Securities Act of 1933. These two pieces of legislation are the basis of securities regulation in the twentieth century. —See also FOREIGN CORRUPT PRACTICES ACT; WILLIAMS ACT.

Securities Industry Association (SIA) A trade group of broker-dealers whose primary function is to lobby for its members' interests in Congress and before the SEC. The SIA is the successor to the Association of Stock Exchange Firms and the Investment Bankers Association.

Securities Industry Automation Corporation (SIAC) A firm that processes and checks clearing data on securities transactions sent by purchase and sales departments of member brokerage firms. The purpose of SIAC, which is owned by the exchanges, is to alleviate much of the confusion and paperwork that ordinarily results from independent actions of an individual brokerage firm. —See also CONTRACT SHEET.

Securities Information Center (SIC) An organization established in 1977 to operate the Securities and Exchange Commission's Lost and Stolen Securities Program. Securities that are missing, stolen, lost, or counterfeit must be reported to the SIC, which maintains a database of lost and stolen securities. Investors who either have lost securities or have had securities stolen are normally required to purchase a surety or indemnity bond before a replacement security is reissued.

Securities Investor Protection Act of 1970 An act that established the Securities Investor Protection Corporation. The legislation responded to the generally unstable condition of the brokerage industry in the late 1960s.

Securities Investor Protection Corporation (SIPC) A government sponsored organization created in 1970 to insure investor accounts at brokerage firms in the event of the brokerage firms' insolvency and liquidation. The maximum insurance of $500,000, including a maximum of $100,000 in cash assets per account, only covers customer losses due to insolvencies, not losses caused by security price fluctuations. SIPC coverage is similar in concept to Federal Deposit Insurance Corporation coverage of customer accounts at commercial banks.

Securities Law Enforcement Remedies Act Federal legislation enacted in 1990 that provides the SEC with additional enforcement powers, especially over corporate officers and directors who demonstrate "substantial unfitness."

securities loan 1. A loan made to an investor for the purpose of buying securities. The loan is secured by the securities. 2. The lending of securities by one broker-dealer to another broker-dealer. Securities loans generally occur when broker-dealers need to borrow securities for delivery on customers' short sales.

Securities Transfer Association (STA) The trade association for bank and independent transfer agents and corporate transfer agents who undertake the service for their own corporations.

securitized Of, related to, or being debt securities that are secured with assets. For example, mortgage purchase bonds are secured by mortgages that have been purchased with the bond issue's proceeds.

> **⋀⋀ CASE STUDY** Tobacco companies agreed in the late 1990s to provide states with billions of dollars in cash payments over many years. The huge monetary settlements came in response to lawsuits filed by the states for health-related expenses resulting from their citizens' tobacco use. Unwilling to wait for all the promised money, politicians in several states proposed issuing debt securities backed by the promised revenue

streams. Promised cash flows from the settlement would be securitized with bonds sold to investors. Florida governor Jeb Bush proposed that his state sell half its $17.4 billion settlement to be received over many years for approximately $2.4 billion. Some financial analysts worried potential lawsuits could force tobacco companies into bankruptcy, in which case promised payment from the settlements would be at risk. Securitizing the settlement payments would transfer the risk from the states to investors who purchased the bonds. Buying the bonds that were backed by promised tobacco company payments would allow individual investors to participate in the settlements.

security 1. An instrument that, for a stock, shows ownership in a firm; for a bond, indicates a creditor relationship with a firm or with a federal, state, or local government; or signifies other rights to ownership. 2. Collateral used to guarantee repayment of a debt.

security depository A centralized location in which security certificates are placed and stored for later transfer. (Transfers usually take place by book entry rather than by physical movement.) —Also called *depository.* —See also DE-POSITORY TRUST COMPANY.

security market line A line used to illustrate the relationship between risk and return for individual securities. The security market line shows a positive linear relationship between returns and systematic risk as measured by beta.

Security Traders Association (STA) A professional trade organization of approximately 7,000 individuals engaged in the buying and selling of securities. Founded in the mid-1930s, the STA provides members with educational opportunities and information relative to the member interests.

security valuation model An analytic tool for valuing securities in which a series of mathematical relationships is used to determine the price at which a security should sell. Accuracy using a model depends not only on the validity of the relationships, but also on the precision of the estimates of other variables required by the model. One widely used security valuation model discounts estimated cash flows, such as dividends or interest, from holding an investment.

seed money Funds provided to finance the initial stages of a new venture. Seed money may be utilized to conduct research, develop the prototype for a product, or determine if an idea is workable or economically viable.

seek a market To search for someone to complete a transaction, as when a buyer searches for a seller or a seller searches for a buyer.

segment An identifiable part of a business organization. For example, a large corporation might have a number of segments including industrial, aerospace, and leisure products. —Also called *business segment.*

segment reporting A type of financial reporting in which the firm discloses information by identifiable industry segments. For example, Union Pacific Corporation reports revenues, income, assets, depreciation, and capital expenditures for each of four segments: transportation, oil and gas, mining, and land. Segment reporting is required by the SEC in an attempt to provide stockholders and the public with better financial data. —Also called *line-of-business reporting.* —See also INDUSTRY SEGMENT.

segregation The safekeeping of a customer's securities in a separate location when the securities have been paid for in full. Segregated securities may not be commingled with the securities of the broker-dealer and they may not be used by the broker-dealer to collateralize loans. —See also RULE 15C3-3.

selected dealer agreement   An agreement by members of a selling group that specifies the rules under which the group will operate in selling an issue of securities.

self-correcting   Of, relating to, or being a security price movement that is excessive and likely to be at least partially retraced.

self-directed IRA   An individual retirement account that permits its owner to have wide latitude as to types of assets and control over the investments within the account. A self-directed IRA generally refers to IRAs established at brokerage firms in which customers may buy and sell securities. Brokerage firms frequently charge an annual fee of up to $50 in addition to commissions on any trades in an account.

self-regulatory organization (SRO)   A member-operated organization that establishes and enforces minimum standards and rules of conduct. The National Association of Securities Dealers, the National Futures Association, and the New York Stock Exchange are examples of self-regulatory organizations.

self-tender   An offer by a firm to repurchase some of its own securities from stockholders, generally on a pro rata basis from those shares offered for sale. A self-tender may be preferable to purchase of the securities in the open market because a self-tender is quicker and will not disrupt public trading in the securities. Firms frequently repurchase their own stock from investors holding fewer than a set number of shares in order to eliminate the high cost of servicing small stockholders. A self-tender is similar to a buyback except that buybacks often refer to repurchases from special groups or a few large holders. —Also called *stock repurchase plan.*

sell   To dispose of an asset. —Compare BUY.

sell a spread   In options trading, to establish a spread position in which the premium on the option sold exceeds the premium on the option purchased. The spread may be on the basis of a difference in expiration or a difference in strike price. An example of selling a spread would be to sell an August call ($20 strike) on Goodyear for a premium of $137 and to buy a February call ($20 strike) for $25.

sell away   Selling a client's stock without proper authorization.

sellers' market   A market in which the demand for an asset swamps supply to the point that prices rise above the level that would have been expected under more usual circumstances. A new issue in great demand by investors is an example of a sellers' market. Underwriters may have to allocate available shares of the issue to their clients, resulting in sharply higher prices once the shares begin trading in the secondary market. —Compare BUYERS' MARKET.

seller's option contract   A security transaction in which the date of settlement is delayed beyond the five business days in a regular-way contract. This very unusual transaction is generally caused by the unavailability of a certificate for regular delivery. The settlement date will be specified. —See also CASH CONTRACT.

selling climax A period of very high volume and sharp downward movement in the stock market. A selling climax generally signals the end of a prolonged bear market. —Compare BUYING CLIMAX. —Also called *climax*.

selling concession —See CONCESSION.

selling group A group of investment bankers that assists a syndicate or an underwriter in the sale of a new security issue but is not responsible for any unsold securities. Because members of a selling group do not assume the risk of syndicate members, their fees are correspondingly lower than the fees of the syndicate members. —See also SELECTED DEALER AGREEMENT.

selling panic A period of rapidly falling stock prices on very large volume as investors, speculators, traders, and institutions attempt to liquidate investment positions without regard to price. Selling panics occur when individuals and institutions believe they must sell securities at once before prices fall further. —Compare BUYING PANIC.

selling plan —See RULE 105B-1.

selling short —See SHORT SALE.

selling short against the box —See SHORT AGAINST THE BOX.

sell-off A general decline in security prices. This term generally refers to a short- or intermediate-term decline rather than to an extended period of falling prices.

sell order A brokerage order to sell a specified amount of a security.

sell out Selling securities by a broker on behalf of a client when the client has failed to settle a trade in a timely manner. For example, a broker may sell stock when a client has failed to meet a margin call.

sellout The distribution of all the securities in a new issue by the selling group.

sell plus A customer order to sell a security only at a price higher than the most recent price it sold at. Thus, the order is to be executed only on an uptick.

sell side The portion of the securities business in which orders are transacted. The sell side includes retail brokers, institutional brokers and traders, and research departments. If an institutional portfolio manager changes jobs and becomes a registered representative, he or she has moved from the buy side to the sell side. —Compare BUY SIDE.

sell signal An indication provided by a technical tool, such as a chart of a stock's price, that the stock should be sold. For example, the fall of a stock below its upward trendline is often interpreted as a sell signal. —Compare BUY SIGNAL.

sell stop order A customer order to a broker to sell a security if it sells at or below a stipulated stop price. This type of stop order can be used to protect an existing profit or to limit the potential loss on an owned security. —Compare BUY STOP ORDER.

sell the book A customer order to a broker to sell as much of a security as possible at the current bid. Purchases also may be made by a specialist or other interested broker-dealers. The phrase derives from the book of existing orders that a specialist keeps.

sell the spread —Used to refer to a hedge transaction in which the contract sold carries a larger premium than the contract purchased. When selling a spread, an investor might write a call option that would expire six months after the expiration date of the call option on an otherwise identical contract that is purchased.

sell-to-cover The selling of sufficient stock acquired through an incentive stock option to cover the total exercise cost of the remaining shares. For example, an employee might exercise options for 800 shares at a cost of $30 per share when the market price of the stock is $60. The employee would sell 400 shares at the market price to cover the cost of the remaining 400 shares.

semistrong form A component of the theory of efficient markets that holds that security prices adjust nearly instantaneously to publicly available information relevant to valuation of securities. If security markets are efficient in the semistrong form, investors cannot earn extraordinary returns by activities such as perusing financial reports, investigating financial ratios, or reading investment newsletters. —See also WEAK FORM.

senior debt A class of debt that has priority with respect to interest and principal over other classes of debt and over all classes of equity by the same issuer. In the event of financial difficulties or liquidation of the borrower's assets, holders of senior debt will have a priority claim. Most loans from financial institutions and certain high-grade debt securities such as mortgage bonds are senior debt. Because senior debt has a relatively secure claim, it is less risky from the point of view of the lender and it pays a lower rate of interest compared with debt of the same issuer having a subordinate claim. —Compare JUNIOR DEBT.

seniority The condition or status of a security that has priority over other securities by the same issuer with respect to the payment of income (that is, interest or dividends) and repayment of principal. As an example, for the same issuer, bonds have seniority over preferred stock and preferred stock has priority over common stock. —See also JUNIOR SECURITY.

sentiment index A numerical guide to investor feeling toward the securities markets that is constructed to determine whether certain segments of the investment community are bullish or bearish. The index is used by technical analysts to determine whether stock should be bought or sold. Sentiment is measured in a variety of ways including short sales by specialists, mutual fund cash positions, and the amount of margin debt. —Compare ADVISERS' SENTIMENT.

SEP —See SIMPLIFIED EMPLOYEE PENSION PLAN.

separate customer For purposes of insurance coverage by the Securities Investor Protection Corporation, an account entitled to full insurance coverage. A husband and wife, each with individual accounts and also a joint account, are viewed as three separate customers for insurance purposes. Each one of the accounts, including the joint account, is covered in full.

separate property The property that is entirely owned by one spouse, even in a community property state. Separate property generally includes property received as an inheritance or as a gift or property owned by one spouse before marriage.

separate return A tax return filed separately by each spouse, in which income and deductions attributable to that spouse are listed. Spouses may choose to file separate returns or to file a joint return combining incomes and deductions. —Compare JOINT RETURN.

Separate Trading of Registered Interest and Principal of Securities (STRIPS)
Treasury securities that have had their coupons and principal repayments separated into what effectively become zero-coupon Treasury bonds. The parts, issued in book-entry form, carry the full backing of the U.S. Treasury. Like other zero-coupon bonds, these securities are subject to wide price fluctuations. They also subject the owner to an annual federal income-tax liability even though no direct interest is paid.

⋀⋀ CASE STUDY | The acronym STRIPS derives from stripping, or peeling, interest payments from Treasury bonds and selling the interest payments and principal amounts as separate zero-coupon securities. Zero-coupon securities were created in the early 1980s when investment firms stripped interest coupons from Treasury bonds and sold interest payments and principal amounts at their current discounted values. These firms acquired large blocks of regular coupon-paying Treasuries that were placed in trust with commercial banks. The banks then issued certificates against each of the interest payments as well as against the principal amount of each bond. Thus, a group of ordinary Treasuries was converted into numerous zero-coupon securities, each with a different maturity. For example, an investment firm might purchase a large number of 15-year Treasury bonds, deposit the bonds with a commercial bank, and the commercial bank would issue a series of zero-coupon securities with maturities ranging from six months (the date of the first interest payment) to 15 years (the date of the last interest payment and the payment of principal). Thus, the 15-year bonds are converted into 30 separate zero-coupon bonds. The new zero-coupon securities became so popular with investors that, in 1985, the U.S. Treasury introduced STRIPS. With these securities, interest and principal payments from U.S. Treasury securities are registered separately through the Federal Reserve. Each interest payment and the principal amount can then be sold to investors as a zero-coupon bond maturing on the date of the scheduled payment.

serial bonds Bonds issued under a single indenture simultaneously with groups of the bonds that are scheduled to mature periodically. For example, a municipality may issue $40 million of bonds with $2 million scheduled to mature each year for 20 years. Many bond issues are a combination of serial bonds and term bonds.

⋀⋀ CASE STUDY | The Private Colleges and Universities Authority of Georgia in fall 2001 issued $211,815,000 of tax-exempt bonds for Emory University, a privately endowed research university located in Atlanta. The Private Colleges and Universities Authority was created to facilitate the financing and refinancing of facilities for use by private institutions for higher education within the state of Georgia. Proceeds from the bond issue were to be used by the university to finance several projects, including a cancer center, a performing arts center, a primate research center, and equipment for an existing university hospital. The bond issue consisted primarily of series bonds that matured annually from 2002 through 2021. Yields to maturity ranged from 2.18% for bonds of the shortest maturity to 5.09% for bonds maturing in 2021. In addition to serial bonds, the issue included $17 million of term bonds maturing in 2031 that yielded 5.21%, and an additional $2 million of term bonds scheduled for maturity two years later in 2033. Like many municipal bond offerings, this issue offered a wide variety of maturities so that investors could choose bonds with maturities that best fit their portfolio requirements. For example, investors with a long investment horizon could lock in a tax-exempt yield for 15 to 20 years while other investors who might need their funds relatively soon were able to choose bonds scheduled for repayment in 4 or 5 years. These bonds were particularly attractive to Georgia residents, who were not required to pay either state or federal income taxes on the interest income.

serial correlation The relationship that one event has to a series of past events. In technical analysis, serial correlation is used to test whether various chart formations are useful in projecting a security's future price movements.

series —See OPTION SERIES.

Series EE savings bond A U.S. Treasury obligation that pays a variable interest rate and is sold to investors in denominations as low as $50 at a 50% discount from face value. Series EE bonds earn interest at 90% of the average yield on five-year Treasury securities for the previous six months. Bonds may be redeemed after six months early, but a three-month interest penalty is assessed for redemptions during the first five years. Federal income taxes on interest earned may be paid each year or may be deferred until the savings bond is redeemed. Interest earned on savings bonds is exempt from state and local taxation. —See also PATRIOT BOND.

Series HH savings bond A U.S. Treasury obligation issued in multiples of $500 that pays interest every six months. The security has a maturity of ten years but may be redeemed after being held six months. This security has not been as popular as the Series EE bond. Now it may be obtained only by swapping the Series EE at its maturity.

Series I savings bond A nonnegotiable U.S. Treasury obligation that pays semiannual interest based on a combination of a fixed rate established by the Treasury and the semiannual inflation rate as measured by changes in the Consumer Price Index. Series I bonds are issued at face value in amounts that range from $50 to $10,000. The bonds have a maturity of 30 years but may be redeemed beginning 6 months after issuance. —See also TREASURY INFLATION-PROTECTED SECURITIES.

〽️ **CASE STUDY** U.S. savings bonds, normally considered very conservative investments offering substandard returns, occasionally rise to the surface as a smart investment choice. This occurred in October 2001 following a yearlong Federal Reserve campaign to drive down short-term interest rates in order to help revive the sluggish economy. The Fed push for lower interest rates continued following the September 11 economic disruptions caused by the terrorist attacks on New York City and Washington, D.C. With savings accounts paying an annual return of 1% to 2%, money market funds yielding less than 3%, and certificates of deposit offering annual returns of 3% to 4%, investors seeking liquidity, safety, and income found an alternative in Series I savings bonds. Series I savings bonds are issued at face value and pay a composite return composed of a fixed rate and an inflation rate. Interest accrues monthly and compounds annually. The fixed rate established each May and November applies to all Series I bonds issued during the subsequent six months and remains unchanged for the life of those bonds. The inflation rate is subject to change twice a year for both new and outstanding bonds. In other words, buy a Series I bond and the fixed component is determined for the life of the bond but the inflation component is likely to change every six months. Series I bonds were a good investment in October 2001 because the fixed component had been established five months prior, when short-term rates were considerably higher. Series I bonds purchased during the month earned a current rate of 5.92%, substantially higher than could be earned from money market funds, certificates of deposit, and U.S. Treasury bills. The inflation component would subsequently decline, but the fixed rate had been established at 3% in May and would remain unchanged on all bonds issued prior to November 1. Thus, the combination of the fixed and the inflation segments offered investors a higher return than could be earned on alternative investments of equal safety. Series I bonds have a maturity of 30 years but can be redeemed 6 months after the issue date. Redemptions prior to 5 years incur a penalty of the most-recent 3 months' interest; redemptions after 5 years incur no penalty.

Series 7　An examination required of potential registered representatives and designed to test the candidates' basic understanding of the securities industry. The multiple-choice test, developed by the New York Stock Exchange, is administered by the National Association of Securities Dealers. —Also called *General Securities Registered Representative Examination.* —See also UNIFORM SECURITIES AGENT STATE LAW EXAMINATION.

⋏⋏ CASE STUDY | The Series 7 is only the best known of many examinations administered by the National Association of Securities Dealers. Other examinations include:

Examinations for Registered Principals
    Series 4: Registered Options Principal
    Series 9 and 10: General Securities Sales Supervisor
    Series 24: General Securities Principal
    Series 26: Investment Company Products/Variable Contracts Limited Principal
    Series 27: Financial and Operations Principal
    Series 28: Introducing Broker-Dealer Financial and Operations Principal
    Series 39: Direct Participation Programs Limited Principal
    Series 53: Municipal Securities Principal

Examinations for Registered Representatives
    Series 6: Investment Company Products/Variable Contracts Limited Representative
    Series 11: Assistant Representative—Order Processing
    Series 22: Direct Participation Programs Limited Representative
    Series 42: Registered Options Representative
    Series 52: Municipal Securities Representative
    Series 55: Equity Trader Limited Representative
    Series 62: Corporate Securities Limited Representative
    Series 72: Government Securities Limited Representative
    Series 82: Limited Representative—Private Securities Offerings Representative

Other Examinations
    Series 3: National Commodity Futures Examination
    Series 5: Interest Rate Options Examination
    Series 15: Foreign Currency Options Examination
    Series 30: Branch Managers Examination—Futures
    Series 31: Futures Managed Funds Examination
    Series 32: Limited Futures Exam
    Series 33: Financial Instruments Examination
    Series 63: Uniform Securities Agent State Law Examination

Series 65: Uniform Investment Adviser Law Examination
Series 66: Uniform Combined State Law Examination

settle To complete a securities transaction.

settlement The transfer of the security (for the seller) or cash (for the buyer) in order to complete a security transaction. —See also DELAYED SETTLEMENT; EARLY SETTLEMENT.

settlement date The date on which either cash (for a buyer) or a security (for a seller) must be in the hands of the broker in order to satisfy the conditions of a security transaction. —Compare TRADE DATE. —See also DELAYED SETTLEMENT.

settlement month The month in which delivery is to take place in a futures contract. Most futures positions are reversed (that is, long positions are sold and short positions are covered) before their respective settlement months.

settlement period The period between the trade date and the settlement date. The settlement period on most securities is five business days.

settlement price In futures trading, an official price established at the end of each trading day by using the range of closing prices for a particular contract. This price, similar to the closing price for stock, is used to determine margin requirements and the following day's price limits.

severally and jointly —See JOINTLY AND SEVERALLY.

severally but not jointly Of or relating to a security offering in which individual underwriters are responsible for selling their initial allocations but are not responsible for any unsold securities allocated to other underwriters. —Compare JOINTLY AND SEVERALLY.

SG&A —See SALES, GENERAL, AND ADMINISTRATIVE EXPENSES.

SGL —See SPECULATIVE GRADE LIQUIDITY RATING.

shadow calendar The security issues in the SEC registration process with no firm offering date.

shakeout A reduction in the number of firms that operate in a particular industry. An example of a shakeout is the decline in the number of commercial banks in the United States. Shakeouts often occur after an industry has experienced a period of rapid growth in demand followed by overexpansion by manufacturers. Large, diversified companies able to survive a weak business climate tend to benefit from shakeouts.

share **1.** A single unit of a class of ownership in a corporation, represented by a stock certificate. **2.** A single unit of ownership in a mutual fund. **3.** The portion of a market controlled by a particular firm.

shareholder —See STOCKHOLDER.

Shareholder Communications Improvement Act Federal legislation passed in 1990 that requires banks and brokers holding shares for beneficial owners to forward proxy and information statements received from investment companies.

shareholder derivative suit A special type of class action lawsuit filed by one shareholder or by a limited number of shareholders on behalf of all of the other shareholders in a firm. An example is such a suit filed against a mutual fund's management in which the litigants claim excessive management and distribution fees.

shareholder of record —See HOLDER OF RECORD.

shareholder proposal A proposal that is submitted by a shareholder for action at a forthcoming annual meeting. If the holder gives timely notice of his or her intentions, the firm's management must include the proposal in the proxy statement and must give the other shareholders a chance to vote for or against the proposal. Typical shareholder proposals involve voting rights, management compensation, and corporate charitable contributions.

shareholders' equity —See OWNERS' EQUITY.

share repurchase plan A corporation's plan for buying back a predetermined number of its own shares in the open market. Institution of a share repurchase plan derives from management's view that the company has limited outside investment opportunities and that its shares are undervalued. Repurchase of the shares will decrease the amount of outstanding capital stock, increase earnings per share, and, it is hoped, result in an increase in the price of the stock.

shares authorized —See AUTHORIZED CAPITAL STOCK.

shares outstanding —See OUTSTANDING CAPITAL STOCK.

shark An investor or firm that is hostile to the target firm's management and that is interested in taking over the firm.

shark repellent A strategy used by corporations to ward off unwanted takeovers. Examples of this antitakeover measure include making a major acquisition, issuing new shares of stock or securities convertible into stock, and staggering the election of directors. Shark repellents often benefit corporate officers more than the stockholders. —Compare SHOW STOPPER. —Also called *takeover defense.* —See also POISON PILL.

shark watcher A company that monitors market rumors and trading activity in an effort to identify takeover attempts.

Sharpe performance measure A measure of risk-adjusted portfolio performance developed by William Sharpe. The index is calculated by dividing the risk premium return (average portfolio return less average risk-free return) divided by risk (standard deviation of portfolio returns). The Sharpe measure adjusts portfolio performance for total risk rather than market risk. —Compare TREYNOR PERFORMANCE MEASURE.

shelf offering A new security issue that is part of a larger issue that has been registered with the Securities and Exchange Commission. Companies are permitted to sell securities that are part of a shelf offering for up to two years without re-registering the issue with the SEC.

shelf registration A simplified method of registering securities that permits corporations to file a relatively uncomplicated registration form with the SEC and, during the subsequent two years, issue the securities. Shelf registration is supposed to provide more flexibility for corporations when they are raising funds in the capital markets. Shelf registration is permitted by SEC Rule 415.

shell corporation A corporation that has no active business operations and few or no assets.

shelter —See TAX SHELTER.

shelter To protect one's income from taxation. Some taxpayers shelter their income by investing in such activities as oil drilling ventures.

Sherman Antitrust Act An 1890 federal antitrust law intended to control or prohibit monopolies by forbidding certain practices that restrain competition. In the early 1900s, the U.S. Supreme Court ruled that the Act applied only to unreasonable restraints of trade and thus could be used only against blatant cases of monopoly.

Shogun bond A bond denominated in currency other than yen and issued in Japan by a non-Japanese borrower. For example, a U.S. firm issuing dollar-denominated bonds in Japan would be selling Shogun bonds.

shop A dealership in securities.

shop To contact a number of dealers in a security in an effort to obtain the most advantageous bid or ask price.

short —See SHORT POSITION 1, 2; SHORT SALE.

short against the box To sell an owned security short, usually in order to carry a profit on the security into the next tax year. Delivery may be made by using the owned shares or by purchasing new shares in the market. The Taxpayer Relief Act of 1997 largely eliminated shorting against the box as a means to defer a gain into a future year. —Also called *against the box; selling short against the box.*

short bond A debt security with a short period remaining until maturity. —Compare LONG BOND. —Also called *short coupon.*

short coupon 1. —See SHORT BOND. 2. The first interest payment on a newly issued bond that includes less than the usual six months' worth of interest. For example, a bond issued on February 1 with interest payment dates of June 1 and December 1 would make an initial interest payment equal to four months' interest.

short cover To purchase a security that has previously been sold short in order to close out the position. Although short covering may occur at any time, the term is often used in reference to investors with short positions who repurchase stock in strongly rising markets in order to cut their losses or protect their profits. This procedure produces even more strength in the market. —Also called *cover.* —See also SHORT SQUEEZE.

short exempt A short sale exempt from the rule that short sales must occur on upticks. Short exempts include some arbitrage transactions. Owning a security that will be converted into the common stock that will be sold allows a short exempt sale.

short hedge An investment transaction that is intended to provide protection against a decline in the value of an asset. For example, an investor who holds shares of Nextel and expects the stock to decline may enter into a short hedge by purchasing a put option on Nextel stock. If Nextel does subsequently decline, the value of the put option should increase.

short interest The number of shares of a particular stock that have been sold but have not yet been repurchased. Many analysts consider a large short position in a given stock bullish, because it represents future demand for the security as purchases are made to replace borrowed certificates. —See also CUSHION THEORY.

short-interest ratio A ratio that is used for market analysis and is calculated by dividing short interest by average daily volume. Technicians use the short-interest ratio as a tool to determine market direction. A relatively high ratio is generally considered bullish because it indicates significant future buying pressures as short sellers cover their short positions. A low ratio is considered bearish. —Also called *days to cover.*

short leg The side of an option spread that has been sold short. With a spread made up of owning a September 30 call and being short a December 30 call, the December 30 call is the short leg. —Compare LONG LEG.

short position 1. A net investment position in a security in which the security has been borrowed and sold but not yet replaced. Essentially, it is a short sale that has not been covered. —Compare LONG POSITION. —Also called *short.* 2. An investment position in which the investor either has written an option or has sold a commodity contract, with the obligation remaining outstanding. —Also called *short.*

short sale The sale of a security that must be borrowed to make delivery. Short sales usually, but not always, entail the sale of securities that are not owned by the seller in anticipation of profiting from a decline in the price of the securities. A short sale is not permitted when the last preceding different price was higher than the current price. —Also called *selling short; short.* —See also FICTITIOUS CREDIT; GHOST STOCK; LENDING AT A PREMIUM; LENDING AT A RATE; ODD-LOT SHORT SALES; RULE 10A-1; SHORT AGAINST THE BOX; SHORT COVER; SYNTHETIC SHORT SALE.

short squeeze The pressure on short sellers to cover their positions as a result of sharp price increases or difficulty in borrowing the security the sellers are short. The rush to cover produces additional upward pressure on the price of the stock, which then causes an even greater squeeze. —Also called *squeezing the shorts.*

short straddle The short sale of an equal number of call options and put options with identical strike prices and expiration dates. A short straddle produces a profit only when the price of the underlying asset remains within a limited range.

short tender A technique for capitalizing on a tender offer by using borrowed shares acquired through a short sale. A short tender is prohibited by SEC Rule 10b-4.

short-term 1. Of or relating to a gain or loss on the value of an asset that has been held less than a specified period of time. For individual tax purposes, an asset held for a year or less is classified as short-term. —Compare LONG-TERM 1. —See also HOLDING PERIOD. 2. Of or relating to a debt security in which a short period of time remains until the face value is paid to the investor. Exactly what constitutes short-term is subjective, although five years and under may be considered the norm. 3. Of or relating to business assets that are expected to be converted to cash within one year and to business liabilities that are due within one year.

short-term discount notes The promissory notes issued by municipalities at a discount from face value. Essentially, short-term discount notes are a form of tax-exempt commercial paper.

short-term municipal bond fund —See TAX-EXEMPT MONEY MARKET FUND.

short-term trading index A technical trading indicator that is calculated by dividing the volume of advancing stocks relative to the volume of declining stocks by the number of advancing stocks relative to the number of declining stocks. An index value above 1.30 is considered a buy signal, while a value below 0.70 is a sell signal.

show stopper A legal barrier to a takeover attempt that is virtually impossible for the suitor to overcome. For example, a target company might convince state legislators to pass various antitakeover laws that would preclude the takeover. —Compare SHARK REPELLENT.

shrinkage The loss of inventory encountered in the regular course of business. A firm engaged in transporting grain can expect to lose part of its product to weather, careless handling, and various other factors.

shrinking asset —See WASTING ASSET.

SIA —See SECURITIES INDUSTRY ASSOCIATION.

SIAC —See SECURITIES INDUSTRY AUTOMATION CORPORATION.

SIC 1. —See SECURITIES INFORMATION CENTER. **2.** —See STANDARD INDUSTRIAL CLASSIFICATION SYSTEM.

side-by-side trading The simultaneous making of a market in a stock and in its associated options. The SEC has long frowned on this practice because of the possibility of price manipulation inherent in it. —Also called *integrated market making.*

sideline —See ON THE SIDELINES.

sideways market —See FLAT MARKET.

sight draft A draft that is payable on demand. —Compare TIME DRAFT.

signal To provide information to. For example, an unexpected dividend increase may signal investors that a firm's directors are more optimistic about future profits than previously thought. Likewise, the announcement of a new equity issue may signal investors that directors consider a firm's stock to be fully valued.

signature guarantee A written guarantee by a financial institution (nearly always a commercial bank or stock exchange member firm) that a particular signature is valid. A signature guarantee is often required on a certificate or other official document to be mailed.

silent partner A member of a partnership who does not take active part in management and who is not publicly recognized as a partner.

silver parachute An agreement for employee severance benefits in the event control of the firm changes hands. A silver parachute is less lucrative and is extended to more employees than is a golden parachute.

SIMPLE A savings incentive match plan for employees that is similar to but more flexible than an IRA for businesses with 100 or fewer employees. Employees enter into a qualified salary reduction agreement to contribute a percentage of their annual compensation to a tax-deferred retirement account.

simple interest The interest that is paid on an initial investment only. Simple interest is calculated multiplying the investment principal times the annual rate of interest times the number of years involved. —Compare COMPOUND INTEREST.

simplified employee pension plan (SEP) A special type of joint Keogh plan–individual retirement account that is created for employees by employers and that permits contributions from each party. The SEP was developed to give small businesses a retirement plan easier to establish and administer than an ordinary pension plan.

simulation A mathematical exercise in which a model of a system is established, then the model's variables are altered to determine the effects on other variables. For example, a financial analyst might construct a model for predicting a stock's market price and then manipulate various determinants of the price including earnings, interest rates, and the inflation rate to determine how each of these changes affects the market price.

simultaneous transaction —See RISKLESS TRANSACTION.

single-country fund A mutual fund that invests in securities of one country. A single-country fund, for example, might invest only in securities issued in Australia.

single-premium deferred annuity A deferred annuity purchase having one lump-sum premium payment. Single-premium deferred annuities offer the tax benefit of increasing in value tax-free until distribution takes place. Thus, an investor could pay a large single premium, have the investment build up free of taxes for a period of years, and then receive partially taxable annuity payments at retirement. A single-premium deferred annuity is more flexible than an individual retirement account, but unlike contributions by some individuals to an IRA, a premium to purchase a deferred annuity is not deductible for tax purposes. —Compare PERIODIC PURCHASE DEFERRED CONTRACT.

single state municipal bond fund —See DOUBLE-EXEMPT FUND.

single stock future A contract in which opposite parties agree to buy and sell a stock at a set price on a certain date. Unlike a stock option in which the owner of the option has a right to either buy (call) or sell (put), both parties in a single stock future contract have an obligation. Trading in single stock futures was pioneered in Europe on the London International Financial Futures and Options Exchange and was banned in the United States until repeal of the Shad-Johnson Accord in 2000. —See also NASDAQ LIFFE MARKETS; ONECHICAGO LLC.

sinker —See SINKING FUND BOND.

sinking fund The assets that are set aside for the redemption of stock, the retirement of debt, or the replacement of fixed assets.

sinking fund bond A bond issue for which the issuer is required to establish a sinking fund to provide for the orderly retirement of the bonds. —Also called *sinker*.

sinking fund call An issuer's call of a portion of an outstanding bond issue to satisfy the issue's sinking fund requirement. A sinking fund call is generally at par value with the bonds to be called determined by lot. Most bond issues provide investors with a period of protection between the date on which the issue is originally sold and the date on which the first sinking fund call takes place. For low-coupon bonds that sell at discount from par value, issuers will usually satisfy sinking fund requirements by purchasing bonds in the open market rather than calling them from investors. —See also EXTRAORDINARY CALL; OPTIONAL CALL.

sinking fund provision A stipulation in many bond indentures that the borrower retire a certain proportion of the debt annually. The retirement may be effected by calling the bonds from the investors (if interest rates have declined) or by purchasing the bonds in the open market (if interest rates have increased). This orderly retirement may be advantageous to a bondholder because it creates some liquidity; however, it also may cause the holder to give up a high-yielding bond at the call price (often at par) during a period of reduced interest rates. —Compare DOUBLING OPTION. —Also called *bond sinking fund.* —See also FUNNEL SINKING FUND.

sinking ship A mutual fund that has a substantial outflow of funds because of its weak investment performance.

SIPC —See SECURITIES INVESTOR PROTECTION CORPORATION.

sixteenth One sixteenth of a point. For bond quotes, a sixteenth represents $1/16$ of 1%. Thus, a bond quoted at $98^{1}/_{16}$ would indicate a price of $98^{1}/_{16}$% of par, or $980.62.

size 1. The market for a security in which a relatively large volume is being offered for sale or in which a large volume can be absorbed. Size in a security is more important for institutional investors than it is for individuals, because most individuals usually do not trade in sufficiently high volume to warrant concern about the size of the market. 2. The number of units bid for and offered in the current quote, usually expressed in abbreviated form, such as, BP 5.10–.15, 2,000 by 1,000.

size effect The effect of firm size, as measured by market value, on investment returns. Some studies indicate that investments in small companies provide higher risk-adjusted returns.

sizing The determination of the number of shares or bonds to be included in a new issue.

skip-day settlement The settlement of a security trade one business day beyond the usual settlement date. For example, a trade that usually requires next-day settlement would require payment and delivery two business days following the trade date using skip-day settlement.

SLD 1. —Used on the consolidated tape to indicate a transaction that is reported out of sequence. For example, a transaction that occurred earlier in the day may be reported late: *IBM.SLD 6s35.* 2. —Used on transaction slips to indicate the side of a trade in which securities are sold. —Compare BOT.

SLD LAST SALE —Used on the consolidated tape to indicate a large price change in the indicated security since the time at which the security was last traded.

sleeping beauty A firm with valuable assets not effectively used by its management. Such a firm has high profit potential and value and is therefore a prime candidate for takeover.

SLOB —See SECURED LEASE OBLIGATION BOND.

SMA —See SPECIAL MISCELLANEOUS ACCOUNT.

small business issuer An issuer of securities that has less than $25 million in annual revenues and outstanding publicly held stock worth no more than $25 million. Public offerings by small businesses are subject to special SEC registration rules.

small-cap 1. Of or relating to the common stock of a relatively small firm having little equity and few shares of common stock outstanding. Small-caps tend to be subject to large price fluctuations; therefore, the potential for short-term

How can I determine whether a small-cap stock is reasonably valued?

A reasonably valued small-cap stock should be a company that has the potential to increase its earnings at a rate higher than the general growth of the economy. Because small-cap stocks generally have unusually high price-earnings ratios, the investor needs to look at each stock individually and compare its price-earnings ratios with the average price-earnings ratio of the appropriate small-cap stock index, such as the Russell 2000.

George Riles, First Vice President and Resident Manager, Merrill Lynch, Albany, GA

gains and losses is great. **2.** Of or relating to mutual funds that invest in the stock of small-cap companies. —See also MICROCAP.

small-firm effect The theory that the stock of small firms tends to outperform the stock of large firms. Some analysts attribute the small-firm effect to the fact that small firms have more room to grow than large firms do.

small investor A person who occasionally buys and sells securities, generally in relatively small amounts. —See also ODD-LOTTER.

small-issue bond A bond that is part of a small-sized municipal bond issue for private purposes such that interest on the bond qualifies for federal tax exemption. Municipalities are limited as to the size of such an issue and the total number of issues if the bonds are to pay tax-exempt interest.

Small Order Execution System (SOES) A computerized linkup of Nasdaq market makers that allows orders of 1,000 shares or less to bypass brokers and receive automatic execution at the best available price. SOES was implemented in late 1987 in response to the 1987 stock market crash. Nasdaq market makers in the National Market System are required to participate in the SOES. —Compare AUTOMATED STOCK TRADING. —See also SOES BANDIT.

CASE STUDY In January 2002 the Securities and Exchange Commission charged iCapital Markets LLC, formerly Datek Securities Corporation, with securities fraud and violations of the SEC's broker-dealer reporting provisions. According to the charge, Datek Securities had for at least five years executed proprietary trades through the Nasdaq Stock Market's Small Order Execution System (SOES), which Nasdaq designed for small public customers. Until 2001 broker-dealers were prohibited from using SOES to trade for their own accounts. SOES served as the only Nasdaq trading system offering automatic execution at the best available price. The SEC charged that Datek fraudulently utilized SOES to execute millions of trades using nominee accounts to hide its proprietary trading. From 1995 through March 1998 the firm's trades constituted over 30% of all SOES trades. As punishment for misusing the Small Order Execution System, the SEC censured iCapital and ordered the firm to pay a $6.3 million penalty. iCapital consented to the order without admitting or denying the findings.

smart money The funds controlled by investors who should have special knowledge of the right kinds of investments to make. Essentially, the term refers to funds controlled by insiders or to institutional money. The implication is that if the individual investor can figure out where the smart money is going, he or she can follow suit and make above-average profits. Many researchers believe that smart money is no more likely to earn above-average returns than funds invested by typical investors.

social investing

Investing in socially responsible mutual funds: Is performance usually sacrificed for the sake of ideology?

No, it appears that mixing money and ethics is not lethal to your financial health. One indication is that the Domini 400 Social Index, a broad-based equity index of socially screened corporations, showed a five-year return of 18.08% versus 18.33% for the Standard & Poor's 500 (for the period ending 2000). Perhaps more important, as socially responsible or ethical investing has become a growing factor in the mutual fund business, this sector's performance has come to mirror the rest of the mutual fund industry, dominated by the talents (or ineptitude) of individual money managers and market sentiment toward a particular investment style. No question, investors now have plenty of choice among socially responsible mutual funds, ranging from money market funds to international equities. Socially oriented mutual funds typically use a set of financial and social concerns to exclude certain kinds of investments: no defense companies, tobacco sellers, or gambling enterprises, for instance. Other ethical investing funds generate additional criteria for picking companies that further valued social goals, such as environmentally conscious firms or companies with strong community relations.

Christopher Farrell, Economics Editor
Minnesota Public Radio, heard nationally on Sound Money®

smokestack industry A basic manufacturing industry, such as the automobile, rubber, and steel industries, that has limited growth potential, and earnings and revenues that vary cyclically with general economic activity.

social investing Limiting one's investment alternatives to securities of firms whose products or actions are considered socially acceptable. For example, an investment manager might decide to eliminate from consideration the securities of all firms engaged in the manufacture of tobacco or liquor products. —Also called *ethical investing.* —See also GREEN INVESTING.

SOES —See SMALL ORDER EXECUTION SYSTEM.

SOES bandit A trader who exploits Nasdaq's Small Order Execution System by taking advantage of market inefficiencies. The bandit typically first enters a relatively small order to manipulate a security's price and then quickly enters a second, larger order to take advantage of the new price.

soft dollars Payment for brokerage firm services that is provided by commissions generated from trades. Thus, an investor who does significant trading might be provided with "complimentary" subscriptions to market letters or an at-home quote system. Payment is disguised in the form of large commissions paid to the brokerage firm. —Compare HARD DOLLARS.

soft landing A slowing of economic growth that avoids a recession and the accompanying high unemployment. The Federal Reserve may pursue a restrictive monetary policy to achieve a soft landing when the economy has been expanding at an unsustainable rate.

soft market A securities market having declining prices and little trading.

solvent Able to meet debts or discharge liabilities. —Compare INSOLVENT.

sources and uses of funds statement —See STATEMENT OF CASH FLOWS.

sovereign risk The risk of owning the security of an issuer in a country other than the one in which the investor lives. For example, an investor residing in the

United States incurs sovereign risk in purchasing a bond issued by the government of Brazil. This risk stems from the fact that a foreign country may nationalize its private businesses, stop paying interest, or repudiate its debt.

SPARQS^{SM} —See STOCK PARTICIPATION ACCREDITING REDEMPTION QUARTERLY-PAY SECURITIES^{SM}.

SPDR —See STANDARD & POOR'S DEPOSITARY RECEIPT.

SPE —See SPECIAL PURPOSE ENTERPRISE.

special arbitrage account A brokerage account in which a customer is limited to hedged positions requiring significantly lower margin than ordinary unhedged positions do.

special assessment bond A municipal bond with debt service limited to revenues from assessments against those who directly benefit from the project the funds have been used to finance. This type of bond is more risky than a general obligation bond of the same issuer if it is not also secured by a full-faith-and-credit pledge.

special bid A bid by an exchange member to fill an order to buy a block of a security. The member generally must find a number of sellers to accrue the required amount of the security.

special bond account A brokerage account in which a customer is limited to transactions in bonds. Special low margin requirements apply to a special bond account because bond prices are generally less volatile than those of most other securities.

special call —See EXTRAORDINARY CALL.

special cash account —See CASH ACCOUNT.

special dividend —See EXTRA DIVIDEND.

specialist A member of a securities exchange who is a market maker in one or more securities listed on the exchange. The specialist is the person on the exchange floor to whom other members go when they wish to transact or leave an order. Specialists are assigned securities by the exchange and are expected to maintain a fair and orderly market in them. —Also called *assigned dealer.* —See also BOOK 1; RULE 104.

specialist's book —See BOOK 1.

specialists' sentiment The view of specialists as to the future direction of a stock or of the stock market itself. Some investors, believing specialists have an inside, or a particularly informed, view of the market, try to make their own investment decisions based on their perceived interpretation of specialists' sentiment, in hopes of gaining above-average profits. Specialists' sentiment is sometimes measured by studying the specialists' short sales.

specialists' short-sale ratio A ratio that compares specialists' short sales with total short sales. Technical analysts use this ratio to measure the market sentiment of the specialists. A high ratio indicates that the specialists are bearish.

specialist unit A group of people or firms acting together to maintain an orderly market in securities assigned by an exchange. Specialist units may act as agent or as principal in executing trades on the floor of the exchange. —Also called *unit.*

special miscellaneous account (SMA) An account in which balances in excess of the amount required under Regulation T are placed. Funds in an SMA may be used to purchase more securities on margin or they may be withdrawn in cash. Suppose a customer purchases $10,000 of securities and puts up the minimum 50% margin required by the Federal Reserve under Regulation T. If the securities subsequently rise in value to $14,000, the new $7,000 loan value (50% of the market value) is $2,000 more than is currently borrowed on the securities. The $2,000 in the special miscellaneous account may be withdrawn in cash as a loan or it may be used to purchase up to $4,000 in additional securities. —See also ADJUSTED DEBIT BALANCE.

special offering A secondary distribution on the floor of the New York Stock Exchange by an exchange member. A special offering is generally priced at the current market price of the security being offered, with the seller absorbing all costs. Thus, members buying parts of the offering for their clients or their own inventory can avoid any fees. The selling member is able to sell a block of stock without having to give a price concession to buyers.

special purpose enterprise (SPE) A semi-independent business organization formed to carry out a specific function. For example, a company might form an SPE to purchase some of the firm's assets. The SPE uses the assets as collateral for a loan with proceeds going to pay the company for the purchased assets. The assets and corresponding debt become balance sheet entries of the SPE, not the corporation. Companies that wish to eliminate troublesome assets and/or debts from their financial statements sometimes abuse the use of special purpose enterprises.

special-purpose fund —See SECTOR FUND.

special situation A currently undervalued stock that can suddenly increase in value because of imminently favorable circumstances. For example, a firm may be about to bring a new, potentially profitable product to market. If everything turns out favorably, the gains in the firm's stock could be quite large. Another special situation might derive from the impending liquidation of a company. Special situations are usually quite risky.

special subscription account A brokerage account opened for the purpose of purchasing stock issued by use of preemptive rights.

special tax bond A municipal bond with debt service limited to the revenues generated by a special tax. A bond issue to finance a convention center with the interest and principal payments limited to taxes received from a levy on motel and restaurant sales is an example of a special tax bond. Certain special tax bonds are also secured by the full faith and credit of the issuer; they have the additional security of being general obligations.

specialty fund —See SECTOR FUND.

spectail A securities dealer who undertakes speculative trading for his or her own account while simultaneously handling retail accounts.

speculation The taking of above-average risks to achieve above-average returns, generally during a relatively short period of time. Speculation involves buying something on the basis of its potential selling price rather than on the basis of its actual value.

speculative Of or relating to an asset or a group of assets with uncertain returns. The greater the degree of uncertainty the more speculative the asset.

Speculative Grade Liquidity Rating (SGL) Assessment of a firm's ability to meet obligations coming due during the next twelve months. The SGL rating system was developed by Moody's Investors Service to provide guidance regarding a company's liquidity risk and the possibility of default. Rating assignments range from SGL–1 (very good) to SGL–4 (weak).

speculator A person who is willing to take large risks and sacrifice the safety of principal in return for potentially large gains. Certain decisions regarding securities clearly characterize a speculator. For example, purchasing a very volatile stock in hopes of making a half a point in profit is speculation, but buying a U.S. Treasury bond to hold for retirement is an investment. It must be added, however, that there is a big gray area in which speculation and investment are difficult to differentiate. —Also called *punter.*

spider —See STANDARD & POOR'S DEPOSITARY RECEIPT.

spike A sudden, short-term change in the price of a security that just as suddenly returns close to its previous level. For example, a stock that has consistently traded in a $10 to $12 per share range may suddenly move to a price of $14 and then return to $12. The sudden rise to the $14 price is a spike.

spinning The allocating of shares of a hot initial offering by a securities firm to the personal account of a corporate executive in anticipation of gaining future business from the executive's firm.

spinoff The distribution to stockholders of the stock of a subsidiary held by a parent company. Usually the distribution is not taxable to the stockholders until the new shares have been sold. —Compare SPLITOFF. —See also PARTIAL SPINOFF.

spin off To distribute stock of a subsidiary to stockholders of the parent company. For example, directors of Union Pacific Corporation voted to spin off the firm's natural resource operations by distributing to Union Pacific stockholders shares of Union Pacific Resources.

⋀⋀ CASE STUDY In October 2001 consumer products giant Procter & Gamble announced an agreement to sell two of its major brands, Jif peanut butter and Crisco cooking oils, to jelly and jam maker J.M. Smucker Company. Acquisition of the two brands doubled the sales of Ohio-based Smucker, whose stock price closed up 20% on the announcement. The acquisition made Smucker a market leader in three major consumer categories. In an unusual move, the sale was accomplished by first spinning off Jif and Crisco assets to P&G shareholders, who then exchanged the assets with Smucker in a stock swap. The agreement called for one Smucker share to be exchanged for each 50 shares held by a P&G stockholder. Thus, the owner of 1,000 shares of Procter & Gamble received 20 Smucker shares in the exchange. An acquisition for stock rather than cash is tax-exempt until shares are eventually sold, an advantage to Procter & Gamble shareholders. Procter & Gamble would have been required to pay taxes on any gain had Smucker paid P&G for the purchase in cash rather than stock. Procter & Gamble decided to spin off Jif and Crisco to its stockholders rather than conduct the exchange directly with Smucker because P&G had no interest in holding Smucker stock. P&G shareholders owned slightly over 50% of Smucker following the share exchange.

split   A proportionate increase in the number of shares of outstanding stock without a corresponding increase in assets or in funds available, as would be the case in a new stock offering or in an acquisition that uses stock as payment. Essentially, a firm splits its stock to reduce the market price and make the shares attractive to a larger pool of investors, although it is questionable if the firm's stockholders actually benefit from a split because share prices are reduced proportionately with the increase in shares outstanding. A 4-for-1 split would result in an owner of 100 shares receiving 300 additional shares, or an after-split total of 4 shares for every 1 share owned before the split. —Compare REVERSE STOCK SPLIT. —Also called *split up; stock split.*

⋀ CASE STUDY | In April 1996, directors of the Coca-Cola Company approved a 2-for-1 split, the firm's fourth stock split in a decade. The announcement stated that trading in the split shares would begin on May 13, approximately a month after the split was announced. Shares of the firm's common stock fell by $1.25 with the announcement. Shareholders of Coca-Cola could expect that the stock price would decrease by half when the securities commenced trading on a post-split basis. A stock split results in additional shares of ownership without a corresponding change in total income or assets. All per-share financial statistics decline in proportion to the size of the split. Thus, a 2-for-1 split results in twice the outstanding shares, each with half the book value and half the earnings as prior to the split. In general, stock splits create more paper but not more value for shareholders, because the market value of the stock can be expected to fall in proportion to the size of the split. A stock trading at $60 per share just prior to a 4-for-1 split should trade at approximately $15 per share following the split. Academic research investigating how or when investors can profitably invest in stock split situations offers mixed results. Some research indicates that trading stock just prior to a split may create unusual profit opportunities. One well-known study finds that unusual returns can be earned in the days before and after the announcement, but not on the date of the actual split. Other research indicates investors will earn unusually low returns by investing in stock in the year or two following a split. This variability of results means the individual investors cannot expect to earn unusual profits by purchasing a stock just prior to or following a split. By the time a split occurs, any unusual profit opportunity has already passed.

split commission   A sales fee divided among two or more people.

split down   —See REVERSE STOCK SPLIT.

split-fee option   —See COMPOUND OPTION.

split funding   The purchase of more than one financial product with the same payment. For example, some financial programs combine life insurance and a mutual fund into the same package, with each customer payment being split between the two.

split gift   A gift from one partner in a marriage to someone outside the marriage when one-half of the gift is assumed by law to have been made by each spouse. A split gift permits the $10,000 annual gift tax exclusion per recipient to effectively be $20,000 per recipient when the gift originates from a married couple.

splitoff   An exchange of the stock of a subsidiary for a pro rata surrender of stock in the parent corporation. A splitoff is similar to a spinoff, but in the case of the splitoff a smaller (or no) decline in the stock of the parent corporation should take place. —Compare SPINOFF.

split offering 1. The sale of a new bond issue that is composed of serial bonds and term bonds. Many municipal issues are sold as split offerings. **2.** A security offering that consists of new and previously issued securities of the issuer. For example, a corporation may undertake an issue of common stock that is composed of new shares and shares being held as Treasury stock.

splitoff IPO —See EQUITY CARVE-OUT.

split order A relatively large single order that is executed in two or more transactions to minimize its effect on the market price of the security being bought or sold.

split rating A condition that occurs when the same bond is rated differently by the rating agencies. An example is a bond rated AA by one agency and A by another agency. A split rating may occur because one rating agency places a different emphasis on certain variables or because it views a particular item (such as a recent acquisition by the issuer) differently than the other rating agency.

split ratio The ratio by which the number of a firm's outstanding shares of stock are increased following a stock split. For example, a two-for-one split results in twice as many outstanding shares, with each share selling at half its pre-split price. The higher the split ratio, the greater the reduction in the price of the stock.

split up The distribution of all of a firm's assets, generally in the form of stock distributions, such that the firm ceases to exist.

split-up value The aggregate dollar value of a firm's various parts if they were to be sold separately. Many takeovers occur because of a difference between the stock market values and the split-up values of the target companies.

sponsor 1. An institutional investor or a brokerage firm that has a position in a security and influences other investors to establish a position in that security. **2.** —See UNDERWRITER.

sponsored American Depositary Receipt An American Depositary Receipt in which the company whose shares are held in custody has direct involvement in issuance of the ADRs. The foreign company registers the receipts with the Securities and Exchange Commission and chooses a single depositary bank. Holders of sponsored ADRs have all the rights of common stockholders, including the right to receive reports, the right to vote, and the right to receive dividends. —Compare UNSPONSORED AMERICAN DEPOSITARY RECEIPT.

spot commodity A commodity that is available for immediate delivery.

spot market —See CASH MARKET.

spot month The nearest month in which a currently traded futures contract is due for delivery.

spot price —See CASH PRICE.

spot secondary distribution A secondary distribution by security holders not affiliated with the issuer such that the distribution does not require registration with the SEC.

spousal IRA An individual retirement account in the name of a nonworking spouse. A spousal IRA may be funded by the working spouse up to a maximum amount established by law. There is also a limit on annual contributions to the combination of IRAs of the working and nonworking spouses.

spousal remainder trust An irrevocable trust that may be set up for any length of time in order to pass assets to a spouse. Between the time that the trust becomes effective and the time that the assets are passed, income earned by the trust is taxable to a named beneficiary at the beneficiary's tax rate.

spread **1.** A position taken in two or more options or futures contracts to profit through a change in the relative price relationships. Purchasing an option to expire in October and selling an option on the same asset expiring three months earlier is one example of a spread. **2.** The difference in price between two futures contracts that are identical except for delivery date. **3.** The difference between the bid and ask prices for a particular security. A large spread often indicates inactive trading of the security. —Also called *markup.* —See also EFFECTIVE SPREAD; GROSS SPREAD; NARROW THE SPREAD. **4.** The difference in yields between two fixed-income securities. —See also BASIS POINT.

spreading The establishment of a long position in an option and a short position in another option of the same class but with a different strike price or expiration date, or both. Spreading is supposed to achieve profit from a difference in relative price movements of two options of the same class.

spread-load contractual plan A contractual plan for purchasing shares of a mutual fund in which sales charges are not concentrated in the first payment or in the first few payments made by the investor.

spread order An order to buy and to sell options of the same class but with different strike prices and/or expiration dates in which the customer specifies a spread between the option sold and the option purchased. For example, an investor might enter a spread order to buy a March call and sell a September call, both on AOL Time Warner and with a strike price of $30, if a spread of $2 can be obtained. The order will be executed only if a floor broker can sell the September call for $2 more than the price at which the March call can be purchased.

spreadsheet A worksheet on which financial data are laid out in rows and columns for comparative purposes. For example, a financial analyst might use a spreadsheet to determine how a firm's sales and profit margins have varied throughout a period of quarters or years.

spread to Treasury The difference in yield between a fixed-income security and a Treasury security of similar maturity.

springing convertible A convertible security that includes warrants to purchase additional shares of the issuer's common stock. Certain prescribed events, such as a hostile tender offer or the accumulation of a large block of stock by a single group, cause the exercise price of the warrants to drop or spring. This unusual security is issued primarily to deter a corporate takeover by making the takeover more expensive.

sprinkling trust A family trust in which the trustee has the power to distribute income to the beneficiaries according to their individual needs rather than according to a specified formula.

SPX —Used to identify Standard & Poor's 500 Stock Index options.

squeeze-out The forcing of stockholders to sell their stock. Majority holders of a company's stock may attempt a squeeze-out of minority stockholders in order to take complete control of the firm.

squeezing the shorts —See SHORT SQUEEZE.

SRO —See SELF-REGULATORY ORGANIZATION.

$\frac{s}{s}$ —Used on the consolidated tape to indicate a transaction of less than a round lot: *AEPPr 5$\frac{s}{s}$47.*

STA 1. —See SECURITIES TRANSFER ASSOCIATION. **2.** —See SECURITY TRADERS ASSOCIATION.

stabilization period The time elapsing between the offering of a security issue for sale and its final distribution, during which the underwriter enters the secondary market in order to stabilize the price of the security. The underwriter attempts to keep the secondary market price of the security from falling below the offering price. —Also called *price stabilization.*

stabilize —See PEG 1.

stagflation An economic condition that is characterized by slow growth, rapidly rising consumer prices, and relatively high unemployment.

staggered maturities In an investor's portfolio, bonds with differing maturity dates. For example, an investor may accumulate a $250,000 portfolio of bonds such that $10,000 face value of bonds matures each year for 25 years.

staggered terms Membership terms for a firm's directors that expire in different years. A firm with 12 directors might have 4-year terms with 3 seats up for election each year. Staggered terms make it more difficult for a raider to gain control of a board.

staggering maturities —See LADDERING.

STAIRS® A registered trademark for a type of municipal convertible bond.

stakeholder Any party that has an interest in an organization. Stakeholders of a company include stockholders, bondholders, customers, suppliers, employees, and so forth.

stake-out investment An investment that provides an initial stake in a company in anticipation of additional investments in the same firm.

stand-alone company An independent operating firm. For example, a large diversified firm may consider spinning off a subsidiary because, as a stand-alone company, the subsidiary would command a higher price-earnings ratio than the parent.

Standard & Poor's® (S&P®) A registered service mark for a service that furnishes financial and statistical data derived from computer tapes and punch cards for use in computers to the specifications and/or orders of others. Standard & Poor's Corporation is an investment advisory service that publishes financial data. This subsidiary of McGraw-Hill also rates debt securities and distributes a series of widely followed stock indexes. Major publications include *The Outlook, Stock Reports, Industry Survey,* and *Stock Guide.*

Standard & Poor's Confidence Indicator An investor confidence indicator in the securities markets that is calculated by constructing an index of low-priced to high-grade common stock. A rising index indicates increased investor willingness to assume risk and therefore indicates increased investor confidence. —Compare BARRON'S CONFIDENCE INDEX.

Standard & Poor's Depositary Receipt (SPDR) An interest in a trust that holds shares of all stock in the S&P 500. Ownership of an SPDR allows an investor to track the entire market through a single investment. These receipts trade on the

American Stock Exchange at about one-tenth the value of the S&P 500. —Also called *spider.*

Standard & Poor's 400 Stock Index (S&P 400) A broad-based index of 400 industrial stock prices weighted on the basis of market value (stock price multiplied by shares outstanding). It includes listed and over-the-counter stock but is heavily influenced by the stock of large corporations. The index is based on a value of 10 during the period 1941–43.

Standard & Poor's 500 Stock Index (S&P 500) An inclusive index made up of 500 stock prices including 400 industrials, 40 utilities, 20 transportation, and 40 financial issues. The index is constructed using market weights (stock price multiplied by shares outstanding) to provide a broad indicator of stock price movements.

> ⋀ **CASE STUDY** Being added to a popular stock index such as the S&P 500 can have a positive effect on a company's stock price. For example, the common stock of Federated Department Stores experienced heavy trading and jumped in price by nearly 9% in the four days following Standard & Poor's announcement that the firm would add Federated's stock to its widely followed index. Most of this activity was apparently generated by index funds holding portfolios that mimic the indexes. Thus, the announcement by S&P caused index funds to begin adding the stock to their portfolios. Likewise, dropping a stock from an index is likely to have a negative effect on its price. Most of the seemingly unusual returns that result from adding or deleting a stock from an index can be expected to occur between the day of the announcement and the day when the stock is actually added to the index.

Standard & Poor's Midcap Index An index designed to measure price movements of the stock of medium-sized companies. The index comprises the market values of the stock of 400 medium-sized companies.

Standard & Poor's 100 Stock Index (S&P 100) A market-capitalization-weighted measure of 100 major, blue chip stocks representing diverse industry groups. It is best known by the ticker symbol OEX.

standard deduction The minimum deduction from income allowed a taxpayer for calculating taxable income. Individuals with few itemized deductions elect the standard deduction in place of itemizing deductions. —Formerly called *zero bracket amount.*

standard deviation A statistical measure of the variability of a distribution. An analyst may wish to calculate the standard deviation of historical returns on a stock or a portfolio as a measure of the investment's riskiness. The higher the standard deviation of an investment's returns, the greater the relative riskiness because of uncertainty in the amount of return. —See also RISK; VARIANCE.

standard industrial classification system (SIC) A classification of businesses and business units by type of economic activity. The system uses from a one-digit to a four-digit classification depending on how narrowly the business unit is defined. There are 11 one-digit groupings and more than 1,000 four-digit groupings.

standard opinion —See CLEAN OPINION.

standby fee The fee paid to an underwriter that agrees to purchase unsold securities as part of a standby underwriting agreement.

standby underwriting   An agreement by underwriters to purchase the portion of a new securities issue that remains after the public offering. Standby underwriting eliminates the issuer's risk of not selling the issue out, but it increases the investment bankers' risk.

standstill agreement   A written agreement between two firms whereby the actions of one firm with respect to the other are limited until a specified date. For example, Firm A may sell Firm B a block of Firm A's stock with the stipulation that Firm B will acquire no additional shares in Firm A for five years.

CASE STUDY In February 1996, the Chrysler Corporation reached a standstill agreement with dissident stockholder Kirk Kerkorian. Over several years, Kerkorian had accumulated nearly 13.6% of Chrysler's common stock in an unsuccessful takeover attempt. At the time of the agreement, the investor was threatening Chrysler management with a proxy fight. As part of the standstill agreement, Kerkorian said he would not accumulate additional Chrysler shares, not attempt a hostile takeover, and not launch a proxy fight for a period of five years. In turn, Chrysler management agreed to give a board seat to a Kerkorian ally. The firm also agreed to double the size of its planned 1996 share-repurchase program to $2 billion and to repurchase an additional $1 billion of Chrysler shares the following year. The standstill agreement rewarded Kerkorian with a boost in the value of his Chrysler shares, and at the same time it permitted Chrysler's management to eliminate a problem that was consuming substantial amounts of the firm's time and resources.

stapled stock   —See PAIRED SHARES.

start-up company   A new business.

stated capital   —See LEGAL CAPITAL.

stated value   A value assigned to common stock by the firm's management for purposes of financial statements. Stated value, used in place of par value, is calculated on a per-share basis by dividing the stated capital resulting from a new issue of common stock by the number of new shares issued. Stated value is unrelated to the stock's market price and is of little importance to the shareholders.

statement   A written presentation, as of financial data. —See also ACCOUNT STATEMENT; FINANCIAL STATEMENT.

statement analysis   An analysis of an organization's financial and operating condition through the use of financial statements. Statement analysis is used by financial analysts in an attempt to determine the value of a firm's securities.

statement of additional information   A document that contains detailed supplementary information for investors. The statement is available from a mutual fund at no charge but generally will not be sent unless specifically requested. —Also called *Part B*.

statement of cash flows   A financial statement listing how a firm has obtained its funds and how it has spent them within a period of time. This statement, developed from changes in balance sheet entries between two dates, provides insights into the ways in which the firm's management raises and invests money. —Also called *application of funds statement; flow of funds statement; funds statement; sources and uses of funds statement.*

statement of financial condition   —See BALANCE SHEET.

statement of financial position —See BALANCE SHEET.

statement of retained earnings A financial statement that lists a firm's accumulated retained earnings and net income that has been paid as dividends to stockholders in the current period. —Also called *retained earnings statement.*

statutory investment —See LEGAL INVESTMENT.

statutory voting —See MAJORITY VOTING.

step-out trading A brokerage firm execution in which credit for the trade is given to another firm.

stepped coupon bond A bond with interest coupons that change to predetermined levels on specific dates. Thus, a stepped coupon bond might pay 9% interest for the first 5 years after issue and then step up the interest every fifth year until maturity. Issuers often have the right to call the bond at par on the date the interest rate is scheduled to change. —Also called *dual coupon bond; rising-coupon security; step-up coupon security.*

stepping in front —See FRONT RUNNING.

step-up A scheduled increase in the exercise or conversion price at which a warrant, an option, or a convertible security may be used to acquire shares of common stock. For example, a warrant may permit its owner to purchase ten shares of stock at $20 per share up to a specified date and at $22.50 per share thereafter until the warrant expires. The step-up works to the disadvantage of the holder, however. It is not a feature of most of these securities.

step-up coupon security —See STEPPED COUPON BOND.

sterile investment An investment vehicle that provides no current income. Examples of a sterile investment include a stock without a dividend, a bond that trades flat, or tangible assets such as gold, art, and baseball cards.

sticky deal A new securities issue that an investment banker may find difficult to sell.

stock An ownership share or ownership shares in a corporation. —See also BEARER STOCK; COMMON STOCK; PREFERRED STOCK; STOCK CLASS.

stock ahead —Used to describe limit orders that have been placed earlier and that take precedence over subsequent orders at the same price. An investor may find that a limit order has not been executed even though the specified price has been reached because orders with the same limit have been placed earlier than his or hers. Limit orders at a specific price are executed in the sequence in which they are received.

stock appreciation right Executive compensation that permits an employee to receive cash or stock equal to the amount by which the firm's stock price exceeds a specified base price.

stock average —See AVERAGES.

stockbroker —See REGISTERED REPRESENTATIVE.

stock buyback —See BUYBACK.

stock certificate —See CERTIFICATE.

stock class 1. A category of capital stock issued by a company and having specific rights or characteristics. Most firms have only a single class of stock outstanding. Thus, every share has exactly the same rights as every other share. But some companies have two or more classes of capital stock designated as class A, class B, and so forth. For example, one class may have controlling voting rights but both classes may share equally in dividends. In general, a firm issues different classes of stock when it wishes to sell one class to the public and reserve another class for its founders. —Also called *class; classified stock.* —See also COMMON STOCK. **2.** A category of stock issued by a mutual fund. Funds sometimes issue multiple classes of stock. A fund, for example, may have one class of shares that carries a sales fee and another class of shares that has a contingent deferred sales fee and a 12b–1 fee, but no initial sales fee. Both classes of shares would be based on the same portfolio of securities.

> **Mᴀ CASE STUDY** In early 1996, fabled investor Warren Buffett announced that Berkshire Hathaway planned its first equity offering in 30 years and would create a new class B common stock. At the same time, the company would designate existing shares as class A stock. The new shares would be offered to investors at one-thirtieth the price of a class A share, which, at the time of the announcement, was trading at an unbelievable $31,500. Approximately $100 million worth of the new shares were expected to be offered, so that they would qualify for listing on the New York Stock Exchange. Owners of class A shares could exchange their shares for class B stock at a rate of 30 shares of class B stock for each share of class A stock, but owners of class B stock would not be permitted to exchange shares for class A stock. At the time of the announcement, Buffett owned 40% of Berkshire Hathaway common stock. He said the decision to issue the lower-priced class B shares was a response to activity by investment trusts that specialized in owning shares of Berkshire Hathaway stock.

stock company A company owned by stockholders, with the ownership evidenced by transferable certificates. —Compare MUTUAL COMPANY.

stock dividend A dividend made up of shares of the paying firm's stock. A stock dividend is often used in place of or in addition to a cash dividend if the firm wishes to conserve cash. Unlike a cash dividend, a stock dividend is usually not taxable to the shareholder when it is received, but rather when it is sold. Stockholders who are supposed to receive a fractional share will often receive a check for the amount equal to the market value of the fractional share. Payment of a stock dividend is indicated in stock transaction tables in newspapers by the symbols *b* and *t*. —See also SCRIP DIVIDEND.

stock exchange —See SECURITIES EXCHANGE.

stockholder An individual or organization that owns common stock or preferred stock in a corporation. —Also called *shareholder.*

stockholder derivative suit A lawsuit filed by one or more of a company's stockholders in the name of the company. A derivative suit is filed when the firm's management will not or cannot sue in the name of the company. For example, a stockholder may enter a derivative suit against the firm's chief executive officer to recover funds from a questionable or an improper act by that officer. —Also called *derivative suit.*

stockholder of record —See HOLDER OF RECORD.

stockholders' equity —See OWNERS' EQUITY.

stock index —See INDEX.

stock-index arbitrage The strategy of buying or selling a basket of stock while making an offsetting trade in stock-index futures or options. Stock-index arbitrage is designed to take advantage of the temporary discrepancies in value between stock and the index futures or options.

stock index future A contract for the future delivery of a sum of money based on the value of a stock index (in most cases, 500 times the index). Unlike other futures contracts, in which a given commodity is specified for delivery, stock index futures call for cash settlements, because it is not possible to deliver an actual index. This future can be used to speculate on the future direction of the stock market (rather than just a few stocks) or to hedge a portfolio of securities against general market movements. —See also SECTION 1256 CONTRACTS.

stock index option A contract that gives its owner the right to buy (call option) or sell (put option) a stock index at a fixed value until a specified date. Options are traded on the S&P 500, the S&P 100, the NYSE Composite Index, and the Major Market Index, along with specialized indexes. These options work exactly like regular stock options except that an index rather than a particular stock is the underlying asset. As with stock index futures, delivery must be in cash because it is not possible to deliver an index. —See also SECTION 1256 CONTRACTS.

stock list The department of a securities exchange that takes care of new listings and delistings of securities on the exchange. —Also called *listing department*.

stock option An option to buy or sell a specific number of shares of stock at a fixed price until a specified date. —See also CALL 1; CAPPED-STYLE OPTION; INCENTIVE STOCK OPTION; PUT 1.

stock outstanding —See OUTSTANDING CAPITAL STOCK.

Stock Participation Accrediting Redemption Quarterly-Pay Securities^SM **(SPAROS**^SM**)** Callable medium-term debt securities issued by Morgan Stanley that pay quarterly interest based on the issue price and at maturity exchange for a specific number of shares of the underlying security.

stock power A form, separate from a stock certificate, that can be used to transfer stock. A stock power is useful when an investor wishes to deliver an unsigned certificate in one envelope and the stock power form for transfer of the certificate in another envelope. —Compare BOND POWER.

stock rating The grading of a stock, generally with respect to its expected price performance or safety. A number of publications, such as *Value Line,* publish stock ratings regularly. Of the major ratings firms only Standard & Poor's rates stocks. —Compare BOND RATING.

stock record An account of the securities being held by a brokerage firm.

stock register A record listing the issues, transfers, and retirements of a firm's stock.

stock repurchase plan 1. —See BUYBACK. 2. —See SELF-TENDER.

stock right —See RIGHT.

stock split —See SPLIT.

stock symbol The letter or sequence of letters used to identify a security. For example, on the consolidated tape, T is used for AT&T Corporation, CVG for Convergys Corporation, and XOM for ExxonMobil. Symbols are also used to identify securities on video display terminals.

stock warrant —See WARRANT.

Stock Watch A New York Stock Exchange system used to monitor trades on the floor of the exchange and to flag those trades that exceed predetermined parameters. Essentially, Stock Watch is designed to spot unusual activity in a security's trading pattern so that exchange officials can investigate the cause of the activity.

stop-and-go tactic The tax reduction or deferment technique in which income and deductions are moved from one year to another. This technique involves advancing deductions and delaying income. For example, an investor may wait to recognize stock gains by selling early in the next year.

stop-limit order A specialized order in which a limit order and a stop order are combined. Once the specified stop price has been reached or exceeded, the stop-limit order becomes a limit order. A stop-limit order differs from a stop order, which becomes a market order when the stop price has been reached or exceeded. A stop-limit order to buy must have a stop-limit price above the market price; conversely, a stop-limit order to sell must have a stop-limit price below the security's market price. In response to a stop-limit order specifying "sell 100 GY 15 stop limit," once the stock sells at or below $15, the order becomes a limit order to sell 100 shares at a price of $15. A variation of the stop-limit order specifies a limit price lower than the stop price.

stop-limit price The price specified in a stop-limit order at which the order becomes a limit order. A stop-limit order to buy must have a stop-limit price above the security's current market price and a stop-limit order to sell must have a stop-limit price below the security's current market price. —See also STOP PRICE.

stop order **1.** An order to buy or to sell a security when the security's price reaches or passes a specified level. At that time the stop order becomes a market order and the executing broker, usually the specialist, obtains the best possible price. A stop order to buy must be at a price above the current market price and a stop order to sell must have a specified price below the current market price. —See also BUY STOP ORDER; ELECTING SALE; PROTECTIVE STOP; SELL STOP ORDER; STOP-LIMIT ORDER; STOP PRICE; TRAILING STOP. **2.** An order from the SEC suspending a registration statement when an omission or a misstatement has been found.

stop-out price The lowest price (highest yield) accepted for new securities issued in a U.S. Treasury auction.

stopped out Having an order executed at a specified stop price. For example, suppose Union Pacific stock trades at $65 and an investor enters a stop order to sell 500 shares at $62. If the stock price subsequently falls and the order is executed at $62, the customer is stopped out.

stopped stock A broker's order with a specialist in which the specialist guarantees a specific price or better.

stop price The price specified in a stop order at which the stop order becomes a market order. A stop price at which to buy is entered above the current market price and a stop price at which to sell is entered below the current market price.

stop transfer An order to stop the transfer of ownership of a particular stock or bond certificate, a situation that generally occurs after an investor has notified a transfer agent that a certificate has been lost or stolen.

story bond A bond so unusual or having such complicated features that salespeople are frequently called on to explain its intricacies to customers. Story bonds sometimes offer slightly higher yields than ordinary bonds as a way of convincing investors that they are worth holding.

straddle 1. In futures, the purchase of a contract for delivery in one month and sale of a contract for delivery in a different month on the same commodity. 2. In options, the purchase or sale of both a call and a put, generally with the same strike price and expiration date. The buyer of a straddle benefits from large price fluctuations in the underlying asset, while the seller of a straddle, who collects the premiums, benefits from small price changes in the underlying asset.

straight debt Debt that cannot be exchanged for another asset. Because most bonds are not convertible, they are examples of straight debt. —See also CONVERTIBLE SECURITY.

straight life annuity An annuity that makes payments to the recipient only for the duration of his or her lifetime. No minimum number of payments and no minimum sum to be paid are guaranteed. All payments end upon the recipient's death. This annuity is desirable for someone with no dependents who wishes to obtain the largest possible payments.

straight-line depreciation A method of recording depreciation such that the original cost minus the estimated salvage value of an asset is written off in equal amounts during each period of the asset's life. For example, a machine costing $10,000 with an estimated life of five years and no salvage value would be depreciated $2,000 ($10,000/5) annually, using straight-line depreciation. If the machine had an estimated salvage value of $4,000, annual straight-line depreciation would amount to $1,200. —Compare ACCELERATED DEPRECIATION.

straight-through processing The direct exchange of cash and securities. Straight-through processing is a major objective for cross-border transactions that are generally much more costly to settle compared to domestic transactions.

strangle strategy The strategy of selling both an out-of-the-money call and an out-of-the-money put. Profits are greatest when relatively small price movements occur in the underlying asset and neither option is exercised. In case the value of the underlying asset moves in one direction, the loss on one side of the spread is at least partially offset by a gain on the other side.

strap A combination option made up of two calls and one put. The buyer of a strap profits from large variations in the price of the underlying asset, especially if it moves upward.

street name —Used to describe registration of a customer-owned security in the name of the brokerage firm holding the certificate. A security is held in street name to simplify trading because no delivery of or signature on the certificate is required, or because the certificate is being used as collateral in a margin account. —See also DELIVERY INSTRUCTIONS.

street-side trade A security trade between brokers.

street sweep An investment strategy in which large amounts of a company's stock are quickly purchased. Street sweeps generally occur in the stock of a company involved in a takeover attempt. —Also called *market sweep*.

strength —See RELATIVE STRENGTH.

stretch IRA An individual retirement account in which the period of tax-deferred earnings within the IRA stretches beyond the lifetime of the person who set up the IRA. Stretch IRAs can result in huge accumulations and payouts depending on the assumptions regarding the rate of return that will be earned and the length of time funds are to accumulate.

strike price The exercise price at which the owner of a call option can purchase the underlying stock or the owner of a put option can sell the underlying stock.

strike spread —See MONEY SPREAD.

strip A combination of two put options and a call option. The buyer of a strip profits from large variations in the price of the underlying asset, especially if it is moving downward.

stripping —See COUPON STRIPPING.

STRIPS —See SEPARATE TRADING OF REGISTERED INTEREST AND PRINCIPAL OF SECURITIES.

strong dollar A dollar that is valuable relative to foreign currencies. A strong dollar exchanges for more units of other currencies compared with the units for which it could be exchanged in the past. A strong dollar tends to hurt U.S. firms that rely heavily on foreign sales because the firms' products will cost more in terms of the foreign currencies. —Compare WEAK DOLLAR. —See also EXCHANGE RATE.

strong form A component of the theory of efficient markets that holds that security prices fully incorporate all public and most private information relevant to valuation of securities. The strong form component infers that professional portfolio managers and insiders are consistently unable to earn extraordinary returns in the security markets. —Compare WEAK FORM. —See also SEMISTRONG FORM.

structured note A medium-term derivative debt security that has one or more special features such as an interest payment based on an equity index, a foreign exchange index, or a benchmark interest rate. Issuers of structured notes often hedge these securities with their own transactions in the derivatives market. Structured notes tend to be complex and are aimed primarily at sophisticated investors.

stubs The shares of equity in a firm that is financed almost completely with debt. Stubs are often created when firms go through a leveraged buyout or pay big cash dividends in order to fend off a takeover.

Student Loan Marketing Association A subsidiary of privately owned USA Education that provides a secondary market in student loans, the majority of which are government guaranteed. This organization, popularly known as *Sallie Mae*, was the first government-sponsored enterprise to be transformed into a private company. As such, the firm lost the implied government backing of its debt that is enjoyed by Fannie Mae and Freddie Mac. USA Education is also the parent company of Nellie Mae, a major provider of higher education loans for students and parents.

style investing An active portfolio management strategy that uses certain signals to determine whether to switch into identifiable equity segments, in particular, whether to move from growth stock to value stock or the reverse, or from small-cap stock to large-cap stock or the reverse.

⋀⋀ CASE STUDY | Style investing became increasingly popular in the 1980s and 1990s as a growing number of investment managers decided they could improve performance by rotating their portfolios among various investment segments. Rather than limiting their investments to only growth stock or only value stock, managers attempt to make gains by moving from one segment to another as conditions warranted. Style investing is based on the belief that certain identifiable equity segments do well over time but do not necessarily do well at the same time. For example, growth stock beats value stock during some periods, while value stock outperforms growth stock during other periods. Likewise, small-cap stock outperforms large-cap stock during certain market periods, with the converse also being true. A portfolio manager who practices style investing rotates from one equity segment to another depending on that manager's view of the market. For example, a manager may feel that a substantial decline in consumer confidence indicates a portfolio should be heavily weighted toward value stock. Successful style investing assumes the portfolio manager can accurately forecast which segments of the market will produce superior returns. Critics argue that style investing increases transaction costs and relies on the faulty assumption that investment managers have predictive abilities.

Subchapter M The portion of the Internal Revenue Service Code that addresses the ways by which investment companies and investment trusts may pass income through to owners in order to avoid double taxation.

subindex An index based on a particular category of components that make up a larger index. For example, the Nasdaq Composite Index is subdivided into 11 subindexes for categories including banks, computers, industrials, insurance, and telecommunications. Subindexes provide an indication of how particular segments of the market are performing.

subject quote —See NOMINAL QUOTE.

subject to opinion An audit opinion by a certified public accountant that a firm's financial statements are fairly presented subject to the outcome of an uncertain future event. A major lawsuit, the outcome of which could significantly affect the firm, may be unresolved at the time of the audit; such a situation is an example of a factor influencing the opinion.

subordinated debenture An unsecured bond with a claim to assets that is subordinate to all existing and future debt. Thus, in the event that the issuer encounters financial difficulties and must be liquidated, all other claims must be satisfied before holders of subordinated debentures can receive a settlement. Frequently, this settlement amounts to relatively little. Because of the risk involved, the issuers have to pay relatively high interest rates in order to sell these securities to investors. Many issues of these debentures include a sweetener such as the right to exchange the securities for shares of common stock. The sweeteners are included so that interest rates on the subordinated debentures can be reduced below the level that would be required without them. Subordinated debentures without the conversion option appeal to risk-oriented investors seeking high current yields. —See also CONVERTIBLE SECURITY.

subscribe To use rights for ordering securities sold as a new issue.

subscription period The span of time during which a new issue of securities may be bought by investors. A subscription period will typically last a week or two, after which the rights to subscribe will expire at no value.

subscription price The price at which rights holders may acquire shares in a new securities issue. The subscription price is usually set at slightly less than the market price so as to ensure that it will be successfully sold. —Compare OVERSUBSCRIPTION PRIVILEGE. —See also RIGHTS OFFERING.

subscription privilege —See PREEMPTIVE RIGHT.

subscription ratio The number of rights required to purchase a single share of a security in a rights offering.

subscription right —See RIGHT.

subscription warrant —See WARRANT.

subsidiary A company controlled or owned by another company. For example, the trucking company Overnite Transportation is a wholly owned subsidiary of Union Pacific Corporation. If a subsidiary is wholly owned, all its stock is held by the parent company. —Compare HOLDING COMPANY; PARENT COMPANY.

substitute —See SWAP.

substitution bond swap The sale of one bond combined with the purchase of another virtually identical bond that offers a slightly higher yield.

sucker rally A sharp, abbreviated upturn in stock prices that occurs during a major bear market.

suicide pill A poison pill provision so devastating to the target of a takeover attempt that the target company may have to be liquidated to satisfy its creditors. For example, the company's directors may institute a suicide pill giving stockholders the right to exchange their stock for debt if a raider acquires more than a specified percentage of the company's outstanding shares. The tremendous increase in debt will effectively doom the target company if the takeover attempt is successful.

suitability rule A National Association of Securities Dealers guideline that requires a brokerage firm to have reasonable grounds for believing a recommendation fits the investment needs of a client. —See also RULE 405.

suitor A company that offers to purchase another firm.

sunk cost A past outlay or loss that cannot be altered by current or future actions.

Super Bowl rule A technical indicator that holds that if a team from the American Football Conference wins the Super Bowl, the stock market will decline during the year, but if a team from the National Football Conference wins the Super Bowl, the stock market will experience an up year.

SuperDOT A New York Stock Exchange system for automatically routing market and limit orders to the appropriate specialist. SuperDOT eliminates the need for clerks and floor brokers to handle modest-sized orders.

super DRIP A dividend reinvestment plan that offers direct purchase of a firm's shares. A super DRIP allows an investor to buy initial shares from the firm, often with no transaction charge. —Also called *no-load DRIP*.

supermajority provision A part of a corporation's by-laws that requires an unusually high percentage of stockholder votes in order to bring about certain changes. For example, a firm may require that 80% of shares approve a resolution to call a meeting of stockholders for any purpose other than the annual meeting. This provision makes a corporate takeover more difficult. —See also BOARD-OUT CLAUSE.

SuperMontage A Nasdaq trading platform introduced in late 2002 to compete with systems used by electronic communications networks such as Instinet. The new platform was designed to provide better organization of data for security traders.

super NOW account An interest-bearing checking account that pays a higher return and requires a higher minimum balance than a standard NOW account. These accounts have not gained much popularity.

super sinker A housing revenue bond issue in which mortgage prepayments are used to retire a specified maturity. Although this particular maturity is far in the future, the bond is likely to be paid off in a relatively short period. Even though an investor in the specified maturity bond is unsure when the security may be retired, the annual return is likely to be relatively high for a short- to intermediate-term holding period.

supervoting stock A class of stock that provides its holders with larger than proportionate voting rights compared with another class of stock issued by the same company. For example, Dow Jones & Company has two classes of common stock: supervoting Class B has ten votes per share compared to the firm's regular common stock with one vote per share. At the end of 2001 Class B shares composed only about 20% of outstanding common stock but enjoyed nearly three quarters of the total voting power. Supervoting stock permits a limited number of stockholders to retain or gain control of a company without having to own more than 50% of all common stock outstanding. —Compare LIMITED-VOTING STOCK. —Also called *control stock.*

supply-demand analysis A technical evaluation of securities on the basis of factors affecting the supply of and demand for a particular security or securities in general. Supply-demand analysis is supposed to determine if an imbalance exists or will exist between supply and demand for securities. For example, if the supply of a security is expected to exceed demand, the security should be sold or not purchased because its price can be expected to decline. Supply-demand analysis incorporates information on new stock offerings, government borrowing, contributions to pension funds, mutual fund cash balances, and a number of other similar factors.

supply-side economics The branch of economics that concentrates on measures to increase output of goods and services in the long run. The basis of supply-side economics is that marginal tax rates should be reduced to provide incentives to supply additional labor and capital, and thereby promote long-term growth.

support Increased demand for a security. —Compare RESISTANCE.

support level A price at which a security or the market will receive considerable buying pressure. Technical analysts believe demand at the support level will tend to keep a stock's price from falling below the support-level price. A support level develops as investors miss purchasing a stock just before a price rise and resolve to buy the stock if it again reaches that level. —Compare RESISTANCE LEVEL.

surety bond An insurance fee required before a duplicate security is issued to replace one that has been lost. The fee is approximately 4% of the market value of the security to be replaced.

surplus 1. Equity in excess of par value. Surplus includes additional paid-in capital and retained earnings. 2. —See RETAINED EARNINGS.

surrender value —See CASH SURRENDER VALUE.

surveillance department The division of a securities exchange charged with ensuring that individuals associated with the exchange operate in an ethical manner and according to established regulations.

surviving company The company that emerges in control following a business combination. The surviving company is generally one of the firms entering the combination but may be a new company formed by the combination. For example, BP, formerly British Petroleum, was the surviving company from the merger of British Petroleum and Amoco Corporation.

suspended trading The temporary suspension of trading in a security. Trading in a security may be suspended if, for instance, a major announcement by the issuing company is expected to influence significantly the security's price. The temporary halt in trading is intended to give the financial community enough time to hear the news. —Also called *trading halt.*

swap A contract in which two parties agree to exchange periodic interest payments. In the most common type of swap arrangement, one party agrees to pay fixed interest payments on designated dates to a counterparty who, in turn, agrees to make return interest payments that float with some reference rate such as the rate on Treasury bills or the prime rate. —Also called *interest rate swap.* —See also COUNTERPARTY RISK.

swap To trade one asset for another. —Also called *exchange; substitute; switch.*

swap order A specialized security order in which a customer specifies that two transactions be made only if a given price differential can be achieved. For example, an investor might specify that 500 shares of one security be purchased and 500 shares of another security be sold only if the former can be executed for $5 per share less than the latter. —Also called *switch order.*

swaption An option taken on an interest-rate swap. A swaption buyer has the right to enter into an interest-rate swap agreement by a specified date.

sweep To automatically move cash balances into an interest-earning money market fund. Certain brokerage firms offer to perform this activity for some or all of their accounts.

sweep account —See ASSET MANAGEMENT ACCOUNT.

sweetener An addition to a security that makes it more appealing to investors. One popular sweetener is the addition of warrants (options to buy stock) to a bond in order to make the bond marketable with a lower interest cost.

sweetheart deal A collusive, unethical transaction between two parties.

swing loan —See BRIDGE LOAN.

switch 1. —See SWAP. 2. To move funds out of one mutual fund and into another mutual fund. —See also TELEPHONE SWITCHING.

switch order —See SWAP ORDER.

SWX Swiss Exchange An all-electronic securities exchange formed from the 1995 merger of exchanges in Geneva, Basel, and Zurich. The exchange offers trading in equity securities, investment funds, exchange-traded funds, bonds, Eurobonds, and options.

syndicate A combination of investment banking firms that bids on a new security issue and then sells it if the bid is successful. The syndicate disbands when the security offering has been completed. Syndicates are needed to spread the risk and obtain greater financial and marketing resources for large issues. —Also called *purchase group; underwriting syndicate.* —See also AGREEMENT AMONG UNDERWRITERS; BREAKING THE SYNDICATE; SELLING GROUP.

syndicate To distribute shares of ownership in a partnership or joint venture. For example, a brokerage firm may syndicate ownership in certain oil and gas properties.

syndicate manager A major underwriting firm that forms a syndicate in order to distribute a security issue to the public. The manager allocates the securities among other firms in the group but is itself generally responsible for the largest share of the issue.

synergy An increase in the value of assets as a result of their combination. Expected synergy is the justification behind most business mergers. For example, General Motors purchased Electronic Data Systems in 1984 with the expectation that considerable synergy would result.

synthetic asset The combination of securities and/or assets in such a way that they produce the same financial effect as the ownership of an entirely different asset would. For example, selling a put option and buying a call option on a commodity produce the same financial effect as actually owning the underlying commodity.

synthetic call The combination of a commodity and a put option on the commodity with the effect being the same as owning a call option.

synthetic lease A financing method that confers certain aspects of ownership to the lessee, who, for accounting purposes, treats the arrangement as an operating lease. Neither the asset nor the lease is included on the lessee's balance sheet. A synthetic lease is a type of off-balance-sheet financing that results in a company understating its financial obligations.

synthetic put The combination of a call option on a commodity and the short sale of the same commodity with the effect being the same as the purchase of a put option.

synthetic short sale The purchase of a put and the simultaneous sale of a call on the same security. This combination produces the same results as a short sale of the underlying stock; that is, unlimited potential gains for a downward price movement of the stock and unlimited potential losses for an upward movement of the stock.

synthetic stock The purchase of a call and simultaneous sale of a put on the same stock. This combination produces unlimited potential gains if the stock rises but unlimited potential losses if the stock falls—the same results as if the stock were owned.

systematic risk Risk caused by factors that affect the prices of virtually all securities, although in different proportions. Examples include changes in interest rates and consumer prices. Although it is not possible to eliminate systematic risk through diversification, it is possible to reduce it by acquiring securities (for example, those of utilities and many blue chips) that have histories of relatively slowly changing prices. —Compare UNSYSTEMATIC RISK. —Also called *market risk; nondiversifiable risk.* —See also BETA.

systematic withdrawal plan —See WITHDRAWAL PLAN.

T

t 1. —Used in the dividend column of stock transaction tables in newspapers to indicate the market value as of the distribution date of stock dividends paid during the preceding 12 months. Stocks with this listing paid no cash dividends: *Jetron .71t.* **2.** —Used in bond transaction tables in newspapers to indicate a floating-rate bond or note: *Amoco 8.05s89t.*

TAB —See TAX ANTICIPATION BILL.

TAC bond —See TARGETED AMORTIZATION CLASS BOND.

tag ends The remaining securities in a new issue that has been largely sold.

tail 1. In a bid for a new security issue, the portion of the bid price that follows the decimal. For example, a bid of $92.125 has a tail of .125. **2.** The difference between the average bid and the lowest bid at an auction for Treasury securities.

tailgating The placement of an order by a registered representative for the registered representative's own account on the basis of an order that has been received from a client. Suppose a customer calls a registered representative with an order to sell 1,000 shares of stock. If the representative sells the stock for the customer and follows it by selling additional shares of the same stock for his or her own personal account, the representative is tailgating.

take To accept the price at which a dealer offers a security.

take a bath To lose a large portion of the money invested in a particular asset, such as during a prolonged bear market.

take a position —See POSITION.

take-away acquisition The purchase of a company that has an outstanding offer to be acquired by another firm. For example, General Electric attempted to acquire Honeywell International for $45 billion shortly after Honeywell had received a $40 billion offer from United Technologies. Take-away acquisitions can be risky for the acquiring firm, which often has insufficient time to conduct a thorough analysis of the acquired company.

take delivery 1. To accept a commodity to be delivered as part of a long futures contract. For example, the buyer of a gold futures contract who will need the metal on the delivery date may plan to take delivery rather than close out the contract. **2.** To accept certificates for securities that have been purchased.

takedown 1. An investment banker's share of a new security offering. **2.** The price paid by an underwriter for securities to be sold as part of a new issue.

take-or-pay agreement A contractual agreement in which one party agrees to purchase a specific amount of another party's goods or services or to pay the equivalent cost even if the goods or services are not needed. Take-or-pay contracts are frequently employed by electric utilities, which use the agreements as collateral for loans to build electric generating plants.

take out **1.** The extra funds generated in an account when an investor sells one block of securities and buys another block at a lower total cost. For example, a customer may sell $50,000 face amount of bonds at 85 and then purchase $50,000 face amount of a different bond at 80. **2.** A bid for a seller's remaining position in a security.

take-out merger —See CLEANUP MERGER.

takeover The acquisition of controlling interest in a firm. Although the term is often used to refer to acquisition by a party hostile to the target's management, many takeovers are friendly. —See also FRIENDLY TAKEOVER; RAIDER; UNFRIENDLY TAKEOVER.

takeover defense —See SHARK REPELLENT.

takeover stock A stock that, for various reasons, has good potential for being taken over by another firm. In 1985, companies engaged in radio and television broadcasting were considered potential takeover targets; as a result, their stock achieved significant price gains. —See also IN PLAY; SPLIT-UP VALUE.

takeover target —See TARGET COMPANY.

taking off a leg —See LEG LIFTING.

taking profits —See PROFIT TAKING.

TAN —See TAX ANTICIPATION NOTE.

tandem The entering into two trades at the same time. An investor who sells a July futures contract and buys a September futures contract is engaging in a tandem trade.

tangible asset An asset such as a building or piece of equipment that has physical properties. —Compare INTANGIBLE ASSET. —Also called *hard asset.* —See also NET TANGIBLE ASSETS PER SHARE.

tape —See TICKER TAPE.

tape is late —See LATE TAPE.

tape racing An illegal transaction technique in which a registered representative takes advantage of a large customer order by transacting business for a personal account before transacting the customer's order. A registered representative with a significant order likely to affect the price of a security can take personal advantage of that situation by tape racing.

tape reader A trader who reads the consolidated tape in order to observe stock price and volume reports and then uses the information to make trading decisions.

target company A firm that is the object of a specific action unwanted by its management, such as a takeover attempt or an antitrust suit. —Compare RAIDER. —Also called *takeover target.* —See also IN PLAY; TAKEOVER; TOEHOLD PURCHASE.

targeted amortization class bond (TAC bond) A debt security that is a specific tranche from a collateralized mortgage obligation. A TAC bond is protected against prepayments and has greater cash flow certainty than the underlying collateralized mortgage obligation.

Targeted Growth Enhanced Terms Securities^{SM} **(TARGETS**^{SM}**)** Trust-issued preferred stock issued by Smith Barney that provides the growth potential of an underlying stock subject to a quarterly appreciation cap of approximately 20%. TARGETS cannot be redeemed by the holder or called by the issuer prior to the scheduled maturity.

target fund A specialized self-liquidating mutual fund that invests in bonds maturing around a specific date. After the last maturity, the fund distributes its assets to the owners and ceases business. The limited life of the fund makes it much like a unit trust except that the portfolio is managed. An annual management fee is charged.

target-payout fund An investment company that distributes a minimum percentage of its assets each year. In years of poor investment performance, a target-payout fund will be required to return to shareholders a portion of their capital since income is unlikely to cover the required payout. These funds are aimed at investors seeking current income.

target price **1.** The price that an investor or a security analyst expects a security to achieve. Generally, when a security achieves the target price, it is time to close out a position in it. **2.** The price at which an investor hopes to purchase an asset. For example, a company desiring to take over another firm may set a target price for the firm.

TARGETS^{SM} —See TARGETED GROWTH ENHANCED TERMS SECURITIES^{SM}.

tariff A tax levied on a good imported into a country. In most instances, tariffs are intended to make imported goods more expensive and thus less competitive with domestic products. —Also called *duty*. —See also GENERAL AGREEMENT ON TARIFFS AND TRADE; TRIGGER PRICE.

taxable income The income that is subject to taxation. Taxable income remains after accounting for adjustments and deductions.

taxable municipal bond A municipal bond in which interest paid to the bondholder does not qualify as tax-exempt for federal tax purposes because of the use to which the bond proceeds are put by the municipal borrower. Taxable municipal bonds were reissued in 1986, the first issue since 1913, because of limitations placed on municipal obligations by tax reform. Although taxable municipal bonds are subject to federal taxation, most are not subject to taxation by the state in which the municipal issuer is located. Taxable municipal bonds are generally more appropriate for pension funds and other tax-exempt investors than for individual investors.

tax anticipation bill (TAB) A short-term U.S. Treasury obligation that is issued at a discount and that may be used at face value upon maturity or a few days before to pay a federal tax obligation. These securities appeal primarily to corporations and relatively large investors with significant tax obligations.

tax anticipation note (TAN) A short-term municipal obligation that is sold to provide funds for government operations until taxes have been received. At that time the receipts are used to repay the debt. These generally low-risk securities appeal primarily to larger investors.

tax avoidance The reduction of a tax liability by legal means. For example, high-income individuals avoid significant federal income taxes by purchasing and holding municipal bonds. —Compare TAX EVASION.

tax base The resources that are available for taxation. An evaluation of the tax base is of particular importance in certain municipal bond issues secured by tax revenues.

tax basis —See BASIS 2.

tax bracket —See MARGINAL TAX RATE.

Tax Court A federal court established to resolve disputes between taxpayers and the Internal Revenue Service.

tax credit A reduction in the amount of taxes owed. For example, corporations are permitted a credit on U.S. taxes for taxes paid to foreign governments, and individuals could, for a number of years, claim a tax credit for a portion of expenditures for certain energy-saving home improvements. A tax credit is more valuable than a deduction of an equal amount because the credit results in a reduction in tax owed rather than a reduction in taxable income. —See also FOREIGN TAX CREDIT.

tax deduction —See DEDUCTION.

tax deferral The delay of a tax liability until a future date. For example, an IRA may result in a tax deferral on the amount contributed to the IRA and on any income earned on funds in the IRA until withdrawals are made. At the corporate level, accelerated depreciation of assets results in a delay in tax liabilities. Tax deferral, which is legal, means a postponement, not an elimination, of a tax liability.

tax-deferred annuity —See TAX-SHELTERED ANNUITY.

tax-deferred income The income that is earned but that is neither received nor taxed until a later date. For example, interest earned on U.S. Treasury bills is received and taxed at maturity. Likewise, U.S. savings bonds provide appreciation of value on which holders may defer paying taxes until the security is cashed in. —Compare TAX-FREE INCOME; TAX-SHELTERED INCOME.

tax-efficient fund A mutual fund that manages its investment portfolio so as to minimize the tax liability of its shareholders. A tax-efficient fund attempts to minimize capital gains distributions by reducing portfolio turnover and to minimize dividend payments to shareholders by concentrating on investments in companies with low dividend payouts.

tax-equivalent yield The pretax yield that provides the same return as a specified aftertax yield. Tax-equivalent yield is calculated by dividing tax-free yield by the difference obtained from subtracting the applicable tax rate from 1. For example, for an investor who pays taxes at a rate of 40%, an aftertax yield of 6% has a tax-equivalent yield of $0.06/(1 - 0.4)$, or 10%.

tax evasion The illegal avoidance of taxes. The intentional omission of a gain from the sale of stock in reporting income to the Internal Revenue Service is an example of tax evasion. —Compare TAX AVOIDANCE.

tax-exempt bond —See MUNICIPAL BOND.

tax-exempt money market fund An open-end investment company that invests in short-term tax-exempt securities. These funds usually pay relatively low current income (free of federal taxes) but are very liquid. They appeal to higher-income investors who seek a temporary investment. —Also called *short-term municipal bond fund.*

tax-free exchange An exchange of assets between taxpayers in which any gain or loss is not recognized in the period during which the exchange takes place. Rather, taxpayers are required to adjust the basis of assets exchanged.

tax-free income The income received but not subject to income taxes. For example, interest from most municipal bonds is free of federal income taxes and often from state and local income taxes as well. —Compare TAX-DEFERRED IN-COME; TAX-SHELTERED INCOME.

tax haven A country or other political entity that offers outside businesses and individuals a climate of minimal or nonexistent taxation. In some cases, the low taxes apply not only to those levied by the tax haven itself but also to the possibility of reducing or avoiding taxes levied in the investor's home country.

tax indexing —See INDEX.

tax loss carryback —See CARRYBACK.

tax loss carryforward —See CARRYFORWARD 1.

tax-loss selling The sale of securities that have declined in value in order to realize losses that may be used to reduce taxable income. Tax-loss selling occurs near the end of a calendar year so that the loss can be used in that tax year to offset ordinary income or gains on other security transactions. Thus, tax-loss selling occurs mainly among stock that has declined in price. —Compare TAX SELLING.

tax-managed mutual fund A mutual fund that is managed so as to maximize the aftertax return rather than the pretax return of its shareholders. Capital gains distributions are minimized by low portfolio turnover and an attempt by the portfolio manager to offset realized gains with realized losses.

taxpayer identification number (TIN) For an individual, his or her Social Security number. For a business or fiduciary, its Employer Identification Number.

tax preference item An item that can be legally omitted in order to reduce taxable income when calculating an individual's tax liability by ordinary means. However, the item must be included when calculating the individual's alternative minimum tax. For example, interest paid by certain municipal bonds that is ordinarily omitted in calculating taxable income must be included when calculating the alternative minimum tax.

tax rate The proportional amount of taxes paid on a given income or the given dollar value of an asset. If the tax is calculated on the basis of total income, it is the average tax rate. If the tax is calculated only on extra units of income, the rate is the marginal tax rate.

Tax Reform Act of 1986 Tax legislation that significantly reduced marginal income tax rates for individuals and corporations as well as curtailed many deductions and eliminated numerous preference items. The Act was designed to be revenue-neutral and, in general, it benefited high-income and low-income individuals and corporations that do not spend large amounts of money on long-lived equipment. Although an original goal had been to simplify the tax system, no simplification was evident in the final legislation.

tax selling The sale of securities to establish gains or losses for income-tax purposes. Significant tax selling often occurs in December, especially following a bear market, as investors seek losses to offset previous gains or other income. An investor may engage in tax selling to establish gains when he or she expects to be paying a higher marginal tax rate the following year. —Compare TAX-LOSS SELLING.

tax shelter   An investment that produces relatively large current deductions that can be used to offset other taxable income. Popular tax shelters include real estate projects and gas and oil drilling ventures. —Also called *shelter.* —See also ABUSIVE TAX SHELTER.

tax-sheltered annuity (TSA)   A retirement plan that permits an employee of a tax-exempt charitable, educational, or religious institution to contribute a certain portion of wages or salary into a tax-sheltered fund. Contributions serve to reduce taxable income in the year they are contributed. Taxes on income earned in the plan are deferred. Both past contributions and income are fully taxable when withdrawals are made. —Also called *403(b) plan; tax-deferred annuity.*

tax-sheltered income   The income that is received and would ordinarily be taxable but, because of certain noncash deductions such as depreciation, is protected from taxation. For example, rent that has been earned from a rental property is generally sheltered by depreciation on the property. —Compare TAX-DEFERRED INCOME; TAX-FREE INCOME.

tax straddle   A combination of two similar futures contracts (one bought and one sold) that tend to move in opposite directions so that a loss on one is offset by a gain in the other. The contract showing the loss is sold in the current year (shortly before year's end), while the contract showing the gain is sold in the next year. The net effect is to push taxes back one year. This practice ended with legislation that requires all gains and losses in futures contracts to be realized for tax purposes at the end of each year. —Compare MARK TO THE MARKET.

tax swap   The sale of a security that has declined in price since the purchase date and the simultaneous purchase of a similar, but not substantially identical, security. The purpose of the swap is to achieve a loss for tax purposes while continuing to maintain market position. —See also WASH SALE 1.

tax umbrella   A corporation's tax loss carryforwards that may be used to shelter profits in future years.

tax year   The 12-month period for which tax is calculated. For most individual taxpayers, the tax year is synonymous with the calendar year.

T bill   —See TREASURY BILL.

tear sheet   A page from one of the security reports published by Standard & Poor's in loose-leaf binders. Customers frequently ask registered representatives to send them tear sheets on particular securities.

technical analysis   The study of relationships among security market variables, such as price levels, trading volume, and price movements, so as to gain insights into the supply and demand for securities. Rather than concentrating on earnings, the economic outlook, and other business-related factors that influence a security's value, technical analysis attempts to determine the market forces at work on a certain security or on the securities market as a whole. —Compare FUNDAMENTAL ANALYSIS.

technical correction   A temporary downturn in the price of a stock or in the market itself following a period of extensive price increases. A technical correction takes place in a generally increasing market when there is no particular reason that the increases should be interrupted other than the fact that investors have temporarily slowed securities purchases.

technical default Default under an indenture agreement for other than non-payment of interest or principal. For example, a borrower may fail to maintain a stipulated level of net working capital.

technical indicator A variable used when technically analyzing the market to determine when to invest and which stocks to select. Technical indicators include chart formations, volume, and odd-lot sales.

technically strong —Used to describe a security or the whole market when most technical indicators point toward a price rise. For example, a stock may be technically strong because it has twice attempted and failed to break through a support level.

technically weak —Used to describe a security or the whole market when technical indicators point toward a price decline. For example, small investors may step up odd-lot purchases of securities, the number of stocks hitting new highs may be small, and market volume on days the averages are rising may be light. Together these things indicate a technically weak stock market.

technical rally A temporary rise in a security price or in the general market during a downward trend. Technical rallies are considered interruptions to a general trend.

technician A person who uses technical analysis to determine the selection and timing of security purchases and sales. —Compare FUNDAMENTALIST. —Also called *market technician.* —See also CHARTIST.

TEDIS An acronym for a type of municipal convertible bond.

TED spread The price spread that occurs when opposing transactions are made in Treasury bill futures and Eurodollar futures as, for example, a long position in Treasury bill futures coupled with a short position in Eurodollar futures. A long spread that anticipates the price spread between the two contracts will widen could involve buying a T-bill future and simultaneously selling a Eurodollar future. A short spread in which a Eurodollar future is purchased and a T-bill future is sold short would anticipate a narrowing of the price spread.

telephone booth One of several telephone-containing cubicles located around the perimeter of the trading floor of the New York Stock Exchange. Telephones in these booths are used by member firms to receive orders that are to be executed on the floor. Once the orders have been executed, the telephones are used to transmit information back to the members' offices.

telephone switching The movement of an investor's funds from one mutual fund to another mutual fund on the basis of an order given via telephone.

tenancy by the entirety A type of asset ownership limited to married couples in which each spouse holds an equal share of the asset but neither may sell or give away an interest without the other's permission. If one spouse dies, the deceased's share automatically passes to the surviving spouse. —Compare TENANCY IN COMMON.

tenancy in common A type of asset ownership for two or more persons in which, upon the death of one owner, his or her share passes to heirs if a will is left or to the estate if no will is left, rather than to the co-owners. Transactions

involving the property require written permission of all owners. —Compare
JOINT TENANCY WITH RIGHT OF SURVIVORSHIP; TENANCY BY THE ENTIRETY.

ten-day window The span of time between the point when an individual or a
company buys 5% or more of a firm's stock and the point at which the purchase
must be publicly reported.

tender To offer a security for sale to a party that is making an offer to buy it.
For example, a stockholder may decide to tender shares to the issuing firm as
part of the company's buyback. —See also HEDGED TENDER.

tender offer An offer made directly to stockholders to purchase or trade for
their securities. A tender offer often contains restrictions such as the minimum
number of shares required to be tendered for the offer to be effective or the
maximum number of tendered shares that will be accepted. A tender offer may
be made by a firm to its own shareholders to reduce the number of outstanding
shares, or it may be made by an outsider wishing to obtain control of the firm.
—Compare HOSTILE TENDER OFFER. —See also CREEPING TENDER OFFER; EXCLUSION-
ARY TENDER OFFER; MINI-TENDER OFFER; PARTIAL TENDER OFFER; SELF-TENDER; TWO-TIER
TENDER OFFER; WILLIAMS ACT.

10-K An annual report of a firm's operations filed with the SEC. Compared
with the typical annual report sent to stockholders, a 10-K is much less physically attractive; however, it contains many more detailed operating and financial statistics, including information on legal proceedings and management
compensation. A firm's stockholders may obtain a free copy of the 10-K by writing to the corporate treasurer. —Also called *Form 10-K.*

1099-DIV An annual statement to investors and to the Internal Revenue Service by payers of dividends that lists the amount of taxable dividend payments
for the year. Also included, if appropriate, is any backup withholding required
by law.

1099-INT An annual statement to savers and the Internal Revenue Service that
shows the amount of taxable interest payments received from an institution
during the year. Interest included on 1099-INT forms includes interest paid on
savings accounts, money market funds, interest-bearing checking accounts,
and taxable bonds. Municipal bond interest is not included on a 1099-INT form.

1099-OID An annual report sent to investors and the Internal Revenue Service
that lists interest income from taxable original-issue discount securities. The
form, which originated during the 1984 tax year, reports the amount of implied
and real income derived from original-issue discount securities such as Treasury bills, zero-coupon bonds, and commercial paper. Income shown on a
1099-OID is to be included on Part I in Schedule D of an investor's federal income tax return.

10-Q A quarterly unaudited financial report filed by firms that have securities
listed with the SEC. The 10-Q is a less detailed, more frequently filed version of
the 10-K. —Also called *Form 10-Q.*

tentative order A customer order that is made for part of a new securities issue
before all the terms of the issue have been set. Underwriters take tentative orders to determine investor interest in a new issue. This practice assists the underwriters in pricing and sizing the issue.

term **1.** The period during which a bond will remain outstanding. **2.** The length of time that a person is to serve in a usually official capacity. For example, a firm's directors may be elected for terms of three years each.

term bonds Any of various bonds that mature on the same date. Corporate bond issues are often of the term variety because all the bonds of a given issue are scheduled to mature simultaneously. Municipalities often issue a combination of serial and term bonds with periodic retirements of serial bonds and then a redemption of a block of term bonds during the final year. —See also SERIAL BONDS.

term certificate A certificate of deposit with a maturity of one year or more.

terminable marital trust A trust in which the surviving spouse has use of the trust's income but not its assets. These assets will pass to others (most likely children) at the death of the spouse.

terminal value The dollar value of an asset at a specific future time. For example, a $1,000 certificate of deposit that earns an annual return of 9% has a terminal value of $1,539 in five years.

termination fee The one-time charge for terminating or transferring an individual retirement account. If a financial institution charges a termination fee, the fee must be spelled out in the original agreement that is signed when the account is opened. Some institutions, particularly banks and savings and loans, may not charge termination fees.

term insurance A type of life insurance in which the insurance company pays a specified sum if the insured dies during the coverage period. Term insurance includes no savings, cash values, borrowing power, or benefits at retirement. On the basis of cost, it is the very least expensive insurance available, although policy prices can vary significantly among firms. —Compare CASH-VALUE LIFE INSURANCE.

term structure of interest rates —See YIELD CURVE.

term to maturity The number of years within which the issuer of debt promises to meet the requirements of an indenture agreement. Bonds with longer terms to maturity are subject to greater price fluctuations than short-term securities are. —See also YIELD CURVE.

territory bond A bond issued by a U.S. territory such as Guam, Puerto Rico, and the Virgin Islands. Interest from territory bonds is generally exempt from taxation by federal, state, and local authorities anywhere in the U.S.

test The attempt by a stock price or a stock market average to break through a support level or a resistance level. For example, a stock that has declined to $20 on several occasions without moving lower may be expected to test this support level once again. Failing to fall below $20 one more time would be considered a successful test of the support level and a bullish sign for the stock.

testamentary trust A trust created by a person's will, thereby not effective until the death of the testator. Testamentary trusts are used chiefly by wealthy individuals who are concerned about their beneficiaries' ability to administer large amounts of assets.

theme fund An investment company that chooses investments according to a particular issue or theme. For example, a fund built on an agricultural theme might invest in the equities of farm equipment manufacturers, chemical companies, and other firms that sell agricultural products. Likewise, an investment company might choose to invest in equities that would reflect an ecological or baby-boomer theme.

theoretical value The calculated price at which a security should sell. Depending upon investor expectations and market imperfections, a security may sell at a price above or below its theoretical value.

the Street —See WALL STREET.

theta The sensitivity of an option's market value relative to a change in the time to expiration. Theta is a measure of time decay and tends to grow larger as an option approaches expiration.

thinly traded security A security that trades with little volume. Institutional investors usually exclude these securities from their portfolios because of the large price changes that would occur if trades of any significant size took place.

thin market A market for a security in which there are relatively few offers and bids. A thin market causes reduced liquidity and makes it more difficult to buy or sell the security without affecting its price. —Compare DEEP MARKET; TIGHT MARKET. —Also called *narrow market.*

third market The over-the-counter dealer market in stock that is listed on organized exchanges such as the New York Stock Exchange. The third market developed in the 1960s when institutional investors became dissatisfied with the liquidity and brokerage commissions for large security trades on the exchanges. —Compare FOURTH MARKET; SECONDARY MARKET.

third market maker A firm that stands ready to buy or sell at publicly quoted prices a stock listed for trading on an exchange. A broker may send a customer order for stock listed on an exchange to a third market maker for execution.

thirty-day visible supply Municipal securities that will be issued within 30 days.

Thomson Financial A major provider of information, analytical tools, and consulting services to the financial community. The firm, a division of Thomson Corporation, is best known to investors for its First Call segment, which publishes consensus earnings estimates. —See also FIRST CALL.

three steps and stumble rule The principle that security prices will decline following three consecutive increases by the Federal Reserve in the discount rate it charges commercial banks. The rule stems from the negative effect rising interest rates have on security prices.

thrift A financial institution that derives its funds primarily from consumer savings accounts. The term originally referred to those institutions offering mainly passbook savings accounts. But the industry evolved through financial deregulation to the point where these accounts often provide only a small source of funds for many thrifts. The term often refers to savings and loan associations, but can also mean credit unions and mutual savings banks.

throwaway —See FOR YOUR INFORMATION.

Thundering Herd A commonly used reference to the firm Merrill Lynch, Pierce, Fenner and Smith, Inc., that derives from the firm's large size and its use of bulls in its advertising.

tick A movement in the price or price quotation of a security or contract. —See also DOWNTICK; MINIMUM TICK; UPTICK.

TICK A short-term technical indicator that describes the difference between the number of stocks whose last sale occurred on an uptick and the number of stocks whose last sale occurred on a downtick. A high positive TICK is generally considered a short-term signal of a strong market. Contrarians consider a high positive TICK to have bearish implications.

ticker An automated quotation system on which security transactions are reported after they occur on an exchange floor. Even though the newer systems are electronic and no longer actually tick, the name of the old mechanical device has stuck.

ticker symbol The abbreviation by which a security appears on stock quotation machines. For example, T represents AT&T, GY represents GenCorp, C represents Citicorp, and CVG represents Convergys. Booklets containing the symbols are available at most brokerage offices, and symbols can also be found on many Internet sites.

ticker tape The narrow continuous rolls of paper on which stock transactions were printed before the electronic age made the old system obsolete. The term now refers to the flow of prices appearing on the tickers of brokerage firms. —Also called *tape.*

ticket —See ORDER TICKET.

tick test A test to measure the extent to which a floor trader has stabilized security prices by trading against market trends, such as the extent to which transactions have been made against the trend as measured by purchases on downticks and sales on upticks.

tie-in agreement A requirement that investors purchase additional shares in the aftermarket as a condition of being allowed to acquire shares that are part of an initial public offering. Reports of this illegal activity by investment bankers were common during the new-issue boom of the late 1990s and early 2000s.

᠕᠕ **CASE STUDY** Initial public offerings can be a lucrative business for underwriters, especially during strong bull markets when capital-hungry companies want to tap the capital markets at the same time that individual and institutional investors are clamoring to acquire shares that are part of new stock issues. The heady days of the dot-com boom during 1998 through 2000 brought an increased level of investor demand for new common stock issues. Watching as new issues soared in price on initial trading immediately after they were brought to market caused even normally conservative investors to join the IPO mania. The huge demand for new issues apparently caused some underwriters to take advantage of the leverage they enjoyed in allocating shares among investors. Following up on investor complaints, the Securities and Exchange Commission, the regulatory unit of the National Association of Securities Dealers, and the U.S. Attorney's Office in Manhattan commenced an investigation of the allocation process in initial public offerings. In addition to charging certain underwriting firms with demanding inflated commissions or taking kickbacks, firms allegedly were also promoting tie-in agreements whereby customers who got IPO shares were required to purchase in the aftermarket additional shares of the same stock. The purpose of the tie-in was to create artificial demand to drive the price of the IPO higher in the secondary market. Tie-ins had for years been illegally used by retailers to earn extra income when particular items were in short supply. Now tie-ins were being used in initial public offerings.

tier A grouping of securities, usually by company size or security quality. —See also SECONDARY STOCK.

tiered market A securities market in which investors favor certain groups or types of stock, with the result that the favored securities sell at higher price-earnings ratios than do other securities with similar characteristics. Favored groups tend to rotate as investors' interests and perceptions change.

tight market A market for securities in which competition is intense and spreads are narrow. In a tight market, dealers must make up in volume what they lose on a narrowing of the spread. —Compare DEEP MARKET; THIN MARKET.

tight money A condition of the money supply in which credit is restricted and interest rates, consequently, are relatively high. Tight money generally has a negative effect on security prices, at least in the short run. —Compare EASY MONEY.

TIGR^{SM} A registered service mark of Merrill Lynch for financial investment services, namely, providing zero-coupon obligations evidencing an interest in U.S. government bonds. —See also COUPON STRIPPING.

time deposit An interest-bearing savings deposit or certificate of deposit at a financial institution. Although the deposits formerly included only deposits with specific maturities (such as certificates of deposit), they now are considered to include virtually all savings-type deposits. —Compare DEMAND DEPOSIT.

time draft A draft that is payable a certain number of days after it has been presented. —Compare SIGHT DRAFT.

time horizon The interval during which an investment program is to be completed. An investor's time horizon is very important in determining the types of investments that should be selected. For example, investments that would be appropriate for an individual's retirement in 30 years are seldom suitable for reaching a short-term goal. —Also called *horizon*.

time series A set of variables with values related to the respective times the variables are measured. Thus, a weekly record of a stock's price throughout a period of years is a time series. Time series are often used to project future values by observing how the value of a variable has changed in the past.

times fixed charges —See FIXED-CHARGE COVERAGE.

times interest earned —See INTEREST COVERAGE.

time spread —See CALENDAR SPREAD.

time stamping The stamping of order tickets with the time of entry and execution. For example, options exchanges require stamping of order tickets with the times of execution to the nearest minute.

time value The portion of an option premium in excess of the option's intrinsic value. A call option that allows the holder to buy 100 shares of a $25 stock for $20 (the strike price) has an intrinsic value of $500. The time value is $150 if the option trades for $650.

time value of money The concept that holds that a specific sum of money is more valuable the sooner it is received. Time value of money is dependent not only on the time interval being considered but also the rate of discount used in calculating current or future values.

time-weighted return A rate-of-return measure of portfolio performance that gives equal weight to each period included in the study regardless of any differences in amounts invested in each period.

timing —See MARKET TIMING.

timing difference The time difference between the point at which a transaction affects items for financial reporting purposes and the point at which it affects the same items for tax purposes. For example, purchase of a fixed asset depreciated by an accelerated method for tax purposes, but by straight-line for reporting purposes, creates a timing difference for depreciation expense.

TIN —See TAXPAYER IDENTIFICATION NUMBER.

tin parachute An employee-protection plan that guarantees severance pay, outplacement assistance, and health and life insurance benefits to all employees who lose their jobs because of a corporate takeover. A generous tin parachute serves to make a takeover more expensive and less likely.

tip Information unavailable to the general public that, if accurate, could produce extraordinary profits for an investor who acts on it in a security transaction.

tippee A person who is given inside information.

TIPS —See TREASURY INFLATION-PROTECTED SECURITIES.

tipster A person who provides inside information.

Tobin's Q —See Q RATIO.

toehold purchase The purchase of less than 5% of the outstanding common shares of a target company before establishing a much larger stake. A toehold purchase allows a party to buy stock in a company without filing a notice with the SEC and with the target company.

Tokyo Stock Exchange (TSE) The largest of six securities exchanges in Japan. The Tokyo Stock Exchange, established in 1878, trades equities electronically in four sections: the first section for stocks of the largest Japanese companies, the second section for stocks of smaller companies with lower trading volumes, the third section for foreign securities, and the fourth section for growth and emerging stocks. The Tokyo Stock Exchange also trades bonds, options, and futures.

tombstone An advertisement for a securities issue. The ad lists the security, some of the security's specifics, and a bracketed list of the members of the syndicate selling the issue in the order of the members' importance. The term derives from the fact that the notice appears as a matter of record after the sale has been completed.

top The highest level to which a stock, a market index, or some other asset will rise. A top may be short-term or long-term, depending upon the type of price movement being evaluated. —Compare BOTTOM.

top a bid To make a bid higher than the prevailing bid.

top-down investing Making investment decisions by first focusing on economic forecasts and then evaluating prospects for individual industries and companies. —Compare BOTTOM-UP INVESTING.

topper fee The penalty fee paid to a potential acquirer by a target company that accepts a higher subsequent offer from another firm. This special type of breakup fee is included in the acquisition agreement between the target company and the original acquiring firm that has been spurned.

CASE STUDY | In November 2001 Houston-based Dynegy, Inc., offered to buy crosstown rival Enron Corporation in an all-stock deal. At the time of the offer Enron was experiencing financial difficulties that grew worse later in the month. Both firms had the right to scuttle the deal in the event one or more of several specified events occurred. For example, Dynegy was permitted to change the terms or cancel the agreement if Enron faced a specific amount of litigation liabilities. The merger agreement permitted Enron to terminate the deal if the firm received a substantially better offer from another company. To terminate the agreement for a better offer Enron was required to pay Dynegy a $350 million topper fee.

Toronto Stock Exchange (TSE)   The main Canadian exchange for trading large-cap equity securities. The TSE moved from traditional floor trading to electronic trading in 1997 and in April 2000 demutualized to become a for-profit corporation. The Toronto Stock Exchange accounts for approximately 95% of all equity trading in Canada. Small-cap Canadian stocks are traded in Vancouver on the Canadian Venture Exchange.

total asset turnover   A financial ratio that indicates the effectiveness with which a firm's management uses its assets to generate sales. A relatively high ratio tends to reflect intensive use of assets. Total asset turnover is calculated by dividing the firm's annual sales by its total assets. Sales are listed on the firm's income statement and assets are listed on its balance sheet. —Also called *asset turnover.*

total capitalization   —See CAPITALIZATION.

total cost   The total amount of money expended to establish an investment position. Total cost includes commissions, accrued interest, and taxes, in addition to the principal amount of securities traded.

total return   The sum of dividend or interest income and any capital gain. Total return is generally considered a better measure of an investment's return than dividends or interest alone.

total volume   The aggregate amount of trading in a security on a particular security exchange, or in a specific type of security such as stocks, bonds, options, or futures contracts. —Also called *rate of return.*

Totten trust   A trust in which the assets are deposited for a beneficiary but the grantor has complete control of the trust, including the right to reclaim the assets. The assets pass to the beneficiary upon the death of the grantor but are taxed as part of the grantor's estate.

tout   To foster interest in a particular company or security. For example, a broker might tout a security to a client in the hope that the client will purchase the security.

tracking error   The difference in the return earned by a portfolio and the return earned by the benchmark against which the portfolio is constructed. For example, if a bond portfolio earns a return of 5.15% during a period when the portfolio's benchmark (say, for example, the Lehman Brothers Index) produces a return of 5.06%, the tracking error is .09%, or 9 basis points.

tracking stock   A common stock that provides holders with a financial interest in a particular segment of a company's business. Essentially, a tracking stock is a proxy for the value of the subsidiary if it were independent and publicly traded. Tracking stocks are generally issued by corporations that feel their firms are not being fully valued by investors.

⋀ CASE STUDY | In April 2000 General Motors Corporation offered owners of its $1²⁄₃ par value common stock an opportunity to exchange each of their shares for 1.065 shares of the firm's class H common stock. The company stated it would accept tenders of up to 86,396,977 shares, or approximately 14% of its outstanding common stock. Class H common was a tracking stock designed to provide holders with financial returns based on the financial performance of GM subsidiary Hughes, which General Motors would continue to control. Dividends to class H shareholders depended on the portion of Hughes's earnings allocated to the class H stock. Hughes's earnings were to be allocated based on a formula that incorporated the proportion of the class H stock outstanding (rather than held by GM). Dividends on class H stock were to be determined by the directors of General Motors. Owners of the class H shares had no claim on the assets of Hughes. Rather, they had rights in the assets of General Motors as common stockholders of GM, not Hughes. At the time of the exchange the company stated that GM directors had no plans to pay dividends on the class H shares in the foreseeable future. It also warned that under certain circumstances the class H shares were subject to being recapitalized into shares of the $1²⁄₃ par value common stock. In other words, GM shareholders who exchanged for the class H stock might be forced to convert back to the same stock they had given up in the initial exchange. General Motors later put its Hughes subsidiary up for sale.

trade The purchase or sale of an asset. —Also called *transaction.*

trade To buy or sell an asset, frequently with only short intervals of ownership.

trade date The date on which an order is executed. Payment or delivery must be made within five business days of the trade date. —Compare SETTLEMENT DATE. —Also called *transaction date.*

trade deficit The amount of goods and services that a country imports that is in excess of the amount of goods and services it exports. Large trade deficits may result in unemployment and a reduction in economic growth in the country with the deficit. —Compare TRADE SURPLUS.

trade-for-trade settlement A securities transaction that is directly settled by the buying and selling firms.

trademark A distinctive proprietary emblem, insignia, or name that identifies a particular product or service. A trademark is an intangible asset that may be protected from use by others.

trader A person who buys and sells securities with the goal of profiting from short-term price swings.

trade surplus The amount of goods and services that a country exports that is in excess of the amount of goods and services it imports. A trade surplus increases economic activity in a country but also may result in higher prices and interest rates if the economy is already operating at near capacity. —Compare TRADE DEFICIT.

trade through To transact an order on an exchange when a more advantageous price is available through another source.

trading authorization A written document that gives another party the power to enter orders for an investor's account. The other party may be an employee of the broker-dealer handling the account, a spouse, or someone else designated by the client in the trading authorization.

trading dividends   The purchase and sale of equity securities with the goal of maximizing dividend income. This practice is used primarily by corporate investors for which 80% of dividend income is tax-exempt.

trading gap   A period of time during which a security is not traded because of a wide gap between the bid and ask or because of an official halt triggered by a technical factor, such as the expected release of a major news story relating to the security.

trading halt   —See SUSPENDED TRADING.

trading limit   The number of commodity contracts that a person may trade during a single day. The limit is established by the Commodity Futures Trading Commission or by the exchange on which the particular contract is traded. —Compare POSITION LIMIT.

trading on the equity   The use of borrowed money to increase the return on an investor's capital. Suppose an investor is able to borrow 50% of the funds required for a $10,000 investment that returns 16% annually. If interest on the loan is 6%, the investor can earn $1,600 ($10,000 at 16%) minus interest of $300 ($5,000 at 6%), or $1,300 on an investment of $5,000 ($10,000 minus $5,000 borrowed), for a return of 26% ($1,300/$5,000).

trading on the perimeter   The trading of a security in the crowd around a specialist's post. When trading in a security becomes particularly active and floor brokers are unable to gain access to the specialist, trading on the perimeter may occur.

trading pattern   The systematic movement of a security's price during a period of time. Traders attempt to discover trading patterns and profit from them when buying and selling.

trading pool   A pool in which the stock is manipulated by purchases and sales in the open market. For example, pool operators affect a stock's price and volume by making purchases in the open market, thereby attracting the interest of other investors.

trading post   —See POST.

trading profit   The income derived from buying and selling a security at a profit within a relatively short-term period.

trading range   The high and low prices between which a specific stock or some stock average has been traded or is expected to trade.   —See also HISTORICAL TRADING RANGE.

trading ring   The area in the bond room of the New York Stock Exchange within which trading in bonds must take place.

trading unit   —See UNIT OF TRADING.

trading variation   —See MINIMUM TICK.

traditional governmental purpose bond   —See ESSENTIAL FUNCTION BOND.

trailer fee   —See TRAILING COMMISSION.

trailing commission   A commission paid annually to a sales agent for as long as a client's money remains in an account.   —Also called *trailer fee*.

transfer

Is it difficult to transfer my brokerage account to a different firm?

Transferring an account to another firm is relatively easy. The first step is to open an account at the new firm. Then sign an account transfer form, which will be provided by the new firm. A representative at the new firm should be able to provide assistance if you encounter any difficulties. The transfer should be completed within two weeks.

George Riles, First Vice President and Resident Manager, Merrill Lynch, Albany, GA

trailing earnings The earnings per share for a firm's most recently completed fiscal year.

trailing P/E The price-earnings ratio of a firm's common stock calculated as the current stock price divided by the previous year's earnings per share. —Compare FORWARD P/E.

trailing stop A stop order to sell (or to buy) a security in which subsequent stop orders are placed at progressively higher (or lower) levels as the stock price increases (or decreases). For example, an investor may purchase shares of Union Pacific Corporation at $60 and simultaneously place a stop order to sell the stock if it drops to $58 or below. If the stock rises to $63 without going through the $58 stop price, the investor raises the stop price to $61. Thus, the stop price trails the market price of the stock.

tranche A class of bonds. Collateralized mortgage obligations are structured with several tranches of bonds that have various maturities.

transaction —See TRADE.

transaction costs The expense incurred in buying or selling a security. Transaction costs include commissions, markups, markdowns, fees, and any direct taxes. Transaction costs, which are of special significance to investors who frequently trade securities, can vary substantially depending upon the firm with which the investor conducts business. —See also DISCOUNT BROKERAGE FIRM.

transaction date —See TRADE DATE.

transaction exposure The risk of loss caused by changes in currency exchange rates when a company's payables and receivables are denominated in a foreign currency. Derivatives are used to hedge against changes in currency exchange rates and reduce transaction exposure.

transfer 1. To record a change of ownership in a security on the issuer's books. 2. To deliver a security to the buyer's broker by the seller's broker.

transferable put right An option granted by a corporation to its shareholders that permits the shareholders to sell stock at a stipulated price back to the corporation. Shareholders who do not wish to exercise the options are permitted to sell the put rights to other investors. Issuing transferable put rights is an alternative to a tender offer or open market purchases as a form of share repurchase.

CASE STUDY In August 1988 Gillette Corporation announced the firm would issue transferable put rights in order to carry out the repurchase of a substantial amount of its common stock. The put rights were issued to Gillette shareholders of record as of August 12, 1988, and could be used to sell stock back to the company at $45 per share until September 19 of the same year. Gillette stock was trading for slightly less than $40 per share on the New York Stock Exchange at the time of the put issue. The right to sell shares back to the company for more than market price caused the puts to have substantial value on the date they were issued. The put rights were issued as part of a settlement with Coniston Partners, a firm that had initiated a proxy fight with Gillette. Gillette issued one put for each seven of its 112 million outstanding shares. Under the plan a shareholder with 1,000 Gillette shares received 143 puts (one for each seven shares owned) that permitted the shareholder to sell 143 shares for $45 each back to the firm. Alternatively, the shareholder could choose to sell the actively traded puts to another investor.

transfer agent A company, generally a bank or trust company, appointed by a firm to transfer that firm's securities. Security holders may send the security certificates directly to the transfer agents by registered mail. The security should be endorsed with a letter of instruction included. The firm's agent is listed on its certificates. The transfer agent is also likely to maintain the current record of security owners for transmitting dividends, reports, security distributions, and so forth.

transfer notice —See DELIVERY NOTICE.

transfer of account An authorization by a customer to transfer the assets of his or her brokerage account at one firm to a brokerage account at another firm. It is generally easier and safer for one to transfer securities this way instead of requesting delivery and then sending the certificates to the new firm by oneself.

transfer on death A legal agreement that, upon the death of its maker, passes ownership of certain assets to beneficiaries while bypassing probate. A transfer-on-death agreement generally results in assets passing with minimal delay and may result in reduced probate fees. Assets passed through this agreement remain subject to estate taxation.

transfer price The price at which an item is transferred internally between two units of the same company. An oil company engaged in drilling, refining, and marketing must determine the price of the product as it is passed through the chain from oil field to service station in order to determine the profitability of each stage.

transfer tax **1.** A tax on the transfer of securities that is paid by the seller. The SEC also imposes a small fee (1¢ per $500 value) on securities that are sold. **2.** A tax on the transfer of assets by gift or by death.

translation The expression of amounts denominated in one currency in terms of another currency by using the rate at which two currencies are exchanged. For example, a firm with foreign operations might express sales made in German marks in terms of U.S. dollars. —Also called *foreign currency translation.*

translation gain The gain that results when a firm translates amounts stated in one currency into terms of another currency. A U.S. company that translates German marks into U.S. dollars following a period of a weakening dollar will report a translation gain because the marks exchange for a greater number of dollars.

translation loss The loss that results when a firm translates amounts stated in one currency into terms of another currency. The loss is incurred when the firm translates from a currency that has declined in value relative to the currency into which the amounts are being converted.

transparency The full, accurate, and timely disclosure of information.

> ᴍᴀ **CASE STUDY** | Ford Motor Company executives indicated in spring 2001 that the company planned to provide shareholders and analysts with greater transparency of the firm's financial results. As part of the improved transparency, Ford was expected to report separate results from its Premier Automotive Group (PAG), comprising Aston Martin, Jaguar, Lincoln, Land Rover, and Volvo Cars. In the prior year Ford reported an operating loss of $35 million in Europe only because income from PAG and customer services mostly offset operating losses of nearly $1 billion in its other European operations. At the time Ford did not report profits for individual brands or product groups. Transparency permits shareholders and analysts a greater understanding of a firm's operations, including which parts of the firm are most and least profitable. This, in turn, places greater pressure on the firm's management to produce acceptable results in all facets of a company's operations.

transparent market A market in which current quotation and trade information is readily available to the public.

treasurer A corporate financial officer who often has the responsibility for preparing financial reports, releasing financial information, and filing tax returns. The treasurer may or may not be the firm's main financial decision maker.

Treasuries All bonds backed by the U.S. government that are issued through the Department of the Treasury. The safety of Treasuries is the benchmark against which all other debt securities are measured.

Treasury bill A short-term debt security of the U.S. government that is sold in minimum amounts of $10,000 and multiples of $5,000 above the minimum. Bills with 13-week and 26-week maturities are auctioned each Monday, and 52-week bills are sold every 4 weeks. These obligations, which are very easy to resell, may be purchased through brokers, commercial banks, or directly from the Federal Reserve. —Also called *T bill.* —See also BANK-DISCOUNT BASIS; CERTIFICATE OF INDEBTEDNESS; FORM PD 4633-1.

Treasury bill auction The weekly Monday auction for 13-week and 26-week Treasury bills and the monthly auction for 52-week Treasury bills. The auctions are conducted on a competitive-bid basis by the Federal Reserve. Securities are also set aside for investors who do not wish to enter a specific bid but who will purchase the securities at the average price paid by competitive bidders. —See also FORM PD 4632.

Treasury bond Longer-term, interest-bearing debt of the U.S. Treasury. Treasury bonds are quoted and traded in thirty-seconds of a point.

Treasury Bond Receipts Receipts to Treasury bond interest and principal payments. —See also COUPON STRIPPING.

Treasury Direct The direct purchase by noncompetitive bid of newly issued Treasury securities. By buying these securities directly from the U.S. Treasury, the purchaser can bypass brokers and dealers and avoid paying commissions. Treasury securities that have already been issued can only be purchased through brokers or dealers in the secondary market.

Treasury Inflation-Protected Securities (TIPS) Negotiable bonds issued and guaranteed by the U.S. Treasury with returns that are indexed to compensate bondholders for inflation. Indexing is accomplished by adjusting the principal amount of TIPS upward to adjust for changes in the consumer price index.

These securities were first issued in 1997 and represent a relatively small portion of U.S. government debt. —See also SERIES I SAVINGS BOND.

Treasury note Intermediate-term (1–10 years), interest-bearing debt of the U.S. Treasury that may be purchased through a bank or brokerage firm or directly from the Federal Reserve. An active secondary market makes it easy to resell a Treasury note.

treasury stock The shares of a firm's stock that have been issued and then repurchased. Treasury stock is not considered in paying dividends, voting, or calculating earnings per share. It may be retired or reissued. —See also RETIREMENT 2.

trend The relatively constant movement of a variable throughout a period of time. The period may be short-term or long-term, depending upon whether the trend itself is short-term or long-term. For example, a rising market is taken to mean that prices of most stocks are in an upward trend.

trend analysis The analysis of a variable's past value changes to determine if a trend exists and, if so, what the trend indicates. A technical analyst may graph a stock's price throughout a period of time to determine whether a trend has been established. Analysts often attempt to determine if trends exist for a firm's earnings per share. —Compare RATIO ANALYSIS.

trendline In technical analysis, a straight line or two parallel straight lines that indicate the direction in which a security has been moving, and, many chartists believe, the direction in which it will continue to move. When a security price breaks through a trendline, the beginning of a new trend is indicated.

Treynor performance measure A gauge of risk-adjusted portfolio performance. The measure is calculated by dividing the portfolio beta (a measure of market, or systematic risk) into the average difference between the portfolio's returns and returns on a risk-free asset. A higher number represents better performance by the portfolio manager. —Compare SHARPE PERFORMANCE MEASURE.

triangle In technical analysis, a chart pattern indicating the convergence in the movement of successive high and low prices and characterized by a formation that resembles a triangle turned on its side. A triangle indicates a period of combat between bulls and bears with the technical analyst having to determine the winner. If prices break out of the triangle on the upside, it is a bullish sign. A breakout on the downside indicates the bears are winners. The closer the breakout occurs to the point of the triangle, the less conclusive the signal to buy or sell. Refer to the *Technical Analysis of Chart Patterns* for an example of this chart. —Also called *coil; flag; pennant; wedge.* —See also ASCENDING TRIANGLE; DESCENDING TRIANGLE.

trigger point The event or condition that initiates a predetermined action. For example, the New York Stock Exchange halts trading in stocks when the Dow Jones Industrial Average declines by a specified number of points (the trigger point) in a trading session.

trigger price The specific price of an imported item below which a quota or tariff will be put into effect. A trigger price is imposed to keep foreign competitors from undercutting prices charged by domestic companies in the domestic firm's home market.

TRIN —See ARMS SHORT-TERM TRADING INDEX.

triple A —See AAA.

triple bottom In technical analysis, a chart formation of a stock or a market index that has attempted to penetrate a lower price level on three different occasions. If the stock price or index actually breaks through on the downside during the third attempt, it is a bearish signal and the investor should sell or sell short the stock or index. If the stock or index is unable to penetrate the price level, it is a bullish sign that the price is at a strong support level. —Compare TRIPLE TOP.

triple tax exempt Of, relating to, or being a municipal bond, trust, or fund paying interest that is free of federal, state, and local income taxation for individuals residing in certain localities. This situation results from the fact that most but not all states and localities exempt municipal bond interest from taxation if the bonds are issued within that particular state. Triple tax exemption is of particular interest to investors residing in high-tax states and localities, such as New York City.

triple top In technical analysis, a chart pattern that indicates that a stock or a market index has attempted to penetrate an upper price level on three different occasions. If the stock price or index actually breaks through on the upside during the third attempt, it is a bullish signal. If the stock price or index fails on the third attempt and pulls back, it is a bearish signal. Refer to the *Technical Analysis Chart Patterns* section for an example of this chart. —Compare TRIPLE BOTTOM.

triple witching hour The hour before the market closing when options and futures on stock indexes expire on the same day, thereby setting off frenzied trading in futures, options, and underlying securities. Traders and arbitrageurs unwind investment positions and produce large price movements in securities. The triple witching hour occurs on the third Fridays of March, June, September, and December. —See also EXPIRATION EFFECT.

troubled debt restructuring —See DEBT RESTRUCTURING.

trust A legal arrangement whereby control over property is transferred to a person or organization (the trustee) for the benefit of someone else (the beneficiary). Trusts are created for a variety of reasons, including tax savings and improved asset management. —See also CHARITABLE LEAD TRUST; CHARITABLE REMAINDER TRUST; CLIFFORD TRUST; MARITAL-DEDUCTION TRUST; QTIP TRUST.

trust deed —See INDENTURE.

trustee An appointed person or institution that manages assets for the benefit of someone else. Trustees are most often trust corporations or trust departments of commercial banks that manage the assets for a fee based on a percentage of the size of the trust (usually under 1%). A trust may be very restrictive or it may allow the trustee wide discretion, depending upon the grantor's wishes.

Trust Indenture Act of 1939 The legislation that established rights for security holders under indenture agreements. The Act sets standards for trustees, requires financial reports by the issuers to the trustees, and mandates disclosure of owners' rights under the indenture agreements.

trustor The person or organization that creates a trust.

TSA —See TAX-SHELTERED ANNUITY.

TSE **1.** —See TOKYO STOCK EXCHANGE. **2.** —See TORONTO STOCK EXCHANGE.

turkey An investment that has performed poorly.

turnaround 1. The process of moving from a period of losses or low profitability into a more profitable stage. A turnaround may be triggered by a number of factors including a better use of assets or the development of new products and services. **2.** A security that is in the process of reversing a declining price trend. **3.** The purchase and sale of a security on the same day.

turn-of-the-month effect The tendency of stock prices to increase during the last two days and the first three days of each month. Some researchers ascribe the effect to the timing of monthly cash flows received by pension funds and reinvested in the stock market.

turnover 1. The trading volume of the market or of a particular security. **2.** The number of times that an asset is replaced during a given period. For example, an inventory turnover of five indicates that the firm's inventory has been turned into sales and has been replaced five times.

turnover rate 1. The trading volume in a particular stock during a time period (generally one year) as a percentage of the total number of shares of that stock outstanding. The turnover rate adjusts for the differences in outstanding shares and provides a measure of the relative activity in a stock. **2.** For an investment company, the volume of shares traded as a percentage of the number of shares in the company's portfolio. A high turnover rate may indicate excessive trading and commissions.

12b–1 fee A type of mutual fund expense in which the fund's operators use a portion of the firm's assets to pay for costs of distributing the fund. The fee is included in the fee table of a fund's prospectus. National Association of Securities Dealers' rules establish an annual limit on the size of the fee. The name is derived from the SEC rule that describes the fee. —Also called *distribution fee.*

twenty-day period —See COOLING-OFF PERIOD.

twenty-five percent rule A guideline for municipal bond buyers that indicates that if a municipality's total long-term debt exceeds 25% of its annual budget, the debt is excessive.

twisting An attempt to convince an individual to sell one product and purchase another product, primarily so the salesperson can earn additional commissions. In the brokerage business, twisting is usually called churning. Twisting, the more general term, applies to the sale of other products as well, such as insurance policies.

two-dollar broker A member of a securities exchange who executes orders for other members. A two-dollar broker performs essentially the same function as a commission broker except that he or she is independent rather than a representative of a specific firm. —Also called *independent broker.*

200-day moving average A technical indicator compiled as a statistical series of a security's closing prices throughout 200 consecutive trading days. A 200-day moving average is designed to discover changes in a trend. Generally, a moving average is superimposed on a stock's line chart. If the stock price penetrates the moving average on the upside after a downward trend, the penetration is a signal to buy. But if the stock price penetrates the moving average on the downside following an upward trend, the penetration is a bearish sign.

two-sided market The market for a security in which a bid price and an ask price are both quoted. —Compare ONE-SIDED MARKET. —Also called *two-way market.*

two-tier tender offer An offer to purchase a sufficient number of stockholders' shares so as to gain effective control of a firm at a certain price per share, followed by a lower offer at a later date for the remaining shares. For example, an investor may offer $50 per share for up to 51% of a firm's outstanding stock and then, having gained control, offer $40 for each of the remaining shares. —Compare ANY-AND-ALL BID. —See also APPRAISAL RIGHT; BACK-END VALUE; BLENDED PRICE; FAIR PRICE AMENDMENT.

two-way market —See TWO-SIDED MARKET.

two-way trading The ability to convert ordinary shares into American Depositary Receipts or Global Depositary Receipts following an earlier conversion of ADRs or GDRs into ordinary shares. In February 2002 the Indian government for the first time approved two-way trading of ADRs. Until then ADRs could be placed in the United States but, if converted back into ordinary shares for trading in India, could not again trade as ADRs. Two-way trading improves the liquidity of ADRs and GDRs.

U

u —Used in the daily or weekly high column of stock transaction tables in newspapers to indicate that the price of a security has reached a new 52-week high: *u75.*

UGMA —See UNIFORM GIFTS TO MINORS ACT.

un —Used in stock transaction tables in newspapers to indicate unit shares: *WebD un.* —Also called *ut.*

unamortized bond discount When a bond is originally sold at a discount from par value, the difference between the par value and the proceeds from selling the bond that has not yet been assessed as an interest expense to the borrower. A firm issuing a bond at below par value must charge off the difference to interest expense throughout the issue's life. Unamortized bond discount is the portion of the discount that has not yet been shown as an expense. —Also called *bond discount.*

unamortized bond premium When a bond is originally sold at a premium to par value, the difference between the par value and the proceeds from selling the bond that has not yet been subtracted from interest expense.

unaudited statement A financial statement prepared by an auditor but not in accordance with generally accepted auditing standards. Unaudited statements are prepared to less rigorous standards than audited statements. —Compare AUDITED STATEMENT.

unbundling The separation and separate pricing of products and services by financial institutions. When deregulation resulted in price competition and the introduction of new products, financial institutions found it increasingly necessary to offer and price each product separately.

uncollected funds A deposit or a portion of a deposit that has not yet been collected by a financial institution. Financial institutions typically prohibit customers from writing checks on uncollected funds.

uncovered option —See NAKED OPTION.

underbanked Of, relating to, or being a new security issue for which the managing underwriter has difficulty obtaining commitments from other underwriters.

underbooked Of, relating to, or being a new security issue in which investment bankers find a general lack of interest among investors before the issue date.

undercapitalized Of, relating to, or being a firm that has insufficient long-term equity to support its assets. A rapidly growing company that finds itself financing its operations primarily with short-term loans may be undercapitalized.

underdepreciation **1.** Depreciation that is insufficient to allow for the eventual replacement of the asset being depreciated. Underdepreciation is generally caused by rising prices on replacement assets. —Compare OVERDEPRECIATION 1. **2.** Depreciation that causes an asset to be carried on a firm's books at a greater value than it would have if it were sold. Underdepreciation results in overstated earnings and assets on the firm's financial statements. —Compare OVERDEPRECIATION 2.

underleveraged Of, relating to, or being a firm that has insufficient debt in its capital structure. Because bond interest is deductible for tax purposes and is generally fixed in amount for a long period of time, some use of debt can often result in greater earnings per share for stockholders. Determining whether a company is underleveraged is usually a matter of opinion.

underlying asset **1.** The physical and financial asset to which a security holder or a class of security holders has a claim. An analyst may believe that a stock is underpriced on the basis of the value of the firm's underlying assets and the potential earning power of those assets. **2.** The asset that underlies and gives value to a security. The underlying asset of a stock option is the stock that the option can be used to purchase. Likewise, the underlying asset of a convertible bond is the stock for which the bond can be exchanged. The market value of a security is directly affected by changes in the value of any underlying asset into which it may be exchanged.

underlying debt Debt of a municipal organization for which a higher municipal organization is at least partially responsible. For example, debt of a hospital authority may be guaranteed by a county such that the hospital debt is underlying the debt of the county. —Compare OVERLAPPING DEBT.

undermargined Of or relating to a brokerage account in which the dollar value of the margin (market value of the assets minus the amount owed) has fallen below the percentage of value set by the maintenance margin requirement.

underperforming asset An asset that earns a lower rate of return than it would be capable of earning if it were properly used. A firm with underperforming assets is a prime target for takeover. —Compare NONPERFORMING ASSET.

underpricing The pricing of a new security issue at less than the prevailing price of the same security in the secondary market. Underpricing helps ensure a successful sale.

undersubscribed Of or relating to a new issue of securities for which demand from investors is less than the number of securities to be issued.

undervalued Of, relating to, or being a security that trades at a price lower than it logically should trade. Determining whether a security is undervalued is a subjective judgment. —Compare OVERVALUED.

undervalued company A firm whose assets and potential earning power are not adequately reflected in its stock price. Although such firms are more likely to be subject to takeover attempts than others, determining whether a particular firm is actually undervalued can be quite difficult. —See also ASSET VALUE.

underwater Of or relating to a stock option for which the option exercise price is higher than the market price of the stock.

underwrite To assume the risk of securities' sale by purchasing the securities from the issuer for resale to the public. Investment bankers often assume this underwriting function in order to guarantee that the issuer will receive all the funds needed from the sale. —See also BEST-EFFORTS BASIS 1; FREED UP; HOT ISSUE; INVESTMENT BANKER; PEG 1; STANDBY UNDERWRITING.

underwriter An investment banker that acts to guarantee the sale of a new securities issue by purchasing the securities for resale to the public. —Also called *sponsor.* —See also AGREEMENT AMONG UNDERWRITERS; INVESTMENT BANKER; LEAD UNDERWRITER.

underwriting agreement A written contract between a company planning a public securities issue and the managing underwriter of that issue. The agreement specifies the particulars of the issue such as dates, fees, offering price, and the responsibilities of the parties. —Compare AGREEMENT AMONG UNDERWRITERS.

underwriting spread —See GROSS SPREAD.

underwriting syndicate —See SYNDICATE.

undigested securities The portion of a new security issue that remains unsold because of insufficient investor demand at the offering price.

undistributed profits —See RETAINED EARNINGS.

undivided account The account of an underwriting syndicate in which sales and liability are shared jointed rather than apportioned individually. —Compare DIVIDED ACCOUNT.

undivided profit The undistributed net income that has not yet been included as part of retained earnings.

unearned income Individual income, such as dividends, pension payments, and capital gains, that is derived from something other than personal services. —Compare EARNED INCOME.

unencumbered Of or relating to an owned asset that does not have a claim against it. Real estate not being used as collateral for a loan and on which all taxes are current is unencumbered. —Compare ENCUMBRANCE 1.

unfriendly takeover The acquisition of a firm despite resistance by the target firm's management and board of directors. —Compare FRIENDLY TAKEOVER. —Also called *hostile takeover.* —See also KILLER BEE; RAIDER.

unified credit A credit used against federal taxes due on estates and large gifts. Under current law, the unified credit is sufficient to offset taxes on values of approximately $1 million in estates and large gifts. Thus, the combination of estate value and large gifts must exceed $1 million during a person's lifetime before any taxes must be paid to the federal government.

Uniform Gifts to Minors Act (UGMA)   Uniform state laws that facilitate irrevocable gifts to a minor by eliminating the requirement of a guardian or trust. A custodian, who may be the donor, is appointed to manage the gift, but full rights to the principal and income reside with the minor. Under 1986 tax reform, only the first $1,000 of income from these custodial accounts will be taxed at the child's rate if the child is under 14 years of age. Income above $1,000 is taxed at the donor's rate. When the child turns 14, all income from the trust is taxed at the child's rate.

Uniform Practice Code   A set of standards for use by members of the National Association of Securities Dealers when settling securities transactions. The Code covers technical items such as the ways by which interest is computed and the times at which settlements are to occur.

Uniform Securities Act   A 1956 act designed to bring uniformity to state regulation of securities. The Act deals with fraud and the registration of securities and dealers. States are free to adopt all, parts, or none of the Act.

Uniform Securities Agent State Law Examination   A test required by many states of people who want to become registered representatives. In addition to passing this test, the National Association of Securities Dealers requires candidates to pass the Series 7.

unissued capital stock   Corporate capital stock that has been authorized but not yet issued. Management of a firm will often ask its stockholders to authorize many more shares of stock than are actually needed in order to provide flexibility for the issuance of more shares later without stockholders' approval.

unit   —See SPECIALIST UNIT; UNIT OF TRADING; UNIT SHARE.

unitary tax   A state corporate income tax on worldwide income. Although they are unpopular with corporations, unitary taxes are instituted by governments to foil firms that use creative accounting techniques to transfer their income to states or countries with low income-tax rates.

unit convertible   A security that is convertible into a package of assets or securities rather than into a specified number of shares of a single common stock.

United States government securities   —See GOVERNMENTS.

United States savings bond   —See SAVINGS BOND.

unit growth   The growth in sales in terms of the actual number of units as opposed to the dollar value of the units that have been sold. Measuring growth in units, rather than in dollars, eliminates the effects of inflation and shows real growth.

unit investment trust   An unmanaged portfolio of investments put together by an investment adviser and sold in units to investors by brokers. Units of a trust usually sell for $1,000 including a sales commission of approximately 4% at the time of the initial offering. Sponsoring brokers usually maintain a secondary market for the units, the value of which depends on the value of the securities held by the trust. Because of the initial sales charge, unit investment trusts are usually not attractive for short-term trading.   —Also called *fixed trust*.

unit of trading The minimum quantity of a security required for regular trading purposes. The unit of trading for most stocks is 100 shares. —Also called *trading unit; unit.*

unit sales Sales measured in terms of physical units rather than dollars. Unit sales data are often used by financial analysts when evaluating the health of a company.

unit share A combination of securities that is traded as a single package. For example, a share of common stock and a warrant may be traded as a unit. —Also called *unit.*

universal life insurance A combination of term life insurance and a tax-deferred savings plan paying a variable return. This combination was developed during the early 1980s when interest rates rose to very high levels and caused the public to view regular whole life policies unfavorably.

unlimited liability The liability of the owner of a business for all the obligations of the business. An owner's personal assets can be seized if the business's assets are insufficient to satisfy claims against it. The placement of personal assets at risk is a great disadvantage of proprietorships and general partnerships. The ability to limit the amount of liability to which an owner is subject is a major reason for the formation of corporations and limited partnerships. —Compare LIMITED LIABILITY.

unlisted security A security that trades only in the over-the-counter market. —Compare LISTED SECURITY.

unlisted trading The trading of a security on the floor of an exchange when the security is not listed on that exchange. Unlisted trading occurs when members of an exchange wish to trade the security but the issuing company has not applied for listing. Unlisted trading requires approval of the SEC.

unload To sell an investment, generally at a loss.

unpaid dividend 1. A declared dividend that has not yet been paid. 2. —See PASSED DIVIDEND.

unqualified opinion —See CLEAN OPINION.

unrealized gain The increased market value of an asset that is still being held compared with its cost of acquisition. Unrealized gains are not usually taxable. —Compare REALIZED GAIN. —Also called *paper gain; paper profit.*

unrealized loss The reduction in value of an asset that is being held compared with its original cost. An unrealized loss usually must be realized by closing out the position before it can be recognized for tax purposes. —Compare REALIZED LOSS. —Also called *paper loss.* —See also WASH SALE 1.

unregistered exchange A securities exchange that has been exempted from registration by the SEC. Unregistered exchanges are generally quite small and trade local issues in moderate volume. The Honolulu Stock Exchange is unregistered. —Compare REGISTERED EXCHANGE.

unregistered security —See RESTRICTED SECURITY.

unsecured creditor A creditor with a claim for which no specific assets are pledged. A debenture holder is an unsecured creditor. —Compare SECURED CREDITOR.

unsecured liability A liability for which no specific collateral is held by a creditor. Essentially, payment on an unsecured liability is assured by the promise of the borrower.

unsponsored American Depositary Receipt An American Depositary Receipt representing shares of a foreign company not directly involved in issuance of the ADR. Unsponsored ADRs are originated by a bank(s) that independently purchases the foreign firm's shares, holds the shares in trust, and sells the ADRs through brokerage firms. The depositary bank rather than holders of the ADRs retains the right to vote shares held in trust. —Compare SPONSORED AMERICAN DEPOSITARY RECEIPT.

unsystematic risk The risk that is specific to an industry or firm. Examples of unsystematic risk include losses caused by labor problems, nationalization of assets, or weather conditions. This type of risk can be reduced by assembling a portfolio with significant diversification so that a single event affects only a limited number of the assets. —Compare SYSTEMATIC RISK. —Also called *diversifiable risk*.

unweighted index A stock price index that is calculated with equal weighting for each component. Unweighted indexes such as the Value Line averages are useful for individuals who invest an equal dollar amount in each stock.

unwelcome assignment The assignment of an option to a writer when the writer does not yet wish to fulfill the terms of the contract. For example, for tax reasons, an option writer may want assignment to occur near the expiration. Unwelcome assignment is a possibility for calls when the underlying asset sells at or above the strike price, and it is a possibility for puts when the underlying asset sells at or below the strike price. Unwelcome assignment can be avoided by purchasing an offsetting contract and closing out a position. —See also ASSIGN.

unwind 1. To close out a relatively complicated investment position. For example, an investor who practices arbitrage by taking one position in stocks and the opposite position in option contracts would have to unwind by the date on which the options would expire. 2. To rectify a transaction in which a mistake has been made. For example, because of a misunderstanding, a brokerage firm may have bought the wrong stock for a customer. The firm must then unwind the erroneous trade by selling the stock just purchased and buying the correct stock.

up-and-in option An option that comes into being only when the price of the underlying asset reaches a specified value.

up-and-out option An option that terminates when the value of the underlying asset reaches a specified value.

up/down volume ratio A stock's aggregate trading volume during days when the price increases divided by the aggregate trading volume during days when the price declines. This technical tool attempts to provide guidance as to whether a stock is being accumulated or distributed. A high up/down volume ratio is considered a bullish indicator.

upgrading 1. An increase in the quality rating of a security issue. An upgrading may occur for a variety of reasons, including an improved outlook for a firm's products, increased profitability, or a reduction in the amount of debt the firm has outstanding. As circumstances change, upgrading or downgrading of a security takes place once the issue has been initially rated and sold. An upgrading generally can be expected to have a positive influence on the price of the security. —Compare DOWNGRADING. **2.** An increase in the quality of securities held in a portfolio.

upside potential The potential price or gain that may be expected in a security or in a security average, generally stated as the dollar price or the dollar amount of gain that may reasonably be expected in the particular security or security average. For example, an analyst may feel that a stock currently selling at $25 per share has an upside potential of $40. —Compare DOWNSIDE RISK.

upstairs market The trading of securities within a broker-dealer firm rather than taking a trade to an exchange floor or trading with another broker-dealer in the over-the-counter market. In the upstairs market, the broker-dealer acts as a dealer or as an agent for both parties.

upstream Of or relating to earnings or operations at a firm that are near or at the initial stages of producing a good or service. For example, exploration and production are upstream operations for a large integrated oil company. —Compare DOWNSTREAM.

uptick An upward price movement for a security transaction compared with the preceding transaction of the same security. —Compare DOWNTICK. —Also called *plus tick*.

uptick/downtick ratio A relative measure of the degree to which block transactions take place at increasing prices as opposed to declining prices. Transactions that occur on upticks are considered to be initiated by buyers, and sellers are considered to initiate transactions on downticks. Technical analysts consider a high ratio to be bearish because it indicates an overbought market.

uptick/downtick rule —See RULE 80A.

uptick rule An SEC rule that prohibits the sale of borrowed stock when the last price change in the stock was downward. Part of the Securities Exchange Act of 1934, the uptick rule is designed to keep investors from manipulating stock prices downward by borrowing and selling shares in a declining stock. —See also SHORT SALE.

uptrend A series of price increases in a security or in the general market. Some investors believe a security tends to take on a certain inertia; as a result, these investors search for stock in an uptrend, thinking that it will probably continue to move in the same direction. —Compare DOWNTREND.

usable bond A bond that may be used at face value in combination with a warrant to purchase shares of common stock. Essentially, the issuer allows warrant owners to substitute the bond for cash when the warrants are exercised. Ownership of this type of bond is, like ownership of a convertible bond, a speculation on the direction of interest rates and on the direction of the price of the underlying stock.

usury law A state law that restricts the interest rate that can be charged on specified types of loans.

ut —See UN.

utility bond

Please compare the risk and return on utility bonds vis-á-vis risk and return on industrial bonds.

Utility bonds, like industrial bonds, range the full spectrum with regard to credit quality. Some utility companies have been able to successfully overcome more difficult times associated with bringing large construction projects into their ratepayers' rate base, thus enabling the companies to pass on to these ratepayers the costs of constructing the projects. Other companies have been forced to pass some or all of these costs on to their stockholders, meaning that these companies' earnings have been hurt severely. (The harm to earnings, of course, also adversely affects the utilities' bondholders because these companies' financial ratios—that is, interest-coverage ratios and debt to equity ratios—are reduced and credit rating agencies are likely to reduce credit ratings as a result. Lower credit ratings translate into higher bond yields and lower bond prices for bondholders.) This is an extremely abbreviated and simplistic explanation of why utility bonds at one time traded at relatively wide yield spreads to industrial bonds. The utility companies' financial ratios were influenced by political factors—such as whether the elected public utility commissioners would permit their reelection chances to be harmed by passing on unpopular rate increases to those same ratepayers who elected them—in addition to all the other factors that were almost beyond the control of the utilities, for example, high interest costs, energy conservation efforts, and environmental concerns. These factors all contributed to the market's perception of greater risk in the utility industry. Some of the factors have changed; others have been overcome by time, as projects have been completed and put into the rate bases of the utility companies of the nation. Still other very positive trends have occurred (such as high interest costs having been reduced through refinancing at lower interest costs). Now we observe that many utility companies are becoming cash cows. The excess cash flows generated by some of them have enabled them to buy companies in nonregulated industries, thus reducing their vulnerability to political influences and allowing them to participate in more growth-oriented businesses. In short, in many cases utility companies are turning the corner on their past problems, and their bonds are trading more and more like industrial bonds in those selected cases.

Stephanie G. Bigwood, CFP, ChFC, CSA, Assistant Vice President
Lombard Securities, Incorporated, Baltimore, MD

utility   A business that provides an essential service, generally under government regulation. Electric companies, gas transmission firms, and local telephone companies are utilities.

utility bond   A long-term debt security that is issued by a utility.

V

valuation   A process for calculating the monetary value of an asset. Valuation is subjective and results in wide disparities for the values of most assets.

value-added tax (VAT)   A tax levied on increases in a product's value at each stage of production and distribution. The value-added tax, essentially an invisible sales tax included in the final price, is ultimately paid by consumers. For example, a candy maker paying $10,000 for ingredients used in the manufacture of chocolate bars that are resold for $15,000 would be required to pay a tax on the $5,000 of value added to the product. Proponents of the value-added tax argue that it should be substituted for the current federal income tax to stimulate consumer saving. —Compare CONSUMPTION TAX.

value investing The selection of securities to be bought and sold on the basis of the value of a firm's assets. For example, an investor may look for a stock in which current assets exceed total liabilities on a per share basis by more than the market price of the stock. Value investing emphasizes asset value more than earnings projections. —See also ASSET VALUE.

Value Line Composite Index An overall measure of stock market performance based on approximately 1,700 stocks covered by the *Value Line Investment Survey*. The index includes stocks listed on the New York Stock Exchange, the American Stock Exchange, the regional and Canadian exchanges, the Nasdaq National Market, and the over-the-counter market. Unlike most indexes, which are weighted by market capitalization or stock price, the Value Line Composite Index assigns equal weight to each component. In other words, it provides an indication of the performance of a portfolio with equal amounts of money invested in each stock covered by Value Line. In 1988 Value Line started publishing the Value Line Arithmetic Index, which tracks the performance of the average stock rather than the median stock. Both the Value Line Composite Index and the Value Line Arithmetic Index serve as indicators for the performance of the overall stock market as opposed to large-cap stocks or particular segments of the market.

Value Line, Inc. A New York–based financial information company best known for its *Value Line Investment Survey*, a weekly analysis of approximately 1,300 stocks. Academic research suggests the Value Line rating system for stocks included in the *Investment Survey* can be used to earn risk-adjusted returns that beat the market. Value Line also operates mutual funds, calculates and distributes a comprehensive stock index, and publishes the *Value Line Convertible Survey* and the *Value Line Mutual Fund Survey*.

Value Line ranking The relative ranking of the short-term price performance for a particular stock that appears in the *Value Line Investment Survey*. Value Line rankings range from 1 to 5, with 1 indicating the greatest potential for short-term gains. The service also ranks stocks for safety.

Vancouver Stock Exchange —See CANADIAN VENTURE EXCHANGE.

variable Something, such as stock prices, earnings, dividend payments, interest rates, and gross domestic product, that has no fixed quantitative value. —See also DEPENDENT VARIABLE; INDEPENDENT VARIABLE.

variable annuity An annuity with payments to the annuitant that vary depending upon the investment success of a separate investment account underlying the annuity. Because the invested funds are primarily in common stock, this annuity offers greater potential rewards and greater attendant risks than annuities supported by fixed-income securities. —Compare FIXED ANNUITY. —See also HYBRID ANNUITY.

variable cost The costs of production that vary directly in proportion to the number of units produced. Variable costs often include labor expenses and raw material costs, because labor and raw material usually must be increased to increase output. Firms for which variable costs represent a high proportion of total costs are usually less likely to experience large fluctuations in earnings, because changes in sales and revenues are accompanied by nearly equal changes in costs. —Compare FIXED COST.

variable coupon renewable note (VCR) A renewable note on which interest is reset on a weekly basis according to a predetermined formula. A VCR continues to renew at quarterly intervals unless the owner directs the issuer to repay the principal.

variable life insurance Life insurance that relates benefits to the value of a separate investment account underlying the annuity. This insurance is designed to prevent erosion of benefits by inflation. The size of the benefits will vary.

variable-rate certificate of deposit A certificate of deposit that pays a rate of interest that changes at predetermined intervals according to a specified formula or a key interest rate. This savings instrument is most appropriate if the investor expects short-term interest rates to rise before the certificates mature.

variable-rate demand obligation A floating-rate debt obligation that has a nominal long-term maturity as well as an option allowing the investor to put (sell) the obligation back to the trustee, generally at par plus accrued interest.

variable-rate note —See FLOATING-RATE NOTE.

variable-rate preferred stock —See FLOATING-RATE PREFERRED STOCK.

variable ratio option writing The writing of options when only some of the underlying assets that may be called for delivery are owned by the writer. Professional option writers use variable ratio option writing to generate profits if the underlying asset price moves within an established range. —Also called *ratio writing.*

variance A statistical measure of the variability of measured datum from the average value of the set of data. A high variance, indicating relatively great variability, also indicates that the average is of minimal use in projecting future values for the data. Standard deviation is the square root of variance. Financial analysts use both statistical measures to weigh investment risk. —Compare COVARIANCE. —See also RISK.

VAT —See VALUE-ADDED TAX.

VCR —See VARIABLE COUPON RENEWABLE NOTE.

vega The change in an option's premium for a 1% change in the volatility of the underlying futures contract.

venture arbitrage —See RAIDING.

venture capital A pool of risk capital, typically contributed by large investors, from which allocations are made available to young, small companies that have good growth prospects but are short of funds. Small investors can buy new issues or participate in mutual funds that specialize in the supply of venture capital. —Also called *risk capital.*

venture capital fund An investment company that invests its shareholders' money in new, very risky, but potentially very profitable, business ventures. —See also NONDIVERSIFIED MANAGEMENT COMPANY.

venture investing The acquiring of a stake in a start-up company by a brokerage firm or analyst by obtaining discounted, pre-IPO shares. Critics claim venture investing causes analysts to have a vested interest in seeing a stock appreciate in value and so are more likely to issue favorable recommendations.

vertical analysis The comparison of an item on a financial statement with a different item on the same statement. For example, an analyst may study a firm's balance sheet to compare the level of current assets with the level of current liabilities in order to measure liquidity. Analysts often study a firm's income statement to compare net income with total sales. —Compare HORIZONTAL ANALYSIS.

vertical line chart —See BAR CHART.

vertical merger A merger between two firms involved in the same business but on different levels. As an example, an automobile company may purchase a tire manufacturer or a glass company. The merger permits the firm to gain more control of another level of the manufacturing or selling process within that single industry. —Compare HORIZONTAL MERGER.

vertical security exchange The exchange of one security for a different security (that is, stock for debt or debt for stock). Exchange offers involving unlike securities are generally tax-free unless the investor only receives debt in exchange for stock.

vertical spread —See MONEY SPREAD.

vested benefits Pension benefits that belong to an employee independent of his or her future employment. An employee usually becomes vested after five years of employment with the same firm, although there are numerous exceptions requiring longer employment. —Compare PENSION PLAN.

V-formation In technical analysis, a chart formation caused by a sharp extended decline followed by a sudden upward movement. Some chartists believe a V-formation is not generally a good indicator of a major change of direction in a security's price. These people believe that a major price reversal requires a period of testing low prices with succeeding price advances and declines. Only after this consolidation phase takes place can a new bull movement be assured.

viatical settlement The purchase of a terminally ill person's life insurance policy for a certain percentage of the policy's face value. The amount paid depends on the size of the policy and the length of time the policyholder is expected to live. The company that purchases the policy begins paying the premiums at the time of purchase and collects the death benefits when the insured dies.

visible supply New security issues, primarily bonds, scheduled for sale during the next month.

VIX Index An equity volatility measure developed in 1993 by the Chicago Board Options Exchange. The index is calculated using eight S&P 100 (OEX) option contracts, four calls and four puts, with an average time to maturity of 30 days. Many traders use the VIX as a general measure of index option volatility. —Also called *CBOE Volatility Index.*

vj —Used in listed stock and bond transaction tables in newspapers to indicate that the firm issuing the security is in bankruptcy or receivership, or that the firm is being reorganized under bankruptcy. It also indicates securities assumed by such companies: *vj Robbins.*

volatile Tending to be subject to large price fluctuations. Traders generally prefer volatile securities if they buy and sell on short-term price movements. —See also BETA.

volume The amount of trading sustained in a security or in the entire market during a given period. Especially heavy volume may indicate that important news has just been announced or is expected. —See also AVERAGE DAILY VOLUME.

volume deleted —Used on the consolidated tape to mean that volume data for trades of 10,000 shares and fewer will be omitted until further notice. The deletion of volume, the next step following the deletion of certain digits of price information, is intended to speed the reporting of trades during periods of very heavy volume. With volume and all data but the digits and fractions deleted, a trade that ordinarily appears as XOM 5s41.3 will be reported as XOM 1.3.

volume-weighted average price The average price of a stock calculated by dividing the daily trading volume into the dollar value of daily transactions. Institutional investors sometimes use the volume-weighted average price to determine if a particular trade was at a favorable or unfavorable price.

voluntary accumulation plan A plan to acquire additional shares in a mutual fund on a more or less regular basis, at the discretion of the shareholder.

voluntary bankruptcy A bankruptcy initiated by the organization entering the bankruptcy rather than by that organization's creditors. Organizations generally enter voluntary bankruptcy to protect themselves from creditors' claims. —Compare INVOLUNTARY BANKRUPTCY. —See also CHAPTER 7; CHAPTER 11.

voting rights The type of voting and the amount of control held by the owners of a class of stock. —See also CUMULATIVE VOTING; MAJORITY VOTING; NONVOTING STOCK; PROXY; SUPERMAJORITY PROVISION.

voting stock Stock for which the holder has the right to vote in the election of directors, in the appointment of auditors, or in other matters brought up at the annual meeting. Most common stock is voting stock. —Compare NONVOTING STOCK. —See also SUPERVOTING STOCK.

voting trust certificate A trust-issued certificate that evidences stock ownership but reserves voting rights for the trust. Voting trust certificates are exchanged for stock when voting power must be consolidated. Thus, holders of certificates have all the usual rights of stockholders with the exception of voting rights.

vulture fund A pool of investment money used to purchase distressed financial assets or real estate at bargain prices. Vulture funds are relatively risky but offer large potential profits. The performance of a vulture fund is dependent upon the skill of the fund's managers in identifying and purchasing undervalued assets that can be turned into profitable investments.

vulture investor An investor who attempts to profit by buying debt of bankrupt or credit-impaired companies. Vulture investors are generally interested in the debt of problem companies that hold substantial tangible assets.

waiting period —See COOLING-OFF PERIOD.

walk-in A new brokerage customer who simply walks into the office. Although walk-ins are generally assigned to brokers, they have the right to specify a preferred broker.

wallflower An out-of-favor security, company, or industry.

Wall Street The main street in New York City's financial district. The term is often used to denote the entire financial district in New York or the world of U.S. finance and investments. —Also called *the Street*.

wanted for cash A notice on the ticker tape that an investor is interested in purchasing a particular security for immediate delivery and payment, in contrast with a regular transaction in which five business days are permitted for delivery and payment.

war chest Liquid assets accumulated by a firm to use in a potential acquisition or in defending itself against a takeover attempt. A substantial war chest adds security and enhances investment opportunities but is likely to be a drain on short-term profitability.

warrant A security that permits its owner to purchase a specific number of shares of stock at a predetermined price. For example, a warrant may give an investor the right to purchase 5 shares of XYZ common stock at a price of $25 per share until October 1, 2007. Warrants usually originate as part of a new bond issue, but they trade separately after issuance. Warrants usually have limited lives. Their values are considerably more volatile than the values of the underlying stock. Thus, investment in warrants is not for the timid. —Also called *equity warrant; stock warrant; subscription warrant.* —See also DEBT WARRANT; PERPETUAL WARRANT; USABLE BOND.

warrant agreement A written statement of the terms of a warrant issue. Although the information in these agreements is quite important, their technical nature is such that they are more appropriate for use by financial analysts and sophisticated traders than by individual investors.

warrant leverage ratio An indication of the degree of change in a warrant price for a given change in the price of the underlying stock. If a warrant doubles for a 50% increase in the stock that the warrant can be used to purchase, the warrant leverage ratio is 100%/50%, or 2. A warrant with a high leverage ratio offers large potential profits at the expense of relatively large potential losses, because the leverage operates in both directions.

warrant premium The excess of a warrant's market price over its minimum value in exchange for shares of common stock. For example, a warrant to purchase 3 shares of stock at $10 each has a minimum value of $45 if the shares trade at a price of $25 (3 × [$25 − $10]). If the warrant has a market price of $55, the premium will be equal to $10 ($55 − $45). Although a warrant usually trades at a premium, the size of the premium declines as its price climbs and as it approaches expiration.

wash sale The illegal purchase or repurchase of an asset within 30 days of the sale date of a basically identical asset that was sold in order to take a tax loss.

For example, if an investor sold a security at a loss and then immediately repurchased the same security or a basically identical security, the Internal Revenue Service would consider the transaction a wash sale.

wash trade　A transaction designed to make it appear that a purchase and sale has occurred even though no change in ownership occurred. For example, an investor might simultaneously buy and sell shares in one company through two different brokerage firms in order to create the appearance of substantial trading activity that will draw in other investors. Wash trades are illegal.

wasting asset　An asset that tends to decline in value over time as its expected life is used up. A factory machine or an automobile is a wasting asset. Some individuals also consider options or warrants wasting assets because they have a limited life after which they are valueless. —Also called *shrinking asset.*

watch list　A roster of securities that are under scrutiny for a special reason. For example, a watch list may be established for stock that has exhibited an unusual trading volume or for debt securities that have reduced quality ratings.

water and sewer bond　A revenue bond issued by a municipality to finance the building or extension of water and sewer systems. Interest and principal payments on the bond are derived from and are limited to revenues received from charges to the users of the systems.

watered stock　Stock that is issued with a value considerably in excess of the value of the assets that support it. The term may be derived from the practice of feeding cattle salt to induce them to drink large amounts of water just before they are sold, thereby increasing their weight. Thus, the buyer—whether of stock or of livestock—pays for more than is actually received.

wd　—Used in stock and bond transaction tables in newspapers to indicate that a security is trading on a when-distributed basis: *ColgP wd.*

WD　—Used on the consolidated tape to indicate that a stock is trading on a when-distributed basis: *GY.WD 52.*

weak dollar　A dollar that is of smaller value relative to foreign currencies. A weak dollar exchanges for fewer units of other currencies compared with the units for which it could have been exchanged in the past. A weak dollar tends to help U.S. firms that rely heavily on foreign sales because the firms' products will cost less in terms of the foreign currencies. A weak dollar hurts consumers of foreign goods because these goods cost more in terms of U.S. dollars. —Compare STRONG DOLLAR. —See also EXCHANGE RATE.

weak form　A component in the theory of efficient markets that holds that successive changes in security prices are independent of one another. If security markets are efficient to the extent of the weak form, existing prices reflect all the information contained in historical market data. Therefore, the charting of security prices and volume is not useful in projecting future price movements. The weak form of efficient markets supports the random-walk hypothesis. —Compare STRONG FORM.

wealth effect　The relationship between personal wealth and consumer spending. According to the wealth effect consumers have a tendency to spend a larger proportion of personal income as their wealth increases. The wealth effect was used to explain increases in consumer spending in the late 1990s when stock prices boomed.

wedge —See TRIANGLE.

weekend effect The tendency of securities to perform better on Fridays than on Mondays. Some technical analysts contend the weekend effect is primarily the result of the Monday auctions of U.S. Treasury securities.

weighted-average coupon rate A valuation of mortgage loans pooled into a mortgage pass-through security and calculated by multiplying the amount of the mortgage that is outstanding by the weighting of each mortgage loan in the pool.

weighted-average maturity A valuation of mortgage loans pooled into a mortgage pass-through security and calculated by multiplying the amount of the mortgage that is outstanding by the weighting of the remaining number of months to maturity for each mortgage loan in the pool.

weighting The assigning of a measure of relative importance to each of a group of variables that are combined. If an investor has 70% of his or her invested funds in stock A, which provides a current yield of 6%, and the remaining 30% of the invested funds in stock B, which provides a current yield of 12%, the weighted current yield of both securities is $(0.70)(0.06) + (0.30)(0.12)$, or 7.8%.

> ⋏⋏ **CASE STUDY** The weighting of individual securities included in an index or average can have a major impact on the market price of both the individual securities included in the index as well as on movements in the index or average itself. Although a few averages are weighted according to each component's price (for example, the Dow Jones Industrial Average), and even fewer are unweighted (the Value Line Average), most are weighted on the basis of market capitalization. That is, the index or average is calculated using a combination of each component's security price and number of outstanding shares. In May 2001 Morgan Stanley Capital International (MSCI), the world's largest indexing company, announced its intention to alter the composition of the indexes the firm calculated and published. In addition to adding and deleting companies, the firm would alter the weighting of most of the securities included in the index. At the time of the announcement MSCI was using full market capitalization to weight the components. That is, the firm was using the total number of shares outstanding, even if some of these shares were unavailable for trading. The new weighting would use "free float," or the number of shares that were actually available to investors. This change was particularly important to shareholders of companies such as Deutsche Telekom and France Telecom because the significant portion of each firm's shares was owned by its government and would not be included under the revised weighting system. The revised weighting would make each of these securities less important in the calculation. It would also likely cause a decline in the price of each security as index funds sold the stocks to rebalance their portfolios. At the same time, other stocks that assumed greater weighting under the new system could be expected to increase in price as index funds accumulated the securities for their portfolios.

W formation In technical analysis, a chart formation caused by a sharp decline, a sharp upward movement, and then a second sharp decline and sharp upward movement. The resultant chart pattern is similar to the letter *W*. In general, if the second upward movement surpasses each of the two previous high points, the W formation is a bullish sign.

when-distributed **1.** —Used to refer to a security that trades after the date of issue but before the time at which the certificates are delivered. **2.** Of or relating to a security on which a distribution is scheduled but has not yet occurred.

> ᴍ̌ᴧ CASE STUDY | AT&T's divestiture of its operating companies, the Baby Bells, was followed a decade later by a second major divestiture, this time of its computer and equipment operations. The firm sold 20% of its equipment subsidiary, Lucent Technologies, early in 1996. In the fall of the same year, the parent company distributed the remaining 80% of Lucent Technologies stock to AT&T stockholders on the basis of approximately 1 new Lucent share for each 3 shares of AT&T that were owned. In other words, the owner of 100 shares of AT&T received approximately 33 shares of stock in Lucent Technologies. Because AT&T distributed the 525 million remaining shares of Lucent without receiving any compensation in return, the distribution caused the value of AT&T common stock to decline by the value of the distribution. The New York Stock Exchange, the major secondary market for AT&T stock, commenced trading the new AT&T stock (AT&T without Lucent) on a when-distributed basis September 13, 1996, a month before the actual distribution. The new shares were listed on stock pages just below the regular AT&T shares. The new shares closed the first day at a price of $42.75, a discount of $12.50 compared with regular AT&T shares' closing price of $55.25. Listing AT&T stock on a when-distributed basis allowed investors to trade the stock on the basis of the company as it would be after the distribution was completed, even though the new Lucent Technologies shares would not be distributed for another month. The new shares were listed as *AT&T Cp wd* while the regular shares were listed as *AT&T Cp.*

when-issued —Used to refer to a security that has not yet been issued but that will be issued in the future. Trading in when-issued securities often occurs between the time a new security is announced (for example, the time when a stock is split) and the time the certificates are actually issued.

whipsaw A quick price movement followed by a sharp price change in the opposite direction. An investor expecting a continuation in the direction of a security's price movement is likely to experience whipsaw in a volatile market. This risk is very important to short-term traders but inconsequential to long-term investors.

whisper number An unofficial estimate of a financial variable (generally, earnings or revenues) that will be reported by a corporation. A whisper number may be different from published estimates by financial analysts or earnings guidance provided by corporate management.

> ᴍ̌ᴧ CASE STUDY | Whisper numbers frequently proved a major factor in moving stock prices during the stock market boom of the late 1990s. A corporate earnings announcement that met consensus estimates by analysts but fell short of the whisper number often resulted in a major price decline in the price of the firm's stock. Likewise, an earnings announcement that exceeded the whisper number could push a stock price higher. Whisper numbers often originated in Internet chat rooms, where individual investors shared rumored information with fellow investors. These rumors were occasionally believed to have corporate insiders as a source. In particular, investors were searching for companies that were likely to report earnings that were higher or lower than expected by Wall Street analysts. Whisper numbers lost their clout following the 2001 implementation of Regulation Fair Disclose, which prohibited companies from making selective disclosures.

whisper stock Shares in a firm that is rumored as a takeover target.

white knight A person or company that rescues a target firm from a takeover attempt by buying the firm. —Compare RAIDER. —See also HOSTILE TENDER OFFER; SHARK REPELLENT; WHITE SQUIRE.

whitemail A takeover target's sale of a large number of its own shares at a bargain price to a friendly party. Whitemail causes a takeover to become more difficult and expensive because a corporate raider must purchase additional shares from a party friendly to the target company.

white sheets A National Quotation Bureau listing of prices for regional over-the-counter stock traded in Chicago, Los Angeles, and San Francisco.

white squire An investor sympathetic with management who holds a block of stock in a company that is or could be subject to an unfriendly takeover.

white squire defense An antitakeover strategy in which a takeover target places a block of its stock in the hands of an investor deemed sympathetic to management. Having a white squire decreases the possibility of a takeover because the suitor must acquire a significantly greater proportion of the remaining shares in order to complete the takeover. However, the white squire may become disenchanted and put its block of stock up for sale, or it may itself mount a takeover attempt.

White's Ratings A rating service for tax-exempt bond issues in which a relative market value index is constructed from bond trading patterns rather than from credit analysis. A bond's yield is scaled on an index of 1 to 100.

whole life insurance —See CASH-VALUE LIFE INSURANCE.

wholesale The sale of securities among broker-dealers and to large institutional investors. Securities sold at wholesale go for slightly lower prices than those paid by individual investors. —Compare RETAIL.

wholesale price index A largely outdated reference to the *producer price index*.

wholly owned subsidiary A company that is totally owned by another company. For example, American Airlines is a wholly owned subsidiary of AMR Corp. A wholly owned subsidiary may have publicly traded preferred stock and debt, but all of its common stock is owned by a parent company and is unavailable for purchase.

w $_i$ —Used on the consolidated tape to indicate the transaction of a security on a when-issued basis: *GMPrE* $_i^w$*10s47¹/₂.*

wi —Used in stock transaction tables in newspapers to indicate securities traded on a when-issued basis: *BltGE wi.*

wide basis A market condition in which there is a relatively large difference between a spot price and futures prices for the same type of contract. —Compare NARROW BASIS.

wide opening A large spread between the bid and ask for a security at the opening of a session's trading.

widow-and-orphan stock A stock characterized by smaller than average price movements, a relatively high dividend, and little likelihood of dividend reduction or serious financial problems. A widow-and-orphan stock is a conservative investment with limited possibility for large gains or losses.

Williams Act A 1968 addition to the Securities Exchange Act of 1934 that requires investors who own or tender more than 5% of a firm's stock to furnish certain information to the SEC. The act also established a minimum period during which a tender offer must be held open. Required information includes the reason for the acquisition, the number of shares owned, and the source of the funds used for the purchase.

Wilshire 5000 Total Market Index A very comprehensive market-capitalization-weighted index composed of over 6,500 stocks. Stocks traded on the New York Stock Exchange represent approximately 77% of the value of the index. The Wilshire 5000 included 5,000 stocks when it was created in 1974 but has since been expanded. Wilshire Associates calculates numerous other indexes, including the Wilshire 4500, which excludes stocks composing the S&P 500.

windfall An unexpected profit or gain. An investor holding a stock that increases greatly in price because of an unexpected takeover offer receives a windfall.

window A period of time during which an action can be expected to generate a successful result. For example, underwriters may have a window for corporate debt issues sandwiched between two periods of heavy U.S. Treasury offerings.

window dressing An adjustment made to a portfolio or financial statement to create false appearances. For example, a manager may decide to provide window dressing to a portfolio by selling stock that has declined in value and replacing it with stock that has increased in value. Such activity creates the impression of successful portfolio management.

window period The time interval during which a company permits its executives and key employees to trade its stock. —See also BLACKOUT PERIOD.

window settlement The physical settlement of transactions between dealers. Window settlement is used when one or both participants are not members of a clearing firm such as the National Clearing Corporation. Settlement entails an actual physical comparison.

winner's curse The likelihood the winning bidder in an auction of several bidders will pay too high a price. From an investor's standpoint, the winner's curse implies the stockholders of the firm acquired in a merger will benefit at the expense of the stockholders of the acquiring firm when several potential acquirers are involved in the bidding.

wire house A relatively large, multioffice brokerage firm that uses electronic communications to transmit customer orders for execution.

wire room The area in a broker-dealer firm in which customer orders are received from retail offices and are relayed to an exchange floor for execution. Following execution, that information is relayed from the wire room back to retail offices.

wire transfer —See ELECTRONIC FUNDS TRANSFER.

withdrawal plan An option offered by some open-end investment companies whereby an investor can receive payments at regular intervals. Withdrawal plans are generally used by people who wish to use their accumulated funds for retirement purposes. —Also called *systematic withdrawal plan.*

withholding 1. The holding back of a portion of wages, dividends, interest, pension payments, or various other sources of income for payment of taxes to the U.S. Treasury. —See also BACKUP WITHHOLDING. 2. The illegal holding back of a portion of securities allocated as part of a new issue to a member of an underwriting syndicate. The underwriter may wish to keep the securities or resell them to a designated party so as to profit from an expected price rise soon after the issue has been offered to the public.

with or without (WOW) —Used to designate an odd-lot order in which the customer asks for an immediate execution. An odd-lot purchase order marked *WOW* will be executed at the current offering price plus any odd-lot differential, and an odd-lot sell order will receive the current bid price minus any odd-lot differential. An odd-lot order marked *with or without* is likely to result in a lower sale price or in a higher purchase price than an ordinary odd-lot order.

without —Used to indicate that no quotation is offered. For example, a dealer might quote a security as a $45 bid without, which means the dealer is willing to buy at $45, but no ask price is currently available. A dealer quotation that includes a without indicates a one-sided market.

with warrants —Used to designate a stock that trades with the right to a declared distribution of warrants. The buyer of a stock trading with warrants will be entitled to receive them if the stock is held until traded ex-warrants. The warrants will later trade separately from the stock. —Compare EX-WARRANTS.

worker capitalism A system in which employees own part or all of the firm for which they work. Proponents of worker capitalism believe employees will be more productive if they have a stake in the profits resulting from their labor. Employee Stock Ownership Plans were developed on this premise.

working capital The amount of current assets that is in excess of current liabilities. Working capital is frequently used to measure a firm's ability to meet current obligations. A high level of working capital indicates significant liquidity. —Also called *net current assets; net working capital.* —See also CURRENT RATIO; QUICK RATIO.

working control The ownership of a sufficient amount of a firm's voting stock (not necessarily more than 50%) to determine corporate policy. —Compare MAJORITY STOCKHOLDER.

work in process The partially finished goods that are held in inventory for completion and eventual sale. —Also called *goods in process.*

workout 1. The process of a debtor's meeting a loan commitment by satisfying altered repayment terms. For example, a firm in Chapter 11 bankruptcy proceedings might reach an agreement with its creditors for ways in which the firm's obligations can be worked out. 2. A range of prices within which a transaction or a series of transactions is likely to take place. For example, a market maker might quote a price range within which he or she would attempt to buy or sell a large order of securities.

World Federation of Exchanges A Paris-based trade organization that encourages and establishes standards for cross-border capital flows. The federation comprises operators of 56 of the world's largest securities exchanges. —Formerly called *International Federation of Stock Exchanges.*

world fund —See GLOBAL FUND.

WOW —See WITH OR WITHOUT.

wrap account A special investment account in which all of the account's assets are entrusted to a professional money manager. All expenses relating to the account, including professional advice and commissions, are wrapped into a single annual fee that generally ranges from 1 to 3% of the total market value of assets in the account. Wrap accounts are designed for individual investors who choose to have a professional money manager handle a part or all of their investments. These accounts usually require minimum initial investments of at least $25,000.

wraparound annuity An annuity contract in which the investor has a measure of control regarding the investments that are in the plan, and in which the income generated by those investments is sheltered from taxation until withdrawal. Tax deferral through a wraparound annuity is no longer permitted by the Internal Revenue Service.

wrinkles —See BELLS AND WHISTLES.

writedown A reduction in the value of an asset carried on a firm's financial statements. For example, the firm's accountants, believing the inventory is overvalued, may decide to take a writedown by reducing inventory valuation. Unlike a writeoff, a writedown does not result in elimination of the asset.

write off To reduce the balance (that is, the book value of an asset or a group of assets) in an account to zero by recognizing the recorded value as an expense. For example, a firm may write off a technologically obsolete asset shown on its balance sheet as having monetary value. The asset will then be deleted from the balance sheet, and income during the period will be reduced (or losses will be increased) by an equivalent amount. —Also called *charge off.*

CASE STUDY In September 2001 Blockbuster, Inc., announced it would write off $450 million in the value of its videotape inventory. Tapes that, depending on age, had each been carried at a value of $4 to $8 would be valued at $2 under the new policy. In addition, Blockbuster said it would reduce the number of old tapes in each store from 8,000 to 6,000, thereby eliminating a quarter of its inventory of older tapes. More profitable DVD rentals had become an increasing part of Blockbuster's business, and the firm decided to devote more shelf space to these items. The charge, taken against second-half earnings, caused Blockbuster to report a large loss when Wall Street analysts had been expecting positive earnings. The unexpected news caused the firm's common stock to fall in price by over 8% on the day of the announcement.

writeoff A reduction to zero in the value of an asset carried on a firm's financial statement. Companies often hesitate to make writeoffs because profits reported to stockholders are reduced.

writer The person who creates an option by selling an option contract in an opening transaction. An investor may be the writer of a call or a put. —See also NAKED WRITER.

writeup An accounting increase in the book value of an asset without an accompanying expenditure of funds. For example, if a firm accounts for inventory on the basis of market value, the firm may need a writeup of inventory during a period of price inflation.

writing The sale of an option in an opening transaction. The option writer incurs a potential obligation to buy (if a put is written) or to sell (if a call is written) an asset at a particular price.

WS —Used on the consolidated tape to indicate a warrant: *G.WS 23.50.*

wt —Used in stock transaction tables in newspapers to indicate that the security is a warrant to buy shares of the common stock: *AExp wt.*

ww —Used in stock and bond transaction tables in newspapers to indicate a security traded with warrants: *RokInd ww.*

X

x —Used in stock transaction tables in newspapers to indicate a stock that trades ex-dividend or ex-rights: *Gencp x212.*

XD —Used on the consolidated tape to indicate a stock that is trading ex-dividend: *GY.XD 16.*

XDIS —Used on the consolidated tape to indicate a stock that is trading ex-distribution: *WIN.XDIS 15.*

Xetra Deutsche Borse electronic trading platform that commenced operation in 1997.

XRT —Used on the consolidated tape to indicate a stock that is trading ex-rights: *GY.XRT 16.*

xw —Used in stock and bond transaction tables in newspapers to indicate securities that are trading ex-warrants: *RokInd xw.*

Y

Yankee bond A dollar-denominated bond sold in the United States by a foreign-domiciled issuer. U.S. investors can therefore purchase the securities of foreign issuers without being subject to price swings caused by variations in currency exchange rates. Yankee bond prices are influenced primarily by changes in U.S. interest rates and the financial condition of the issuer.

year bill A 12-month U.S. Treasury bill. Unlike 13- and 26-week Treasury bills, which are auctioned weekly, year bills are auctioned only once a month.

year-end dividend —See FINAL DIVIDEND 2.

year-end rally —See SANTA CLAUS RALLY.

year to date (YTD) January 1 until the current date. Financial publications frequently provide information for a security's YTD return, or the return provided by the security since the beginning of the calendar year.

Yellow Sheets A privately owned centralized electronic and printed quotation service for corporate, convertible, high-yield, and foreign bonds. Yellow Sheets derives its name from the yellow paper on which taxable debt quotations are distributed. Electronic quotations are in real time, and printed quotations are distributed weekly. —See also PINK SHEETS.

yield The percentage return on an investment. A given investment can have a variety of yields because of the many methods used to measure yield. For example, a bond's yield may be stated in terms of its returns if held to maturity, if held to the call date, or if held to the put date; or the yield may be calculated simply on the basis of the interest the bond pays compared with its current market price. —Also called *return*. —See also CURRENT YIELD; DIVIDEND YIELD; YIELD TO AVERAGE LIFE; YIELD TO CALL; YIELD TO MATURITY; YIELD TO PUT.

yield advantage The additional current return from holding a convertible security as opposed to owning the stock into which the convertible can be exchanged.

yield basis A method of quoting a bond's price in terms of its yield rather than in terms of its dollar value. Because bonds are bought and sold on the basis of yield, yield is generally a more informative measure of value than a bond's dollar price is. Treasury securities are usually auctioned on a yield basis.

yield burning Marking up the prices by underwriters and thereby reducing, or burning, the yields of bonds to be placed in escrow as part of a municipal bond refunding. Yield burning benefits the underwriters at the expense of their clients.

yield curve At any particular time, the relation between bond yields and maturity lengths. The yield curve usually has a positive slope because yields on long-term bonds generally exceed yields on short-term bonds. The shape of a yield curve is influenced by a number of factors including the relative riskiness between long-term and short-term securities and by investors' expectations as to the level of future interest rates. —Also called *term structure of interest rates.* —See also EXPECTATIONS HYPOTHESIS; FLAT YIELD CURVE; NEGATIVE YIELD CURVE; POSITIVE YIELD CURVE; RIDING THE YIELD CURVE.

〜〜 **CASE STUDY** Long-term interest rates are generally higher than short-term rates, resulting in a yield curve that slopes upward. An upward-sloping yield curve was in place in fall 2001 when six-month Treasury bills were yielding 2% at the same time that 30-year Treasury bonds were selling to yield slightly over 5%. Despite the relatively steep slope of the curve, many bond traders were convinced the slope would grow even steeper. That is, they believed short-term interest rates would continue to fall at the same time long-term rates remained steady or moved upward. The Federal Reserve was actively pursuing an easy money policy to stimulate a weakening economy. The September 11 terrorist attacks on the World Trade Center and Pentagon accelerated the economic decline with major corporate layoffs, reductions in industrial output, and increased business bankruptcies. The attack also made it likely that the U.S. Treasury would increase spending, thereby borrowing more and selling more Treasury bonds. The increased borrowing would result in higher long-term interest rates and reduced prices for Treasury bonds. At least, that was the theory. In this environment many bond traders decided to take an investment position that allowed them to profit

---

yield to call / yield to maturity

When is yield to call more relevant than yield to maturity?

Yield to call is more relevant than yield to maturity when interest rates are declining and you are concerned about the yield on a premium-priced bond. What you really want to know is how much you will make on an investment that is going to pay you an above-market rate of income for some period of time but then may produce only a partial return of your original principal at a later date when the bond is called. If the income flow to you is sufficiently above the going rate for par-priced bonds, and if it lasts long enough, then the loss of principal that might result from a bond being called is not a problem. In any case, the yield to call formula takes this principal loss into account: the shorter the time period a premium-priced bond has before its first call date versus its maturity date, the greater the disparity between the bond's yield to call and its yield to maturity.

Stephanie G. Bigwood, CFP, ChFC, CSA, Assistant Vice President
Lombard Securities, Incorporated, Baltimore, MD

---

from a steeper yield curve. Traders took a bullish position (bought) in short-term Treasuries they thought would increase in price, and at the same time they assumed a bearish position (sold) in long-term Treasuries they thought would decline in price. This investment strategy came tumbling down on October 31, when the U.S. Treasury made a surprise announcement that it would quit selling 30-year bonds. The announcement caused a major price increase in these bonds that in a two-day period reduced yields from 5.25% to about 4.8%. What seemed a sure thing among sophisticated investors turned into a nightmare as a bearish bet on long-term Treasuries went bad for a reason none of the participants had foreseen.

yield curve note A floating-rate note on which yields increase when interest rates decline and yields decline when interest rates increase. Yield curve notes appeal to investors who want to hedge falling interest rates.

yield equivalence Equal aftertax returns on different investments. As an example, for an investor in a 25% marginal tax bracket, a corporate bond with a taxable return of 8% has yield equivalence with a tax-free bond returning 6%.

yield spread The difference in yield, at a given time, between two bonds or between different segments of the bond market. For example, the yield spread between AAA-rated bonds and A-rated bonds may be one half of 1% at a particular time. Likewise, the yield spread between long-term taxable and nontaxable bonds may be 2%. Yield spread may be caused by any of various factors including maturity difference, risk difference, or taxability difference.

yield to average life The average yield on a fixed-income security assuming an average life for the security. In the case of bonds, average life may be significantly less than the number of years until maturity because of sinking fund requirements. Thus, the investor may be forced to sell the bond back before maturity.

yield to call The annual return on a bond, assuming the security will be redeemed at the call price on the first date permitted. This measure of yield includes interest payments and price depreciation because bonds are quoted in this way only if they sell above the call price.

yield to current call The annual return from owning a bond assuming the earliest possible call.

yield to maturity (YTM) The annual return on a bond held to maturity when interest payments and price appreciation (if priced below par) or depreciation (if priced above par) are considered. When a bond sells at par, the yield to maturity is the same as the current yield because price appreciation or depreciation is zero if the security is held to maturity. Bond quotations are generally on a yield-to-maturity basis, although an investor who sells a bond before maturity may earn a yield different from the yield to maturity as calculated at the time the security was purchased. —See also INTERNAL RATE OF RETURN; MATURITY BASIS.

yield to par call The annual return from owning a bond assuming a redemption on the first date the bond can be called at face value.

yield to put The annual yield on a bond, assuming the security will be put (sold back to the issuer) on the first permissible date after purchase. Bonds are quoted in this manner only if they sell at a price below the put price. Therefore, the yield includes interest and price appreciation. —Compare PREMIUM PUT.

yield to worst The lowest possible yield from owning a bond considering all potential call dates prior to maturity.

YTD —See YEAR TO DATE.

YTM —See YIELD TO MATURITY.

Z

z 1. —Used in stock transaction tables in newspapers to indicate that the volume reported is the actual number of shares transacted, not the number of round lots: *z150.* **2.** —Used in over-the-counter stock transaction tables to indicate that no representative quote is available: z.

Zacks Investment Research A firm that compiles earnings estimates and brokerage firm investment recommendations for thousands of publicly traded firms.

zero —See ZERO-COUPON BOND.

zero bracket amount A largely outdated reference to the *standard deduction.*

zero-cost collar The investment position of being short a call option and long a put option for stock already owned. The premium received from selling the call option is used to pay for purchase of the put. The collar is designed to protect an investor against a decline in the price of the stock without the investor being required to sell the stock and pay a tax on capital gains.

zero-coupon bond A bond that provides no periodic interest payments to its owner. A zero-coupon bond is issued at a fraction of its par value (perhaps at $3 to $5 for each $100 of face value for a long-term bond) and increases gradually in value as it approaches maturity. Thus, an investor's income from a zero-coupon bond comes solely from appreciation in value. Zero-coupon bonds are subject to very large price fluctuations. The tax consequences of taxable issues often make zero-coupon bonds more suitable for tax-deferred accounts such as IRAs than for regular investments. —Also called *accrual bond; capital appreciation bond; zero.*

〽 CASE STUDY | Zero-coupon bonds offer advantages, at least to some investors. Zero-coupon bonds present an investor with the certainty that the rate of return earned on reinvested interest payments will be zero because no payments will be available for reinvestment. Zero-coupon bonds accumulate interest each period until they become worth their face value on the scheduled maturity date. Buy a 7% zero and you will earn 7% both on your original investment and also on the interest that is added to your original investment every six months. A fixed reinvestment rate is an advantage if you believe interest rates are likely to fall—there is no concern about reinvesting interest payments at a rate lower than 7%. Of course, if interest rates subsequently increase, the owner of a zero-coupon bond will be worse off because interest payments could have been reinvested at a rate higher than 7%. This is a downside to earning the guaranteed rate. Zero-coupon bonds, especially issues with long maturities, tend to have very volatile prices. Buy a zero-coupon bond with a 25-year maturity and watch the price plummet if market interest rates increase. Of course, the opposite also holds true. A long-term zero-coupon bond will produce substantial gains in value when market rates of interest decline. Invest in a 7% zero-coupon bond before a major decline in interest rates and you will own a very valuable asset. The price volatility of long-term zero-coupon bonds subjects an investor to substantial risk in the event the bond must be sold prior to maturity. Zero-coupon bonds also often suffer from a lack of liquidity and so may be difficult to sell at a fair price before maturity. Again, liquidity is important if you may be required to sell the security on relatively short notice. However, if you plan to hold the bond to maturity, a lack of liquidity is not a problem. It is important to recognize that interest accumulations on corporate and U.S. government zero-coupon bonds must be reported as taxable income each year even though you do not receive any interest payments. This may result in a cash flow problem since money (specifically, taxes) will be going out and no money (for example, interest income) will be coming in. If interest from the bond is exempt from taxes (such as with an obligation of a state or municipality), or if a taxable issue is held in a tax-sheltered retirement account, taxability will not be an important issue.

zero-coupon certificate of deposit A certificate of deposit that pays no periodic interest and that is sold at a discount from face value (that is, maturity value). A zero-coupon CD is essentially the same as any other CD in which the investor leaves interest to compound.

zero-minus tick The sale of a security when the price is the same as the security's preceding sale price but is below the last different sale price. A short sale of a security is not permitted on a zero-minus tick.

zero-plus tick The sale of a security when the price is the same as the security's preceding sale price but is above the last different sale price. A short sale of a security is permitted on a zero-plus tick.

zero-sum game A situation in which one person's gain must be matched by another person's loss. Without considering taxes and transaction costs, many types of investing, such as options and futures, are examples of zero-sum games.

zero tick   A security transaction in which the sale price is identical to the price of the immediately preceding transaction in the same security.

zombie   A company that remains in business even though it is technically bankrupt and almost surely headed for the graveyard.

Z-tranche   The last tranche in a collateralized mortgage obligation. A Z-tranche accrues periodic interest but receives no cash payments until previous tranches from the same CMO are retired.

zero-coupon bond

What are the advantages and disadvantages of buying zero-coupon bonds? Who should buy them?

Zero-coupon bonds are quite useful in financial planning because they permit you to plan with certainty for specific rates of growth on the monies invested in them, provided that those monies will be left intact until maturity. If, however, you need to liquidate your zero-coupon bonds before their maturity, you will find that since you purchased your bonds, their prices will have moved dramatically in a direction opposite that of interest rates. These bonds have the most volatile price movements of any bonds in their respective credit quality and maturity group because they pay no coupon interest to cushion the blow of any change in interest rates. Another important aspect of zero-coupon bonds relates to their taxation. Income is accrued on zero-coupon bonds even though they do not pay any interest before maturity. If the bond is taxable (that is, it is a U.S. Treasury bond or a corporate bond), you will have to pay annual federal income tax on the accrued income even though you did not receive any cash flow from the bond before maturity. The income is based on the accretion of the bond from the discount price at which you bought it to the par value it will grow to have at maturity. If your bond is a municipal zero-coupon, the accretion is still calculated each year, but the bond's accretion is not taxed at the federal level. (Consult your state's tax laws regarding the taxation of the accretion.) This accretion affects the municipal bond's book value, however, which in turn influences the portion of any capital gain subject to federal income tax. Taxable zero-coupon bonds are often used in retirement plans and in children's custodial accounts because of the predictability of their values at maturity and the fact that income earned in accounts of this sort is generally able to grow tax-deferred or is taxed at a low federal income tax rate. Tax-exempt zero-coupon bonds are often used to form a "Side-IRA," which means that a pool of money is able to grow, free of taxation, with its anticipated use being to enhance the pool of money that is allowed to grow within an IRA. The obvious result is that more money will be available at the time of retirement because of careful planning for tax savings and the continuous compounding of the tax-favored rate of return.

Stephanie G. Bigwood, CFP, ChFC, CSA, Assistant Vice President
Lombard Securities, Incorporated, Baltimore, MD

Technical Analysis Chart Patterns

TYPICAL EXAMPLES

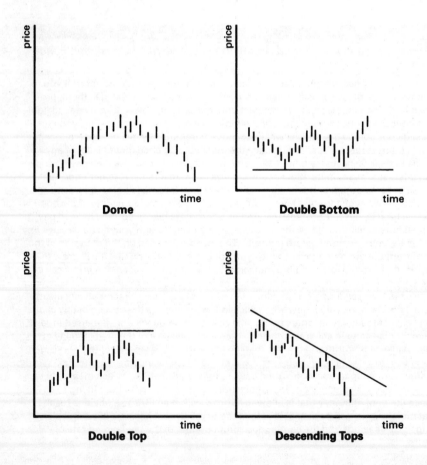

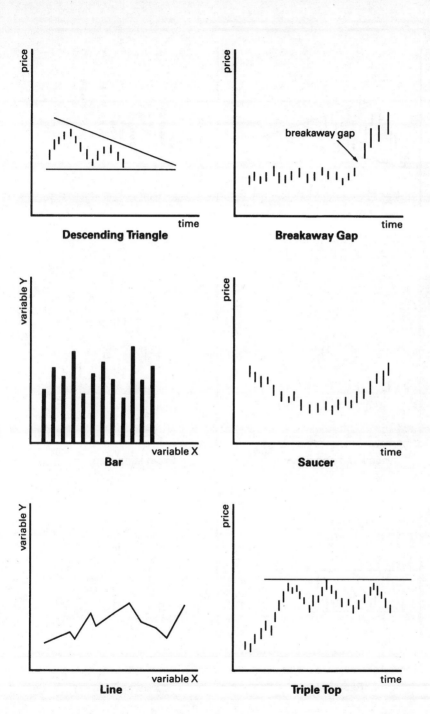

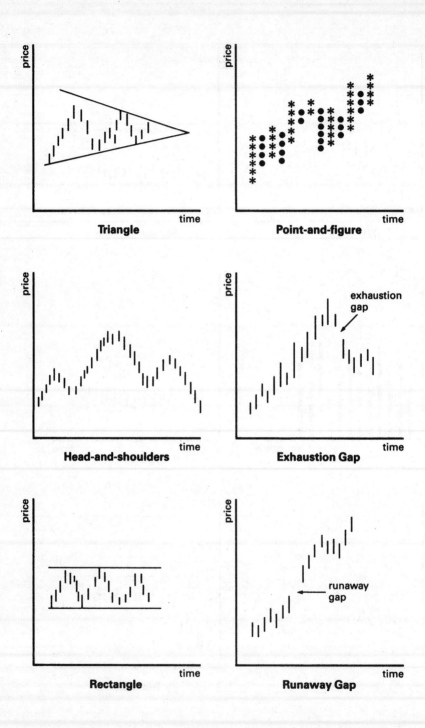

Triangle

Point-and-figure

Head-and-shoulders

Exhaustion Gap

exhaustion gap

Rectangle

Runaway Gap

runaway gap

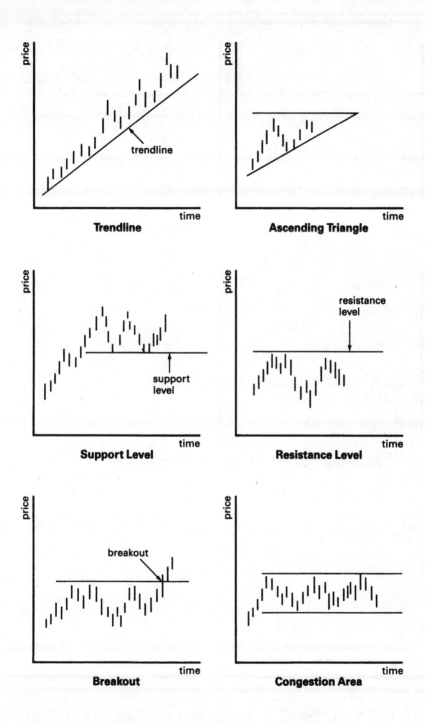

Trendline

Ascending Triangle

Support Level

Resistance Level

Breakout

Congestion Area

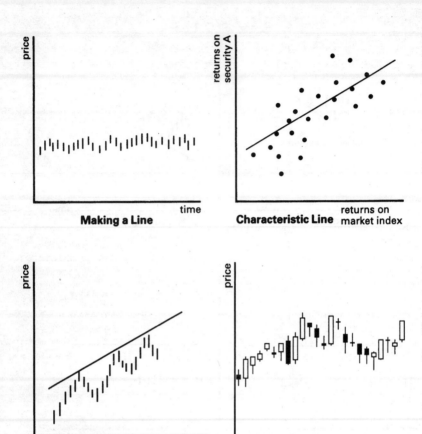

Making a Line

Characteristic Line

Ascending Tops

Candlestick

Selected Investment Websites

Ambac Assurance Corporation	www.ambac.com/aboutus.html
American Association of Individual Investors	www.aaii.com
American Stock Exchange	www.amex.com
Archipelago	www.archipelago.com
Arizona Stock Exchange	www.azx.com
Association for Investment Management and Research	www.aimr.com
Bond Buyer	www.bondbuyer.com
Bond Market Association	www.bondmarkets.com
Boston Stock Exchange	www.bostonstock.com
Bourse de Montreal	www.me.org
Canadian Venture Exchange	www.tsx.ca
Chicago Board of Trade	www.cbot.com
Chicago Board Options Exchange	www.cboe.com
Chicago Mercantile Exchange	www.cme.com
Chicago Stock Exchange	www.chicagostockex.com
Cincinnati Stock Exchange	www.cincinnatistock.com
Clearstream International	www.cedel-bank.com
Commodity Futures Trading Commission	www.cftc.gov
Council of Institutional Investors	www.cii.org
Currenex	www.currenex.com
Deutsche Borse Group	www.deutsche-boerse.com
EDGAR	www.sec.gov/edgar.shtml
Emerging Markets Clearing Corporation	www.e-m-c-c.com
Emerging Markets Traders Association	www.emta.org
Euroclear	www.euroclear.com
Fannie Mae	www.fanniemae.com
Federal Home Loan Bank System	www.fhlbanks.com
Federal Reserve System	www.federalreserve.gov
Financial Accounting Standards Board	www.fasb.org
Financial Guaranty Insurance Corporation	www.fgic.com
Fitch Ratings	www.fitchratings.com
Freddie Mac	www.freddiemac.com
Ginnie Mae	www.ginniemae.gov
Government Securities Clearing Corporation	www.gscc.com
Hulbert Financial Digest	www.hulbertdigest.com

Instinet	www.instinet.com
Institute of Management Accountants	www.imanet.org
Institutional Shareholder Services	www.isstf.com
International Accounting Standards Board	www.iasc.org.uk
International Securities Exchange	www.iseoptions.com
Investment Company Institute	www.ici.org
Investment Counsel Association of America	www.icaa.org
Island	www.island.com
Kansas City Board of Trade	www.kcbt.com
London Stock Exchange	www.londonstockexchange.com
London International Financial Futures and Options Exchange	www.liffe.com
London Metal Exchange	www.lme.co.uk
MBIA	www.mbia.com
MBS Clearing Corporation	www.mbscc.com
Moody's Investors Service	www.moodys.com
Morningstar	www.morningstar.com
Nasdaq	www.nasdaq.com
Nasdaq Liffe Markets	www.nqlx.com
NASD Dispute Resolution	www.nasdadr.com
NASD Regulation	www.nasdr.com
National Association of Investors Corporation	www.better-investing.org
National Association of Securities Dealers	www.nasd.com
National Securities Clearing Corporation	www.nscc.com
New York Board of Trade	www.nyce.com
New York Mercantile Exchange	www.nymex.com
New York Stock Exchange	www.nyse.com
North American Securities Administrators Association	www.nasaa.org
OneChicago LLC	www.onechicago.com
OTC Bulletin Board	www.otcbb.com
Pacific Exchange	www.pacificex.com
Philadelphia Stock Exchange	www.phlx.com
Pink Sheets	www.pinksheets.com
Russell Indexes	www.russell.com/ww/indexes
savings bonds	www.publicdebt.treas.gov/sav/sav.htm
Securities and Exchange Commission	www.sec.gov
Securities Industry Association	www.sia.com
Securities Industry Automation Corporation	www.siac.com
Securities Investor Protection Corporation	www.sipc.org
Securities Transfer Association	www.stai.org
Security Traders Association	www.securitytraders.org
Standard & Poor's Corporation	www.standardpoor.com
SWX Swiss Exchange	www.swx.com
Thomson Financial	www.thomsonfinancial.com
Tokyo Stock Exchange	www.tse.or.jp/english/
Toronto Stock Exchange	www.tse.com
Value Line	www.valueline.com
Wilshire Associates	www.wilshire.com
World Federation of Exchanges	www.world-exchanges.org